CONTRACT AND CONVEYANCE

The author is also the editor of:

Emmet on Title
Conveyancer and Property Lawyer
Wolstenholme & Cherry's Conveyancing Statutes

CONTRACT AND CONVEYANCE

Fourth edition

J T FARRAND, LL D

Solicitor, Professor of Law at the University of Manchester

© Oyez Longman Publishing Limited 1983
21/27 Lamb's Conduit Street
London WC1N 3NJ

ISBN 0 85120 771 5

CONTENTS OF A CONVEYANCE

First published 1963

CONVEYANCING CONTRACTS:
CONDITIONS OF SALE AND TITLE

First published 1964

CONTRACT AND CONVEYANCE

First published 1969
Second edition 1973
Third edition　1980
Fourth edition　1983

Set in Times by Kerrypress

Printed in Great Britain by
Biddles Ltd, Guildford, Surrey

CONTENTS

Book One

CONVEYANCING CONTRACTS

Conditions of Sale and Title

BOOK TWO

CONTENTS OF A CONVEYANCE

PREFACE

LAW and practice are taken in effect as at *Easter 1983*. So this book is now over 20 years old but, never mind, the text has had to age even better than its writer. Thus a further thorough facelift, for this fourth edition, has proved unavoidable: the lack of footnotes to titivate means that all the significant developments of recent years have had to be properly incorporated by appropriate rewriting and even rethinking throughout. The net result in my contemplation remains a readable and relevant account of a substantially serious subject.

As with earlier editions, the objective is to offer a critical scrutiny in adequate detail of the fundamental principles supporting unregistered conveyancing in the context of modern practice coupled with a point-by-point comparative examination of the rules observed where title is registered. Achievement of this objective still seems to demand a bipartite treatment corresponding with the ordinary order of events in the transaction itself. Accordingly Book One considers the rights and duties inter se of the parties to a contract for the sale and purchase of land, including their position before exchange as well as the investigation of title, whilst Book Two deals with the traditional and statutory form and contents of the deed of conveyance or transfer which completes the matter.

May Day 1983   JTF

TABLE OF CASES

TABLE OF STATUTES

TABLE OF STATUTORY INSTRUMENTS

TABLE OF REFERENCES TO STANDARD CONDITIONS OF SALE

BOOK ONE

CONVEYANCING CONTRACTS

CONDITIONS OF SALE AND TITLE

I INTRODUCTION

'"Convey" the wise it call. "Steal!" foh! a fico for the phrase.'
—Shakespeare: 'The Merry Wives of Windsor'

Act I, Sc 3 (Pistol).

IN this book is told a tale of two innocents, one who owned land (he thought) and wished to sell it (he thought) and another who had money to spend (he thought) and wished to buy that land (he thought). Nothing could be simpler (they thought). Little foresaw they the dark and dangerous depths of the 'wide and sometimes largely uncharted sea' to which they entrusted their ship of fortune when first their thoughts they turned to that relation of sympathy or conquest, a contract for the sale and purchase of land (cf per Goff J in *Lee-Parker* v *Izzet* [1971] 1 WLR 1688, at p 1690). They risked their all in 'coming to it dewy-eyed and venturing forth into wholly unknown territory' (per Edmund Davies LJ in *Jaques* v *Lloyd D George & Partners* [1968] 1 WLR 625, at p 632). Could a fate worse than 'gazumping' befall them?

Seriously though, such contracts have always seemed so surrounded by peculiar principles as to be worthy of exploration beyond the place from which they trace their source, that is, beyond the basic law of contract. Thus the call for such an exploration was recently recognised, albeit without any enthusiasm, in the House of Lords:

> The factual situation is commonplace, indeed routine . . . One would think that the law as to so typical a set of facts would be both simple and clear. It is no credit to our law that it is neither. Learned judges in the Chancery Division and in the Court of Appeal have had great difficulty in formulating a rule and have been obliged to reach differing conclusions. That this is so is due partly to the mystification which has been allowed to characterise contracts for the sale of land, as contrasted with other contracts, partly to an accumulated debris of decisions and text book pronouncements which has brought semantic confusion and misunderstandings into an area capable of being governed by principle. I hope that this may be an opportunity for a little simplification

(per Lord Wilberforce in *Johnson* v *Agnew* [1980] AC 367, at pp 390–1, not necessarily having the present book in mind). So let us now burrow into the debris to see if we can tell the difference between sales of land and other contracts in the same simple way as between, say, chalk and cheese.

In the first place, then, the merest mention may be made of the formalities, of the ubiquitous exchange and the mandatory memorandum (see pp 15 and 32), for other more learned lawyers have already commented that 'These requirements put contracts for dispositions of land into a special category by themselves' (Megarry and Wade, *Real Property*, 4th ed, p 542). After this a passing finger may be pointed at the problem of particularising the subject-matter of the sale, the land and the estate or interest sold, both physically and legally (see p 50). Thus in one modern case the site sold 'consisted of at least seven different parcels of land' and was described:

3

from a conveyancing point of view and the conveyancing problems arising as either a conveyancer's dream or a conveyancer's nightmare, depending upon the attitude and enthusiasm with which the particular person entrusted with the conveyance approached the discharge of his functions

(per Mocatta J in *G + K Ladenbau Ltd* v *Crawley & De Reya* [1978] 1 WLR 266, at p 270). Again the circumstances on a sale of land are seldom straightforward. It is true, of course, that though the details are never identical—the parties, the property, the price, etc, enjoying almost infinite variety—one can yet say that the area of material fact has been sufficiently small to become mapped by principles. Nonetheless, even admitting this, one must still recognise that:

Cases on the law of vendor and purchaser are often extremely complex and require minute investigation: and although from some of them general principles may be evolved, they often result merely in the judges' opinion on the particular contract

(per Chitty J in *Ashburner* v *Sewell* [1891] 3 Ch 405, at p 410).

Be that as it may, not all cases call for the evolvement, but rather for the application, of principles. Then the proper approach, as always, is first to investigate the facts, the circumstances, and then to enquire 'what is the nature of the legal principle that regulates the relations of vendor and purchaser in those circumstances' (*Selkirk* v *Romar Investments Ltd* [1963] 1 WLR 1415, at p 1420). In this context, however, this enquiry may be even less easy than the investigation of the circumstances, for the principle is likely to be peculiar in being unlikely to prove pure-bred. Instead, as one writer once graphically explained:

the historical peculiarities of real property law relating to forms of conveyance led to a comparatively late development of contracts for the sale of land, which have in some aspects settled uneasily into common-law principles. Such contracts are hybrid creatures, born of an uneasy marriage of the law of property and the law of contract, and doubtful to which parent they owe their primary allegiance

(RG Rowley (1954) 18 Conv (NS) 301–2). Other writers also, no doubt after 'blood' tests, have found that 'contracts for the sale of land are so much part and parcel of the whole system of conveyancing that they have many peculiarities drawn from the law,' instancing the 'many implied terms as to proof of title and other matters' (Megarry and Wade, *Real Property*, 4th ed, p 542).

Indeed the incompatibility of temperament between common law and conveyancing contractual concepts has been evidenced in two particularly important cases before the House of Lords. First, it now appears clear once again that whilst the commercial lawyer must still regard the doctrine of privity of contract as fundamental, the conveyancer can call in aid not only the counter-doctrine of privity of estate and the equitable rules as to restrictive covenants but also the provisions of s 56 of the Law of Property Act 1925 (see *Beswick* v *Beswick* [1968] AC 58). Secondly, a novel extension of the completely common law doctrine of restraint of trade has become established: the doctrine is applicable notwithstanding that the restriction was imposed in relation to land and notwithstanding even that it was imposed by way of covenant in a mortgage (see *Esso Petroleum Co* v *Harper's Garage* [1968] AC 269). Sacrilege, some would say, but their lordships could not, as Diplock LJ put it in the Court of Appeal, be 'persuaded that mortgages of land are condemned today to linger in a jurisprudential cul-de-sac built by the Court of Chancery before the Judicature Acts from which the robust doctrines of the common law are barred' ([1966] 2 QB 555, at p 578: cp notes at (1975) 39 Conv (NS) 1 and 236). But all is not saved, some barriers still stand: it was explicitly and unanimously indicated in the House of Lords that covenants restricting the use of land imposed as a condition of any sale or lease to the covenantor (or his successors) are not subject to the doctrine. Thus as regards the doctrines both of privity and of restraint of trade, contracts for the sale of land can be said to retain at least some peculiarities of their own.

These two, however, are not the only points at which it becomes a problem to reconcile the rules relating to sales of land with those applicable to other ordinary contracts. For example, has the present fluctuating status of the doctrine of fundamental breach had any effect upon the rule in *Flight* v *Booth* (see p 54)? Again, can a conveyancing contract be frustrated (see p 167)? Can any distinction still be sustained between sales of chattels and sales of real property so as to deny liability in tort in respect of defective premises (see p 67)? Are the consequences of non-registration of land charges to be undermined by the tort of inducing breach of contract? And further will liability for negligent misstatement supersede the anomalous rule in *Bain* v *Fothergill* (see p 58)?

At this stage, the officious and efficacious intervention of equity can no longer be ignored. For it was equity's patent remedies and reliefs—particularly specific performance (see p 215) from which flow the peculiar fiduciary obligations of the vendor and the peculiar equitable ownership of the purchaser (see p 167)—which, inter alia, introduced the term that the vendor should show a good title, a term only afterwards adopted by the common law (see p 83). Yet not too much assistance should be expected here. As Walton J once observed:

> in my view, just as equity mends no man's bargains, so it mends no man's poor conveyancing. There are many areas of the law—and this is one of them—where good intentions alone are not enough. The paperwork must also be at least adequate

(*Re Earl of Coventry's Indentures* [1974] Ch 77, at p 96). And as to certainty being better than justice in property law, see a note at [1982] Conv 396–7.

Equity's particular remedy was recognised alongside a secondary source of distinction by Harman LJ when remarking that:

> Contracts for the sale of real property are unlike other contracts, first, because there enters into them a question of the equitable doctrine of specific performance, which is a discretionary remedy, and, second, because of the difficulties of title

(in *Scheggia* v *Gradwell* [1963] 1 WLR 1049, at p 1062).

The learned lord justice's second point leads us to perhaps the most peculiar of the peculiarities: this is, that no vendor has ever been lowered in the estimation of right-thinking members of the judiciary generally simply because he did not know he did not own his own land! Thus Romer J:

> Now when I consider the state of the laws of this country concerning land, and the difficulties under which even a perfectly honest and careful vendor labours, it does not appear to me to be reasonable to impute to him knowledge of all possible defects of title for the purpose of such a clause as this

(in *Re Woods and Lewis' Contract* [1898] 1 Ch 433, at p 436: the clause concerned 'wilful default' causing delay, see p 194). Again Tomlin J:

> Now it seems to me, having regard to the general law as to contracts for the sale of real estate, and to the fact that the provisions of that law are really based upon this that title to land is an uncertain matter and that nobody can be quite sure until the last moment (that is, at any rate, before January, 1926) whether he had any title to land at all: that it would be a strange construction to imply in any contract for the sale of land—unless absolutely driven to it by the language—a warranty by the vendor that he was making title in a particular form.

(in *Re Spencer and Hauser's Contract* [1928] Ch 598, at pp 606–7).

The most anomalous aberration produced by this attitude occurs with the remedy of damages for breach: the general rule of the law of contract is, of course, that substantial damages may be recovered,

> but to this rule there is an exception, as the law as to real property is such that a vendor may well be in doubt whether he had a good title or not

(per Blackburn J in *Lock v Furze* (1866) 15 LT 161, at p 162), the exception being that a purchaser may in such a case recover only nominal damages for loss of bargain (see p 214). Elsewhere, other aberrant exceptions to other rules can be found, for example with regard to the question as to when a vendor should have title: as Harman J once said, at common law:

> it matters not at all that at the date of the contract [the vendor] had no interest if he obtain it in time to fulfil the bargain. To this doctrine equity made a qualification in cases of specific performance of contracts for the sale of land. The exception arises, I think, out of the peculiar difficulty of making a title to land in England which is also recognised in the rule as to damages on failure to make a good title

(in *Elliott v Pierson* [1948] Ch 452, at p 455). The exception is that a purchaser may in equity at once repudiate whilst remaining liable at common law (see per Buckley LJ in *Price v Strange* [1978] Ch 337, at p 364) but cp p 111.

Now, as everybody knows, the rules of real property were much simplified as recently as 1925 (see Tomlin J's parenthesis, above) and since then there spreads apace, a peculiarity in itself, the official registration of title—'the necessary process,' as Wilberforce J referred to it in *Re Hewitt's Contract* [1963] 1 WLR 1298, at p 1305. Although 'necessary' to what end seems less clear than it used to: as Donaldson J once observed:

> The title was in fact registered, but it was common ground that nowadays, when in unregistered cases short title can be made, there is little, if any, saving in time or effort in dealing with a registered title

(*Property and Reversionary Investment Corporation Ltd v Secretary of State for the Environment* [1975] 1 WLR 1504, at p 1507). But though the vendor may, therefore, be much more likely to know his own title, some difficulties do remain, and this is so even though he be a registered proprietor (see p 141). Also, on the other side of the coin, commonsense, if nothing else, commands that a purchaser ascertain for himself that the vendor has made no mistake about ownership notwithstanding the passing of 1925.

This last truism, more than anything else, accounts in the end for the very existence of the subject-matter of this book, since from it sprang the practical dictate that any conveyance of land should be preceded by a more or less formal contract. This is, of course, especially so where payment of a lump sum is in prospect, for then the object of the contract is to afford the purchaser what may be called a 'pay pause,' that is, simply a time after the conclusion of the negotiations and before he pays his money during which to investigate the vendor's title. Where no lump sum is to change hands, eg, on the grant of a lease at a rack rent, no delay for this reason (there may be others) will be at all necessary. Also the suggestion has been made, but by no means accepted, that registered titles are so straightforward that again no preliminary contract is needed (see p 147). Further, not all purchasers take the same view of what constitutes commonsense:

> I summoned up my decision and bought a mews house off Queensborough Terrace in Bayswater. I did not mess about with searches and deposits, subject to contract and all that jargon, so beloved of lawyers and estate agents. I simply wrote a cheque for the £25,000 the owner asked and the house was mine

(per Kenneth More, *More or Less*, an autobiography, p 194). Legally, of course, this was not true, pending a deed of conveyance or twelve years adverse possession. And apart altogether from the investigation of title, the sale and purchase of land is today such a major transaction for so many people that time has to be spent anyway on extraneous arrangements, such as raising the money, removal estimates and dates, and so on. When this sort of thing is multiplied, as it might be many times by each of the parties to each sale and purchase also purchasing or selling other land, respite really is required.

Whatever the reason, however, for a pay pause, the obvious result is that the rights and duties of the vendor and purchaser between and at contract and completion have to be clearly defined. If the parties do not do this for themselves, their positions will be entirely regulated by implied terms and provisions. Yet more usual is the introduction of express terms, either specially or by way of common form general conditions of sale. The hotch-potch thus created is considered in a later chapter all to itself (see p 76) and the writer would only stress here that the whole story is never to be found solely in the express terms: as will be seen, however comprehensive the conditions of sale, they will rarely if ever cover all the ground, and the extent to which they may exclude or modify the implied terms is strictly limited. Even so, it is thought that in this respect a contract for the sale of land has, for the lawyer, a considerable edge over one for the sale of goods, the suggestion being that many of the difficulties experienced with the latter are due to the lack of a real as opposed to a notional distinction between contract and transfer.

In addition to actually defining the rights and duties of the parties, some difficulty is always experienced in sorting these out into separate legal categories for the purpose of exposition. For example, the disclosure of defects in title (see p 62) is for the vendor a pre-contract duty appropriately put with misrepresentation, whilst for the purchaser it is an aspect of the post-contract deduction of title. Again the vendor's inability to give vacant possession (see p 174) may be due to a defect in his title or to a breach of his duty as a trustee (see p 167). Then there are various places in which the payment of a deposit could be considered (see p 203), eg, on formation, or as a condition of sale, or amongst the remedies—also the payment is not itself an implied term, but if made, terms are implied. Fortunately, however, an exponent's arrangement can conveniently follow as near as may be the almost immutable order of events prescribed by practice.

This leads on to another aspect peculiar to the contract for the sale of land, namely, the influence exercised over its development and operation by what conveyancers are accustomed actually to do. Since practice tends to constitute the skeleton of the subject, its general shape has to emerge from any book on the law of conveyancing, but its particular niceties, neither depending on nor affecting general principles, can be largely assumed and left to be grasped from doing (ie, whilst in articles of clerkship) rather than by reading (although Moeran's *Practical Conveyancing*, currently in its 8th ed, may always be referred to with great advantage).

How, one may wonder, has practice achieved its influence? The answer in essence is that conveyancers have gone through the same motions for so long that something had to happen. From a game without rules, a game with rules has emerged. And if you think this analogy a trifle disrespectful to what Viscount Radcliffe once called 'the whole elaborate and protracted transaction' (in *Selkirk* v *Romar Investments Ltd* [1963] 1 WLR 1415, at p 1422), please to remember that Evershed MR is reported as saying that an answer to a requisition provided the purchaser:

with a heaven-sent opportunity to resile from a bargain of which he had
already repented and he embraced that opportunity with alacrity . . . he
undoubtedly took advantage of the rigour of the game and the loss must fall
upon the vendor

(in *Simmons* v *Pennington & Son* [1955] 1 WLR 183, at p 186). Even an editor of so
august a periodical as the *Conveyancer and Property Lawyer* once referred to 'this
game of chicken' (1961) vol 25, p 90). Nonetheless there is no denying the more
elevating dignity inherent in the mention by Buckley J of:

the time within which any particular step must be taken in the stately saraband
which takes place between vendor and purchaser on a purchase of land

(in *Re Stone and Saville's Contract* [1962] 1 WLR 460, at p 465: on appeal [1963]
1 WLR 163).

Whether a game or a dance, however, the point is that practice makes perfect:

The uniform opinion and practice of eminent conveyancers has always had
great regard paid to it in all courts of justice

(per Lord Hardwicke in *Basset* v *Basset* (1744) 3 Atk 203, p 208); and:

For the exposition of our very complicated real property law, it is proper in
the absence of judicial authority to resort to textbooks which have been
recognised by the courts as representing the views and practice of conveyancers
of repute

(per Byrne J in *Hallis's Hospital and Hague's Contract* [1899] 2 Ch 540, at p 551).
Again, in considering a pre-1926 device adopted for the suppression of equities,
Chitty J observed:

The difficulty I really feel about this part of the case is the danger of doing
anything which may imperil what has been going on for centuries among
conveyancers

(in *Cavitt* v *Real and Personal Advance Co* (1889) 42 Ch D 263, at p 272).

Accordingly, in this book the derivation purely from practice of a number of now
well-established rules is from time to time indicated—eg, as to the root, period and
abstract of title (see pp 95, 96 and 112, and as to other more general terms of an open
contract, see p 77). Indeed, the basic rule as to the formation of a contract for the
sale of land by exchange was authoritatively endorsed by the Court of Appeal
largely because it represented the customary procedure of conveyancers so that the
practical inconveniences of rejecting it would be formidable (*Eccles* v *Bryant &
Pollock* [1948] Ch 93: see p 15 et seq). Again Evershed MR, in finding a scintilla
temporis between conveyance and mortgage within which to feed an estoppel, said:

It is no doubt true to say that in one sense the transaction was one transaction:
but it is equally true to say that it consists necessarily of certain defined steps
which must take place in a certain defined order, if the result intended is
eventually to be achieved. That seems to me not an artificiality, but a necessary
result of the law and of the conveyancing practice which was involved

(*Church of England Building Society* v *Piskor* [1954] Ch 553, at p 561). Further of
course, the implication of terms into agreements very often depends upon practice:
for example, in determining what are the 'usual covenants' to be incorporated into
any particular lease, it is clear that 'it is proper to take the evidence of conveyancers
and others familiar with the practice in reference to leases, and that it is also
permissible to examine books of precedents' (per Maugham J in *Flexman* v *Corbett*
[1930] 1 Ch 672, at p 678: see also *Sweet & Maxwell* v *Universal News Services* [1964]
2 QB 699 and per Foster J in *Chester* v *Buckingham Travel Ltd* [1981] 1 WLR 96, at
p 101; for reference to precedent books, see as well *Re Neeld* [1962] Ch 643).

Thus, as Denning LJ once said:

The practice of the profession in these cases is the best evidence of what the
law is—indeed it makes law

(in *Re Downshire Settled Estates* [1953] Ch 218, at p 279). Yet it is not without significance that the learned lord justice was not in this case upheld on appeal (*Chapman v Chapman* [1954] AC 429), statute having to step into the breach (Variation of Trusts Act 1958). In other words, the potency of practice as an extra-judicial source of law may be thought to have waxed and be now waning. For one thing, it can only fill the gaps left by an absence of other authority of which there is now more than there was, if not yet enough: after all practice cannot by itself *un*make the law (although, as the reader will observe, it has not infrequently led to statutory changes). For another thing, it appears to depend on a uniformity evidenced by a certain authoritative formulation by writers that may be lacking today.

Fifty years or so ago Sargant LJ destructively concluded a judgment by adding that 'the learned judge [Astbury J] attached undue weight to certain expressions in a text book written by a well known conveyancer' (*Re Ryder and Steadman's Contract* [1927] 2 Ch 62, at p 84; it should perhaps be mentioned that the text-book was *Wolstenholme & Cherry's Conveyancing Statutes*, now in its 13th edition, that Sir Benjamin Cherry was not only a well known conveyancer but was also closely concerned in the drafting of the 1925 property legislation and that the case concerned a point of construction of that legislation: see also per Jenkins LJ in *Pawson v Revell* [1958] 2 QB 360, at pp 369–70, but for a number of more reverential references see the citations in the Preface to *Wolstenholme & Cherry's Conveyancing Statutes*, 13th ed, vol 1, p ix, note 1 and more recently and gratifyingly per Ormrod LJ in *Williams & Glyn's Bank v Boland* [1979] Ch 312, at p 337). Then our dear Lord Wilberforce quoted from 'a well-known book of reference on conveyancing matters' and commented:

> My Lords, this passage is almost a perfect illustration of the dangers, well perceived by our predecessors but tending to be neglected in modern times, of placing reliance on textbook authority for an analysis of judicial decisions. It is on the face of it a jumble of unclear propositions not logically related to each other

(in *Johnson v Agnew* [1980] AC 367, at p 395, speaking of the otherwise revered *Williams on Vendor and Purchaser*, 4th ed, 1936; as to credit but not authority being accorded to *Megarry & Wade* in particular, and to judicial authors in general, see a note at (1975) 39 Conv (NS) 384–6). This mention of modern times seems a trifle Chaplinesque in this context where the judiciary increasingly rush in where angels once feared to tread with ex cathedra pronouncements about conveyancing although, as a former editor of the *Conveyancer and Property Lawyer* has commented:

> One of the difficulties today is that the Bar and Bench no longer seem familiar with the "practice of conveyancers", for this is now the almost exclusive province of solicitors and the Land Registry. Who would have thought of arguing about a notional *scintilla temporis* if he had attended a completion or even if he had not been able to find a Latin phrase to help him?

((1963) 27 Conv (NS) 318; but see, for the regard paid to certain expert evidence, *Sykes v Midland Bank Executor and Trustee Co Ltd* [1969] 2 QB 518, on appeal [1971] 1 QB 113). Attention has been drawn elsewhere to:

> A curiosity of judicial administration . . . that, although the case is exclusively about equity and real property law, none of the nine judges involved was a Chancery lawyer

(HWRW at (1974) 90 LQR 433, commenting on *Steadman v Steadman* [1976] AC 536, the significant conveyancing inferences from which were noted at (1974) 38 Conv (NS) 388–91). The gifted amateur approach was more recently exemplified in a case where counsel had 'laid great stress upon the importance of these and other conveyancing difficulties': first Ormrod LJ remarked, 'It is not easy for one whose experience has been acquired in a different branch of the law to assess the real significance of these contentions but they must be taken seriously' and then he dismissed the contentions as exaggerated (in *Williams & Glyn's Bank Ltd* v *Boland* [1979] Ch 312, at p 339; on appeal [1981] AC 487).

In consequence, perhaps, of this lack of expertise, the judiciary appear particularly ready to reject current practice: our judges seem unduly impressed by the immemorial. Thus even in the last century, James LJ held the view that:

> though the settled practice of conveyancers is to be looked upon as part of the common law, I do not think that a modern practice in which some conveyancers differ from others is to be treated as a part of the law of the land

(in *Re Ford & Hill* (1879) 10 Ch D 365, at p 370). What then of twentieth-century practice? In the course of finding a solicitor guilty of negligence, Danckwerts J, with regard to evidence called to show conduct 'in accordance with the usual practice of solicitors,' expressed himself as follows:

> Counsel for the defendant contended that I was bound to accept their evidence of the proper practice in these matters, and (if I understood him correctly) I was not at liberty to draw on my own conveyancing experience or reach conclusions from cases. . . which would suggest that their practices were below standard. This I cannot accept

(in *Goody* v *Baring* [1956] 1 WLR 448, at p 455). Consistent with this was the treatment accorded to a practice 'developed by solicitors of their own initiative over recent years' and 'adopted for good or ill by experienced solicitors in the London area, at any rate, in a significant and by no means insubstantial minority of cases' in the firmly-held belief that they could by this practice best carry out their client's instructions: in *Domb* v *Isoz* (1978) 248 EG 783–6, a deputy judge was reported as follows: 'While he fully appreciated the considerations which had led solicitors to adopt the practice of exchanging contracts by telephone, his lordship's opinion was that it was a bad practice'. But on appeal Buckley LJ did not agree: in his view happily the procedure would not involve 'any undesirable degree of risk' ([1980] Ch 548, at p 558; see further p 19).

A more awful example had already occurred in *Re King's Will Trusts* [1964] Ch 542, where Pennycuick J, as he recognised, considered a question:

> which is of some general importance to conveyancers and has given rise to uncertainty among the learned authors of textbooks

([1964] 1 All ER 833, at p 834, a dictum omitted, perhaps significantly, from the text of the *Law Reports*). The question was whether a signed written assent was essential even though given by personal representatives in their own favour (eg, as trustees). The established answer according to the prevailing practice of conveyancers as evidenced by the clear better view of writers was that an implied assent was possible (ie, despite s 36(4) of the Administration of Estates Act 1925). Over the years many titles have been accepted as good on this basis. Yet the learned judge paid not even lip-service to the practice of conveyancers as an indication of the law, and equally never had in mind the inconvenient conveyancing consequences, in coming to a different answer (cp per Goulding J in *Oakley* v *Boston* [1976] QB 270 (CA), at pp 283–4).

In the first edition of this book the suggestion was made parenthetically (at p 7) that sufficiently authoritative formations of current conveyancing practice might be found in the published Opinions of the Council of The Law Society (*Digest*, 1954, vol 1, with Supplements, also *Law Society's Gazette* from time to time). However, this idea has since received rather a rebuff in no less a place than the House of Lords.

In *Brown* v *Inland Revenue Commissioners* [1965] AC 244, reliance was firmly placed by a solicitor on an Opinion expressed by the Council of The Law Society, but this reliance proved misplaced. Lord Reid pronounced:

> This opinion, coming from so responsible a body, negatives any suggestion of professional malpractice by the appellant or any other solicitor who has acted in accordance with it. But it was not argued that it has any binding force and I do not think it can be supported in law

(at p 258); and Lord Guest added:

> I have come to the conclusion that the opinion given by the Society is not well-founded. But whether the opinion is sound or not, it could not in any case be the basis upon which a general custom of the profession could be founded

(at p 264).

Of course, if it were not for the latter part of each of these quotations, it could have been contended that the case only invalidated the particular Opinion in point (that is, as to retention of interest earned by client account). But as it is, their lordships appear to make it clear that this sort of Opinion, whatever aspect of practice it may concern, will not in any event be regarded as making law (cp notes entitled 'Suspect Opinions' at [1978] Conv 85 and 178 et seq; also 'Our Masters' Voices' at [1982] Conv 171 and 326 et seq).

It becomes pertinent at this point, therefore, to enquire whether the practice of registered conveyancing will ever make law. An aspect of this question has already been commented on by the courts. In *Strand Securities Ltd* v *Caswell* [1965] Ch 958 (reversing [1965] Ch 373), Cross J at first instance observed that:

> Just as in general conveyancing matters the court always gives weight to the practice of conveyancers, so in questions under the Land Registration Act 1925 the court ought to give weight to any established practice in the Land Registry which is not clearly inconsistent with the wording of the Act or the Rules

(ibid, p 386). Thus the practice, not of private conveyancers, but that dictated by the Land Registry, was to become a new source of law, an extension by analogy which was strongly criticised by Dr A R Mellows in the *Law Society's Gazette* (1964) vol 61, at p 724, and as strongly defended (notwithstanding the view of the Court of Appeal, below) by the then Chief Land Registrar at ibid (1965) vol 62, at p 507. But this new source was soon stemmed. In the Court of Appeal, Lord Denning MR uttered the counter-observation that:

> The judge was much influenced by the practice of the Land Registry. He thought he ought to give weight to it, just as to the practice of conveyancers. I do not agree with this. We cannot allow the registrar by his practice to make bad law

(ibid, p 977). Harman and Russell LJJ permitted themselves no such general observations but concurred in holding erroneous the particular practice in question (one of requiring production by a lessee of his lessor's land certificate). Further reference should also be made to a case in which Goulding J respectfully read and firmly rejected as wrong in law certain passages in Curtis and Ruoff on *Registered Conveyancing* describing practice as to the protection of mortgages (*Barclays Bank Ltd* v *Taylor* [1973] Ch 63; reversed without contradiction at [1974] Ch 137).

Even if practice of conveyancers is in fact no longer *laying* the rails upon which sales of land in general are to travel, such practice can still be said to *constitute* the rails upon which any particular sale of land will run, usually with mechanical efficiency, to a mutually satisfying terminus, the parties living happily ever after. Nonetheless, just as principles without practice may get you nowhere, so practice without principles will be of little help if you go off the rails, that is, if some dispute arises. Now the truth can hardly be concealed that the pure conveyancing question coming to court has been a comparative rarity. As one very learned writer has written:

> One merit of the traditional English system of conveyancing is that it gives rise to so little litigation. This is not because all its principles are too clear for argument—there are indeed astonishingly few decisions on the absolute fundamentals of title—but more probably because negotiations between vendor and purchaser are so commonly handled under legal advice from before the stage of contract, and this is in practice the best (if not the cheapest) precaution against the kind of unpleasant surprise which may drive the parties into court

(HWR Wade in [1954] Camb LJ 89). Whilst not denying the dangers of 'doing-it-yourself,' the present writer feels that legal advice is *not* the real reason for the lack of litigation—save in so far, that is, as another writer's view can be accepted, that

> most conveyancing solicitors are busy and pressed for time and therefore reluctant to engage in litigation if it can be avoided

(GA Grove (1961) 24 MLR 124). Rather, the real reason would appear to be that once the game has begun, the formation and formalities over and the parties bound to play, thereafter they are playing on the same side: they each have in mind the same result and either do not want or else cannot afford to have the game interrupted by technical offences. Thus in *Property and Bloodstock* v *Emerton* [1968] Ch 94, Danckwerts LJ was able to observe (at p 117):

> In the present case, the purchaser is not insisting upon his strict rights. As I have already observed, both vendor . . . (the mortgagees) and purchaser are in agreement. They look forward to that happy moment when, freed from the unhappy interference by the mortgagor at the eleventh hour, their contract, which they both regard as still in force, will proceed to completion and the purchaser will obtain the property sold to him and the mortgagees will receive the purchase price.

In other words, the conveyancing machinery is either oiled 'by the goodwill of both parties,' being willing, or else forced along by one or other's desperation to complete, ie, to move in or to get the money and to effect other transactions (see (1961) 25 Conv (NS) 90, preferring the latter 'game of chicken' to the former view of GA Grove, loc cit). Whatever the explanation, however, strength and support may be sought to justify the rarity of litigation from the probably greater rarity of the actually bad title.

This latter rarity appears largely attributable to the fact that the health of most titles has for very many years been submitted to regular medical check-ups. The repeated investigation of unregistered titles by qualified persons on each disposition has produced a considerable cumulative preventive effect so far as legal defects are concerned. Equally the all-seeing eyes at HM Land Registry continue to perform a similar function for registered titles on each transfer so as to preserve intact the curative effect of registration itself (see pp 145, 156). So titles to land generally speaking are not too bad.

Granted all this, the fact still remains that disputes can and do arise. Surely most solicitors would concede that they have clients who are litigation prone even in this prosaic context. Thus Devlin J described the defendants in one case as 'very old and not very reliable' (*Parker* v *Clark* [1960] 1 WLR 286, at p 291), and in another Danckwerts LJ remarked that 'both plaintiff and defendant are women, and the defendant, Mrs Sweet, is an elderly woman between seventy and eighty years of age, who appears to have been liable to change her mind from time to time' (in *Davies* v *Sweet* [1962] 2 QB 300, at p 305). Again, the sort of man who hopes to rest in peace with a 'home-made' will may now more often turn his hand to conveyancing either for himself or even for others. Indeed examples of this species have been spotted in a number of modern cases. In one, the vendor 'went to an estate agent and got a standard form which he typed out filling in the blanks and this form was signed by both parties over a 6d stamp' (*Gavaghan* v *Edwards* [1961] 2 QB 220, per Danckwerts LJ at p 222). In another 'the parties did not go to solicitors. The agent produced a photographic standard form of agreement into which he typed the names of the parties and so forth, and the parties signed it in his presence and he witnessed their signatures' (*Scheggia* v *Gradwell* [1963] 1 WLR 1049, per Lord Denning MR at p 1052). Then fairly recently, Templeman J contemplated 'a deal between laymen in a hurry . . . simple chaps, I do not suppose that they will have the slightest idea of the full meaning and consequences' (*Re Wallis & Simmonds (Builders) Ltd* [1974] 1 WLR 391, at p 403).

Laymen and estate agents, what else can one expect? At least, you think all that can ever truly be said of solicitors, despite any dispute, is to echo the words of Wilberforce J:

> No doubt—and I fully accept this—the solicitors acting for the vendors were doing their best to get the matter through. There was a pleasant spirit of co-operation between them and the solicitors for the purchasers; they acted in sympathy, and so far as it was possible for them to do so, expeditiously in trying to get the matter completed

(in *Re Hewitt's Contract* [1963] 1 WLR 1298, at p 1305). Unhappily, however, this is not always echoable [sic]: resounding instead may be the words of Younger J speaking of a long correspondence between solicitors:

> much of which, I regret to say, magnifies difficulties which were really non-existent and operated to keep apart this vendor and purchaser, who were both, I am sure, eager to conclude their bargain

(in *North* v *Loomes* (1919) 120 LT 533, at p 536, not reproduced at [1919] 1 Ch 378), and Danckwerts J:

> At this stage there was a willing vendor and a willing purchaser, and I cannot understand why the two solicitors could not have got together in a reasonable manner and settled the matter without further controversy and so saved the expense of these actions

(in *Finkielkraut* v *Monohan* [1949] 2 All ER 234, at p 236G; see also at p 238B). Again, in a more modern conveyancing case, Harman LJ commented that:

> Letters passed through the hands of two sets of solicitors who, during the course of negotiations, both distinguished themselves by the dilatory nature of their proceedings. It is really rather lamentable to see the leisurely way in which these matters seem to have been attended to

(in *Wilkinson (AL)* v *Brown* [1966] 1 WLR 194, at p 197). And rather more recently the correspondence between the two solicitors acting in a conveyancing matter was described as 'desultory' and 'inconsistent' by Widgery LJ (in *Griffiths* v *Young* [1970] Ch 675, at p 682, F and G: the two solicitors hardly redeemed themselves by offering to the court conflicting versions of their telephone conversation which had begun the correspondence). No wonder Danckwerts J felt able to differentiate, as he once did, between 'reasonable behaviour' and 'mere conveyancing' (in *Re Barr's Contract, Moorwell Buildings Ltd* v *Barr* [1956] Ch 551, at p 558). But in a case concerning conveyancing costs, Donaldson J was able to give credit where credit was due by recognising that 'A skilful lack of expedition may also on occasion be in the interests of the client, and might on an exceptional occasion justify some increase in the remuneration' (*Property and Reversionary Investment Corporation Ltd* v *Secretary of State for the Environment* [1975] 1 WLR 1504, at p 1511; for the concept of the benevolent mistake, see notes at (1974) 38 Conv (NS) 311 and 392, about *Harrison* v *Battye* [1975] 1 WLR 58, CA).

Beyond all this 'litigation prone' becomes too light a label if, as in some cases, there is in addition to a litigious client, 'a failure by the solicitor to appreciate the proper legal position' (per Danckwerts LJ in *Smith* v *Mansi* [1963] 1 WLR 26, at p 34). This utterance indicates where lies the solution, without litigation, of every dispute. It brings us back with a bump to the dangers of practice without principle. Following on from this, but more in order to explain his approach and purpose, the writer would borrow passages from the works of two most eminent conveyancers, one of the early nineteenth century and the other of the early twentieth century. First, one must not overlook:

> the misfortune of a person who, either as a clerk to a solicitor or as a student in a conveyancer's chambers, begins to study the practice of conveyancing, [which] is, that he is taught by form or precedent, rather than principle. He is made to copy precedents, without knowing either their application, or those rules on which they are grounded. When he begins to prepare drafts, he is led to expect all his information from those forms: and his knowledge is, in the end, as limited as the means by which he has been instructed

(*Preston's Conveyancing*, vol 1, p ix; see (1950) 14 Conv (NS) 346–9). Secondly, perhaps those who are already 'experienced conveyancers'—the practitioner's counterpart of the mythical 'reasonable man'—may also submit to being led, where only the late T Cyprian Williams would have dared otherwise to lead them:

> to discard the prejudices which are apt to become encrusted on their minds— like barnacles on the bottom of an old wooden ship—in the course of a lifetime given up to practice, and to regard the law of sale of land from the point of view of a jurist. The writer thinks, indeed, that it is the plain man and the student who are more apt to observe the anomalies and absurdities of the law, and often get nearer to the juristic point of view than the lawyer immersed in practice. But it will do lawyers of long experience no harm to try to regain the layman's or the student's freshness of outlook

(*Sale of Land*, p xxix).

In the ensuing chapters, therefore, an endeavour is made to present the basic but peculiar principles both in general and as they affect practice on a sale and purchase of land.

II FORMATION

THE initial peculiarity of a contract for the sale of land lies in the manner of its formation, ie, in the way in which it becomes binding upon the parties. Before proceeding, however, let it be conceded that this is a pseudo-peculiarity, produced not by principle, but by practice. For the principle is plain: whether or not such a contract has been constituted depends primarily upon the true construction of what the parties have said or written, looked at in the light of all those elementary rules about offer and acceptance (see *Gibson* v *Manchester City Council* [1979] 1 WLR 294, HL, reaffirming this approach despite an alternative test based on mere intention adopted in the Court of Appeal: cp *Storer* v *Manchester City Council* [1974] 1 WLR 1403, CA, which was distinguished). But the practice is a little peculiar.

A EXCHANGE

In the ordinary sale of residential property, the parties tend to meet on the property, mostly at the instance of an estate agent, and after the customary conducted tour, they then and there agree on a price. Prima facie, therefore, the essentials of a binding contract have already emerged. But fortunately laymen, having perhaps perused one of the proliferating paperback guides to house-purchase, now often know enough to agree only 'subject to contract'. If they do not, their estate agents should, and in any case the writing requirements of s 40 of the Law of Property Act 1925 (see p 32) may provide an eleventh hour.

Do the parties appreciate the legal significance of agreeing 'subject to contract'? The judicial view is that they do:

> Ever since the case of *Winn* v *Bull* (1877) 7 Ch D 29, if not long before, it has been well settled that the result of an offer "subject to contract" means that the matter remains in negotiation until a formal contract is executed, that is, if the contract is recorded in two parts until the formal contracts are exchanged. . .
> Taught by experience in these courts it is everyday practice for intending purchasers of property who are making an offer to make their offer "subject to contract" with the result that they are not at that time bound and have a *locus poenitentiae* until the formal contracts are exchanged

(per Maugham LJ in *George Trollope & Sons* v *Martyn Bros* [1934] 2 KB 436). This statement has received the approval of the Court of Appeal in *Eccles* v *Bryant & Pollock* [1948] Ch 93, where it was reaffirmed that either party in law may resile even after agreement of the terms, engrossment and signature of a formal contract provided exchange has not yet taken place.

A critical illustration occurred in *King* v *O'Shee* (1951) 158 EG 83, where:

> By 1st June 1950, each party had signed one part of the contract, its terms having been agreed by their solicitors. Plaintiff's part was posted to defendants who received it on 2nd June. They later received a telephone message from plaintiff saying he withdrew. Defendant's solicitors had not posted their part of the engrossment to plaintiff's solicitors. For the defence it was contended

15

that the contract to purchase had been concluded on 1st June. His lordship said that there having been no concluded exchange, either party might recall his words.

Equally fatal were the facts of *Sim* v *Griffiths* (1963), commented on at 107 SJ 462 (where the vendor died after signing her part of the contract and after the purchaser's part plus deposit had been received but before her part was posted; Cross J held that no contract existed; contrast the position where a deed has been delivered in escrow: see *D'Silva* v *Lister House Development Ltd* [1971] Ch 17, and p 322).

This established ability to resile led eventually to the imaginatively named and much maligned sub-practice of 'gazumping,' ie, of potential vendors increasing the agreed price of property (especially houses) sold 'subject to contract' and the ignominy seems to extend also to selling at an increased price to a different purchaser. The original prospective purchaser will nowadays have a tendency to flaunt his disappointment and indignation—for one thing he will likely enough have been hit in the pocket (eg, surveyor's fees) and for another he may not be willing or able to pay more. Is the potential vendor to be blamed? It is true that most solicitors and many clients will say that they regard an agreement 'subject to contract' as morally, if not legally, binding (see, eg, *Pimms Ltd* v *Tallow Chandlers in the City of London* [1964] 2 QB 547, at p 552). Yet much more worthy of notice is Sachs J's penetrating judgment on:

> this hybrid type of "subject to contract" transaction, which is so often referred to as a gentleman's agreement but which experience shows is only too often a transaction in which each side hopes the other will act like a gentleman and neither intends so to act if it is against his material interests

(*Goding* v *Frazer* [1967] 1 WLR 286, at p 293). And, for example, the duty of trustees to sell only at the best price reasonably obtainable will override commercial morality, ie, on receiving a higher offer before exchange, they must 'gazump'. This is subject, of course, to the dictates of proper prudence which would permit trustees to 'pray in aid the common sense rule underlying the old proverb: "A bird in the hand is worth two in the bush" ' (per Wynn-Parry J in *Buttle* v *Saunders* [1950] 2 All ER 193, at p 195). Nevertheless, any inflation of the housing market must surely lead even common prudence to speak in almost all cases for the better price.

Nevertheless, 'gazumping' by vendors attracted so many newsworthy attacks that the Law Commission was hastily asked to concoct some legislative solution. But after three years deliberation all that emerged was a recommendation of no change in law:

> In the context of house purchase it is in our view of paramount importance that the law should place no fetter on the freedom of each of the parties, and in particular the buyer, to refrain from binding commitment if he so wishes

(*Report on 'Subject to Contract' Agreements* 1975 Law Com No 65, para 7). This quasi-authoritative view does not mean that private anti-gazumping devices have not been attempted with the idea of binding one side only. Thus in *Pateman* v *Pay* (1974) 232 EG 457, following an agreement on the property as to price, the vendor signed a so-called option agreement at the insistence of the purchaser—'a rough diamond, frightened of gazumpers', according to Templeman J—but to no effect: a degree of 'sharp practice' and a lack of contractual intent were found. Again in *Damm* v *Herrtage* (1974) 234 EG 365, the device involved an immediate oral contract sufficiently evidenced by a deposit receipt signed by the vendor—this was to be relied on only if the vendor tried to resile before exchange in the ordinary way. But this too failed: the vendor had not intended to be bound, held Pennycuick V-C who also observed: 'Whatever the ethical merits of gazumping, it seems to me that this counter-device comes very near sharp practice and could easily be used as an engine of fraud' (ibid p 369). In other words, all appear agreed that here any cure must be worse than the disease (but see a comparison of English and Scottish practice by J Gilchrist Smith at (1979) 76 *Law Society's Gazette* 492).

The actual method of exchange calls for some comment. In the leading case on the significance of 'subject to contract' namely *Eccles* v *Bryant & Pollock* [1948] Ch 93, a rather dated reference was made to:

> the ceremonial form of exchange, namely, the meeting of solicitors in the office of one of them—the vendor's solicitor's office as a rule—and the passing of the two signed engrossments over the table, [which] may be taken to have fallen—and, indeed, no doubt it has—into disuse to a certain extent, particularly when there are firms of solicitors in different parts of the country

adding that:

> an exchange by post would, in many cases, take the place of the old more ceremonial exchange, but that an exchange was contemplated by both firms of solicitors from beginning to end appears to me to be clear from what took place and from the correspondence

(per Lord Greene MR [1948] 1 Ch 97). In practice today exchange of contracts does most commonly occur by post but is still not quite free from unsettled queries, in particular as to the precise moment at which the contract is concluded. Thus one query was raised but not decided in *Eccles* v *Bryant & Pollock* itself, Lord Greene MR saying:

> When an exchange takes place by post and a contract comes into existence through the act of exchange, the earliest date at which such a contract can come into existence, it appears to me, would be the date when the later of the two documents to be put in the post is actually put in the post. Another view might be that the exchange takes place and the contract thereby comes into existence when, and not before, the respective parties or their solicitors receive from their "opposite numbers" their parts of the contract. It is not necessary here to choose between these two views

(at pp 97–8, see also per Cohen LJ at p 107 appearing to favour the former). Posting rather than receipt would certainly be consistent with the ordinary contract rule (remember *Household Fire Insurance Co* v *Grant* (1879) 4 Ex D 216), but it is not of universal application. For a relevant example, it was not applied by the Court of Appeal in *Holwell Securities Ltd* v *Hughes* [1974] 1 WLR 155, where an option to purchase land was exercisable by notice in writing: the option was not effectively exercised by a letter which went astray after posting. Likewise actual delivery surely represents substantially what was envisaged by 'exchange'—as Lord Greene MR has explained:

> When you are dealing with contracts for the sale of land, it is of the greatest importance to the vendor that he should have a document signed by the purchaser, and to the purchaser that he should have a document signed by the vendor. It is of the greatest importance that there should be no dispute whether a contract had or had not been made and that there should be no dispute as to the terms of it. This particular procedure of exchange ensures that none of these difficulties will arise. Each party has got what is a document of title, because directly a contract in writing relating to land is entered into, it is a document of title

(in *Eccles* v *Bryant & Pollock* [1948] Ch 93, at pp 99–100).

Until the other party's part is actually held and inspected, its signature and sufficiency must still be suspect. Thus if the parties' parts happen not to be identical, no contract will have been concluded (as in *Harrison* v *Battye* [1975] 1 WLR 58, CA, where the discrepancy was only as to the amount of the deposit). Again the absence of one party's signature will be fatal (as in *Beck* v *Box* (1973) 231 EG 1295, concerning a contract between two couples where one husband had not signed). Equally any uninitialled alterations may render the contract either not binding at all (*Earl* v *Mawson* (1974) 232 EG 1315, CA) or at least unenforceable (*New Hart Builders Ltd* v *Brindley* [1975] Ch 342—ie, no memorandum within s 40(1) of the Law of Property Act 1925).

Yet ignoring such persuasive points, the Law Society's Conditions of Sale still stipulate that where exchange is by post 'the contract shall be made when the last part is posted' (1980 edition, No 10(1)). Could this be a 'chicken or egg' condition? Unless and until the parties become bound according to law, it is simply a term of a non-existent contract. But afterwards it may serve the different purpose of dating the contract so that the general time for completion can be conveniently calculated (ibid, No 21(1); cp National Conditions of Sale, 20th ed, No 1(7) which restricts itself to dating not making). And in any dispute as to the conclusion of contract, the condition might be referred to as 'an indication of what was in the contemplation of the parties' (per Blackett-Ord V-C in *Harrison* v *Battye* [1974] 2 All ER 1201, at p 1204; on appeal [1975] 1 WLR 58). Nevertheless this reference might itself mislead.

In the last cited case, the vendor's solicitors had made a little mistake and posted back the purchaser's part instead of forwarding the vendor's part. At first instance, Blackett-Ord V-C applied the *Eccles* case and held that 'The parties contemplated entering into a contract by exchange and exchange only, and as no exchange had in fact taken place, no contract had come into existence' (headnote at [1974] 2 All ER 1201). He also rejected, without reasons, an argument that the vendor's solicitors had become trustees for the purchaser of the vendor's part of the contract (ibid, p 1205). His decision was affirmed by the Court of Appeal on the quite different ground that the two parts were not in identical terms. The absence of any actual exchange was *not* seen as fatal: thus Sir Eric Sachs, whilst expressly reserving his opinion, said (at [1975] 1 WLR 61):

> It is, however, right, in view of the full and helpful argument, to record my having been much impressed with the view that upon the posting by the vendor's solicitors of the second letter of October 9, there was communicated to the purchasers an unequivocal appropriation to him (sic) of the counterpart signed by the vendor; that accordingly as between the vendor and the purchasers the latter became entitled to possession of the document, and that accordingly an effective exchange of contract and documents occurred despite the clerical error in the vendor's solicitors' office.

Even Lord Denning MR would have 'overlooked' the absence of an actual exchange, regarding this view as 'a telling point' (ibid, p 60). So the eventual posting of the last part would presumably have been strictly irrelevant to the making or dating of the contract.

But there is more to be said about the mechanics: postal exchanges, having superseded ceremonial exchanges, are in course of being replaced by telephonic exchanges. The problem in practice is to achieve simultaneous exchanges in a chain of transactions. Clients buying and selling usually want to own one house at a time, neither more nor less, and will instruct their solicitors, expressly or perhaps impliedly, not to exchange contracts in either without the other. Failure to observe such instructions has already led to liability for professional negligence (*Buckley* v *Lane Herdman & Co* [1977] CLY 3143). A solution has been found in a new-fangled device called the telephone: solicitors speak into the mouthpiece saying, 'Let us deem an exchange'. Surprise, surprise—it works. In *Domb* v *Isoz* [1980] Ch 548, the Court of Appeal held that a constructive exchange of contracts by telephone was both authorised and effective: contrary to the view at first instance, there was no purported dispensing with exchange and the machinery was of no interest to a client who 'impliedly authorises, and ostensibly authorises, his solicitor to effect exchange of contracts in such manner and by such agents as the solicitor may think fit' (per Templeman LJ at p 563). In this case, the two parts of the contract were in the possession of the vendor's solicitor at the time of the exchange by telephone, but this does not appear to be an essential element: the decision should cover the case where solicitors each still retain their own client's part and undertake by telephone to hold it to the other's order.

At first instance, deputy judge Dillon had thought that telephone exchanges were not only unauthorised but also 'bad practice' largely because of the ample scope left for conflicts of evidence, everything turning 'on an oral conversation and possibly on the precise inflection of the words used' (at (1978) 248 EG 783, 786). On appeal however Buckley LJ saw the practice as good enough if not foolproof: the handling of telephones by solicitors 'does not, in my view, involve any undesirable degree of risk of it leading to errors or confusion' (at [1980] Ch 558). Nevertheless readers should appreciate that risks are involved in such constructive exchanges, in particular the signature and sufficiency of the other side's part cannot be ascertained without actual possession. Further Templeman LJ, with foolproofing in mind, suggested that exchanges by telephone should only be carried out by partners and that a short formula for attendance notes should be adopted (at p 564; see also 'Council News' at *Law Society's Gazette* vol 77, No 6, p 144 and a note at [1980] Conv 87–92).

Exchange of contracts by telephone is now expressly provided for in the 1980 Edition of The Law Society's Conditions of Sale, No 10(2) and also by the 20th Edition of the National Conditions of Sale, No 1(6). Each of these conditions should be regarded strictly as terms of unmade contracts (ie, in contemplation of exchange) and as unnecessary in the light of the decision in *Domb* v *Isoz* [1980] Ch 548, CA, which recognised the practice of telephonic exchanges by solicitors as generally valid anyway.

Exchange of contracts by telex is also provided for but may still give rise to technical hitches. Where a contract is made by instantaneous communication, such as telex, the general rule applies that the contract is made when and where the acceptance was received: *Brinkibon Ltd* v *Stahag Stahl GmbH* [1982] 2 WLR 264, HL. However this general rule may only be applicable where the vendor and purchaser themselves, rather than their solicitors, make the contract by telex and the application of the rule may be affected by other factors (see per Lord Wilberforce at p 267). Further the question may occur where a contract for the sale of land is made by telex of whether there is sufficient evidence of signed writing to satisfy s 40(1) of the Law of Property Act 1925. As to the sufficiency of signatures in such transactions, see a note at [1979] Conv 157–8.

Quite apart from the mechanics of exchange, various other more or less marvellous mysteries can be conjured up by the magic words 'subject to contract'. For a substantial instance, the Court of Appeal has recently told us twice, so it must be true, that an overwhelming principle exists. Once an agreement has been made 'subject to contract' (eg, in the first letters between the parties) the words will, even without being repeated, continue to qualify everything which is subsequently said or done unless and until the parties expressly or by necessary implication agree that the qualification should be expunged. In *Sherbrooke* v *Dipple* (1980) 255 EG 1203, CA, there had been an interruption in negotiations of over a year but the magic lasted: no contract. In *Cohen* v *Nessdale Ltd* [1982] 2 All ER 97, CA, the interruption was of eight months and it might have been reasonable to suppose a binding agreement, but no: the original qualification remained effective. Note notes at [1981] Conv 165–7 and [1982] Conv 396–7 and reconcile *Griffiths* v *Young* [1970] Ch 675, CA, post pp 22–3 by presuming that the waiver there must have amounted to an expungement within the principle here.

Incidentally in *Sherbrooke* v *Dipple* supra it was not contemplated that 'subject to contract' should lead in the ordinary way to exchange of contracts but that 'no one was to be bound unless and until the vendors executed and delivered a conveyance' (per Templeman LJ at p 177). An unusual but not impossible thing for the parties to intend. Thus, rather similarly, the magic words are applicable but peculiarly qualified where the agreement is for a term of years and the transaction proceeds directly towards the grant of the lease itself. The primary position is that the state of negotiation continues and there will be no contract to enforce until exchange of lease and counterpart (see most recently *Derby & Co Ltd* v *ITC Pension Trust Ltd* (1977) 245 EG 569). But the secondary prevailing position is that if the grantor happens actually to execute the lease as an unconditional deed then it is immediately binding as such even without any exchange (see *D'Silva* v *Lister House Development Ltd* [1971] Ch 17). This conflict in consequences clearly constitutes a trap in practice which may be fallen into whenever the efficient preparation for completion involves the execution of documents under seal in advance, ie, particularly where a company is concerned.

Another point just worth mentioning is the question of construing the contract once it has been made by exchange. The theoretical proposition is that, although the court is entitled to look at the factual background and the aim of the transaction, no evidence either of the negotiations, or of the parties' intentions, should be received (see *Prenn* v *Simmonds* [1971] 1 WLR 1381, HL). Thus the introduction into an agreement of the words 'subject to contract' would not only mean that there is no contract until exchange, but also that the formal written contract eventually produced must be construed alone ignoring any preceding correspondence and conversations, because until its parts were exchanged all was negotiation. This proposition, however, must be made without prejudice to any potential liabilities for misrepresentation or non-disclosure. It is also subject, of course, to the possibility of the court finding and enforcing an oral antecedent promise which induced the written contract, ie, in effect an overriding collateral contract (see *City & Westminster Properties (1934) Ltd* v *Mudd* [1959] Ch 129: also *Mendelssohn* v *Normand Ltd* [1970] 1 QB 177). However, the evidence will have to be clear and compelling in order to qualify a formal written document of the present sort (see per Goulding J in *Lee-Parker* v *Izzet (No 2)* [1972] 2 All ER 800, at p 803). Further the proposition can hardly prevent the application of the equitable remedy of rectification where appropriate which necessarily calls for evidence of prior negotiations and intentions (see per Russell LJ in *Joscelyne* v *Nissen* [1970] 2 QB 86, at p 98). Again, in a tax case, Megarry J remarked:

> A bargain struck "subject to contract" creates no legally enforceable contract, yet I cannot think that it would be right to exclude all evidence of such a bargain in arriving for fiscal purposes at what is the true nature of the contract subsequently made

(in *IRC* v *Church Commissioners* [1975] 1 WLR 251, at p 268; on appeal [1977] AC 329).

Consequently, despite theoretical lip-service paid to the exclusive and sacrosanct words of the formal contract, it is never too difficult to discover some practical excuse for scrutinising the 'subject to contract' negotiations. Nevertheless, it should still not be assumed that such a scrutiny will always prove fruitful (see *Lloyd* v *Stanbury* [1971] 1 WLR 535, in which the written contract 'professionally drawn' and 'in unambiguous terms' prevailed over the unestablished intentions of the vendor; also *Hill* v *Harris* [1965] 2 QB 601, where discussions and letters in the course of negotiation were superseded by the formal documents).

Here a relevant reference might be made to *Clark* v *Follett* (1973) 48 TC 677, where a taxpayer argued that an intending purchaser of land 'subject to contract' had during discussions with his intending vendor already acquired a proprietary interest or right by estoppel prior to exchange. This argument was not accepted by Goulding J, who also held that a transaction remains a bargain made at arm's length for capital gains tax purposes despite the vendor's honourable refusal to gazump. Unfortunately no reference was made to this case in *Salvation Army Trustee Co Ltd* v *West Yorkshire Metropolitan County Council* (1980) 41 P & CR 179 where Woolf J regarded 'the principle of proprietary estoppel as being capable of extending to the disposal of an interest in land where the disposal is closely linked by an arrangement that also involves the acquiring of an interest in land' (at p 192). Accordingly two separate but connected sales 'subject to contract' became binding on both sides irrespective of exchange. True this happened in somewhat abnormal circumstances, but the principle as stated may seem applicable to an entirely normal chain of residential purchases. Further reference should be made to a note at [1983] Conv 85–7.

More important perhaps is the fact that the Court of Appeal has occasionally shown a rather derisory attitude towards the understandably prevalent idea that an agreement 'subject to contract' always requires an 'exchange of contracts' to become binding. In *Smith* v *Mansi* [1963] 1 WLR 26, the vendor and purchaser, having agreed 'subject to contract,' instructed the *same* solicitor who drew up *one* formal document which the purchaser signed first and passed on to the vendor who also signed it, before handing it back to the solicitor. Later the vendor, encouraged by the solicitor, contended that he was not bound because the contract had not been formally exchanged. Said Danckwerts LJ (at p 32):

> This, in my view, was a mistaken view of the law, based on the practice where two separate solicitors act for persons who have bought and sold "subject to contract" and there are two documents, see *Eccles* v *Bryant, supra*; but *Eccles* v *Bryant* was a case of the very ordinary type where there was a sale "subject to contract" and there were two solicitors and two documents to be exchanged. Where there is only one document as the contract and only one solicitor, acting for both parties, the idea of exchange, in my opinion, can only be described as artificial nonsense. It is impossible to carry out. Once a complete contract has been signed by both parties there is nothing more to be done.

This strongly worded statement is now more indicative of attitude than it is significant in practice, for it has become the rule that one solicitor alone may not act for both parties (see Practice Rule, with exceptions, published in *The Law Society's Gazette* (1972) vol 69, p 1117). Compare, however, *Beck* v *Box* (1973) 231 EG 1295, where an unqualified go-between acted, and *Earl* v *Mawson* (1974) 232 EG 1315, CA, where different offices of the same firm of solicitors acted; in each a top copy was to be signed by one side and the carbon copy by the other side but in neither was actual exchange regarded as a requisite (in fact both the contracts failed for want of due signatures or initials). Presumably the situation remains the same where there happens to be only one document despite two separate solicitors acting, ie, once signed by both parties it will be binding without waiting for 'some mysterious rite . . . labelled "exchange"' (cp per Russell LJ in *Smith* v *Mansi* [1963] 1 WLR 26, at p 34).

Bearing some little resemblance to this attitude is the proposition that 'subject to contract' negotiations do not necessarily negative the possibility of some collateral liability subsisting between the parties (eg, in quasi-contract). For example, where a prospective purchaser has requested the prospective vendor to make alterations to the property and has agreed (expressly or, presumably, by implication) to accept responsibility for the cost, then if the negotiations for a contract of sale break down the cost of the alterations made can nevertheless be recovered from the prospective purchaser (see *Brewer Street Investments Ltd* v *Barclays Woollen Co Ltd* [1954] 1 QB 428, CA). This would clearly be so if the blame for the breakdown of negotiations could be placed on the prospective purchaser alone and apparently would remain true if no blame attached to either party, but not if the blame was the prospective vendor's alone since he would also be taking the benefit of the alterations (see ibid). It will be appreciated that in referring in this way to blame, the Court of Appeal was obliged to disregard the submission that where an agreement is made 'subject to contract' it should follow that each side has an absolute right to withdraw from the negotiations and could not be said to be at fault in doing so (see per Denning LJ, in ibid at p 437).

Further evidence of this attitude was encountered in *Griffiths* v *Young* [1970] Ch 675. In this case a solicitor's letter expressly contemplating 'subject to contract' negotiations was held by the Court of Appeal to have been superseded by a subsequent unconditional offer and acceptance over the telephone. Put another way, the suspensive condition embodied in the words 'subject to contract' was treated as having been waived so as to produce there and then and most informally a binding contract. Thus an agreement 'subject to contract' could hardly be said any more to stand or fall solely by reference to a formal exchange, which some people found surprising (eg, the solicitors in the case itself had actually continued to conduct an ineffectual correspondence about a formal contract). Since then the majority decision in *Law* v *Jones* [1974] Ch 112 has underlined the fact that the unilateral insertion of the words 'subject to contract' into correspondence between the solicitors acting cannot cancel out any already existing contract, whether oral or written. In addition, producing a painful problem for practitioners, who never want their letters held against them or against their clients, it was decided that such 'subject to contract' correspondence can constitute a memorandum within the Law of Property Act 1925, s 40(1), and so render an oral contract enforceable.

However, Lord Denning MR led a charge to the rescue, having heard 'an alarm bell in the offices of every solicitor in the land,' and was extraordinarily concerned that 'the legal profession should be freed from the anxieties which beset them', in *Tiverton Estates Ltd* v *Wearwell Ltd* [1975] Ch 146. There the Court of Appeal, differently constituted, held that inclusion of the words 'subject to contract' effectively prevented correspondence from satisfying the statute (purporting to follow *Thirkell* v *Cambi* [1919] 2 KB 590 in preference to *Law* v *Jones*). The Council of The Law Society in consequence and contentment announced: 'The problem has now been solved' (*The Law Society's Gazette* (1973) vol 70, p 2637), and indeed the convenient *Tiverton Estates* decision has since been followed at first instance in *Jones* v *Morgan* (1974) 231 EG 1167.

Nevertheless, there are difficulties in accepting the opinion that, in effect, *Law* v *Jones* has been overruled by *Tiverton Estates*. To begin with, only the House of Lords can overrule a Court of Appeal decision, and *Law* v *Jones* does enjoy the implicit approval of the House of Lords in that the Appellate Committee refused leave to appeal (see at [1974] Ch 129); no notice of appeal was lodged within the week allowed in *Tiverton Estates* (see *The Law Society's Gazette* (1973) vol 70, p 2609). Moreover the two cases technically concerned different issues: application for specific performance in *Law* v *Jones* and a motion for cancellation of a caution in *Tiverton Estates*. Also *Griffiths* v *Young*, which raised much the same problem, was described as justifiable on other grounds (per Lord Denning MR in *Tiverton Estates* at [1975] Ch 160). And what is more the judiciary still disagree; Buckley and Orr LJJ, who decided *Law* v *Jones*, have not been persuaded to recant but on the contrary quickly seized an obiter occasion for discounting *Tiverton Estates* and restating at length their own decision: see *Daulia Ltd* v *Four Millbank Nominees Ltd* [1978] Ch 231, at pp 249–51. So The Law Society's announcement of a final solution of the *Law* v *Jones* problem seems somewhat premature.

An analogous inconvenience for solicitors emerged briefly from *Michael Richards Properties Ltd* v *St Saviour's Wardens* [1975] 3 All ER 416: a letter accepting a tender by clerical error bore the words 'subject to contract'. Nevertheless, Goff J held that since the tender document set out all the terms of the contract, nothing remained to be negotiated and there was no need for any further formalities and that therefore the words were meaningless and could be ignored. Bearing in mind that his decision did not rest on the clerical error, the implications for ordinary conveyancing transactions appeared obvious and disturbing. Happily, however, the learned judge himself hastened to explain it away. In *Munton* v *GLC* [1976] 1 WLR 649 the Court of Appeal considered a 'subject to contract' agreement as to compensation for compulsory acquisition and, although such agreements do not normally involve any exchange of contracts, held it not binding. Goff LJ took the opportunity of undermining his *Michael Richards* decision as based on facts which were strong, exceptional and rare and as 'not throw[ing] any doubt upon the well established and well settled sanctity of the words "subject to contract"' (ibid, p 656). A similar 'subject to contract' compensation agreement was seen with a difference in *Dutton's Breweries Ltd* v *Leeds City Council* (1981) 43 P & CR 160, CA. The difference was that the crucial letter also stated, 'I agree that contracts may be dispensed with and will let you have draft conveyance for approval in due course.' Never mind, the meaningful words won by one: the majority merely held that 'to dispense with a contract cannot *make* a contract' (per Oliver LJ at p 180). But they had particularly borne in mind the fact that the writer of the letter was 'a skilled and experienced conveyancer, with the most complete familiarity with the invariable— or almost invariable—and certainly the natural and *prima facie* meaning and effect of the expression "subject to contract" in any conveyancing correspondence' (per Oliver LJ again at p 179). So variable to meaningless for laymen may seem an obvious inference (see eg, per Lord Denning MR in *Howard Marine Ltd* v *Ogden & Sons Ltd* [1978] QB 574, at p 590).

One last aspect of exchange concerns the so-called 'contract race'. This begins when a vendor's solicitor forwards draft contracts to more than one prospective purchaser intimating, expressly or impliedly, that 'the vendor . . . will sell to the purchaser who returns a signed contract first' (cp *The Law Society's Gazette* (1971) vol 68, p 358). In response to mounting complaints, the profession's Council has recognised rather than condemned the practice subject to certain track rules, the principal one being that the fact of the race must be fully disclosed in writing to all the participants (see ibid (1979) vol 76, p 1177). But this step could trip a vendor up. The mere participation by any prospective purchaser in the race seems to give rise at once to a contract; ie, the vendor has bound himself to sell to whosoever satisfies the stated condition.

A firm basis for this last proposition can now be found in *Daulia Ltd* v *Four Millbank Nominees Ltd* [1978] Ch 231, where a promise had been made to enter a contract for the sale of certain land if, in effect, a prospective purchaser tendered his part of the contract plus a banker's draft for the deposit; but when this condition was satisfied, the vendor refused to exchange contracts. The Court of Appeal held that the facts established a valid 'unilateral or "if contract"', ie, 'a contract to enter into a proper written contract for the sale of land' (per Goff LJ, ibid at pp 238 and 241). In the case the 'if contract' was actually unenforceable because it was not evidenced in writing (as required by the Law of Property Act 1925, s 40(1)), but with contract races the Council's rule about written disclosure should incidentally ensure enforceability. Further, the automatic inclusion of the magic formula 'subject to contract' will not necessarily preclude an 'if contract', ie, there can be a binding contract to exchange contracts in due course (per Buckley LJ at ibid, p 246). Therefore the eventual winner of the race should receive the prize of a contract before exchange and there may be other advantages and disadvantages. Thus once the race is on, the vendor appears bound not to 'gazump' whilst all the runners might register estate contracts (ie, as enjoying 'any other like right' to a right of pre-emption within the Land Charges Act 1972, s 2(4), Class C(iv); cp the Land Registration Act 1925, s 54, as to lodging a caution).

B   CONSTRUCTION

Although the terse 'subject to contract' is the hallowed formula, other qualifying expressions have, as a matter of construction, had exactly the same effect of leaving matters in negotiation. Indeed, in *Winn* v *Bull*, itself (ante, p 15) the expression was 'subject to the preparation of a formal contract' (see also, eg, *Spottiswoode, Ballantyne & Co* v *Doreen Appliances Ltd* [1942] 2 KB 32). Again in *Riley* v *Troll* [1953] 1 All ER 966, the words used were 'this agreement is subject to formal contract to be prepared by the vendors' solicitors *if the vendors shall so require.*' The purchaser having resiled, the plaintiff-vendors contended that the italicised words qualified the whole sentence so that, as they had made it clear that they did not require a formal contract, the agreement amounted to a binding contract. Ormerod J, however, rejected this, holding that the italicised words related merely to who should prepare the formal contract with the result that the purchaser was able to escape.

Sometimes, however, the courts seem to go beyond actual construction towards pure implication. Thus in *Tevanan* v *Norman Brett (Builders) Ltd* (1972) 223 EG 1945 (a decision approved and adopted by the Court of Appeal in *Sherbrooke* v *Dipple* (1980) 255 EG 1203, ante p 19) Brightman J remarked:

> It was true that none of the relevant letters contained the actual formula "subject to contract", but they contained abundantly and repeatedly the meaning of that formula, which was that the contract was to be brought about by the exchange of the two parts signed by the respective parties.

What the letters contained were references to preliminary enquiries and a draft contract. Again in *Tiverton Estates Ltd* v *Wearwell Ltd* [1975] Ch 146, CA, the vital letter upon which the rescue decision turned (see ante p 22) did not itself say 'subject to contract' but referred to 'your letter' (which did so say) and said, 'We now send you draft contract for approval . . .'. In Stamp LJ's judgment: 'whatever else may be said about that letter, it is clear beyond doubt, that, *whether it be read in isolation*, or together with the letter to which it was a reply, it did not recognise the existence of . . . any contract' (at p 163, italics supplied). Compare also *Edgewater Developments Co* v *Bailey* (1974) 118 SJ 312, CA, where a vendor was not bound because 'the words "deposit upon receipt of contracts" contemplated a future contract' (per Lord Denning MR).

Apart from the construction of words actually used by the parties, an intention to remain in negotiation may apparently be inferred from conduct (see per Danckwerts LJ in *Smith* v *Mansi* [1963] 1 WLR 26, at p 31, also per Stamp J in *Goldsmith Ltd* v *Baxter* [1970] Ch 85, at pp 89–90). In particular, a judicial readiness has sometimes been seen to imply the words 'subject to contract' into any informal oral agreement for the sale of land if it would otherwise be binding (see, eg, *Pateman* v *Pay* (1974) 232 EG 457, also *Glessing* v *Green* [1975] 1 WLR 863, at p 865B). Thus Pennycuick V-C after mentioning the complexities normally involved in sales of land, concluded:

> It is not necessary, although obviously prudent, in this connection that the parties should expressly use the words "subject to contract", or the like, if they wish to exclude the implication of a contractual intention

(*Damm* v *Herrtage* (1974) 234 EG 365, at p 371: see further (1975) 39 Conv (NS) 229–36). This attitude to the oral would have stifled at birth the problems of *Law* v *Jones* (where the factual finding of a contract was not challenged on appeal; see per Russell and Buckley LJJ at [1974] Ch 118 and 121). But it is not a consistent attitude. Thus Pennycuick V-C has also observed that:

> He (his lordship) was well aware of the difficulty of establishing an oral contract for the sale of land. Parties who acted prudently did not enter into an oral contract in this complicated sphere. But if they liked to do so, and words of unconditional contract were established by evidence, then subject to the requirement of the memorandum under section 40, there was no doubt that it was a contract which was valid and would be enforced by the court

(in *Farrell* v *Green* (1974) 232 EG 587, decided after *Damm* v *Herrtage*; see also per Plowman V-C in *Tweddell* v *Henderson* [1975] 1 WLR 1496, at p 1500).

Beyond all this unpredictability there is another aspect; 'subject to contract' is not the only expression adopted. Agreements to buy land made subject to more specific qualifications than that of exchange of formal parts are not infrequently encountered. For example, 'subject to satisfactory survey' has also been held to leave the matter in negotiation (see *Marks* v *Board* (1930) 46 TLR 424: *Graham & Scott (Southgate) Ltd* v *Oxlade* [1950] 2 KB 257). As Russell J somewhat cynically explained:

> The surveyor's report, which could be described as not only covering without qualification every conceivable aspect of building, but also giving each aspect 100 per cent marks (even if 100 per cent is capable of definition), has yet to be seen—certainly if he is instructed by a proposed purchaser. It is easy to see, therefore, why such a phrase is properly regarded as a badge of no contract

(*Batten* v *White (No 2)* (1960) 12 P & CR 66, at p 70). These cases were followed where a ship was sold 'subject to a satisfactory survey'; (*Astra Trust* v *Adams and Williams* [1969] 1 Lloyd's Rep 81) but then doubted and distinguished where such a sale was 'subject to superficial inspection afloat' (per Lord Denning MR in *The Merak* [1976] 2 Lloyd's Rep 250, at pp 254–5).

Now most recently the earlier authorities were rejected, although hardly overruled, by Walton J in *Ee* v *Kakar* (1979) 40 P & CR 223 (applying the decision, not the dicta, in *Batten* v *White* supra). In this latest case, there was a written agreement for the sale of land at a specified price 'subject to survey of the property' and the vendor wished to resile. His lordship held that the quoted words constituted a condition precedent (or a suspensory condition); that the purchaser was obliged to obtain a survey with due diligence (ie, to spend money so that there was consideration); that the purchaser must consider the report bona fide (ie, acting reasonably and objectively); and that the purchaser could waive the condition (ie, as being wholly in his favour) and then enforce the contract as binding.

· In contrast to this qualification as to physical quality, an offer to sell accepted 'subject to the title being approved by our solicitors' has been said in the House of Lords to constitute a binding contract straightaway since nothing more was meant than a good title should be shown which would in any case be implied (per Cairns LC in *Hussey* v *Horne-Payne* (1879) 4 App Cas 311, at pp 321 and 322, followed in *Chipperfield* v *Carter* (1895) 72 LT 487). However, the more general view has been that such a qualification goes beyond the implied term (under which the quality of the title could be determined by the court) to leave the contract unenforceable if the title be disapproved by the purchaser's solicitor acting in good faith (see the consideration of the cases by Farwell J in *Caney* v *Leith* [1937] 2 All ER 532). But against this, without relevant citation, where a sale had been agreed 'subject [*inter alia*] . . . to questions of Title being to our approval,' Cross J held that the contract would have been binding in this respect—'if the title was in order so that no reasonable objections could be taken to it' (in *Re Longlands Farm* [1968] 3 All ER 552, at p 555). The point was, admittedly, marginal to his decision between the parties, so it is perhaps not surprising that this finding lacks focus: the language seems to be that of *Hussey* whilst the approach appears to favour *Caney*. Let us look to Lord Denning MR for a sort of reconciliation:

> Similarly when a man agrees to buy property "subject to the title being approved by our solicitor", there is a binding contract. There is an implied promise by the buyer that he will appoint a solicitor and shall consult him in good faith, and that the solicitor shall give his honest opinion. If the solicitor honestly disapproves, the contract does not bind. But until he does disapprove, the contract binds

(*Smallman* v *Smallman* [1972] Fam 25, at p 32 citing *Hussey*). Due (or not) to such uncertainties, the practical answer is obvious: no good purpose will be served by an attempt to make approval of the vendor's title an express condition of the contract (but see *Edginton* v *Clark* [1964] 1 QB 367, at p 376, as to a purchaser, merely by virtue of the contract, acknowledging that the vendor has a better title than he has).

More commonly today agreements may be met made 'subject to answers to preliminary enquiries and to searches,' this being usually stipulated (if at all) in the correspondence passing between the parties' solicitors when the parts of the formal contract are exchanged (ie, both exchange and expenditure on local searches having been held back until mortgage arrangements were made). In *Smith and Olley* v *Townsend* (1949) 1 P & CR 28, which concerned the words quoted, Roxburgh J held there to be no binding contract, but expressly did not decide whether the condition was void for uncertainty, so that there was no contract at all, or whether there was a concluded contract upon the sufficiently certain condition of the answers received to the searches being satisfactory to a reasonable man (which on the facts the answers were not). The learned judge apparently did not contemplate the matter simply being still in negotiation in the same way as with 'subject to contract' or perhaps 'to survey'. Therefore, where there are outstanding searches and enquiries at exchange, each case would seem to depend upon the certainty with which the condition is expressed in, usually, the solicitor's letter accompanying the purchaser's part of the contract. The parties, particularly the vendor, may be content with a conditional contract but disappointed to find a non-existent contract.

Another modern qualification is found with agreements 'subject to mortgage' (or words to this intent). Indeed, in 1959, the 17th Edition of the National Conditions of Sale introduced a new general condition (No 9) aimed at enabling the contract to be made conditional upon the purchaser arranging a mortgage (as to the risks of exchanging contracts before a mortgage is arranged, see *Buckland* v *Mackesy* (1968)

112 SJ 841, where the purchaser lost his deposit and sued his solicitor). Although this 'let-out' condition was attributable to popular demand (see the explanation at (1961) 105 SJ 497) it was apparently little used in practice and has now been dropped altogether from all subsequent editions of the National Conditions, which was probably wise. The difficulties attending such a qualification or condition were highlighted in a case where the formal contract included the Special Condition; 'This sale is subject to the purchaser obtaining a satisfactory mortgage' (*Lee-Parker* v *Izzet (No 2)* [1972] 2 All ER 800). Goulding J held that the condition was void for uncertainty and that this avoided the whole contract. He said (ibid, p 803 G/H):

> it seems to me that in the circumstances of the present case the concept of a satisfactory mortgage is too indefinite for the court to give it a practical meaning. Everything is at large, not only matters like rate of interest and ancillary obligations, on which evidence might establish what would be usual or reasonable, but also on these two most essential points—the amount of the loan and the terms of repayment.

The Special Condition in question was in fact written into the 17th Edition of the National Conditions of Sale but was inaptly drawn so far as the relevant general condition (No 9) was concerned since that required an express reference to 'an advance of a specified sum from a named person'. Even so, one wonders now whether that general conditon would have sufficed without mention also of the terms of repayment, the rate of interest and ancillary obligations.

Goulding J was able to follow specifically the decision of Russell J in *Re Rich's Will Trusts* (1962) 106 SJ 75, that a contract for sale providing that the vendor's solicitors should 'be instructed to obtain and fix a suitable mortgage advance on this property' thereby failed for uncertainty (both followed generally *Scammell* v *Ouston* [1941] AC 251, concerning the vagueness of 'on hire-purchase terms'). However, in doing so he swam rather against the more recent tide in the courts which shows a growing reluctance to hold void for uncertainty any provision that was intended to have legal effect (see especially the anthology of warnings collected by Megarry J in *Brown* v *Gould* [1972] Ch 53, at pp 56–7). Further, Goulding J also differed directly from a decision of Goff J in earlier proceedings involving somewhat similar words (in *Lee-Parker* v *Izzet* [1971] 1 WLR 1688, relating to different parties and properties). The case is reported on other points, but it is noted (in brackets at [1971] 3 All ER 1099, p 1105, but not at all in the WLR) that Goff J, rejecting a submission that the contract failed for uncertainty, held that '"arranging . . . a satisfactory mortgage" meant a mortgage to the satisfaction of the purchaser acting reasonably'. This objective approach might well commend itself as a means of binding the parties and as a flowing away from states of uncertainty and negotiation. Nevertheless, the position in practice is simply unsatisfactory: there will always be the risk of failure for uncertainty if Goulding J is right, and even if he is wrong the difficult question of the purchaser's reasonableness on the facts may remain until a court rules. The only perfect solution lies in the drafting of a condition so indisputably definite that the courts could not conceivably be called upon to consider its certainty. But lacking such a paragon, if it proves impracticable to spell out in detail the anticipated mortgage terms, any lesser condition which had actually been tried and tested successfully before the courts would do. At this moment there seems to be neither sort of condition available, so that parties who wish to be bound in all respects bar the mortgage arrangements are merely left to linger in uncertainty (perhaps for as long as five years, as in *Lee-Parker* v *Izzet (No 2)* [1972] 2 All ER 800). Further reference should be made to 'Agreements "Subject to Finance"' by Brian Coote in (1976) 40 Conv (NS) 37–50.

This really leads to the crucial question which is the one of construction. Where the parties to a prospective sale and purchase have reached what at least looks like agreement but have added some prima facie conditional or qualifying words to the offer or to the acceptance then there are four possibilities. First, there may be a complete failure for uncertainty (see *Smith and Olley* v *Townsend* ante and *Lee-Parker* v *Izzet (No 2)*, ante). Secondly, as with 'subject to contract,' there may be no concluded contract at all on account of the elementary principle of the law of contract that offer and acceptance must be unconditional. In each of these two possibilities, since there is no contract, any deposit paid can be recovered, this usually being the object of any proceedings (*Chillingworth* v *Esche* [1924] 1 Ch 97). Thirdly, there may at once be a binding contract despite the qualifying words. The leading example of this occurred in *Branca* v *Cobarro* [1947] KB 854, where the added words were: 'This is a provisional agreement until a fully legalised agreement drawn up by a solicitor and embodying all the conditions herewith is signed.' A layman might have thought this to be the equivalent of 'subject to contract' and if so he would have been in good company, for Denning J at first instance so decided. However, the Court of Appeal held that the words (especially the word 'until') implied that the agreement was intended to be fully binding immediately and to remain so unless and until merged into a subsequent more formal contract. Here the task of construction was particularly delicate since had 'tentative' been used instead of 'provisional' an opposite decision would apparently have been reached! Another, perhaps more likely, instance of an immediate binding contract by surprise would occur where the vendor writes to accept the purchaser's offer to buy at a particular price and adds that he is asking his solicitors 'to prepare a contract'; there will already be a contract (see *Bournewell* v *Jenkins* (1878) 8 Ch D 70; *Rossiter* v *Miller* (1878) 3 App Cas 1124). These last cases were more recently followed by the Court of Appeal where a letter of acceptance had concluded: 'Perhaps you will kindly instruct your solicitor to write to my solicitors . . . with the necessary agreement'; the argument that there was not a binding contract but merely a contract to make a contract or a conditional contract was rejected (*ER Ives Investment Ltd* v *High* [1967] 2 QB 379).

C   CONDITIONAL CONTRACT

The fourth possibility is that the court will find that the parties have concluded a conditional contract (see, eg, *Smith and Olley* v *Townsend*, ante). The distinction to be drawn is between an offer or an acceptance subject to a condition, when there will be no concluded contract at all, and an agreement subject to an agreed condition, when there will be a concluded contract although it will not be enforceable unless and until the condition is fulfilled (see per Farwell J in *Caney* v *Leith* [1937] 2 All ER 532, at p 533). The importance of the distinction is that in the latter case the parties are not free to resile according to their whim but must await fulfilment or not of the condition. In this sense the contract is binding. Thus the purchaser under a conditional contract has been held by the Court of Appeal to become the owner in equity of the land pending even fulfilment of the condition (*Gordon Hill Trust Ltd* v *Segall* [1941] 2 All ER 379: also p 111).

However, possibly to be preferred is the nicer distinction more recently suggested, namely that this sort of contract is to be regarded as a binding agreement containing a condition precedent to the formation of the actual contract of sale and purchase (see per Ungoed-Thomas J at first instance in *Property and Bloodstock Ltd* v *Emerton* [1967] 2 All ER 839, at pp 847–8). On appeal in this last mentioned case it was emphasised that this sort of conditional contract is to be distinguished from the ordinary absolute contract of sale and purchase which incorporates what are traditionally called 'conditions of sale' but which are really no more than the terms of that contract (see per Danckwerts and Sachs LJJ [1968] Ch 94, at pp 112 and 121; also post, pp 50 and 76). This last distinction will it seems be particularly applicable to a requirement that one or other of the parties should perform some obligation before completion. Buckley LJ has observed that, even though couched in conditional language:

> That is not, in my judgment, a condition precedent to the contract at all, it is part of the terms of the contract. You may call it a condition if you please, but it does not make it a condition precedent to the existence of a contract, it merely indicates that it is part of the terms of the bargain, just as in all contracts for sale the terms of the bargain are customarily described as conditions of sale

(in *Eastham* v *Leigh London and Provincial Properties Ltd* [1971] Ch 871, at p 891; see also *Brickwoods* v *Butler and Walters* (1970) 21 P & CR 256 and 317; cp S Robinson in (1970) 34 Conv (NS) 332, contending without quite convincing that where the event is in the control of either party there is a condition *subsequent* and the contract is voidable). For further more refined analyses of conditional contracts happily not in a conveyancing context, reference should be made to the judgments of Diplock LJ in *United Dominions Trust (Commercial) Ltd* v *Eagle Aircraft Services Ltd* [1968] 1 WLR 74, and of Goff J in *Wood Preservation Ltd* v *Prior* [1968] 2 All ER 849, on appeal [1969] 1 WLR 1077).

Common examples of such agreed conditions precedent are that the vendor should procure a surrender of a lease or obtain someone's consent, eg, a reversioner's licence (see *Scheggia* v *Gradwell* [1963] 1 WLR 1049, but contrast *Property and Bloodstock Ltd* v *Emerton* [1968] Ch 94, where such a licence was regarded as a mere 'matter of title'), or that approval of the price by a third party be forthcoming (see *Manchester Diocesan Council of Education* v *Commercial and General Investments Ltd* [1970] 1 WLR 241). Beyond these examples, a modern near rash of cases has occurred concerning contracts conditional, in effect, upon the purchaser being allowed to build a small fortune on the land. Thus in *Re Longlands Farm* [1968] 3 All ER 552, a common form letter to a farmer (in duplicate, stamped and signed all round) included the statement that 'my company is agreeable to the purchase from you . . . [for £114,000] . . . subject to my company obtaining Planning Permission to its entire satisfaction . . .' Despite arguments that this letter merely conferred an option terminable by the farmer by reasonable notice, Cross J held that there was a conditional contract which would become absolute in the event of the condition being fulfilled (on the facts it clearly had not been so, which may explain why no questions as to certainty of terms seem to have crossed anyone's mind). In two contemporary cases, the contractual condition had indicated the requisite planning permission with indisputable detail, but in one, outline permission only was given (approval of the detailed plan being refused) and in the other only a conditional consent was granted (see respectively *Hargreaves Transport Ltd* v *Lynch* [1969] 1 WLR 215 and *Richard West and Partners* v *Dick* [1969] 2 Ch 424). The Court of Appeal held in the former case that the purchasers could treat the contract as 'off' and recover the deposit (ie, the condition could be treated as unfulfilled without pursuing an appeal to the minister) and in the latter case that the conditional consent sufficed in the circumstances to prevent the purchaser from resiling. Then lastly by way of comparison reference may be made to *Guiness* v *Pearce* (1971) 22 P & CR 998, in which a contract for the sale of land provided for an abatement of the price if planning permission should be refused within six months; in fact, an application for permission was refused by the local planning authority within that period but an appeal was later allowed by the minister with the consequence that Foster J held the provision for abatement to be inapplicable. Further reference for the precise position of the parties should be made to 'Sale of Land "Subject to Planning Permission"' by HW Wilkinson at (1974) 38 Conv (NS) 77–9.

These planning cases often appear to blur the distinction between conditions precedent and conditions of sale, especially when they concern the question of waiver in relation to a 'conditional contract'. Thus in *Heron Garage Properties Ltd* v *Moss* [1974] 1 WLR 148, one clause in the contract provided for its determination by either party by notice in the event of planning permission not being duly granted (which it was not); the purchaser purported to waive the benefit of this clause and enforce the contract as 'unconditional' but was held unable to do so unilaterally because the clause was not for its exclusive benefit. This decision was followed in *Federated Homes Ltd* v *Turner* (1974) 233 EG 845; see also *Cutts* v *Heron Garage Properties Ltd* (1974) 232 EG 459 and cp *Usanga* v *Bishop* (1974) 232 EG 835. In none of these cases was it made clear precisely what the court was considering, but logically at least questions of waiver ought only to arise in relation to a right to repudiate in accordance with a term of an unconditional contract. For example, in *Aquis Estates Ltd* v *Minton* [1975] 1 WLR 1452, CA, the contract for sale was subject to 'a good title and property being found free from adverse entry on the purchaser's local land charge, land charge and land registry searches'; there was an adverse entry, tested objectively, but this was treated as 'a breach of condition' conferring a right to repudiate which had been waived by conduct. Had there been a condition precedent, the presence of the adverse entry should simply have meant that there was no contract.

Whenever a conditional contract for sale is encountered, it may become necessary to know how long the parties are bound to wait on tenterhooks for fulfilment or non-fulfilment. This question of 'time-limits' has been authoritatively considered by the Privy Council in *Aberfoyle Plantations Ltd* v *Cheng* [1960] AC 115. The condition in the case was that the vendor should obtain renewal of several leases or else the contract should become void. Renewal of all the leases had not been obtained by the date fixed for completion and shortly afterwards the purchaser sued to recover the deposit paid. The principal question on which this depended was: within what period of time did the condition have to be performed? The Privy Council, deciding that the deposit was recoverable, stated the following general rules (at pp 124–5):

> The answer to that question must plainly depend on the true construction of the agreement, or in other words on the intention of the parties as expressed in, or to be implied from, the language they have used. But, subject to this overriding consideration their lordships would adopt, as warranted by authority and manifestly reasonable in themselves, the following general principles: (i) Where a conditional contract of sale fixes a date for the completion of the sale, then the condition must be fulfilled by that date; (ii) where a conditional contract of sale fixes no date for completion of the sale, then the condition must be fulfilled within a reasonable time; (iii) where a conditional contract of sale fixes (whether specifically or by reference to the date fixed for completion) the date by which the condition is to be fulfilled, then the date so fixed must be strictly adhered to, and the time allowed is not to be extended by reference to equitable principles.

Thus if a date is fixed for completion or for fulfilment of the condition, time will, without more ado, be of the essence under principles (i) or (iii) above, despite the well-known equitable rule that it usually is not. Making time of the essence beyond peradventure (particularly as to the giving of vacant possession) is a familiar difficulty of conveyancers. It might, therefore, be thought that the Privy Council has indicated a possible way of by-passing the difficulty in advance by the simple expedient of framing the term in question as a condition precedent to be performed by a fixed date. But if the condition amounts really to a term of the contract, ie, a condition of sale, then this will not work. For example, if the so-called condition is merely an aspect of showing title, then its performance is due not by the contractual completion date but simply 'by the date at which title has to be established, normally actual completion' (see per Ungoed-Thomas J in *Property and Bloodstock Ltd* v *Emerton* [1967] 2 All ER 839, at p 848; on appeal [1968] Ch 94). The Privy Council's rules were considered in the Court of Appeal without being approved and with some suggestions of disapproval, but as Danckwerts LJ said:

> The *Aberfoyle Plantation* case is nothing to do with the present case and the arguments based on it are fallacious

(at [1968] Ch 117; the point of distinction was that in the later case the vendor and purchaser were not in conflict inter se; see also per Russell LJ in *Hargreaves Transport Ltd* v *Lynch* [1969] 1 WLR 215, at p 220).

General principle (ii) from the *Aberfoyle Plantation* case was further explained by Cross J in *Re Longlands Farm* [1968] 3 All ER 552, at pp 555–6, where the two points were made:

> that the reasonableness of the time must be determined as at the date of the contract and that what is reasonable must be judged by an objective test applicable to both parties.

In the case, a period of over three and a half years for the purchaser to obtain planning permission was held to be far more than a reasonable time.

Incidentally notice the query as to whether conditional contracts are registrable under the Land Charges Act 1972 before fulfilment of the condition (see RJ Smith at [1974] Camb LJ 211–4 taking the view that until then no equitable interest is created but cp *Gordon Hill Trust Ltd* v *Segall* [1941] 2 All ER 379, CA). In answer to the query, it may be contended that conditional contracts are covered by the words 'or any other like right' in the definition of estate contract (s 2(4)(iv) of the 1972 Act), and in *Haslemere Estates Ltd* v *Baker* [1982] 1 WLR 1109, Megarry V-C, no less, declined to vacate a registration, saying (at p 1118): 'Indeed, as at present advised I incline to the view that a conditional contract relating to land is registrable as an estate contract if the condition is one that is to be satisfied not by the parties but by some extraneous person or event. I say nothing about other conditional contracts.' However, it is clearly safer and therefore better conveyancing practice to register all such contracts (as in *Re Longlands Farm* supra; see also *Wood Preservation Ltd* v *Prior* [1968] 2 All ER 849 as to an equitable interest passing if the condition is one which can be waived by the purchaser).

III MEMORANDUM

THE concept of the unenforceable although valid contract originated with the Statute of Frauds in 1677. Expressly enacted 'for prevention of many fraudulent practices, which are commonly endeavoured to be upheld by perjury and subornation of perjury', that Statute (ss 4 and 17) required a large but miscellaneous selection of contracts to be supported by signed writing as a matter of evidence rather than substance. Now after some three centuries of general abuse and judicial evasion this requirement applies to only two of these contracts (see the Law Reform (Enforcement of Contracts) Act 1954). The more important of the two survivors is, of course, the contract for the sale or other disposition of an interest in land, and this survival may perhaps now be justified by the comparative complexity of the transaction rather than by reference to fraudulent practices.

The relevant portion of s 4 of the Statute of Frauds 1677 was repealed by the Law of Property Act 1925 (s 207 and Sched 7), and reproduced with only slight linguistic differences, as follows (s 40(1)):

> No action may be brought upon any contract for the sale or other disposition of land or any interest in land, unless the agreement upon which such action is brought, or some memorandum or note thereof, is in writing and signed by the party to be charged, or by some other person thereunto by him lawfully authorised.

The rules shown by case law since 1677 to emerge from this provision may be conveniently covered by a phrase-by-phrase commentary. Throughout the commentary, however, bear in mind that the first question to be considered is always whether or not there exists a valid contract at all to be evidenced in writing.

A 'SALE OR OTHER DISPOSITION'

By the statutory definition of 'disposition' (s 205(1)(ii)), the provision applies to contracts not only for the sale but also, inter alia, for the mortgage (see also *Pottle* v *Anstruther* (1893) 69 LT 175), lease (see also *Thursby* v *Eccles* (1900) 70 LJQB 91), release, devise or bequest of an interest in land (see *Re Gonin* [1979] Ch 16). Thus the provision would apply to contracts for the creation as well as the transfer of such an interest. It should be noted that, although s 54(2) of the Law of Property Act 1925 permits the actual grant of certain short leases to be by parol, a *contract* to grant such a lease nonetheless falls within the present provision (see *Rollason* v *Leon* (1861) 7 H & N 73; also *Biss* v *Hygate* [1918] 2 KB 314).

For a more modern example, a contract to exchange contracts for the sale of land in due course has been held to be a contract for the disposition of an equitable interest in the land and so caught by s 40(1) (see particularly per Buckley LJ in *Daulia Ltd* v *Four Millbank Nominees Ltd* [1978] Ch 231, CA, at p 246; cp ante, p 23). Equally a contract containing a right of pre-emption in respect of land ought to be within the section despite not itself creating an interest in land: see per Walton J in *Pritchard* v *Briggs* [1980] Ch 338, at p 369; sed quaere in view of his reversal on appeal. But contrast *Munton* v *GLC* [1976] 1 WLR 649, CA: an agreement as to the price of a compulsory acquisition, despite constituting a contract for the conveyance of land, does not require writing because apparently it involves 'not an ordinary contract but a statutory contract' (per Lord Denning MR at p 653).

B 'LAND OR ANY INTEREST IN LAND'

The definition of 'land' for the purposes of the Law of Property Act 1925 is extremely wide (s 205(1)(ix)) comprising a curious but familiar assortment of physical descriptions and concepts of law, including the very word being defined, and expressly excluding only 'an undivided share in land.' In the teeth of this one express exclusion, however, s 40(1) has been regarded as applicable to a contract for the sale of an undivided share in land: *Cooper* v *Critchley* [1955] Ch 431, CA (sale by one co-owner to the other co-owner). To put it another way, a beneficiary's entitlement under a trust for sale was treated as an interest in land rather than as a mere interest in the proceeds of sale (cp *Irani Finance Ltd* v *Singh* [1971] Ch 59, at pp 79–80). This attitude now seems well-established, at least for present purposes. Thus in *Steadman* v *Steadman* [1976] AC 536 an oral agreement compromising various matrimonial matters included a provision that the wife should transfer to the husband her interest in their jointly owned home for £1,500: both the Court of Appeal and the House of Lords accepted without argument that the transfer provision was within s 40(1). Again in *Liddell* v *Hopkinson* (1974) 233 EG 512, the subsection caught a husband's oral agreement to pay his divorced wife two-thirds of the proceeds of sale of a house if she left (see also *McDonald* v *Windaybank* (1975) 120 SJ 96). A similar attitude to interests behind a trust for sale has been adopted in registered conveyancing (see, eg, *Elias* v *Mitchell* [1972] Ch 652, as to beneficiaries lodging cautions) and quite recently Lord Denning MR felt able to say that he found *Cooper* v *Critchley* more compelling than *Irani Finance Ltd* v *Singh*: see *Williams & Glyn's Bank Ltd* v *Boland* [1979] Ch 312, at p 331: upheld on appeal [1981] AC 487 (as to beneficiaries enjoying overriding interests).

The phrase 'land or any interest in land,' for the purposes of s 40(1) of the Law of Property Act 1925 (and its predecessor), has had to be tried for size on to other interests than the undivided share in land, sometimes with as much uncertainty as to the fit (see A Kiralfy (1956) 20 Conv (NS) 12–14). The following, for better or for worse, have been held within the phrase:

(i) A right of shooting over land *and* taking away game is within this, having been held to be an incorporeal hereditament (*Webber* v *Lee* (1882) 9 QBD 315) and so within the statutory definition of 'land' itself (s 205(1)(ix)). However, this right, as a profit à prendre in gross, may no longer be a legal interest, despite the usual textbook statement to the contrary. Section 187 of the Law of Property Act 1925, a new section, provides that such a legal right 'shall enure for the benefit of the land to which it is intended to be annexed'. This section has not been considered judicially, but its framers state that 'legal sporting rights can be granted by annexing to them a keeper's or bailiff's cottage included in the grant' (see *Wolstenholme & Cherry's Conveyancing Statutes*, 13th ed, vol 1, at p 312). Even so, although only an equitable profit, any such sporting right would at least still be an 'interest in land' (see ss 1(8) and 205(1)(x)). As to the nature of profits à prendre in gross, further reference may be made to the judgment of Megarry J in *Lowe* v *Ashmore* [1971] Ch 545.

(ii) A contract for the sale of debentures charged on land is within s 40(1) (*Driver* v *Broad* [1893] 1 QB 744).

(iii) With contracts to take a furnished room or rooms, the distinction usually made is between a letting (a lease) and lodgings (a licence), the former necessarily involving exclusive occupation, and being within s 40(1), and the latter not.

However, in passing, remember that this simple distinction is today so blurred that recognition approaches the impossible: the fact of exclusive possession is no longer conclusive of a lease and the description of the agreement as a licence is also not conclusive the other way (see per Lord Denning MR in *Marchant* v *Charters* [1977] 1 WLR 1181, at p 1185, as to the 'stake in the room' test).

(iv) Following aptly on, one may observe that certain somewhat controversial cases seem to indicate that the irrevocable licence is today approaching the status of an interest in land (see most recently *ER Ives Investment Ltd* v *High* [1967] 2 QB 379, also the judgment of Lord Denning MR in *Binions* v *Evans* [1972] Ch 359 and the decision in *Midland Bank Ltd* v *Farmpride Hatcheries Ltd* (1980) 260 EG 493, CA, as noted by Ruth E Annand at [1982] Conv 67, but cp still *National Provincial Bank Ltd* v *Ainsworth* [1965] AC 1175). Accordingly a minor matter inevitably to be raised is whether a contract relating to such a licence falls within s 40(1).

Thus in the obscurely reported case of *National Provincial Bank Ltd* v *Moore* (1967) 111 SJ 357 a father had orally promised his daughter that if she continued to care for her parents until they died she need never leave and his bungalow would be hers. Part of Cross J's judgment is reported as follows:

What was the legal effect of the words used by him? Did they create an immediate irrevocable licence or was it a promise to make a will? If it were the latter it would be a contract to create a legal interest and as such would need to be evidenced by writing. If it were the former, a licence to live in the house for the remainder of her life . . ., it might be that it would not require to be so evidenced on the grounds that it was a personal interest and not an interest in land, but his lordship left the question open in view of *National Provincial Bank Ltd* v *Hastings Car Mart Ltd* [1965] AC 1175.

In the event, the learned judge found that the promise was to make a will and was therefore unenforceable for lack of written evidence. But there is certainly a flaw in this decision.

Surely the promise in this sort of case should not stand or fall by reference to writing alone. Assuming that s 40(1) is, prima facie, applicable whether the promise is to make a will or to create an irrevocable licence, then a solution to the problem was indicated years ago by the Court of Appeal in *Errington* v *Errington* [1952] 1 KB 290 (a licence case) namely, to find that the occupation involved amounted to a sufficient act of part-performance so excluding s 40 (see especially per Somervell LJ at ibid, p 294). This solution can also be strongly supported by citing two more recent cases which concerned similar situations and promises (although in neither was a licence found), namely *Kingswood Estate Co Ltd* v *Anderson* [1963] 2 QB 169, CA, and *Wakeham* v *Mackenzie* [1968] 1 WLR 1175 (and see Phillip H Pettit at (1968) 32 Conv (NS) 384 for a full discussion).

(v) Since fixtures are a part of the 'land,' a contract for their sale, even separately from the land, is within s 40(1) (*Jarvis* v *Jarvis* (1893) 63 LJ Ch 10: also *Morgan* v *Russell and Sons* [1909] 1 KB 357, re slag and cinders which had become part of the land). An apparent exception to this occurs with tenants' fixtures since the tenant is treated as dealing not with land but with his right of removal (*Lee* v *Gaskell* (1876) 1 QBD 700). Again, although a contract for the sale of the building materials in a house to be demolished and removed by the purchaser within a given time is within s 40(1) (*Lavery* v *Pursell* (1888) 39 Ch D 508), the converse, a contract to build a house, is not (per Hill J in *Wright* v *Stavert* (1860) 2 El & El 721, at p 728: also *Jameson* v *Kinmell Bay Land Co Ltd* (1931) 47 TLR 593).

The problem of drawing the line between the sale of land and the sale of goods occurred with regard to a sale of turves, that is, of the top two inches of $26\frac{1}{2}$ acres of land. Although the context was quite different (ie, the taxation distinction between capital and income receipts), the decision should still be of present relevance. Since the contract in question was for a limited period and of some informality, Megarry J felt that there were grounds for inferring 'that the intention was not to create any interest in the land at all, but merely to create a contractual obligation and right to enter the land, sever the turf and keep it, being thus a form of contract for the sale of goods' (in *Lowe* v *JW Ashmore Ltd* [1971] Ch 545, at p 557). Unhappily, the application of s 40(1) to a sale of turves was not rendered easier by the learned judge's subsequent refusal to resolve whether the contract should not correctly be classified rather as creating an equitable profit à prendre in gross (loc cit, pp 557–8) which would, of course, be an interest in land.

Finally, it should just be mentioned as well-established that fructus naturales (natural crops), as opposed to fructus industriales (cultivated crops), are to be regarded as 'land' within s 40(1) unless necessarily to be severed on sale. Nothing further will be said here of this odd byway which is of little if any practical interest and on which there has been no reported decision for over a century (*Marshall* v *Green* (1875) 1 CPD 35, reviewing the earlier decisions; cf *Saunders* v *Pilcher* [1949] 2 All ER 1097; see further AH Hudson at (1958) 22 Conv (NS) 137).

C 'UNLESS THE AGREEMENT . . . OR SOME MEMORANDUM OR NOTE THEREOF . . .'

The initial point to appreciate here is that the contract itself need not be in writing: mere written evidence of it is sufficient (*Re Holland* [1902] 2 Ch 360). This evidence, the memorandum, must have been brought into existence before the particular action on the contract commenced, ie, by the time the writ was issued (see *Lucas* v *Dixon* (1889) 22 QBD 357; cf *Farr, Smith & Co* v *Messers Ltd* [1928] 1 KB 397). Apart from this, however, there is no time-limit after the contract within which to make the memorandum (eg, *Barkworth* v *Young* (1856) 4 Drew 1—over fourteen years later).

Further, in one circumstance, the memorandum may even be made *before* the contract: s 40(1) may be satisfied by a written offer accepted orally but unconditionally: *Parker* v *Clark* [1960] 1 WLR 286 (here the plaintiff's acceptance was, in fact, written, but (1) had since been destroyed, and (2) presumably was not signed as required 'by the party to be charged'). Devlin J emphasised that anything less than an offer proper will not do (see also *Munday* v *Asprey* (1880) 13 Ch D 855). Accordingly, the elementary law of contract distinctions must be remembered between an offer and an invitation to treat (see *Grainger* v *Gough* [1896] AC 325) or a mere preliminary statement of fact (see *Harvey* v *Facey* [1893] AC 552). Thus, for a modern example, a letter which not only indicated the parties and the property but also said: 'For a quick sale I would accept £26,000 . . .' was held by the Court of Appeal to constitute an offer capable of acceptance so as to create a binding contract of which specific performance was ordered (*Bigg* v *Boyd Gibbins Ltd* [1971] 1 WLR 913). It follows that the acceptance in that case could effectively have been oral.

The 'written offer accepted orally' position rests on well-settled authority but is usually thought to push the evidential requirements of s 40(1) to their furthest limit (see per Lord Denning MR in *Tiverton Estates Ltd* v *Wearwell Ltd* [1975] Ch 146, at pp 158–9). Nevertheless a hint could be taken from elsewhere that this is not the only circumstance in which the memorandum may be made before the contract. In *Daulia Ltd* v *Four Millbank Nominees Ltd* [1978] Ch 231, Buckley LJ said that 'if the parties subsequently enter into a new and distinct oral agreement, the fact may be such that the earlier letter may form part of a sufficient note or memorandum of the later oral agreement' (at p 250). However, in the context of the cases he cited, this passage appears to envisage a post-agreement letter incorporating by reference the earlier correspondence.

A memorandum which has been lost or destroyed may still satisfy s 40(1) since proof of it by oral or other secondary evidence will be accepted, although with care (see *Barber* v *Rowe* [1948] 2 All ER 1050). Thus the ordinary rule as to missing documents is allowed to make a cautious inroad into s 40(1) (see also *Last* v *Hucklesby* (1914) 58 SJ 431).

1   Form

The memorandum need not have been meant to satisfy s 40(1): 'the question is not one of intention of the party who signs the document, but simply one of evidence against him' (*Re Hoyle, Hoyle* v *Hoyle* [1893] 1 Ch 84, at p 99: also per Sargant J in *Daniels* v *Trefusis* [1914] 1 Ch 788, at p 799). Therefore, no special form of memorandum is necessary (see, eg, *Hill* v *Hill* [1947] Ch 231, where the defendant, to acknowledge receipt of rent, had initialled a rent book in which the plaintiff had written 'Renewed lease Dec 25, 1941', and this sufficed). Examples are numerous and varied, but the commonest inadvertent memoranda found to satisfy s 40(1) have been receipts for deposits (as in *Davies* v *Sweet* [1962] 2 QB 300) and mere letters (as in *Parker* v *Clark* [1960] 1 WLR 286). The scope of the latter of these was illustrated by *Smith-Bird* v *Blower* [1939] 2 All ER 406, where the only sufficient memorandum of the contract was a letter by the defendant to his solicitors which was held not privileged from disclosure as not written to obtain legal advice but to provide information. This may be thought a dangerous precedent, but it does not stand alone. Since then in *Smith* v *Mansi* [1963] 1 WLR 26, a 'completely satisfactory memorandum' was found by the Court of Appeal to be supplied by an incomplete formal contract in conjunction with two letters, one written by the vendor to his solicitor and the other written by the solicitor to the vendor at the latter's request to set out the history of the events (see per Danckwerts LJ at p 34).

Another catch here is that a letter repudiating the contract may constitute a sufficient memorandum to support it (*Dewar* v *Mintoft* [1912] 2 KB 373); contrast a simple denial of a contract (*Thirkell* v *Cambi* [1919] 2 KB 590). And an even more subtle trap was sprung originally in *Griffiths* v *Young* [1970] Ch 675, where the written evidence (solicitors' letters) contained the phrase 'subject to contract' but the oral evidence showed that its effect had been waived and the Court of Appeal held there to be a valid and enforceable contract. Then this was followed in *Law* v *Jones* [1974] Ch 112, CA, where the majority of the court took the view that it is the terms agreed on, not the fact of agreement, which must be found recorded in writing and held that the phrase did not prevent there being a sufficient memorandum. Against this a completely contrary decision was at once reached in *Tiverton Estates Ltd* v *Wearwell Ltd* [1975] Ch 146, CA: the writing relied on must acknowledge the existence of the contract and the words 'subject to contract' are equivalent to a denial. In this respect, as one of the *Law* v *Jones* majority has remarked, these two Court of Appeal decisions 'are undoubtedly in conflict' (per Buckley LJ in *Daulia Ltd* v *Four Millbank Nominees Ltd* [1978] Ch 231, at p 250). The present writer suspects that only an extreme distaste for defences resting on s 40(1) could surmount the surely persuasive submission that letters stating 'subject to contract' evidence, according to principle, not a contract but a state of negotiation and he wonders why solicitors do not now substitute the more potent incantation 'contract denied'.

2   Several documents

The written evidence supporting a contract is often not to be found in any single document, but rather embodied, for example, in correspondence between the parties. Nonetheless, a memorandum within s 40(1) clearly may be constituted by several documents (see *Long* v *Millar* (1879) 4 CPD 450). If the several documents when physically placed side by side can be seen to refer to the same transaction and each is signed by the defendant, then they may be simply read together as a memorandum without any more patent connection (see *Sheers* v *Thimbleby & Son* (1897) 76 LT 709). This last may apparently extend even to cases where the defendant has signed only one of the documents provided that the reference to the same transaction can be 'manifestly' seen when the documents are placed side by side—whatever this means (*Burgess* v *Cox* [1951] Ch 383).

Apart from these cases where the cross-references in the documents need not be patent and may depend on physical juxtaposition, the well-established rule was restated by Jenkins LJ (in *Timmins* v *Moreland Street Property Co Ltd* [1958] Ch 110, at p 130, and see GHL Fridman at (1958) 22 Conv (NS 275):

> that there should be a document signed by the party to be charged which, while not containing in itself all the necessary ingredients of the required memorandum, does contain some reference, express or implied, to some other document or transaction. Where any such reference can be spelt out of a document so signed, then parol evidence may be given to identify the other document referred to, or as the case may be, to explain the other transaction, and to identify any document relating to it. If by this process a document is brought to light which contains in writing all the terms of the bargain so far as not contained in the document signed by the party to be charged, then the two documents can be read together so as to constitute a sufficient memorandum for the purposes of s 40 of the Law of Property Act 1925.

This passage was accepted by the Privy Council as a correct statement of the modern law in *Elias* v *George Sahely & Co* [1982] 3 WLR 956. In that case a receipt for money 'being deposit on property at Swan Street B'town agreed to be sold . . .' was taken as clearly referring to a transaction. This let in parol evidence which led to the letter with which the deposit cheque had been enclosed. This letter then sufficed for present purposes.

From this it is clear that the cross-reference may be indirect to the point of vagueness, and a fairly flagrant example occurred in *Stokes* v *Whicher* [1920] 1 Ch 411. In that case, on a carbon copy of the plaintiff's agreement to purchase (expressed in the first person) the defendant's agent had signed both (*a*) the agreement and (*b*) a receipt for the deposit of £50: in order to find the purchaser's name to complete the memorandum Russell J held (*a*) that the carbon copy indicated the top copy, and (*b*) that the receipt referred to a cheque for £62 [sic], both of which were signed by the plaintiff! Again the words 'our agreement' have been held a sufficient reference to a transaction to let in documents completing the memorandum (*Cave* v *Hastings* (1881) 7 QBD 125; see also per Evershed MR in *Fowler* v *Bratt* [1950] 2 KB 96, at pp 101–2). A much more common example, so ordinary as to appear hardly worth mentioning, occurs where a letter is written explicitly in reply to another letter; the earlier letter will be regarded as incorporated by reference into the later letter and the two together may therefore constitute a memorandum signed by the writer of the later letter (as in *Griffiths* v *Young* [1970] Ch 675 and *Law* v *Jones* [1974] Ch 112, CA).

Further it now seems likely that references to transactions may even let in documents unknown to the defendant (cp *Peirce* v *Corf* (1874) LR 9 QB 210, disapproved in *Elias* v *George Sahely & Co* supra). However, there can be no reference to a document not yet in existence when the defendant signed (*Turnley* v *Hartley* (1848) 3 New Pract Cas 96), except that:

> where two documents relied on as a memorandum are signed and exchanged at one and the same meeting as part of the same transaction, so that they may fairly be said to have been to all intents and purposes contemporaneously signed, the document signed by the party to be charged should not be treated as incapable of referring to the other document merely because the latter, on a minute investigation of the order of events at the meeting, is found to have come second in the order of preparation and signing

(per Jenkins LJ in *Timmins* v *Moreland Street Property Co Ltd* [1958] Ch 110, at p 123). In this, the leading case, the Court of Appeal in fact held that a cheque, the only document signed by the defendant, could *not* be read with the receipt so as to constitute a memorandum, since the only transaction referred to by the cheque was its own order for payment. With respect, however, was this not a little unrealistic? One might have thought that the drawing of a cheque in favour of the vendor's solicitors for 10 per cent of the purchase price called for some sufficient explanation outside itself. Further, it should be noticed that, whereas the cheque was made payable to the plaintiff-vendor's solicitors, the receipt was given by the plaintiff himself. A clear inference to be drawn from the judgments in the case is that if there had in fact been no discrepancy between the payees of the cheque and the signatory of the receipt, then the two documents might have been read side by side so as to constitute a sufficient memorandum (see per Romer LJ at pp 135-6). As it was, a contract was broken with impunity.

3   All terms

As a rule the writing relied on to satisfy s 40(1) of the Law of Property Act 1925 must contain all the terms of the parties' agreement (see *Beckett* v *Nurse* [1948] 1 KB 535). If the agreement itself is in writing, eg, where a formal contract is drawn up and the parts exchanged by solicitors, then this rule will almost inevitably be observed (see *Hutton* v *Watling* [1948] Ch 398). Where, however, the writing is merely a memorandum of the parties' prior oral agreement, it will normally be insufficient unless it simply records neither more nor less than the terms of that agreement (see ibid; also *Smith* v *MacGowan* [1938] 3 All ER 447). In other words, the memorandum must specify the four 'P's—the parties, the property, the price plus any other provisions.

(a)   Parties

Obviously a memorandum will be incomplete if the parties and their respective functions (eg, which is the vendor and which the purchaser) are not indicated with certainty (see *Dewar* v *Mintoft* [1912] 2 KB 373). The names of the parties, however, need only be ascertainable, not stated—id cerum est quod certum reddi potest— and a statement of the party's capacity may well be less uncertain than his name (how many John Smiths are there?). Thus a sufficient indication of a party's identity has been a reference simply to 'mortgagees' (in *Allen (AH) & Co Ltd* v *Whiteman* (1920) 89 LJ Ch 534). Even the familiar clause that the 'Vendor will convey as personal representative', although not saying of whom, has sufficed for the Court of Appeal (in *Fay* v *Miller, Wilkins & Co* [1941] Ch 360; but compare *Re Spencer & Hauser's Contract* [1928] Ch 598, at p 608, where Tomlin J stated that 'a contract containing a clause indicating how the title is to be made is indicative only of the vendor's intention and is not a warranty to make good title in the particular form that is mentioned', ie, the clause is not a certain statement that the vendor is anyone's personal representative at all).

Further even where the names are stated but wrongly, the rule remains the same: the memorandum will suffice in this respect if the parties can be identified from the inaccurate description in the light of the surrounding circumstances and known facts (*F Goldsmith (Sicklesmere) Ltd* v *Baxter* [1970] Ch 85). In that case, specific performance was ordered of a contract for sale where the plaintiff-vendor had been named in the memorandum as 'Goldsmith Coaches (Sicklesmere) Ltd' (Stamp J followed *Cummins* v *Scott* (1875) LR 20 Eq 11, where there was no indication of the vendor in the contract except that it was a company in possession of the property and this sufficed). See further as to the description of parties to deeds, p 240).

On the other side of the line, however, such descriptions as 'the vendor' (in *Potter* v *Duffield* (1874) LR 18 Eq 4) and 'my clients' (in *Lovesy* v *Palmer* [1916] 2 Ch 233) have not sufficed on their own as being indefinite. Nonetheless, more recently in *Davies* v *Sweet* [1962] 2 QB 300, Lord Evershed MR somehow felt able to point out (at p 308) that:

> The statutory language requires that there should be a sufficient note or memorandum of the contract alleged, that is, of its essential provisions. It does not in terms require that the contracting parties should be named or identified, but rather that the note or memorandum should be signed by the party sought to be charged or by his duly authorised agent.

Whatever the learned Master of the Rolls may have meant by this obiter dictum, the Court of Appeal actually decided that a memorandum will be sufficient if, although *not* identifying one of the parties to the contract, it does identify someone who will be bound by the contract, as, for example, an agent who has incurred personal liability. In the case, an estate agent, acting for the vendor, signed a receipt written on his own headed notepaper for a deposit paid by the plaintiff. Apart from not mentioning the vendor, the receipt contained all the terms of the agreement for sale which had been concluded orally by the estate agent on behalf of the vendor (he evidently forgot to incant 'subject to contract'). The estate agent was held to have incurred personal liability and the receipt to be a sufficient memorandum, on the proposition of law that where an agent contracts in his own name without mentioning the agency both he and his principal are bound even though the other party knows of the agency (see *Basma* v *Weekes* [1950] AC 441, and the cases there discussed; cp as to an undisclosed principal being unable to enforce a tenancy agreement *Hanstown Properties Ltd* v *Green* (1977) 246 EG 917, CA).

(b) Property

It is obvious really that a memorandum, to be complete, must indicate the property which is the subject-matter of the agreement. However, as with the parties, the property also need only be described so as to be identifiable. Thus, although 'property' alone has not sufficed (in *Vale of Neath Colliery Co* v *Furness* (1876) 45 LJ Ch 276), 'my house' has sufficed (in *Cowley* v *Watts* (1853) 17 Jur 172), the possessive adjective apparently creating certainty. But even without this or any other particularising adjective, 'twenty-four acres of land, freehold, at Totmons-low' has succeeded with the Court of Appeal (in *Plant* v *Bourne* [1897] 2 Ch 281). The question is one not of law but of construction and fact combined, which depends on individual circumstances. In *Davies* v *Sweet* [1962] 2 QB 300, for example, no difficulty was found with 'land on which Evans Row houses previously stood' as a description of the property (see per Danckwerts LJ at p 306), nor was any found with 'this chalet' in *Smith* v *Mansi* [1963] 1 WLR 26 (see per Russell LJ at p 30).

The property need only be described in a physical sense. As Romer LJ put it (in *Timmins* v *Moreland Street Property Co Ltd* [1958] Ch 110, at p 132):

> The memorandum is not insufficient if it omits to mention the particular interest which the vendor is selling in the property, provided that the property itself is sufficiently described. If no interest is mentioned, then prima facie an unencumbered freehold interest will be implied. No such implication arises, however, if the purchaser knew at the time of the contract (as the defendant company knew in the present case) that some lesser interest or some encumbered interest was to be the subject of the sale. I cannot think that a memorandum fails in point of sufficiency if it omits an explanation of why the implication of an unencumbered fee simple is displaced or if it fails to specify the precise legal interest in the identified property which the vendor has agreed to sell and the purchaser agreed to buy, or if it makes no reference to encumbrances affecting the property. A right of way, for example, over land agreed to be sold is not a term of the contract of sale but a matter of title, and need not be mentioned in the memorandum.

However, Jenkins LJ (ibid at pp 118–19), put this on the slightly different basis of the knowledge of the purchaser implying a term into the agreement, implied terms not having to be mentioned in the memorandum (see post).

(c) Price

Again obviously the consideration for the contract must be indicated (*Hawes* v *Armstrong* (1835) 1 Scott 661), a price being stated if fixed or else the method of its ascertainment (see *Smith* v *Jones* [1952] 2 All ER 907, where the sale was agreed at 'the controlled price fixed by the government'; also *Selkirk* v *Romar Investments Ltd* [1963] 1 WLR 1415, where the purchase price was to be precisely ascertained by measurement of the area before completion), together with any special terms as to payment (*Neale* v *Merrett* [1930] WN 189). An illustration of all this occurred in *Savage* v *Uwechia* [1961] 1 WLR 455, although not in connection with s 40 of the Law of Property Act 1925. In effect, Mr S signed a document headed 'Promissory Note' which read: 'I promise to pay to [Mr U] or order three months after date the sum of £780 for value received or in default to convey to him all those messages together with appurtenances thereto situate at 6 New Market Road in the township of Onitsha, to hold the same unto [Mr U] or order in fee simple.' The £780 was not paid and Mr U sought specific performance on the ground that the document constituted a conditional contract to convey. The Privy Council, allowing the appeal, refused specific performance, first, because no price for the land was stated or ascertainable, and second, because 'for value received' indicated past consideration which is insufficient to support a contract. Again in *Cross* v *Hetenyi* (1978) 129 NLJ 250, as Lawton LJ sorted it out: 'By way of compromise, it was agreed that there should be a contract for the sale of the land forthwith, followed by a conveyance, at a price of £9,000, and that two years later the defendant should pay another £500'. Five years afterwards the vendor failed to get his further £500. The Court of Appeal could not swallow the idea here of a collateral contract (as at first instance) and also refused to read a post-completion piece of paper promising to pay the £500 with the rest of the contractual documents on the grounds of patent inconsistency.

The accepted view has long been that where the parties to a sale of land have not themselves determined the price, no term will be implied that the purchaser must pay a reasonable price (see per Cranworth LC in *Morgan* v *Milman* (1853) 3 De GM & G 24, at pp 34 and 37: also Grant MR in *Gowlay* v *Somerset* (1815) 19 Ves 429, at p 431). Yet at the same time it has also been accepted that an explicit agreement to buy land at a 'fair price' or a 'reasonable valuation' will be valid and enforceable. In the hope of explanations, reference should now be made to *Sudbrook Trading Estate Ltd* v *Eggleton* [1982] 3 WLR 315, HL, which concerned an option to purchase at a valuation price in which each side (landlord and tenant) had to appoint valuers and in default of agreement the valuers were to appoint an umpire, but where one side (the landlord) refused to appoint a valuer. Overruling earlier authority, it was held that the breakdown of the valuation machinery should not defeat the contract *unless* that machinery was expressly or impliedly of the essence; ie, generally the court could substitute its own machinery for that agreed abortively by the parties. Further, it was held that the description 'valuer' necessarily implied that the price to be fixed should be 'fair and reasonable' as between the parties. The accepted view was accepted that the use of such formulae simpliciter, ie, without any valuation machinery, would render the price sufficiently ascertainable by appropriate enquiries for the contract to be valid and enforceable (see also per Grant MR in *Milnes* v *Gery* (1807) 14 Ves 400, at p 407 and per Harman LJ in *Talbot* v *Talbot* [1968] Ch 1, at p 12).

However, do not forget that if anything essential is left to be settled by agreement between the parties there will in principle still be no contract (*May & Butcher* v *The King* [1934] 2 KB 17, 21n). Thus in *Courtney Ltd* v *Tolaini Bros Ltd* [1975] 1 WLR 297 the Court of Appeal considered an agreement to 'negotiate fair and reasonable contract sums' in respect of certain development projects and decided that no contract had been concluded since there was no agreement on the price or on any method by which the price was to be calculated. The court also rejected the proposition that there might be an enforceable contract to negotiate. Again in *Bushwall Properties Ltd* v *Vortex Properties Ltd* [1976] 1 WLR 591, the Court of Appeal held unenforceable for uncertainty a contract for the sale of 51½ acres of land for £500,000 payable in three unequal instalments because of the provision that on each payment 'a proportionate part of the land shall be released'. The Court decided that the purchaser could not cure the uncertainty by claiming an implied power to select the land to be conveyed on each occasion. Accordingly it may never be safe to assume that a memorandum will satisfy s 40(1) if it states neither the price nor the method of ascertainment but leaves the court to supply the machinery of valuation.

Incidentally, where the contract is for the sale of land at a price to be fixed by an agreed valuer, the parties will be bound by an honest valuation notwithstanding that other valuers may produce different figures: *Campbell* v *Edwards* [1976] 1 WLR 403, CA. The only possible escape from this binding position is 'if a valuer gives a speaking valuation—if he gives his reasons or his calculations—and you can show on the face of them that they are wrong it might be upset' (per Lord Denning MR at p 407H; see also *Baber* v *Kenwood Manufacturing Co Ltd* [1978] 1 Lloyds Rep 175, CA). Otherwise where the valuation was negligent as well as wrong damages may be recoverable from the valuer (ibid; also *Arenson* v *Casson, Beckman Rutley & Co* [1977] AC 405).

(d)   Other provisions

Contrary to a quite common supposition, a memorandum which merely states the parties, the property and the price will be quite sufficient, if, and only if, no other provisions have been agreed. For example, if the parties have orally agreed, inter alia, as to when completion should take place and vacant possession be given, a later memorandum which omits to mention this will not satisfy s 40(1): *Hawkins* v *Price* [1947] Ch 645 (see also *Burgess* v *Cox* [1951] Ch 383). Again in *Tweddell* v *Henderson* [1975] 1 WLR 1496 the memorandum was insufficient because no reference was made to an undertaking to make up the road or to payment of the price by stages.

4 Implied terms

However, any terms which are not expressly agreed, but which are implied into the agreement between the parties—and there are, of course, many such terms on a sale of land—do not have to be mentioned in the memorandum to satisfy s 40(1). For example, if the parties express no thoughts as to a date for completion or for giving vacant possession, then vacant possession on completion, and completion within a reasonable time, will both be implied terms and neither need be mentioned (*Farrell v Green* (1974) 232 EG 587). The situation will be the same where there is such a term agreed which happens to be identical with the term which would otherwise be implied (ibid).

Much more usually, though, where a formal contract is drawn up by solicitors, the sale will be made subject to some standard form of general conditions, which will almost certainly provide for the completion date if none be fixed by the special conditions. Thus both the National Conditions of Sale, 20th ed (Conditions 5(1) and 9(1)) and The Law Society's Conditions of Sale, 1980 (Condition 22(1)), provide for completion to be seven weeks (in effect) or five weeks respectively after the date of the contract. Nonetheless, in practice, four weeks only is often agreed between the parties' solicitors, but even so, the special condition fixing the completion date is not infrequently left blank on exchange of the two parts of the formal contract. This latter sloppy practice having first become questionable, has now fortunately for sloppy practitioners been vindicated.

The courts have twice rejected the argument that if the usual special condition (ie, 'The date fixed for completion is the   day of   19 ') should be neither filled in nor deleted on exchange then it would override the general conditions and indicate that there was no concluded contract (*Smith* v *Mansi* [1963] 1 WLR 26, CA, and *Lee-Parker* v *Izzet* [1971] 3 All ER 1099, at p 1105, a point not noted at [1971] 1 WLR 1688). However, the argument might well revive if the special condition unusually provided that 'the date fixed for completion is to be agreed between the parties' (as in *Gavaghan* v *Edwards* [1961] 2 QB 220). But even then an argued obiter should save the day. In *Walters* v *Roberts* (1980) 41 P & CR 210, at pp 215–6, Nourse J strongly inclined to the view that although such an express provision for agreeing the completion date would render inoperative a general 'fall-back' condition, 'the court would imply a reasonable time in default of agreement' (cf similarly *Simpson* v *Hughes* (1897) 76 LT 237 and *Fowler* v *Bratt* [1950] 2 KB 96).

Perhaps at this point mention should be made that, if the contract is not for the sale of land but for the grant of a lease, there can be no implication that the term should commence within a reasonable time. In a case concerning such a contract, Lord Denning MR has stated that:

> It is settled beyond question that, in order for there to be a valid agreement for a lease, the essentials are not only the parties to be determined, the property to be determined, the length of the term and the rent, but also the date of its commencement. This document does not contain it. It is not sufficient to say that it can be supplied by an implied term as to reasonable time

(in *Harvey* v *Pratt* [1965] 1 WLR 1025, at p 1027). Nor would the Court of Appeal accept a suggestion that the date of the agreement be the date of commencement. However, the main basis of the decision was that the property which was the subject-matter of the agreement had not been adequately indicated (see p 39):

In the case of the sale of freehold, the subject-matter is ascertained, namely the land. In the case of an agreement for a lease, unless the length of the term and the commencement of the term are defined, then the subject of the agreement or contract is uncertain. Therefore there is no agreement
(per Davies LJ at p 1027; see also per Russell LJ at pp 1027–8 to the same effect).

5 Waived provision

Another exception to the general rule that the memorandum must contain all the provisions of the agreement in order for the agreement to be enforceable rests on waiver by the plaintiff. The exception simply is that if the memorandum is complete apart from some provision solely benefiting him, then the plaintiff may waive that provision and enforce the rest of the contract: *North* v *Loomes* [1919] 1 Ch 378 (see per Younger J in a postscript at pp 385–6, concerning a provision that defendant should pay plaintiff's costs; see also *Von Hatzfeldt-Wildenburg* v *Alexander* [1912] 1 Ch 284, and per Astbury J in *Morrell* v *Studd and Millington* [1913] 2 Ch 648, at p 660). This exception presupposes, of course, that there is a concluded contract to enforce (see *Allsopp* v *Orchard* [1923] 1 Ch 323; cp *Heron Garage Properties Ltd* v *Moss* [1974] 1 WLR 148 as to the waiver of the condition of a 'conditional contract').

However, there are two vital restrictions on this exception. First, it is always emphasised that the provision must be for the exclusive benefit of the plaintiff: *Hawkins* v *Price* [1947] Ch 645. Second, the provision to be waived apparently must not be of such great importance as to be a material term of the agreement: see *Hawkins* v *Price*, ante. In this case, Evershed J held that a provision as to the date for completion and vacant possession could not be waived, first, because it might be for the benefit of both parties, and second, because it was of 'real' importance to the agreement in question. However, omission of the date for possession may not, in the circumstances of a particular case, always be so devastating (see *Fowler* v *Bratt* [1950] 2 KB 96).

6 Stipulation submitted to

The converse of the above waiver exception, namely, 'that if a stipulation, which is to the detriment . . . of one of the parties exclusively, be omitted from the memorandum, that party may submit to perform it . . . and may with such submission . . . enforce the contract as stated in the memorandum' was laid down in *Williams on Vendor and Purchaser*, 3rd ed, at pp 4–5, on the authority of *Martin* v *Pycroft* (1852) 22 LJ Ch 94. In that case, the Court of Appeal in Chancery refused, on equitable principles, to allow the defendant to resist specific performance by setting up an omitted provision for the plaintiff to pay a premium of £200, the plaintiff submitting to pay the £200. Then, a century later, Harman J brusquely denied the existence of this submission exception (in *Burgess* v *Cox* [1951] Ch 383; criticised at 67 LQR 299 by 'REM') on the ground that whilst the waiver exception leaves a term out altogether, the submission exception would involve asking the court to assert a term which is not in the memorandum at all.

Now, however, after a scant twenty further years, the rule in *Williams*, the authority of *Martin* v *Pycroft* and the criticisms of 'REM' have all been followed by Plowman J in *Scott* v *Bradley* [1971] 1 Ch 850 (where the plaintiff, submitting to perform the missing term that he pay half the defendant's costs, was held entitled to specific performance). But what will happen next time round?

7   Rectified mistake

Another exception to the 'all terms' rule exists where the equitable remedy of rectification is applicable. If any of the provisions of the prior oral agreement are omitted from the memorandum thereof due to a mistake common to both parties, then the court may, in one action, both rectify the memorandum and decree specific performance of the true agreement: *Craddock Bros Ltd* v *Hunt* [1923] 2 Ch 136 (see also *United States of America* v *Motor Trucks Ltd* [1924] AC 196, at p 201). Further, after a recent re-examination of this remedy by the Court of Appeal, it now appears clear that there is jurisdiction to rectify on the basis of a common continuing intention of the parties, such intention having some outward expression, even though no prior concluded agreement existed (see *Joscelyne* v *Nissen* [1970] 2 QB 86). Consequently, considerable inroads into the 'all terms' rule of s 40(1) could be achieved with sales of land where the negotiations customarily proceed throughout on a basis of various common continuing intentions expressed in correspondence up to a formal exchange of contracts.

8   Collateral contract

Lastly the damning effect of s 40(1) may be evaded by setting up the omitted provision or promise as a separate contract in its own right, collateral to the principal contract with only the latter needing to be evidenced with all its terms in writing (*Jameson* v *Kinmell Bay Land Co* (1931) 47 TLR 593). The provision or promise must, of course, have on its own all the elements of a valid contract and in this respect the consideration is usually found, if at all, in the making of the principal contract (see per Lord Moulton in *Heilbut Symons & Co* v *Buckleton* [1913] AC 30, at p 47). In addition, contractual liability in respect of the promise must have been intended by the parties (ibid, p 51)—in reality this is a question of the court being able or not to attribute the appropriate intention to the parties ex post facto.

D   'IN WRITING'

Continuing the phrase-by-phrase commentary on the formal requirements of s 40(1) of the Law of Property Act 1925, the next phrase is 'in writing.' However, the only point to mention on this requirement that the memorandum should be 'in writing' is that ' "writing" includes typing, printing, lithography, photography and other modes of representing or reproducing words in a visible form': Interpretation Act 1978, Sched 1. A modern illustration would be a contract by telex (as in *Aquis Estates Ltd* v *Minton* [1975] 1 WLR 1452, 1454). The next one-word requirement of the section has more to it.

E   'SIGNED'

A great deal of latitude has been allowed by the courts as to this requirement that the memorandum should be signed. The minimum which seems necessary is that the name (or initials) of the party to be charged should appear in *some form* (handwritten, typewritten, printed, rubber stamped) *somewhere* ('subscribed' is not specified) in or on the memorandum provided that that party has *somehow* indicated that he recognised not the name as a signature but the memorandum as being of the alleged agreement (see *Hill* v *Hill* [1947] Ch 231 and *Leeman* v *Stocks* [1951] Ch 941, cf *Goodman* v *Eban Ltd* [1954] 1 QB 550). Thus, an early and obvious example, 'I, *A*, agree' has sufficed without other signature (*Knight* v *Crockford* (1794) 1 Esp 190). Further, this minimum has even been held satisfied despite the fact of the name having been written in *before* the agreement was made (*Leeman* v *Stocks*, ante).

However, this minimum should not be taken as satisfied if the memorandum on the face of it shows that the name in question was not inserted as a signature. For example, where formal articles of agreement containing the full names of the parties concluded 'As witness our hands,' without any signatures being subscribed, there was held to be no signed memorandum: *Hubert* v *Treherne* (1842) 3 Man & G 743. That case would appear to fit current conveyancing practice, yet it was distinguished by Roxburgh J in *Leeman* v *Stocks* [1951] Ch 941. There a printed 'memorandum of agreement' in which the names of both parties had been inserted by an auctioneer concluded, as is usual: 'As witness the hands of the parties hereunto the day and year first before written', but only the plaintiff-purchaser had signed beneath. This was nonetheless held to be a memorandum signed by the vendor on the grounds that (1) only the purchaser had been intended to subscribe, and (2) the vendor had recognised the memorandum through his agent, the auctioneer, having procured the purchaser's signature to it. Thus there is still room for a measure of uncertainty on the facts of particular cases.

Also where a contract is reduced to writing and signed any alterations thereto subsequently added and agreed by the parties have been held to have the consequence that there will be no memorandum satisfying s 40(1) of the Law of Property Act 1925 in the absence, in effect, of the customary initialling (*New Hart Builders Ltd* v *Brindley* [1975] Ch 342). Distinguish the position where the signed document is altered in order to correct a mistake in the written statement of an existing contract (*Bluck* v *Gompertz* (1852) 7 Exch 862) or when the signed document is altered before the parties are contractually bound at all (*Stewart* v *Eddowes* (1874) LR 9 CP 311; *Koenigsblatt* v *Sweet* [1923] 2 Ch 314). In these cases the altered document is sufficiently signed by the original signature. But, illogically, where the alterations amount to a variation by consent of a concluded contract appropriate words or gestures must be directed to the original signature to achieve the same authentication: *New Hart Builders Ltd* v *Brindley*, ante. Consequently in practice due initialling of alterations should always be insisted upon; see also *Earl* v *Mawson* (1974) 232 EG 1315, CA. Further reference may be made to an article entitled 'Statute of Frauds: The Authenticated Signature Fiction—An Illogical Distinction' by CT Emery in (1975) 39 Conv (NS) 336–42).

1 'By the party to be charged'

Section 40(1) of the Law of Property Act 1925 does not require both parties' signatures but only that of the defendant. Accordingly, where there is a concluded agreement for sale and only, say, the purchaser has signed a memorandum thereof, then the agreement will be enforceable by action by the vendor and not by the purchaser (*Bays* v *Ayerst* (1822) 6 Madd 316). The vendor here may even maintain an action for specific performance despite the apparent lack of mutuality (*Flight* v *Bolland* (1828) 4 Russ 298) and despite payment of damages being for him a complete remedy (*Cogent* v *Gibson* (1864) 33 Beav 557). This may well seem an oddity since the latter is generally explained away by the desire of equity for mutuality, but no doubt the vendor can be said to make the remedy mutual by bringing the action. Nevertheless, a purchaser's action to take advantage of a memorandum signed by the vendor alone (as an anti-gazumping device), although obtaining an order for specific performance, was also criticised as 'distasteful to one's ideas of fairness' (per Pennycuick V-C in *Farrell* v *Green* (1974) 232 EG 587).

2 'Or by some other person thereunto by him lawfully authorised'

Since no statutory definition of 'lawfully authorised' is provided, the ordinary principles of agency appear to be applicable. Accordingly, the authority to sign may be conferred on the 'some other person' (*a*) expressly, even by an undisclosed principal (see *Davies* v *Sweet* [1962] 2 QB 300): (*b*) impliedly (see *Keen* v *Mear* [1920] 2 Ch 574; also *Davies* v *Sweet*, ante, at p 305, where Danckwerts LJ said that authority 'should be inferred from the circumstances of this case' in the absence of rebutting evidence; and see *Smith* v *Mansi* [1963] 1 WLR 26, at pp 34 and 35); or (*c*) retrospectively by ratification (*Maclean* v *Dunn* (1828) 4 Bing 722). Additionally, although there is no clear authority to this effect, a signature within an agent's apparent or ostensible authority should suffice unless s 40(1) be held to refer only to actual authority. However, the limiting maxim delegatus non potest delegare clearly applies, a signature by an auctioneer's clerk having been held ineffective on this ground (*Bell* v *Balls* [1897] 1 Ch 663), and presumably the same would go for a solicitor's legal executive or other clerk.

The authority which has to be conferred on the 'some other person' need not amount to entering into the agreement for sale itself, but may simply be to sign the document which happens to constitute the memorandum relied on by the plaintiff (*Thirkell* v *Cambi* [1919] 2 KB 590; *Hoover* v *Walker* [1923] 2 Ch 788). It matters not a jot that the agent had no intention at all of constituting a memorandum or even of binding his principal in any way (see *Grindell* v *Bass* [1920] 2 Ch 487). Further, the same person, may, if duly authorised, sign as agent for both parties (as in *Gavaghan* v *Edwards* [1961] 2 QB 220), except that one party is not permitted, for an obvious reason, to sign for the other (*Sharman* v *Brandt* (1871) LR 6 QB 720).

The position of two particular sorts of agent may be briefly mentioned here. First, in accordance with the ordinary principles of agency, a solicitor may not sign the writing (whether constituting the contract itself or only a memorandum of it) which makes an enforceable contract within s 40(1) unless this is within his authority received from his client. Whether he has such authority or not is, as always, a question of fact and/or construction, and it is well settled law 'that a solicitor has no ostensible or apparent authority to sign a contract of sale on behalf of a client so as to bind him when there is no contract in fact' (per Lord Denning MR in *H Clark Ltd* v *Wilkinson* [1965] Ch 694, at p 702). Further, no implication that he has authority to sign the contract itself appears to arise merely from the solicitor-client relationship, although instructions to a solicitor to act would seem sufficient for him to sign a memorandum of an already negotiated oral contract (*North* v *Loomes* [1919] 1 Ch 378). Thus in *Horner* v *Walker* [1923] 2 Ch 218 it was held that a letter signed by the lessee's solicitor purporting to enclose an engrossment of the lease formed an adequate memorandum. The lessee's solicitor had authority to carry out the transaction in the usual way and so had authority to sign the letter although no-one thought that it might be treated as a memorandum of the oral agreement for the lease. It is suggested that the same rule would be applied to a letter sending requisitions on title or a draft conveyance if the documents together contain all the terms of the contract. Similarly in *Gavaghan* v *Edwards* [1961] 2 QB 220, a note of a telephone conversation with the purchaser confirming what he had already agreed with the vendor, made by the solicitor acting for both parties on a copy letter, was held to amount, with the copy letter, to a memorandum binding on the purchaser. In this case, Danckwerts LJ said (at p 226) that from the way in which the instructions are given to the solicitor, he may by implication be entitled to sign a memorandum which will bind his client. Against this, it must be emphasised again that the courts are still not prepared to find that the giving of instructions to a solicitor to act in a transaction which remains in a state of negotiation (eg, to prepare or approve a draft contract where the parties have agreed 'subject to contract') confers on its own any authority to conclude or sign the contract itself (see per Buckley J in *D'Silva* v *Lister House Development Ltd* [1971] Ch 17, at pp 28–9 and per Widgery LJ in *Griffiths* v *Young* [1970] Ch 675, at p 685). In practice, therefore, it is probably better to assume that a solicitor's authority to sign the contract itself can only be given to him expressly whilst his authority to sign a memorandum of an existing contract may be implied. But contrast the mere machinery of making a contract: a solicitor is impliedly and ostensibly authorised to effect exchange of contracts in such manner as he may think fit (*Domb* v *Isoz* [1980] Ch 548, CA).

Second, an auctioneer has a peculiar position. Primarily, of course, he is the vendor's agent, with at least ostensible or apparent authority to sign the memorandum on his behalf, but the purchaser (the highest bidder) also will be deemed to have conferred authority on him to sign on his behalf (see *Chaney* v *Maclow* [1929] 1 Ch 461). Then this authority to sign cannot be revoked after the fall of the hammer by either the vendor or the purchaser (see ibid). However, whilst the auctioneer's authority to sign for the vendor subsists for the period for which he was expressly made the vendor's agent, his authority to sign for the purchaser is confined to the time of the sale (*Bell* v *Balls* [1897] 1 Ch 663). Further, it has been contended that the auctioneer's implied authority to sign for the purchaser carries with it a duty owed to the purchaser to sign the memorandum on behalf of the vendor to enable enforcement of the contract; this contention was considered and doubted, but not decided, by Pennycuick J in *Richards* v *Phillips* [1967] 3 All ER 876 (affirmed at [1969] 1 Ch 39, where this particular point was not debated).

F NO MEMORANDUM

'No action may be brought' is the stated effect of there being no memorandum in writing within s 40(1) of the Law of Property Act 1925. This does not mean that the contract for sale will be void but simply that the important remedy of enforcement by action will not be available (see *Maddison* v *Alderson* (1883) 8 App Cas 467, also *Delaney* v *Smith Ltd* [1946] KB 393 and per Megarry J in *Thompson* v *Salah* [1972] 1 All ER 530, at p 524E/F). The section, whilst not affecting the essential validity of the contract, thus provides a procedural bar, resembling those provided by the Limitation Act 1980 (see *Leroux* v *Brown* (1852) 12 CB 801).

Consequently, not only may the defendant waive the section's requirements but if he wishes to rely on them, then he must specially plead them in his defence. Further, the contract for sale may be enforced in any available way other than action. For example, a vendor may forfeit any deposit paid if the purchaser defaults (*Monnickendam* v *Leanse* (1923) 39 TLR 445; if the vendor defaults, the purchaser can recover his deposit by a quasi-contractual claim based on failure of consideration: *Pulbrook* v *Lawes* (1876) 1 QBD 284). In addition, it appears that an oral contract can be relied on as a defence notwithstanding the provisions of s 40(1): *Steadman* v *Steadman* [1976] AC 536, HL (see per Viscount Dilhorne at p 551, also per Edmund Davies LJ at [1974] QB 161, 167E); but cp *Thompson's Trustee in Bankruptcy* v *Heaton* [1974] 1 WLR 605, and *McDonald* v *Windaybank* (1975) 120 SJ

96, where such reliance did not succeed. It has also been held that an oral agreement for sale between joint tenants, although unenforceable, may effect a severance of their beneficial joint tenancy (*Burgess* v *Rawnsley* [1975] Ch 429, CA).

The effect of unenforceability by action, introduced by the Statute of Frauds 1677, was soon evaded or supplemented by equity in accordance with its maxim of not allowing a statute 'to be used as an instrument of fraud.' Thus less than ten years later the equitable remedy of specific performance was decreed of an unsigned agreement for the sale of land (*Butcher* v *Stapely* (1685) 1 Vern 363; the common law remedy of damages may now also be awarded: Supreme Court Act 1981, s 50). The commonest example of equitable fraud justifying equity's intervention arises from the performance by the plaintiff of some act under and unequivocally referable to some such agreement as that alleged (see *Maddison* v *Alderson* (1883) 8 App Cas 467). This became known as the doctrine of part performance and now enjoys express statutory recognition in subs (2) of s 40. A detailed introductory discussion of this surely well known doctrine is, rightly or wrongly, taken to be outside the scope of this book (see the exposition in Megarry and Wade, *Real Property*, 4th ed, pp 561–71). However, conveyancers may be particularly concerned with certain recent developments as to the nature of the acts which may be relied on within the doctrine.

In *Steadman* v *Steadman*, supra, the House of Lords re-examined the question at great length and held that mere payment of a sum of money in the circumstances of the case amounted to a sufficient act of part performance so that the contract was enforceable despite the lack of writing (the husband had paid £100 to the wife as arrears of maintenance under the compromise agreement). Further, the majority of the law lords severally indicated that, in the ordinary circumstances of a contract for the sale of land, a sufficient such act could be found in the fact of the purchaser instructing solicitors to prepare and submit a draft conveyance or transfer. In consequence it appears that an oral contract for sale can readily and unilaterally be rendered enforceable by the purchaser (see also a note at (1974) 38 Conv (NS) 388–91). There are suggestions, seemingly both illogical and impractical, that payment of a deposit or tender of the purchase money would suffice for the doctrine only if the vendor was unable to make repayment (see per Lord Salmon at [1976] AC 571; also per Lord Reid at ibid, p 541). On the vendor's side, it is arguable that he could rely on the unilateral act of (part) performance constituted by actually executing a deed of conveyance or transfer and subsequently suing for the price (see Conv (NS) loc cit, where the practical difficulties are dealt with). Reference may also be made to *Re Windle* [1975] 1 WLR 1628, where there was an oral agreement between spouses as to the transfer of property; Goff J applied (at pp 1635–6) the principle laid down in *Steadman* v *Steadman*, ante, and held, first, that payment of mortgage arrears and instalments would not suffice as an act of part performance but, second, that instructing solicitors to prepare the transfer and payment of their costs and disbursements did suffice. For some insufficient acts, see *New Hart Builders Ltd* v *Brindley* [1975] Ch 342 (purchaser's planning application), *Re Gonin* [1979] Ch 16 (looking after parents) and *Daulia Ltd* v *Four Millbank Nominees Ltd* [1978] Ch 231, CA (tendering signed contract plus deposit). In this last cited case, it was emphasised that a plaintiff's acts must be in performance of some contract, not merely in contemplation of making one. See also per Shaw LJ obiter in *Elsden* v *Pick* [1980] 1 WLR 898, at p 905 that acts of part performance 'must still be in furtherance of the contract and not merely a recognition of its existence or its contemplation'.

Finally, two anomalous cases may be mentioned. First, where a contract has been concluded and a complete memorandum of it satisfying the section has been constituted and subsequently a parol variation of the contract is agreed, then the variation may be disregarded, the original recorded contract remaining enforceable by action (see *Morris* v *Baron & Co* [1918] AC 1; cp *New Hart Builders Ltd* v *Brindley* ante where it was unauthenticated alterations rather than the original which was in issue). However, variation must be distinguished from an agreement which amounts to a rescission of the recorded contract and the making of a new contract, since then neither the original nor the substituted contract can be enforced by action (ibid). Also distinguished must be mere further negotiations which if they prove to be abortive do not affect the original contract anyway (see *Davies* v *Sweet* [1962] 2 QB 300). These distinctions unhappily are less easy to recognise in practice than to state in theory.

The second anomaly to note is that a single contract for the sale of land and goods together which does not comply with s 40(1) will not be actionable even as to the goods alone (*Hawkesworth* v *Turner* (1930) 46 TLR 389). This rule was applied rather rigidly where there was an oral agreement for the sale of two farms, two bullocks, two ploughshares plus perhaps a tractor, but the only possible memorandum merely referred to the farms: contract held unenforceable (*Ram Narayan* v *Shah* [1979] 1 WLR 1349, PC, queried at [1980] Conv 92). Bear in mind, however, that things which are prima facie chattels may be included without express mention in a sale of land if found to be fixtures (see *Hamp* v *Bygrave* (1983) *The Times*, 6 January as to garden ornaments where estoppel was an alternative basis of inclusion).

IV PARTICULARS OF SALE

ASSUMING the presence of both a binding agreement and the formality of writing the particulars of sale, which are the first part of the traditional division of the contents of a contract for the sale of land, can be considered. At the outset, however, the second part of this traditional division, namely, the conditions of sale, should be distinguished and this has been done briefly and judicially as follows:

> The proper office of the particulars is to describe the subject-matter of the contract; that of the conditions to state the terms on which it is sold

(per Malins V-C in *Torrance* v *Bolton* (1872) 14 Eq 124, at p 130; see also per Warrington J in *Blaiberg* v *Keeves* [1906] 2 Ch 175, at p 184).

Whilst the conditions of sale owe their existence to the need to provide for the investigation of title and other complexities of conveyancing the special place of the particulars of sale is due to the peculiar difficulty of delimiting land both physically and legally. The particulars ideally should describe the following aspects of the subject-matter of the sale: (1) the physical extent of the land; (2) the estate or interest in that land; (3) the rights, etc, the benefit of which is to pass with that estate or interest, and (4) the rights, etc, to the burden of which that estate or interest is subject. This fourth aspect means, according to the Council of The Law Society, that any charges, onerous covenants, easements, and the like should be referred to in the particulars and not merely in the conditions of sale (*Law Society's Gazette* (1951) vol 49, at p 29): ie, in the large rather than in the small print.

It must be stressed, however, that the distinction between the particulars of sale and the conditions of sale is purely traditional. It is not a matter of substance and need not be regarded too rigidly. Thus Sargant J has said of a general condition expressed to relate to omissions in the particulars of sale that it could not be:

> construed so strictly as to exclude from its purview omissions in that part of the document under which the sale was effected, divided off, and headed "Conditions of Sale"

(*Re Courcier & Harrold's Contract* [1923] 1 Ch 565, at p 572; see also *Cook* v *Taylor* [1942] Ch 349, where a term for vacant possession on completion was found in the 'particulars'). This being so, the effect of relevant conditions of sale will be considered in this chapter whilst dealing with the various aspects of the particulars of sale. Not to do so would be misleading since the contract for sale should be looked at as a whole.

A IDENTITY

Before drafting the particulars of sale, thought should always be given to the vendor's eventual obligation to prove the identity of the property sold with that to which the documents of title relate (*Flower* v *Hartopp* (1843) 6 Beav 476; for the position if the title is registered, see p 149). If the contract description differs from the title deeds description, the purchaser will be entitled to require further evidence establishing that the latter comprises the former (ibid). In practice, however, the conditions of sale will commonly seek to relieve the vendor of this burden in one or both of the following two ways.

First, there may be a condition expressed to preclude the purchaser from requiring further evidence of identity than is afforded by comparing the two descriptions (eg, National Conditions of Sale, 20th ed, No 13(1); cp The Law Society's Conditions of Sale 1980, No 13(1)). Such a condition, however, normally implies that the title deeds description *will* substantially identify the property; therefore, if it does not, the vendor will be unable, notwithstanding the condition, to enforce the contract (see per Kindersley V-C in *Curling* v *Austin* (1862) 2 Dr & Sm 129, at p 135; also *Flower* v *Hartopp*, ante). These cases were followed where the most that could be shown was that the property sold was 'probably' described in the parcels of the root of title; Stamp J observed:

> If the root of title is not shown to comprise the land agreed to be sold, how can it be said that it affords any evidence of the identity of the property with that agreed to be sold? The contract that the deeds shall show identity is broken. In my view the identity of the property is far too uncertain and unsatisfactory to force upon the defendants

(in *Re Bramwell's Contract, Bramwell* v *Ballards Securities Investments Ltd* [1969] 1 WLR 1659, at p 1663).

Thus the result of this implication is that a contract is no more enforceable in such cases than an open contract, that is one not containing a condition of sale in the form currently used. However, the implication may be nullified by the condition referring to the evidence of identity, 'if any', to be afforded by the title deeds description (as in The Law Society's 1953 ed, No 17(2)(*a*), but *not* in the 1980 ed or the National Conditions of Sale, ante). Again the condition may provide that the title deeds description should be 'conclusive' evidence of identity (as in *Nicoll* v *Chambers* (1852) 11 CB 996). In either of these cases the purchaser would be legally bound by the condition, and liable to forfeit his deposit, but the vendor would nonetheless be unlikely to obtain the equitable remedy of specific performance if no identity be actually shown (see *Beyfus* v *Lodge* [1925] Ch 350).

Secondly, as a reinforcement, there may also be a condition requiring the purchaser, in effect, to accept certain specified evidence of identity (see *Curling* v *Austin*, ante). Commonly the evidence specified is a statutory declaration (to be paid for by the purchaser) that the property sold has been enjoyed according to the title for the last twelve years (eg, National Conditions of Sale, 20th ed, No 13(1); cp The Law Society's Conditions 1980, No 13(2)). On this three points may be made: (1) twelve years will not be satisfactory where the failure to identify occurs in an older title deed; (2) the purchaser can insist on the declaration being made by an independent person unless the condition provides, as the two referred to above do not, for the vendor to make it (*Hobson* v *Bell, Glynn* v *Bell* (1839) 2 Beav 17): and (3) the purchaser may, despite the condition, still be able to insist upon better evidence of identity than the declaration being given if this is possible (*Bird* v *Fox* (1853) 11 Hare 40).

The practical answer is to avoid difficulties by ensuring that the contract description does in fact tie in with the title deeds description. This, however, should not mean the thoughtless copying of the latter description:

> it is the duty of the conveyancer in framing a description upon sale not to take it for granted that he is to follow the exact terms of the description of the existing title but to make full enquiry into the facts in order that he may be able to describe correctly the subject intended to be disponed

(per Lord Kinnear in *Gordon-Cumming* v *Houldsworth* [1910] AC 537, at p 547). Performance of this duty is considered elsewhere (see p 280 et seq), leaving non-performance of the duty—better known as misdescription—as the next topic in this chapter.

B MISDESCRIPTION

If a vendor is unable to convey a property corresponding exactly with the property described in the contract for sale, then necessarily there has been a misdescription. Since the particulars of sale are a part of the contract for sale, then necessarily a misdescription involves the committal of a breach of contract by the vendor.

Misdescriptions take many forms. There may be a physical inaccuracy such as an overstatement of the area of the land (see *Watson* v *Burton* [1957] 1 WLR 19), or a legal inaccuracy such as describing leasehold land as freehold or land held by underlease as leasehold or vice versa (see *Re Russ and Brown's Contract* [1934] Ch 34 and *Re Thompson and Cottrell's Contract* [1943] Ch 97; but *not* describing a 'sub-underlease' as an 'underlease' since the former term is not really a conveyancing expression in established use and since the latter is in some senses an accurate description anyway: see *Becker* v *Partridge* [1966] 2 QB 155). Again four freehold houses were held to be misdescribed as 'freehold decontrolled tenancies' where two rooms in one of the houses were still subject to the Rent Acts (*Ridley* v *Oster* [1939] 1 All ER 618). Further the description need not be positively inaccurate but may simply be misleading for it to amount to a misdescription. Thus a description of land as 'registered' simpliciter will not suffice where the vendor has only possessory title (*Re Brine and Davies' Contract* [1935] Ch 388). Again, in a more recent case, land was sold subject to and with the benefit of a protected tenancy and although the particulars of sale stated the rent payable correctly as at the date of the contract, mention was neglected of a prospective abatement of the rent in consequence of a certificate of disrepair (*Re Englefield Holdings Ltd and Sinclair's Contract* [1962] 1 WLR 1119: followed in *Pagebar Properties Ltd* v *Derby Investment Holdings Ltd* [1972] 1 WLR 1500, where the contract particulars had stated the wrong tenant, term and rent).

However, for there to be a misdescription there must be a statement which purports to be of fact. A mistaken opinion, even though written into the particulars of sale, will not give rise to a misdescription (but see *Brown* v *Raphael* [1958] Ch 636). Thus the following adjectival expressions used in the particulars, namely 'valuable and extensive,' 'in a first-class position' and even 'suitable for development,' have been dismissed by Wynn-Parry J, 'with no disrespect, as typical auctioneers' "puff" ' not to be regarded as part of the contract (in *Watson* v *Burton*, ante, at pp 21 and 24).

1 Position of the parties

Assuming a misdescription has been shown, what is the position of the parties consequent upon the breach of contract? In the absence of any condition of sale affecting the position, the rules appear to be as follows:

(1) If the misdescription is substantial, the vendor will be unable to enforce the contract, either at law or in equity, even with an abatement of the price (*Flight* v *Booth* (1834) 1 Bing NC 370—the leading case; see also *Re Weston and Thomas's Contract* [1907] 1 Ch 244, purchaser not compelled to accept personal indemnity from vendor). A misdescription will be substantial if the purchaser would not, in effect, get what he wanted, ie, if the misdescription is as to a point

> so far affecting the subject-matter of the contract that it may be reasonably supposed, that, but for such misdescription, the purchaser might never have entered into the contract at all

(per Tindal CJ in *Flight* v *Booth*, ante, at p 377). What the purchaser wants, in this context, is not simply value for money; Eve J has said:

A vendor could not fulfil a contract to sell Whiteacre by conveying Blackacre, although he might prove to demonstration that the value of the latter was largely in excess of the value of the former. Value, no doubt, is an element to be taken into account in determining whether an error in description is substantial or material, but it is certainly not the only element, nor, in my opinion, the dominant one

(in *Lee* v *Rayson* [1917] 1 Ch 613, at p 618).

The question whether a misdescription is substantial is clearly one of fact for the court to decide in the circumstances of each particular case (*Watson* v *Burton* [1957] 1 WLR 19). What is not so clear is whether the court should apply a subjective or an objective test. The earlier cases appear to prefer the former; Tindal CJ, in his dicta quoted from *Flight* v *Booth*, ante, indeed, referred to '*the* purchaser' not getting what he wanted. However, in this century, Oliver J has said that 'the test laid down by Tindal CJ is an abstract one, and the standard to be applied is general and not individual' (in *Ridley* v *Oster* [1939] 1 All ER 618, at p 622). Again in *Watson* v *Burton*, ante, Wynn-Parry J apparently regarded the test as objective since he treated separately the two questions of whether the misdescription was substantial and of whether the purchaser in question was prejudiced. The test applied, subjective or objective, could vitally affect the decision reached. Thus, although in this last case a 40 per cent over-statement of the area sold was held (objectively *and* subjectively) to be a substantial misdescription, a different decision as to a similar overstatement had been reached (subjectively) in an earlier case where the purchaser had apparently wanted what he saw without relying on the statement of area for the price he agreed to pay (*Re Fawcett and Holmes' Contract* (1889) 42 Ch D 150).

(2) If the misdescription is *not* substantial (ie, the purchaser would get what he wanted), then provided it was made innocently the vendor will be able to enforce the contract, although subject to an abatement of the price by way of compensation for the insubstantial deficiency (see *Jacobs* v *Revell* [1900] 2 Ch 858). This is so even though the purchaser would now rather not get what he once wanted (*Re Brewer & Hankin's Contract* (1899) 80 LT 127) but is presumably dependent upon the misdescription actually affecting adversely the value of the property (see *Pagebar Properties Ltd* v *Derby Investment Holdings Ltd* [1972] 1 WLR 1500).

(3) The purchaser's position is stronger than the vendor's. Whether the misdescription is substantial or not the purchaser 'may elect to take all he can get, and to have a proportionate abatement from the purchase-money' (per Viscount Haldane in *Rutherford* v *Acton-Adams* [1915] AC 866, at p 870). In other words, the vendor may be compelled to convey whatever he can, and to suffer compensation, even though the purchaser will not thereby get what he originally wanted. A qualification of this has, however, been indicated. Viscount Haldane's proposition will not apply where the misdescription is as to a defect in title preventing the vendor from conveying without committing a breach of contract with a third party (*Lipmans Wallpaper Ltd* v *Mason & Hodghton Ltd* [1969] 1 Ch 20, at pp 37–8). Nor can the proposition ever be applied where the vendor has and effectively exercises a right of rescission of the contract (ibid).

Further, the purchaser will be taken to have waived any compensation by way of an abatement of the price (see rules (2) and (3), ante) if he fails to make a claim before completion (*Joliffe* v *Baker* (1883) 11 QBD 255) unless the misdescription was not discoverable before completion (*Clayton* v *Leech* (1889) 41 Ch D 103). Nonetheless, after completion and assuming the misdescription to be embodied in the conveyance, the purchaser would probably be able to sue the vendor on his implied covenants for title (see *Re Wallis and Barnard's Contract* [1899] 2 Ch 515: cf *Willson* v *Greene* [1971] 1 WLR 635; also p 258). Also the purchaser will not be entitled to compensation either if it is not open to fair assessment (*Rudd* v *Lascelles* [1900] 1 Ch 815—restrictive covenants; as to the mode of assessment, see *Re Chifferiel, Chifferiel* v *Watson* (1889) 40 Ch D 45, and *Aspinalls to Powell & Scholefield* (1889) 60 LT 595), or if he was aware of the misdescription at the date of the contract (*Castle* v *Wilkinson* (1870) LR 5 Ch App 534). Nor, it seems, will a purchaser be entitled to compensation where the misdescription simply does not affect the value of the property—the test of what is substantial appears not relevant to the amount of compensation (see *Pagebar Properties Ltd* v *Derby Investment Holdings Ltd* [1972] 1 WLR 1500).

(4) If the misdescription is *against* the vendor, ie, the purchaser would get *more* than he bargained for, the vendor cannot claim an increase in price by way of compensation (see *Re Lindsay and Forder's Contract* (1895) 72 LT 832). This is equally true where the vendor finds that he would be conveying more than he intended. As Brightman J has clearly explained:

> It must be borne in mind that it lay entirely within the power of the [vendors] to define with precision what land they wished to retain and what land they wished to sell. If they failed to do that accurately in the contract they have only themselves to blame

(in *Lloyd* v *Stanbury* [1971] 1 WLR 535, at p 544). However, if such a misdescription were substantial, the court might refuse specific performance in respect of the whole on the ground of hardship (see *Manser* v *Back* (1848) 6 Hare 443, where an auctioneer forgot to sell subject to the reservation of a right of way; see also Jessel MR's judgment in *Cato* v *Thompson* (1882) 9 QBD 616). Nonetheless, in a case of hardship, the purchaser would still be able to obtain specific performance in respect of what the vendor intended to sell, but only if he does not also claim compensation in respect of the rest (see *Alvanley* v *Kinnaird* (1849) 2 Mac & G 1). Alternatively, instead of seeking specific performance at all, the purchaser would be entitled to recover substantial damages for loss of bargain (see *Lloyd* v *Stanbury* [1971] 1 WLR 535).

2   Conditions of sale

Since the vendor's position is comparatively weak, conditions of sale relieving him from the consequences of any misdescription are only to be expected. These conditions may take many special forms, so that only the more general varieties can be considered here.

Conditions of sale directed to the consequences of a misdescription are most commonly found to be to the following effect:

(*a*) *That no misdescription shall annul the sale* (cp The Law Society's Conditions of Sale, 1980, No 7(1); also National Conditions of Sale, 20th ed, No 17). The purport of this condition is that the vendor should be able to enforce the contract despite rule (1) above. Unfortunately, perhaps, for the vendor, the condition is simply unlikely to have this effect. The accepted rule here is that where the misdescription is substantial the purchaser will be able, notwithstanding such a condition, to avoid the contract both at law and in equity, recovering his deposit with interest and costs (*Flight* v *Booth* (1834) 1 Bing NC 370; see also per Harman LJ in *Yeoman Credit Ltd* v *Apps* [1962] 2 QB 508, at p 523).

(*b*) In addition to (*a*) above, *that the purchaser or the vendor, as appropriate, shall be entitled to compensation.* It follows from the rule in *Flight* v *Booth*, ante, that this condition can only apply where the misdescription is not substantial or where the purchaser chooses not to avoid the contract. The only significant alteration of the general law position appears to be that the condition provides for compensation for the vendor where the misdescription is against him (cf rule (4) above).

If the condition simply provides for compensation without being confined to misdescriptions pointed out before completion, a claim could be made under it for misdescriptions discovered even after completion (*Palmer* v *Johnson* (1884) 13 QBD 351; cf the position under rule (3) ante, where there is no express provision for compensation).

(*c*) In addition to (*a*) above, but instead of (*b*) above, *that the purchaser shall not be entitled to compensation for any misdescription*. Although the combination of conditions (*a*) and (*b*) may well be said to hold the balance between the parties reasonably fairly, the present combination of conditions (*a*) and (*c*) might appear at first sight to tip the scales formidably far in the vendor's favour. This, however, is an illusion. If the misdescription is substantial, the vendor will still be unable to enforce the contract against the purchaser at law or in equity (see *Jacobs* v *Revell* [1900] 2 Ch 858 and *Lee* v *Rayson* [1917] 1 Ch 613) and this is so even though the vendor is willing to waive the exclusion of compensation (*Watson* v *Burton* [1957] 1 WLR 19). Therefore, the application of this condition is limited to preventing the purchaser from obtaining compensation if he asks for specific performance (see *Re Terry and White's Contract* (1886) 32 Ch D 14) or from recovering damages for breach of contract (see *Curtis* v *French* [1929] 1 Ch 253). The condition will not apply even to this extent if it states that 'the property is believed to be correctly described' when the description was, to the knowledge of the vendor, incorrect (see *Re Englefield Holdings Ltd and Sinclair's Contract* [1962] 1 WLR 1119).

This last-mentioned case points as strongly as any other case to the only possible conclusion. The courts have no sympathy at all for a vendor who not only misdescribes the property sold but also seeks to escape the consequences by reliance on conditions of sale. Therefore:

> every precaution should be taken to ascertain that the land described in the particulars of sale is not in point of quantity, tenure, estate, or in any other respect more extensive than or different from that which the vendor is able or intends to convey in performance of the agreement

(*Williams on Vendor and Purchaser*, 3rd ed, p 64).

C MISREPRESENTATION

Very little indeed can justifiably be said here of either the elements or consequences of misrepresentation in contract (or tort), since these are almost entirely *not* peculiar to the sale of land. However, perhaps the following few observations may be forgiven.

The two vendor's transgressions of misdescription and misrepresentation, always closely related, have now become confusingly alike since the passing of the Misrepresentation Act 1967, and though they can still be distinguished one from another there is now less point in so doing. The essential distinction remains reasonably clear cut: a misdescription is only to be found in the contract itself, whilst a misrepresentation necessarily precedes the making of the contract. Not surprisingly this distinction tends to blur with sales of land in that in practice a misrepresentation may well be written into the contract and thus become also a misdescription. Nevertheless it should be remembered that the elements of the two slightly, but sometimes significantly, differ. Both involve a false statement of fact, but for misdescription the statement need appear merely in the contract, whilst for misrepresentation it must have been an inducement to the purchaser to enter into the contract. It is true that without any inducement to contract a misdescription might not be regarded as substantial (for the importance of this, see p 52 et seq), but the test of inducement for misrepresentation is certainly subjective whereas the test of a substantial misdescription is probably objective.

Illustrations of the mixing of misrepresentations and misdescriptions seem easy to find. Thus most recently in *Laurence* v *Lexcourt Holdings Ltd* [1978] 1 WLR 1128 an informal contract involved a description of the property as 'offices', which was not right because the only planning permission for use as such was extremely limited, and rescission was allowed on the ground of misrepresentation rather than misdescription (alternatively it would have been allowed for common mistake). Similarly in *Mapes* v *Jones* (1974) 232 EG 717 the contract had described a lease as for twenty-one years whereas, in effect, it would only be for nineteen years; rescission for misrepresentation, not mentioning misdescription, was granted.

The tendency of misrepresentations to become misdescriptions used to produce the first point of distinguishing between the two. In such a case, assuming an absence of fraud, the purchaser was at common law permitted to proceed only in respect of the misdescription into which the misrepresentation was taken to have merged (per Branson J in *Pennsylvania Shipping Co* v *Compagnie Nationale de Navigation* [1936] 2 All ER 1167, at p 1171; see also *Leaf* v *International Galleries* [1950] 2 KB 86).

However, s 1(*a*) of the Misrepresentation Act 1967 now provides that a contract may be rescinded for an innocent misrepresentation notwithstanding its being reproduced as a term of the contract. It would appear to follow from this provision that in such a case the purchaser is supposed to have available the two courses of pursuing both the misrepresentation and the misdescription. But this may not be so in that the remedies for misrepresentation seem no longer available: if a representation by one party is reproduced as a term of the contract (ie, not merely in the writing but as a substantive part of the contract) this must be taken as negativing any reliance on it by the other party, so that the essential element of inducement will be lacking. As a clear expression of this, in *George Wimpey & Co* v *Sohn* [1967] Ch 487, Russell LJ began his judgment:

> Before the contract the vendors through their solicitor represented to the purchaser that [the vendors] had been in exclusive undisputed possession of [the garden] since their purchase in 1952 and that to the best of their knowledge, information and belief the title thereto of their predecessors had not been disputed for a period of twenty years. *That was quite plainly a misrepresentation, though it cannot be said to have induced the contract because the contract itself contained an equivalent provision*

(ibid, p 509, italics supplied; see also per Harman LJ ibid, p 502).

A real change apparently made by the 1967 Act is that a contract may now be rescinded for innocent misrepresentation notwithstanding that it has been performed (s 1(*b*)). Thus a purchaser of land no longer loses his right to rescind merely because the contract has been completed by execution of a conveyance or lease (ie, contrary to the rule established by *Wilde* v *Gibson* (1848) 1 HL Cas 605 and *Angel* v *Jay* [1911] 1 KB 666, which was generally criticised as to sales of goods, but recognised as sound as to sales of land). It is assumed that this change will be a matter of no concern to any third party acquiring an interest in the land in good faith and for value without notice of any claim to rescind (*Oakes* v *Turquand* (1867) LR 2 HL 325). Indeed the Act only enables a purchaser to rescind after completion for innocent misrepresentation 'if otherwise he would be entitled to rescind' (s 1).

Accordingly, it may be suggested that in the commonest case of a purchase of land today where a mortgage by the purchaser is contemporaneously completed, the right to rescind will still prima facie be lost, ie, because of the acquisition of third party rights by the mortgagee.

Incidentally, where rescission is possible, one may wonder what must be done in respect of the legal estate. The Act refers only to rescission of the contract after it has been performed, from which a possible inference is that the conveyance at least will stand, the grantee holding the legal estate as trustee for the grantor unless and until a reconveyance or surrender be executed. However, before the Act where a sale of land was rescinded despite completion because the misrepresentation was fraudulent, the court would order not a reconveyance but that the conveyance be set aside or cancelled (see *Edwards* v *M'Leay* (1818) 2 Swan 287, also *Wilde* v *Gibson* above). From this the inference surely is that on rescission for misrepresentation the legal estate revests by operation of law. Nonetheless it is clearly desirable that an effective rescission of a sale or other disposition of land be supported by documentary evidence for the benefit of future investigations of title.

Section 2(2) of the Misrepresentation Act 1967 gave the court a discretion, in any proceedings where it is claimed a contract ought to be or has been rescinded for innocent misrepresentation, to declare the contract subsisting and award damages in lieu of rescission. As if one new remedy was not enough, the 1967 Act additionally made damages recoverable in any case notwithstanding that the misrepresentation was not fraudulent unless the person making the misrepresentation proves that he had reasonable ground to believe and did believe up to the time the contract was made that the facts represented were true (s 2(1)). In effect, this provision imposed on the lay vendor much the same duty of care as that discovered in the novel tort of negligent misstatement in *Hedley Byrne & Co Ltd* v *Heller & Partners Ltd* [1964] AC 465. A nice illustration of how careful a vendor should now be in what he says to a prospective purchaser occurred in *Esso Petroleum Co Ltd* v *Mardon* [1976] QB 801 where employees of the owner of a petrol filling station made a careless misstatement as to its throughput potential which induced entry into a tenancy agreement of the station. A claim for damages was based on three grounds: (1) misrepresentation, which failed only because the transaction occurred before the Misrepresentation Act 1967, which has no retrospective application (s 5)—for the future, such a claim would appear to be within s 2(1) of that Act; (2) breach of warranty, which succeeded (for reasons difficult to distinguish from those supporting the next ground) and (3) negligence within the *Hedley Byrne* principle. From the judgment of Lord Denning MR (at p 820), the inference may be drawn that vendors will frequently profess sufficient special knowledge about the property to run the risk of tortious liability. Thus in *Jackson* v *Bishop* noted at [1982] Conv 324, the Court of Appeal incidentally held that a vendor-developer owed a duty of care to purchasers to ensure accurate site plans. Nevertheless, a vendor may very often be saved from liability by practice; ie, either his statements will not amount to representations (see as to replies to preliminary enquiries, p 60) or the purchaser will not rely on them.

The provisions of the Act so far mentioned all apply 'where a person has entered into a contract *after* a misrepresentation has been made to him' (ss 1, 2(1), (2)). It can only be presumed that the common law element of inducement is to be found implicit in the context although not made explicit. If so, the Act would seem to be of little if any assistance to the cautious and otherwise well-advised purchaser who has not relied on his vendor's representations but instead employed both a solicitor and a surveyor to make full enquiries, investigations and reports about the property in all its aspects (*Attwood* v *Small* (1838) 6 Cl & Fin 232; but cp *Gosling* v *Anderson* post).

At this point a relevant reference may be made to *Gross* v *Lewis Hillman Ltd* [1970] Ch 445 (the misrepresentation involved occurred before the 1967 Act but becomes comparable because it was alleged to be fraudulent). There the Court of Appeal decided that a sub-purchaser was not entitled to rescind as against the original vendor on account of a misrepresentation made only to the original purchaser even though the sub-purchaser had known of the misrepresentation and had taken a conveyance of the property directly from the original vendor. Presumably this decision will be applicable also to the statutory consequences of innocent misrepresentations so that one can say that the right to rescind does *not* run with the land as if it were an attached equity.

However, practice will not always prove to be the vendor's saviour as was illustrated in the very first case under the 1967 Act to reach the Court of Appeal. In *Gosling* v *Anderson* (1972) *The Times*, 6 February, a purchaser of a flat recovered damages because of an innocent misrepresentation by the vendor's estate agent that planning permission for a garage had been granted. This vendor was not saved from liability either by a letter from her solicitors indicating that an application for planning permission was still necessary (the terms of this letter managed to suggest that it was a mere formality) or by the purchaser's solicitors properly pointing out to their client before contract that the garage position was not cleared up.

Another illustration of the practical utility of s 2(1) of the 1967 Act occurred in *Watts* v *Spence* [1976] Ch 165. In effect, one joint tenant contracted to sell a house without any authority or estoppel on the part of the other joint tenant. Accordingly the purchaser's action for specific performance did not succeed, even in respect of the one joint tenant's own beneficial interest. As a result the question became one of a remedy in damages for the disappointed purchaser. So far as concerns breach of contract the default of the one joint tenant lay in his inability to make title and Graham J held that, since fraud on his part was not alleged, the case came within the principle of *Flureau* v *Thornhill* (1776) 2 Wm Bl 1078 and *Bain* v *Fothergill* (1874) LR 7 HL 158 (post, p 214); ie, the purchaser could only recover for expenses and not for loss of bargain. The learned judge proceeded to consider misrepresentation, starting by stating that he was satisfied that the one joint tenant, '*by his conduct*, clearly made a false representation to the [purchaser] that he was the owner of the house in question and therefore able to sell to the [purchaser]' (at p 175; italics supplied). Since the representation was false to the knowledge of the one joint tenant, it was indicated that had it been pleaded the true position would have been that he was guilty of fraud within the definition of deceit in *Derry* v *Peek* (1889) 14 App Cas 337. However, it was held that damages were recoverable within s 2(1) of the Misrepresentation Act 1967 since the representation even though not treated as fraudulent was nonetheless false and the one joint tenant had no defence under the subsection because he neither believed it to be true nor had any reasonable grounds for so doing (following *Gosling* v *Anderson*, ante). Further, such damages under the statute extended to recovering for loss of bargain. This decision was applied in *Errington* v *Martell-Wilson* (1980) 130 NLJ 545, noticed at [1981] Conv 167.

A peculiarity with sales of land worth mention here is that the standard conditions of sale designed to relieve vendors from the consequences of their misdescriptions were not before the 1967 Act normally drafted to relate also to their misrepresentations (see *Bellotti* v *Chequers Developments Ltd* [1936] 1 All ER 89). But now, not surprisingly, some general attempts are made to cover misrepresentations as well. Thus the National Conditions of Sale, 20th ed, No 17, provides that 'no error, mis-statement or omission *in any preliminary answer concerning the property* . . . shall annul the sale . . .' (italics supplied); the condition further proceeds with a restriction upon the recovery of damages or compensation and with a definition of preliminary answer which would appear to include any statement made in any circumstances by the vendor or by the estate agents or even solicitors acting for him. Equally, The Law Society's Conditions of Sale, 1980 ed, No 7, is expressed as extending similar protective cover to 'any plan furnished or statement made in the course of the negotiations leading to the contract'.

The question, however, is the efficacy of such conditions of sale, since any provision in any agreement excluding liability or remedies for misrepresentation is supposed to be of no effect (s 3 of the 1967 Act as replaced by s 8 of the Unfair Contract Terms Act 1977). But exclusion clauses are allowed in so far as 'the term shall have been a fair and reasonable one to be included having regard to all the circumstances which were, or ought reasonably to have been, known to or in the contemplation of the parties when the contract was made' (s 11 of the 1977 Act). The onus of showing that these requirements are satisfied in respect of the standard conditions of sale will be on the vendor (cf s 3 as amended). Note that ss 2–4 of the 1977 Act as to avoidance of liability for negligence and breach of contract, do *not* apply to 'any contract so far as it relates to the creation or transfer of an interest in land, or to the termination of such an interest, whether by extinction, merger, surrender, forfeiture or otherwise' (Sched 1, para 1(*b*)); semble these sections may apply to a contract for the sale or other disposition of land in so far as it relates to other matters, eg chattels, or compliance with covenants.

Condition 17 in the 19th Edition of the National Conditions of Sale was held *not* to satisfy the statutory requirements of reasonableness, and also to be ineffective in equity, in *Walker* v *Boyle* [1982] 1 WLR 495 (concerning an inaccurate reply to an enquiry about boundary disputes). In response to this decision, Condition 17 in the 20th Edition has been redrafted by deletion of a restriction to written answers and by insertion of the following: '(2) Paragraph (1) of this condition shall not apply to any error, mis-statement or omission which is recklessly or fraudulently made, or to any matter or thing by which the purchaser is prevented from getting substantially what he contracted to buy'. Whether the condition as redrafted will satisfy both the equitable and statutory tests of validity remains to be litigated. However, it may be noted that Dillon J spoke (at p 506) of the equitable bar as applicable to any innocent misrepresentation where the facts were within the vendor's knowledge unless perhaps the misrepresentation was 'trifling' (ie, not just to reckless, fraudulent or substantial misrepresentations as envisaged by the new para (2)). The 1980 Edition of The Law Society's General Conditions of Sale, Condition 7(5) incidentally provides: 'The purchaser acknowledges that in making the contract he has not relied on any statement made to him save one made or confirmed in writing.' In *Walker* v *Boyle* the purported exclusion of compensation for any oral misstatement however grave or even fraudulent was described, obiter, as strange (at p 503). Hence the amendment mentioned to Condition 17 of the National Conditions of Sale. It is accordingly thought that the new Condition 7(5) (at least) of The Law Society's 1980 Edition should be regarded as unreliable.

However, there are dicta in *Walker* v *Boyle* indicating that the position might have been different had the condition of sale in question not been a standard general condition but a special condition which both sides' solicitors would have particularly considered and as to which the purchaser's solicitor should have advised him: then the argument 'would have great force' that it ought to be regarded as fair and reasonable in the circumstances (per Dillon J at p 507).

Further s 3 of the Misrepresentation Act 1967, as amended, may be indirectly avoided, since it has been held that the section does not invalidate a provision in a contract for sale that an agent has no authority to make any representation (*Overbrooke Estates Ltd* v *Glencombe Properties Ltd* [1974] 1 WLR 1335, applied *Collins* v *Howell-Jones* (1980) 259 EG 331, CA). Against this, it also appears that a statement that the particulars do not form part of any contract does not avoid liability for error in the particulars, and a general provision that the vendor shall be deemed not to have made any representation would not be effective: *Cremdean Properties Ltd* v *Nash* (1977) 244 EG 547. In this case, Bridge LJ said (at p 551) that 'if the ingenuity of a draftsman could devise language which would have that effect [ie of excluding liability for a representation which has undoubtedly been made], I am extremely doubtful whether the court would allow it to operate so as to defeat section 3 [of the Misrepresentation Act 1967]'. Thus an otherwise effective exclusion clause in an auctioneer's conditions of sale failed to satisfy the reasonableness requirements in the circumstances of the auction itself, ie, the purchaser had attended without time to make full enquiries: *South Western General Property Co Ltd* v *Marton* (1982) 263 EG 1090. Accordingly it appears that a distinction has to be drawn between the vendor's own misrepresentations and those of his agents: the vendor's liability for the latter but not the former can be effectively excluded by an *Overbrooke* condition to the effect that agents have no authority to make any representations. Sed quaere: if the agent in question did in fact have such authority, might the condition be treated as ineffective as being itself a misrepresentation? In any case would not the agent be liable to be sued himself for negligent misstatement as indicated by *Wilson* v *Bloomfield* (1979) 123 SJ 860?

1   Replies to preliminary enquiries

A sale of land, as a rule and as might be expected, produces a fine crop of representations. The prospective purchaser will naturally wish to know a great deal about the merits and demerits of the property. However, the prospective vendor, albeit forthcoming about the merits, may be reluctant to disclose demerits and is only under a limited duty to do so (the limits will be discussed in the next section in this chapter). This explains, if explanation be needed, Sachs J's delightful reference to a prospective purchaser 'fresh from the recurrent joy of comparing the realities of some property with the benign description in the estate agent's "particulars"' (in *Goding* v *Frazer* [1967] 1 WLR 286, at p 292). As to matters outside the vendor's duty of disclosure, the rule is that the purchaser will enter into the contract at his own risk. Hence the established modern practice is for 'enquiries before contract' to be made on behalf of the purchaser, usually on a standard form with any particular enquiries added and (occasionally) inappropriate enquiries struck out. If the vendor's replies are correct but unsatisfactory, the purchaser simply need not enter into the proposed contract. What, however, if the replies are satisfactory but incorrect? Assuming an absence of fraud or, one must now say, negligence, what remedies will the purchaser have after entering into the contract?

The replies form no part of the contract, so there is no question of misdescription. One might have hoped to contend that the vendor had warranted the truth of his replies which would at least enable damages to be recovered (as in *De Lassalle* v *Guildford* [1901] 2 KB 215, where in correspondence it was enquired whether, and replied that, the drains were in good order; cp *Hill* v *Harris* [1965] 2 QB 601, where one side, instead of enquiring, made an incorrect statement of the position as they understood it, which the other side simply left uncontradicted, and no warranty was found). Unfortunately, this hope has been dashed by the Court of Appeal in so far as replies to the standard forms of preliminary enquiries are concerned. In *Mahon* v *Ainscough* [1952] 1 All ER 337 the vendor's solicitor had replied 'I understand not' to the then standard enquiry 'Has the property suffered war damage?' and no warranty of truth was found to have been intended by the parties (see the like decision in *Terrene Ltd* v *Nelson* [1937] 3 All ER 739, in which there was perhaps the earliest judicial reference to printed forms of enquiry, at p 742).

Never mind about damages for breach of warranty, you think, the purchaser will always be able to pursue his equitable and statutory remedies for innocent misrepresentation. True the vendor's replies to preliminary enquiries may be representations which if incorrect and relied on by the purchaser would enable rescission; indeed, this was assumed in *Gilchester Properties Ltd* v *Gomm* [1948] 1 All ER 493. Unfortunately again, however, this case also shows that everyday conveyancing practice probably manages to stymie any intervention by equity or, therefore, by statute. Romer J stated that he was 'not entirely satisfied that the replies to the preliminary enquiries did constitute sufficiently definite statements of fact to amount to a representation' (at p 495). His primary reason for saying this was that the replies in question (allegedly giving details of tenancies subject to which the property was sold) were 'cautiously qualified by the phrase, "so far as the vendor knows"' (see ibid). Well, are not all vendor's solicitors cautious enough to have a string of like phrases with which, interchangeably, they qualify their replies? This indeed is the practice (see Danckwerts J in *Goody* v *Baring* [1956] 1 WLR 448, at p 456).

Further, solicitors acting for vendors may nowadays be equally concerned to exclude their own liability in respect of answers to preliminary enquiries. The possibility of liability to the purchaser for the tort of negligence appeared from *Wilson* v *Bloomfield* (1979) 123 SJ 860, CA (cf *JEB Fasteners Ltd* v *Marks Bloom & Co* (1982) *The Times*, 24 July, CA). The disclaimer on the standard form of enquiries before contract has, since this decision, been expanded on the initiative of The Law Society to read as follows: 'These replies are given on behalf of the proposed Vendor and without responsibility on the part of his solicitors their partners or employees. They are believed to be correct but the (sic) accuracy is not guaranteed and they do not obviate the need to make appropriate searches, enquiries and inspections.' It may be observed that this form does not purport to protect the vendor against the purchaser, so that a vendor made liable in respect of replies might have recourse against his solicitors. Also the disclaimer depends upon the replies being believed to be correct, without saying whose belief and affording no protection to solicitors who have no grounds for such belief. See *Re Englefield Holdings Ltd and Sinclair's Contract* [1962] 1 WLR 1119 concerning a condition of sale excluding liability but prefaced with the words 'The properties are believed to be correctly described . . .'; it was regarded as clear that the condition could have no operation where the description was to the knowledge of the vendor incorrect. See also *Coats Patons (Retail) Ltd* v *Birmingham Corporation* (1971) 69 LGR 356 concerning local authority enquiries where it was in effect treated as a fundamental condition precedent to a belief in the accuracy of replies that appropriate enquiries of persons having information should actually have been made. Further, the earlier form of disclaimer (ie, not excluding responsibility of solicitors) has been considered in *Walker* v *Boyle* [1982] 1 WLR 495, at p 501, where a standard enquiry about boundary disputes had received an inaccurate reply ('Not to the vendor's knowledge'). Dillon J expressly ignored the disclaimer stating, 'A person who makes a representation of fact cannot negative the representation by words such as those in the small print'. In addition the application of s 3 of the Misrepresentation Act 1967 to such a disclaimer remains unsettled. See also JEA [1980] Conv 401–3 suggesting inter alia that the expanded form might be ineffective to protect the vendor's solicitor by virtue of s 2 of the Unfair Contract Terms Act 1977.

2 Purchasers

To the surprise of some, it seems, the rules may be applied equally to statements, etc, made by a purchaser to the vendor: see *Goldsmith* v *Rodger* [1962] 2 Lloyd's Rep 249, CA. In that case the submission that only misrepresentations justified rescission was rejected. The purchaser had made a misrepresentation about inspection of the property being sold and finding its condition defective, which induced a sale at a substantially reduced price. Accordingly the vendor was held entitled to rescind. The case actually concerned a boat but the principles should be applied to sales of land. Cp *Mayer* v *Pluck* (1971) 223 EG 33, 219 where a prospective purchaser at an auction sale asked publicly whether the auctioneer was aware that the house was built over an underground stream and had a flooded cellar; in consequence the property was regarded as unsaleable and the prospective purchaser was held liable in damages for malicious falsehood.

D NON-DISCLOSURE

The topic of non-disclosure in relation to contracts for the sale of land resembles, but may be distinguished from, the topics of misdescription and misrepresentation. Apart from the obvious point that non-disclosure, an omission, is negative whilst both misdescription and misrepresentation, involving statements or acts, are positive, the distinguishing lines may be drawn as follows.

First, a misdescription appears in the contract itself, whereas both misrepresentation and a non-disclosure precede and induce (positively or negatively) the contract. Secondly, a misrepresentation does not cause a breach of contract but merely an intervention of equity assisted now by statute, whereas both a misdescription and a non-disclosure (where there was a duty to disclose) do cause a breach of contract. As will be seen, in this context a duty to disclose arises where otherwise there would be a breach of the term implied (if not expressed) into a contract for the sale of land that the vendor is entitled to and is selling the fee simple absolute in possession free from incumbrances (see per Greene MR in *Re Ossemsley Estates Ltd* [1937] 3 All ER 774, at p 778, also *Timmins* v *Moreland Street Property Co Ltd* [1958] Ch 110). Thus the drawing of a distinction would seem preferable to the view that non-disclosure is simply the equivalent of a positive misrepresentation that the land is not subject to the undisclosed defect in title or incumbrance in question (for this view, see *Williams on Vendor and Purchaser*, 3rd ed, at p 807, but cp Megarry and Wade, *Real Property*, 4th ed, p 592, note 10). An apparent flaw in this latter view is that non-disclosure probably can result in recovery of damages at common law (see consequences later) whilst the remedy of damages for misrepresentation was only introduced by statute. Again, unlike misrepresentation, the topic of non-disclosure enjoys special rules constituting a variation from those applying on the sale of property other than land.

1 Duty to disclose

The general rule of contract is caveat emptor—'the failure to disclose a material fact which might influence the mind of a prudent contractor does not give the right to avoid the contract' (per Lord Atkin in *Bell* v *Lever Bros Ltd* [1932] AC 161, at p 227). To this rule there are three well-known exceptions where non-disclosure of material facts is a ground for relief: (1) where the contract requires uberrima fides (eg, insurance, family arrangement); (2) where a fiduciary relationship exists between the parties (eg, solicitor and client, trustee and beneficiary); and (3) where a positive representation thereby becomes distorted.

The second of these exceptions, in particular, often occurs with sales of land, and the third (like misleading conduct) is really more a case of misrepresentation or misdescription than non-disclosure (see *Re Ossemsley Estates Ltd,* ante). Thus, despite his words, Pennycuick J was dealing with a case of misdescription in *Re Englefield Holdings Ltd and Sinclair's Contract* [1962] 1 WLR 1119. There a house had been sold at an auction subject to and with the benefit of a protected tenancy and the particulars of sale stated the rent to be £1 8s 3d per week shortly to rise to £1 9s per week. The learned judge held that the vendor had been 'bound to disclose' a certificate of disrepair already served on him in consequence of which the stated rent would even more shortly sink to 15s 7d per week until the repairs were carried out, and he declared that the contract ought, therefore, to be completed at a reduced price (other points arising are mentioned below; see also *Pagebar Properties Ltd* v *Derby Investment Holdings Ltd* [1972] 1 WLR 1500 but contrast *Schlisselmann* v *Rubin* [1951] WN 530). Again in *Laurence* v *Lexcourt Holdings Ltd* [1978] 1 WLR 1128, a failure to disclose a restricted planning permission falsified the description of property as 'offices'.

Contracts for the sale of land go beyond all three of these exceptions and occupy a somewhat ambivalent position. The general caveat emptor rule does apply (see *Terrene Ltd* v *Nelson* [1937] 3 All ER 739, at p 744). Yet some, if not the utmost, good faith is expected in that the vendor must disclose some, if not all, of the material facts. This half-exception to the general rule imposes on a vendor of land a duty to disclose to a prospective purchaser any *latent defects in title.* These are incumbrances and other adverse matters of title which the purchaser could not discover for himself by inspecting the property with reasonable care; discovery is reasonably possible, and defects *patent,* only where there is some visible indication on the property of the existence of third party rights. As Sargant J explained generally in *Yandle & Sons* v *Sutton* [1922] 2 Ch 199, at p 210:

> In all these cases between vendor and purchaser, the vendor knows what the property is, and what the rights with regard to it are. The purchaser is generally in the dark. I think, therefore, that, in considering what is a latent defect and what a patent defect, one ought to take the general view that a patent defect, which can be thrust upon the purchaser, must be a defect which arises either to the eye, or by necessary implication from something which is visible to the eye. It would not be fair to hold that a purchaser is to be subjected to all the rights which he might have found out if he had pursued an inquiry based upon that which was presented to his eye. I think he is only liable to take the property subject to those defects which are patent to the eye, including those defects which are a necessary consequence of something which is patent to the eye.

Thus rights of way are commonly apparent on inspection; as Lord Loughborough said in *Bowles* v *Round* (1800) 5 Ves 508:

> Certainly the meadow is very much the worse for a road going through it; but I cannot help the carelessness of the purchaser who does not choose to inquire. It is not a latent defect.

See also fanciful dicta throughout *A–G* v *Shonleigh Nominees* [1974] 1 WLR 305, HL, as to purchasing an airfield bisected by the Great North Road.

But the mere presence of a visible way, ie, a road or path, is not sufficient unless it necessarily implies third party rights, rather than, say, simply an exercise of ownership by the vendor (see *Ashburner* v *Sewell* [1891] 3 Ch 405; it seems to depend largely on where the way goes!). Again a road or path may indicate at least a private, but not necessarily a public, right of way, so that a purchaser who only discovered after exchange of contracts the existence of a more onerous public right of way over the property would be able to rescind or resist specific performance (see per Sargant J in *Yandle & Sons v Sutton* [1922] 2 Ch 199, at p 209). Another decided example of a patent defect not requiring disclosure was a notice to carry out private street works where an inspection of the property would have shown that such a notice was likely to be served at any time (*Re Leyland and Taylor's Contract* [1900] 2 Ch 625; contrast a party wall notice on which an award had been made which required disclosure as being a latent defect in title: *Carlish v Salt* [1906] 1 Ch 335; also *Re Englefield Holdings Ltd and Sinclair's Contract* [1962] 1 WLR 1119).

It should be noticed, however, that if the vendor has misled the purchaser by a representation as to a patent defect, then there is in effect a duty to disclose the true position: the purchaser would be justified in relying on the vendor and the court would grant relief (*Bascomb v Beckwith* (1869) 20 LT 862; *Denny v Hancock* (1870) 23 LT 686). For example, where a plan attached to auction particulars of sale did not show a footway over the property, the purchasers were granted relief for misrepresentation even though the footway constituted a patent defect (*Dykes v Blake* (1838) 4 Bing (NC) 463).

Are people on the property patent? To put it differently, the question arises whether or not a vendor need disclose any rights or interests of which a purchaser will have constructive notice from the fact of occupation of the land by the person claiming them (ie, as under the rule in *Hunt v Luck* [1902] 1 Ch 428; see also the limited s 14 of the Law of Property Act 1925 and the unlimited s 70 (1) (*g*) of the Land Registration Act 1925). Thus in *James v Lichfield* (1869) LR 9 Eq 51, a purchaser, who had known that part of the property was occupied by a tenant, was held to have constructive notice of the tenant's rights (a lease with fourteen years unexpired) and to be thereby precluded from insisting upon vacant possession. However, that decision was not followed by the Court of Appeal in *Caballero v Henty* (1874) LR 9 Ch 447. There a public house had been sold 'as the same is in the occupation of' a named tenant but the contract did not refer to the lease; James LJ observed that the constructive notice cases apply only to 'equities between the purchaser and the tenant when the legal estate has passed, and have nothing to do with the rights and liabilities of vendors and purchasers as between themselves' (at p 450; see also *Phillips v Miller* (1875) LR 10 CP 420).

This is surely the correct approach: the rights and interests of an occupier should not constitute patent defects in the absence of actual knowledge of them on the part of the purchaser (as of the lease in *Timmins v Moreland Street Property Co* [1958] Ch 110). The doctrine of constructive notice obviously would involve that pursuance of enquiries which Sargant J stigmatised in the present context as unfair (see the quotation from *Yandle & Sons v Sutton* [1922] 2 Ch 199, at p 210). Accordingly the position can be summarised by adopting the distinction indicated by Knight-Bruce V-C in saying that a purchaser's knowledge of his vendor's mother's occupation of the land:

> may well, as between herself and [the purchaser], have carried with it constructive notice of her [equitable] rights, supposing that material to her: but it does not follow that it was notice as between [the vendor] in his character of vendor, and [the purchaser] in the character of purchaser

(in *Nelthorpe v Holgate* (1844) 1 Coll 203, at p 215; see also per Cottenham LC in *Penny v Watts* (1849) 1 Mac & G 150, at p 164 and *Cook v Taylor* [1942] Ch 349, as to the implication of vacant possession; cp *Wroth v Tyler* [1974] Ch 30 where the sale was expressly with vacant possession).

2 Defects in title

Defects in title, to which if latent the duty of disclosure applies, tend to come in three convenient but by no means clear-cut varieties (bear in mind that essentially involved here is the implication that the vendor is able to sell the fee simple free from incumbrances; the expression 'defects in title' may have a more restricted significance in other contexts: see, eg, *A–G* v *Shonleigh Nominees Ltd* [1974] 1 WLR 305, HL). First there are those defects which detract from the vendor's good right to convey the estate he is selling, ie, they affect his ownership itself. Mostly these defects are discovered on the investigation of title, dealt with in the ordinary way by requisition on title, and not thought of in 'non-disclosure' terms (eg, a previous conveyance on sale by trustees to one of themselves; cf *Pilkington* v *Wood* [1953] Ch 770). Nonetheless, there is still a duty to disclose such defects, for example, that the vendor's title depends on adverse possession and that extinction of the earlier title cannot be proved (see *Re Brine and Davies' Contract* [1935] Ch 388, sale of registered land, vendor who failed to disclose that his title was possessory and not absolute unable to enforce the contract; see also *Wimpey (George) & Co* v *Sohn* [1967] Ch 487). Again the Privy Council has said in passing that:

No doubt the law imposes on a vendor of land certain obligations of disclosure with regard to a matter so peculiarly within his own knowledge as the title to his own land

(in *Selkirk* v *Romar Investments Ltd* [1963] 1 WLR 1415, at p 1423; the defect was a deficiency of evidence with regard to the descent of title, but the purchaser was seeking specific performance and the vendor rescission in preference to complying with a requisition).

Secondly, there are those defects which mean that the vendor cannot convey free from incumbrances. Obvious examples of what must be fully disclosed are easements (see *Yandle & Sons* v *Sutton* [1922] 2 Ch 199), tenancies (see *Re Englefield Holdings Ltd and Sinclair's Contract* [1962] 1 WLR 1119), restrictive covenants (see *Re Stone and Saville's Contract* [1963] 1 WLR 163) and some overriding interests. The vendor need not, however, disclose anything of this sort unless it will in fact bind the purchaser (see *Smith* v *Colbourne* [1914] 2 Ch 533, licence granted to vendor by which light to windows enjoyed and which purported ineffectively to oblige successors to brick up windows on termination; note conversely that the fact that windows in the property sold are not ancient lights is not a defect in title requiring disclosure: *Greenhalgh* v *Brindley* [1901] 2 Ch 324). Another example of something which need not be disclosed would be a restrictive covenant with regard to which the vendor has been a bona fide purchaser for value of a legal estate without notice for his purchaser also will not be bound (*Wilkes* v *Spooner* [1911] 2 KB 473). Again there can no longer be any question of a vendor having to disclose his deserted wife's equity in respect of the property since we now know that this is purely personal, not binding a purchaser (*National Provincial Bank Ltd* v *Ainsworth* [1965] AC 1175)—unless protected by registration by virtue of s 2 (7), (8) of the Matrimonial Homes Act 1967 when she will *not* be treated as a removable defect in title: *Wroth* v *Tyler* [1974] Ch 30 (cp *Williams & Glyn's Bank Ltd* v *Boland* [1981] AC 487, HL, for the situation where a wife enjoys not a mere equity but an equitable interest under a constructive trust). Nevertheless it may occasionally be in a vendor's best interests to disclose matters even though the purchaser will not be bound by them. For example, it may be that the vendor himself will remain personally liable and so will wish to make disclosures with a view to securing an indemnity covenant from the purchaser (see Law Society's Conditions of Sale, 1980 ed, No 5 (2) (c); cp *Eagon* v *Dent* [1965] 3 All ER 334, concerning an unregistered option to renew a tenancy).

Thirdly, where the property sold is leasehold, any onerous or unusual covenants in the lease must be disclosed (*Re White and Smith's Contract* [1896] 1 Ch 637; see also *F & H Entertainments Ltd* v *Leisure Enterprises Ltd* (1976) 120 SJ 331 as to the service of notices under a rent review clause requiring disclosure as a latent defect in title).

The ideal way of disclosing latent defects is to set out the facts fully and fairly in the contract itself (see *Williams* v *Wood* (1868) 16 WR 1005; *Re Cumming to Godbolt* (1884) 1 TLR 21). But the method more often adopted is to give the purchaser an opportunity of discovering the details of the defect by inspection of a document referred to by the contract (eg, as to tenancies, see National Conditions of Sale, 20th ed, No 18(1) and The Law Society's Conditions of Sale, 1980 ed, No 6(2)). This method may well not work. The test of an adequate disclosure is whether an ordinary purchaser would understand what the difficulty is — rejected as too good for present purposes would be a condition of sale 'which set out the defect in title, set it out absolutely accurately, so that the trained equity conveyancer, reading it, would know, after he had put on a wet towel and consulted all the works available, precisely and exactly what the trouble was': per Walton J in *Faruqi* v *English Real Estates Ltd* [1979] 1 WLR 963, at p 967. There, in the merest essence, land was sold at auction expressly subject to the entries on the register of title; one familiar entry related to restrictive covenants contained in a deed dated 1883 not produced on first registration; requisitions on title were answered by saying that no copy of the deed could be supplied. It was held that the purchaser was not bound in equity because the vendor had failed to disclose his defective title. Nevertheless, the test propounded only makes sense so long as solicitors are not supposed to be instructed until after exchange of contracts, if at all. In any case, his lordship's idea of an ordinary purchaser might be thought a pretty esoteric chap: he would read the contract reference to entries on the register and assume that 'those entries were only of what I may call the usual sort, which do not in any way affect the value of the property adversely' (p 968); he would thereafter raise no question about entries as to matters 'such as the use of the property and support from neighbouring buildings' or even as to rights of way granted by leases (p 966). Yet this clever fellow could not be expected to seek a sight pre-contract of a copy of the entries even though another condition of sale generally invited inspection at the vendor's solicitors' offices. In other words, a potential purchaser neglected elementary precautions to the peril not of himself but of his vendor.

Further, *in*effective for the purpose of disclosure, as affording at most constructive notice, should be the increasing but questionable practice of providing with the draft contract a full abstract of title in which, of course, will be secreted all defects in title. Yet a recent judicial obiter analogy appears to contradict this. In *Holder* v *Holder* [1968] Ch 353, where a beneficiary was seeking rescission of a sale to an executor who had purported to renounce probate, Cross J considering the question of acquiescence, said:

> If the plaintiff had been a prospective purchaser of the property from [the executor], who had instructed his solicitor to examine [the executor's] title before entering into a contract to buy, and subsequently wished to get out of his contract on the ground that the renunciation was invalid, it may be that the court would hold that the plaintiff had contracted with constructive notice of the invalidity

(ibid, p 370; on appeal at ibid, p 379). Nevertheless, this dictum ought to be confined to the somewhat unlikely case it envisages, namely, of a purchaser actually authorising his solicitor to vary the order of events established by practice and investigate title fully before rather than after the exchange of contracts. Otherwise such a pre-contract concern with the validity of the vendor's title is surely not something which ought reasonably to have been displayed by the purchaser's solicitor within s 199 (1) (ii) (*b*) of the Law of Property Act 1925 (which states certain restrictions on constructive notice). Further it may be submitted that actual investigation of title, not mere authorisation, should be necessary before a vendor could be deemed to have made all due disclosures, for in principle a purchaser owes no duty of care to his vendor to make the usual, prudent searches and enquiries (per Mr Brian Dillon QC in *Laurence* v *Lexcourt Holdings Ltd* [1978] 1 WLR 1128, at p 1138). Notice too that The Law Society's Conditions of Sale, 1980 ed, No 12(3) now expressly provides that a purchaser should not in general be deemed to have notice of any matter of title disclosed by 'any abstract, epitome or document' delivered before contract.

Notwithstanding the above it appears clear that where the sale is subject to matters contained in a particular document, the provision of a copy before contract would constitute an adequate disclosure. Thus in *Faruqi* v *English Real Estates Ltd* if, in accordance with common practice, office copies of the register of title had actually been supplied with the draft contract, then the purchaser would have been 'bound to take the property subject to the entries on the register of title, whatever they may be' (per Walton J at [1979] 1 WLR 966; sed quaere: could this conceivably cover removable defects such as registered charges?).

3 Defects in quality

Unnecessarily perhaps, at this point readers may be reminded that a prospective vendor need not disclose defects in the quality of the land, whether these are patent or latent (see *Turner* v *Green* [1895] 2 Ch 205; *Greenhalgh* v *Brindley* [1901] 2 Ch 324; cp *Shepherd* v *Croft* [1911] 1 Ch 521). In other words, physical defects are within the general caveat emptor rule. At its most extreme, this rule fully covers physical defects which are actually known to the vendor, even though they might endanger the purchaser (the Law Commission's recommendation to the contrary failed to achieve legislative consecration: compare the draft clause 3 on p 38 of the *Report on Civil Liability of Vendors and Lessors for Defective Premises*, Law Com No 40 (1970) with the final version of the Defective Premises Act 1972). Apparently there was enough of a lobby to convince that 'anything which encouraged house purchasers to dispense with a proper survey would be contrary to the public interest' (see para 17 of the Law Commission Report cited above). Thus a purchaser could direct no complaint against his vendor if the house turns out to be undermined by tree roots or even bombed by cricket balls emanating from neighbouring land (cp *Masters* v *Brent London BC* [1978] QB 841 and *Miller* v *Jackson* [1977] QB 966, noted (1978) 41 Conv (NS) 1-2).

Nevertheless, it should be noted that a defect in physical quality may also involve a defect in title (*Re Belcham and Gawley's Contract* [1930] 1 Ch 56, sewers vested in local authority). If so, and if latent, it should be disclosed. Again, as already noticed, a non-disclosure may falsify a positive representation or description of physical quality of the property (see *Re Puckett and Smith's Contract* [1902] 2 Ch 258). Further, where the vendor himself has caused the defect he can be liable to the purchaser in negligence. This was decided as a matter of law in *Hone* v *Benson* (1978) 248 EG 1013 which concerned the 'do-it-yourself' installation of an allegedly faulty central heating and hot water system; in effect, the duty of care lying upon professional builders was extended to amateurs (for this duty, see *Dutton* v *Bognor Regis UDC* [1972] 1 QB 373 and *Anns* v *Merton London BC* [1978] AC 728). The learned judge (Judge Edgar Fay QC) recognised as a substantial point that:

It has been the case over the centuries that on sales of real property *caveat emptor* and there is no doubt that that principle which is dear to conveyancers, is in collision with this extension—and it is an extension—of the law of negligence to cases of this kind

(at p 1014). But he remained unmoved by it: all builder-vendors, great and small, owe a common law duty, not of disclosure but of care, to all purchasers (and their successors) in respect of physical defects. The novel risks involved seem to call for fresh conditions of sale effectively excluding liability in negligence (nothing in The Law Society's Conditions of Sale, 1970 edition, was found apt for this purpose). Further reference should be made to an article by Eric L Newsome at [1980] Conv 287 suggesting a duty in tort to disclose dangerous defects to purchasers pre-contract.

User

Is the user of the property an aspect of quality or of title? There is some authority supporting an implied obligation on the part of a vendor to disclose planning restrictions (see per Harman J in *Sidney* v *Buddery* (1949) 1 P & CR 34; but cp *Mitchell* v *Beacon Estates (Finsbury Park) Ltd* ibid 32). Thus Graham J after saying that the value of the land would be affected, stated: 'Nondisclosure of the position in respect of planning permission might therefore in some circumstances give rise to a misrepresentation' (*Sinclair-Hill* v *Southcott* (1973) 226 EG 1399, at p 1401). This authority may be better explained not as indicating an extension of a vendor's duty of disclosure of latent defects in title but merely as illustrating that misrepresentations can be made by conduct as well as words (cp *Gosling* v *Anderson* (1971) 220 EG 1117, on appeal (1972) 223 EG 1743, and *Laurence* v *Lexcourt Holdings Ltd* [1978] 1 WLR 1128). Otherwise it would appear to be in conflict with the general principle that it is the business of the purchaser

if he does not protect himself by an express warranty, to satisfy himself that the premises are fit for the purposes for which he wants to use them, whether that fitness depends on the state of their structure or the state of the law or any other relevant circumstances

(per Devlin J in *Edler* v *Auerbach* [1950] 1 KB 359, at p 374). This statement of the law now enjoys the express approval of the Court of Appeal (*Hill* v *Harris* [1965] 2 QB 601, concerning a head lease covenant) but is still not applicable where there has been a positive misrepresentation as to user (*Laurence* v *Lexcourt Holdings Ltd* [1978] 1 WLR 1128, at p 1134).

4 Effect of purchaser's knowledge

The vendor generally need not have disclosed any defects of title, even though latent, of which the purchaser knew when he entered into the contract. This is because generally no breach of contract will ensue:

If no interest is mentioned [in the contract] then prima facie an unencumbered freehold interest will be implied. No such implication arises, however, if the purchaser knew at the time of the contract . . . that some lesser interest or some encumbered interest was to be the subject of the sale

(per Romer LJ in *Timmins* v *Moreland Street Property Co Ltd* [1958] Ch 110, at p 132, where the purchaser knew that the property was subject to a lease; but cp a note at (1975) 39 Conv (NS) 313). Equally, no such implication arises where the purchaser, although actually ignorant, ought to have known of the defect in title because it was patent.

However, a distinction must be made between the purchaser knowing of an *irremovable* defect and of a *removable* defect. The implication that the vendor is entitled to and is selling an unincumbered freehold interest is rebutted only by the purchaser's knowledge of an irremovable defect (*Timmins* v *Moreland Street Property Co Ltd* ante; cf an article at (1954) 18 Conv (NS) 301). Knowledge of a removable defect is no rebuttal and the purchaser can, subject to express provision in the contract, require the vendor to remove the defect before completion (*Re Gloag and Miller's Contract* (1883) 23 Ch D 320). Examples of removable defects would be a mortgage which could be discharged, or a certificate of disrepair, which could be complied with (cf *Re Englefield Holdings Ltd and Sinclair's Contract* [1962] 1 WLR 1119).

Also, if the contract *expressly* provides that 'a good marketable title' or 'a valid title' should be conveyed, then the existence of any defects in title not mentioned in the contract will result in a breach of contract even though they are irremovable as of right and were known to the purchaser (*Cato* v *Thompson* (1882) 9 QBD 616, also *Re Gloag and Miller's Contract* (1883) 23 Ch D 320). This seems to be based simply on the rule that parol evidence is inadmissible to imply an act of waiver by the purchaser of his rights by entering into a contract containing such a provision; he may, for example, have assumed that the vendor had been able, although not as of right, to arrange for removal.

As an esoteric refinement of this same theme of the effect of a purchaser's knowledge, it also used to be arguable that the vendor need not disclose any defect in title which is an instrument or matter registered under the Land Charges Act 1925. The point was that such registration 'shall be deemed to constitute actual notice of such instrument or matter . . . to all persons and for all purposes connected with the land affected' (s 198 (1) of the Law of Property Act 1925), ie, whether or not the register had in fact been searched. Consequently, the argument ran, mere registration might rebut the implication of an unincumbered freehold interest in just the same way as the purchaser's actual knowledge. This argument had received the stamp of judicial approval from Eve J at first instance in *Re Forsey and Hollebone's Contract* [1927] 2 Ch 379, at p 387, where he said of an undisclosed planning resolution:

> even if it were an incumbrance, it was an incumbrance, of which the purchaser, under s 198 of the Law of Property Act 1925, had notice, of a nature which precluded him from repudiating his purchase.

These words were clearly obiter since both he and the Court of Appeal adopted the ratio decidendi that the resolution was not an incumbrance or any defect in title; further the judgments in the Court of Appeal contain no mention at all of Eve J's obiter dictum. Further this view of the effect of registration was subjected to considerable criticism (see especially HWR Wade at (1954) CLJ 89, also RG Rowley (1964) 28 Conv (NS) 114 et seq). Nevertheless it could not be disregarded in practice with a clear conscience (see *Law Society's Digest*, Opinion No 135, as to the advisability of making full land charge searches before exchange of contracts). Then, after standing abused but largely believed for over forty years, the so-called rule in *Re Forsey and Hollebone* was both recognised and knocked down in 1969 (for which we have to thank again the Law Commission: see generally the recommendations in *Transfer of Land—Report on Land Charges Affecting Unregistered Land*, Law Com No 18).

The Law of Property Act 1969, s 24, provides that a purchaser's knowledge of a registered land charge at the time of the contract is to be determined by reference to 'his actual knowledge' without regard to s 198 of the 1925 Act. The vital quoted expression is left lamentably undefined, but the idea appears clear: so far as concerns registered land charges, the vendor's duty of disclosure is not qualified either by the fact of registration or by the fact that the purchaser ought reasonably to have had knowledge. Remembering the meaning attached in this context to latent defects in title, the odd incidental conclusion can be reached that a vendor is now also under a duty to disclose any defects in title which happen to be registered as land charges (see further AM Prichard at [1970] JPL 494-6, instancing equitable easements as the most likely candidates).

For the purposes of s 24 of the 1969 Act, two special definitions have been offered. First 'purchaser' is to include 'a lessee, mortgagee or other person acquiring or intending to acquire an estate or interest in land' (s 24 (3)). Apart from extending to prospective purchasers, this definition is somewhat special in omitting to make either good faith or valuable consideration an element (cp s 205 (1) (xxi) of the 1925 Act). Secondly 'registered land charge' here means an instrument or matter registrable under the Land Charges Act 1925 (see now the 1972 consolidating Act) but expressly excluding local land charges (s 24 (3) of the 1969 Act). Accordingly this definition may be seen as saving the rule (if it really was one) in *Re Forsey and Hollebone*, in relation to local land charges, ie, if registered, there is no duty of disclosure by the vendor. However, searches before contract for local land charges are not only standard conveyancing practice but also a sufficient safeguard in that their registration will be against the land rather than the possibly unascertainable names of previous estate owners.

It is to be observed that s 24 (1) of the 1969 Act expressly does not apply where title is registered. This will be because the argument resulting in pre-contract searches (apart from local land charges) was never equally applicable to registered titles. The reason is the absence from the Land Registration Acts of any provision that the registration of incumbrances constitutes 'actual notice . . . to all persons and for all purposes' (as in s 198 (1) of the Law of Property Act 1925). Thus in a case concerning an undisclosed restrictive covenant which was entered on the charges register of the vendor's title, there was no suggestion that disclosure was unnecessary (*Re Stone and Saville's Contract* [1963] 1 WLR 163). If, however, the usual practice is followed of supplying with the draft contract copies of the entries on the charges register, then the prospective purchaser may well be fixed with actual or imputed notice thereof, even if the entries are not expressly incorporated by reference in the contract (see ante p 66).

5   Consequences of non-disclosure

Where a latent defect in title not disclosed by the vendor or known to the purchaser comes to light after a contract for the sale of land has been made, the prima facie position of the parties is very much the same as that pertaining where a misdescription is shown. In the absence of any conditions of sale affecting the position, (1) if the non-disclosure is of a substantial defect, the vendor simply cannot enforce the contract (*Phillips* v *Caldcleugh* (1868) LR 4 QB 159); 'substantial' here appears to have much the same meaning as with misdescription, ie, of the purchaser, in effect, not getting what he wanted (*Shepherd* v *Croft* [1911] 1 Ch 521); (2) if the defect is not substantial, the vendor can enforce the contract but only subject to a reduction in price (*Re Belcham and Gawley's Contract* [1930] 1 Ch 56); and (3) the purchaser may, where the defect is substantial, either avoid the contract or obtain specific performance with (semble) a reduction in price (cf *Rudd* v *Lascelles* [1900] 1 Ch 815).

In addition, the purchaser can, it seems, recover damages for breach of contract, independently of obtaining specific performance: non-disclosure of a latent defect in title results in a breach of the implied term that the vendor has an unincumbered title (as in *Baines* v *Tweddle* [1959] Ch 679). Nonetheless there seems to be some general feeling that innocent non-disclosure, like innocent (non-negligent) misrepresentation, does not give rise to common law remedies. Some indirect support for this feeling might be derived from the fact that a statutory provision was thought necessary to give a purchaser a right to damages for the fraudulent concealment of 'any instrument or incumbrance material to the title' (s 183 of the Law of Property Act 1925; this was also made a misdemeanour). But this provision goes far beyond any contractual position, extending rights to persons deriving title under the purchaser and liability to the solicitor or agent of the vendor. However, even though damages may be recoverable by the purchaser, these could often prove less substantial than he might have wished in view of the anomalous rule considered post, p 214.

6 Vendor's knowledge

It should be noted that the vendor's own knowledge of the existence of the defect in question is almost irrelevant; the duty to disclose is, in essence, absolute and the consequences of non-disclosure do not, with three exceptions, seem to be affected by the vendor's innocence (see *Re Brewer and Hankin's Contract* (1899) 80 LT 127, but cf conditions of sale below). The three exceptions are, first, if the non-disclosure is not innocent, the vendor will be unlikely to obtain specific performance, even subject to a reduction in price where the defect is not substantial (see above); second, intent to defraud has to be shown for a statutory claim to damages to succeed (*District Bank Ltd* v *Luigi Grill Ltd* [1943] Ch 78); and third, the vendor would not be held reasonable in rescinding in the face of requisitions under conditions of sale otherwise permitting this (see p 122).

Further, if the vendor has actually represented to the purchaser that he has a good title, then his failure to disclose a defect in title known to him has been held to amount to fraudulent misrepresentation (*Edwards* v *M'Leay* (1815) Coop G 308; (1818) 2 Swan 287). There are dicta in this last case which might be taken (and have so been taken in the headnote at (1818) 2 Swan 287) as suggesting that mere non-disclosure of a known defect, without any representation as to title, suffices: thus Grant MR said:

> Whether it would be fraud to offer as good a title which the vendor knows to be defective in point of law, it is not necessary to determine. But if he knows and conceals a fact material to the validity of the title, I am not aware of any principle on which relief can be refused to the purchaser

(at (1815) Coop G 312). But the decision proceeded entirely on the basis of an admitted representation as to title.

Thus *Edwards* v *M'Leay,* ante, was distinguished by Lord Cottenham LC in *Wilde* v *Gibson* (1848) 1 HL Cas 605, at p 626, which also concerned an undisclosed defect in title, on the grounds that in the later case the vendor had neither actually known of the defect (as opposed to having constructive notice) nor made any false representation (see also *Legge* v *Croker* (1811) 1 Ball & B 506 and *Gordon Hill Trust* v *Segall* [1941] 2 All ER 379). Yet in uttering what became known as the rule in *Wilde* v *Gibson* (subsequently reversed by s 1 of the Misrepresentation Act 1967), Lord Campbell firmly placed misrepresentation and non-disclosure on the same footing, as follows:

> If there be, in any way whatever, misrepresentation *or concealment* which is material to the purchaser, a court of equity will not compel him to complete the purchase, but where the conveyance has been executed, I apprehend, my lords,

that a court of equity will set aside the conveyance only on the ground of actual fraud. There would be no safety for the transactions of mankind if, upon a discovery being made at any distance of time of a material fact *not disclosed* to the purchaser of which the vendor had merely constructive notice, a conveyance which had been executed could be set aside

((1848) 1 HL Cas at pp 632–3).

In addition, there is modern authority supporting the proposition that merely entering into a contract to sell land as owner may amount to a representation as to title by conduct: see *Watts* v *Spence* [1976] Ch 165. This was followed in *Errington* v *Martell-Wilson* (1980) 130 NLJ 545 where an elderly lady agreed to sell for £500 a site which was worth £3,400, but to which she no longer had any title, a fact which she had forgotten; Latey J held that there had been a representation implicit in everything she had done, including instructing solicitors, so that the purchaser was entitled to recover substantial damages for loss of bargain under s 2 (1) of the Misrepresentation Act 1967. Although there are also dicta from which the contrary could be deduced (see *Malhotra* v *Choudhury* [1980] Ch 52, at p 70) these can be balanced by a comparatively early statement to the effect that a mere offer to sell real property constituted an implied representation as to the vendor's title (per Farwell J in *Rudd* v *Lascelles* [1900] 1 Ch 815, at pp 818–9). However, that stated implication was then held to be qualified or rebutted in any case where the purchaser knows that the vendor is ignorant as to the title (in the case, the defendant was both a widow and a mortgagor and so obviously ignorant).

Consequently, the effect of non-disclosure is not as clear in this respect as it ought to be. Further, of course, if the mere non-disclosure of a defect in title is to be taken as the equivalent of a positive misrepresentation as to title, then the purchaser will presumably enjoy all the alternative remedies afforded by the Misrepresentation Act 1967, that is of damages and post-completion rescission. Thus not only need he no longer allege fraud but he would also be thankfully relieved from reliance on the usual covenants for title (see p 258).

7 Remedies before completion

The purchaser must seek his remedies, of avoiding the contract or compensation by ways of a reduction in price, before completion (cf innocent misrepresentation but for s 1 (*b*) of the Misrepresentation Act 1967). The reason is that a non-disclosure necessarily involves breach of a term of the contract which, not being collateral, merges in the conveyance (see *Greswolde-Williams* v *Barneby* (1900) 83 LT 708). However, since it will also be necessarily a defect in title which has not been disclosed, rights of action may well be available under the usual implied covenants for title (s 76 of the Law of Property Act 1925; see *Eastwood* v *Ashton* [1915] AC 900).

8 Conditions of sale

As with misdescription, since the vendor's prima facie position is comparatively vulnerable, naturally protection is sought through more or less carefully drafted conditions of sale. The relevant principle of law, however, is adamant: the vendor will not be permitted to mislead the purchaser by concealing known defects in title behind conditions of sale (*Re Banister, Broad* v *Munton* (1879) 12 Ch D 131). Therefore, conditions to the effect that the purchaser should accept the vendor's title or that he should make no requisition or objection as to any defects or incumbrances there may be, will not enable a vendor who has failed to disclose what he knows to enforce the contract (*Re Haedicke and Lipski's Contract* [1901] 2 Ch 666). Equally ineffective for this purpose is a condition that the title should commence with an instrument subsequent to the defect (cf *Re Nisbet and Potts' Contract* [1906] 1 Ch 386). Again those conditions which commence 'the purchaser shall assume as is the case . . .' will not do if what has to be assumed is not the case, or even may not be the case, to the knowledge of the vendor (see *Wilson v Thomas* [1958] 1 WLR 422, where the state of affairs to be assumed depended on the proper construction, with the aid of extrinsic evidence, of a latent ambiguity in a will).

Consequently, what the prudent vendor ought to do to protect himself is, in the condition, first to indicate sufficiently the nature of the defect in title, and then to provide that the purchaser should make no requisition or objection as to that particular defect (see *Re Sandbach and Edmondson's Contract* [1891] 1 Ch 99). With this the purchaser would go into the contract with his eyes open and could not later complain of having been misled. Further, even if the vendor were to make a mistake, so that the purchaser be in fact misled, although innocently, such a condition would nonetheless be effective (ibid, also *Blaiberg v Keeves* [1906] 2 Ch 175). However, in this last circumstance, the vendor would probably still be denied the discretionary remedy of specific performance (see *Beyfus v Lodge* [1925] Ch 350 and cp *Faruqi v English Real Estates Ltd* [1979] 1 WLR 963, ante p 66).

9 General conditions

In addition to any special conditions, the standard forms of conditions of sale do contain several general conditions purporting to affect the consequences of non-disclosure. These general conditions are of three main types:

(1) The first type provide that the purchaser is 'deemed to buy with full notice in all respects of the actual state and condition of the property' (see National Conditions of Sale, 20th ed, No 13 (3); also The Law Society's Conditions of Sale, 1980 ed, No 5 (2)(*a*)). Although such a condition will certainly cover a defect in the physical quality of the land, eg, disrepair (see *Butler v Mountview Estates Ltd* [1951] 2 KB 563), it seems that it may not extend to a connected defect in title, eg, a certificate of disrepair, since this is 'not an element in the "actual state and condition of the property"' (see per Pennycuick J in *Re Englefield Holdings Ltd and Sinclair's Contract* [1962] 1 WLR 1119, at p 1123; there is some conflict here with the previous case cited where the condition was held to cover breaches of a tenant's covenant to repair).

Incidentally, it may be noticed that this present condition of sale does not derogate from the implied term that a newly built house should be fit for human habitation (see *Hancock v B W Brazier* [1966] 1 WLR 1317). Nor will it exclude or restrict in any way the statutory duty under the Defective Premises Act 1972 (see s 6(3) thereof). Further, it has not been allowed to protect a negligent builder-vendor from liability in tort (*Hone v Benson* (1978) 248 EG 1013).

(2) The second type of relieving conditions provide that 'without prejudice to the duty of the vendor to disclose all latent easements and latent liabilities known to the vendor to affect the property, the property is sold subject to any rights of way and water, rights of common, and other rights, easements, quasi-easements, liabilities and public rights affecting the same' (see National Conditions of Sale, 20th ed, No 14). The opening phrase of this condition merely restates the position at law in any case so far as known defects are concerned (see *Nottingham Patent Brick & Tile Co v Butler* (1886) 16 QBD 778). What is more, however, the position at law is exactly the same with regard to defects of which the vendor ought reasonably to have known

(see *Heywood* v *Mallalieu* (1883) 25 Ch D 357, where the vendor's solicitor would have discovered the defect, an easement, had he made proper enquiries into claims made). Nonetheless, this condition will be effective to alter the ordinary law by protecting the vendor where there are defects of which he neither knew nor ought to have known (see *Simpson* v *Gilley* (1922) 92 LJ Ch 194).

(3) The third and most potent type of relieving conditions provide, in effect, that the vendor may rescind the contract if the purchaser does not withdraw any requisition as to title with which the vendor is unwilling to comply. This, however, is dealt with fully and more appropriately later (see p 122). Here note only that a vendor guilty of a breach of his duty of disclosure is not ipso facto precluded from taking advantage of a contractual right of rescission (*Selkirk* v *Romar Investments Ltd* [1963] 1 WLR 1415, at p 1423).

By way of astonishing contrast to such relieving conditions, attention is drawn to the extensive warranties of disclosure on the part of a vendor now contained in the 1980 ed of The Law Society's Conditions of Sale, No 3 (3) (written communications relating to relevant matters) and No 5 (1) ('all easements, rights, privileges, and liabilities affecting the property, of which the vendor knows or ought to know'). It is thought that the latter condition is capable of comprehending patent defects in title, matters discoverable by searches or enquiries and overriding interests, all of which ought to be known to the vendor; the only exclusion is of matters actually known to the purchaser.

10   Non-disclosure by purchasers

Hitherto in this section non-disclosure of material matters by the vendor alone has been envisaged. Nevertheless, a purchaser too may have reason to be secretive and generally he can be with impunity. Since there is no question of his concealing latent defects in title, the general rule of caveat vendor applies free from that particular sub-exception. See *Williams on Vendor and Purchaser*, 3rd ed, p 757:

mere silence on the purchaser's part as to some fact known to him alone and enhancing the value of the property sold (such as the existence of valuable minerals) is no ground in equity for the vendor to avoid or resist specific performance of the contract.

As a general rule, therefore, a potential purchaser not already in a fiduciary relationship owes no duties to his vendor, whether of disclosure or of reasonable care (cf *Laurence* v *Lexcourt Holdings Ltd* [1978] 1 WLR 1128, at p 1138, where the purchaser had deliberately neglected to make the usual, prudent searches and enquiries before contract). However, against this, Slade J has enunciated two general propositions of sufficient importance to justify verbatim repetition here:

(1) Where during the course of negotiations for a contract for the sale and purchase of property, the proposed purchaser, in the name of and purportedly as agent on behalf of the vendor, but without the consent or authority of the vendor, takes some action in regard to the property (whether it be the making of a planning application, a contract for the sale of the property, or anything else) which, if disclosed to the vendor, might reasonably be supposed to be likely to influence him in deciding whether or not to conclude the contract, a fiduciary relationship in my judgment arises between the two parties.

(2) Such fiduciary relationship gives rise to the consequences that there is a duty on the proposed purchaser to disclose to the vendor before the conclusion of the contract what he has done as the vendor's purported agent, and correspondingly, in the event of non-disclosure, there is a duty on him to

account to him for any profit made in the course of the purported agency, unless the vendor consents to his retaining it. In such circumstances, the person who, for his own private purposes, uses the vendor's name and purports to act as his agent cannot reasonably complain if the law subjects him to the same consequences *vis à vis* his alleged principal as if he had actually had the authority which he purported to have

(in *English* v *Dedham Vale Properties Ltd*[1978] 1 WLR 93, at p 111). In the case, by virtue of these propositions, a purchaser became accountable to a vendor for profits ultimately received as a result of a successful but undisclosed planning application.

V CONDITIONS OF SALE

THE last chapter dealt with certain topics arising out of and around particulars of sale, ie, directly concerning the subject-matter itself of contracts for the sale of land. Now conditions of sale may be considered, ie, the terms on which the land is sold (see per Danckwerts LJ in *Property and Bloodstock Ltd* v *Emerton* [1968] Ch 94, at p 118 as to the word 'condition' being 'traditional rather than appropriate'). The reader will, perhaps, recall that some of these terms, alias conditions of sale, have already been examined, for comprehension's sake, where relevant to the earlier chapters.

Any discussion of the terms of contracts for the sale of land must have much in common with the house that Jack built: that is the agreement that incorporates the special conditions that refer to the general conditions that modify the statutory provisions that vary the equitable principles that mitigate the rules of the common law. If you doubt this, have another glance at the agreement drawn on the National Conditions of Sale, 20th ed. Faced with an unexciting illustration of this 'down-the-line' effect, Eve J permitted himself the observation:

> I cannot help thinking it would be prudent, especially in the case of sales held in the country, when a sale is made subject to general conditions, that a copy of those conditions should be circulated with the particulars

(in *Curtis* v *French* [1929] 1 Ch 253, at p 260). His words are now generally heeded; the standard sets of general conditions of sale do accompany the rest of the agreement albeit in the form of small print on the back. But the resulting amalgam has a tendency to mislead. Already the general use of comprehensive conditions of sale may effectively obscure the fact that every agreement for sale is made on the terms of an open contract as more or less but never completely modified. None of the general conditions of sale makes any attempt to state the basic duties and rights of the vendor and purchaser. Consequently the position under an open contract should never be neglected; it is at once the background and the basis of all else. Even if an open contract point be dealt with expressly by the conditions of sale, this is *not* the furthest one need look: as Wilberforce J said:

> In approaching the question of the construction of the conditions of sale, it is well-established that the court should have regard to the normal rules of equity as regards the respective rights of vendor and purchaser

(in *Re Hewitt's Contract* [1963] 1 WLR 1298, at p 1301, see also Romer J in *Re Priestley's Contract* [1947] Ch 469, at p 482).

Consistently with this, there happens to be a significant collection of cases in which perfectly clear conditions of sale are not permitted to prevail over the principles of equity. Examples of these are conditions that no misdescription should annul the sale (see p 54), that no requisitions should be made as to non-disclosed defects (see p 72), that the vendor may rescind if he be unwilling to comply with a requisition (see p 122), or that the deposit should be forfeited if completion be delayed (see p 203). In addition to these, the court will look right through any conditions of sale in considering any request for the equitable decree of specific performance (see p 215). So one should never slip into the shoddy habit of imagining sales of land as the subject of standard forms divine, for then even more would be bodied forth the forms of things unknown! Therefore, the pedestrian approach is adopted in this book of always considering first the terms of an open contract and thereafter the extent to which these can be modified, negatived or supplemented in practice. In this way the heresy may best be avoided of thinking that there are three separate sorts of contract—open, with conditions, and by correspondence. These are really three in one. Before going any further, however, perhaps a short statement of what is meant by an open contract and why and how conditions of sale are incorporated would be advisable.

A OPEN CONTRACTS CLOSED

A contract for the sale of land is said to be 'open' when it provides expressly for nothing beyond the parties, the property, and the price. All the rights and duties of the parties are then prescribed by the general law which is to be found in decisions of the courts and in s 42 et seq of the Law of Property Act 1925 (as amended, eg, by the Law of Property Act 1969, Pt III), plus perhaps the practice of conveyancers. As already seen, all negotiations for the sale of land must aim at producing not merely an agreement but also the signed and written embodiment thereof (s 40 of the Law of Property Act 1925). This affords that opportunity, so eagerly grasped in other fields of contract, of limiting liability by way of the still small print on the back. Since a vendor of land both has the greater prima facie liability and normally proffers the draft contract, the opportunity is his, but the practice in grasping it has fluctuated (see *Williams on Vendor and Purchaser*, 3rd ed, at p 79 et seq). Until the mid-nineteenth century vendors apparently were content to enter by way of express condition into exactly those obligations then imposed on them by the general law under an open contract, obligations which were much more onerous than those of today. Then a more general prosperity gave land a seller's market and purchasers came passively to accept conditions drawn with the simple aim of removing the inconveniences experienced by vendors under open contracts. Thus the commencement of and objections to title would be restricted; the expenses of obtaining evidence of title or the concurrence of necessary parties would be passed to the purchaser; the vendor would be given the trump-card of rescission in response to requisitions; a deposit and interest on any delay in completion would have to be paid; time-limits for requisitions and completion would be provided and made of the essence; and so on.

Many of these conditions in favour of vendors became so much the practice that some of them had even received statutory recognition by the last quarter of the nineteenth century (ie, in ss 1 and 2 of the Vendor and Purchaser Act 1874 and s 3 of the Conveyancing Act 1881), a recognition which still holds good, with some amendments, today (ie, in ss 44 and 45 of the Law of Property Act 1925). Despite this recognition, however, where there was an open contract the sales remained, and remain, on the whole, tipped decidedly in the purchaser's favour. Consequently, conditions tipping the scales back down in the vendor's favour were still incorporated. Then, at the beginning of the present century practitioners apparently became more appreciative of their responsibilities when acting for purchasers and began to contest any conditions going too far. As a result, sets of conditions of sale were drafted which could be applied to any sale and which endeavoured to adjust the balance more fairly between the vendor and the purchaser. The use of such sets by means of printed forms gradually became general after the 1925 property legislation, which indeed seems to have caused such uncertainty amongst conveyancers that, for safety's sake, the forms contained many conditions having little or no application to most transactions, a nuisance which has since been aggravated by conditions providing for the spate of post-war planning legislation. Nonetheless, too much is probably better than too little; the busy practitioner finds it easier to strike out the unnecessary than to think up the necessary.

Clearly the incorporation by reference of familiar standard sets of conditions of sale can simplify and make certain the law and practice of conveyancing. Yet even in this there are at least two pitfalls. One lies in the old adage that familiarity breeds contempt: business efficiency, streamlining, may lead to unthinking acceptance and legal inefficiency. In an interesting article concerning the history of the National Conditions of Sale (at (1961) 105 SJ 497) reference was made to:

> the main body of stalwart practitioners, who tread the familiar paths of practical conveyancing firmly, and often with but light regard to what the National Conditions of Sale have actually said, either in their current edition or previous editions, but who nevertheless turn to them in moments of difficulty, in the expectation of discovering that the draftsman has happened to foresee some crisis, which in a particular case they have omitted to foresee themselves.

Since the question in the crisis will always be whether these great expectations about the draftsman's foresight are fulfilled and, if so, who his foresight favours, steps should surely be taken to avoid in anticipation the charge of the 'light regard.' Conveyancers ought actually to have in mind the precise provisions of any conditions they incorporate into the contract—after all, the parties themselves may be assumed to have had them in mind (see per Simonds J in *Re Debenham & Mercer's Contract* [1944] 1 All ER 364, at p 366c). Such an incorporated condition 'must be given its full status as a contractual term and cannot just be ignored because it is one of a number of printed conditions which the parties may well not actually have read' (per Oliver LJ in *Squarey* v *Harris-Smith* (1981) 42 P & CR 118, at p 128).

But contrast dicta in a case where it had been submitted that a *general* condition covering misrepresentations should be accepted as fair and reasonable (ie, within s 3 of the Misrepresentation Act 1967, see ante p 59) because of the particular circumstance that the purchaser had instructed a solicitor. The submission was rejected in the following words (which seem right in practice but wrong in principle):

> It is, of course, the duty of a solicitor to advise his client about any abnormal or unusual term in a contract, but I think it is perfectly normal and proper for a solicitor to use standard forms of conditions of sale such as the National Conditions of Sale. I do not think he is called on to go through the small print of those somewhat lengthy conditions with a toothcomb every time he is advising a purchaser to draw the purchaser's attention to every problem which on a careful reading of the conditions might in some circumstances or other conceivably arise. I cannot believe that purchasers of house property throughout the land would be overjoyed at having such lengthy explanations of the National Conditions of Sale ritually foisted upon them

(per Dillon J in *Walker* v *Boyle* [1982] 1 WLR 495, at pp 507–8). Yet, a *special* condition evolved by the solicitors acting for each side in the individual transaction might have been different: then the submission would have had 'great force, no doubt' (ibid).

The second pitfall is that any familiarity may prove somewhat one-sided. The most commonly met standard sets are still the National and The Law Society's Conditions of Sale. The choice between these two sets in practice seems to be dictated largely by local traditions (eg, London conveyancers mostly incorporate the National Conditions, whilst in Manchester the preference has been for The Law Society's), although after a detailed comparison of the sets in their latest editions (20th and 1980 respectively) the writer concluded in effect that the latter set was now significantly less favourable for vendors (see [1982] Conv 85–93). Further, local law 23);societies have increasingly been issuing their own pet sets of conditions which purchasers' solicitors practising in other localities have, however hardpressed, perforce to peruse and digest, then accept or reject in detail and in general. What is worse, these local sets occasionally constitute a compromise, themselves incorporating, subject to exceptions, one or other of the standard sets (see, eg, the conditions of sale in *Re Birmingham, Savage v Stannard* [1959] Ch 523); considerable conundrums of construction could be caused (see below). Also worth incidental notice at least is a new set which appeared like an eagle on the horizon during 1978 to be called 'The Conveyancing Lawyers' Conditions of Sale' (assessed anonyously at [1981] Conv 38–54).

An effective incorporation is necessary for these standard sets of general conditions of sale to apply to the contract. In *McKay v Turner* (1975) 120 SJ 367, special condition 1 in the auction particulars stated that the property was sold 'subject to the general conditions printed within so far as they are not varied by or inconsistent with those conditions, but the rate of interest under condition 16 shall be 15 per cent'. In fact no conditions were printed within, though the defendant vendors intended to have incorporated The Law Society's Conditions of Sale, 1973 Revision. Fox J said that special condition 1 could only be construed on its actual wording, in the light of any admissible surrounding circumstances, of which the defendants' intention to have included The Law Society's Conditions of Sale was not one. So those conditions were not incorporated. Nevertheless it was held that a notice to complete purportedly served under those conditions of sale was valid. Cp a note at [1978] Conv 81.

B   CONSTRUCTION

Now that the incorporation of general conditions of sale almost goes without saying and as they also embody what is thought to be a fair balance between the parties, it would seem doubly important to remember that these conditions still constitute adjustments, most often in the vendor's favour, from the open contract position. The first point is that:

> If a vendor means to exclude a purchaser from that which is a matter of common right, he is bound to express himself in terms the most clear and unambiguous, and if there be any chance of reasonable doubt, or reasonable misapprehension of his meaning, I think that the construction must be that which is rather favourable to the purchaser than to the vendor

(per Knight-Bruce V-C in *Symons v James* (1842) 1 Y & C Ch Cas 487, at p 490). This was recently re-emphasised by Slade J in *Leominister Properties Ltd v Broadway Finance Ltd* (1981) 42 P & CR 372, at p 387 where he stated that if the words of a particular standard condition of sale (ie, National Condition 10) could be said to give rise to an ambiguity, they should be construed against the vendor 'because it was the grantor, and the rights of the plaintiff as purchaser were thereby restricted'. Thus the contra proferentem principle of construction will most often apply to general conditions as it did to special conditions.

The second point is that the general conditions of sale were not drafted by prophets: for any particular transaction, they may go either too far or not far enough. As Pearson LJ has fairly recently said:

even a good standard form, however well drafted in the past by a competent lawyer, may not be appropriate to the particular case unless suitably adapted (in *Scheggia* v *Gradwell* [1963] 1 WLR 1049, at p 1066). The remedy lies, therefore, with the drafting and incorporating of special conditions for the particular transaction. These should deal with any peculiar matters of title, with any out of the ordinary provisions desired in the conveyance, and indeed with anything at all that the parties may wish. The general conditions are invariably incorporated 'so far as not inconsistent' with the special conditions, and any undesired general condition may be deleted simply by a special condition saying that it 'shall not have effect.' One must beware, however, of upsetting a delicate construction. The arguments arising from inconsistencies between the completion date in the special conditions and that in the general conditions have already been adumbrated in this book (p 42). The apparently simple deletion of a condition of sale may cause arguments, first, because other conditions may either suffer or give rise to unlooked for consequential effects, and secondly, because the general law may simply fill the gap and apply to much the same effect as the deleted condition would have applied (see *Re Priestley's Contract* [1947] Ch 469, illustrating both these points, exhaustively considered at (1947-8) 12 Conv (NS) 40). Consequently, the only careful counsel is to reinforce any deletions or variations with a positive statement of precisely what is to happen in the circumstances envisaged by the condition concerned.

A third point to appreciate perhaps is that the courts have demonstrated a disturbing tendency to dislike and discount general conditions of sale. Already mentioned is the unprincipled argument that a special condition might be 'fair and reasonable' where a general condition would not because a lay client's knowledge and approval of the latter should not apparently be presumed (see *Walker* v *Boyle* [1982] 1 WLR 495, ante p 78). Another case concerned a not uncommon form of general condition as to purchasers being deemed to take with full knowledge of the contents of certain documents expressly available for inspection: this condition was judicially described as 'very special and ferocious' and counsel's reliance on it dismissed as 'an argument to which I cannot in any circumstances pay any regard whatsoever' (per Walton J in *Faruqi* v *English Real Estates Ltd* [1979] 1 WLR 963, at pp 965, 967). And other illustrations of this attitude can certainly be seen in *Hone* v *Benson* (1978) 248 EG 1013, ante p 73, and especially in *Topfell Ltd* v *Galley Properties Ltd* [1979] 1 WLR 446, post p 176. In other words, you cannot confidently rely upon the small print.

Does this mean that standard, general conditions of sale are always to be regarded as unreliable as exclusion clauses? Yes, apparently, with one conceivable exception:

> Of course it is true that there are common form clauses which have been evolved by negotiation between trade associations, associations of merchants or associations of growers or trade unions or other such bodies concerned to protect the rights of their members which can be regarded as representing what consensus in the trade regards as fair and reasonable. Again, the National Conditions of Sale are not the product of negotiation between such bodies

(per Dillon J in *Walker* v *Boyle* [1982] 1 WLR 495, at p 508). Nor, needless to say, are the Law Society's Conditions such a product, unless being drafted by a committee counts. But perhaps for the next editions of each set, solicitors could divide their clients up into notionally separate bodies of vendors and purchasers which could then nominate representatives to negotiate judicially acceptable conditions of sale. Why, in Lord Denning's final fling, with cabbages and whatnots, he indicated that even he might have swallowed such a negotiated exclusion clause (see *George Mitchell Ltd* v *Finney Lock Seeds Ltd* [1983] 1 All ER 108, at pp 112,

117). Yet this is wholly fanciful: the standard sets of conditions of sale should properly be regarded already as 'negotiated within the trade' (cp per Kerr LJ, ibid p 126).

C BY CORRESPONDENCE

No solicitor would advise a vendor to do without the shelter of conditions when entering into a contract for the sale of land. Happily, the layman who does without a lawyer is not left entirely out in the open (although both the National and The Law Society's Conditions of Sale are protected by copyright and theoretically obtainable only by solicitors). If the contract is 'by correspondence' then the Lord Chancellor's Statutory Form of Conditions of Sale will apply in all its insignificant glory (SR & O 1925 No 779, promulgated under s 46 of the Law of Property Act 1925). This further statutory recognition of the inconveniences of an open contract achieves a result which is in principle the same as if some standard set of conditions had been expressly incorporated, ie, an open contract plus modifications. The statutory form provides a time-table for the steps leading from the contract to completion, deals with a few incidental matters, and best of all gives the vendor the contractual remedies of rescission and resale. Nonetheless the shelter afforded, although better than nothing, is much slighter than that provided by the usual general conditions, and the statutory form must rarely, if ever, be adopted expressly. So the problem is to say precisely when this form is impliedly adopted, ie, what does the phrase 'contracts by correspondence' mean? There is no statutory definition and despite initial predictions of a harvest of litigation there has still been no judicial interpretation. Therefore the meaning can be briefly questioned, untrammelled by authority.

The primary sense of 'correspondence' according to *The Oxford English Dictionary* involves essentially 'congruity, harmony, agreement.' Since this would leave the phrase as a tautology, the sixth sense there given may be preferred of 'intercourse or communication by letters.' Therefore it can be said that 'if parties exchange letters by post, and such letters constitute a clear offer for sale of a specified property and an unqualified acceptance of such offer, no doubt a contract has arisen by correspondence' (Walford, *Sale of Land*, 2nd ed, p 1). Such a contract would then be subject to the statutory conditions of sale mentioned; ie, whatever the parties' intentions they will *not* have achieved a purely 'open' contract (pace Russell LJ in *Bigg* v *Boyd Gibbins Ltd* [1971] 1 WLR 913).

If the parties in their haste exchange telegrams, a contract by correspondence would still arise (see *Holland* v *Tolley* [1952] CPL 34), but they might well be too hasty for present purposes if they were to use telex or some other modern form of instantaneous communication (cf *Entores Ltd* v *Miles Far East Corporation* [1955] 2 QB 327 and *Aquis Estates Ltd* v *Minton* [1975] 1 WLR 1452 at p 1454). What, however, if an oral offer is accepted by letter, or vice versa (cf *Parker* v *Clark* [1960] 1 WLR 286)? Or if the parties exchange. letters by hand rather than through the post? Or if an oral contract is confirmed and evidenced by letters? The present writer would suggest that, since the statutory form resulted from an intention to relieve the inconvenience of an open contract, the widest possible relief should be given, even accepting if needs be the tautological primary meaning of 'contracts by correspondence'. Thus the statutory form could even be applied where formal parts of a contract are exchanged by post so long as it is borne in mind that the application gives way to any express conditions (cf Williams, *Sale of Land*, p 26, note (*p*), and (1937) 56 LN 369).

D   CONCLUSION

This conclusion, which anticipates the detailed discussion of particular conditions
of sale in the ensuing chapters, is borrowed from *Williams on Vendor and Purchaser*,
p 100 of the 4th ed, which appeared in 1936:

> On the whole, it seems advisable for an intending purchaser always to offer,
> and if he can, to procure the signature of an open contract. If the vendor is
> anxious to sell and satisfied with the price proposed, such an offer will bring
> home to him the advantage of binding the purchaser definitely and at once
> instead of disputing over special stipulations, each of which gives the buyer an
> opportunity of retiring.

True though this is, the dispute mentioned is not now the principal cause of delays.
The four realities for a modern purchaser have been his pre-contract enquiries
(including survey), his financial arrangements, his own sale, and his completion and
removal date. He has always been advised not to rush into any quick contract until
the first three are dealt with and he might not be happy with the 'completion within
a reasonable time' of an open contract. So the completely open contract has become
a comparative rarity. However these realities have of late rather shrunk before the
overriding truth of today: the market has become the mistress. Sometimes house
prices inflate fast so that a purchaser may find himself 'gazumped' unless he hurries
into an instant contract. Other times, house sales stagnate so that vendors are
anxious to grasp at almost any offer and purchasers can look for bargains. Either
way the temptations to contract quickly are often irresistible. But such a quick
contract will still rarely be an open one: it will be on the terms imposed by the party
currently favoured by the market. Nevertheless, as indicated at the outset, in each of
the ensuing chapters, as in practice, convenience and logic require any discussion of
conditions of sale of land to work from the open contract position up to the
modifications thereof.

VI TITLE

A THE OBLIGATION DEFINED

ASSUMING the existence of that comparative rarity, the completely open contract for the sale of land, then 'the most prominent term of the contract is that which requires the vendor to show a good title' (*Williams on Vendor and Purchaser*, 3rd ed, at p 34; and see per Jessel MR in *Lysaght v Edwards* (1876) 2 Ch D 499, at p 507). The quotation continues: 'this obligation is the cause of most of the disputes and litigation between buyers and sellers of land' (ibid). This might once have been true, but now that the simplifying legislation of 1925 has withdrawn well beyond the current fifteen-year fishing limits, the courts, conveyancers and their clients are in truth less exercised than they were by the technicalities of title. Nonetheless, the purchaser must always see that the vendor can show a good title, the mere fact of present possession not sufficing, for as Lord Erskine has said 'no man in his senses would take an offer of a purchase from a man merely because he stood on the ground' (in *Hiern v Mill* (1806) 13 Ves 114, at p 122; although a mere possession can be sold: *Rosenberg v Cook* (1881) 8 QBD 162).

1 Origin

For the purchaser the rule that title must be shown originates in common prudence. For the vendor, however, the origin seems to be his conscience. Medieval common law knew nothing of the rule, since feoffees looked for security simply to the feoffor's warranty of title which afforded a remedy in rem. Then the Courts of Equity, as a condition of granting to a vendor their special remedy for specific performance, held it to be only equitable that he should first show a good title (see *Jenkins v Hiles* (1802) 6 Ves 646, at p 653; *Purvis v Rayer* (1821) 9 Price 488, at pp 518–19). Once given birth to by equity, the rule was adopted also by the common law (see *Doe d Gray v Stanion* (1836) 1 M & W 695, at p 701).

The rule is now established in law, but whether it represents the imposition of a rule of law or merely the implication of a contractual term has enjoyed some few instances of judicial indecision. Initially, Grant MR uttered the view that:

> The right to a good title is a right not growing out of the agreement between the parties, but which is given by law. The defendant insists on having a good title, not because it is stipulated for by the agreement, but on the general right of a purchaser to require it

(in *Ogilvie v Foljambe* (1817) 3 Mer 53). Although authority for the view that the right to a good title is only an implied term could be found (eg, *Souter v Drake* (1834) 5 B & Ad 992 but cp *Hall v Betty* (1842) 4 M & G 410 where both the preceding cases were cited as if consistent), the next pronouncement was plain: 'Now the right of a vendee to a good title is a right, not merely growing out of the agreement between the parties, but is given by the law' (per Pollock B in *Want v Stallibrass* (1873) LR 8 Ex 175, at p 185). In this last case the point mattered: the purchaser was able to raise out-of-time objections to a bad title despite a condition of sale to the contrary. Nevertheless the next judicial consideration was much more inconclusive: Cotton LJ contented himself with the extraordinary comment that 'it might under some circumstances have been necessary for us to decide on which of these two grounds the right to a good title rests, whether it depends on an implied term in the contract or is a collateral right given by the law' (*Ellis* v *Rogers* (1885) 29 Ch D 661, at p 671).

More likely, however, the so-called different grounds are really different expressions for the same thing; the distinction between obligations imposed by law and objectively implied terms seems to have no essential validity. Certainly the courts have never attached any importance to any such distinction in the present context. Thus Finlay LC seeming to use both views, has said that:

> if the contract is open, the obligation which *the law would import into it* to make a good title in every respect may be rebutted by proving that the purchaser entered into the contract with knowledge of certain defects in the title. The inference in such a case is that he was content to take a title less than *the law would otherwise have given him by implication*

(in *McGrory* v *Alderdale Estate Co Ltd* [1918] AC 503, at p 508). More recently in *Timmins* v *Moreland Street Property Co Ltd* [1958] Ch 110, the terminology and citations of Jenkins LJ's judgment (pp 118–9) seem to be a reliance on the implied term view, whilst Romer LJ seemed to accept the imposition of law view (at p 132) by saying that 'a right of way, for example, over land agreed to be sold is not a term of the contract of sale but a matter of title.' However, none of these were considered opinions on the present question, but merely observations passed whilst gyrating either to avoid s 40 of the Law of Property Act 1925 or to give effect to a purchaser's pre-contract knowledge of defects in title.

2   Meanings

Whatever the view taken, however, the vendor's obligation to show a good title is an immutable part of the scenery of an open contract. But what precisely is a 'good title'? It is proposed to discuss the meaning of this expression as a general conception before dealing in ensuing parts of this chapter with the method of showing it—is not the proper order of enquiry 'what' before 'how'? True the everyday duties of conveyancers involve certifying as to title, usually that someone has or has not 'a good and marketable title' (see, eg, *Law Society's Gazette* (1966) vol 63, at p 185, and (1971) vol 68, at p 338, as to the form of reports on title to banks) and conveyancers surely know what they are doing, perhaps not with jurisprudential precision, but at least for everyday purposes. Nevertheless, a gentle attempt at dissecting the meaning should do no harm, especially as the opening incision reveals only that ' "title" is an ambiguous word' (per Kindersley V-C in *Felkin* v *Lord Herbert* (1861) 30 LJ Ch 798, at p 799; theorists may find more meat in an article by Bernard Rudden, 'The Terminology of Title' (1964) 80 LQR 63, to which some comparative salt can be added through 'The Concepts of "Property", "Title" and "Owner" used in the Sale of Goods Act 1893' by G Battersby and A D Preston (1972) 35 MLR 268).

Putting aside for the moment its adjectival varieties, by 'title' the conveyancer unconsciously confuses more often than not three separate but closely connected ideas. The first of these is the vendor's ownership, the right to property. The second is simply the evidence of that ownership (see glossary, Megarry and Wade, *Real Property*, 4th ed, at p cxvi). Whilst the third is the property itself, which in this context is necessarily some estate or interest in land (remember the doctrine of tenure).

Quick disposal at this stage of the third idea is possible. Under an open contract the implication is always that an unincumbered freehold is being sold (see *Timmins* v *Moreland Street Property Co Ltd* [1958] Ch 110; the rebuttal of this implication was discussed in the section on non-disclosure at p 62). If the element of the freehold being unincumbered, ie, free from defects in title, were not invariably tacked on, this implication would probably form no part in anybody's mind of the good title idea. Nothing more will be said of this here.

The first idea, ownership, has its varieties, of which the essence is always possession (or more properly with freeholds 'seisin'), the lowest variety being bare possession and the next the right of possession (English land law admits of no abstract ownership, as the mere right of property without either possession or the right of possession). The conveyancer, however, is little troubled by these lesser varieties; he assumes, quite rightly, the meaning of 'a complete legal title [which] exists where the right of possession is joined with the right of property' (2 Bl Comm 196). The conveyancer also tends, mistakenly, to assume that this ownership is capable of being absolute, ie, good against the whole world, whereas English land law is such that, save in the rare case of a grant of ownership by or under Act of Parliament, the possibility always exists of someone turning up with competing and better rights in the property. Borrowing, perhaps, a word from the lips of a purposive face, Holroyd Pearce LJ once explained:

> Title to land is pragmatic. It is true if and so long as it works. It works if it only comes up against a weaker title. But if it is challenged by a stronger title, it ceases to be a true title and must give way . . . Thus even a fee simple is only good as long as no better title can be shown

(in *St Marylebone Property Co Ltd* v *Fairweather* [1962] 1 QB 498, at p 513; affirmed at [1963] AC 510). There is no novelty in this approach; it echoes the words of Jessel MR at the end of the nineteenth century:

> Now the title of the disseiser is in this country a freehold title, and therefore, although the vendor had a very bad title, and a title liable to be defeated, he had still a title good against all the world, except against those who might be proved to have a better one

(in *Rosenberg* v *Cook* (1881) 8 QBD 162, at p 165). Any such better title will generally be legal rather than equitable, and for present purposes need only involve rights adverse to an unincumbered estate ownership.

In particular, ownership of land must almost always be regarded as not absolute, but relative, because conveyancing practice and law has limited the proof of ownership, in effect, to possession for a period long enough only to make better legal rights improbable, not impossible (see, eg, *Wyld* v *Silver* [1963] Ch 243, where a purchaser, who took without notice, who had investigated title properly and who was without a remedy on the covenants for title, was restrained from acts, eg, building, which would interfere with the legal but 'ancient and outmoded right' to hold a fair on the land on Fridays in Whitsun week in every year). To make better rights impossible the proof would have to start with the grant to Adam and Eve, but even this was save and except the Garden of Eden, and one is not even sure whether they took as joint tenants or tenants in common (cf *Selkirk* v *Romar Investments Ltd* [1963] 1 WLR 1415, at p 1418, where the dates of certain title deeds were qualified in the contract for sale by the letters 'AD').

Apart altogether from ancient rights (which need not be very old in view of the 1969 reduction in the period of title, see p 95), title to unregistered land is always less than absolute simply because the traditional methods of investigation of title used in practice are not directed towards the discovery of all defects. For a fearful example, the absence of fraud seems to be assumed; no steps are taken in the ordinary way to reveal such ungentlemanly behaviour as the forgery or suppression of title deeds (cp *Re A Solicitor* (1976) 120 SJ 353 and *Weston* v *Henshaw* [1950] Ch

510). Thus the liberally commended reform of having wives on titles (ie, instead of leaving them to override as in *Williams & Glyn's Bank* v *Boland* [1981] AC 487, HL) could actually encourage fraud and forgery: two cases have already occurred where the husband had the other woman sign the wife's name on a consequently abortive mortgage (*Cedar Holdings Ltd* v *Green* [1981] Ch 129, CA and *First National Securities Ltd* v *Hegarty* (1982) *The Times*, 2 November). The normal conveyancing practices followed in these cases simply failed to reveal the fundamental flaw in the whole transaction to the loss of the lenders (as to Attestation see pp 328–329). As to a solicitor's potential liability for merely lodging forged transfers, compare *Yeung Kai Yung* v *Hong Kong and Shanghai Banking Corporation* [1981] AC 787, PC.

Again the competence of those investigating title will not often extend to checking faults in the plans or verbal descriptions of the land comprised in the title deeds; uncertainties as to boundaries and even double conveyances of land, especially of overlapping estate plots, are by no means unknown (see a note at [1982] Conv 324). Then there may be nasty surprises on the land itself, such as squatters or easements by prescription, not to mention overriding wives, which are not readily apparent from an office chair. All in all, therefore, even the best of titles to unregistered land may turn out to be riddled with unknown flaws and hazards (see further Stephen Cretney at (1969) 32 MLR 494–5; also a note at (1974) 38 Conv (NS) 226–9).

Against this, it must be conceded that registered titles are not subject at all to the risk of many of these undiscoverable defects: the mere fact of registration greatly reduces the possibility of better titles or rights. But even so the proposition remains generally valid: ownership of registered land, notwithstanding a statutory description as 'absolute,' is still strictly relative (or pragmatic) in that there are provisions permitting rectification of the register (see p 162). And also, of course, registered conveyancing practice is just as naïve as the traditional investigation of title when it comes to conduct unbefitting a gentleman: see, for example, *Robson-Paul* v *Farrugia* (1969) 113 SJ 346, CA, where a transfer of registered land had been declared null and void due to forgery of a signature following the failure of a bigamous marriage (cf also Theodore B F Ruoff at (1969) 32 MLR 140–1, as to the consequences of being clever with forgery as well as with acid baths).

3 Evidence

This unhealthy preoccupation with the relative nature of ownership of land leads to the second more acceptable idea of title, namely, the evidence supporting the vendor's claim to own the property (estate or interest) which he has contracted to sell. If the land is unregistered, this evidence is directed to the mode of acquisition of ownership which may be either original (eg, by creation, as on the grant of a lease) or derivative (ie, by taking the place of a predecessor either by an act of the parties, eg, a conveyance, or by operation of law). If the land is registered, the evidence is simply of registration. For conveyancers the object of this exercise in evidence is to show ownership with a view to transfer. Hence a rough and confusing terminology for titles has arisen varying with the extent to which the evidence offered of the transferor's ownership makes better rights than the transferee's improbable.

In the first place, the vendor has to show a 'good title' which, at its very best, seems to mean simply that the purchaser will actually get a legal estate free from adverse interests. The difficulty here is lack of judicial definition (although Fletcher-Moulton LJ has provided us with: 'Now it is said that a good title is a good title. It may be so', in *Re Atkinson and Horsell's Contract* [1912] 2 Ch 1, at p 15).

The courts are rarely asked to pronounce upon perfection; the titles they see almost all have something wrong with them, the question being: how bad may good be?

The answer which lies to that is that what a purchaser is entitled to is to be satisfied that his vendor is seised of the estate which he is purporting to sell, in this case the fee simple, and that he is in the position, *without the possibility of dispute or litigation*, to pass that fee simple to the purchaser

(per Wilberforce J in *Re Stirrup's Contract, Stirrup* v *Foel Agricultural Co-operative Society Ltd* [1961] 1 WLR 449, at p 454). The italicised words indicate the rule and the rub. Faced with a less than perfect title one has to decide whether 'the risk cannot be said to be so remote or so shadowy as to be one to which no serious attention need be paid': per Sir L Stone V-C in *Manning* v *Turner* [1957] 1 WLR 91, at p 94, who proceeded:

In my opinion, the test must always be: would the court, in an action for specific performance at the instance of the vendors, force a title containing the alleged defect upon a reluctant purchaser?

Unfortunately this test enables no definite line to be drawn; each particular title must be looked at, some will be clearly good and some not, but the problem will remain that 'there is no possibility of mistaking midnight for noon; but at what precise moment twilight becomes darkness is hard to determine' (per Cranworth LC in *Boyse* v *Rossborough* (1857) 6 HL Cas 2, at p 45). Happily, however, with registered land all seems black or white: on a sale of freeholds under an open contract an absolute title must be shown, no other being good (*Re Brine and Davies' Contract* [1935] Ch 388). But even here some shadows may be thrown: does an open sale of registered leaseholds also imply nothing less than an absolute title? The writer's view is that a good leasehold title should also be a good title, in the present sense, simply because a purchaser from a lessee is not ordinarily entitled to concern himself with the freehold title (s 44 (2) of the Law of Property Act 1925 and p 133), a position which a good leasehold registration merely reflects (see s 10 of the Land Registration Act 1925). Nonetheless a contrary view is, at least, indicated in Ruoff and Roper, *Registered Conveyancing*, 4th ed, at pp 87 and 308). Again, how far may the light of an otherwise absolutely good title be cut off by overriding interests and rectification?

A good title, therefore, is not necessarily perfect. In practice, any imperfections, although not thought serious, would be taken care of, no doubt, by a special condition in the contract. From this follows the somewhat better nature of a 'marketable title', a nature which, despite the next quotation, may not be entirely shared by a 'good title' simpliciter (see observations in *Re Atkinson and Horsell's Contract* [1912] 2 Ch 1). Thus Luxmoore J has said:

The purchaser having bought on an open contract, was entitled to have a good marketable title, which, as I understand it, is a title which will enable him to sell the property without the necessity of making special conditions of sale restrictive of a purchaser's rights

(in *Re Spollon and Long's Contract* [1936] Ch 713, at p 718). In other words, for a title to be 'marketable' the vendor's estate ownership must be supported by the maximum evidence requirable by conveyancing practice and law which must suffer no blot to which a prudent purchaser might properly object. Consequently, if the copybook (or abstract) is not reasonably clean, the result is likely to be either a 'doubtful title' or a 'bad title.'

A 'doubtful title', which will not be forced on a reluctant purchaser under an open contract, occurs where the vendor is not shown with certainty to have the ownership he contracted to sell, ie, his ownership on the evidence may or may not be good. The doubt may be because of uncertainty (1) as to the law itself at some point, or (2) as to the application of a settled rule of law, or (3) as to some fact or construction on which the title depends (*Nottingham Patent Brick & Tile Co* v *Butler* (1886) 16 QBD 778, as to whether a vendor had taken without notice of restrictive covenants: see also the question in *Selkirk* v *Romar Investments Ltd* [1963] 1 WLR 1415, at p 1419, and further *Choppy* v *Bibi* [1967] 1 AC 158, where the bastardisation of children was sought in an attempt to establish title to certain land). Then the vendor can only clear his title by embarking upon the litigation or enquiry for evidence necessary to disperse the doubt not just against the purchaser but, as it were, against the world (see *Wilson* v *Thomas* [1958] 1 WLR 422, a latent ambiguity in a will would not be resolved without having all the beneficiaries represented before the court).

An excellent illustration of a doubtful title and its consequences can be found in *Re Hollis' Hospital Trustees and Hague's Contract* [1899] 2 Ch 540. The purchaser sought a declaration that a good title had not been shown because of a reverter clause in the title deeds. Byrne J first held that the clause constituted a common law condition subsequent which was void for remoteness but because the point was 'one of some obscurity and difficulty' and because 'the purchaser, if he completes, will be in danger of immediate litigation' he concluded that the title was not such as ought to be forced upon an unwilling purchaser (ibid, p 555; see also the quotations from *Re Stirrup's Contract* [1961] 1 WLR 449, 454, given ante, p 87, and from *Re Bramwell's Contract, Bramwell* v *Ballards Securities Investments Ltd* [1969] 1 WLR 1659, 1663, given ante, p 51).

Again more recently in *Horton* v *Kurzke* [1971] 1 WLR 769, where land had been sold with vacant possession, an agricultural grazing right tenancy had been claimed but eventually the claim was effectively rejected by an arbitrator. Before this rejection the vendor served a notice to complete. Goff J said (at p 772):

It is a fundamental part of the vendor's obligations to prove his title, and he is not, in my judgment, able to complete when he is not in a position to discharge that duty. Now, when [the vendor] served the notice, and when it expired, the position was that there was an adverse claim to the property which was either a question of fact or of mixed law and fact, the facts being . . . within the knowledge of [the vendor] and the claimant and not that of [the purchaser]. It seems to me, therefore, that it was the duty of [the vendor] to clear her title, either by a vendor and purchaser summons, or probably more aptly by awaiting the determination of the arbitration.

The vendor's title subject to the adverse claim was not bad and was eventually good but in the meantime was sufficiently doubtful not to be forced upon a purchaser.

A 'bad title' means that the vendor is shown with certainty *not* to have the full ownership he contracted to sell. In other words, the evidence produced by the vendor reveals no uncertainty but the actuality of a defect in title. This may be something which strikes directly at the vendor's ownership (eg, that he has no valid power of sale: *Re Holmes (W & R) and Cosmopolitan Press Ltd's Contract* [1944] Ch 53), or something which establishes third-party rights enforceable against future owners (eg, an incumbrance: cf *Manning* v *Turner* [1957] 1 WLR 91). Lord Denning MR extracted the essence of such situations with the words:

On the face of the title which [the vendor] produced, it was a thoroughly bad title with this restrictive covenant still imposed on it . . . He was guilty of a breach going to the root of the contract, because he was not, on the face of his documents, able to make a good title

(*Re Stone and Saville's Contract* [1963] 1 WLR 163, at p 169, where the vendor's ownership was in fact good although his evidence was bad).

Such a situation must be distinguished, however, from that where there is something which can be dismissed as merely a 'technical' defect in title. This appears to envisage some hitch in the smooth showing of title to the legal estate which nonetheless does not detract from the vendor's beneficial ownership. In other words, a conveyancing mistake has occurred which is open to correction by a general rule of law. If it only *may* be corrected, then the title would be doubtful. If it clearly *is* corrected, then there would be a good, though not perfect, title (as in *Re Stirrup's Contract, Stirrup* v *Foel Agricultural Co-operative Society Ltd* [1961] 1 WLR 449, where an inappropriate word of grant—'assents'—had been used in a conveyance). The distinction is again one of uncertain degrees. Some modern examples may help.

In one case the mortgagee's receipt endorsed on a mortgage was dated two days after a conveyance on sale by the mortgagor which recited legal ownership 'free from incumbrances'; in the circumstances, the receipt operated not as a discharge but as a transfer (s 115 (2) of the Law of Property Act 1925) and consequently a subsequent purchaser objected. Ungoed-Thomas J held that the doctrine of feeding the estoppel applied to prevent any enforcement of the mortgage and that as the subsequent purchaser 'would get a perfectly good equitable title and could not be disturbed, it was not a matter which went to the root of the title' (*Cumberland Court (Brighton) Ltd* v *Taylor* [1964] Ch 29, at p 37; following *Pryce-Jones* v *Williams* [1902] 2 Ch 517, where all the assets of a company in liquidation had been sold to a new company of the same name but no formal assignments had been made of certain leases and on a later sale of the leases the purchaser objected, unsuccessfully, that no legal title had been shown by the new company). The learned judge's distinction, easily stated but less easily applied, was between defects which go to the root of the title and technical defects which do not (in this context 'the root of the title' does not mean the first instrument (cf p 96), but beneficial ownership itself, and Joyce J is thought to have expressed the distinction imprecisely in *Pryce-Jones* v *Williams* ante, when saying, at p 522, that the objections 'were not as to the root of title but as to the subsequent devolution').

In another modern case, one of the title deeds conveying settled land to the tenant for life was, on the face of it, voidable as being a sale by executors to one of themselves; in the light of the facts Buckley J found:

> On equitable grounds the transaction is not open to any criticism whatever. It is only open to criticism on purely technical conveyancing grounds relating to the machinery employed, and since it seems to me that the statutory powers conferred by s 68 (2) [of the Settled Land Act 1925] were available to the parties, and since the transaction was one which could not properly be carried out without the leave of the court except by the use of those statutory powers: it is right . . . that I should treat this conveyance as made in the exercise of those statutory powers, notwithstanding that these powers were clearly not in the minds of the parties . . .
>
> For these reasons, I am of opinion that the conveyance was an effective conveyance to confer an absolute and indisputable title

(in *Re Pennant's Will Trusts* [1970] Ch 75, at pp 83–4; as to the relative nature of titles, cf ante, p 85).

These cases (including *Re Stirrup's Contract*, ante) are all examples of intention prevailing over form, of the courts correcting conveyancing mistakes notwithstanding even statutory technicalities, and other instances of this approach have been reported (see, eg, *Grangeside Properties Ltd* v *Collingwoods Securities Ltd* [1964] 1 WLR 139). Unhappily this is a welcome but not a predictable approach: there are other notorious cases where the strict technicalities have triumphed (see, eg, *Re King's Will Trusts, Assheton* v *Boyne* [1964] Ch 542, post, p 106; also *Weston* v

Henshaw [1950] Ch 510 and *Barclays Bank Ltd* v *Taylor* [1974] Ch 137).
Accordingly, a title which stands or falls upon the courts adopting this approach
may have to be treated as doubtful unless and until the wisdom of hindsight has
produced a decision that its defects are technical and itself good.

With the cases in this state, two examples ancient and modern may afford a more
comprehensible reminder of the principles governing the finding of technical
defects. In *Re Heaysman's and Tweedy's Contract* (1893) 69 LT 89, concerning a
contract for sale in fee simple free from incumbrances, the land had been subject to
a lease which had been determined by a judgment in ejectment but the vendor could
not produce the lease because it was still held by an equitable mortgagee of the
ejected tenant; the purchaser's objections to the title were, however, rejected by the
Court of Appeal. As Lindley LJ put it (ibid, p 91):

> It is a general principle that a purchaser ought not to be forced to accept a
> doubtful title or buy a law suit. In applying that principle, however, we must
> exercise our common sense, and see if the supposed law suit has any basis
> whatever. We must see if there is the slightest reasonable chance of any such
> law suit being instituted. If we come to the conclusion that the supposed law
> suit exists only in the imagination of the purchaser, we ought to disregard it,
> giving him the advantage of every reasonable doubt. . . I think the facts are
> such that this supposed blot is a purely theoretical and not a practical blot.
> Nothing could be made of it at law or equity.

Similarly in *Darvell* v *Basildon Development Corporation* (1969) 211 EG 33 the
previous purchaser, now selling, had been not only an infant but also the daughter
of her vendor's estate agent; after a confirmatory conveyance (to cure the infancy)
and hearing the vendor's evidence on subpoena, Megarry J concluded that there
was 'mere conjecture of an attack by what would be idle litigation' and decreed
specific performance plus costs and interest. This approach was adopted in effect by
the House of Lords, although without actually citing the earlier cases, in *MEPC Ltd*
v *Christian-Edwards* [1981] AC 205. There freehold property was sold at auction for
£710,000: the vendors sold as trustees for sale under the will of a Mr Metchim who
had died in 1911; examination of title revealed that in 1912 the then trustees had
contracted to sell the property to the deceased's son; no copy of that contract was
available but it was referred to in deeds dated 1912 and 1930, the latter reciting its
suspension but not the terms thereof. The applicable principle was pronounced to
be that where the facts and circumstances of a case were so compelling that a court
would conclude that the purchaser would not be at risk of a successful assertion
against him of the incumbrance, then a good title should be declared as shown.
Accordingly, in the case it was held that a good title had been shown because it was
established beyond reasonable doubt that the 1912 contract had been abandoned
and also that specific performance of it could not have been obtained.

However, the writer does not consider this principle to be an entirely satisfactory
one on which to rely in similar cases of doubtful incumbrances appearing on a title.
Thus the third party potential claimant would not be bound by the decision, so that
the possibility of future litigation remains, albeit probably unsuccessful. Nor would
HM Land Registry be bound by the decision (the property in the case was in an area
of compulsory first registration of title). True it was said to be inconceivable that,
where higher courts had held that a vendor had shown a good title, the Chief Land
Registrar should take a different view (per Lord Russell of Killowen at p 221). But
attaining this position involves first taking the apparently doubtful title to court
and also on appeal perhaps for a ruling. And this represents the real practical
difficulty: how can solicitors be quickly and sufficiently certain, whilst clients are
pressing for progress, that the facts and circumstances will or will not appear

compelling to the courts after a full hearing? Take the *Darvell* decision: short of such litigation how could the title have been safely accepted? Compare *Faruqi* v *English Real Estates Ltd* [1979] 1 WLR 963 where certain undisclosed and unknown restrictive covenants imposed in 1883 rendered a title defective irrespective apparently of any likelihood of litigation. In practice, solicitors must continue to raise requisitions as to doubtful incumbrances and might also perhaps seek indemnities from the other side (cf below).

Let us now turn again to what Lord Denning called a 'thoroughly bad title' (see ante, p 88), only to find that:

> There are bad titles and bad titles; bad titles which are good holding titles, although they may be open to objections which are not serious, are bad titles in a conveyancer's point of view, but good in a businessman's point of view

(per Lindley LJ in *Re Scott and Alvarez's Contract, Scott* v *Alvarez* [1895] 2 Ch 603, at p 613). A 'holding title' is one which looks back to the origin of ownership, namely possession. The expression envisages a doubtful title or one suffering from a merely technical defect, under which there has been undisturbed possession. This becomes a 'good holding title' if the possession is likely to continue to be undisturbed. Twelve years' possession normally leads to this likelihood, but where a trustee had purchased trust property in 1937, the position in 1953 still was that:

> for a number of years it would be impossible to say with certainty that no claim could arise to upset the transaction, although hitherto no claim has been made. This is clearly a serious blot on the title, and not one that can be described with any propriety as a technical defect. There is a real danger that anyone acquiring this property with notice may be dispossessed of it hereafter

(per Harman J in *Pilkington* v *Wood* [1953] Ch 770, at p 775); as to the lack of limitation of actions in respect of trust property, see s 20 of the Limitation Act 1980, also *Re Landi* [1939] Ch 828; and as to avoiding purchases of trust property by trustees and the like, see *Holder* v *Holder* [1968] Ch 353. Nonetheless, twelve years' possession can even become not just a good holding title but a good title in its own right if sufficient evidence of the defeated ownership is forthcoming (*Re Atkinson & Horsell's Contract* [1912] 2 Ch 1, but cf *George Wimpey & Co Ltd* v *Sohn* [1967] Ch 487, discussed post, p 109), and now a mere fifteen years' possession covering the period of title may have to be accepted (see *Jacobs* v *Revell* [1900] 2 Ch 858). Notwithstanding the principle that 'however bad the title may be the purchaser has a right to accept it' (per Jessel MR in *Lysaght* v *Edwards* (1876) 2 Ch D 499, at p 507), until a holding title (whether or not a 'good holding title') becomes a good title it will not be forced on a reluctant purchaser under an open contract (*Pyrke* v *Waddingham* (1852) 10 Hare 1).

In practice it may be pertinent to enquire whether or not a vendor can cure any shortcomings in his title by the simple expedient of offering to indemnify the purchaser. How far may the provision of an indemnity be the complete reply to a purchaser's requisition as to any particular defect in title? In *Re Heaysman's and Tweedy's Contract* (1893) 69 LT 89 (ante, p 90) where the defect was merely technical or theoretical, the vendor had offered an indemnity which the purchaser had refused. The Court of Appeal held that the purchaser was not bound to accept the indemnity (see per Lindley LJ at p 91) but somewhat paradoxically indicated that it ought to have been offered and ought not to have been refused, and that this was material on the question of costs. More recently in *Manning* v *Turner* [1957] 1 WLR 91, where the defect was *not* merely technical, Sir Leonard Stone V-C observed that it was a case where 'the title would not be forced on [the purchaser] *unless* the defect were first removed by an indemnity policy offered by a reputable insurance company insuring against the risk involved' (at p 94). However, it is submitted that this later case should be confined to its own facts, in particular that the defect in question was only a possible money liability (a charge to estate duty) not affecting possession of the property, and also that it was the purchaser initially who requested the indemnity. Otherwise the general rule must be that supported by the Court of Appeal in the earlier case, namely that the purchaser is not bound to accept an indemnity as curing a defective title.

4   Matters of conveyance

At this point the distinction may conveniently be drawn between matters of title and matters of conveyance. Anything which detracts from the vendor's ownership according to the contract is strictly a defect in his title. If, however, the defect is removable as of right by the vendor, then it is said to be a matter of conveyance rather than of title. The point is that:

> a vendor is considered to have shown an acceptable title if it appears from the abstract that on doing certain acts which he can perform immediately and independently of others' consent, he will have the right to direct a conveyance of the whole estate contracted for. But by his own showing he has no good title except he do such acts. It is therefore a matter of course that he shall perform them; and it is unnecessary for the purchaser to address any requisition to this point

(*Williams on Vendor and Purchaser*, 3rd ed, p 170; see also *Re Scott and Eave's Contract* (1902) 86 LT 617 and *Halkett* v *Dudley* [1907] 1 Ch 590). The commonest example of this is the discharge of a mortgage of the property (see *Re Daniel, Daniel* v *Vassall* [1917] 2 Ch 405); others would be the appointment of a second trustee of a trust for sale or Settled Land Act trustees to receive the consideration (*Hatten* v *Russell* (1888) 38 Ch D 334; cp *Cole* v *Rose* [1978] 3 All ER 1121, at p 1127). Again where an equitable mortgagee has contracted to convey a legal estate in the mortgaged property *and* has the benefit of one of the standard devices which would enable him to do so, then procuring and conveying the legal estate can properly be described as a question of conveyancing rather than title (see *Sopher* v *Mercer* [1967] CLY 2543).

In a comparatively modern case on the borderline of the distinction between matters of conveyance and of title, Mr *A* and Mr *B* contracted to sell a house as trustees for sale; in fact, the trustees in whom the house was vested were Mr and Mrs *A*, no deed replacing Mrs *A* by Mr *B* having been executed, although it was said that such a deed would have been handed over on completion. Romer J nonetheless held this to be a matter of title, saying:

> The concurrence of a mortgagee who is immediately redeemable is simply a matter of conveyancing and is not comparable to the due execution of a deed, such as the deed of appointment, which constitutes the very title of one of the vendors and without which he had no interest in the property at all

(*Re Priestley's Contract* [1947] Ch 469, at p 477).

The vendor's obligation to procure a lessor's licence to assign is generally regarded as a matter of conveyance rather than of title, so that the vendor ordinarily has until completion for this (*Ellis* v *Rogers* (1885) 29 Ch D 661; *Smith* v *Butler* [1900] 1 QB 694; also *Ellis* v *Lawrence* (1969) 210 EG 215; see further, post p 140). Yet this is illogical since such a licence is, by definition almost, not within the vendor's sole control and command. The confusion thus caused is reflected in the following imprecise passage from a judgment of Danckwerts LJ:

> As it has sometimes been expressed, the need for obtaining the landlord's consent to the assignment is a "matter of title", or, as it has sometimes been

expressed, "a matter of completion", or "matter of conveyance" (in *Property and Bloodstock Ltd* v *Emerton* [1968] Ch 94, at p 118).

5 Conditions of Sale

Since a vendor may feel his obligations as to title under an open contract to be particularly onerous it is the custom of conveyancers, where there is any shadow of doubt, to deny the purchaser his corresponding rights. This indeed is not improper; judicial encouragement has been forthcoming, for as Simonds J once said:

> It is a salutary rule, of which many examples are to be found in this branch of the law, that the purchaser is not bound to be put to a risk of that kind [ie, of a doubtful title], particularly as the vendor can, by appropriate provisions in the contract, enormously safeguard himself against any undue trouble to which he might be put by inquiries about facts which took place some time ago

(in *Re Holmes (W & R) and Cosmopolitan Press Ltd's Contract* [1944] Ch 53, at p 57; cf *Selkirk* v *Romar Investments Ltd* [1963] 1 WLR 1415, at pp 1423–4). Conditions for sale, general or special, incorporated with a denial of this sort in mind, are almost invariably directed to particular matters, such as non-disclosure, commencement of title, or requisitions, and these have been or will be considered in the sections of this book most relevant. Largely, these conditions content themselves with cautiously lighting the unpredictable twilight zone of doubtful titles and technical defects. However, special conditions may be encountered which boldly and baldly disclaim completely the vendor's obligation to show a good title. These disclaimers are often expressed in some such incantation as 'the purchaser shall take such title as the vendor has', although the notorious title 'well known in the neighbourhood' formula may still confront and confound one.

These conditions, whatever their form, are all subject to the overpowering principle that the vendor must not mislead the purchaser in any way; this means that a sufficient indication of the risk must be given before the contract is made (*Re Haedicke and Lipski's Contract* [1901] 2 Ch 666). Thus even where a purchaser has agreed to accept such title as the vendor has, he is entitled to assume that the vendor has fully fulfilled his duty of disclosure; ie, the condition can only be taken as precluding objections to defects in the title on that basis (ibid). For example, a vendor who contracts to sell only such right or interest, if any, as he has, will still be bound to convey such interest free from any *undisclosed* incumbrances (*Goold* v *Birmingham, Dudley and District Bank* (1888) 58 LT 560; contrast *Fowler* v *Willis* [1922] 2 Ch 514, where a similarly worded contract was held to extend only to the vendor's equity of redemption, a decision rendered dubious both by the judge's failure to advert to the question of disclosure and now by s 85 of the Law of Property Act 1925). More recently, in *Becker* v *Partridge* [1966] 2 QB 155, the Court of Appeal was faced with the following special condition: 'The vendor's title has been accepted by the purchaser and the purchaser shall raise no requisition or objection thereon.' In consequence of his constructive knowledge of defects in his title, the vendor was held unable to rely on the special condition so that the purchaser was entitled to rescind (see also *Heywood* v *Mallalieu* (1883) 25 Ch D 357, ante, p 74).

Apart from this general caveat against misleading, special conditions of this sort will bind any purchaser who accepts them (*Hume* v *Pocock* (1866) 1 Ch App 379). This means that, although the vendor still has to give what evidence of ownership he can, objections are precluded if the result happens not to be a good title. Occasionally, for example, on a sale by a public authority, or for small consideration, the condition may even go further and also exempt the vendor from giving any evidence at all of ownership (*Southby* v *Hutt* (1837) 2 My & Cr 207). In either case, however, the purchaser, although bound, will not have put himself entirely at the vendor's mercy. Unless the vendor shows at least a holding title, with the holding not about to cease, specific performance will not be ordered (*Re Scott and Alvarez's Contract, Scott* v *Alvarez* [1895] 2 Ch 603). Nonetheless, a purchaser thus released in equity does not escape at law, being at least liable to lose his deposit (ibid; the court now has a discretion to order repayment of the deposit in such a case: s 49 (2) of the Law of Property Act 1925; see *James Macara Ltd* v *Barclay* [1945] KB 148, and post, p 205). Presumably he is also liable to an action for damages (see ibid), which might perhaps be a large sum if he not only accepted the risk of a bad title but also agreed to a price commensurate with a good title, for then the worse the vendor's title the greater his loss of bargain (see further, p 214).

Another point on the purchaser's side occurs if a special condition of sale not only relieves the vendor from showing a good title but also specifies precisely what other evidence supporting ownership will be offered. Apparently strict compliance by the vendor with the terms of the condition will be regarded as an essential of the contract, and failure will enable the purchaser to rescind (see *George Wimpey & Co Ltd* v *Sohn* [1967] Ch 487, considered, p 109).

Finally, ex abundante cautela no doubt, mention may be made that these conditions of sale precluding objection to title do not enable the vendor to introduce any defects in title not already existing at the date of the contract (*Re Crosby's Contract, Crosby* v *Houghton* [1949] 1 All ER 830, concerning an option to purchase, the relevant date being that of the grant not of its exercise).

B COMMENCEMENT OF TITLE

Under an open contract for the sale of land the vendor is obliged to show a good title. What this means as a general conception has been discussed in the preceding part of this chapter. Now, therefore, we can turn to the principles governing the method by which the vendor performs this obligation. Without a consideration of these principles the meaning of title itself is difficult to grasp fully, not least because the primary meaning thereof in conveyancing is the evidence supporting the vendor's ownership. At this stage, the basic and essential divergence between the systems of registered and unregistered conveyancing emerges by reason of which the two simply cannot be considered pari passu. Consequently, age must come before beauty and the system of unregistered conveyancing will be dealt with in this and ensuing parts, followed in due but belated course by its heir apparent. Also for convenience sake, the special rules relating to leasehold titles will be segregated but treated kindly in a later section all to themselves. In other words the reader should now have in mind, as does the writer, a sale of unregistered freehold land. However, bear also in mind that in the present context, as in the Law of Property Act 1925 (see s 205 (1) (ix)), the word 'land' can comprehend more than the physical subject-matter of the sale. Consequently the obligation upon the vendor extends to showing a good title to any easements or other rights the benefit of which is to pass with the estate or interest sold, and all the rules discussed in the following pages as to period, root, chain and deduction of title are applicable (compare *Jones* v *Watts* (1890) 43 Ch D 574). This point, easily overlooked, occasionally becomes inconvenient where the initial grant of the right in question and ownership of the land with which it is sold depend upon separate titles.

1 The period of title

To support his claim to own the property he is selling, a vendor must direct his evidence towards acquisition, ie, he must give a convincing historical account of how the property came to be owned by him. He might say, therefore, that he got it from Tom who got it from Dick who got it from Harry and so on and so on back even through biblical begats to the beginning, and the proof of what he said would lie in the instruments which would (since medieval times at least) have been brought into existence to effect and record each change of ownership. But there are limits. As will be seen, a vendor is not required to give anything like a complete history of the property's ownership; instead, a purchaser is limited to a period (immediately before the contract) regarded as sufficiently lengthy to provide a plausible picture. Of course, without the complete history, the account may not be of ownership at all, some third party being the true owner all the time. What is shown essentially are certain successive acts of ownership, ie, dispositions of the land, during the selected period; these acts imply possession (or seisin) throughout that period and give rise to a presumption of ownership of the estate or interest concerned. This means simply that an earlier and better ownership is shown to be unlikely, ie, the presumption is rebuttable (cp *Whitfield* v *Gowling* (1974) 28 P & CR 386—where a conveyance of property to someone can be shown, there is a presumption that it remains his which may be rebutted).

The changes in the length of the select period during which acts of ownership over the land have to be shown afford an excellent illustration of the practice of conveyancers influencing the law. The initially established practice became the law for open contracts by receiving judicial recognition: 'It is a technical rule among conveyancers to approve a possession of sixty years as a good title to a fee simple' (per Heath J in *Barnwell* v *Harris* (1809) 1 Taunt 430, at p 432; this period, which appears arbitrary, may have been selected either because experience had shown it to be enough or because sixty years had been the maximum statutory limitation period for the various real actions: (1540) 32 Hen 8, c 2, and see per Cockburn LJ in *Bryant* v *Foot* (1867) LR 2 QB 161, at pp 179–81). Then in the mid-nineteenth century the wind veered and conditions shortening the sixty-year period became common. This practice received statutory recognition, and forty years was substituted as the period for open contracts by s 1 of the Vendor and Purchaser Act 1874. Conveyancing practice, however, did not remain satisfied with this relief and further nibbling at the period was recognised by the substitution of thirty years by s 44 (1) of the Law of Property Act 1925.

But even this 1925 reduction has not been enough for practitioners. Thus by the 1940s there were suggestions of a movement towards a twenty years period of title (see EO Walford in (1943–4) 8 Conv (NS) 135). This movement flowed from the proposition that a purchaser was bound to accept as true a recital of the then vendor's ownership in a conveyance twenty years old (ie, because of s 45 (6) of the Law of Property Act 1925, re-enacting the second rule in s 2 of the Vendor and Purchaser Act 1874, see p 248). However, the idea that such a conveyance should therefore constitute a good root of title never achieved uncontroversial acceptance in practice or theory (see *Re Wallis and Grout's Contract* [1906] 2 Ch 206, and cp *Bolton* v *London School Board* (1878) 7 Ch D 766). Then in 1965 there occurred a shift in professional opinion which has proved decisive although not previously representing practice.

The Non-Contentious Business Committee of The Law Society in June 1965 issued a *Report on Conveyancing Practice*, which after other more radical and rejected proposals (ie, the ill-starred Title Certificate Scheme), actually recommended that 'the statutory minimum period for investigation of title to any unregistered land back to a good root should be reduced from thirty to fifteen years' (para 63). This recommendation was heard and echoed on high and all around by the Law Commission which in December 1966 published an Interim Report embodying an outstanding outline, explanation and consideration of this and allied topics, and concluding with a brief draft clause which would achieve the recommended reduction. The draft clause was enacted as s 23 of the Law of Property Act 1969 and takes the oddly textual form of providing that s 44 (1) of the 1925 Act should have effect in its application to contracts made after 1969 'as if it specified fifteen years instead of thirty years as the period of commencement of title which may be so required'. This reduction naturally remains subject to the expression of a contrary intention in the contract (see s 44 (11) of the 1925 Act). For some far from unrestrained enthusiasm over the original recommendation, reference may be made to an editorial note in (1966) 30 Conv (NS) 157–9, and a penetrating article at (1966) 110 SJ 179, 201 (by VGH Hallett and EG Nugee) and for a critical account of its enactment see Stephen Cretney at (1969) 32 MLR 478–82. Nevertheless, the period of title under a contract for the sale of land, assuming it to be 'open' in this respect, does now stand at fifteen years.

2   The root of title

> And when I say a [fifteen] years title, I mean a title deduced for [fifteen] years and for so much longer as it is necessary to go back in order to arrive at a point at which the title can properly commence. A title cannot commence *in nubibus* at the exact point of time which is represented by 365 days multiplied by [fifteen]. It must commence at or before the [fifteen] years with something which is in itself . . . a proper root of title

(per North J in *Re Cox and Neve's Contract* [1891] 2 Ch 109, at p 118, who, of course, really said 'forty'; this rule appears to have been first formulated out of conveyancing practice in *Dart on Vendors and Purchasers*, see 5th ed, vol 1, p 296). No comment is called for beyond the query: what is a 'proper root of title' under an open contract? Certainly this is a query which can be seen as assuming an even more substantial significance in view of the provisions of the Law of Property Act 1969. If an improper root of title is accepted by a purchaser, a drastically reduced investigation of title will occur with, in consequence, a possible loss not only of protection against constructive notice of equities (pp 103–105) but also of compensation for undisclosed registered land charges (see p 100).

There is neither any statutory nor any judicial definition to be tendered of a good or proper root of title. What is more, the Law Commission in its *Interim Report on Root of Title to Freehold Land* accepted the view that a statutory definition 'might do more harm than good by introducing an undesirable rigidity' and so recommended that none be enacted (paras 40 and 41) and none was (see further 'Roots of Title Today' by AM Prichard, *Current Legal Problems* 1975, pp 125–49). However, the good root of title never languished without authoritative description: reference is invariably made to the definition offered by one textbook. In the classic words of *Williams on Vendor and Purchaser*, 3rd ed, at p 39, though the division into three parts is the present writer's own, a good root of title is an instrument of disposition which must:

> (i) *'deal with or prove on the face of it, without the aid of extrinsic evidence, the ownership of the whole legal and equitable estate in the property sold'*

Therefore, such instruments as leases and equitable mortgages would not be good roots of title. Also a transfer of mortgage without the mortgagor's concurrence in the reservation of a fresh equity of redemption would be a bad root. Equally, a conveyance subject to a mortgage, ie, of the equity of redemption, was regarded as a bad root, but since 1925 it may be a good root as the mortgagor now retains a legal estate; nonetheless, the mortgage, ownership of which has to be shown, would still be a more convenient root. Another doubtful root of title would be a conveyance from which words of limitation have been omitted in reliance upon s 60(1) of the Law of Property Act 1925, since it would not show on its face exactly what was the 'whole interest' of the grantor. This particular lack may, of course, be found supplied by an appropriate recital (see p 242).

That the equitable interest should also be dealt with on the face of the instrument is now probably more of an exception than a rule in that, since 1925, the legal estate generally carries the equitable interest with it. Thus a post-1925 conveyance on trust for sale or vesting deed under a strict settlement may often be accepted as good roots. Nonetheless, the statutory provisions do envisage cases where equitable interests are not overreached (see ss 10 and 43 of the Law of Property Act 1925 and s 1 of the Law of Property (Amendment) Act 1926). For these cases the old rule remains: on the sale of a legal estate, the root must purport to deal with both the legal and equitable interest.

(ii) 'contain a description by which the property can be identified'

This aspect is not so easy to apply as to state, the parcels and plans in aged instruments, usually disposing of properties rather larger than the tiny plots of present purchasers, not being all they might. However, an example of a bad root here would be a general devise in a will, when the property sold can only be identified as belonging to the testator by extrinsic evidence (*Parr* v *Lovegrove* (1858) 4 Drew 170). A specific devise did not infringe this rule and was accepted as a good root of title before 1898. Between 1897 and 1926 such a devise would still be a good root although the assent of the deceased's personal representative was also necessary to make the devise operative as to the legal estate (s 3 of the Land Transfer Act 1897; *Attenborough* v *Solomon* [1913] AC 76). After 1925 wills operate purely in equity, and whether the devise was general or specific, only the assent can become a good root, although the probate or letters of administration should also be produced to show both the title to assent and the absence of endorsements (s 36 (5) of the Administration of Estates Act 1925; also *Re Miller and Pickersgill's Contract* [1931] 1 Ch 511).

(iii) 'show nothing to cast any doubt on the title of the disposing parties'

Thus there should not, for instance, be any too revealing recitals in the instrument (see *Re Duce and Boots Cash Chemists (Southern) Ltd's Contract* [1937] Ch 642). More important, however, doubt will be cast if the instrument depends for its effect on an earlier instrument. For example, a subsidiary vesting deed will not suffice, since reference back must always be made to the principal vesting instrument (see ss 10 (2) and 110 (2) of the Settled Land Act 1925). Again the exercise of a power, of appointment or otherwise, which is a disposition by a delegate and not by an owner, will not do (cf *Re Holmes (W & R) and Cosmopolitan Press Ltd's Contract* [1944] Ch 53). This is so despite the provision that a pre-root instrument is taboo for a purchaser 'even though the same creates a power subsequently exercised' within the period of title (s 45 (1) (a) of the Law of Property Act 1925). The point is that this provision has only the effect of a contractual condition (s 45 (11)) which would not bind the purchaser to accept an instrument exercising a power as a root of title unless its nature had been clearly indicated in the contract *(Re Marsh and Earl Granville* (1882) 24 Ch D 11; also *Re Copelin's Contract* [1937] 4 All ER 447; see further below).

A conveyance for value of the freehold estate in the land is the *'best root'* of title because of the probability that the then purchaser will have thoroughly investigated his vendor's title. A mortgage is often accepted as equal best on the same ground and, indeed, is sometimes regarded as even better than best since a mortgagee would have been less likely to take a doubtful title than would a purchaser. However, the acceptance of a mortgage as a root of title at all now has a theoretical flaw. Before 1926 a mortgage by conveyance of the fee simple was the commonly used method and such a mortgage was and is a good root of title. The then disused alternative was to mortgage by means of a lease to the mortgagee which could be enlarged; this sort of mortgage, like any other lease, was a bad root on sale of the fee simple, although it might be accepted if it recited the mortgagor's ownership in fee simple. Since 1925 no mortgage can be by conveyance of the fee simple (s 85 (1) of the Law of Property Act 1925) so that 'the whole legal and equitable estate' is no longer dealt with by a mortgage and one of the elements of a good root is missing. Nonetheless, post-1925 mortgages will no doubt continue to be accepted as good roots in practice particularly where the mortgagor's fee simple ownership is recited (see *Williams on Vendor and Purchaser*, 4th ed, at p 124). All the same there is surely no denying the usual rule that a recital is no substitute for a proper root (see *Re Wallis and Grout's Contract* [1906] 2 Ch 206).

A voluntary disposition, on which the title would not have been investigated, although not the best, will pass muster as a good enough root under an open contract when the fully statutory period of title is shown (per Cotton LJ in *Re Marsh and Earl Granville* (1882) 24 Ch D 11, at p 24).

Again, infrequently in practice, there may be no root of title in the sense of an instrument at all:

> I am perfectly satisfied that there are good titles in which the origin cannot be shown by any deed or will; but then you must show something that is satisfactory to the mind of the court—that there has been such a long uninterrupted possession enjoyment and dealing with the property as to afford a reasonable presumption that there is an absolute title in fee simple

(per Lord Langdale MR, in *Cottrell* v *Watkins* (1839) 1 Beav 361, at p 365). The length of such possession is not the twelve years of s 15 of the Limitation Act 1980 but will be the fifteen years of the current statutory period of title under an open contract (*Jacobs* v *Revell* [1900] 2 Ch 858). Possessory titles will be mentioned more fully in a later section (p 108) but note that such a title does not suffice in place of instruments known to be lost, secondary evidence of the documentary title being required (*Re Halifax Commercial Banking Co Ltd and Wood* (1898) 79 LT 536).

3 Pre-root title

If the vendor has proffered a sufficiently aged and good root of title, the purchaser has to restrain his curiosity as to any remoter ancestry of ownership. Statute provides that he may not see, ask about or object to anything earlier than 'the time prescribed by law or stipulated for the commencement of the title' and must assume later recitals of any such thing to be the truth the whole truth and nothing but the truth (s 45 (1) of the Law of Property Act 1925, replacing s 3 (3) of the Conveyancing Act 1881, which enacted a condition of conveyancing practice favouring vendors). An odd point to note in passing is that the 'whole truth' element in this assumption may occasionally put a purchaser on enquiry. If the later recitals omit, whether or not inadvertently, mention of some material fact or document, it is arguable that since the purchaser must take the recitals as 'correct,' he must also take it that there actually was no such fact or document. This, of course, may well adversely affect acceptance of the prior title.

This statutory provision applies only if the contrary is not expressed in the contract (s 45 (10), ibid). Also it has no greater effect than a condition included and construed in a contract (s 45 (11), ibid: see per Wills J, *Nottingham Patent Brick & Tile Co v Butler* (1885) 15 QBD 261, at p 272; on appeal (1886) 16 QBD 778). Consequently, if the purchaser, by fair means or foul, actually detects some defect in the pre-root title, then *one* he is nonetheless bound to take a doubtful title, since it will with the passage of time have become at least a good holding title (see *Re Scott and Alvarez* [1895] 1 Ch 596 (first appeal); cf per North J, *Re National Provincial Bank of England and Marsh* [1895] 1 Ch 190, at p 192); but *two* he will not be bound to take an indubitably bad title (*Re Scott and Alvarez's Contract, Scott v Alvarez* [1895] 2 Ch 603 (second appeal)), although remaining bound at law to damages (semble) and loss of deposit (subject to s 49 (2) of the Law of Property Act 1925). Thus a purchaser can object if incumbrances, such as restrictive covenants, come to light which he has not accepted and which will bind him even though created before the root of title (see *Re Nisbet and Potts' Contract* [1906] 1 Ch 386). The reason for this is that the vendor has then been shown *not* to have the ownership (ie, unincumbered freehold) which he contracted to sell, notwithstanding that the limited evidence with which he had to support his alleged ownership was in order, since this evidence only shifts to the purchaser the burden of disproving title.

In addition to this general exception for bad titles, the statutory provision putting pre-root matters out of bounds to purchasers when re-enacted, in 1925, had attached to it a new proviso relaxing the entirely pro-vendor character which it had inherited from conveyancing practice. By virtue of the proviso, the purchaser is no longer deprived of the right (which the proviso implies he would otherwise have) of seeing:

(i) any power of attorney under which any abstracted document is executed; or

(ii) any document creating or disposing of an interest, power or obligation which is now shown to have ceased or expired, and subject to which any part of the property is disposed of by an abstracted document; or

(iii) any document creating any limitation or trust by reference to which any part of the property is disposed of by an abstracted document.

Paragraph (i) of this proviso applies however ancient the power of attorney may be and even if the 'abstracted document' in question is the root of title (*Re Copelin's Contract* [1937] 4 All ER 447). In addition, the purchaser enjoys an inalienable right to have at least a free copy of any post-1925 power of attorney affecting the title (s 125 (2) of the Law of Property Act 1925, as amended in 1926 and 1971). Paragraph (ii) apparently was intended to have special reference to pre-root leases (see *Wolstenholme & Cherry's Conveyancing Statutes*, 12th ed, at p 302; cf 13th ed, vol 1, p 115), but would seem also to cover, eg, pre-root restrictive covenants and even pre-root plans referred to by post-root parcels clauses (cf *Llewellyn v Earl of Jersey* (1843) 11 M & W 183 and *Brown v Wales* (1872) LR 15 Eq 142, at p 147). The paragraph does not appear to cover instruments relating to interests which will be overreached by the conveyance to the purchaser (see s 10 of the Law of Property Act 1925). Equally, paragraph (iii) does not cover a trust instrument referred to by either a conveyance on trust for sale or a vesting instrument (s 27 (1) of the Law of Property Act 1925; s 110 (2) of the Settled Land Act 1925).

4   Undisclosed land charges

One of the substantial seeming obstacles to any reduction in the statutory period of title arose directly from the worst flaw of the 1925 property legislation, namely that land charges registration is against not the land but the name of the estate owner for the time being (s 3 (1) of the Land Charges Act 1972, re-enacting s 10 (2) of the 1925 Act). Such registration, of course, constitutes in effect actual notice to all the world, which includes every subsequent purchaser (s 198 (1) of the Law of Property Act 1925). Accordingly the opinion was expressed that a pre-1926 root of title should always be insisted upon by a purchaser so that he could be sure of knowing, for the purposes of searches, the names of all estate owners against whom land charges might have been registered (see *Law Society's Gazette* (1964) vol 61, at p 253; also Megarry and Wade, *Real Property*, 3rd ed, at pp 1128–9, where it was observed that one consequence of registration being against names was that 'it will be impossible to make any further reduction in the minimum period of title'; cp 4th ed, pp 1165–6). Even with the thirty years old root of title, there was at least a theoretical risk to purchasers which was increasing as the gap from 1925 widened.

This obstacle of the unknown estate owner has been dealt with by s 25 of the Law of Property Act 1969, which again enacts a recommendation and draft clause of the Law Commision (see *Transfer of Land—Report on Land Charges Affecting Unregistered Land*, Law Com No 18). The solution adopted amounts merely to a worldly resort to money: all duly registered pre-root land charges remain entirely unprejudiced, but any purchaser bound despite ignorance is to be compensated by the Chief Land Registrar.

More precisely, the essential negative conditions precedent to the recovery of compensation are as follows:

(1) The purchaser must not have had 'actual knowledge' of the registered land charge on the date of completion (s 25 (1) (*b*) of the Law of Property Act 1969). Actual knowledge expressly comprehends imputed knowledge (subs (11)) but not the actual notice otherwise stemming from registration (subs (2)).

(2) The land charge must not have been registered against the name of any estate owner who was 'a party to any transaction, or concerned in any event, comprised in the relevant title' (s 25 (1) (*c*) of the Law of Property Act 1969). The intent is obvious: anyone named in the abstract of title ought to be searched against; this can be seen as coupling a limited notion of constructive notice onto the actual or imputed knowledge already mentioned.

For the purposes of condition (2), the 'relevant title' is defined as meaning 'the title which the purchaser was, apart from acceptance by him (by agreement or otherwise) of a short or an imperfect title, entitled to require' (subs (10)). Again the idea is obvious: the abstract should cover at least the statutory fifteen years plus any *longer* contractual period of title. Thus the exclusion of 'shorter' titles may be unlikely to cause trouble. But the same cannot be said for the exclusion of 'imperfect' titles: no doubt this was supposed to preclude compensation claims by purchasers who deliberately—or even accidentally?—accepted less than 'a good and marketable title' (as to which see p 86 et seq). This only illustrates how careful legislation must be to say what is meant since the description of abstracts of title as 'perfect' or 'imperfect' already has an established but different conveyancing significance (see pp 116–117). A 'perfect' title is *not* necessarily a 'good' title; it merely means that the vendor has produced all the evidence of ownership that he was able to. Accordingly, for example, a purchaser who agrees to a bad root of title more than fifteen years old or who accepts a mere holding title could nonetheless contend that the title, although bad or doubtful, was neither short nor imperfect. It would follow that if, after completion, such a purchaser discovers that land charges have been registered against the true estate owners, even within the previous fifteen years, then he should be entitled to compensation. Construed in this way, at least, the statute would accord some small recognition of the relative nature of titles to English land (see p 85), yet this result does have a fortuitous feel about it. Another caprice of construction would occur where an estate has been owned twice by the same person, once within and once without the period of title: if the statute (ie, s 25 (1) (c)) be read as meaning what it says, then a purchaser could claim no compensation for any charges registered during the earlier, unknown ownership (see further AM Prichard at [1970] JPL 498–500).

At this point a practitioner might justifiably protest that these difficulties are all academic. And one would have to agree since the very problem of unknown registered land charges seems itself to be an entirely academic creation. In practice, any registered land charges, so long as possibly still of effect, would be referred to in later title deeds; ie, the land would be conveyed expressly subject to any such subsisting charge. In consequence, subsequent purchasers would be unable either to plead ignorance or to claim compensation (see s 25 (3) of the 1969 Act to this effect). Thus this whole topic of pre-root registered land charges as an obstacle to be overcome before reducing the period of title could well be dismissed as a storm in a teacup (as indeed the Law Commission virtually did in its *Interim Report on Root of Title to Freehold Land*, para 24, Law Com No 9, mentioning an absence of known cases of loss). Nevertheless, the academic does sometimes become practical by happening, when the statutory details of ascertainment and recovery of compensation will have to be read for real!

5 Conditions of sale

'The abstract of title shall begin with . . .' or so says Special Condition E accompanying The Law Society's Conditions of Sale (1980 edition). The almost invariable practice on behalf of vendors is to state in the contract the instrument which is to be the root of title. From the possibilities which emerge represent the combinations of the instrument being or not being older than the statutory period of title and its nature being or not being specified in the condition.

First, if the nature of the instrument is *not* specified but it has attained the age of fifteen years, then the question may be raised of whether the purchaser has agreed that that instrument, whatever its nature may be, shall constitute the root of title. The only acceptable answer appears to be that the instrument, although specified, must in nature be at least a good root; the vendor remains under an obligation to show the ownership of the property at the commencement as well as at the end of the period of title (see *Re Copelin's Contract* [1937] 4 All ER 447).

Secondly, if the nature of the instrument is *not* specified and it is *less* old than the statutory period of title, then the purchaser is clearly only bound if it is in fact a best root of title. In other words, those of Baggallay LJ, the purchaser is entitled to assume that the specified instrument 'was a conveyance to a purchaser for value, the inference from which would be that at that time the title was investigated and approved of' (in *Re Marsh and Earl Granville* (1882) 24 Ch D 11, at p 22). If the instrument was voluntary, then as Fry J more trenchantly had said at first instance: 'you do not look a gift horse in the mouth' (ibid, at p 15).

Thirdly, if in the last possibility considered the nature of the instrument had been specified, then the purchaser would have had what Baggallay LJ held him entitled to, namely, 'an opportunity of deciding whether he would accept a title of this description as a root of title when the title was to commence within the statutory period' (ibid, at p 22). Thus an otherwise good but not best root can still be good despite its immaturity if accepted, which it may not be. After all, there has even been a tendency in practice for purchasers' solicitors not to accept a condition specifying a good but not best root even though the instrument *is* older than the statutory period of title; the moral for vendors' solicitors in such cases is not to specify the root, since no objection to it could be heard after the contract.

But the crucial question really is whether the purchaser should ever contract for any root of title, be it best or specified, less old than the full statutory period which has now, of course, become a mere fifteen years. Certainly, such a shortening of title used not infrequently to be accepted by conveyancers before the 1969 reduction in the statutory period, quite safely, although not, one trusts, without the consent of a client who appreciated the risks.

This mention of the risks involves a reference to the dual purpose of showing title. On the one hand, the vendor is supporting, with a limited amount of evidence, his claim to ownership of the property at law. As to this, even if the full statutory period of title be shown, the result is not conclusive, only a rebuttable presumption of ownership being raised (see, eg, *Wyld* v *Silver* [1963] Ch 243). Thus the position is exactly the same, on this hand, if the purchaser agrees to the supporting evidence being limited to a lesser period, save that the presumption is just that much more likely to be rebutted.

On the other hand, the purchaser's investigation of title affords him an opportunity of discovering the existence of certain equitable interests by which he will be bound. As to this, if the full statutory period of title is properly investigated and reveals nothing, the result is conclusive: unless further investigation is in fact made, the purchaser prima facie becomes one of equity's blue-eyed boys—bona fide, for value, legal estate, without notice—and takes free from earlier unknown equitable interests (*Pilcher* v *Rawlins* (1872) 7 Ch App 259; s 44 (8) of the Law of Property Act 1925; see *Shears* v *Wells* [1936] 1 All ER 832, as to the onus of providing further investigations).

The sort of matters indicated on the face of the documents of title and within this last rule might be, eg, the lack of a necessary concurrence (see *Re Soden and Alexander's Contract* [1918] 2 Ch 258, *Re Balen and Shepherd's Contract* [1924] 2 Ch 365, cf *Re Chafer and Randall's Contract* [1916] 2 Ch 8), or failure to comply with the Settled Land Act conveyancing machinery (see *Re Duce and Boots Cash Chemists (Southern) Ltd's Contract* [1937] Ch 642), or the purchase of trust property by a trustee (see *Pilkington* v *Wood* [1953] Ch 770), or an unexplained conveyance by one trustee to another without any consideration (see AM Prichard at (1972) 36 Conv (NS) 192). The rule has, in the past, tended to arise with restrictive covenants (see *Re Cox and Neve's Contract* [1891] 2 Ch 109; *Re Nisbet and Potts' Contract* [1906] 1 Ch 386), but since 1925 the provisions for registration of land charges and the passage of time have in this respect given rise to other problems than that of investigating the documentary title for the full statutory period.

The risk the purchaser runs, therefore, by agreeing to investigate title for a period stopping short of a good root fifteen years old, is simply of being bound by any equitable interests which he would otherwise have discovered. In other words a purchaser has constructive notice of anything (not void for non-registration) which 'would have come to his knowledge if such inquiries and inspections had been made as ought reasonably to have been made by him' (s 199 (1) (ii) (*a*) of the Law of Property Act 1925). Nothing less than the fullest investigation under an open contract will be recognised as reasonable.

Therefore, to be free beyond peradventure of unknown equitable interests, the purchaser must insist on the full statutory period of title being shown (see per North

J in *Re Cox and Neve's Contract* [1891] 2 Ch 109, at pp 117–18, and *Re Nisbet and Potts' Contract* [1906] 1 Ch 386). And, since that period has become a mere fifteen years, this is no longer the counsel of perfection it once was. On the contrary, thought should now be given by a purchaser (or perhaps his mortgagee) to the question of whether a longer period of title should not be sought. The object would be to strengthen the rebuttable presumption of ownership which is all that arises from any investigation of title.

C CHAIN OF TITLE

The commencement of title—ie, the root and period—with which a vendor of land must begin performance of his obligation to show title has been dealt with. Next to be looked at are the principles (practice is to come later) governing the way in which the vendor must continue and conclude this performance. In short, he must do so by showing the links in the chain of title stretching between the root of title and himself. In long and in general, these links are every document or event effecting or affecting a disposition or devolution of any legal or equitable estate or interest in the property sold during the period of title. Since little purpose is ever served by starkly stating the obvious, such as that conveyances and deaths are links in title within the rule, in the following pages the positive principles will be approached largely from the exceptions, ie, from the links which need *not* be shown.

1 Off with his equities

As stated, the vendor's obligation extends to links in the equitable title where at any time this has parted company with the legal title (eg, a trust). In other words, the general rule is that matters affecting ownership in equity must be shown even if they do not also relate to the legal ownership. However, conveyancers have long striven to blinker their gaze to the antics of the legal estate and to keep all awkward equities out of sight off the title.

Before 1926, particularly where mortgages were made to trustees (a situation now cared for by s 113 of the Law of Property Act 1925), especial advantage had begun to be taken of equity's darling, the bona fide purchaser for value of a legal estate who would take free of all equitable interests of which he had no notice (see *Jared* v *Clements* [1903] 1 Ch 428). The equities were simply suppressed; the land would be conveyed to the trustees, without mentioning the trust in the conveyance, the separate settlement being concealed, so that the trustees might appear to have vested in them the whole legal and equitable interest. And this suppression was acquiesced in by the courts (*Carritt* v *Real and Personal Advance Co* (1889) 42 Ch D 263, at pp 272–3). Then, during the subsistence of the trust, any person not told about the trust and dealing with the trustees as beneficial owners would be fully protected from the beneficiaries (see, eg, *Re King's Settlement, King* v *King* [1931] 2 Ch 294). Whenever there was a change of trustees the practice was for the old trustees to convey to the new trustees reciting baldly that the former had held on trust for the latter (see *Re Harman and Uxbridge & Rickmansworth Railway Co* (1883) 24 Ch D 720).

This sort of device, first used for mortgagee-trustees, was later operated for other cases, and the determination of a trust consequently presented no conveyancing problem at all: the then trustees (although apparently beneficial owners) simply conveyed to or at the direction and with the concurrence of the beneficiary entitled, reciting the bare fact that they held in trust for him (see *Re Chafer and Randall's*

Contract [1916] 2 Ch 8, also *Re Soden and Alexander's Contract* [1918] 2 Ch 258). The device worked because the mere disclosure of a trust by persons apparently both legally and equitably entitled was treated as a binding admission against interest to be accepted at its face value so excluding tedious enquiries as to how the hitherto undisclosed trust arose (but cp *Re Balen and Shepherd's Contract* [1924] 2 Ch 365, also *Re Blaiberg and Abrahams* [1899] 2 Ch 340 and *Re Pope's Contract* [1911] 2 Ch 442 as to purchasers having constructive notice of the contents of trust instruments).

Notwithstanding minor limitations, this device of non-disclosure, developed tentatively by conveyancers in contravention of the general 'disclose all' principle, might have attained quite satisfactorily 'the highly desirable and perfectly honest object of keeping the trust off the title' (per Cozens-Hardy MR in *Re Chafer and Randall's Contract* [1916] 2 Ch 8, at p 19). Since 1925, however, the device has been superseded, somewhat less satisfactorily, by the better-known statutory system for the suppression of equities familiarly known as 'overreaching.' Very briefly indeed, by this system, on a conveyance of a legal estate made, inter alia, under the Settled Land Act 1925 or by trustees for sale, any equitable interests are simply shifted from the land to the proceeds of sale, and the purchaser, *with or without notice*, takes free of them, provided only that he pays the price to the proper persons (see s 2 of the Law of Property Act 1925, not applying to equitable interests, such as restrictive covenants, which would be futile if detached from the land). Consequently, it became neither necessary nor proper to show the title to any equitable (or other) interests overreached by the conveyance of the legal estate (s 10 of the same Act).

During the subsistence of the trust, therefore, this statutory system can effectively keep the equities off the title. A flaw in the system, however, is often encountered on the ending of a trust for sale. Although a direct method was provided for determining strict settlements, without causing investigation of the equitable entitlement (ie, by a deed of discharge: s 17 of the Settled Land Act 1925, also s 110 (5)), no such method, other than an actual sale of the land, was provided for the much more common trust for sale. Therefore, where a trust for sale ends, as by all the equitable interests vesting in a single person, perhaps following a family arrangement, two alternatives confront the conveyancer. First, he could have the land conveyed to or at the direction of the person equitably entitled and so, against all precept, bring the question of that person's entitlement on to the title for ever more (ie, because the conveyance to him would not overreach any other equitable interests). Secondly, he could 'keep the trust alive,' which means doing nothing until the person entitled wishes to sell and then having the trustees convey as if in exercise of the trust for sale, which, to protect the purchaser, will be deemed to be still subsisting (s 23 of the Law Property Act 1925; ie, this would be an overreaching conveyance). The only objections to this latter alternative are the slightly extra expense and complexity involved, usually, in appointing an additional trustee, and the considerable difficulty experienced by the layman in appreciating the artificial arrangement itself.

Before moving on, let the fact be reiterated that all the above devices and systems for keeping the equities off the title constitute exceptions, albeit extensive, to the general rule that all legal and equitable links in ownership must be shown. If the vendor is selling with the concurrence of the owners of equitable interests, then to this extent the equities are on the title. Such concurrence, however, will be rare (though its occurrence is expressly contemplated by, eg, ss 10 and 42 of the Law of Property Act 1925), except for the fairly common case of a purchase of trust property by a trustee which would otherwise be voidable (see s 72(4) of the Law of Property Act 1925). Apart from this, such concurrence is rare because the statutory system for keeping the equities off the title enjoys a complementary provision to the effect that where the trust for sale, Settled Land Act or any other conveyancing machinery is available for overreaching equitable interests, then it must be utilised at the vendor's expense, contrary conditions of sale being made void (see s 42 of the Law of Property Act 1925; note the odd exception in s 1 of the Law of Property (Amendment) Act 1926. This is a reversal of the pre-1926 position, stated as follows:

> The general rule is this, that a man makes a good title by showing a good equitable title and power to get in the legal estate. You are not bound to trace the legal estate further than to show you can get at it

(per Jessel MR in *Camberwell & South London Building Society* v *Holloway* (1879) 13 Ch D 754, at p 763). In other words, the getting in of the legal estate used to be a mere matter of conveyancing not of title (see *Kitchen* v *Palmer* (1877) 46 LJ Ch 611). Occasionally this may still be so, for example, where the purchaser, as often in practice, does not insist on seeing the cumbersome overreaching machinery creak into operation or where, much less often, there happens to be no available overreaching machinery, for example, where nothing more than a bare trust in favour of the vendor is shown (see *Gordon Hill Trust* v *Segall* [1941] 2 All ER 379, also *Re Alefounder's Will Trusts, Adnams* v *Alefounder* [1927] 1 Ch 360 and *Green* v *Whitehead* [1930] 1 Ch 38). But the main maxim remains, so far as possible, keep your eyes on the legal estate and off the equities.

2   Leases

Subsisting leases of the land sold must, of course, be disclosed to the purchaser as affecting the vendor's ownership even though created before the root of title (see s 45 (1), proviso (ii) of the Law of Property Act 1925, and non-disclosure at p 62). Equally, no longer subsisting leases, if created since the root of title, should in theory be shown to the purchaser as dispositions of a legal estate in the land sold. Nonetheless, in practice *expired* leases have always been kept off the title, as not being capable of adversely affecting the purchaser, whilst *surrendered* leases should be put on the title so that the purchaser can satisfy himself that the surrender was effective, since if it were not the lease might revive (see *Knight* v *Williams* [1901] 1 Ch 256; also *Barclays Bank Ltd* v *Stasek* [1957] Ch 28; contrast *Rhyl UDC* v *Rhyl Amusements Ltd* [1959] 1 WLR 465). Thus in *Re Heaysman's and Tweedy's Contract* (1893) 69 LT 89 the Court of Appeal held a vendor to be at fault in not abstracting a lease which had been determined by a judgment in ejectment.

3   Mortgages

Again, subsisting legal mortgages are obviously of concern to the purchaser but generally as matters of conveyance rather than title. In other words, what the purchaser generally has to be shown is that he will take the land unaffected by any old mortgages. Consequently, as with surrendered leases, legal mortgages and their discharges are links in title, the purchaser being entitled to satisfy himself that the discharge was effective (see *Heath* v *Crealock* (1874) LR 10 Ch 22; cf *Cumberland Court (Brighton) Ltd* v *Taylor* [1964] Ch 29 and also *Edwards* v *Marshall-Lee* (1975) 119 SJ 506 as to a simple receipt sufficing). However, on a sale by a mortgagee the conveyance will overreach the mortgagor's and all other interests to which the mortgage had priority, and therefore subsequent mortgages, even though legal and registered, need not in such a case be shown on the title (ss 88 (1) (*b*), 89 (1) (*b*) and 104 (1) of the Law of Property Act 1925 and s 13 (2) of the Land Charges Act 1972).

Again a puisne mortgage no longer protected by registration, ie, because the entry was removed on discharge, strictly need not be shown because the purchaser will not be affected by it (s 199 (1) (i) of the Law of Property Act 1925 and s 4 of the Land Charges Act 1972), but practice tends to disregard this point.

Equitable mortgages, commonly encountered in favour of banks and unregistered because protected by deposit of documents, occupy an ambivalent position. Strictly, whether already discharged or to be discharged on completion, these should appear on the title, with their discharge (see per Wood V-C in *Drummond v Tracy* (1860) John 608, at p 612). Nonetheless the practice is to keep all of this off the title, although handing over the discharged charge with the other deeds on completion (see *The Law Society's Digest*, Opinion No 194). If no such handing over will take place, as is very often the case on the purchase of one plot out of an estate which is being developed with the help of a bank loan, the practice for many years has been for the manager of the local branch to give a letter acknowledging that his bank has no claim on the property sold. This convenient practice appears to operate effectively, but causes considerable theoretical problems (there is a full discussion of these at (1962) 26 Conv (NS) 445). The principal problem is the dilemma caused by the necessary acknowledgment for production: if taken from the vendor himself (as is usual) it may very well be ineffective as not given by the person retaining possession of the documents (see s 64 (1) of the Law of Property Act 1925); if taken from the bank, it would be effective but notice of the equitable mortgage would for ever after be there on the title for all to see and, properly, to investigate. There seems no ready solution.

4 Wills

Following deaths since 1925, wills are like equities: they are to be kept off the title. The legal estate passes to the deceased's personal representatives (ss 1 and 3 of the Administration of Estates Act 1925), and the probate or letters of administration are each conveyancing evidence of his death and their appointment. Equitable interests arising under the will are overreached by a conveyance on sale by the personal representatives (s 2 of the Law of Property Act 1925), and an assent to the person equitably entitled is to be taken by a purchaser as sufficient evidence of its own propriety (s 36 (7) of the Administration of Estates Act 1925, cf *Re Duce & Boots Cash Chemists (Southern) Ltd's Contract* [1937] Ch 642). Since 1925, an assent, to be effectual, must be in writing, must name the person in whose favour it is made and must be signed by the personal representative (s 36 (4) of the Administration of Estates Act 1925); ie, it can no longer be implied, even where personal representatives assent in their own favour (*Re King's Will Trusts* [1964] Ch 542, cf *Re Edwards Will Trusts* [1982] Ch 30, CA, as to equitable interests, also *Beebe v Mason* (1980) 254 EG 987 as to resident landlords).

So the purchaser need only see on the title, first, the probate or letters of administration (see per Goulding J in *Re Crowhurst Park* [1974] 1 WLR 583, at p 594 FG) and any endorsement thereon under s 36 (5) of the Administration of Estates Act 1925 (see *Re Miller & Pickersgill's Contract* [1931] 1 Ch 511) and, secondly, the subsequent assent or conveyance (see ss 10 (2) and 206 (2) of, and Sched 6 to, the Law of Property Act 1925). In practice, however, he tends also to be told of the date of the will, of the appointment of executors, and of the date of death.

5 Voluntary links

The purchaser's task is to test each of the links in the chain offered to him as joining the vendor's claim to ownership to the root of title. Although, as will be seen later his investigation of title will go much further, the purchaser must always see that the links are valid, for the chain of title can only be as strong as its weakest link. Weaknesses may be due to a variety of reasons too vast to be detailed here; after all conveyancing can be defined as an activity carried on within the confines of the whole of the law of property. However, one point on weak links may be made.

Speaking generally, any of the dispositions of the property shown on the title as made without consideration may be liable to be set aside under one of four statutory provisions, namely, s 172 of the Law of Property Act 1925 ('voluntary conveyances to defraud creditors voidable'), s 173 of the same Act ('voluntary dispositions of land how far voidable as against purchasers'), s 42 of the Bankruptcy Act 1914 ('avoidance of certain settlements'), and s 16 of the Matrimonial Proceedings and Property Act 1970 ('avoidance of transactions intended to defeat certain claims'). As a consequence the question may be asked, is a voluntary conveyance necessarily a weak link in title? The answer is no.

A document which falls within any of the four provisions above can nonetheless be a good link. The reason is that avoidance of a conveyance within s 172 of the Law of Property Act 1925 does not affect the rights of a bona fide purchaser for value who, without notice of any intent to defraud acquires any interest, legal or equitable, in the property conveyed (s 172 (3)), and such a purchaser is protected rather than adversely affected by s 173 of that Act. Although the word 'void' is used in s 42 of the Bankruptcy Act 1914, it has been held to mean 'voidable' so that a bona fide purchaser for value before receiving notice of the commencement of the bankruptcy gets a good title (see *Re Carter and Kenderdine's Contract* [1897] 1 Ch 776 and *Re Hart* [1912] 3 KB 6) and a settlement in favour of such a purchaser is expressly not caught (see *Re Abbott* [1982] 3 WLR 86). Reference may also be made to *Re A Debtor* [1965] 1 WLR 1498, in which a conveyance was held void within s 42 without in any way apparently affecting an immediately subsequent mortgage.

Express provision for protecting the bona fide purchaser for valuable consideration without notice of any intention of defeating a claim for financial provision is also to be found in s 16 (2) of the Matrimonial Proceedings and Property Act 1970. The conveyancing consequences of s 16 of the 1970 Act were illustrated (as to a replaced enactment) in *National Provincial Bank Ltd* v *Hastings Car Mart Ltd (No 2)* [1964] Ch 128, 665. There a husband in desertion conveyed the matrimonial home to a private company he owned which immediately mortgaged it to a bank; in earlier unreported proceedings to which the bank was not a party an order was made that the conveyance to the company 'be set aside'; the question of the effect of this order on the bank's mortgage had then to be decided. In the Court of Appeal, referring to the contention that the mortgage was extinguished, Russell LJ said:

> This is indeed a startling proposition. I cannot accept it. Any disposition by a husband is . . . potentially voidable under the section at the instance of the wife if made with the requisite intention. But there is no ground for holding that intermediate bona fide dealings for value are nullified as a result. That would be wholly contrary to principle, and the language of the section is quite inadequate for that purpose

([1964] Ch 665, at pp 701–2; see also per Lord Denning MR, ibid, p 691; quaere: why did not the majority consider whether the wife's occupation could give the bank notice not only of the husband's desertion but also of his intention to avoid alimony?). In the result then, whichever of the four statutory provisions may be applied, the title of a purchaser for value without notice will prevail.

6 Possessory titles

In addition to testing the strength of each link, the purchaser has, of course, also to ascertain that the chain of title does in fact stretch without a break from the root to the vendor. Here, however, one not uncommon case may be mentioned where the chain commencing with the root of title never actually reaches the vendor. This case occurs where the vendor's title is possessory. It was originally held that where the contract was open (ie, not indicating how title is to be made), the purchaser could be compelled to take a title depending on the Statute of Limitations, *provided* only that the vendor could show that the adverse possession has barred all the interests, legal and equitable, otherwise subsisting in the land (*Games* v *Bonnor* (1884) 54 LJ Ch 517). The proviso involves the vendor showing a title commencing with a good root older than the statutory period of title and continuing with the links from that root (dealing with all the equitable interests normally hidden behind trusts for sale or strict settlements, since here there is no overreaching) until the dispossession (see *Jacobs* v *Revell* [1900] 2 Ch 858). In other words the vendor should first show in the ordinary way, by the evidence of instruments, the interests existing in the land at the moment of dispossession and thereafter show by parol evidence possession of a proper nature and sufficient length to defeat all those interests.

Unhappily this is not such a satisfactory principle as it once was now that the statutory period of title has been reduced to a mere fifteen years (Law of Property Act 1969, s 23; see p 95). True, twelve of these fifteen years will be sufficient to bar very many claims (Limitation Act 1980, s 15). Nevertheless certain exceptional claims to the land will remain potentially undefeated—for example, claims by the Crown, by reversioners on leases, or by trustees where there are future beneficial interests (see Sched 1, para 4 et seq of the 1980 Act). Consequently, a prospective purchaser would be well advised not to accept a contractual stipulation for a possessory title which only involves the present short statutory period of title. But after the making of a contract which is open in this respect, it appears that the purchaser can still be compelled to accept the possessory title principle stated above, even though the period is now so short.

Further, the application of this principle has been extended by the Court of Appeal from open contracts to those containing, as most do today, a special condition stating the instrument with which title is to commence (*Re Atkinson and Horsell's Contract* [1912] 2 Ch 1). As Buckley LJ put it (ibid, p 20):

> It seems to me that that case [ie, *Games* v *Bonnor*, ante] necessarily involves that where as between two contracting parties a title is to be shown as from a defined date the purchaser can be compelled to take a possessory title commencing at a later date: in other words, though you cannot in a contract of this kind get away from the proposition that the title to be shown is to be such as stipulated, there is nothing which entitles the purchaser to say that the contract is that he is not to have a possessory title, but is to have some other title, namely, a title commencing with the root of title and showing title therefrom by devolution.

In the case, the title as shown by instruments was not interrupted by a dispossession as such but by a defect which made that title, as the purchaser's solicitor said, 'wholly bad', so that subsequent occupiers, whose successors were selling, started off as trespassers, albeit in good faith. Thus a defective title can be effectively cured by mere possession even though the vendor remained ignorant of the defect until disillusioned by the purchaser. Then at the eleventh hour and in mid-stream, the vendor can change horses and show a documentary title only up to the defect and for the balance rely on parol evidence of possession.

However, more recently the decision in *Re Atkinson and Horsell's Contract,* ante, has been distinguished, but by no means disapproved, by the Court of Appeal in *George Wimpey & Co Ltd* v *Sohn* [1967] Ch 487. This later case concerned a contract for the sale of a hotel and of an adjoining garden for the purposes of development. No trouble was encountered in showing title to the hotel itself, but as to the garden a special condition of sale had been inserted providing that:

> the vendors shall convey all such right, title and interest as they have therein and shall in support of such title and interest make or procure a statutory declaration to the effect that the said property has for a period of twenty years and upwards been in the undisputed possession of the vendors or their predecessors.

This condition was necessary because, on the face of their title, the vendors had only purchased an easement in common with others over the garden (cf *Re Ellenborough Park* [1956] Ch 131) which clearly would not enable development. Unhappily the vendors could not in fact furnish the statutory declaration stipulated because their possession had been and still was consistently disputed. Instead, the vendors claimed that they could show twelve years' adverse (as opposed to undisputed) possession of the garden and force that possessory title upon the purchaser.

The Court of Appeal unanimously held that the purchaser was entitled to rescind for breach of contract. The reasoning was that where a special condition agreed to by the purchaser provides that a good title should *not* be shown but that some particular evidence instead would be offered, then it must be strictly complied with and the offer of other evidence does not perform the contract. In addition, their lordships (Harman and Russell LJJ, Diplock LJ merely concurring) made it plain that even if the vendors had established twelve years' adverse possession (on the facts they even failed in this), specific performance would not have been ordered—it would not have been equitable, since the allegedly dispossessed freeholder was still asserting title to and others were claiming easements over the garden, the whole thing amounted to buying a law suit.

The points of distinction from the earlier case appear to be that in *Re Atkinson and Horsell's Contract*, ante, first, the contract contained no condition relieving the vendor from the obligation of actually showing a good title, but only one indicating its root, and secondly, a good title was shown, although in an unexpected way, beyond the possibility of any dispute. If in *George Wimpey & Co Ltd* v *Sohn*, ante, the vendors had been able to show not only twelve years' adverse possession but also the title dispossessed back to a good root older than the statutory period of title (apparently they made no effort in this direction), then the two cases would surely have become indistinguishable. In other words if the offer of evidence other than that stipulated for amounts to showing a good title in the open contract sense, it is impossible to see how the purchaser could be allowed to object: he would be getting better than he bargained for. Nonetheless, a contrary view was taken by Russell LJ on the ground that the special condition entitled the purchaser to insist upon undisputed, rather than merely adverse, possession (at pp 508–10). Further, it must be borne in mind that the courts have been demonstrating a recent reluctance about the actual finding of any sufficiently 'adverse' possession (see cases cited in *Emmet on Title*, 18th ed, pp 164–7).

7 The end of the chain

In the preceding pages certain of the missing links in the chain of title which the vendor must show to stretch from the root of title down to himself were considered. Since the root and the links have now each had their share of discussion, attention may be turned to the other end of the chain, namely, the proposition that title must be shown down to the vendor, a proposition not quite so self-evident as it might seem.

The rule really is that the title offered 'should end in showing that the vendor can convey *or cause to be conveyed* to the purchaser the whole estate contracted for in the land sold' (*Williams on Vendor and Purchaser*, 3rd ed, p 150, giving the very common example of the vendor being entitled under an uncompleted contract of purchase as satisfying the italicised words; but cp a note at [1978] Conv 1–3). Consequently, the purchaser can object to the title where it appears that the whole title is in some third person whose conveyance the vendor has no *right*, legal or equitable, to direct (ibid, at p 153). It is nothing to the point that the third person with the title is willing to concur if he is not compellable (*Re Bryant and Barningham's Contract* (1890) 44 Ch D 218, where following a contract for sale by Settled Land Act trustees the purchaser was held entitled to decline a conveyance from the tenant for life; cf *Re Thompson & Holt* (1890) 44 Ch D 492; see also *Re Head's Trustees and Macdonald* (1890) 45 Ch D 310). The apparent reasoning is that the court simply will not force on the purchaser a contract different from that into which he entered, namely, to buy from the vendor.

Nonetheless, the courts here have not been too prone to mistake the shadow for the substance. Thus a beneficiary under a bare trust need only show the legal title in his trustee, and a bare trustee selling at his beneficiary's request can make title with the beneficiary's concurrence since the request made this compellable (see *Re Baker and Selmon's Contract* [1907] 1 Ch 238, where the trustee-beneficiary relationship was held to become in substance an agent-principal one). Again, where title was in a company of which the vendor was the controlling shareholder, Harman J said in his judgment that:

> It was objected that, as things stood, [the vendor] had no interest in the freehold by virtue of which he could compel the concurrence of the company, but I do not feel the force of this. It seems to me to be enough that he was in a position, either by exercising his power as sole director, or, if necessary, by winding up the company, to procure it to act as he chose

(in *Elliott* v *Pierson* [1948] Ch 452, at p 457). This decision has since been applied in an extraordinary case where the vendor had, for some unexplained reason, sought to avoid specific performance by selling and conveying the land to a controlled company after the making but before completion of the original contract; his ingenuity was wasted, for Russell J decreed specific performance against both the vendor and the company, describing the latter as 'the creature of the first defendant, a device and a sham, a mask which he holds before his face in an attempt to avoid recognition by the eye of equity' (in *Jones* v *Lipman* [1962] 1 WLR 832, at p 836). It is pleasing, is it not, to see the courts recognising Rachmanite realities in this way?

A corollary may exist to the rule that a vendor must show title in himself or his shadow, namely, that he must also show this title in the capacity stated in the contract (ie, beneficial owner, trustees for sale, or as may be). This corollary emerged somewhat uncertainly from a decision of Eve J that beneficial joint tenants who contracted to sell as statutory trustees could not instead make title as the persons equitably entitled (*Green* v *Whitehead* [1930] 1 Ch 38). The uncertainty is due to the earlier express denial of the corollary by Tomlin J saying that:

> A contract containing a clause indicating how the title is to be made is indicative only of the vendor's intention and is not a warranty to make a good title in the particular form that is mentioned

(*Re Spencer and Hauser's Contract* [1928] Ch 598, at p 608; vendors who contracted to sell as trustees for sale able to compel the purchaser to accept a title made as executors; not apparently cited in *Green* v *Whitehead*, ante). However, this observation of Tomlin J was not followed by the Court of Appeal in *George Wimpey & Co Ltd* v *Sohn* [1967] Ch 487 (considered p 109), a case which concerned not the vendor's capacity but the evidence supporting his possession of the land; it was held that a condition of sale as to how title would be made in this respect did amount to a warranty.

Finally, a question arises as to when the vendor should show that he (or his shadow) has title, ie, whether title must have been possessed when the contract was made or whether the acquisition thereof on or before completion suffices. The answer appears to be supplied by the following propositions.

First, in theory, title on or before completion is the rule; as Harman J has said:

> At law *A* may contract to sell to *B* any defined subject-matter and can enforce the contract if by the time when he is obliged to do so he has obtained a sufficient interest or can compel other interested parties to concur in the sale. It matters not at all that at the date of the contract *A* had no interest if he obtain it in time to fulfil the bargain

(in *Elliott* v *Pierson* [1948] Ch 452, at p 455; see also *Gordon Hill Trust Ltd* v *Segall* [1941] 2 All ER 379, where a proposed vendor was the owner in equity under a contract to purchase; cf *Johnston* v *Heath* [1970] 1 WLR 1567, where a vendor had actually entered into a contract to sell land before he had any contract to purchase it). An example of this would occur where the period of the vendor's adverse possession on which his title depends expires after the contract but before completion (see *Re Atkinson & Horsell's Contract* [1912] 2 Ch 1).

Secondly, however, in practice the rule really appears to be that the vendor (or his shadow) should have title by the time that he endeavours to show that he has, and showing title is an obligation which 'ought properly to be performed by the vendor well before the date fixed for completion' (per Romer J in *Re Priestley's Contract* [1947] Ch 469, at p 476). If the vendor fails in this, the purchaser may repudiate at once, not waiting to see whether the vendor can succeed on or before completion (see per Goff LJ in *Price* v *Strange* [1978] Ch 337, at p 355; also per Romilly MR in *Forrer* v *Nash* (1865) 35 Beav 167, at p 171). However, if the purchaser wishes to repudiate, he must do so immediately and definitely (*Re Hailes and Hutchinson's Contract* [1920] 1 Ch 233). To be more precise:

> If, after ascertaining the defect, the purchaser still treats the contract as subsisting he does not retain the right to repudiate at any subsequent moment he may choose

(per Parker J in *Halkett* v *Dudley* [1907] 1 Ch 590, at p 597), and:

> If he [the purchaser] begins to seek for explanations or to demand the getting in of outstanding interests he will be deemed to have waived the point

(per Harman J in *Elliott* v *Pierson*, ante, but cf *Manning* v *Turner* [1957] 1 WLR 91, at p 98). All this assumes that the title shown *is* necessarily defective, otherwise the vendor must be given an opportunity of dispelling the doubt (see *Re Balen and Shepherd's Contract* [1924] 2 Ch 365).

The general judicial view is that this immediate right to repudiate was introduced by equity as a qualification of the position at law and arose 'out of the peculiar difficulty of making a title to land in England' (see per Harman J in *Elliott* v *Pierson*, ante; also *Proctor* v *Pugh* [1921] 2 Ch 256). This echoes the earlier view of Parker J that the right to repudiate was no more than 'an equitable right affecting the equitable remedy by way of specific performance . . . [arising] out of that want of mutuality which, unless waived, is generally fatal to relief by way of specific performance' (in *Halkett* v *Dudley* [1907] 1 Ch 590, at p 596; see also per Buckley LJ in *Price* v *Strange* [1978] Ch 337, at pp 369–70).

The third proposition follows on from and is dependent on acceptance of the view that the purchaser's right to repudiate before completion is equitable rather than legal. This proposition is that if after the purchaser has repudiated but before the completion date the vendor acquires title, then the vendor should be able to recover damages at common law for breach of contract if the purchaser still refuses to complete (see per Parker J in *Halkett* v *Dudley*, ante; restated per Buckley LJ *Price* v *Strange*, ante, at p 364). However, Megarry V-C has understandably found some difficulty in this distinction in consequences between equity and law: he referred to the vendor's duty of disclosure of defects in title and the purchaser's right to investigate title as rendering the apparent position at law 'strange' (see *Pips (Leisure Productions) Ltd* v *Walton* (1980) 260 EG 601, at p 603). Happily he was able to feel unsure that all the authorities had been duly cited or considered and so, despite some hesitation, actually held 'that upon discovering that a vendor has no title or power to convey what he has contracted to convey, the purchaser may thereupon treat the contract as at an end, both in law and in equity' (ibid, pp 603–4). Accordingly the so-called third proposition must be treated with extreme suspicion (but see further an article by CT Emery at (1977) 41 Conv (NS) 18–34).

D DEDUCING TITLE

1 Abstracts

The preceding sections in this chapter discussed the principles governing the performance by a vendor of land of his obligation to show title; the root, the period and the chain of title have been examined as three of the commandments for conveyancers. After the theory, the practice; what the vendor must actually do is *deduce* his title, which involves the delivery and proof of an *abstract of title*.

By an abstract of title is meant an epitome of the documents and events which, in accordance with the principles discussed in the preceding sections, constitute the vendor's evidence of ownership (cf the epitomes of abstracts in Sched 6 to the Law of Property Act 1925). What is more, to be an abstract of title properly so-called, it must appear in the traditional form. To begin with, it needs to be written, or even typed, on that large unmanageable paper contradictorily called brief, which must be visualised as having no less than four margins. Then the documents and events have to be chronologically laid out with their parts patterned to the appropriate margin. Thus the outer margin is to be intruded upon only by the date and stamp duty on each abstracted document and otherwise preserved for the 'marks' of those perusing or examining the abstract. From that margin are written the names of each of the abstracted documents and their parties and, much lower down, all their residuary clauses containing the various covenants, powers and provisos etc, and the certificate of value; in this second margin, the events affecting the title also are stated. The third margin is an exclusive enclosure for the beginning of any recitals. In the fourth margin the vital *habendum* makes its bow and from this fourth margin are cramped the still vital *parcels*. Also, as a heading to the abstract, will be found a statement of the person whose title is being shown and of the property.

This lay-out, so bewildering to the beginner, is in fact a maze soon mastered so that the margins may be seen not as hiding, but as finding places in which ready perusal may be made of any particular part of any of the abstracted documents. Less easy to dispel is the initial confusion caused by encountering the peculiar past-tense and passive voice and by the esoteric and general abbreviations used; herein unhappily lies the true art of abstracting for which there is no substitute for experience. Happily, however, this so hardily acquired art shows signs of dying out; its health already undermined by a dearth of expert exponents, it may at last succumb to twentieth-century business efficiency. After a few decades of hesitation the Council of The Law Society in 1969 pronounced that:

> an unregistered title may be deduced by supplying an epitome of the title accompanied by copies (which may be machine-made facsimile copies) of the documents shown in the epitome, as an alternative to an abstract of title in traditional form

(*Digest*, Opinion No 94, Fourth Cumulative Supplement). Where approved copying processes are used, the Council say that this 'will be deemed a proper method of deducing title which the purchaser or other recipient may be required to accept in lieu of a traditional typed abstract' (para 4). The judgment on non-approved (photographic) copying processes remains, in effect, as it was before— not enough alone. In the Opinion, it is especially emphasised that care must be taken over the quality and requirements of individual copy documents (paras 1 and 3) and there is also some further explanatory matter as to the form of the epitome (para 2).

So a vendor, or rather his solicitor, who delivers an abstract, traditional or modern as above, and then verifies it, is said to deduce title: see *Re Lacey & Son* (1883) 25 Ch D 301). But this apparently is not precise:

> Now, if we are to examine the word critically, it is quite clear that when you speak of deducing a title, as meaning to express either the delivery of the abstract or the showing of the deeds, whichever it may be applied to, it is not altogether an appropriate expression, or strictly correct. The deducing the title—the appropriate use of that expression would be this: I deduce my title from my great-grandfather; I do not deduce my title by sending you a document; nor do I deduce my title by showing you the deeds, I show you how I deduce my title; but according to the strict meaning of the words "deducing the title", it is stating from whom or from what source the party draws forth his title

(per Kindersley V–C in *Oakden* v *Pike* (1865) 34 LJ Ch 620, at p 622; cf per Cottenham LC in *Southby* v *Hutt* (1837) 2 My & Cr 207, at p 213).

Mean what you may by the word deducing, the lay vendor, incorrigibly lacking the calluses caused by actual conveyancing on the minds of conveyancers, might well wonder whether he cannot by-pass all this abstract nonsense. Why cannot he simply hand over his title deeds for inspection? The popular explanation would put it down to the vendor's own interests: he should not part with his evidence of ownership (even if his mortgagee would let him) until he receives the purchase money. But if the vendor still wishes to gamble the deducing costs against this risk (or demands that the purchaser, like Mahomet, come to his mountain of deeds), then a more authoritative account can be given:

> Evidence of title on sales being for the most part documentary, and such as can be weighed only by skilled legal advisers, it became usual to facilitate the task of judging the effect of the title-deeds by making an abstract of their contents for the perusal of the purchaser's counsel. It appears that formerly deeds were handed over to the purchaser for examination, and any abstract of them which he might require was made at his expense. But afterwards it became established that the vendor was bound to make at his own expense and deliver to the purchaser an abstract of the title to the property sold; and so the law still remains

(*Williams on Vendor and Purchaser*, 3rd ed, p 97). This, indeed, is an interesting illustration of the way the practice of conveyancers made law: at first the matter was purely one of practice in that express contractual provision would be made for delivery of an abstract by the vendor at his own expense, then a rule to this effect was formulated by an eminent text-book writer (ie, *Sugden on Vendors and Purchasers*, 14th ed, at p 406), which was eventually endorsed by the courts as an implied term of an open contract (see *Williams on Contract of Sale of Land*, p xvii, note 20, also *Re Johnson & Tustin* (1885) 30 Ch D 42).

Now although perusal by the purchaser's counsel has gone the way of the dinosaur, the rule of law is established: an abstract of title must be delivered, delivery of the title deeds themselves simply not sufficing (see *Horne* v *Wingfield* (1841) 3 Man & G 33, where only two deeds formed the whole of the vendor's title; cf *Selkirk* v *Romar Investments Ltd* [1963] 1 WLR 1415, at pp 1418–19, as to the practice in the Bahamas). The Council of The Law Society has even prescribed the courses of action for coercing conformity out of our incorrigible lay vendor, namely:

(*a*) to persuade the vendor to consult a solicitor; or

(*b*) to instruct him (the purchaser's solicitor) to prepare the abstract and pay him for the extra work occasioned; or

(*c*) to register the contract as an estate contract and to take such proceedings as were necessary to compel the vendor to deduce his title

(*Law Society's Digest*, Opinion No 93, as amended; presumably, course (*b*) can now only exceptionally be proper in view of the general prohibition on acting for both parties; per *Law Society's Gazette* (1972) vol 69, No 26, p 629). From being a mere conveyancing convenience, the abstract of title has thus acquired a special sanctity of its own as a part of the transaction. For instance, an abstract still has to be delivered where a mortgagor is selling his equity of redemption to his mortgagee even though the latter is already in possession of all the title-deeds (*Law Society's Digest*, Opinion No 88). Again where one solicitor acts for both vendor and purchaser, or mortgagor and mortgagee, an abstract must still be solemnly prepared and supplied (ibid, Nos 78 and 238). Of course, this has an obsolete smell about it: not only are these last two Opinions dated respectively 1890 and 1881 but only exceptionally now may a solicitor act for both parties (see above). The real reason behind all this, however, is no longer the original one of convenient perusal but the fact that abstracts of title tend in time to become something of a substitute for the title deeds themselves. That is, when the abstract is no longer virgin, but is marked as examined (see later), then it becomes acceptable as some evidence of title, using this last word strictly—ie, the abstract is evidence of the evidence of ownership and as such is a useful document for the purchaser to have (see *Law Society's Digest*. Opinion No 76—opined that his solicitor too must hand it over even though it contain private notes on title).

Nonetheless, the courts have not always accorded the same absolute allegiance to abstracts as the Council of The Law Society. Eve J once said in judgment that:

Having regard to the multiplicity of documents to be abstracted and the difficulty at the present time of obtaining the services of skilled persons to abstract documents, I do not·think that the purchasers can reasonably complain if they are supplied, not with abstracts but with full copies

(in *Bond* v *Bassett* (1917) 87 LJ Ch 160). In pursuance of this he declared that the vendor would satisfy his obligations by delivering to the purchasers as part of the abstract the counterparts of certain leases and completed drafts of certain conveyances.

Be that as it may, the accepted obligation is that a vendor prepare and deliver an abstract of title, and that he do so unconditionally (*Law Society's Digest*, Opinion No 95 (*b*) in Fourth (Cumulative) Supplement—purchaser's solicitor cannot be required to hold it to the order of the vendor's solicitor pending completion). Thus the purchaser calls the tune, but who pays the piper, particularly if any of the deeds are not in the vendor's possession? The answer is that the vendor must meet all the cost of abstracting, notwithstanding that the expense of producing any such deeds to verify the abstract may later be thrown on the purchaser (*Re Johnson and Tustin* (1885) 30 Ch D 42, *Re Stamford, Spalding & Boston Banking Co & Knight's Contract* [1900] 1 Ch 287).

Naturally where vendors have a burden one expects to find a readiness to remove it to the purchaser. Here, however, one would be pleasantly surprised: the most used general conditions of sale in fact confirm the obligation to deliver an abstract of title (see now No 9 of the National 20th ed, and No 12 of The Law Society's 1980 edition) and special exclusion is rarely encountered. Occasionally, on the sale of many tiny plots out of a big holding conditions may still be met to the effect that the purchasers may have free conveyances, provided neither abstracts nor investigations of title are pursued (nowadays vendors can more easily sidestep their difficulties in this respect by first registering the title). Are such conditions valid? The condition for a free conveyance without more does not preclude a purchaser from requiring both an abstract and an investigation (*Re Pelly and Jacob's Contract* (1899) 80 LT 45). But there would seem no reason why the condition could not go the rest of the way, so long as the purchaser is allowed to select his own solicitor (see s 48 (1) of the Law of Property Act 1925).

The manner in which documents should be abstracted in traditional form is governed by the idea behind the original practice:

> For the whole object of requiring an abstract of title is to enable the purchaser's conveyancing counsel to examine the title in a convenient way; the abstract is all he sees; and if the very words used are not placed before him, it is impossible for him to exercise his judgment on the title

(*Willliams on Vendor and Purchaser*, 3rd ed, at p 103). Consequently, the rule is that the full wording of all the material contents of any document should be given (cf *Barnaby* v *Equitable Reversionary Interest Society* (1885) 28 Ch D 416). For example, the following contents of a conveyance are generally regarded as material, namely the date, the parties, the recitals (unless of a previously abstracted matter), the premises, the grant, the parcels and the habendum (especially pre-1926); whilst not material in this context are any common covenants (eg, of title), any overreachable trusts of the proceeds of sale, and any powers which will not have been exercised. Naturally, with a modern form of abstract (see p 113) one can only expect that everything will be indiscriminately copied in full. In addition, coloured copies of plans incorporated by reference into the parcels of abstracted documents should always be attached to the abstract, or so the Council of The Law Society tells us (see *Law Society's Digest*, Opinions No 77, 84 and 94 as substituted by the Fourth Supplement; but cp per Parke B in *Blackburn* v *Smith* (1848) 2 Ex 783, at p 792).

Again, endorsements on documents are often material, particularly since 1925, and must be fully abstracted, eg, of assents or of the appointment of new trustees (see *Re Miller & Pickersgill's Contract* [1931] 1 .Ch 511; s 36 of the Administration of Estates Act 1925; s 35 of the Trustee Act 1925; and s 35 of the Settled Land Act 1925). Equally, the abstract should also actually state which of the parties executed any document ('duly executed' will not do, being for the purchaser to judge), adding whether the execution was attested and whether any special formalities were observed.

As with the material parts, a fortiori, all documents material to the title should be abstracted in their own right:

All documents forming part of the title should be abstracted in *chief*; the introduction of them merely as recitals in other abstracted instruments is clearly improper. The omission to abstract a document in chief might proceed from a desire to avoid noticing matters of a suspicious character occurring in such document, but which are not noticed in the recital
(see per North J in *Re Stamford, Spalding & Boston Banking Co & Knight's Contract* [1900] 1 Ch 287). Once again the purchaser is entitled to judge the effect of the document for himself rather than rely on the recitor's view (but cf *Re Ebsworth and Tidy's Contract* (1889) 42 Ch D 23, at p 34, where an objection based on this rule was said to be technically right but of no substance as the purchaser had got as much information from the recital as if the document has been abstracted in chief). However, any events material to the title need only be shortly stated in the abstract (later recital thereof not sufficing), since anything further descends into the realms of proof of the abstract (see *Re Wright and Thompson's Contract* [1920] 1 Ch 191).

2   Time for delivery of abstract

As a rule time is not of the essence of the contract with regard to delivery of an abstract of title (*Roberts v Berry* (1853) 3 De GM & G 284). Nonetheless, if the vendor delays unreasonably in fulfilling his obligation to deliver an abstract, the purchaser may refuse to complete the contract (*Compton v Bagley* [1892] 1 Ch 313: contra if an out of time abstract is accepted: *Hipwell v Knight* (1835) 4 LJ Ex Eq 52). What, however, is the due date for delivery? Under a contract open in this respect, it is simply that old uncertainty, within a reasonable time, except that the purchaser may by giving reasonable notice fix a date (ibid). Most often, however, a time for delivery of the abstract after the date of the contract will be specified by the general conditions of sale incorporated (eg, Statutory, No 5 (1), fourteen days, and National 20th ed, No 9 (1), eleven working days; compare The Law Society's 1980 edition No 12 (1) (*a*), providing for delivery forthwith upon exchange of contracts, which had become common practice).

   In addition, a time calculated by reference to delivery of the abstract will be similarly provided for delivery of requisitions (as to which see later). Without more, such time will only be calculated from delivery of a 'perfect' abstract (*Hobson v Bell, Glynn v Bell* (1839) 8 LJ Ch 241). What a perfect abstract is emerges from the following words of Joyce J:

> With reference to the abstract of title that was delivered, I do not think that it was very seriously contended before me that that abstract was imperfect; indeed it appears to have been the most perfect abstract the vendors could furnish at the time of its delivery; and that being so, the abstract is not imperfect or insufficient because it shows a defective title or even no title at all

(in *Pryce-Jones v Williams* [1902] 2 Ch 517, at pp 521–2). In other words, the vendor need only do the best he can with what he has got (see also *Oakden v Pike* (1865) 34 LJ Ch 620). If the abstract in fact shows a good title, then it is said to be 'complete' as well as perfect (see *Braybrooke v Inskip* (1803) 8 Ves 417, also *Re Wright & Thompson's Contract* [1920] 1 Ch 191). However, perfect suffices for present purposes, and an abstract is presumed to be of this quality unless the contrary is shown by the purchaser (see *Gray v Fowler* (1873) LR 8 Exch 249).

   Despite this presumption in the vendor's favour, conditions of sale have tended to provide that time should run from the *actual* delivery of an abstract which will be *deemed* perfect. General Condition 10 (1) and (3) of The Law Society's Conditions of Sale, 1973 Revision, which contained such a provision, was considered in *Ogilvy v Hope-Davies* [1976] 1 All ER 683, where vendors selling as trustees had delivered an abstract omitting the deed appointing them trustees and the purchaser's requisitions were not delivered within the specified fourteen days. Graham J suggested (at p 686) that revision of Condition 10 (3) ought to be considered, continuing:

Though apparently hallowed by time, it is, to my mind, in its context avoidably obscure and uncertain in scope and, indeed, it seems that such an authority as *Williams on Vendor and Purchaser* (4th ed (1936) p 71), also takes the same view that the scope of the condition is uncertain, though his criticism is perhaps not so harsh as mine. What then does it mean and what is its proper construction? I do not think the condition should be construed so as to make it necessary to deem 'perfect' any so-called abstract, however deficient. This would lead to loose conveyancing with deplorable results. Neither do I think that the argument and construction of counsel for the purchaser can be right. The logical conclusion of his argument is that any deficiency, however small or unimportant, entitles the purchaser to sit back and do nothing until the deficiency is made good.

Giving the matter the best consideration I can, I think that the proper construction (which, incidentally, produces a common-sense result) is that the matter must be looked at as one of substance. An abstract does not cease to be an abstract on which a purchaser must make his requisitions within the time specified if it is only deficient in respects which are unimportant in that a solicitor investigating the title would, or ought to, assume that the gaps could be and would be likely to be filled in a way which he would expect from the information supplied in the abstract. In such a case, he ought to get on with it, raise what requisitions he can on the abstract submitted, and at the same time call for the obvious gaps to be filled. Of course, when these are filled, he will be entitled to make further requisitions if such turn out to be necessary in respect of the new material.

On the facts, therefore, the purchaser had not been entitled to delay his requisitions. Reference may now be made to No 15 (4) of the 1980 edition and also to No 9 (4) of the 20th edition of the National Conditions, which take account of this decision.

3   Requisitions

Once the vendor has completed the first leg of his obligations in deducing title—ie, he has delivered an abstract—what happens next? The ball is in the purchaser's half; he or rather his solicitor (rarely now his counsel) must peruse the abstract to see whether a good title in accordance with the contract for sale is shown; in effect, he is considering the links in the chain of the vendor's title. If any weak links are overlooked, the purchaser's solicitor might well find himself on the end of an action for professional negligence (see *Pilkington* v *Wood* [1953] Ch 770). Consequently, over-much care is taken to discover defects in the title offered, after which the vendor must be compelled to do his duty by putting the defects right in order to show a good title. The procedure traditionally adopted to this end is for the purchaser's solicitor:

to send in written requisitions dealing with the points in which [he] consider[s] the title to be deficient or insufficiently proved or the vendor's obligations to be otherwise imperfectly discharged. To these requisitions the vendor returns written answers confessing or repudiating his liability to comply with them, as the case may be. Unless he accede to every requisition, his answers will evoke replies from the other side; and these again will demand further responses. So the contest continues until all grounds of difference are removed, the title is accepted, and the parties proceed to completion, or the questions on which neither party will give way are submitted to the determination of the court (*Williams on Vendor and Purchaser*, 3rd ed, at pp 34–5). Thus, as Greene MR has said: 'One of the principal functions of a requisition is, in the case of a defect in title, to enable the purchaser to point it out to the vendor, and to require him to get rid of it' (in *Re Ossemsley Estates Ltd* [1937] 3 All ER 774, at p 780). The second leg of the vendor's obligations, proof of the abstract of title—verification by the vendor, examination by the purchaser—will be left for a later look, even though ideally perhaps everything ought to take place in practice before all the purchaser's requisitions have been raised (see *Law Society's Digest*, Opinion No 95 (*a*) in Fourth (Cumulative) Supplement).

May the purchaser, in his requisitions, raise any questions he wishes? Strictly, no. Requisitions on title, if the writer may be pardoned for saying so, should be requisitions *on title* (see per Oliver J in *Ridley* v *Oster* [1939] 1 All ER 618, at p 623; cf per Lord Macnaghten in *London County Council* v *Attorney-General* [1901] AC 26, at p 35). That is to say that in theory requisitions are appropriate only as to matters arising from the perusal of the abstract of title, being confined to stating the purchaser's objections and requirements in respect of such matters. In practice, however, the requisitions on title so-called will almost always be found to include many other statements and enquiries. Thus requisitions should properly be raised and pursued in respect of any adverse interests protected by registration and revealed by searches with a view to their removal from the register before completion. This is so even though it is alleged and appears probable that the interest is void or the registration mistaken, ie, the title remains doubtful. See *Kitney* v *MEPC Ltd* [1977] 1 WLR 981, CA; and *G + K Ladenbau (UK) Ltd* v *Crawley & de Reya* [1978] 1 WLR 266; cp *MEPC Ltd* v *Christian-Edwards* [1981] AC 205, HL, ante p 90.

Requisitions as to matters of conveyance, which the vendor is bound to attend to anyway, are clearly unnecessary in theory (see *Bain* v *Fothergill* (1874) LR 7 HL 158) but just as clearly convenient as reminders in practice (eg, payment off of a mortgage: *Re Daniel, Daniel* v *Vassall* [1917] 2 Ch 405; cp *Cole* v *Rose* [1978] 3 All ER 1121). Again, the published standard forms of requisitions on title have usually dealt first with several general matters (eg, insurance, delivery of title deeds, even vacant possession on completion) and then mostly, if not all, concluded with a note that: 'The requisitions founded on the abstract of title or contract [sic] must, of course, be added to the above.' What is more, if 'enquiries before contract' were not for some reason made, the practice is for enquiries of the same sort to be made with the requisitions (eg, as to tenants, drainage, etc, local authorities, user, and so on). And even where 'enquiries before contract' were made, the practice is to ask with the requisitions for confirmation that the replies would still be the same. Indeed, this practice of raising requisitions *not* on title has been judicially spoken of as the duty of a purchaser's solicitor (per Danckwerts J in *Goody* v *Baring* [1956] 1 WLR 448, at p 456). However, the more important question, which his lordship may have overlooked, surely is what sort of requisitions the vendor need answer.

Commonly, out of courtesy, or because he knows no better, a vendor's solicitor will answer every requisition raised on behalf of the purchaser, albeit that the enigmatic 'subject to contract' which is so often encountered is not much of an answer. But what *need* he answer?

It is conceived that the vendor is, as a rule, bound to answer *all questions relevant to the abstracted title*, that is, the title he is offering for the purchaser's acceptance

(*Williams on Vendor and Purchaser*, 3rd ed, at p 123). Even this comparatively narrow rule pushes hard against the limits indicated by the decision in the leading case of *Re Ford and Hill* (1879) 10 Ch D 365. There, the Court of Appeal held that the vendor was not bound to answer such a searching interrogation as:

> Is there to the knowledge of the vendors or their solicitors any settlement, deed, fact, omission, or any incumbrance affecting the property not disclosed by the abstract?

The rule, therefore, would appear to be more consistent with authority if it were stated to be that the vendor must answer all *specific* questions relevant to the abstracted title. Either way, however, a vendor's solicitor would seem to keep entirely within his client's rights by using, where appropriate, the judicially approved formula 'This question has nothing to do with the title' (see *Re Chafer & Randall's Contract* [1916] 2 Ch 8; see also per Stirling LJ in *Taylor* v *London & County Banking Co* [1901] 2 Ch 231, at p 258, and per Vaughan Williams and Farwell LJJ in *Wilkes* v *Spooner* [1911] 2 KB 473, at pp 484 and 486, respectively). Is this a proper approach to adopt in dealing with questions relating to the property sold rather than its title? As James LJ long ago said:

> The introduction of new-fangled requisitions of this kind is dangerous and ought to be discouraged as tending to increase the expense and delay in the investigation of titles, which already are almost a disgrace to the law of the country

(in *Re Ford & Hill* (1879) 10 Ch D 365, at p 370). And as Dillon J not so long ago said, after referring to the statement in a well-known practitioner's book that a vendor was bound to answer all specific questions put to him in respect of the property sold:

> normal practice was for many questions to be asked, very often reasonable ones, and for which the purchaser's solicitors might be liable in negligence if they failed to ask, but it was plain that they could not all be questions which would entitle a purchaser to refuse to complete (notwithstanding that contracts had been exchanged) until an answer was forthcoming. Once contracts had been exchanged, the vendor's primary duty was to deduce title, and requisitions were normally directed to that or to the form of conveyance. They were not necessarily limited to those matters, but they could not go so far as the passage in *Emmet* sugggested

(*Luff* v *Raymond* (1982) 79 *Law Society's Gazette* 1330; in the case the unanswered requisition concerned insurance and *Emmet* has now been amended).

If the vendor refuses an answer to a requisition properly raised, then clearly the purchaser could either discontinue with the sale or else compel an answer by means of a vendor and purchaser summons (see s 49 of the Law of Property Act 1925). And since the purchaser will almost always think his requisitions proper, only trouble is courted by a straight refusal to answer. But what does the vendor risk by giving a false answer to an improper requisition? Perhaps nothing. It must be remembered that the rights and obligations of the parties have already been defined in a binding form by virtue of the contract for sale. The false answer could not, therefore, be a misrepresentation inducing the purchaser to enter into the contract for sale and so enabling avoidance. Equally, no consideration would seem to be given by the purchaser to support any allegation that the vendor warranted, as a collateral contract, the truth of his answers to requisitions (but cf per Denning LJ in *Simmons* v *Pennington & Son* [1955] 1 WLR 183, at p 186). The false answer itself, as also the matter as to which it was false, might well be said to be a breach of a term implied into the contract of sale that the vendor would not only answer but answer truthfully and properly raised requisitions, but this would hardly cover requisitions *not* on title. Again the vendor might be made liable in damages for the torts of deceit or negligence (see the *Hedley Byrne* case [1964] AC 465) or under the Misrepresentation Act 1967, but then the requisition would have had to relate to something which would have entitled the purchaser to escape from the contract since otherwise he will have suffered no loss by going on in ignorance.

More important both the vendor and his solicitor might find themselves statutorily liable in damages or even prosecuted, with the Attorney-General's leave, as guilty of a misdemeanour, if by the false answer, with criminal intent to defraud, they conceal from the purchaser 'any instrument or incumbrance material to the title' (see s 183 of the Law of Property Act 1925, not, therefore, covering requisition *not* on title). As to this, however, the false answer would, in theory at least, be likely to add nothing to the liability (if any) already incurred by the original concealment involved in the earlier omission of the instrument or incumbrance from the abstract of title (see *Re Ford & Hill* (1879) 10 Ch D 365, at pp 370–1). In any case whether there could be any liability under the section as to pre-root matters has been queried (by Fry J in *Smith v Robinson* (1879) 13 Ch D 148, at p 151; cf *Wolstenholme & Cherry's Conveyancing Statutes*, 12th ed, at p 547, and 13th ed, vol 1, p 310, where it is submitted that there can be if there is the necessary intent). In practice, the section is likely to prove a sanction only against blatant cases because of the near impossibility of establishing the intent to defraud. In what is virtually the only case on the section—*District Bank Ltd v Luigi Grill* [1943] Ch 78—the defendant's solicitors had deduced title and answered requisitions on the mortgage of a certain property without disclosing the important information, which they knew all about, that the rent reserved by a lease of the property had already been paid in advance for the next three years. In these circumstances, nonetheless, not even a suggestion was made on behalf of the plaintiff-mortgagees that there had been any intent to defraud, instead the argument—unsuccessful—was that this was not necessary for the civil liability. In addition, left open by the decision is the extent of 'incumbrance' for the purposes of the section (the word could be confined by s 205 (1) (vii) of the Act to matters involving money payments, and see *District Bank Ltd v Webb* [1958] 1 WLR 148, lease held on the facts not an incumbrance).

Generally, therefore, the conclusion would seem to be that if a vendor incurs any liability at all by a false answer to a requisition, such liability will rarely, if ever, go beyond that which he would risk anyway under his implied covenants for title (see s 76 of the Law of Property Act 1925; the benefit of s 183 also runs with the land). The falsity of the answer is unlikely to be discovered before completion, after which the contract will have merged in the conveyance (but cf the effect of the Misrepresentation Act 1967, mentioned at p 215). Now, the writer is far from advocating deliberate deception as a weapon to be used on purchasers. He is merely hoping to show that unless the object is to get the abstract or proof of title completed in some specific respect in a way which will necessarily be seen to before completion, the general requisitions commonly raised (and directed as a duty by Danckwerts J in *Goody v Baring*, ante) appear to create nothing stronger in the protection of purchasers than a paper shield.

4   Time for delivery of requisitions

The event from which to calculate the time for delivery of requisitions on title is the delivery of the abstract. How long is the time? If the contract makes no provision, then the requisitions must be delivered within a reasonable time (*Spurrier v Hancock* (1799) 4 Ves 667). But the standard sets of general conditions of sale generally provide for this time-limit: fourteen days (Statutory, No 6 (1)) (or eleven working days (National, 20th ed, No 9 (2)) or even six working days (The Law Society's 1980 edition, No 15 (2)). What is more, the latter two of these standard sets make time of the essence of their provisions (see respectively No 9 (3) and No 15 (5)), whilst the absence of this from the Statutory set has been said to deprive the provision of its utility (see T Cyprian Williams on *Contract of Sale of Land*, at p 88, note (*y*)). Nonetheless there is authority for stating a rule that the stipulated time for delivery of requisitions is always of the essence even though the provision does not expressly make it so (*Oakden* v *Pike* (1865) 34 LJ Ch 620; cp the rule that the time for delivery of the abstract is not of the essence, an established rule which was contradicted in the judgment so weakening this case's authority). Although the authority may not be very satisfactory, the rule does appear to be accepted by most textbook writers (see, eg, *Gibson's Conveyancing*, 20th ed, p 135; *Williams on Title*, 4th ed, p 522, note 15; cp Barnsley, *Conveyancing Law and Practice*, 2nd ed, p 367, *n* 15). The present writer (a voice in the wilderness for once in very good company, see T Cyprian Williams, loc cit) inclines gently to the view that this stipulation as to time is no different in principle from any other and should not normally be of the essence without express provision to that effect (and see the support received from Buckley J in *Re Stone and Saville's Contract* [1962] 1 WLR 460, at pp 464–5; on appeal [1963] 1 WLR 163).

Whether of the essence or not, conditions of sale often add, in effect, that out of time requisitions are to be deemed waived (Statutory, No 6 (2); cf National Conditions, 20th ed, No 9 (5) as to deeming the title accepted; The Law Society's 1980 ed, No 15, deems neither waiver nor acceptance). In other words, the position usually is that requisitions cannot be effectively raised out of time (see *Cumberland Court (Brighton) Ltd* v *Taylor* [1964] Ch 29). To this prima facie position, however, there are three established exceptions; they are that requisitions may always be raised out of time:

(*a*) as to defects going to the root of the title (*Want* v *Stallibrass* (1873) LR 8 Ex 175, *Re Tanqueray-Willaume and Landau* (1882) 20 Ch D 465) the nature of these has already been discussed (p 87: but essentially involved is the vendor's inability to convey what he has contracted to (se *Re Brine and Davies' Contract* [1935] Ch 388);

(*b*) as to matters of conveyance (*Re Hughes and Ashley's Contract* [1900] 2 Ch 595, *Re Scott and Eave's Contract* (1902) 86 LT 617); again these have already been discussed (p 92), but in effect they are defects in title removable by the vendor as of right (eg, a mortgage); also mention was made earlier that requisitions as to these matters need not be raised at all; and

(*c*) as to anything affecting the title *not* discoverable from the face of the abstract (*Warde* v *Dixon* (1858) 28 LJ Ch 315); this would apply, for example, where incumbrances (eg, restrictive covenants) emerge from the purchaser's own searches and enquiries elsewhere (see *Re Haedicke and Lipski's Contract* [1901] 2 Ch 666, at p 669) or semble from the later verification of the abstract (see *Southby* v *Hutt* (1837) 2 My & Cr 207; cf *Law Society's Digest*, Opinion No 95 (*a*) in Fourth (Cumulative) Supplement).

Consequently, the customary concluding statement sent with requisitions on title, reserving the right to make further requisitions as to these last aliunde affairs is perfectly proper, save in so far as the contract specifically says not (*Rosenberg* v *Cook* (1881) 8 QBD 162; cp (1946) 11 Conv (NS) 2).

Notwithstanding these three exceptions, practical convenience demands that all requisitions, relating to anything whatever, be raised within time if possible. Conversely, courtesy in practice means that out of time requisitions are often answered. This is unwise: a solicitor may find that he has all unwittingly waived the vendor's right to insist on the time limit (see *Cutts* v *Thodey* (1842) 6 Jur 1027; *Lane* v *Debenham* (1853) 11 Hare 188). Theoretically, therefore, a client's authority should be sought before extending any such courtesies. The speedier practice, however, is to preface the answers with a statement of courtesy and non-waiver.

5   Answering time

At this point attention may be turned briefly to the time-limits, first, for the vendor's answers to requisitions, and secondly, for the purchaser's answers to these answers (more often known as the purchaser's 'observations' on the vendor's 'replies'). As to each of these the scales have usually seemed weighted in favour of the vendor, no time being specified, never mind made of the essence, for his answers. However, The Law Society's Conditions, 1980 ed, does now provide that the vendor shall deliver his replies within four working days and makes time of the essence (No 15 (2), (5)). What happens if the vendor is late is not stated: presumably he could not be excused from complying with properly raised requisitions (but cf *Re Stone and Saville's Contract* [1963] 1 WLR 163). The purchaser's answers, in contrast, have always had to be made within a specified number of days, time being made of the essence (National Conditions, 20th ed, No 9 (2), (3); The Law Society Conditions, 1980 ed, No 15 (3), (5); Statutory Conditions, No 6 (4): otherwise the implication appears to be that the purchaser has as long for these answers as for his original requisitions). But if the vendor's answer to the original requisition has to take the form of a supplementary abstract of title, then further requisitions on this abstract count as original requisitions, the reducing series of time-limits starting all over again (see *Re Ossemsley Estates Ltd* [1937] 3 All ER 774).

This last case also illustrates how easily and drastically the seven-day time limit can be overstepped (counsel's opinion was taken on a difficult point but objections made on the basis of it had become barred). In contrast, when the vendor's solicitors purported to reply to a requisition (as to the statutory acknowledgment regarding documents of title) by writing a letter which gave no answer to the particular question (also failing to reveal the lack of a valid acknowledgment concerning an earlier conveyance), the Court of Appeal held that there had been no 'reply' at all within the meaning of The Law Society's Conditions, 1953 ed, No 9 (4); accordingly time did not run against the purchaser so as to entitle the vendor to serve a notice to complete: *Pratt* v *Betts* (1973) 27 P & CR 398.

6   Rescission resulting from requisitions

Resting on the excuse that titles to land tend to pass the understanding of mortal vendors, the standard conditions of sale are all constructed with an integral escape route from the contract in case the purchaser, mortal or otherwise, not only perceives that the vendor's title is not what it ought to be but is also tactless enough to point this out. In other words, provision is made to the effect that the vendor may rescind the contract whenever he would rather not comply with any of the purchaser's requisitions (see Statutory Conditions, No 7, The Law Society's Conditions, 1980 ed, No 16, and National Conditions, 20th ed, No 10). This is an example of rescission by agreement, as opposed to rescission of a voidable contract or rescission on breach of contract, and provisions to this effect in contracts for the sale of land have 'long been common form' (see *Selkirk* v *Romar Investments Ltd* [1963] 1 WLR 1415, at p 1418).

Such a provision could go so far as to entitle rescission on the 'making' of the unwelcome requisition, the purchaser being given no locus poenitentiae (see *Re Starr-Bowkett Building Society and Sibun's Contract* (1889) 42 Ch D 386). If so, equity will not intervene on the purchaser's behalf; no new term will be implied into the contract that any notice of rescission should be given (see per Cotton LJ in *Re Dames and Wood* (1885) 29 Ch D 626, at p 629). More often, however, the right to rescind is expressed to arise on the purchaser 'insisting' or 'persisting' with regard to the requisition. In this case, there are four conditions precedent to rescission, namely: (1) the purchaser makes the requisition, (2) the vendor is unwilling to comply, (3) this unwillingness is communicated to the purchaser, and (4) the requisition is nonetheless not withdrawn (see per Cairns LJ in *Duddell v Simpson* (1866) 2 Ch App 102, at p 109; also *Mawson v Fletcher* (1870) 6 Ch App 91). Although only the National Conditions use the word 'persist', all three expressly give the purchaser the opportunity of withdrawing within ten days, so that the four conditions precedent would appear to apply anyway.

There would be little point in the vendor jealously reserving his right to rescind, if he could not do so without paying the purchaser any compensation for his conveyancing costs thrown away, never mind for his loss of bargain (for the peculiarly limited circumstances in which substantial damages would be recoverable see p 214). This, not surprisingly, happens to be exactly what the general conditions cited say; the purchaser may only recover, with or without interest depending on the set, any deposit paid. An apparent conflict is capable of occurring here between a provision for rescission and a condition for compensation to be paid (eg, as to misdescriptions, see p 52). In such cases, however, the former will prevail: the vendor by rescinding can always defeat the purchaser's contractual rights (see *Ashburner v Sewell* [1891] 3 Ch 405; *Vowles v Bristol Building Society* (1900) 44 SJ 592).

All this cutting-off of compensation, a weapon not available for the vendor under an open contract, called forth the sternest criticism from that learned conveyancer, the late T Cyprian Williams, essentially because it seemed so one-sided (*Sale of Land*, p xi). With his tirade the present writer would be tempted to concur were it not that the vendor's right to rescind cannot be quite taken at its face value; as Viscount Radcliffe has said in the course of giving the advice of the Privy Council:

> it is not in dispute that courts of equity have on numerous occasions intervened to restrain or control the exercise of such a right of rescission in contracts for the sale of land, despite what, on the face of the contract, its terms seem to secure for the vendor

(in *Selkirk v Romar Investments Ltd* [1963] 1 WLR 1415, at p 1422).

In what way, therefore, will the vendor's reliance on the express provisions of the standard sets of conditions of sale be impliedly circumscribed? If he may, the writer would like to formulate this handy-size rule: the vendor must be reasonable in being unwilling to comply with the purchaser's requisition. Then, to further and better particularise, the vendor will not be regarded as reasonable unless *all* of the following constituents be present:

(*a*) The vendor has at least some title to some of the property sold (*Bowman v Hyland* (1878) 8 Ch D 588; cf *Heppenstall v Hose* (1884) 51 LT 589, title shown to three and one-half out of five acres); ie, the purchaser may be deprived of compensation where there is a defective title, but not where there is a complete absence of title; and

(*b*) The vendor had no knowledge that the title was defective when the contract was made (*Re Des Reaux and Setchfield's Contract* [1926] Ch 178; cf *Selkirk v Romar Investments Ltd*, ante, where an insufficiency of evidence about a pre-1914 intestacy had been known but there was 'no knowledge of any outstanding title or claim to title to the property nor had [the vendor's solicitor] any reason to expect that one would appear'); and

(c) The vendor's lack of such knowledge was not due to 'that element of shortcoming on his part which, though falling short of fraud or dishonesty, might be described as "recklessness"' (per Collins MR in *Re Jackson and Haden's Contract* [1906] 1 Ch 412, at p 422, applied in *Baines* v *Tweddle* [1959] Ch 679, where the vendor had neglected to ensure that his mortgagee would concur in a sale of part of the mortgaged land). Citing these two cases, the Privy Council has explained the term 'recklessness' as connoting 'an unacceptable indifference to the situation of a purchaser who is allowed to enter into a contract with the expectation of obtaining a title which the vendor has no reasonable anticipation of being able to deliver' (in *Selkirk* v *Romar Investments Ltd* [1963] 1 WLR 1415, at pp 1422, 1423). But since the law is not for laymen, the vital question, raised but not decided in *Baines* v *Tweddle*, ante, surely is: what if the vendor had relied on erroneous, even reckless professional advice? In that case, Lord Evershed MR and Romer LJ each seemed to favour the view that the vendor's personal faults only were in point (a view supported by *Re Milner and Organ's Contract* (1920) 89 LJ Ch 315, not mentioned by the Court of Appeal; see also *Merrett* v *Schuster* [1920] 2 Ch 240). Nonetheless, in *Selkirk* v *Romar Investments Ltd*, ante, the Privy Council in fact considered only the conduct of the vendor's solicitor (admittedly the vendor was a limited company) so the question seems still open; and

(d) The defect in the title is either irremovable or removable only at disproportionate expense (*Hardman* v *Child* (1885) 28 Ch D 712; see also *Selkirk* v *Romar Investments Ltd* [1963] 1 WLR 1415, at p 1425); and

(e) The vendor relies on the condition for rescission both definitely and within a reasonable time (*Re Weston and Thomas's Contract* [1907] 1 Ch 244). This does not necessarily mean before the completion date (*St Leonard's Shoreditch Vestry* v *Hughes* (1864) 17 CB (NS) 137), but only that he must not have attempted to answer the requisition or to negotiate with the purchaser unless the condition expressly permits this (*Tanner* v *Smith* (1840) 10 Sim 410). In fact, both the National and The Law Society's Conditions (loc cit) do now include the phrase 'notwithstanding any intermediate negotiation or litigation.' This last word, however, seems strictly unnecessary, being comprehended by 'negotiation' (*Isaacs* v *Towell* [1898] 2 Ch 285, cf *Gray* v *Fowler* (1873) LR 8 Exch 249; see the Statutory Conditions) and in any case would not enable rescission after judgment (*Re Arbib and Class's Contract* [1891] 1 Ch 601) and even before judgment the vendor must either be prompt if it is the purchaser's action, or he may be ordered to pay the costs (see *Re Spindler and Mear's Contract* [1901] 1 Ch 908), or else dismiss the action first if it is his own (see *Public Trustee* v *Pearlberg* [1940] 2 KB 1). On the one hand, the word 'dispute,' which never is added, probably ought to be regarded as also necessary (see *Gardom* v *Lee* (1865) 3 H & C 651); ie, as in the case cited, a vendor might easily fall into the trap of denying the alleged defect, which is a dispute and not a negotiation, and so losing his right to rescind!

Thus one can see that the vendor's ace of rescission is only too liable to be trumped by an allegation of unreasonableness, but do not forget that he has only to be reasonable : 'he does not have to be beyond criticism before he can exercise his right of rescission' (*Selkirk* v *Romar Investments Ltd* [1963] 1 WLR 1415, at p 1425). Even so the vendor may do well to mask his hand by going no further into the reason for his rescission than the bald fact that he is unwilling to comply with a requisition. He is certainly entitled to be so secretive (see *Re Starr-Bowkett Building Society and Sibun's Contract* (1889) 42 Ch D 386), but the risk of this poker play is that the court, seeing no more on the table than eminently reasonable requisitions, may simply take it that the vendor acted arbitrarily and so invalidly (cf *Steer* v *Crowley* (1863) 14 CB (NS) 337).

An incidental point worth noting is that the vendor's escape route may only be open to him where the requisition with which he is unwilling to comply relates 'to the title' (as in the National Conditions, 20th ed, No 10 (1)). If so, he cannot rescind in the face of unwelcome requisitions as to matters of conveyance (see *Leominster Properties Ltd* v *Broadway Finance Ltd* (1981) 42 P & CR 372). Sometimes, however, the provision will expressly extend the cover to requisitions 'as to title, conveyance or otherwise' (as in The Law Society's Conditions, 1973 Revision, No 18 (1); cp 1980 ed, No 16 (1), which is not precise).

In addition, two statutory restrictions on the right to rescind should be noted, both of which are actually mentioned in the two standard conditions just cited. First, rescission cannot be used to refute the purchaser's right to require any outstanding legal estates to be got in by the vendor (see s 42 (8) of the Law of Property Act 1925). Secondly, the right to rescind cannot arise on account of the purchaser's inalienable entitlement to have either the original or a copy of any post-1925 powers of attorney affecting the title (see s 125 (3) of the same Act).

To extract at last the essence of the right to rescind which conditions of sale commonly give to a vendor one can only say paradoxically that they generally confer an option on the *purchaser*. The option is simply whether or not he should accept, by withdrawing his requisition, a defective or doubtful title which the vendor has done his reasonable best to make good. This option remains open until the vendor has actually and properly rescinded (*Duddell* v *Simpson* (1866) 2 Ch App 102, and see *Selkirk* v *Romar Investments Ltd* [1963] 1 WLR 1415, at p 1420).

Finally, by way of painful postscript, vendors should be aware that a successful rescission vis-à-vis the purchaser, leaving him to whistle for his costs, etc, may yet be an expensive failure vis-à-vis the vendor's own estate agent. In other words, depending on the proper construction of the commission formula used, the estate agent may have earned and remain entitled to his commission notwithstanding the vendor's rescission (see per Lord Denning and Pearson LJ in *Scheggia* v *Gradwell* [1963] 1 WLR 1049, at pp 1056, 1065, respectively).

7 Verification

The vendor's obligations to deduce his title involve not only the delivery but also the proof of an abstract thereof. By this latter, in conveyancing parlance, he 'verifies' his title, and as observed by *Williams on Vendor and Purchaser* (3rd ed, at p 131, rising excitedly to italics, but sinking to using the word 'title' in the sense of ownership):

> The extreme importance of the proper verification of the abstract is too often overlooked. The abstract being the chief document delivered and the only document laid before and commented on by counsel, there is always a certain danger of losing sight of the fact, that *the most perfect abstract is no evidence at all of title*. It is only when we turn away from the abstract to the verification of it that the real proof of title begins. The most severe scrutiny of the abstract may be utterly useless if the purchaser's advisers are lax in exacting or examining the evidence in support of it.

In other words, the vendor having shown a good title on the abstract by way of statements must go on to show a good title in the full sense by way of proving the statements true (see per Cottenham LC in *Southby* v *Hutt* (1837) 2 My & Cr 207, at pp 212 and 213). The abstract states the documents and events constituting the vendor's evidence of ownership. How these stated documents and events are proved may perhaps best be indicated successively, giving documentary titles their proper priority.

Rather obviously, the starting step a vendor must take towards proving his documentary title is to produce the documents for the purchaser to examine. He has however, a considerable choice as to where he must do the producing, although expense may exercise some influence. In practice, the documents will tend to be produced at the office of the solicitor acting either for the vendor himself or for his mortgagee. Nonetheless, the proper places for production, according to author-itative authors, include neither of these offices, but are as follows: ' at the vendor's own residence, or upon or near the property sold, or in London as the vendor shall select' (see Williams' *Sale of Land*, p 42, note (i); also *Law Society's Digest*, Opinion No 121). Yet since this is a rule based solely on the practice of conveyancers, it may very well be that modern practice has effectively substituted for the vendor's residence his solicitor's office.

Alternatively the vendor, if he wishes, may produce the documents at some other improper place. The only difference used to be that, if the production was at a proper place, the purchaser had to meet all his own expenses himself (ie, of the examination by his solicitor, of travelling, etc), whilst the vendor had to meet any *extra* expenses caused to the purchaser by production elsewhere (see *Sharp* v *Page* (1815) Sug V & P 430, *Hughes* v *Wynne* (1836) 8 Sim 85, affirmed at (1837) 1 Jur 720). This rule was originally established by the courts in recognition of the practice of conveyancers, but then vendors found it too costly and practice veered away from it, via special conditions of sale, until eventually the change of practice was enacted in the Conveyancing Act 1881. Section 3 (6) of that Act, in effect, threw upon purchasers the full expenses of production of any documents *not* in the vendor's possession (for documents in his possession, the old rule remained). As a result, purchasers found themselves unforeseeably paying the extra expenses of production by the vendor's mortgagees (*Re Willett and Argenti* (1889) 60 LT 735) or by his trustees (see per North J in *Re Ebsworth and Tidy's Contract* (1889) 42 Ch D 23, at p 34). This was felt to veer too far in the vendor's favour, and the re-enactment in 1925 relieved the purchaser of his expenses of production of documents 'in the possession of the vendor *or his mortgagee or trustee*' (s 45 (4) (*a*) of the Law of Property Act 1925). As to such documents, therefore, the old pre-1881 Act rule still stands (thus, in theory, any extra expense occasioned by production, as so often in practice, at the vendor's mortgagee's solicitor's office could be passed on to the vendor). Any other documents not in such possession, however, may merely be produced wherever they can be found, without the vendor having to meet any extra expenses (see *Re Stuart & Olivant & Seadon's Contract* [1896] 2 Ch 328).

Even so the vendor does not, in this respect, have it all his own way. First, he will have to bear any expenses incurred by production of the documents for the purpose of preparing his abstract of title (*Re Johnson & Tustin* (1885) 30 Ch D 42). Secondly, he can be called upon to account for the documents not being in his possession since that is where, prima facie, they ought to be, the purchaser consequently having constructive notice of the possessor's rights (see s 13 of the Law of Property Act 1925). Thirdly, he is not exonerated from the expenses of obtaining possession of documents where necessary for the purpose of handing them over on completion (*Re Duthy and Jesson's Contract* [1898] 1 Ch 419). And fourthly, the purchaser, paying the piper, can call the tune; that is, he can, albeit at his own cost, compel the vendor to procure the production of all and any of the documents of title to the point of impossibility (see per Parker J in *Halkett* v *Dudley* [1907] 1 Ch 590, at pp 603–4). At least, the purchaser would be able to call this tune were it not that vendors have taken some general steps not to dance. The position is entirely subject to anything the contract expressly says about it (see s 45 (10) of the Law of Property Act 1925). Consequently, general conditions of sale might be expected to lift this terrible burden from the vendor's shoulders. And indeed the National Conditions, 20th ed, No 12 (3), do provide that the vendor shall be compelled neither to procure the production of documents of title not in the possession of himself, his mortgagee or trustee, 'nor to trace or state who has the possession of the same' (sic). But in surprising contrast The Law Society's Conditions, 1980 ed, No 12 (2), merely provide that 'the vendor shall at his own expense produce the relevant documents of title or an abstract, epitome of title or copy thereof (bearing in each case original markings of examination of all relevant documents of title or of examined abstracts thereof)'. The present writer finds it quite impossible to read this positive provision as negativing, even by implication, any of the four obligations upon a vendor set out at the beginning of the paragraph. Actually the provision seems to increase the obligations upon a vendor by further relieving the purchaser of the expenses of production of documents which are not in the possession of the vendor, etc, but which ought to be (cp s 45 (4) of the Law of Property Act 1925).

As *Williams on Vendor and Purchaser* (3rd ed, at p 131) points out, 'no part of the verification of the abstract is more important than the examination of the title deeds', adding that 'this is especially the case at the present day [ie, 1922], when abstracts are constantly delivered, which have been drawn in the most slovenly and unskilled manner'. Since the art of abstracting certainly thrives no better at this present day—after all ars longa, vita brevis—the examination at least retains its importance (see *Law Society's Digest*, Opinions No 89 and 95 (*a*) in Fourth (Cumulative) Supplement). The fourfold object with which the purchaser's solicitor examines the documents still is, as it always has been:

> to ascertain, first that what has been abstracted is correctly abstracted; secondly, that what is omitted is clearly immaterial; thirdly, that all the documents are perfect as respects execution, attestation, endorsed receipts, registration, stamps, etc; and fourthly, that there are no endorsed notices, nor any circumstances attending the mode of execution or attestation, etc, which are calculated to excite suspicion

(*Williams on Vendor and Purchaser* (loc cit)). Of course, where the abstract has been delivered in modern form, which involves 'machine-made facsimile copies' of documents of title (see p 113), the examination also may be much more mechanical since machines are expected not to lie.

In addition the practice is for the purchaser's solicitor to mark the abstract as examined—that is, to write on each document in the first margin under the date and stamp duty 'Examined with original' adding where, by whom, and when—and this, solicitors have been reminded from on high, is important (see *Law Society's Digest*, Opinion No 95 (*a*) in Fourth (Cumulative) Supplement). The importance of the marking lies in the fact that thereby the abstract may become a little better evidence of the evidence of ownership.

In practice, of course, production of the original is at least nine points of the proof of any abstracted document (or production of the counterpart on a sale subject to a lease: *Magdalen Hospital (Governors)* v *Knotts* (1878) 8 Ch D 709, affirmed (1879) 4 App Cas 324). Strictly, however, the proof involves not only that there is a document but also that it is the document (deed in writing) of the person alleged to have altered his legal position by it: ie, due execution should be shown (see *Williams on Vendor and Purchaser*, 3rd ed, at p 107). Nonetheless conveyancers rarely require any proof of execution—omnia praesumuntur rite et solemniter esse acta, no doubt they mutter to themselves, and indeed the Council of The Law

Society opined to this effect as early as 1859 (*Law Society's Digest*, Opinion No 125; see, however, per Collins MR in *Jared* v *Clements* [1903] 1 Ch 428, at p 431, as to whether a solicitor who accepted a forged receipt as discharging an equitable mortage had taken reasonable care). Naturally this presumption is rebuttable, so that purchasers would be entitled to have any suspicious circumstances attending the execution or otherwise explained away (see *Hobson* v *Bell, Glynn* v *Bell* (1839) 2 Beav 17). In particular, the presumption will not stand unless the documents are produced from the proper custody, which means any place where the documents might reasonably be expected to be found, which is a question of fact (see per Tindal CJ in *Meath* v *Winchester* (1836) 4 Cl & Fin 445, at p 540; also per Parke B in *Croughton* v *Blake* (1843) 12 M & W 205, at p 208, and *Doe d Jacobs* v *Phillips* (1845) 8 QB 158). Normally documents are produced by some other side's solicitor and no questions asked as to his custody, but might it not be more of a relevant comfort to find out where he found them?

Assuming that the documents are produced from proper custody with an absence of suspicious circumstances, the suggestion has been made that the purchaser is then bound to presume due execution, however recent the document, because this is what the court would do (in *Williams on Title*, 4th ed, p 658; see per Kekewich J in *Re Airey, Airey* v *Stapleton* [1897] 1 Ch 164, at p 169). This might seem reasonable but is perhaps too difficult to marry with the statutory saving that such documents prove themselves *provided* that they are twenty years old (s 4 of the Evidence Act 1938, replacing a like common law rule which required an age of thirty years: *Doe d Oldham* v *Wolley* (1828) 8 B & C 22).

What if the vendor has no documents to produce because they are lost, stolen or destroyed? This occurrence offers no reward to the purchaser in the way of avoiding the contract: provided that the vendor can produce secondary evidence of the contents and execution of the missing documents, the purchase must be completed (see *Re Halifax Commercial Banking Co and Wood* (1898) 79 LT 536; also *Halkett* v *Dudley* [1907] 1 Ch 590; cf per Leach V-C in *Barclay* v *Raine* (1823) 1 Sim & St 449). Of course, there are degrees of secondary evidence, ranging from duplicates, completed copies, examined abstracts, via drafts to mere parol evidence, and the less satisfactory degrees might mean that the vendor could not specifically enforce the contract. Also, the execution of missing documents has to be proved not presumed (*Bryant* v *Busk* (1827) 4 Russ 1; cp *Moulton* v *Edmonds* (1859) 1 De GF & J 246, as to very old documents). Again, the loss itself must be actually proved (see *Re Duthy and Jesson's Contract* [1898] 1 Ch 419), although nothing more in this respect than a statutory declaration of the circumstances and the search is usually required (see *Hart* v *Hart* (1841) 1 Hare 1, also deciding that due stamping will be presumed).

The *events* affecting the vendor's title are a different kettle of fish, their actual production and examination often being no more than a necromantic fancy. Instead, see *Williams on Vendor and Purchaser*, 3rd ed, at p 120:

> With regard to the evidence necessary to prove the facts as distinct from the documents stated in the abstract, *what a purchaser requires is testimony reduced to writing so that it may be preserved as a muniment of title.* So far as the facts may be proved by written evidence admissible in a court of justice, a purchaser is entitled to call for such evidence, if it can be obtained. But if none can be procured, he must accept other evidence such as it is the established practice to receive on sales.

The proper method of proof for each particular event is so much more a matter of commonsense than conveyancing principle, that no attempt at all will be made to give the details here, the reader being referred with relief to the bigger books.

Having thus satisfactorily disposed of the particular, two general topics may be touched upon.

The first topic is that the vendor's burden of evidencing events may be lightened in one of two ways. First, the purchaser may have to make do with a presumption. The general rule is that he will be 'bound to presume whatever a judge would at law direct the jury to presume, but not matters which the judge would leave to the jury to pronounce on the effect of the evidence' (*Williams on Vendor and Purchaser*, 3rd ed, at p 122: see also per Grant MR and Erskine LC in *Hillary* v *Waller* (1806) 12 Ves 239, at pp 254 and 270, respectively, and per Leach V-C in *Emery* v *Grocock* (1821) 6 Madd 54, at p 57; applied in effect in *MEPC Ltd* v *Christian-Edwards* [1981] AC 205, HL, as to abandonment of a contract). Secondly, by statute the expenses of obtaining the evidence of events, where not in the possession of the vendor or his mortgagee or trustee, are passed to the purchaser (s 45 (4) (*b*) of the Law of Property Act 1925). The story of this is so similar to that of the like provision as to production of documents that nothing need be added here (see p 126). Nothing, that is, save to say that neither of the standard sets of conditions seeks to preclude the purchaser from calling the tune and demanding that all and any events be evidenced albeit at his own expense.

The second topic is the evidencing of an absence of events. On a sale of land there are always many varieties of events which if they had happened would affect the vendor's title. For a few examples, easements may have been created, restrictive covenants breached, powers of appointment exercised, powers of attorney revoked, equitable joint tenancies severed (ie, that conundrum of a sale by the survivor which has been solved by the Law of Property (Joint Tenants) Act 1964) and so on. The problem is that, in the nature of things, a negative unlike a positive cannot be proved conclusively. In other words, whilst evidence can be appropriately aimed at abstracted events, unabstracted events which actually have not happened will have nothing to show for themselves but an absence of evidence. Yet if such unabstracted events have happened they may well affect the purchaser whether he knows of them or not. What can he do to satisfy himself of his safety from them? Very little, it might seem, recalling the impropriety of searching requisitions indicated earlier (p 117).

The ordinary rule of evidence seems to be that 'generally the only way of proving a negative is by presumption and the court has to apply the proper presumption' (per Channell J in *Over* v *Harwood* [1900] 1 QB 803, at p 806). Consequently, one learned writer has purportedly laid down the rules for sales of land that 'no proof of a negative can be required and in the absence of any evidence of the positive, the negative must be presumed' (see *Williams on Title*, 4th ed, p 667; immediately after this, however, the suggestion is made that a purchaser would be entitled to an answer to a requisition, which seems contrary to the view taken in *Re Ford & Hill* (1879) 10 Ch D 365). This rule might well appear reasonable since in essence it only means that the purchaser is, first, accepting that neither the vendor nor his solicitor is concealing anything (which might be a little risky for them), and for the rest relying on his implied covenants for title (for what they are worth).

Nonetheless, the older writers' views went further than this, being summed up as follows:

> That an event did not happen is in many cases a matter of inference rather than of positive proof: but if the event be such that its occurrence must necessarily have rendered the title different from that stated, *the purchaser is entitled to require some evidence from which its absence may reasonably be inferred*

(*Williams on Vendor and Purchaser*, 3rd ed, at p 121). The 'some evidence' envisaged consisted of statutory declarations by persons who would be likely to know if the event had happened (see per Lord Ellenborough, *Doe lessee of Banning* v *Griffin* (1812) 15 East 293, at p 294; *Greaves* v *Greenwood* (1877) 2 Ex D 289; *Re Jackson, Jackson* v *Ward* [1907] 2 Ch 354). And this view has gained some judicial support in a conveyancing context (from Fry J in *Re Marsh and Granville* (1882) 24 Ch D 11, at p 19). In other words, sufficient if not conclusive evidence is to be sought going beyond a mere absence of concealment. However, accepting this older view does seem to involve the uncertainty of somewhere drawing a line between the permitted pursuit of specific negatives and the prohibited putting of searching requisitions.

8 Acceptance

The end of a deduction and investigation of title usually occurs when the purchaser capitulates, as it were, and accepts the vendor's title. This is usually the end because by doing this the purchaser is taken to have waived any objections he might otherwise have had to the title as abstracted (*Burnell* v *Brown* (1820) 1 Jac & W 168; *Bown* v *Stenson* (1857) 24 Beav 631). However, the purchaser's waiver will extend neither to anything not appearing on the face of the abstract (see per Romilly MR in *Bousfield* v *Hodges* (1863) 33 Beav 90, at p 94, also *Turquand* v *Rhodes* (1868) 37 LJ Ch 830; see also *Southby* v *Hutt* (1837) 2 My & Cr 207, as to verification at any time), nor to mere matters of conveyance (see per Fry J in *Re Gloag and Miller's Contract* (1883) 23 Ch D 320, at pp 327–8).

The acceptance of title, with its inherent waiver of objections may be, but rarely is, *express*. Most often, in practice, the acceptance will be found *deemed* to have occurred by virtue of contractual provisions as to the time for requisitions and observations on answers thereto (*Re Martin's Bank Ltd's Contract* (1969) 113 SJ 980). Occasionally, the acceptance may merely by *implied* from the purchaser's conduct.

An implied aceptance of title depends on whether it appeared from the purchaser's conduct that he intended to waive any objections. This is a question of fact only to be determined in the light of the whole of the circumstances of the case. The quality of conduct to be looked for involves the performance by the purchaser of acts which a prudent purchaser would not normally perform until a good title has been shown, ie, not until completion would be bound to take place (see *Haydon* v *Bell* (1838) 1 Beav 337; *Hyde* v *Warden* (1877) 3 Ex D 72). In addition, the inference from the acts should not be nullified by a continued insistence on the part of the purchaser on any objections (see *Burroughs* v *Oakley* (1819) 3 Swanst 159).

Conduct implying acceptance of the title may take many forms (eg, payment of the purchase price), two only of which are worthy of especial mention. First, the submission of a draft conveyance for approval by or on behalf of the vendor is significant if not conclusive (see per Plumer MR in *Burroughs* v *Oakley* (1819) 3 Swanst 159, at p 171; the circumstances there were that questions arising on the title had still to be discussed; see also *Sweet* v *Meredith* (1862) 8 Jur (NS) 637). In practice, however, the draft conveyance very often accompanies the purchaser's requisitions, the covering letter stating that it is submitted subject to the answers being satisfactory. This time-saving device should never imply acceptance of the title (see eg, *Re Spollon and Long's Contract* [1936] Ch 713), and both The Law Society's Conditions 1980 ed, No 17 (3), and the Statutory Conditions, No 8 (3), but not the National Conditions, provide expressly that delivery of the draft or engrossment should not prejudice any outstanding requisition.

The second sort of conduct worthy of mention here is the purchaser occupying before completing. In a circumstantial vacuum, this may not be enough—the 'bare fact of taking possession has over and over again been held not to be a waiver of objections to title' (per curiam in *Re Barrington, ex parte Sidebotham* (1835) 2 Mont & A 146; see also *Simpson* v *Sadd* (1854) 4 De G M & G 665). But, like submission of a draft conveyance, occupation before completion has always been treated as most significant (see per Plumer MR in *Burroughs* v *Oakley* (1819) 3 Swanst 159, at p 169; also *Bown* v *Stenson* (1857) 24 Beav 631, at p 637, where Romilly MR even said that taking possession would give rise to a presumption of waiver). If, however, the occupation is taken by virtue of a condition in the contract, then no acceptance of the title can be presumed, whether or not the condition expressly excludes any waiver (see *Bolton* v *London School Board* (1878) 7 Ch D 766; also *Boxhall* v *Jackson* (1825) 2 LJ (OS) Ch 100, *Stevens* v *Guppy* (1828) 3 Russ 171). In practice, the standard sets of conditions of sale do provide for occupation before completion, adding that no acceptance of title should be thereby deemed (see National Conditions, 20th ed, No 8 (3), and Law Society's Conditions, 1980 ed, No 18 (3)). But if the contract makes no such provision, a purchaser would be unwise to take occupation without ensuring that any possible presumption of acceptance is rebutted by stating and continuing to insist on any objections he may have to the title (see *Rellie* v *Pyke* [1936] 1 All ER 345; also *Becker* v *Partridge* [1966] 2 QB 155, where the purchaser seeking and getting rescission was still in possession of the property at the date of the hearing, but apparently by agreement between the parties and without prejudice to the position). For certain other consequences of possession before completion, see pp 177–178.

E   LEASEHOLD TITLE

1   Title

The old conveyancers' practice which became law, of requiring title to be shown for at least a sixty-year period (see p 95), used to apply as much to leaseholds as to freeholds. Hence, the alternatives depended on the age of the lease. On the one hand, if the lease was more than sixty years old, the vendor would always have to show the lease itself but then only the leasehold title for the sixty years before the contract; the freehold title was not shown, leases of that age being presumed validly granted although having themselves to be produced 'in order to prove that the vendor could assign the very interest which he sold' (*Williams on Vendor and Purchaser*, 3rd ed, at p 91; *Frend* v *Buckley* (1870) LR 5 QB 213; also *Williams* v *Spargo* [1893] WN 100). This was not too onerous for vendors. On the other hand, however, if the lease was less than sixty years old, then the vendor would, in addition to both the lease itself and the leasehold title, have to show the freehold title for the balance of the full period (*Purvis* v *Rayer* (1821) 9 Price 488; *Souter* v *Drake* (1834) 5 B & Ad 992). Equally, if the sale was of an underlease not yet sixty years old, the purchaser was entitled to see the title of the underlessor and of every superior lessor for the period between the grant of the underlease and the beginning of the sixty years. The elementary explanation for all this is that unless he sees that the lease or underlease was validly granted, the purchaser simply has not been shown sufficient evidence that he will get the property sold.

This paradise for purchasers of shorter leases was naturally not over long tolerated by, or on behalf of, vendors whose principal difficulty in deducing title often proved to be in inducing the co-operation of lessors. Accordingly, the purchaser's investigation of title would be strictly restricted by the contract, and special stipulations with this object were submitted to so often that statutory recognition was eventually accorded. First, the Vendor and Purchaser Act 1874, after reducing the period of title to forty years, went on to deprive any purchaser of leaseholds of any right to see the freehold title (ss 1 and 2, First Rule, applying to lessees also). Then the Conveyancing Act 1881 went further and deprived purchasers from underlessees of any sight of 'the title to the leasehold reversion,' adding that purchasers should also assume in every case that the lease or underlease (even if less old than the period of title) and all superior leases were validly granted (s 3 (1), (4) and (5), see also s 13 applying to lessees). These statutory provisions have now been re-enacted, substantially the same, by the Law of Property Act 1925, which also reduced the period of title to thirty years (ss 44 (1)–(4) and 45 (2) and (3)), and have not been affected by the Law of Property Act 1969, which further reduced the period of title to fifteen years (s 23).

Illustration rather than information may enable the operation of these statutory provisions to be seen more clearly:

IF:

> F, the freeholder, grants a lease to L;
> L grants an underlease to UL;
> L sells his lease to $P1$;
> $P1$ sells the lease to $P2$;
> UL grants a sub-lease to SL; and
> UL sells his underlease to PU.

THEN:

> $P1$ sees only the lease;
> $P2$ sees only the lease and the assignment to $P1$; and
> PU similarly sees only the underlease (but see below).

ALSO (although title on the grant, as opposed to the assignment, of leases and underleases is not strictly within this book):

> L does not see anything;
> UL sees only the lease; and
> SL sees only the underlease.

This algebraic operation agrees with that ascribed to the statutory provisions in text-books, so far as the writer knows, nem con (see, eg, *Gibson's Conveyancing*, 20th ed, at pp 115–16). It also accords, the writer feels, with the legislative intention. Unfortunately, this, to some extent, involves overcoming or overlooking certain awkward judicial dicta on sales by underlessees. The difficulties all stem from *Gosling* v *Woolf* [1893] 1 QB 39, where the Divisional Court might easily be taken to have decided that the purchaser of an underlease is entitled to see the lease out of which the underlease was granted. Thus Pollock B is reported as saying (ibid, p 40):

> Then by s 3 (1) [of the Conveyancing Act 1881] "Under a contract to sell and assign a term of years derived out of a leasehold interest in land, the intended assign shall not have the right to call for the title to the leasehold reversion." I am of the opinion that these words mean the reversion of that leasehold interest out of which the term of years contracted to be sold and assigned is derived.

Yet if reference is made to the less abbreviated report of the case at 68 LT 89, normally a less authoritative series, it can be seen that, notwithstanding the talk in counsel's argument about the sale and purchase of an underlease, the agreement in question in fact provided for the *grant* of an underlease. In other words the actual unexceptional decision was that a prospective underlessee is entitled to inspect the lease out of which the underlease is to be granted. What is more, from the fuller LT version, Pollock B's dicta are reported as going no further than this. Nonetheless, rather more recently the QB heresy has gained a none-too reluctant adherent in Romer LJ who uttered the obiter that:

> When Wroxhall Estates Ltd took their assignment from Mrs Sykes the position would appear to be (though the point was not argued before us and I do not wish to be taken as expressing any definite opinion upon it) that the company were entitled to see the head-lease to Miss Strutt as well as the sub-lease by her to Mrs Sykes (*Gosling v Woolf*)

(in *Drive Yourself Hire Co (London) Ltd v Strutt* [1954] 1 QB 250, at p 278). However, since then, in *Becker v Partridge* [1966] 2 QB 155, the judgment of the Court of Appeal included the following passages:

> Owing to the provisions of s 44 (2) and s 45 (1) of the Law of Property Act 1925, the underlease of 28 December 1963, provided for as the commencement of title in clause 3 of the agreement, was in fact the same as that provided for by law, and the purchaser's enquiries were restricted accordingly

(at p 169); and later:

> unlike the [plaintiff] purchaser, the vendor was entitled by law to call for the lease out of which the underlease by Mrs Smith to him was to be granted

(at p 169). Each of these passages embodies the accepted and illustrated operation of the statutory provisions. So the vendor or purchaser of an underlease can only say that he knows where he ought to be but is not yet quite sure where he is!

Whatever their precise operation, however, the statutory provisions are not impenetrable. A purchaser of leaseholds may still get some sort of a sight of the higher title if he first manages to detect a defect in it somehow else (see per Cotton LJ in *Jones v Watts* (1890) 43 Ch D 574, at p 584; in fact the purchaser's most specific allegation was that the property was 'subject to divers restrictive covenants' and this was rejected out of hand as mere fishing).

In addition, the provisions that the purchaser should assume that all leases, underleases and superior leases were validly granted only apply 'unless the contrary appears', and in any case are no more effective than a contractual stipulation to the same effect (s 45 (2), (3) and (11) of the Law of Property Act 1925). Thus in *Becker v Partridge* [1966] 2 QB 155 the Court of Appeal's judgment continued the first passage quoted above as follows:

> But the assumptions which s 45 (1) and s 45 (3) require a purchaser to make are only "unless the contrary appears"; and, unless a purchaser is prohibited from raising objection to the title by a bona fide and clear special condition, a purchaser will not be prevented from objecting to the vendor's title by reason of a defect which the purchaser discovers by other means.

(at p 169; the defects in that case were discovered from a letter addressed to the purchaser's solicitors by mistake: see (1967) 110 SJ 795).

2 Notice

Not only may the statutory provisions be penetrated from outside, but by precautions taken in advance they may be escaped altogether, for they also apply in so far as a contrary intention is not expressed in the contract (ss 44 (11) and 45 (10), proviso, of the Law of Property Act 1925; see eg, *Re Pursell and Deakin's Contract* [1893] WN 152, agreement by freeholder to deliver an abstract of his title to potential lessee showed a contrary intention). So the question may be asked what, if any, intention should the parties express in their contract? Since the statutory provisions favour the vendor, the question is really one for the purchaser, the answer depending largely on what risks he runs by submitting to the open contract position. In practice the question occurs more often on the grant than on the sale of a lease, so that this aspect also may be mentioned.

The most obvious risk arising from the restrictions on the investigation of title is simply that the lease may not be validly granted. This is a risk which may well be taken to diminish, without disappearing, with the age of the lease. Whether or not a purchaser or lessee should accept such a risk as this ought to depend largely on how much money, in the way of premium, improvements, repairs, etc, he would be gambling on the lease's validity.

In addition to the invalidity risk, there is the nasty aspect of notice. In the good old days, before the position was complicated by any statutory provisions, a purchaser of leaseholds would suffer constructive notice of any equitable interests which he could have discovered by making the fullest investigation of title then possible under an open contract (see per Turner LJ in *Wilson* v *Hart* (1866) LR 1 Ch 463, at p 467). In other words, by agreeing to any restrictions on his investigation he would run much the same risk of unknown equities that a purchaser of freeholds would do today (see p 101; also s 199 (1) (ii) and (2) of the Law of Property Act 1925). Thus owners of equitable incumbrances appearing on the title to the freehold or superior leasehold before the grant of the lease were not to be prejudiced by the special stipulations submitted to by assignees of the lease (see per Romilly MR in *Peto* v *Hammond* (1861) 30 Beav 495, at pp 507 and 508; after its grant, the lease would, of course, be a legal estate taking priority over any equitable interest subsequently appearing on the higher title).

Then, subject to contract, statute endorsed the restrictions imposed in practice (ie, s 2, First Rule, of the Vendor and Purchaser Act 1874 and s 3 (1) of the Conveyancing Act 1881). This was, essentially, an alteration of the open contract position. Nonetheless, the statutory provisions were held, in the present context, to be no better than the special stipulations which they had superseded. Consequently, purchasers of leaseholds still suffered from constructive notice to exactly the same extent as before even though a condition precedent to their full investigation of title was now a special enabling stipulation in the contract (*Patman* v *Harland* (1881) 17 Ch D 353, especially per Jessel MR at p 359). This was felt to be rather tough on the purchasers and in 1925 some relief was sent to them in the form of a provision that:

> Where by reason of [the statutory provisions], an intending lessee or assign is not entitled to call for the title to the freehold or to a leasehold reversion, as the case may be, he shall not, where the contract is made after the commencement of this Act, be deemed to be affected with notice of any matter or thing of which, if he had contracted that such title should be furnished, he might have had notice

(s 45 (5) of the Law of Property Act 1925). As relief, however, this can be regarded as more soft-headed than soft-hearted.

Although the relieving provision (s 44 (5)) is said to apply 'only if and so far as a contrary intention is not expressed in the contract' (s 45 (11)), it cannot really be regarded as a mere term of the parties' open contract. To be effective at all the provision must be treated as a rule of law adversely affecting all those persons who would otherwise be able to enforce their equitable interests against the purchaser or lessee on the basis of his constructive notice. Thus, to take two particular examples, inconvenient pre-1926 restrictive covenants and any equitable mortgages by deposit of documents (neither being registrable, see below), may be defeated to all intents and purposes by a simple grant or assignment of a lease in pursuance of an open contract (see (1944) 8 Conv (NS) 145, also (1956) 20 Conv (NS) 450-1, the specific s 44 (5) being taken to prevail over the general s 13 of the Law of Property

Act 1925, but cf per Romer LJ in *Drive Yourself Hire Co (London) Ltd* v *Strutt* [1954] 1 QB 250, at p 278). In other words property rights may now be destroyed by unforeseen future arrangements between third parties. This is tougher on these equitable incumbrances than it ever was on purchasers of leaseholds since the latter at least might have mitigated, had they wished, their foreseeable risk by insisting on a full investigation of title.

Equitable incumbrances as a whole, however, are not left so badly off as may seem at first sight, for these interests are mostly registrable under the Land Charges Act 1972. If so registered, then the sweeping effect is that that 'shall be deemed to constitute actual notice . . . to all persons and for all purposes connected with the land affected' (s 198 (1) of the Law of Property Act 1925). The clear conflict between this and the relieving s 44 (5) has never been directly resolved, but we do have the benefit of an obiter observation of Simonds J that s 198 'appears, notwithstanding the unqualified language of s 44 (5), to affect a lessee with notice of all those charges which are registered under the Land Charges Act 1925' (in *White* v *Bijou Mansions Ltd* [1937] Ch 610, at p 621; on appeal [1938] Ch 351). Although almost all writers appear to accept this, in at least one authoritative place a preference has been expressed editorially for the more precise words of s 44 (5) (see (1938) 3 Conv (NS) 116), but the trouble is that neither choice ought to be open. If s 44 (5) be preferred, an exception to the scheme of registration has been created which would severely penalise equitable incumbrances. If s 198 (1) be preferred, which seems more likely, then what the Act has given to lessees and their assigns with one hand it has taken away with the other, for without a sight of the freehold title, no satisfactory search can be made against the appropriate estate owners.

What is more, this vicious flaw, far from being rectified, received recognition in the Law of Property Act 1969. In explicit effect, no compensation is made available to purchasers of leaseholds in respect of unknown land charges registered against freehold or superior leasehold estate owners (see the definition of 'registered land charge' in s 25 (10) of the 1969 Act and generally p 100). Equally, although the compensation provisions are made available to the grantee of an underlease, they are expressly withheld from the grantee of a lease out of the freehold (see s 25 (9) of the 1969 Act; the underlessee's potential compensation is confined to land charges registered against the immediately superior leasehold title which, of course, he can investigate: see s 25 (10) of the 1969 Act). All this unhappy reflection of the unsatisfactory consequences of the restrictions upon the investigation of leasehold titles under an open contract is due directly to the extremely short-sighted view taken by the Law Commission that any hardship arising has 'nothing to do with the system of registration of land charges' (Law Com No 18, p 11). And the worst is yet to come: compensation is still not available to the purchaser of a lease who has contracted out of the restrictions on his investigation of title (as to which see below). In other words, if such a purchaser contracts to investigate title as though he were purchasing the freehold, he will not enjoy any statutory protection against pre-root registered land charges. This discrimination in favour of purchasers of freeholds is surely disgraceful whether deliberate or an oversight (see also Stephen Cretney at (1969) 32 MLR 485).

3   Practice

These then are the risks of invalidity and notice which a purchaser of leaseholds, or a lessee, runs under an open contract. What, therefore, should he do? If the lease is short at a rack rent, little is ventured and little would be gained by insisting on the fullest investigation of title (see *Clayton* v *Leech* (1889) 41 Ch D 103, at pp 105 and

106). If, however, the consideration involves a premium, the lease reserving only a ground rent, the picture and the practice should change. Indeed, the suggestion has even been made that the solicitor who allowed the open contract position to pass untouched might conceivably find himself liable for professional negligence (in Walford's *Sale of Land*, 2nd ed, at p 113, on the strength of certain comments by Lopes and Rigby LJJ in *Imray* v *Oakshette* [1897] 2 QB 218, at pp 225 and 229, respectively, where an underlessee was held to have acted negligently in not looking at his lessor's title and so refused relief against forfeiture). This suggestion, however, would actually appear to have been put per incuriam. Section 182 (1) of the Law of Property Act 1925 affords blanket protection for any solicitor who leaves his client resting on the 'stipulations . . . which . . . are by this Act made applicable to any contract of sale . . .' Yet, first, this should not free his conscience; the section indeed adds that the insertion of other stipulations is not impliedly improper (subs (2)). And secondly, what about any mortgagee's solicitor? If the lessee at a premium, or his assign, seeks financial assistance he rarely gets it under a contract. Therefore his mortgagee is never prevented by the statutory provisions from insisting on the fullest investigation of title, and therefore never statutorily protected from constructive notice if he does not (cf s 8 (2) of the Trustee Act 1925 as to trustee-mortgagees).

Lastly a thought may be spared for what, if anything, the standard sets of general conditions of sale contain affecting the investigation of title on a sale of leaseholds. Are the statutory provisions, by added ingredients, softened or hardened? Well, the Statutory Conditions contain nothing at all relevant to leasehold titles, whilst the National Conditions, 20th ed, No 11, deals only with aspects of leasehold sales other than the investigation of title. But this lack is amply balanced by The Law Society's Conditions of Sale, 1980 ed, No 8 (2) (*a*), which represents a fair attempt at consistency with current practice. It restates the open contract rule that the root of title should be the lease which is being sold but in addition provides that where that lease was granted not more than fifteen years before the contract and for a term exceeding twenty-one years then, in effect, the freehold title must be deduced as well for at least fifteen years (ie, the statutory period). Further, the condition brings in superior leasehold titles for investigation where an underlease is being sold of appropriate age and length and also entitles the purchaser to require an abstract or copy of the immediately superior lease in all cases.

4   Misdescription and non-disclosure

In the preceding pages were seen the confines within which a purchaser of leasehold land may have to conduct his investigation of title. Now a handful of other matters peculiar to leasehold titles may be looked at.

Notwithstanding all the statutory provisions in his favour, a prospective vendor of leaseholds must take care that his descriptions and disclosures are all that they ought to be. Thus, neither may underleases be misdescribed as leases nor even vice versa (see *Re Russ and Brown's Contract* [1934] Ch 34 and *Re Thompson and Cottrell's Contract* [1943] Ch 97). But apparently it is all right to describe a 'sub-underlease' as an 'underlease' since the former is not really a conveyancing expression in established use and since the latter is in some sense an accurate description anyway (*Becker* v *Partridge* [1966] 2 QB 155). Again, where the vendor has an underlease, the purchaser should be given notice before the contract if the head lease comprises more property than that sold (see *Re Lloyds Bank Ltd and Lillington's Contract* [1912] 1 Ch 601); the reason is the risk of forfeiture on breaches of covenant in respect of the rest of the property. However, this objection that the property sold is included with other property in the head lease has been held by the Court of Appeal to be weakened 'by the fact that the property is part of a house, and it is practically obvious that it would almost certainly be the subject of a letting of the whole house' (*Becker* v *Partridge* [1966] 2 QB 155, at p 171). This seems a sensible variation of the rule that a vendor need not disclose patent defects in title.

More important, perhaps, notwithstanding the normal rule that notice of a document is notice of its contents, a vendor of leaseholds is under a duty to disclose any covenants in the lease which are unusually onerous for leases of that sort (*Re White and Smith's Contract* [1896] 1 Ch 637, see also per Tomlin J in *Melzak* v *Lilienfeld* [1926] Ch 480, at pp 490–2; what is unusual here is a question of fact: see *Flexman* v *Corbett* [1930] 1 Ch 672). The vendor may perform this duty either by express disclosure or by giving the purchaser a reasonable opportunity of discovering the covenants, as by proper inspection of the lease (*Molyneux* v *Hawtrey* [1903] 2 KB 487; cf *Hunt (Charles) Ltd* v *Palmer* [1931] 2 Ch 287, where such an opportunity did not suffice since there had been a positive misdescription). In addition, the purchaser may object to the title where the covenants in a head lease are more onerous than those in the underlease he is buying, since the risk of forfeiture arises again (see per Wood V-C in *Darlington* v *Hamilton* (1854) Kay 550, at pp 558–9; as to the position on forfeiture, see s 146 of the Law of Property Act 1925 and *Ewart* v *Fryer* [1901] 1 Ch 499).

In practice, the two matters mentioned in the preceding paragraph should each be catered for by the conditions of sale. Thus the National Conditions, 20th ed, No 11 (2), does shortly state 'The lease or underlease or a copy thereof having been made available, the purchaser (whether he has inspected the same or not) shall be deemed to have bought with full notice of the contents thereof'. The Law Society's Conditions, 1980 ed, contain an equivalent provision: No 8 (2) (*b*).

A purchaser under a contract containing such a condition as this has probably precluded himself from complaining about anything in the lease (see *Lawrie* v *Lees* (1880) 14 Ch D 249, at pp 252 and 257, also *Re Derby and Fergusson's Contract* [1912] 1 Ch 479). He could still complain, however, if the contents of the lease have in any way been misrepresented or misdescribed by the vendor (see *Flight* v *Barton* (1832) 3 My & K 282; *Van* v *Corpe* (1834) 3 My & K 269). Then the National Conditions, 20th ed, No 11 (4), further flatly states that 'No objection shall be taken on account of the covenants in an underlease not corresponding with the covenants in any superior lease'. Here, the Law Society's Conditions, 1980 ed, are much more sporting: there is now no equivalent provision. In this connection reference may be made to two Court of Appeal cases which arose entirely because the solicitors acting for intending underlessees failed to inspect the head lease, namely *Hill* v *Harris* [1965] 2 QB 601 and *Becker* v *Partridge* [1966] 2 QB 155 (concerning covenants restricting user and underletting without consent respectively).

5   Breaches of covenant?

Even if the covenants to be found in the lease or underlease sold and any superior leases are not unusually onerous, the anxious purchaser will still not rest in peace until he is assured that there have been no breaches (this assumes the usual proviso for re-entry to be present). For it is clear that:

> if an interest in leasehold is subject to determination by the exercise of a right of re-entry for breaches of covenant which have already been committed, then that is a title which is not a good title, for it is defeasible

(*Becker* v *Partridge* [1966] 2 QB 155, at p 171). A fortiori a purchaser needs to know about pending proceedings for forfeiture 'for otherwise he might be purchasing something which, on service of the proceedings for forfeiture, had ceased to exist' (per Megarry V-C in *Selim Ltd* v *Bickenhall Engineering Ltd* [1981] 1 WLR 1318, at p 1323, referring to *Pips (Leisure Productions) Ltd* v *Walton* (1980) 260 EG 601 where the title was bad because judgment for forfeiture had already been obtained and it made no difference that relief against forfeiture was being sought). However, such proceedings are registrable as a 'pending land action' (ie, within s 17 (1) of the Land Charges Act 1972: *Selim Ltd* v *Bickenhall Engineering Ltd*, supra). If not registered, the action will not bind a purchaser for value without express notice (Land Charges Act 1972, s 5 (7)) but that does not necessarily mean that he will take free of the breach of covenant and the liability to fresh forfeiture proceedings. Consequently vendors of leaseholds are, as they always have been, under an obligation to show an absence of any breaches of any covenants in their own or any superior lease (see *Palmer* v *Goren* (1856) 25 LJ Ch 841; this includes payment of all rent reserved). One should not be too surprised, however, to learn that the burden of performing this obligation has been eased, if not removed.

To this end of relieving vendors of leaseholds, the original practice of conveyancers was to stipulate in the contract that the production of the receipt for the last payment of rent due before completion should be *conclusive* evidence of the absence of breaches of any covenant right up to actual completion (see *Williams on Vendor and Purchaser*, 3rd ed, at p 340, note (*g*); acceptance of rent, of course, does not necessarily constitute a waiver and never goes beyond the due date for payment, see, eg, *Oak Property Co Ltd* v *Chapman* [1947] KB 886, and *Atkin* v *Rose* [1923] 1 Ch 522). Then statute intervened, wielding this stipulation as a new term of an open contract, but softening the blow by only binding the purchaser to assume an absence of breaches '*unless the contrary appears*', ie, the receipt is now prima facie evidence only (s 3 (4) and (5) of the Conveyancing Act 1881, replaced by s 45 (2) and (3) of the Law of Property Act 1925).

This softening means that the statutory stipulation simply will not apply if the purchaser is able to show the fact of some breach of covenant, in which case the vendor, unless he remedy the breach, will be unable to enforce the contract at law or in equity since his title will have been shown to be defective (*Re Highett and Bird's Contract* [1903] 1 Ch 287). In the case cited, the Court of Appeal held this to be so notwithstanding that the purchaser knew of the breach (which was of a repairing covenant) before the contract and that the vendor had agreed to a lower price in consequence. This would appear to contradict the ordinary rule that a purchaser's pre-contract knowledge of defects in the vendor's title to that extent rebuts the implication that a good title will be shown. Hence, Romer LJ in a later case felt compelled to say of the decision:

> The arguments proceeded on the assumption that the vendor was in the same position as if he had expressly agreed to make a good title. The case was decided on that footing, and it is not to be taken as an authority for any case in which there is not an express contract by the vendor to make a good title

(in *Re Allen and Driscoll's Contract* [1904] 2 Ch 226, at p 231). Nonetheless, a preferable explanation may be to point out that the purchaser's pre-contract knowledge only subjects him to irremovable defects. Breach of a repairing covenant can almost always be remedied and the purchaser may merely contemplate the vendor doing this before completion, ie, there is insufficient to rebut the implication of a good title (see, eg, per Alderson B in *Barnett* v *Wheeler* (1841) 7 M & W 364, at p 367, referred to in *Re Highett and Bird's Contract*, ante). Therefore, if the purchaser knows of and is to accept a remediable breach of covenant, the contract should say so; then if the vendor is in fact compelled to remedy the breach in order to show a good title, he can charge the cost of doing so to the purchaser (see *Lockharts* v *Bernard Rosen & Co* [1922] 1 Ch 433). A similar result was reached in the case of a compulsory purchase of leaseholds where, because the acquiring authority knew of the dilapidations, it was treated as having contracted to buy the property in its existing condition, so that it had to indemnify the 'vendor' against all relevant breaches of covenant (*Re King, Robinson* v *Gray* [1962] 1 WLR 632). Unhappily, in his judgment, Buckley J seemed somehow to insinuate both that an express agreement to take the property in its existing state was necessary for this result and that the purchaser's knowledge of that state would do instead (see ibid, p 655; reversed on other aspects at [1963] Ch 459).

Equally, the statutory stipulation whereby the last receipt is only prima facie evidence, will not cover a continuing breach of covenant even if the landlord actually accepts rent right up to completion, for the lease would remain forfeitable (see *Re Taunton and West of England Perpetual Benefit Building Society and Roberts' Contract* [1912] 2 Ch 381). This reverses the position under the old practice of stipulating that the last receipt should be conclusive evidence, where purchasers had been held unable to object to continuing breaches (see Parker J, ibid, at p 385, also *Bull* v *Hutchens* (1863) 32 Beav 615; and *Lawrie* v *Lees* (1880) 14 Ch D 249). However, even with such a special stipulation of conclusiveness up to completion, the vendor was never able to compel the purchaser to submit to new breaches of covenant committed after the contract (*Howell* v *Kightley* (1856) 21 Beav 331). What is more, such a conclusive stipulation would by no means necessarily enable the vendor to obtain the equitable remedy of specific performance, although keeping the purchaser bound at law (*Beyfus* v *Lodge* [1925] Ch 350, deposit forfeited, cf now s 49 of the Law of Property Act 1925).

In addition, the statutory stipulation is inapplicable where there is a peppercorn rent, or presumably any other rent in kind, which would be rendered without payment (see *Re Moody and Yates' Contract* (1885) 30 Ch D 344). Again, on the sale of an underlease, production of a receipt given by a superior lessor, even though the rent was paid to him by the vendor under threat of distress, does not comply with the statutory provisions; what is required is the last receipt for rent due under the underlease (*Re Higgins and Percival* (1888) 57 LJ Ch 807). Further, if the receipt is not given by the original lessor, then the purchaser may be able to insist on having the title of the person giving the receipt deduced from the original lessor. This is not certain; it would fly in the face of the restrictions on investigation discussed at p 131. Nonetheless, a purchaser was in one case held entitled to see such title (*Turner* v *Marriott* (1867) LR 3 Eq 744), but there the material facts included an actual breach of covenant plus an allegation of waiver, which goes a bit further than the ordinary case (see also *Pegler* v *White* (1864) 33 Beav 403, where there was a doubt as to who was the current lessor which precluded specific performance).

Neither of the standard sets of general conditions of sale, in their current editions, appears much concerned about this aspect of leasehold titles. Both provide for every sale that the property should be taken in its 'actual state and condition' (The Law Society's Conditions, 1980 ed, No 5 (2) (*a*) and National Conditions, 20th ed, No 13 (3)) and this would cover, inter alia, any breaches of a lessee's repairing covenant (see *Butler* v *Mountview Estates Ltd* [1951] 2 KB 563; cf *Re Englefield Holdings Ltd and Sinclair's Contract* [1962] 1 WLR 1119). Apart from this, the National Conditions (20th ed, No 11 (3)) also provide that 'the purchaser' should 'assume without proof that the person giving the receipt, though not the original lessor, is the reversioner expectant on the said lease or underlease or his duly authorised agent'; The Law Society's Conditions (1980 ed, No 8 (6)) are to like effect.

6 Licence to assign

One final aspect of the sale of leaseholds remains, that irritant, the lessor's licence to assign. Where the lease, as it usually will, requires this, the covenant will nonetheless count as 'unusually onerous' within the vendor's duty of disclosure (*Reeve* v *Berridge* (1888) 20 QBD 523; also *Becker* v *Partridge* [1966] 2 QB 155; see further above). Then, following an open contract, the vendor is bound to procure the licence at his own expense, since otherwise he would fail to show a good title (see *Bain* v *Fothergill* (1874) LR 7 HL 158). Even if the lessor seems to be withholding his licence unreasonably when he should not (see, eg, s 29 of the Landlord and Tenant Act 1927), the title might still be found too uncertain to be forced upon an unwilling purchaser, at law or in equity (*Re Marshall and Salt's Contract* [1900] 2 Ch 202; cf *Young* v *Ashley Gardens Properties Ltd* [1903] 2 Ch 112, where a vendor-lessee obtained a declaration against the lessor). Yet in a slightly earlier case (not cited) the title had been forced on the purchaser on the ground that the lessor was with certainty unreasonable (*White* v *Hay* (1895) 72 LT 281; see also per Maugham J, *Curtis Moffat Ltd* v *Wheeler* [1929] 2 Ch 224, at p 236). Alternatively, of course, where the lessor is certainly unreasonable in withholding his licence, the parties could go ahead with the assignment and the purchaser-lessee later seek a declaration of validity (ie, as in *Theodorou* v *Bloom* [1964] 1 WLR 1152). Incidentally, it may be noted that a contract can go 'off' before exchange if a lessor intimates that his licence will be withheld and that this may cause other difficulties, eg, over estate agent's commission (see *Wilkinson* v *Brown* [1966] 1 WLR 194).

Procuring the licence to assign is regarded as a matter not of title but of conveyance, so that the vendor ordinarily has until completion for this (*Ellis* v *Rogers* (1885) 29 Ch D 661; *Smith* v *Butler* [1900] 1 QB 694; *Property and Bloodstock Ltd* v *Emerton* [1968] Ch 94). If by then the vendor has still not succeeded in his procuration, he will prima facie have to repay the deposit plus interest together with the purchaser's expenses incurred in investigating the title (*Re Marshall and Salt's Contract*, ante; *Re Hargreaves & Thompson's Contract* (1886) 32 Ch D 454). However, the contract may well have been made more cautiously as expressly subject to the lessor's licence being forthcoming. In this case, the vendor must, in his procuration, still employ his best endeavours, for if he does not, he may easily find himself paying general damages to the purchaser for loss of bargain (*Day* v *Singleton* [1899] 2 Ch 320), whilst if he does, but unsuccessfully, he will be discharged from the contract without a stain on his purse (*Lehmann* v *McArthur* (1868) LR 3 Ch 496). But the employing of his best endeavours need not involve the expenditure of too much energy by the vendor; it has been held that a vendor may properly give up if his application for a licence be 'met with a refusal on grounds not obviously unreasonable' (see per Goff J in *Lipmans Wallpaper Ltd* v *Mason & Hodghton Ltd* [1969] 1 Ch 20, at p 34). In that case, the grounds for the lessor's refusal of a licence to assign a sub-lease were that the purchaser's proposed user would breach covenants in a head lease; the learned judge held that the vendor could properly rescind without either himself approaching or allowing the purchaser time to approach the freeholder for waiver of the covenants.

Alternatively the vendor need not be discharged, if he has foreseen the difficulty and made provision in the contract for some other course to be pursued, since this will bind both the parties (see *Pincott* v *Moorstons Ltd* [1937] 1 All ER 513, where the vendor was, in lieu of procuring the licence, to declare a trust in favour of the purchaser; also *Gian Singh & Co* v *Nahar* [1965] 1 WLR 412, where leasehold premises became a partnership asset without being assigned).

The standard sets of conditions of sale could not be expected to overlook the lessor's licence to assign and each treats it in substantially the same way. Thus The Law Society's Conditions 1980 ed, No 8 (3), covers the ground carefully. In the first place, it writes in the otherwise implied obligation on the vendor to endeavour to procure the licence. Then it expressly obliges the purchaser, in effect, to co-operate in giving references, which again would be implied anyway (see per Harman LJ in *Scheggia* v *Gradwell* [1963] 1 WLR 1049, at p 1062; cf *Shires* v *Brock* (1977) 247 EG 127, CA). Lastly, it provides that either party may rescind if the licence 'is not granted at least five working days before contractual completion date'. In practice this time-limit may be found too short and strict for comfort: compare *Aberfoyle Plantations Ltd* v *Cheng* [1960] AC 115 with *Property and Bloodstock Ltd* v *Emerton* [1968] Ch 94, discussed ante, p 30. The National Conditions, 20th ed, No 11 (5), essentially only differs in having no time-limit and in purporting to permit the vendor alone to rescind which is evidently otiose, since the condition makes the sale itself subject to a licence being obtained.

Pound-wise, the National Conditions, but not The Law Society's by cross-reference, enable the rescission for lack of a licence to be as if the vendor were unwilling to comply with an unwithdrawn requisition (see p 122); ie, on repayment of the deposit and nothing more. See further as to rescission under general conditions of sale, *Lipmans Wallpaper Ltd* v *Mason & Hodghton Ltd* [1969] 1 Ch 20, where it was also held that the purchaser could not waive the lack of a licence to assign if the vendor wishes to and does rescind, and *Re Davies' Agreement* (1970) 21 P & CR 328, where it was held that the purchaser could not concern himself with the terms on which the vendor performed his duty of obtaining an unconditional licence (in this case, the lessor required a deposit from the vendor as security for dilapidations).

F REGISTERED TITLES

Hitherto in considering the obligation of a vendor of land to show title, deferential attention has been paid exclusively to the ancien régime of unregistered conveyancing, overlooking until now the nouveaux riches of the registered system. This split in any finite treatment of the topic is inevitable, for herein lies the essential parting of two mutually exclusive ways. Thus its leading text book now tells us that the newer system's first 'essential general feature' is that:

> Registration of title gives finality and certainty by providing an up-to-date official record of land ownership. The need to examine the past history of the title on each successive transaction is thus eliminated

(Ruoff and Roper, *Registered Conveyancing*, 4th ed, at p 8; see also per Vaughan Williams LJ in *A-G* v *Odell* [1906] 2 Ch 47, at pp 69–70).

What all this essentially means is that the registrar makes a traditional investigation of any title offered to him (see s 13 of the Land Registration Act 1925 and r 25 et seq of the Land Registration Rules 1925), and then records (registers) the result which is ever after available for inspection instead of anyone else's investigation (see below).

A preliminary question, therefore, is: when will a title be offered up for investigation by the registrar? Or, to put it another way, since such investigation is an obvious condition precedent: when will first registration of the title occur? The short answer is that it should occur following certain dispositions of land situated within an area of compulsory registration (a list of these areas may be obtained free of charge from any regional office of the Land Registry). In all other areas, registration used to be voluntary but has become prohibited with some permissive exceptions (s 1 (2) of the Land Registration Act 1966—all was officially explained at (1967) 31 Conv (NS) 7–12, but very briefly the reason was the effort of extending compulsory registration and the exceptions involved lost or destroyed deeds and building estates; cf the unusual case where a voluntary first registration was permitted because a landowner had defaced his unregistered documents with defamatory remarks about his solicitor, noticed at (1970) 34 Conv (NS) 223).

A small step back from the ideal of registration of all titles has been achieved through the Land Registration and Land Charges Act 1971, s 4, by virtue of which an area may be declared subject to a 'souvenir land scheme' (see the Land Registration (Souvenir Land) Rules 1972). The effect of such a declaration is to exclude the area from compulsory registration (see rr 5, 6 and 7 of the 1972 Rules which in effect provide that souvenir land, whether or not already registered, can thereafter only be dealt with as unregistered). Land becomes 'souvenir' for present purposes when the registrar believes that its disposal is in plots which 'being of inconsiderable size and little or no practical utility, [are] unlikely to be wanted in isolation except for the sake of pure ownership or for sentimental reasons or commemorative purposes' (s 4 (5) of the 1971 Act).

The only aspects of all this particularly within the scope of this book are the 'certain dispositions' which should be followed by first registration and the consequences if they are not. The substance of s 123 (1) of the Land Registration Act 1925 provides that:

> . . . every conveyance on sale of freehold land and every grant of a term of years absolute not being less than forty years from the date of delivery of the grant, and every assignment on sale of leasehold land held for a term of years absolute having not less than forty years to run from the date of delivery of the assignment, shall . . . on the expiration of two months from the date thereof . . . become void so far as regards the grant or conveyance of the legal estate in the freehold or leasehold land comprised in the conveyance, grant or assignment . . . unless the grantee . . . has in the meantime applied to be registered as proprietor of such land.

Thus, the consequence of non-registration is that the legal estate, having passed to the grantee, will automatically pass back to the grantor two months later. And this would seem a fair enough sanction since the grantee can be seen as losing what he has paid for. The subsection, however, does authorise the acceptance of out-of-time applications when the legal estate will re-vest in the grantee on registration (see ss 5 and 69 (1) of the Act). Provision also is made for any dealings in the intermediate period to take effect as if they had taken place after the date of first registration (s 123 (2) of the Land Registration Act 1925 and r 73 of the Land Registration Rules 1925); this protects in particular the mortgage enabling the first registered proprietor to purchase, the mortgagee being expressly permitted to make the appropriate application (as to the position of a sub-purchaser, see a note at [1979] Conv 1–2).

The generally accepted view of the effect of these provisions as to non-registration is that 'the vendor, having been paid his purchase money, will remain trustee of the legal estate for the purchaser' (see Ruoff and Roper, *Registered Conveyancing*, 4th ed, at p 177). Against this the original and unorthodox suggestion has been made that s 123 (1) of the Land Registration Act 1925 has the effect of creating a strict settlement of the land so that the inappropriately cumbersome conveyancing machinery of the Settled Land Act 1925 would have to be operated (see DG Barnsley at (1968) 32 Conv (NS) 391–411). However, this suggestion appears based entirely on the fundamental error in reasoning of equating a *legal estate* liable to be divested with a *fee simple* liable to be divested (see particularly ibid, at p 401, where the argument proceeds as if the two expressions here italicised were synonymous). The true position would appear to be that the purchaser of unregistered freehold land in an area of compulsory registration of title obtains and retains *beneficially* the fee simple absolute in possession conveyed to him notwithstanding non-registration; ie, the purchaser has an estate which, although it may cease to subsist at law, remains *capable* of so doing within s 1 (1) (*a*) of the Law of Property Act 1925 and which does not fall within any of the paragraphs of s 1 (1) of the Settled Land Act 1925. Accordingly the better view must surely still be that, since there is nothing in s 123 (1), ante, to disturb the equitable position as to ownership, non-registration merely produces a bare trusteeship on the part of the vendor for the benefit of the purchaser (this more orthodox approach is also usefully considered in detail in the article referred to). Then, as a sole beneficiary absolutely entitled, the purchaser would always be able to call for a further conveyance from the vendor (ie, under the well-known rule in *Saunders* v *Vautier* (1841) Cr & Ph 240), but would run the risk of being accidentally or deliberately defrauded by intermediate dispositions of the legal estate.

However, a complicating conundrum which sprang one day to the writer's mind may be worth passing mention. Section 123 (1) only renders a conveyance void so far as regards the grant of the legal estate, leaving it entirely effectual in all other respects. If such a conveyance happened to contain a recital of the grantor's ownership of the legal estate, then in favour of the grantee, an estoppel would arise which could be fed much as in *Church of England Building Society* v *Piskor* [1954] Ch 553. Accordingly, on the legal estate passing back to the grantor because of non-registration, the feeding of the estoppel should immediately return it to the grantee. The conundrum is to say where this game of ping-pong will stop and where the legal estate will drop. However, reference may be made to *British Maritime Trust* v *Upsons Ltd* [1931] WN 7, where the grant of a sub-lease within s 123 (1) had not been registered; Clauson J treated the instrument as wholly void and made no mention of any possible effect of the estoppel which would have arisen between the parties by virtue of the grant. Another complication not to be contemplated could occur if a conveyance was delivered in escrow before registration and the condition of the escrow was satisfied afterwards with retrospective effect (see p 322).

Apart from this, it may be noted that s 123 (1) only applies to a conveyance or assignment '*on sale*' which, by s 123 (3), requires 'an instrument made on sale by virtue whereof there is conferred or completed a registrable title' and includes an exchange where equality money is paid, but otherwise lacks any general definition in the Act. The expression 'conveyance on sale' is familiar as the basis of a number of stamp duty cases (ie, turning on s 54 of the Stamp Act 1891) and presumably it is legitimate to adopt the principles of these in the present context. Accordingly, s 123 (1) of the Land Registration Act 1925 would appear *not* to apply to a conveyance made in consideration of services, marriage or property other than money (ie, a mere exchange, see *Littlewoods Mail Order Stores Ltd* v *IRC* [1963] AC 135), or to a conveyance which merely happens after a sale (see *Henty & Constable (Brewers) Ltd* v *IRC* [1961] 1 WLR 1504), or to a conveyance made in contemplation of a sale (see *William Cory & Son Ltd* v *IRC* [1965] AC 1088; cp Finance Act 1965, s 90 (1)). Incidentally, since the special provisions of the Stamp Act 1891 extending the ordinary meaning of 'on sale' are not incorporated, the suggestion that a conveyance of land in exchange for shares causes compulsory registration of title seems erroneously founded (see Ruoff and Roper, *Registered Conveyancing*,

4th ed, p 174; cf ss 55–7 of the 1891 Act and *J & P Coats Ltd* v *IRC* [1897] 2 QB 423).
Of course, a voluntary conveyance, such as an ordinary assent, would not be caught
by s 123 (1) of the Land Registration Act 1925, but against this registration should
follow an assent in favour of a purchaser from the deceased (see *GHR Co Ltd* v *IRC*
[1943] KB 303) or in pursuance of an appropriation by consent (see *Jopling* v *IRC*
[1940] 2 KB 282). Also, a mortgage cannot in this context be treated as a
conveyance on sale (see ss 4 (*b*) and 8 (1) (*a*) of the Land Registration Act 1925).

One other aspect of first registration of passing interest here is the position of
leases granted for a term of *less* than forty years *by a registered proprietor*. First, if
the term does not exceed twenty-one years and rent but not a premium is paid, then
title cannot be registered, the lease existing instead as an overriding interest.
Secondly, for longer terms, it appears that registration is compulsory
notwithstanding the forty-years limit of s 123 (1) and notwithstanding that the area
is not compulsory (see Ruoff and Roper, *Registered Conveyancing*, 4th ed, p 185,
also footnote at (1967) 31 Conv (NS) 7). The reason is that such a lease must be
regarded simply as a disposition of registered land requiring completion by
registration in order to operate at law (ss 19 (2) and 22 (2) of the Land Registration
Act 1925). Incidentally, to obtain registration it is no longer necessary for the
lessee's application to be accompanied by the lessor's land certificate, the
production of which he has no right to call for (*Strand Securities Ltd* v *Caswell*
[1965] Ch 958, concerning a sub-lessee who in *un*registered conveyancing *is* entitled
to see the superior leasehold title; cp ante, p 131 and post, p 153).

Without descending further to the details of obtaining first registration (these
must be sought amongst the ample elsewheres, for this book revolves solely around
the position inter se of the parties to a sale of land, and here intends only to graft the
new principles on to those relating to unregistered conveyancing) one should at
least mention that the registrar must classify the result of his investigation into one
of certain categories. Of these, the best classification is, of course, 'absolute' for
freeholds or leaseholds, followed fairly closely for the latter by 'good leasehold' and
more distantly for either by 'possessory' or 'qualified'. The particular classification
is of importance because registration with each has a special statutory effect (see
ss 5–7 and 9–12 of the Land Registration Act 1925). Consequently, cause for
comfort may be culled from the thought that the registrar, on whose approval the
classification depends (ss 4, proviso (i), 8 (1), provisos (i) and (ii) of the Act, see also
Dennis v *Malcolm* [1934] Ch 244), may approach his investigation as if he were a
very willing, though not too rash, purchaser under an open contract—in other
words he may accept what is known as a 'good holding title' (s 13, proviso (*c*), of the
Act). In addition, however, the policy and presumably practice of successive Chief
Registrars have gone rather further than this in ignoring technical defects:
apparently they have long considered it 'their prime and justifiable aim to
endeavour to cure for all time the greatest possible number of defective titles by the
grant of an absolute title' (Ruoff & Roper, *Registered Conveyancing*, 4th ed, p 228).
Accordingly enquiries are supposed to tend towards the existence not of defects but
of persons who might impugn the title, with the discretion to accept a good holding
title being generously exercised (loc cit; see also per Lord Russell of Killowen in
MEPC Ltd v *Christian-Edwards* [1981] AC 205, at p 221; but cp CT Emery as to 'A
Case of Jurisdiction Exceeded?' at (1976) 40 Conv (NS) 122–38).

In the result, the vast majority of freehold titles, with all their degrees of defects
short of the thoroughly bad, should be squeezed into the category of absolute and
thereafter present proudly a status equivalent to the 'good and marketable title'
sans reproche. Much the same applies to leasehold titles, save that they often got a
'good leasehold' grouping in recognition of the restrictions on the investigation of

title discussed in the preceding section on p 131; cf s 8 (1), proviso (i), of the Act. All this, however, only affects vendors and purchasers inter se in so far as the registrar's confidence in a title may, indeed must, be shared by every future purchaser without question.

1   What is registered?

Assuming then that the registrar has investigated an unregistered title, what precisely is it that he records or registers? Without knowing this, one can hardly expect to understand how the newer system is replacing unregistered conveyancing. Well, the 1925 Act and Rules, under which the registrar operates, are called *Land* Registration; s 1 of the Act continues the keeping of 'a register of *title* to freehold land and leasehold land'; s 2 speaks first of the estates 'in respect of which a *proprietor* can be registered', then later of '*interests* entered on the register'; and other sections throughout the statute ring the changes on registration of one or other of the four italicised words (see especially the gamut run by each of ss 4, 5, 8, 9 and 69). So one must see not what is imprecisely said but what is actually done. In other words, what will the registrar's register reveal on inspection?

By the register, in this context, is meant the whole collection of records kept at HM Land Registry which has taken the physical form of a 'vast card index' (see Ruoff and Roper, *Registered Conveyancing*, 4th ed, p 13), but which may now become metaphysical by computerisation (see Administration of Justice Act 1982, s 66). Whatever the form, it relates to an equally vast number of individual properties each bearing a distinguishing title number and all divided into three parts, called the Property Register, the Proprietorship Register and the Charges Register. Arranged across the three parts of this register is to be found all the information about each property which would be found on a traditional investigation of a documentary title, *less* both the title's history and its defects (except, of course, for defects inherent in the registrar's classification as 'good leasehold', 'possessory' or 'qualified'), and also *less* all equities, these being completely curtained off (see s 74 of the Act). For a context limiting the meaning of 'register' to the 'one or two papers in respect of which a land certificate has already been issued' to an individual proprietor, see *Strand Securities Ltd* v *Caswell* [1965] Ch 958 (re s 64 of the Land Registration Act 1925).

Put another way, an inspection of the register reveals the conclusions a conveyancer would come to as to the present position of an unregistered title after his investigation had run the customary course of abstract, perusal, requisition, reply, and verification, but with the evidence on which he would reach this conclusion replaced by the simple fact of registration. This last fact, indeed, is worth all the rest put together in being able to operate by itself by 'statutory magic' to confer actual ownership of the legal estate in question (see s 69 (1) of the 1925 Act and Ruoff and Roper, *Registered Conveyancing*, 4th ed, p 64; also Simon NL Palk, 'First Registration of Title—Just What Does It Do?' at (1974) 38 Conv (NS) 236–52).

Accordingly, one can say that it is the *title* to each property which is registered (see especially s 3 (xxiv) of the 1925 Act). Thus a Chief Land Registrar once explained that the work of the Land Registry consists of 'registering the titles of specified landowners to particular estates in land' ((1963) *Law Society's Gazette*, vol 6, at p 345). What is more, the word 'title' here can and must be taken in two of its unregistered senses simultaneously; first, the register is *of* title, meaning ownership itself, and secondly, the register *equals* the title, meaning now the evidence of ownership (cf p 86).

Thus, in theory at least, all a purchaser need do is look at the register (or at a land or charge certificate or an office copy, all of which take, most often, the place of examined abstracts in unregistered conveyancing: see ss 68 and 113 of the 1925 Act; although the certificates may on occasion be treated as title deeds themselves: see s 66 as to liens by deposit, also per Lord Evershed MR in *Lee* v *Barrey* [1957] Ch 251, at p 259; cp a note at (1975) 39 Conv (NS) 315–7). As the Privy Council once said: 'The cardinal principle of the statute is that the register is everything' (speaking of the Torrens system in *Waimiha Sawmilling Co Ltd (In Liquidation)* v *Waione Timber Co Ltd* [1926] AC 101, at p 106). Unfortunately, the civilised simplicity of this theory is marred. First, there may be matters affecting the title (ie, ownership) but not revealed by the register (eg, 'overriding interests,' see s 70 of the Act). And secondly, the machinery of practice has achieved an equally civilised complexity—with a farrago of form-filling the spotlight today tends to be turned away from the initial ideals of simplicity and facility (see preambles to the Land Registry Act 1862 and the Land Transfer Act 1875), towards the indemnity insurance aspect (as to the deliberate development of the insurance principle, see the Chief Land Registrar's Report 1971–72, pp 9–10; cf as to title insurance a note at (1975) 39 Conv (NS) 81–8, also an article by John C Payne at (1976) 40 Conv (NS) 11–36). The established emphasis on form-filling may be clearly seen from the *Registered Land Practice Notes*, 1982/83, prepared jointly by The Law Society and HM Land Registry which begin with a warning about choosing the correct one of the 18 varieties of application form currently published for first registration (p 1) and list in an Appendix merely the 55 printed forms most commonly required (pp 58–9). The statutory forms scheduled in the various Land Registry Rules from 1925 onwards actually reach No 102 on top of which the Chief Land Registrar makes considerable use of his power to promulgate further forms (see Ruoff and Roper, *Registered Conveyancing*, 4th ed, pp 268–9).

That our judiciary have no illusions of registered simplicity was evidenced in *Re White Rose Cottage* [1965] Ch 940, where Harman LJ began his judgment with the following notable passage:

> The system of land registration was introduced into our law in response to the lay demand that dealings with land should be assimilated to dealings with chattels and should cease to be a mystery understood only by conveyancers. The process of reform began as long ago as Lord Cairns's Act of 1875 and was enlarged by Lord Halsbury's Act of 1897. When the great change in the law of real property was brought about by Lord Birkenhead's Acts of 1925, it was of course necessary radically to reform the land registration system to match the new régime. At the same time the reformers proposed to introduce various improvements. The preface to Brickdale and Stewart-Wallace's *Land Registration Act 1925*, 4th ed (1939) claims in its first chapter, among other things, that the system of land registration 'provides plain and simple methods for effecting transfers and charges'. It cannot be said that either of these policies emerge from the facts of the present case. No doubt the system has worked very well since 1925 by the efforts of the land registrars and the practice of the office, but the present case shows that there are difficulties and pitfalls in the way of comparatively simple transactions which would not have arisen with unregistered land

(p 951: the decision involved a point of priorities between incumbrances and a point of construction not relevant here; for some critical unenthusiasm inspired by the case see Professor EC Ryder, *Current Legal Problems 1966*, at p 26 et seq).

2 Vendor and purchaser

On a sale of registered land, therefore, the parties perform precisely the play of unregistered conveyancing except that the second act—the investigation of title—has been censoriously curtailed: in effect, the purchaser now sees only the detective registrar's dénouement without having to make his own guesses from the clues cum red herring which have been investigated. Since this should be a mere momentary matter, one may wonder whether a contract for sale is still really necessary, for at the outset of this book the explanation offered for having a contract was 'to give the purchaser what may be called a "pay pause", ie, a time after the conclusion of the negotiations and before he pays his money during which to investigate the vendor's title.' Indeed, the early authoritative view did favour dispensing with contracts; as Brickdale and Stewart-Wallace put it:

> A purchaser of land with an absolute title . . . has *ordinarily* only three things to do: namely (1) to find out who is the registered proprietor of the land; (2) to obtain a transfer . . . from that proprietor; and (3) to procure his own registration. *If there are charges, incumbrances, notices, cautions, inhibitions, or restrictions registered, they must also be dealt with* . . . Where the parties *have confidence in one another, and* desire to save expense and delay, there is no difficulty, and *practically* no risk, in combining the first two of these operations in one. The vendor produces his land certificate, the purchaser peruses it, and, if satisfied, pays the purchase-money at once in exchange for a duly-executed instrument of transfer, and the land certificate

(*The Land Registration Act 1925*, 3rd ed, at p 28; present writer's italics, as to which see below). In reply, the late Professor Potter made four good points against this practice (in *Registered Land Conveyancing*, at pp 318–19). In précis his points were that the purchaser should (i) inspect the register rather than the land certificate, which may be out of date; (ii) draw or at least approve the form of transfer himself; (iii) preserve priority by making an official search, and (iv) compare the registered description with the property and elicit any overriding interests. These points, however, used to be shortly dismissed in the principal authoritative work with the observation, under the heading '*Need for a contract*', that: 'Some academic lawyers have answered this by saying it is more necessary than ever to do so [sic], although this answer is not convincing' (Ruoff and Roper, *Registered Conveyancing*, 3rd ed, p 327, with footnote reference only to Potter). After this, and after quoting Brickdale and Stewart-Wallace as above, and mentioning local searches and enquiries, those official writers concluded with a somewhat difficult distinction between a 'formal contract' which can sometimes be avoided and a 'preliminary agreement' which is sometimes desirable (ibid, p 328). The present writer's feeling was that such a view might conceivably be acceptable if the italicised words could be omitted from the quotation from Brickdale and Stewart-Wallace. However, in their latest edition, Ruoff and Roper have quietly recanted: after noting that a registered proprietor is explicitly permitted to enter into any contract just as if his land (or charge) were not registered (s 107 of the Land Registration Act 1925), they simply assert that the registration system provides simpler conveyancing machinery and then proceed to consider the contractual position (4th ed, p 304 et seq).

In recognition, no doubt, of what actually happens, the advocates of the registered system in general no longer try to deny contracts, but restrict their claims instead to saying, in substance, that a registered proprietor wishing to sell 'can speedily offer proof of his title' which a purchaser 'can quickly and safely accept' (Ruoff and Roper, ibid, p 9, 'characteristic advantages', Nos (8) and (9)). Yet even this seems a little disingenuous and not only as to overriding interests; decided cases have illustrated the risks. Thus in *Re Stone and Saville's Contract* [1963] 1 WLR 163, only after an open contract for the sale of registered land had been made did the purchaser learn that the charges register referred to a relevant although released restrictive covenant; a successful rescission resulted. Again in *Faruqi* v *English Real Estates Ltd* [1979] 1 WLR 963 a special condition at an auction sale provided that the property was sold subject to entries on the register of title; one entry referred to certain restrictive covenants contained in a deed of 17 May 1883 which had not been available on first registration. Although the condition was binding, Walton J did not agree that the purchaser had been given a fair opportunity to discover what he was letting himself in for:

> Any purchaser reading these general and special conditions of sale would be entitled, I think, to assume that of course there were entries on the register but that those entries were only of what I may call the usual sort, which do not in any way affect the value of the property adversely. He would be most surprised to learn, as I am certain that the purchaser here was most surprised to learn, that he was literally buying a pig in a poke because he was taking the property subject to the contents of a deed which could not even be produced

(at p 968). Accordingly, instead of specific performance, return of the purchaser's deposit was ordered. Does this not sound an awful echo of that which registration of title was to have saved us all from?

Assuming, therefore, that the solicitors acting for the vendor and the purchaser consider it necessary to have a formal contract, how should the subject-matter of the sale be described? The only acceptable answer appears to be: when on the register, do as the registrar does. Thus the authoritative form is to head the contract in the familiar Land Registry way and to sell and buy 'the land comprised in the title referred to above' (Ruoff, *Land Registration Forms*, 2nd ed, Precedent No 16, at p 57). Yet, a moment's thought—no purchaser of *un*registered land would ever agree to buy 'the property which happens to be comprised in the vendor's title deeds subject not only to the incumbrances mentioned therein but to any others there may turn out to be'. Surely the vendor's responsibility remains of particularising by description the property he is selling, be it registered or not? Naturally he should not depart one iota from the description on the register and a purchaser should certainly be completely satisfied by getting, as he very often does with the draft contract, an office copy of the register.

Further, in relation to 'overriding interests', the vendor will be under a general duty to disclose not all (as is sometimes suggested), but any of them which may be latent defects in title, ie, only those not discoverable on a reasonably careful inspection of the property (see p 62). Obviously the vendor would have some difficulty in actually disclosing any overriding interests of which he is ignorant. Nonetheless The Law Society's Conditions of Sale, 1980 ed, No 5 (1), has the vendor warrant disclosure of the existence of certain overriding interests (ie, easements etc) of which he 'knows *or ought to know*'. In contrast a former Chief Land Registrar himself drafted a contractual clause to the effect that the land is sold subject to all unknown overriding interests (see Ruoff, *Land Registration Forms*, 2nd ed, Clause 6, on pp 58 and 61).

3   Investigation

Having none too quickly concluded a formal contract for the sale of registered land, the time has come to consider exactly how the vendor should show his good title. The most practical approach to this would seem to be to adopt the unregistered order of events so as to facilitate those comparisons without which the essential nature of registration of title cannot really be appreciated.

Well, the first event here is that registered conveyancing entertains no real equivalent to the laborious learning embodied in the lengthy sections on the commencement and chain of title to unregistered land. The essence of the register is in needing only stirring to produce 'instant title'. As a rule, the history of the vendor's ownership of his registered land is, in Ford's famous phrase, 'bunk'. Not even the conveyance or transfer to the vendor himself need to be seen as a document of title (see The Law Society's *Registered Land Practice Notes,* 1982/83, No C3 and C4 but cp *Lee* v *Barrey* [1957] Ch 251). However, the register does not always purport to be all things to all men; that is, the vendor's registered title may be less than absolute: for example if it be possessory or qualified, the pre-registration title must be treated as unregistered (see s 110 (2) of the Land Registration Act 1925).

Nonetheless, the real question remains; how does one deduce an instant title? Is redundancy the fate of our titular abstracts, requisitions and verifications? The answer in general is that their functions are fulfilled by the automation of the register. Yet this answer becomes something of a sheep in wolf's clothing: its naked simplicity is clothed by the comparative complexities caused by the purchaser's primary problem of seeing the register without actually going to look at it. So the answer must be given more in particular.

(a) Abstracts

Initially, then, the Act has said, let there be no more abstracts, and this 'notwithstanding any stipulation to the contrary' (s 110 (3) of the Land Registration Act 1925). Instead, the vendor is to furnish the purchaser—'notwithstanding . . .', as before—with two things:

(i) *An authority to inspect the register* (s 110 (1)) without which there can be no inspection and which carries the right to take pencil copies, to obtain office copies and to make official searches (s 112 of the Act and rr 287–97 of, and Form 80 in the Schedule, to, the Land Registration Rules 1925). The practice is to confer the authority to inspect on the purchaser, or more often on his solicitor, as a specified person (see Ruoff, *Land Registration Forms,* 2nd ed, Precedent No 18, at p 62) and the official attitude clearly is that this authority is not transferable (see Ruoff and Roper, *Registered Conveyancing,* 4th ed, at pp 318 and 671 envisaging only a named purchaser), so that an extra authority for any expected mortgagee has to be asked for, which an awkward minded vendor might conceivably withhold arguing that his statutory duty relates only to the purchaser. Yet the section (s 110 (1)) refers to 'an authority to inspect the register' and the prescribed form confers its authority on 'the bearer' (Schedule, Form 80 to the Rules, which 'shall be used': r 74). True, alterations to the prescribed forms are possible, if desired (r 74, see also r 289 which seems too discretionary to marry with the imperative s 110 (1)), but since the purchaser has an inescapable right to an authority he should be entitled, if he wishes, to insist strictly on the prescribed form whatever the vendor may desire. In other words, the submission is that the only proper practice is for the vendor to supply a bearer authority which would then be transferable by delivery to mortgagees or anyone else. Nevertheless, it is obviously the more convenient practice for the vendor to give an authority both to the purchaser and to any mortgagee who may advance money to the purchaser in connection with the particular purchase (see as to this The Law Society's Conditions of Sale, 1980 ed, No 12 (1) (*b*) (ii) referring to sub-purchasers and prospective lessees as well as mortgagees). The authority to inspect, according to the prescribed Form 80, has 'To be signed by *AB* or his solicitor'. Since 'neither a facsimile "signature" applied by means of a rubber stamp nor any other form of printed or typed "signature" is acceptable' to HM Land Registry (see *Wontner's Guide to Land Registry Practice*, 14th ed, at p 171), it is preferable practice for the solicitor (or his legal executive or clerk) acting for the vendor to use a pen to sign the firm's name (but cp notes at [1975] Conv 153–6 and [1979] Conv 7–8).

Under the 1981 Official Searches Rules, solicitors no longer need to lodge an authority to inspect at HM Land Registry, certifying instead that such an authority is held. Accordingly it would appear possible for an appropriate authority to be incorporated as a standard condition of sale on a disposition of registered land (see further a note at [1981] Conv 393–4).

(ii) '*A copy of the subsisting entries in the register and of any filed plans and copies or abstracts of any documents or any part thereof noted on the register*' (s 110 (1)). These need only be furnished 'if required' (ibid), but no effective contracting not to require would seem possible (cf Brickdale and Stewart-Wallace, *Land Registration Act 1925*, 3rd ed, at p 629). The obligation does not extend to filed settlements (s 110 (1) proviso (*b*)), nor to anything that does not affect the land to be dealt with (s 110 (1); eg, on a sale of part, matters affecting the remainder), nor to charges or incumbrances which will be discharged or overridden on completion (ibid, not of course relating to overriding interests. This last seems distinctly odd: one would have thought that a purchaser ought to be entitled to satisfy himself as to the discharge or overriding being possible, yet the statute forbids him.) Filed abstracts or copies referred to by the register are, as between vendor and purchaser, to be assumed to be the whole material truth without production of the original documents (s 110 (4)), and all expenses are to be borne by the vendor unless the purchase price does not exceed £1,000 when, subject to contract, the purchaser is to foot the bill (s 110 (1), proviso (*a*)).

In practice, whatever the strict obligations, office copies of everything tend always to be supplied at the vendor's expense (the fees are negligible) on or before exchange of contracts as a matter of course (this has been recommended by the Council of The Law Society: see Opinion No 316 (i) in *The Law Society's Digest*, Fourth (Cumulative) Supplement). The Law Society's Conditions of Sale, 1980 ed, No 12 (1) (*b*) (i), provides for the delivery of office copies forthwith on exchange of contracts in accordance with the above recommendation. However, in view of the duty of adequate disclosure, in substance, the vendor's obligation appears to be to supply copy entries *before* contract: (see *Faruqi* v *English Real Estates Ltd* [1979] 1 WLR 963). Nevertheless under Condition 12 (3) such pre-contract delivery will not fix the purchaser with notice of any matters of title.

Now certain more general observations may be made about this twofold statutory substitute for the old abstract of title.

First, some queries are raised by the fact of its applying only 'on a sale or other disposition of registered land to a purchaser other than a lessee or chargee' (s 110). Obviously a chargee must be allowed to make his own terms, but the mention of this seems to imply that the section otherwise applies whether or not the transfer is preceded by a contract, although it is difficult to see how. Again, lessees had to be excluded since under an open contract they are not to see their lessor's title (s 44 (2) of the Law of Property Act 1925; see p 131), but since 'lease' is defined to include 'underlease' (s 3 (*x*) of the Land Registration Act 1925), probably 'lessee' should be taken to include 'underlessee' even though an underlessor's title ordinarily may be investigated (s 44 (4) of the Law of Property Act 1925; *Gosling* v *Woolf* [1893] 1 QB 39).

Secondly, 'subject to any stipulation to the contrary', title to anything as to which the register is not conclusive or which is excepted from the effect of registration must be deduced by the vendor at his own expense in the unregistered way (s 110 (2)). The main 'things' within this are the pre-registration position of a possessory title, overriding interests, and incumbrances entered on the register as subsisting on first registration (r 160 of the Land Registration Rules 1925).

Thirdly, if the vendor is only in the position of being entitled to be registered (ie, he is relying on s 37 of the Act and rr 81 and 170 of the Rules), then the purchaser would wish to be satisfied of his entitlement. Commonly, this would mean seeing the first contract on a sub-sale or the grant to the personal representatives of a deceased registered proprietor. However, the purchaser actually is entitled to have the vendor procure either his own registration or a disposition from the registered proprietor, and this 'notwithstanding any stipulation to the contrary' (s 110 (5)), so that the vendor would hardly be able to cover the point in the contract despite authoritative suggestion to this effect (Ruoff and Roper, *Registered Conveyancing*, 4th ed, pp 315–6). However, it is not made clear by the provision whether the vendor's statutory obligation should be performed before completion of the contract or merely before completion of the purchaser's registration, though the former is generally taken to be the more natural construction. Nor does the provision make clear which of the vendor or the purchaser is entitled to decide whether the vendor procures his own registration or whether he procures a disposition directly from the registered proprietor (cp a note at [1979] Conv 1–3). Incidentally, in one odd case, s 110 (5) was unsuccessfully called in aid by the 'difficult' purchaser of a piece of registered land together with appurtenant easements over unregistered land: he was held unable to compel the vendors to procure their registration as proprietors of the easements (by Stamp J in *Re Evans' Contract* [1970] 1 WLR 583). The reasoning for this decision embodies peculiarly unprincipled alternatives: either the easements were not registered land and so not within s 110 at all or they were registered land and so the vendors were already the registered proprietors. In view of the statutory definition of registered land (s 3 (xxiv)), the latter might appear the slightly more acceptable alternative, but it produces the inherent contradiction of an unregistered title to registered land.

So much then for artificial abstracts. What next about the raising of requisitions?

(b) Requisitions

The question occasionally occurs of whether requisitions on title can find a corner in registered conveyancing. The authoritative answer remains adamant: '*Requisitions on title are unnecessary*' (sub-heading in Ruoff and Roper, *Registered Conveyancing*, 4th ed, at p 320). Yet acceptance of this answer may become a little difficult if reference be made to the decision in *Re Stone and Saville's Contract* [1963] 1 WLR 163 where a perfectly proper requisition on a sale of land registered with an absolute title led to a perfectly proper rescission by the purchaser. Again in *Re Evans' Contract* [1970] 1 WLR 583 (see above) concerning a sale of registered land, the declaration granted was 'that requisitions on title had been sufficiently answered by the vendors and that a good title to the property had been shown in accordance with the contract of sale.'

The truth is that freedom from technical defects is not the whole story. Even the much-vaunted absolute title is only a good title as between vendor and purchaser in so far as it accords with the contract for sale. Otherwise requisitions are properly raisable, eg, as to any adverse entries on the register (see FR Crane's summary at (1937) 2 Conv (NS) 49–50; also Potter's *Registered Land Conveyancing*, p 311 et seq). Further, the register is *not* conclusive as to ownership albeit that it may replace the evidence of ownership; even an absolute title is relative in so far as it may be rectified and the possibility of overriding interests is hardly conducive to completeness. Again, whatever the merits of the register there is surely no denying that anything untoward revealed by the purchaser's official search before completion could cause requisitions to be raised, which leads to the next question, the whereabouts of the verification.

(c)   Verification

In unregistered conveyancing, the verification of an abstract of title primarily involves examining it against the title deeds. In registered conveyancing the register (*not* the land certificate or office copies) takes the place of the title deeds and the nearest thing to an abstract becomes a copy of the register. Does the purchaser have to examine the copy against the register? Is that what the authority to inspect is for? The Land Registry view, which represents the common practice, is that the purchaser should be quite content either with a sight of the land certificate or with possession of an office copy of the register *plus* an official search as to entries since the date noted as being when the land certificate was last officially made to correspond with the register or since the date of the office copy. Although this view was not entertained by the late Professor Potter, who preferred personal inspection, his reasons would appear better directed to a preference for an office copy rather than a sight of the land certificate (see *Registered Land Conveyancing*, p 310; cf Key & Elphinstone, *Precedents in Conveyancing*, 15th ed, vol 3, p 327). Indeed, as against a personal inspection, the official search enjoys a number of cogent conveniences, not least of which are the absence of attendance or fee and the presence of priority and indemnity (ie, under the Land Registration (Official Searches) Rules 1981; also s 83 (3) of the Land Registration Act 1925).

Care must, of course, be taken that the purchaser's application for registration be made within the period of protection afforded by an official search (cf *Strand Securities Ltd* v *Caswell* [1965] Ch 958 and *Elias* v *Mitchell* [1972] Ch 652, in each of which a prejudicial delay occurred). But if this is done, this verification of a registered title ought to be entirely adequate and acceptable (see to this effect per Russell LJ in the *Strand Securities* case at p 987). This necessarily assumes, however, that the purchaser is 'in good faith', as well as for value, as required now by r 2 (1) of the Land Registration (Official Searches) Rules 1981. However, the quoted words call only for honesty and an absence of ulterior motive: *Smith* v *Morrison* [1974] 1 WLR 659, where the purchaser had known of an adverse claim but thought it was a try-on—this was classified as an honest doubt not interfering with the priority conferred by a clear official search. In addition, although the purchaser's application need not be in perfect order it must be 'in due course completed by registration' (r 5 (iii) of the Official Searches Rules 1981, as to applications not in order, see now r 317 of the 1925 Rules, as substituted by r 11 of the Land Registration Rules 1978, permitting requisitions and rejection; cp *Smith* v *Morrison*, ante).

Further, any completely unqualified acceptance of the Land Registry view that a purchaser is able to rely on an official search as an absolute verification of title must still be withheld in so far as the Land Registry itself remains humanly (or even computerly) unreliable. Thus in *Parkash* v *Irani Finance Ltd* [1970] Ch 101 an official search, due to an unexplained mistake, failed to reveal the existence of a caution which had been duly lodged; Plowman J held that the cautioner retained priority notwithstanding the ignorance of the purchaser.

Finally, a fleeting mention may be made, for the benefit of all those building societies from which the glad tidings have been kept, that searches either under the

Land Charges Act 1972 or in the companies registry have been relegated in registered conveyancing to the category of the unnecessary (the former notwithstanding the observation of Evershed MR in *City Permanent Building Society* v *Miller* [1952] Ch 840, at pp 849–50, rebutted by the Chief Land Registrar at (1953) 17 Conv (NS) 39, see also per Ungoed-Thomas J in *Webb* v *Pollmount* [1966] Ch 584, at p 603; the latter notwithstanding *Re Overseas Aviation Engineering (GB) Ltd* [1963] Ch 24, see (1962) 26 Conv (NS) 408). The justification for requiring a strictly unnecessary land charges search is often said to be to discover the existence of any pending bankruptcy proceedings as reflecting on the financial soundness of the proposed borrower. However, for this purpose it is possible to make a 'bankruptcy only', rather than a full, search (see (1964) 28 Conv (NS) 420–2). Incidentally, do not forget that a *local* land charges search must still be made because these charges are overriding interests (s 70 (1) (i) of the Land Registration Act 1925).

(d) Conditions of sale

That then is what the investigation of a registered title essentially involves (viz, authority to inspect, office copies and official search), a procedure of such newborn simplicity that no reader could possibly pine for the fuller flavour, for all its faults, of the mature unregistered methods. Do the standard sets of conditions of sale purport to add or subtract anything to or from the statutory stipulations? Not much. Both the National and The Law Society's Conditions of Sale now refer to s 110 of the Land Registration Act 1925 in connection with abstracts of title (see 20th ed, No (11) and 1980 ed, No 12 (1) (b) respectively). Then the latter set, as noted, specifies office copies, whilst the former attempts to anticipate the rights of occupiers (which may well be 'overriding interests') by allowing fishing requisitions and completion at the property (see 20th ed, Nos 9 (2) and 5 (4)).

(e) Leaseholds

Before finally parting from the investigation of title, a word or two should be said of sales of registered leaseholds. There is much here that is the same as in unregistered conveyancing (see p 131). Thus, although the lease, as well as a certified copy of it, will accompany the application for first registration, eventually the lease itself will be returned, being only noted in the Property Register (see rr 21, 310 and 5 of the Land Registration Rules 1925). Consequently, the vendor will retain possession of the lease which will remain the essential root of title as in, unregistered conveyancing, the register only replacing the subsequent chain of title, and the purchaser will be as much concerned with its contents as ever.

Again, the purchaser must not only be shown the covenants in the lease but must also be satisfied of an absence of breaches. This involves exactly the same evidence, by way of last receipts for rent, and consequences as in unregistered conveyancing, (see p 137). Only the covenant against unlicensed assignments calls for any particular comment. Where there is such a covenant, an entry must be made excepting from the effect of registration the rights arising on an unlicensed assignment (r 45 of the Land Registration Rules 1925; see also s 8 (2) of the Act). This simply saves the registrar from having to investigate the title in each case of the person giving the licence (although this would only be a problem where the reversion remained unregistered).

Apart from the above, the point may be put of how far a purchaser of registered leaseholds may, or need, see any superior title. This depends on the quality of his vendor's title, which may be either absolute or else good leasehold (or, of course, possessory or qualified, which would be an extraordinarily rare and different matter). An absolute leasehold title means that the registrar has investigated and approved the title not only to the leasehold but also to the freehold and to any intermediate leasehold (s 8 (1), proviso (i), of the Land Registration Act 1925). Accordingly, where the vendor has secured an absolute title, whether originally or by conversion (see s 77 of the Act), its nature is obviously such that the purchaser need never concern himself with any superior title, the registrar has seen it for him (s 9 of the Act). What is more, any restrictive covenants or other entries on the superior will also appear on the leasehold title so that no problem should arise of the purchaser being affected by what he cannot discover.

If, however, the vendor is registered with merely a good leasehold title, this means that the registrar has only investigated and approved the leasehold title itself (s 8 (1), proviso (ii), of the Act) so that the purchaser is as much concerned with the superior title as in *un*registered conveyancing (see s 10 and p 131, ante). This involves not only the question of the validity of the lease's grant but also that of notice of equitable incumbrances appearing on the superior title. Indeed, this latter calls for some comment here in connection only with cases where the superior title *is* registered (if it is not registered, all is as in unregistered conveyancing).

On the one hand, a lessee of registered land who registers his title takes subject, inter alia, 'to the incumbrances and other entries, if any, appearing on the *register*' (s 20 (1) (*a*) of the Land Registration Act 1925) and purchasers from him do likewise (s 23 (1) (*a*)). On the other hand s 50 of the Act provides that notice of restrictive covenants may be entered 'on the *register*' after which 'the proprietor of the land and the persons deriving title under him . . . shall be deemed to be affected with notice of the covenant or agreement as being an incumbrance on the land.' Of this, Simonds J has said:

> That section appears to me to be the proper complement to s 20, and so far it appears to me to be clear beyond all doubt that when an incumbrance has been registered [sic] on the *register* it is notice to all persons deriving title from the proprietor, though it may be perhaps a blot, that the lessee, unless he makes some bargain to that effect, is not permitted to inspect the register. The answer is: He is at liberty, if he thinks fit, to make such a bargain and to refuse to enter into any contract or lease unless he first obtains the permission of the lessor, who can grant it to him, to inspect the register

(in *White* v *Bijou Mansions Ltd* [1937] Ch 610, at p 621; he proceeded to reject an argument based on s 52 of the Act; on appeal [1938] Ch 351). From these words and the decision in the case it emerges that the '*register*' referred to is not confined, as it might have been, to that of the leasehold title itself but includes that of the superior title(s).

This risk of notice which a purchaser of registered leaseholds runs under an open contract may even be regarded as more of a blot here than on the *un*registered system for two reasons. The first is that the Land Charges Register, unlike the register of the superior title, can be searched without the lessor's co-operation provided only that the estate owners' names are available. The second is that a new rational system, whether of conveyancing or anything else, should discard rather than preserve the anomalies of the old (see p 133; also (1952) 16 Conv (NS) 180–1).

4   A statutory estate

Having peered at the purchaser's investigation of title on a sale of registered land, it may be pertinent to enquire what he is looking for. He will, of course, be looking at the register of title as being the evidence of the vendor's ownership, but ownership of what? Once upon a time, an academic controversy arose as to whether the registered proprietor owned an ordinary common law legal estate or a special statutory estate. The latter was first intimated by the late Professor H Potter in 1941 in his *Principles of Registered Land* (Ch VI), then eventually challenged by the late Professor AD Hargreaves in 1949 in a review of the second edition (12 MLR 139), after which these two learned lawyers completed their engagements with, respectively, a defending and a counter-attacking article (at 12 MLR 205 and 447). Unfortunately, perhaps, this controversy was unable to achieve anything conclusive since it essentially took the form of conflicting declarations of faith followed by a disputing over details so detailed as to obscure the issues. The whole affair further fails to convince in two ways. On the one hand, Professor Potter's argument seems flawed by his (mis)taking certain of the incidents of an estate (particularly the powers of disposition) for the estate itself. Then, on the other hand, the very basis of Professor Hargreaves's differing views has since been undermined by later decisions: that is, in challenging Professor Potter's preference for a new threefold classification of interests (ie, into registrable, overriding and minor), which challenge was why he wrote, he made the 'root' point that an agreement for the lease 'cannot possibly refer to an interest in land, nor can it "be" an overriding, or any other, interest in land' (see at 12 MLR 142, 478 and 481-2; also (1952) 16 Conv (NS) 38-40), yet now we all know it can be within para (g) of s 70 (1) of the Land Registration Act 1925 (see *Grace Rymer Investments Ltd* v *Waite* [1958] Ch 831, CA, also *Webb* v *Pollmount* [1966] Ch 584).

One or two other contributions to the controversy can be found elsewhere. The strongest statement of the statutory estate theory is by RC Connell seeking strength from the persuasive authority of Australian and New Zealand decisions on their comparable systems of registered conveyancing (in (1947) 11 Conv (NS) 184 and 232). This statement, however, seems to suffer some weaknesses, principally, that although title and estate are treated separately, the latter still seems to be confused with the former as well as with its incidents. Again, the statutory estate theory is not only doubted by Megarry and Wade, with a mere footnote reference, for their reasons presumably, to Professor Hargreaves's views (*Real Property*, 4th ed, p 1064), but is also roundly rejected by Ruoff and Roper (*Registered Conveyancing*, 4th ed, pp 68-9). Yet since the nature of the controversy seems such that none of its contributors is likely to be proved to be wrong the present writer feels free to dip in his oar, albeit both briefly and tentatively.

The solution, it is suggested, lies in seeing the problem as appellative rather than substantive. Thus the word 'estate' connotes an interest in land of some particular duration, a time in the land, a quantum of interest (see Megarry and Wade, *Real Property*, 4th ed, at pp 14-15). There are two classes of estates, freeholds and less than freeholds, the former comprehending the fee simple, the fee tail and the life estate, and the latter only the term of years, and each of these denotes a different duration (ibid, pp 40-1). Before 1926, all these estates could be legal, but now only the fee simple and the terms of years can be (s 1 (1) of the Law of Property Act 1925). These two legal estates, so statute says, first, are the only interests in respect of which a proprietor can be registered (s 2 (1) of the Land Registration Act 1925, see also s 3 (xi) but cf s 3 (xxiii) and (xxiv)), and secondly, are the interests which will be vested in the registered proprietor (ss 5, 9, 20, 23 and, most of all, 69 (1) of the Act, though these sections do not always use the precise expressions of s 1 (1) of the Law of Property Act 1925). Since the registered proprietor's interest will be both enforceable at law and of exactly the same duration as before, there is surely no denying it the name of 'legal estate'. This christening, however, does not conclude the discussion.

Having thus given the registered proprietor's interest a general status, in the same sense as persons are provided with convenient classification in law, eg, minor, married woman, solicitor (indeed the word 'estate' is derived from the 'status' of the tenant holding the interest), attention may now be turned to the more important aspect of the particular incidents—the rights, duties, powers and disabilities which define enjoyment— attending that interest. At this point the need for new names begins to become apparent, for whilst the enjoyment of the legal estate is substantially the same whether or not the title to it is registered, there do seem to be sufficient differences of detail to make it desirable to distinguish between the two. Take, for example, the legal estate which a registered proprietor calls his own: (1) his ownership of the estate comes to him solely from the statutory magic of registration (see Ruoff and Roper, *Registered Conveyancing*, 4th ed, p 64); (2) his evidence of ownership is prescribed by statute in order to supersede any non-statutory form (see p 149); (3) his powers of disposition are expressly enumerated by statute (ss 18 and 21 of the Land Registration Act 1925), which is always liable either to cause an accidental change on construction from the non-statutory powers or else to exclude by implication any omitted powers otherwise inherent in the legal estate (this point appears purely academic, the writer being as yet unaware of any acceptable illustrations, mention of testamentary powers, eg, to devise land, being completely misconceived since wills now operate only in equity no longer affecting the legal estate directly; see an article at (1962) 26 Conv (NS) 169); (4) the manner of exercising the powers of disposition is prescribed by statute (see ss 69 (4) and 109 of the Act, also *Spectrum Investment Co v Holmes* [1981] 1 WLR 221 where this point was not academic); and (5) the machinery set up by statute for protecting interests adverse to the registered proprietor's legal estate leads to the threefold classification of interests in registered land, the other two being overriding interests and minor interests (see s 2 (1) of the Act), and although the members of each of the three classes bear a resemblance to interests in unregistered land, not only is this sometimes superficial but the classification tends not to coincide with any unregistered classification, even to the point of including legal estates and interests in one or other of the latter two classes.

Since the legal estate in registered land enjoys or suffers so many peculiar statutory incidents, an improvement in communication would surely be achieved by calling it 'statutory' (or 'registered' if you like). This improvement would simply be in making explicit the distinction from the legal estate in *un*registered land, the incidents of which derive from the common law (and from statutes other than the Land Registration Act 1925). After this a lawyer's natural propensity for abbreviation might lead comfortably to the contractions: 'statutory estate' and 'legal estate', respectively, meaning thereby the same estate with some different incidents.

In earlier editions a crude challenge was thrown down to anyone to controvert this conclusion. The glove has only once been picked up in print, examined briefly and put firmly down again: Professor David Jackson, in the course of a comparatively penetrating article, managed only to find that—'While the conclusion is, it is suggested, not to be queried, the approach is to be lamented' (see (1972) 88 LQR 93, at p 96; cf Paul B Fairest who found in this discussion 'the breath of life' at [1969] CLJ 303).

5 Quality of title

Having decided what sort of estate the purchaser of registered land is looking for, the next question is: how sure can he be of getting it? In other words, how far can he be sure of the vendor's ownership? Here the reader will recall the proposition advanced much earlier that ownership in English land law is rarely absolute and generally relative (see p 85). Probably this is indisputable in unregistered conveyancing, but what the purchaser now needs to appreciate is the quality of a registered title (taking this in the combined senses of ownership and the evidence thereof). Since such a title will most commonly (for freeholds at least) be called 'absolute' by order, the riddle arises: how absolute is an absolute title? As to this, a renowned Chief Land Registrar has written that 'whereas the quality of an unregistered title is a matter of opinion about which differing views may be held, the quality of a registered title is one of hard fact' (Ruoff, *The Torrens System*, 1957). So let us face the facts, which may best be done from the purchaser's post-registration point of view.

The reason for this awkward attitude rests on the opinion of a full Court of Appeal that the statutory provisions (ss 20 and 23) as to the effect of registration of a disposition:

> are designed to protect a purchasing transferee from defects in the transferor's title . . . and not to relieve such a transferee from a defect in the transferee's own title

(*Morelle* v *Wakeling* [1955] 2 QB 379, at p 411, overruled in effect on other points in *Attorney-General* v *Parsons* [1956] AC 421; see also *Gibbs* v *Messer* [1891] AC 248, at p 254, and cp *Frazer* v *Walker* [1967] 1 AC 569). In other words, each registered proprietor's title stands or falls entirely on its own merits.

However, this individual quality, independent of any predecessor's position, can remain unsullied in so far only as the following two of the three fundamental principles of any system of registration of title are observed, namely: (1) the mirror principle, and (2) the curtain principle (see Ruoff, *The Torrens System*, at p 8; the third, the insurance principle, though valuable, is but a consolation prize for non-observance of the first two).

(a)   Mirrors

The first fundamental principle:

> involves the proposition that the register is a mirror which reflects accurately and completely and beyond all argument the current facts that are material to a man's title. This mirror does not reveal the history of the title, for disused facts are obliterated. It does not show matters (such as trusts) that are incapable of substantive registration. And it does not allow anyone to view and consider facts and events which are capable of being registered and ought to have been registered. In other words a title is free from all adverse burdens, rights and qualifications unless they are mentioned on the register

(Ruoff, *The Torrens System*, at p 8). This, it is added, is what we mean in England when we speak of an absolute title whilst others use the word 'indefeasibility' when describing the conclusive state of the title (loc cit). Thereafter it is recognised that 'in this imperfect world the mirror does not invariably give a completely reliable reflection' and a few examples are given of matters (including certain of the overriding interests) which would lead to rectification of the register.

The view may be taken by conveyancers that it is these two topics (ie, overriding interests and rectification) which render the mirror image seriously and unacceptably incomplete, but they generally enjoy detailed discussion as aspects of basic land law and will not be re-examined here. However, the most shattering illustration ought not to be overlooked. This can occur whenever a trust for sale comes into conjunction with the occupational hazard, which is, of course, the inclusion in the list of the overriding interests of:

The rights of every person in actual occupation of the land or in receipt of the rents and profits thereof, save where enquiry is made of such person and the rights are not disclosed;

(para (g) of s 70 (1) of the Land Registration Act 1925).

The position of the beneficiaries under a trust for sale in relation to para (g) has appeared uncertain. No problem should arise where the overreaching machinery has been operated by payment to two trustees in compliance usually with the restriction on the register. For in such cases an occupying beneficiary's only rights would be against the proceeds of sale, beating the air so far as any purchaser of land is concerned. Consequently the only case requiring consideration was where a sole unrestricted proprietor appeared on the register and was selling as beneficial owner whilst in fact a trust for sale subsisted (eg, because of contributions to the purchase price: *Bull* v *Bull* [1955] 1 QB 234). In *un*registered conveyancing the answer would depend on notice, the bona fide purchaser for value of a legal estate taking free of any equitable interest of which he had no notice (*Pilcher* v *Rawlins* (1872) 7 Ch App 259). In registered conveyancing, however, para (g) makes the consequences of occupation absolute, and the strict position has now been made clear in *Williams & Glyn's Bank Ltd* v *Boland* [1981] AC 487. The material facts were that a husband was registered as sole proprietor of the matrimonial home where he lived with his wife; the wife had made a substantial contribution to the acquisition of the house but had not entered any caution, restriction or notice on the register; the husband, to secure business debts, charged the house to the plaintiff bank without the wife knowing; the bank made no enquiry as to any interest of the wife. The combined effect of the decisions (unanimous) of the Court of Appeal and the House of Lords was as follows: *first*, that the wife, because of her contribution, was an equitable tenant in common under a trust for sale, the husband being a sole trustee of the legal estate; *second*, that the wife's interest, although technically in the proceeds of sale, was capable of constituting an 'overriding interest' within para (g); and *third*, that the wife was 'in actual occupation' for the purposes of the paragraph notwithstanding that the sole legal owner was also in occupation. Accordingly, the bank's charge was subject to the wife's interest. Arguments about inconvenient conveyancing consequences were dismissed as exaggerated: Lord Wilberforce observed (at pp 508–9) that 'What is involved is a departure from an easy-going practice of dispensing with enquiries as to occupation beyond that of the vendor and accepting the risks of doing so. To substitute for this a practice of more careful enquiry as to the fact of occupation, and if necessary, as to the rights of occupiers can not, in my view of the matter, be considered as unacceptable except at the price of overlooking the widespread development of shared interests of ownership.'

However, readers should appreciate that the consequences of the decision are not confined to spouses and mortgagees, but would cover any contributory occupier and also affect purchasers and lessees from the sole registered proprietor. So obviously thought ought to be given to developing an effective enquiry procedure; merely directing enquiries to the registered proprietor himself about other occupiers and their interests will not suffice to protect purchasers or mortgagees (except that remedies for misrepresentation may become available). Some such thought was given in a quasi-official note at [1980] Conv 85–7.

Most building societies and other institutional lenders have issued 'supplementary instructions' to their solicitors essentially involving not only enquiry of the borrower but also forms of consent, acknowledgment or waiver to be signed by other disclosed occupiers. However, doubts are felt about the efficacy of these precautions. Para (g) is expressly only avoided 'where enquiry is made of such persons and the rights are not disclosed'. So enquiry of the borrower is irrelevant and consents, etc, are not envisaged but simply non-disclosure with absolute consequences. The difficulties with consents, etc, appear to be fourfold, *first*, they are purported transactions dependent for their validity on the presence of legal and mental capacity and of consideration and on the absence of duress or undue influence (cp *Re Pauling's ST* [1964] Ch 303, as to the presumption of undue influence on the part of a parent not only enduring for a time after full age has been attained but also invalidating consents given to a bank which knew or ought to have known thereof); *second*, the transactions involved in these consents, etc, may technically constitute assignments of equitable choses in action and, as such protection by entry of a priority caution on the 'minor interests index' should strictly be required (s 102 (2), see note at [1981] Conv 323–5); *third*, the 'supplementary instructions' only contemplate current actual occupiers whereas it is clear that para (*g*) comprehends constructive occupation (see *Strand Securities Ltd* v *Caswell* [1965] Ch 958, CA) as well also as persons 'in receipt of the rents or profits'; *fourth*, the consents, etc, are required on the basis that the occupier signing does have an interest or right but allows priority. This last difficulty in itself seems to constitute defective conveyancing. If the occupier actually has such an interest as in the *Williams & Glyn's* case, this means that there is a statutory trust for sale so that the sole proprietor is, to the knowledge of the lender, a trustee for sale with a limited power to mortgage and no power alone to give a valid receipt for capital money arising (see s 27 (2) of the Law of Property Act 1925 and *Suenson-Taylor's ST* [1974] 1 WLR 1280). Therefore, instead of it being a mere matter of priorities, the mortgage itself might be held to be void. Accordingly, it is suggested that the better practice would be to operate the overreaching machinery in all cases by the appointment of a second trustee for sale (see also a note at [1980] Conv 313–8 but cp a letter at ibid, pp 458–9). Further reference may usefully be made to articles by Jill Martin at [1980] Conv 316–87, by Colin Sydenham at ibid, pp 427–32 and by Sydney M Clayton at [1981] Conv 19–31. Incidentally it may be just noticed that the implications have also been considered in detail by the Law Commission who have reported that they can see no satisfactory solution without legislation (Law Com No 115); see further, as to the plaintive pigeonholing of this report, notes, etc, at [1982] Conv 393–6 and [1983] Conv 5–8 and 87–8.

Aside altogether from this notorious crack, it should also be understood that the mirror may reveal shadows on a title of no substance. The point is that the mere entry of a matter on the register does not necessarily mean that it is valid and enforceable (see *Kitney* v *MEPC Ltd* [1977] 1 WLR 981, CA, as to a void option, also s 52 (2) of the Land Registration Act 1925 and *Willé* v *St John* [1910] 1 Ch 325, as to positive covenants).

(*b*) *Curtains*

Turning to the second principle, we find that it merely means keeping the equities off the title:

> The curtain principle is one which provides that the register is the sole source of information for proposing purchasers, who need not and, indeed, must not concern themselves with trusts and equities which lie behind the curtain

(Ruoff, ibid, at p 11; cf as to unregistered conveyancing, ante, p 103). In general, the equities are 'offed' by s 74 of the Land Registration Act 1925, which provides that no person 'dealing with a registered estate . . . shall be affected with notice of a trust express implied or constructive' (see also s 59 (6)). In particular, the equities are 'offed' by ss 20 (1) and 23 (1) of the Act by which registration confers the legal estate on the transferee subject to any entries on the register and to overriding interests 'but free from all other estates and interests whatsoever'. These very wide words have been said judicially to 'embrace prima facie not only all kinds of legal interests but all kinds of equitable interests' (per Bridge J in *Miles v Bull (No 2)* [1969] 3 All ER 1585, at pp 1589–90).

In this last cited case, it had been contended that the novel interest conferred on spouses by the Matrimonial Homes Act 1967 should be treated as enforceable against purchasers who took with constructive notice. This contention was rejected as follows:

> it does not seem to me that it is for the court to say that Parliament really did not mean what it said, that Parliament has not provided adequate or effective protection, or that the old equitable doctrines of the court can be introduced for the purpose in effect of widening the protection to extend it to those who have not protected themselves by taking the appropriate statutory steps

(per Bridge J in *Miles v Bull (No 2)* [1969] 3 All ER 1585, at p 1590). Indeed, the judicial line has seemed quite consistent. As Cross J forcefully observed:

> It must be borne in mind, first, that it is vital to the working of the land registration system that notice of something which is not on the register of title

in question shall not affect a transferee unless it is an overriding interest (*Strand Securities Ltd v Caswell* [1965] Ch 373, at p 390; echoed clearly per Russell LJ on appeal [1965] Ch 958, at p 987; per Plowman LJ in *Parkash v Irani Finance Ltd* [1970] Ch 101, at p 109; per Walton J in *Freer v Unwins Ltd* [1976] Ch 288, at p 297). Thus in *De Lusignan v Johnson* (1973) 117 SJ 854 a registered chargee took free of an estate contract, even though he knew of its existence, because it was not protected on the register.

So far the curtain seems thick, does it not? The statutory machinery has apparently superseded all equitable principles. Accordingly, most recently, Lord Wilberforce has given his opinion that 'the law as to notice as it may affect purchasers of unregistered land, whether contained in decided cases, or in a statute (. . . Law of Property Act, s 199) has no application even by analogy to registered land' (in *Williams & Glyn's Bank Ltd v Boland* [1981] AC 487, at p 504; see also to like effect, per Simonds J in *White v Bijou Mansions Ltd* [1937] Ch 610, at p 620; affirmed [1938] Ch 351; cf per Harman J in *Hollington Bros v Rhodes* [1951] 2 All ER 578, at p 580). Unhappily, however, the curtain has not proved impenetrable. To begin with, a volunteer, hardly surprisingly, will take subject to the same equities, if any, as his transferor (ss 20 (4) and 23 (5) of the Act). Then, naturally, the trustee-transferee will certainly remain tied to his own trust, ie, he will take subject to the equities of his own beneficiaries, although a purchaser for value from him should take free of them. But beyond those two unexceptional chinks a larger hole has now been torn to let a great shaft of darkness through into the light otherwise preserved by the curtain principle.

Neither of the sections which directly keep equities off registered titles (ie, ss 20 (1) and 23 (1) of the 1925 Act) explicitly calls for good faith but only for the registration of a 'transferee' for valuable consideration. However, in *Peffer v Rigg* [1977] 1 WLR 285, Graham J managed to treat 'transferee' and 'purchaser' as synonymous for present purposes and then looked to the definition of the latter word in order to import the requirement of good faith (see s 3 (xxi)). He did this by reading s 20 (1), which uses the undefined word 'transferee', with s 59 (6), which provides, fraud and bankruptcy apart, that '. . . a *purchaser* acquiring title under a registered disposition shall not be concerned with . . .' in effect, any matter not protected by entry on the register. Having done this, he pronounced that a transferee purchaser 'cannot in my judgment be in good faith if he has in fact notice of something which affects his title as in the present case' (ibid, p 294; the something there was a trust producing a mere 'minor interest' protectable by entry on the register). In other words, a purchaser with notice cannot rely on the registered title.

This proposition is most unsatisfactory. Doubtless the pronouncement was confined to actual notice but even so it appears difficult to justify. None of the cases supporting the curtain principle was cited. No mention was made of s 74 of the Act, or of the definition of 'minor interest' in s 3 (xv)—'. . . capable of being overridden (whether or not a purchaser has notice thereof)'. Nor, even, was the rest of s 59 (6) itself quoted: 'whether he has or has not notice thereof, express, implied or constructive'. Nor was there any reference to *Smith* v *Morrison* [1974] 1 WLR 659 for the meaning of 'good faith' in this context (ie, despite actual notice 'acts honestly . . . no ulterior motive . . . honest doubt': per Plowman J at p 676). The only decision referred to in support was *Jones* v *Lipman* [1962] 1 WLR 832, where between contract and completion a vendor of property registered with an absolute title transferred that property for value to a limited company which he owned and which obtained registration; the purchaser sued for specific performance both the vendor and his company, and Russell J, inter alia, held that:

> The defendant company is the creature of the first defendant, a device and a sham, a mask which he holds before his face in an attempt to avoid recognition by the eye of equity . . . an equitable remedy is rightly to be granted against the creature in such circumstances

(at p 836). In so holding he did no more than mention the submission of counsel for the defendants that this 'ran counter to the express statutory provisions as to title to be found in ss 20 and 59 of the Land Registration Act 1925' (loc cit). The decision might well be distinguishable in that it did not in substance and reality involve any transferee or purchaser at all (see further Jill Martin, 'Constructive Trusts of Registered Land' [1978] Conv 52–9).

The *Peffer* v *Rigg* proposition also appears to be in traumatic contrast to the position in unregistered conveyancing. There the House of Lords has recognised that 'good faith' is *not* an element in the definition of 'purchaser' for the purposes of the provisions of the Land Charges Acts (*Midland Bank Trust Co Ltd* v *Green* [1981] AC 513). Therefore an estate contract was held void for non-registration as against a purchaser, notwithstanding actual notice and a collusive sale for a near nominal consideration (ie, by virtue of now the 1972 Act, s 4 (6)). However, Lord Wilberforce no less did incidentally admit that 'Addition of a requirement that the purchaser should be in good faith would bring with it the necessity of inquiry into the purchaser's motives and state of mind' (ibid). So the true question might seem to be: was Graham J justified in adding that requirement? Surely not: the conflict with other dicta of Lord Wilberforce about the system of land registration would prove intolerable (see again *Williams & Glyn's Bank Ltd* v *Boland* [1981] AC 487, at pp 503–4: '. . . designed to free the purchaser from the hazards of notice—real or constructive . . . the law as to notice . . . has no application . . .').

However, Graham J did shortly suggest an alternative basis for his decision in *Peffer* v *Rigg*, namely that the transferee's knowledge of the existing trust gave rise to a constructive trust:

> Even if, therefore, I am wrong as to the proper construction of sections 20 and 59, when read together, and even if section 20 strikes off the shackles of the express trust which bound the [transferor], this cannot invalidate the new trust imposed on the [transferee]. On this assumption it seems to me that the ground is properly laid for granting rectification of the register under section 82

(at [1977] 1 WLR 294). This alternative approach has since been followed, quite independently, by the Court of Appeal. In *Orakpo* v *Manson Investments Ltd* [1977] 1 WLR 347 concerning an unpaid vendor's lien, Buckley LJ appeared to reject the contention that s 20 (1) 'should be read in a modified manner, so as not to free a registered proprietor from liabilities or encumbrances to the creation of which he has himself been privy' whilst accepting that 'if the present entries on the register do not reflect the true position, the register is open to rectification' (ibid, p 360; see also per Goff LJ at p 370; affirmed on other aspects [1978] AC 95). This approach certainly seems more consistent with the principles of registration of title: bad faith would not necessarily escape unscathed but it would have to be judged under the specific statutory provisions as to rectification of the register (ie, s 82 of the Act as amended) rather than under general equitable principles affecting the disposition itself (cp notes at (1977) 41 Conv (NS) 1 and 221 and see further DC Jackson 'Security of Title in Registered Land' (1978) 74 LQR 239-54).

Nevertheless the worst was yet to come. Regretful reference must also be made to *Lyus* v *Prowsa Developments Ltd* [1982] 1 WLR 1044 in which a plot of land was sold expressly subject to the plaintiff's contract to purchase so far, if at all, as it might be enforceable; the plaintiff was not in occupation so as to claim an overriding interest and his contract had not been protected by registration and was not mentioned in the transfer. Dillon J held that the plaintiff's contract was specifically enforceable against the registered proprietor on the basis of not allowing the Land Registration Act 1925 to be used as an instrument of fraud: the sale subject to the contract gave rise to a constructive trust in the plaintiff's favour. Yet perhaps this is not so bad: no reliance was placed on the illicitly imported words 'good faith' nor simply on the fact of actual notice, and his lordship accepted that there was no fraud in relying on legal rights conferred by statute; instead all turned on there being equitable fraud involved in reneging on a positive contractual stipulation whereby a purchaser expressly or impliedly undertook a trust (see ibid, pp 1054-5).

But even that is not quite the end of the matter. With resignation, readers should appreciate that there may be a collateral liability on indemnity covenants notwithstanding the statutory consequences of non-registration (see *Eagon* v *Dent* [1965] 3 All ER 334 as to No 18 (3) of the National Conditions now in the 20th ed; cf The Law Society's Conditions, 1980 ed, No 5 (1) (*c*)). Further borne in mind should be the possibility of a remedy in tort, ie, conspiracy to induce breach of contract (see *Esso Petroleum Co Ltd* v *Kingswood Motors Ltd* [1974] 1 QB 142). And do not forget to plead the point of voidness for non-registration, for the courts may then not allow it to be raised on appeal (*Balchin* v *Buckle* (1982) *The Times,* 1 June, CA).

Against all this, where good faith is not disputed, a transferee for value *without notice* may nonetheless take subject to some equities. This applies especially to those equities which can be squeezed into the classification as 'overriding interests', which are more a breach of the first fundamental principle than of the present curtain principle. There is, however, another instance in which a bona fide purchaser of registered land can be prejudiced by unknown equities. This is where an equitable interest has been properly protected on the register but the transferee for value fails to discover the entry: he will take subject to that equity even though the fault was not his. Thus Plowman J rejected a submission that the doctrine of purchaser of a legal estate without notice could be prayed in aid so as to confer priority over a charge protected by a caution which, due to a Land Registry mistake, had not been revealed by an official search (in *Parkash* v *Irani Finance Ltd* [1970] Ch 101).

Finally, one or two lesser queries may occur about whether certain other equitable rules have really been superseded by the statutory machinery of registration of title. For example, is it true that, in the absence of an appropriate restriction on the register, the general limits of the powers of joint proprietors can be ignored (see the editorial divergence in Key and Elphinstone, *Precedents in Conveyancing*, 15th ed, vol 3, at pp 255–8; cf an article by the present writer in *Law Society's Gazette* (1963), vol 60, at p 419)? Again, the moot point has been mentioned of whether a registered proprietor of leaseholds could be liable to another lessee under a building scheme without any notice of the equitable obligation appearing on the register of his title (see per Atkinson J in *Newman v Real Estate Debenture Corporation Ltd and Flower Decorations Ltd* [1940] 1 All ER 131, at pp 149–50).

G STAMPING ON THE TITLE*

Let us, at least, begin logically: *First*, the most likely meaning, in a conveyancing context, of the vital word 'title' is *evidence of ownership*. *Second*, an instrument which is not duly stamped is neither admissible in evidence (except in criminal proceedings) nor available for any other purpose whatever (s 14 (4) of the Stamp Act 1891). *Therefore*, if such an instrument were to form the root of or a link in a vendor's chain of the title then the title—the evidence of ownership—would be defective. Thereafter the purchaser's requisition and the vendor's compliance at his own expense (duty plus penalties for late stamping) should follow as the night the day. For as the courts have said:

the question of the proper stamping of a deed is an important matter of title, because, if the owner of the property is called on either to defend his right or to attack a wrong-doer with regard to the property, it is necessary for him to be able to produce his title deeds in evidence without further trouble

(per Luxmoore J in *Re Spollon and Long's Contract* [1936] Ch 713, at p 718); and so:

A purchaser is entitled to have every deed forming a step in his title in such a shape that he can, if he needs it, give it in evidence

(per Lush LJ in *Whiting to Loomes* (1881) 17 Ch D 10, at p 12; see also per James LJ, ibid, p 11). In other words, the purchaser can insist on the due stamping of every instrument which the vendor has, or ought to have, abstracted. Thus the rule extends not only to instruments disposing of the estate sold but also to those relating to interests to which the estate sold is or has been subject, eg, a lease or tenancy agreement (*Smith v Wyley* (1852) 16 Jur 1136; *Coleman v Coleman* (1898) 79 LT 66) or a mortgage deed (*Whiting to Loomes,* ante). In the mentioned case the vendor was bound to effect due stamping even though the mortgagee was to join in the conveyance, since :

the court is not entitled to speculate whether the purchaser may or may not have occasion to use the deed

(per Lush LJ, loc cit).

So the purchaser's entitlement in respect of stamping on the title is, prima facie, pretty absolute. What is more the vendor cannot anticipate and avoid his obligations in the usual way, for statute has forestalled him with the provision that:

Every condition of sale framed with the view of precluding objection or requisition upon the ground of absence or insufficiency of stamp upon any instrument executed after 16 May 1888 and every contract, arrangement, or undertaking for assuming the liability on account of absence or insufficiency of

---

*This section is concerned only with the stamp duty position as between vendor and purchaser. Otherwise readers may be pleased to refer to *Emmet on Title*, 18th ed, pp 1105–39.

stamp upon any such instrument or indemnifying against such liability, absence or insufficiency shall be void

(s 117 of the Stamp Act 1891; for the practice as to instruments executed on or before 16 May 1888 see *Williams on Vendor and Purchaser*, 3rd ed, vol 1, pp 72, 119). This provision should even proscribe a condition of sale to the effect that any instrument should be left to be duly stamped by the vendor only if and when this becomes necessary (cf *Nixon* v *Albion Marine Insurance Co* (1867) LR 2 Exch 338).

The prima facie absolute rule as to a purchaser's stamping rights outlined above has suffered some seemingly severe denting from two rather peculiar decisions. In the first of these—*Ex parte Birkbeck Freehold Land Society* (1883) 24 Ch D 119— the basic facts were that a vendor-society, instead of duly stamping the reconveyances to it of the land in question from its members, suggested joining them in the conveyance to the purchaser. Pearson J agreed with this suggestion, saying that the result would be as effective as proper reconveyances, since 'the entire legal estate, free from any claim, legal or equitable [would be vested in the purchaser] under a conveyance to which [the members] were parties' (ibid, p 125). The learned judge distinguished *Whiting to Loomes* on the ground that a mortgagee cannot be joined in a conveyance without the purchaser being obliged subsequently to show why he was joined, for which the duly stamped mortgage deed would be required. Nonetheless, this decision does indicate a possible way, if ever need arises, for a vendor to avoid due stamping (plus penalties) of, eg, a discharge of a mortgage or a surrender of a lease or such like. One should add, however, that Pearson J was evidently much influenced in his decision by the surely immaterial fact that the purchase in question was compulsory.

The other peculiar decision—*Re Weir and Pitt's Contract* (1911) 55 SJ 536—has been cited without comment as authority for the reasonable-sounding proposition that:

the onus of showing that a document is improperly stamped lies on the person alleging this, and if consistently with all the known facts the document may be properly stamped, a purchaser cannot call upon the vendor to show that it is

(Monroe and Nock, *Stamp Duties*, 5th ed, at para 335; also Alpe, *Stamp Duties*, 25th ed, p 64; and compare *Law Society's Digest*, Opinion, No 268, with the apparently contradictory Opinion No 209 (*a*) in the Fourth (Cumulative) Supplement). From the short, somewhat confusing report of the case, the material facts which emerge are that the land in question had been sold and conveyed first for £520 to *W* senior, then for £200 from *W* senior to *W* junior. After this, *P*, buying from *W* junior for £530, objected that the latter conveyance was not duly stamped, being ad valorem only on £200 rather than on the full value of the land as a voluntary disposition within s 74 of the Finance (1909–10) Act 1910. With regard to this objection, Warrington J is reported (loc cit) as saying:

Section 74 (1) of the Act lays down general provisions as to the mode of ascertaining the amount of the stamp duty on voluntary transfers. Subsection (5) lays it down that any transfer or conveyance shall be deemed voluntary if, in the opinion of the commissioners, the consideration is inadequate, or if the transferee, under the circumstances, receives a substantial benefit. It is said that this means that at any time hereafter a subsequent purchaser for value may be attacked, on the ground that a previous conveyance was not properly stamped. The section only means that at the time a conveyance comes to be stamped the commissioners may raise a question whether the consideration mentioned in it is adequate, or whether under the circumstances the transfer confers a substantial benefit. Once the conveyance is stamped, the provisions of the subsection are at an end as far as any subsequent purchaser is concerned.

It would be intolerable that he should have his conveyance prejudiced by what had taken place between other parties and the commissioners at a previous sale.

Now this judgment, far from containing a general proposition, clearly relates only to the particular question of the stamping of instruments of title which may or may not be deemed voluntary within s 74 (5) of the 1910 Act. For, as a rule, there can be little doubt that the mere stamping of an instrument in accordance with the stated consideration is *not* conclusive against any future stamp duty objections (see per Collins MR in *Maynard* v *Consolidated Kent Collieries Corporation* [1903] 2 KB 121, at p 129, and per Bennett J in *Conybear* v *British Briquettes Ltd* [1937] 4 All ER 191, at p 196).

In addition, Warrington J was surely led to error by assuming that stamping a conveyance always involves an opinion of the commissioners. Apart from the possibility, which accords with the theory of the Stamp Act, that the conveyance may have been engrossed on already stamped paper, there can again be little doubt that an opinion of the commissioners within the meaning of s 74 (5) is only obtained by way of adjudication under s 12 of the 1891 Act, when, and only when, future stamp duty objections really would be precluded (see s 12 (5)). This certainly was the view taken of the legislature's intention by Lord Greene MR in *Re Robb's Contract* [1941] Ch 463, at pp 473, 475 (which view remains valid for present purposes even though the decision itself was not allowed to stand: see s 44 of the Finance Act 1942). Further, in *Lap Shun Textiles Industrial Co Ltd* v *Collector of Stamp Revenue* [1976] AC 530 the Privy Council decided that it is still open to the commissioners to treat a conveyance as a voluntary disposition if they ever form the opinion that the stated consideration conferred a substantial benefit on the purchaser, even though that consideration was agreed in good faith by way of an arm's length bargain. It has as a result been suggested that practitioners should insist upon adjudication: see a note in (1976) 40 Conv (NS) 250.

The proposition attributed to *Re Weir and Pitt*, ante, is true in that in the absence of any evidence at all either way, the onus clearly does lie upon the person raising the stamp objection (see per Wigram V-C in *Hart* v *Hart* (1841) 1 Hare 1 at p 6). This onus, however, is not thought to amount to showing that the instrument actually is improperly stamped. Rather the purchaser has only to point to some evidence which contradicts the initial presumption of due stamping, and thereafter the onus will have been shifted (see per Lord Cairns in *Marine Investment Co* v *Haviside* (1872) LR 5 HL 624, at p 633). In the result therefore the more correct proposition would appear to be that where any cause is discovered to doubt the due stamping of an instrument of title, then the purchaser *is* able to call upon the vendor to show that the instrument actually is duly stamped, the doubt and any difficulty being 'got over by the vendor's willingness to have the deed adjudicated' (see per Younger J in *Re Soden and Alexander's Contract* [1918] 2 Ch 258, at p 267; also *Law Society's Digest*, Opinion No 209 (*a*) in Fourth (Cumulative) Supplement).

An additional curiosity of the decision in *Re Weir and Pitt's Contract*, ante, is that title to the land was registered, the purchaser noticing the discrepancies in price from the land certificate. Although there may be nothing inconsistent with what has been said above in a purchaser of registered land checking the due stamping of earlier transfers, for these may be needed in evidence for rectification purposes, such an excessively cautious course would certainly be inconsistent with the principles of registration of title. The present writer could hardly advise any change in the practice of leaving all questions of the stamping of the earlier title to the registrar, who is, after all, under a statutory duty to satisfy himself in this respect (s 14 (3) of the Land Registration Act 1925; also s 17 of the Stamp Act 1891).

Lastly, mention may be made that any lost instruments of which satisfactory secondary evidence has been produced are to be presumed duly stamped (*Hart* v *Hart* (1841) 1 Hare 1; but cp per Chitty LJ and per Williams LJ in *Re Halifax Commercial Banking Co and Wood* (1898) 79 LT 536, at pp 539 and 540, respectively). This presumption arises because of the lack of evidence for or against due stamping and is, of course, rebuttable, for example, by evidence that the instrument had remained unstamped when it should have been stamped (*Marine Investment Co* v *Haviside* (1872) LR 5 HL 624). This is really no more than an application of the proposition mentioned above that when any cause to doubt due stamping appears, the vendor must remove it.

VII VENDOR AS TRUSTEE

ONE of the more important peculiarities of a contract for the sale of land is the availability almost as of right to either party of the equitable remedy of specific performance. This availability allows the application of the equitable maxim that equity looks on that as done which ought to be done, ie, the contract ought to be performed. And from this application flow consequences considerably affecting the rights and duties inter se of the vendor and purchaser.

The heart of the matter is that in the eyes of equity the purchaser has become the owner of the land and the vendor the owner of the purchase money just as if the contract had been completed by a conveyance (see eg, per Vaisey J in *Hillingdon Estates Co* v *Stonefield Estates Ltd* [1952] Ch 627, at p 631; also per Pennycuick J in *Capital Finance Co Ltd* v *Stokes* [1968] 1 WLR 1158, at pp 1162–3; on appeal [1969] 1 Ch 261). Hence the doctrine of conversion raises its often ugly head, though this is of more concern to those around the parties than to the parties themselves (see, eg, *Re Birmingham, Savage* v *Stannard* [1959] Ch 523; also articles by Phillip H Pettit at (1960) 24 Conv (NS) 47 and by John Tiley at (1969) 33 Conv (NS) 43). Also hence, however, comes the description of the vendor as a constructive trustee, for whilst the equitable ownership is in the purchaser the legal ownership remains outstanding in the vendor and that is almost a definition of the trust relationship. But—there is, of course, a but—this relationship subsists 'subject to the paramount right of the vendor and trustee to protect his own interest as vendor of the property' (per Lord Cairns in *Shaw* v *Foster* (1872) LR 5 HL 321, at p 338, see also per Jessel MR in *Lysaght* v *Edwards* (1876) 2 Ch D 499, at p 506). The vendor's interest, which qualifies his trusteeship, is in actually getting the purchase money and once he has got it he will become fully a trustee for the purchaser (see, eg, *Bridges* v *Mees* [1957] Ch 475). All this as a general proposition appears clear enough; nonetheless its actual application to the rights and duties of the parties may still need spelling out.

A PURCHASER'S POSITION

1 Losses

As the beneficial owner of the land, the purchaser is privileged to bear both losses and gains of, as it were, a capital nature (those of an income nature are the vendor's pigeon). That is to say, taking losses first, that the risk passes to the purchaser on the making of the contract in so far as concerns anything *not* caused by a breach of the vendor's duties (see *Rayner* v *Preston* (1881) 18 Ch D 1). Thus no simple contract for the sale of land has, so far as the writer is aware, ever been held discharged as frustrated, although apparently the possibility cannot be ruled out. This is a matter of deduction from the decision of the House of Lords that the doctrine of frustration is in principle applicable to executed leases as well as to agreements for leases (*National Carriers Ltd* v *Panalpina (Northern) Ltd* [1981] AC 675). Nevertheless the doctrine's application here in practice must be rare (cp per Lord Hailsham at p 691 envisaging coastal erosion as well as a 'vast convulsion of nature' as causing 'houses, gardens, even villages and their churches to fall into the North Sea'). Accordingly, no frustration was in fact found where a compulsory purchase order intervened (*Hillingdon Estates Co* v *Stonefield Estates Ltd* [1952] Ch 627, cp *Korogluyan* v *Matheou* (1975) 239 EG 649 as to the vendor's consequent inability to give vacant possession), nor where the property was listed as of architectural or historical interest, so precluding the purchaser's planned development (*Amalgamated Investment & Property Co Ltd* v *John Walker & Sons Ltd* [1977] 1 WLR 164, CA) nor where the purchaser's money was stuck in Nigeria (*Universal Corporation* v *Five Ways Properties Ltd* [1979] 1 All ER 552, CA).

Catastrophic and hypothetical events apart, those losses to land which are entirely the purchaser's look out may range the whole spectrum from act of God (eg, earthquake: *Cass* v *Rudele* (1693) 2 Vern 280) to act of man (eg, bombing: cf *Killner* v *France* [1946] 2 All ER 83). Even so, the riskiest risk is destruction by fire (this not frustrating the contract: *Paine* v *Meller* (1801) 6 Ves 349) and with this more in mind than anything else, insurance questions may be raised (but see a note at [1978] Conv 183–5 suggesting that the onus should be on the vendor to show that the fire was not his fault; cp per Goddard LCJ in *Sochaki* v *Sas* [1947] 1 All ER 344, at p 345, rejecting res ipsa loquitur for fire).

The primary *insurance* question is: what happens if the vendor has insured (being unpaid, he has an insurable interest; *Collingridge* v *Royal Exchange Assurance Corporation* (1877) 3 QBD 173) but the purchaser has not? Who gets any insurance money in respect of a loss occurring between contract and completion? Fair's fair requires that the purchaser, as risk-bearer, gets the money, but this would be too simple. Apart from statute, first, the vendor would be able to recover the money from the insurance company (*Collingridge* v *Royal Exchange Assurance Corporation*, ante); secondly, the purchaser would be unable to recover the money from the vendor, a sale of land not normally including the benefit of insurance policies (*Rayner* v *Preston* (1881) 18 Ch D 1, see further below); and thirdly, the insurance company would be able to recover the insurance money out of the purchase money either from the vendor, he having after completion suffered no loss to be indemnified against, or from the purchaser, the insurance company being subrogated to the vendor's rights (*Castellain* v *Preston* (1883) 11 QBD 380).

By statute two possibilities are now open to the purchaser. The first, which has been open for a long time, applies only where buildings have been destroyed or damaged by fire. It enables a purchaser, as a person interested, to require the insurance company to lay out the insurance money towards rebuilding or reinstating the building in question (s 83 of the Fires Prevention (Metropolis) Act 1774). This possibility, on the face of it fairly satisfactory, is generally considered to be under a cloud by conveyancers, as having so many doubts about it that reliance should not be placed on it (see, eg, *Gibson's Conveyancing*, 20th ed, at p 150). So let us hurry on to the second possibility which was introduced amongst the 1925 property legislation. In effect, a purchaser may, on or after completion, recover from the vendor any money coming to him under an insurance policy 'in respect of any damage to or destruction of property included in the contract,' ie, not just fire (s 47 (1) of the Law of Property Act 1925). But this is subject to:

    (*a*) any stipulation to the contrary contained in the contract,

    (*b*) any requisite consent of the insurers, [and]

    (*c*) the payment by the purchaser of the proportionate part of the premium from the date of the contract

(s 47 (2)). The contract mentioned in (*a*) must, one supposes, be that between the vendor and purchaser, not that between vendor and insurance company. Otherwise comment is called for only on (*b*): whilst most policies do contain terms indicating general consent, this, first, may not be known to the purchaser, secondly, will not enable him to sue on an insurance contract to which he is not a party, and thirdly, on the safety-first precept, does not mean dispensing with giving notice for the purchaser's interest to the insurance company. All this is catered for, so far as possible, by the National Conditions, 20th ed, No 21, but even these emphasise that the vendor is not bound to keep up with any insurance. Compare The Law Society's Conditions, 1980 ed, No 11, which is designed instead to deal with the position when both parties insure and certainly the better practice would seem to be that of having the purchaser insure for himself (see further JE Adams in (1971) *Law Society's Gazette* vol 68, at p 224; also Adams and Aldridge at ibid (1980) vol 77, p 376).

2 Gains

Leaving losses, the other side of the scales bears the rule that the purchaser is entitled to all 'capital benefits'—such as improvements or appreciation—accruing to the land 'twixt contract and completion (see per Plumer V-C in *Harford* v *Purrier* (1816) 1 Madd 532, at p 539). And this is so even if the benefit arises by virtue of the vendor's expenditure (see per Wigram V-C in *Monro* v *Taylor* (1848) 8 Hare 51, at p 60; and see *Sherwin* v *Shakspear* (1854) 5 De GM & G 517). Then, however, the question may be asked whether the vendor is entitled, like all good trustees, to be indemnified for this expenditure. Ordinarily he is not, for as Simonds J put it, after stating that the vendor was a constructive trustee for the purchaser:

> but this statement must not be pressed so far as to give to the vendor all the rights of indemnity to which a trustee in the full sense is entitled from his trust estate, for the vendor has his own personal and substantial interest in the property, which he is entitled to protect, and it is, in my judgment, impossible to concede to him in respect of payments made by him, whether voluntarily or, as this payment was made, compulsorily [a war damage contribution], the right of indemnity which an ordinary trustee can claim. This is a payment which might in certain circumstances enure for the vendor's own benefit, as, for example, if the purchaser made default in completion and the contract was rescinded

(in *Re Watford Corporation's and Ware's Contract* [1943] Ch 82, at p 85). Nonetheless, the conflicting suggestion has been made judicially that a vendor who makes permanent improvements at a cost exceeding income merely to preserve the property may recover from the purchaser (see per Lord Selborne in *Phillips* v *Silvester* (1872) LR 8 Ch 173, at p 176, and per Kekewich J in *Bolton Partners* v *Lambert* (1888) 41 Ch D 295, at p 302). As put, this suggestion seems dubious and in the former case it probably went no further than saying that the vendor might give the purchaser the choice of paying for essential improvements or permitting the deterioration to continue (see also *Golden Bread Co* v *Hemmings* [1922] 1 Ch 162, which would support this).

The rule as to gains may have been expressed deceptively at the beginning of the preceding paragraph—please reread it as though the words '*to the land*' were italicised. The point is that the purchaser is only entitled to physical accretions and not to financial benefit coming to the vendor. This was illustrated by a most ingenious vendor not so long ago; Mr H-S, occupying a requisitioned house, on one day contracted to buy it, subject to the requisitioning, and to resell it for a much higher price without mentioning the requisitioning; three days after the conveyance to Mr H-S and seventeen days before the conveyance to his purchaser, the house was derequisitioned and a substantial sum became payable to Mr H-S as the then 'owner' under the Compensation (Defence) Act 1939; the purchaser not surprisingly claimed that Mr H-S held the sum as a trustee; Upjohn J however, held that:

> The contract of sale did not, in my judgment, include or comprehend this compensation money. Had that been intended, then, in my view, it should have been expressly put in as part of the subject-matter of the sale. I cannot see how it is possible to say in the circumstances of this case, that [Mr H-S], who is entitled to receive it under the terms of the Act, becomes in some way a constructive trustee of that sum which he has not contracted to sell to the purchaser

(*Re Hamilton-Snowball's Conveyance* [1959] Ch 308, at pp 314–15, following *Rayner* v *Preston* (1881) 18 Ch D 1 and *Re Lyne-Stephens & Scott-Miller's Contract* [1920] 1 Ch 472, respectively relating to insurance money and dilapidations arising between contract and completion, and distinguishing *Re Armitage's Contract, Armitage* v *Inkpen* [1949] Ch 666, where compensation for requisitioning was held to belong to a vendor solely on a construction of the contract; cf also *Henshall* v *Fogg* [1964] 1 WLR 1127 as to a refund of surplus road costs).

So a vendor, at best, is only a trustee of that which was sold and the general rule that a trustee may not make any profit out of his trust cannot be relied on as between vendor and purchaser (see per Upjohn J in *Re Hamilton-Snowball's Conveyance*, ante, at p 312; his insinuation that only an express trustee becomes a constructive trustee of profits would seem untenable). But in odd contrast another general rule of the law of trusts may permit the recovery of financial profits by a purchaser from his vendor, namely the doctrine of tracing. In *Lake* v *Bayliss* [1974] 1 WLR 1073 it was held that if a vendor wrongfully but effectively sells and conveys the land to a third party he must account for the proceeds to the first purchaser. The basis for this decision was that the vendor is a trustee of the land and the purchaser has a beneficiary's remedy in rem of tracing the trust property into its new form, money. Ordinarily this remedy would only be of use where the first contract for sale had not been protected by registration and the second contract was at a sufficiently higher price (ie, so that the profit would exceed the measure of damages otherwise recoverable). An incidental and ironic aspect of this was the suggestion that it might in certain circumstances be within a vendor's duty to pass better offers on to the purchaser (see per Walton J at p 1076).

B   VENDOR'S POSITION

On the one, non-trustee, hand, stemming from his understandable anxiety about the purchase money, the vendor enjoys certain valuable rights (see generally per Jessel MR in *Lysaght* v *Edwards* (1876) 2 Ch D 499, at p 506). Thus he is impliedly entitled to remain in possession of the property until actual completion when the purchase money is paid (*Gedye* v *Montrose* (1858) 26 Beav 45; *Phillips* v *Silvester* (1872) LR 8 Ch 173). And if he parts with possession before actual completion, or even conveys the land to the purchaser, he may always fall back on the lien on the land that equity gives him until he is actually paid (see *Winter* v *Lord Anson* (1827) 3 Russ 488; *Nives* v *Nives* (1880) 15 Ch D 649; *Re Birmingham, Savage* v *Stannard* [1959] Ch 523 and *London and Cheshire Insurance Co Ltd* v *Laplagrene Property Co Ltd* [1971] Ch 499). In addition, a vendor will be entitled to receive and keep for himself the rents and profits of the land, less outgoings, accruing before the contractual completion date (*Cuddon* v *Tite* (1858) 1 Giff 395; for the position pending actual completion see Apportionment and Interest, p 192).

On the other, more trustee-like, hand, there is the rule that:

> during the interval prior to completion the vendor in possession is a trustee for the purchaser, and as such has duties to perform towards him, not exactly the same as in the case of other trustees, but certain duties, one of which is to use reasonable care to preserve the property in a reasonable state of preservation, and, so far as may be, as it was when the contract was made

(per Lord Coleridge CJ in *Clarke* v *Ramuz* [1891] 2 QB 456, at pp 459–60, see also per Kay LJ ibid, at p 462, and per Jessel MR in *Lysaght* v *Edwards* (1876) 2 Ch D 499, at p 507). These duties continue so long as the vendor retains possession of the property, which may be past the contractual completion date up to actual completion (see *Phillips* v *Silvester* (1872) LR 8 Ch 173, also per Kay LJ in *Clarke* v *Ramuz*, ante, at p 463). Unlike a trustee, however, the duties must be performed without hope of any indemnity (see *Re Watford Corporation's and Ware's Contract* [1943] Ch 82, and cases cited above) except in so far as outgoings as well as income are apportionable to the purchaser after the contractual completion date (see p 192). In truth the vendor is as much entitled as bound to perserve the property since he himself will benefit if the sale is not completed, which explains the lack of indemnity (see *Ecclesiastical Commissioners* v *Pinney* [1899] 2 Ch 729, at p 736, also per Simonds J in *Re Watford Corporation's and Ware's Contract*, ante, at p 85).

The duration of the vendor's duties calls for some comment. At one end, since the obligations arise not under but after the contract, they will not normally merge in the conveyance and, in the absence of waiver, the vendor can be sued even after completion for breach of them (see per Bowen LJ in *Clarke* v *Ramuz* [1891] 2 QB 456, at p 461, also *Cumberland Consolidated Holdings Ltd* v *Ireland* [1946] KB 264, at p 269). At the other end, there has recently been something of an extension, as Judge Edgar QC explained with regard to a vendor's duty not to remove fixtures and to take reasonable care of the property sold:

> This duty arises strictly only as at the date of the contract, but where there are representations made prior to the contract that certain items will be included or that certain states of affairs exist, then it seems to me that there would be a breach of the representation, which would be much the same in effect as the breach of duty of care. So that there is some duty before contract as well as after it

(*Ware* v *Verderber* (1978) 247 EG 1081, at p 1083).

There is little more that can be done here than indicate aspects of the duty of a vendor in possession to look after the property with much the same care that a trustee owes to his beneficiaries. To think of it in other terms, such a vendor will be liable for both permissive and voluntary waste. Thus he must keep the property repaired (*Royal Bristol Permanent Building Society* v *Bomash* (1887) 35 Ch D 390), and neither allow other persons to cause damage (*Clarke* v *Ramuz*, ante, a mysterious stranger removed several hundred cartloads of top soil) nor, needless to say, cause damage himself (*Cumberland Consolidated Holdings Ltd* v *Ireland*, ante, abandoning rubbish on the land; *Phillips* v *Lamdin* [1949] 2 KB 33, replacing an ornate Adam door by a plain white wood door).

However, with the common or garden dwellinghouse conveyance, the problems in practice seem to be of two sorts—both exemplified by that common man, who, after exchange of contracts, does nothing in the garden except for digging up the rose trees on the day of his departure—(1) what may a vendor take with him? and, (2) what care should he take of the property? In principle the answers are easy. As to (1), he may not remove anything that is a part of the property sold and he must remove everything else, ie, fixtures should be left and fittings or chattels taken (see, eg, the last two cases cited; trees and plants belong to the former). Of course the preliminary question of whether ornamental 'things' such as statues are fixtures or chattels may not always be so easy to answer (see *Hamp* v *Bygrave* (1983) *The Times*, 6 January and cp *Berkley* v *Poulett* (1976) 120 SJ 836, CA). And as to (2), he must, until actual completion, take reasonable care to preserve the property (see above), and Jessel MR has said of a vendor that 'as a trustee it is his duty to keep the property in a proper state of cultivation' (in *Egmont* v *Smith* (1877) 6 Ch D 469, at pp 475–6; see also as to cultivation *Foster* v *Deacon* (1818) 3 Madd 394; *Lord* v *Stephens* (1835) 1 Y & C Ex 222).

One other aspect of the preservation of the property requires special mention and that is the position arising where property, sold subject to subsisting tenancies, becomes wholly or partly vacant before completion. Should the vendor relet or leave vacant? In itself the only answer is unhelpful, being the dusty 'it all depends'. In one case a vendor was not liable for reletting when he would have been liable for not reletting; in another case vice versa exactly (see respectively *Egmont* v *Smith* (1877) 6 Ch D 469, agricultural land, and *Abdulla* v *Shah* [1959] AC 124, controlled reletting; cf *Vartoukian* v *Daejan Properties* (1969) 20 P & CR 983). This being so, the conclusion has been drawn that:

> Every case of this kind must therefore depend on its own facts but the moral for vendors is, in the light of *Abdulla* v *Shah*: if in doubt or when opportunity permits notify the purchaser that you intend to relet. Having notified the purchaser the moral derived from *Egmont* v *Smith* is: if he does not reply promptly go ahead with the reletting

(VG Wellings (1959) 23 Conv (NS) 178). In other words, shift the onus to the purchaser by consulting him, but bear in mind that his desire should not necessarily be the vendor's command, for the latter 'has to consider his own position in case the purchase does not go through' (per Sargant J in *Golden Bread Co* v *Hemmings* [1922] 1 Ch 162, at p 174). The purchaser's desire will, however, become virtually a command if accompanied by an offer of indemnity against loss (see per Jessel MR in *Egmont* v *Smith*, ante, at p 476, also *Abdulla* v *Shah*, ante).

Similarly, it has been held that after contract a vendor was under an obligation not to withdraw a planning application, which must be assumed to be of value to the purchaser, without his consent (*Sinclair-Hill* v *Southcott* (1973) 226 EG 1399). However, this did not mean that the vendor was under any obligation to prosecute the application for the benefit of the purchaser or to be responsible for costs incurred after contract (ibid). Nevertheless it has also been held that the vendor's duty of care extends to enforcing any post-contract breaches of covenants by tenants, although the vendor's failure to carry out this duty will only make him liable in damages (ie, by abatement of the price) and not preclude him from serving an effective notice to complete (*Prosper Homes Ltd* v *Hambros Bank Executor and Trustee Co Ltd* (1979) 39 P & CR 395).

C   QUALIFIED

By way of conclusion, the writer wishes to re-emphasise that the vendor is not normally a trustee for the purchaser in the fullest sense. Apart from the vital fact of having his own interest in the property to protect, there are two other major matters which qualify the vendor's trusteeship. The first of these is that the specific enforceability of the contract is a sine qua non (see *Howard* v *Miller* [1915] AC 318, at p 326; but cp *Lake* v *Bayliss* [1974] 1 WLR 1073, concerning tracing). From this fact alone fly all the shrapnel doctrines, of conversion, of the purchaser's equitable ownership and risk, and of the vendor's duties (see, eg, *Simmons* v *Pennington & Son* [1955] 1 WLR 183, especially per Denning LJ at ibid, p 187, where in the absence of specific performance the risk of fire was the vendor's). The second matter is that if the transaction be never completed, even though the discharge of the contract does not occur for months or even years, then again none of the doctrines can arise, so that the vendor cannot be held liable to the purchaser for any failure to preserve the property (see *Plews* v *Samuel* [1904] 1 Ch 464; *Ridout* v *Fowler* [1904] 1 Ch 658; 2 Ch 93). Completion, in this context, means merely payment of the purchase price ignoring any conveyance of the legal estate. On this essential event, therefore, the vendor makes two chameleonic changes of character: change one, he can be seen retrospectively to have been all along a qualified trustee as above for the purchaser (see the judgment of James LJ in *Rayner* v *Preston* (1881) 18 Ch D 1, also per Lord Hatherley in *Shaw* v *Foster* (1872) LR 5 HL 321, at p 356); change two, he is henceforth revealed as the fullest bare trustee imaginable, remaining such until he decently clothes the purchaser with the legal estate by conveyance (see, eg, *Bridges* v *Mees* [1957] Ch 475).

And more by way of postscript, a query may be put: does the vendor's duty of care as a trustee last until actual completion or only until the contractual completion date? The latter might seem fair whenever any delay in completion was due to the purchaser's default but perhaps this only causes common law consequences (cp *Raineri* v *Miles* [1981] AC 1050, HL).

VIII VACANT POSSESSION

WHAT the purchaser is entitled to get in the way of possession on completion depends, of course, on what the contract says. Thus if the sale were made expressly subject to some tenancy or other, then the purchaser would only be entitled to constructive possession, ie, in the sense of receipt of rents and profits (cf s 205 (1) (xix) of the Law of Property Act 1925). Again, if the sale were made expressly with vacant possession on completion, then the purchaser would be entitled to actual possession, ie, in the sense of occupation (*Beard* v *Porter* [1948] 1 KB 321). But what if the contract says nothing either way? Simonds J has held as a matter of law that:

> where a contract is silent as to vacant possession, but also silent as to any tenancy to which the property is subject, there is impliedly a contract that vacant possession will be given on completion

(in *Cook* v *Taylor* [1942] Ch 349, at p 352; followed by Romer J in *Re Crosby's Contract, Crosby* v *Houghton* [1949] 1 All ER 830).

The clarity of this, however, becomes occasionally obscured because this initial implication may be rebutted by implication (see *Lake* v *Dean* (1860) 28 Beav 607, also *North* v *Loomes* [1919] 1 Ch 378, see below). It is therefore desirable to provide expressly for vacant possession on completion, as indeed is usual, but this does not mean that there is no initial implication to that effect.

Obviously, the term, whether expressed or implied, for vacant possession would be breached if on completion anyone else is found to have a right to occupy prior to the purchaser's. The most common example of this is the still subsisting tenancy (eg, *Leek and Moorlands Building Society* v *Clark* [1952] 2 QB 788, surrender by one joint tenant insufficient), although there are, of course, other possibilities (see, eg, *Macara (James) Ltd* v *Barclay* [1945] KB 148, where the property was requisitioned after contract and before completion).

Less obviously, however, the vacant possession term goes beyond prior *rights* to occupy:

> Occupation by a person having no claim of right prevents the giving of "vacant possession", and it is the duty of the vendor to eject such a person before completion . . . The reason for this, it appears to us, is that the right to actual unimpeached physical enjoyment is comprised in the right to vacant possession

(*Cumberland Consolidated Holdings Ltd* v *Ireland* [1946] KB 264, at pp 270–1). The actual decision in the case was that a vendor who left enough rubbish behind to interfere substantially with the user of the property did not give vacant possession (the cellars of a warehouse were two-thirds filled with bags of solidified cement). The court indicated that this physical impediment aspect was subject to the rule de minimis and that such cases will be rare (loc cit), but the ratio decidendi has since been applied where a property was left full of furniture (*Norwich Union Life Insurance Society* v *Preston* [1957] 1 WLR 813).

Now, not obviously at all, the meaning of vacant possession has been extended beyond both prior rights and physical emptiness. In *Topfell Ltd* v *Galley Properties Ltd* [1979] 1 WLR 446 a house was sold with 'vacant possession of ground floor', there being a first floor tenancy, but a Housing Act notice limited occupation of the house to one household. Templeman J accepted the contention that vacant possession means 'the right to occupy and enjoy the property either by the purchaser himself or by his tenants or licensees' (at p 449) although adding that the meaning can 'vary from context to context' (loc cit). Then he looked at the background and concluded that the mere right to possession of a flat empty of persons and rubbish did not satisfy the contractual obligation in the case, which contemplated actual occupation and enjoyment for the future.

1   Latent defects?

The principles applicable to this vacant possession term bear a strong resemblance to those applicable to the vendor's duty to disclose any latent defects in his title (see p 62). The duty arises from the implied (if not expressed) term that the property is being sold 'free from incumbrances' (see *Timmins* v *Moreland Street Property Co* [1958] Ch 110). If anyone has a prior right to occupy, then there is a breach of that implied term also (see *Re Englefield Holdings Ltd and Sinclair's Contract* [1962] 1 WLR 1119, cf *District Bank Ltd* v *Webb* [1958] 1 WLR 148, where a lease was not treated as an incumbrance). Thus fairly recently where an agricultural grazing right tenancy had been claimed over the property sold, Goff J observed:

> The [purchaser] opened her case on the footing that in the circumstances the [vendor] was not at any material time able to give vacant possession. I doubt whether that is an entirely correct way of approaching it. I think the real question is whether the [vendor] was able to prove her title. As, however, there is no sufficient evidence that the alleged claimant was in actual occupation, and the inability to give vacant possession, therefore—if there were such inability—was based upon the right to possession, I think whether one looks at it as a question of vacant possession or of title, one gets back to the same position and must apply the same test

(in *Horton* v *Kurzke* [1971] 1 WLR 769, at pp 771–2).

After this further points of similarity can be detected. If the property is not in fact vacant when inspected by the purchaser the implication of vacant possession may not arise (this is an inference from rather than the decision in *Cook* v *Taylor* [1942] 2 All ER 85, see per Simonds J at p 87 B/C, omitted from [1942] Ch 349). Equally, *one*, there is no duty to disclose patent defects in title (see *Yandle* v *Sutton* [1922] 2 Ch 199), and *two*, the purchaser takes subject to defects of which he knew before the contract (see *Timmins* v *Moreland Street Property Co* [1958] Ch 110). Further, if the contract expressly provides for vacant possession there will be a breach even though the occupation is apparent or known to the purchaser before the contract (see *Hissett* v *Reading Roofing Co Ltd* [1969] 1 WLR 1757; cf *Re Gloag and Miller's Contract* (1883) 23 Ch D 320). Again, if the occupier is either without right or inanimate (eg, rubbish), then he, she or it can be likened to a removable defect in title which the vendor can be required to remove (see *Re Gloag and Miller's Contract*, ante; note that even rubbish, not being a fixture, is not a defect in the quality of the land itself: *Cumberland Consolidated Holdings Ltd* v *Ireland,* ante).

The only discernible difference of any substance between the two implications is in the post-completion position. Whilst the purchaser must pursue his remedies for non-disclosure before completion, thereafter relying on any covenants for title, it now appears established that damages for a failure to give vacant possession may be recovered even after completion. In *Hissett* v *Reading Roofing Co Ltd* [1969] 1 WLR 1757 a contract for the sale of property comprising offices, depot space and a flat had contained a special condition for vacant possession on completion, yet a protected tenant remained in occupation of the flat, and the purchaser succeeded in an action for damages for breach of contract. Stamp J rejected the argument put for the vendor that the contractual term for vacant possession had disappeared by merger into the conveyance; he took the view that this was not a matter with which the conveyance was concerned. Semble the result would be the same even though the term for vacant possession was implied rather than express.

2   Remedies

A failure to give vacant possession, again like a non-disclosure, renders the contract enforceable by the vendor neither at law nor in equity, the purchaser being entitled to the return of any deposit paid (see *Cook* v *Taylor* [1942] Ch 349, also *James Macara Ltd* v *Barclay* [1945] KB 148, decided independently of s 49 (2) of the Law of Property Act 1925). Alternatively, the purchaser may complete and then recover substantial damages in respect of the breach (*Beard* v *Porter* [1948] 1 KB 321). In *Cumberland Consolidated Holdings* v *Ireland* [1946] KB 264 the actual cost of removing the rubbish had been awarded and this measure of damages was not questioned in the Court of Appeal. Another alternative for a purchaser would be to seek specific performance with abatement of the price as in *Topfell Ltd* v *Galley Properties Ltd* [1979] 1 WLR 446, where Templeman J asserted that the proper measure of abatement or damages was the difference between the prices of the property with and without vacant possession (at p 451; cp *Beard* v *Porter*, ante, in which additional items of loss were recoverable).

3   Conditions of sale

Next, a care may be had for the effect of conditions of sale. Nothing now is said about vacant possession in The Law Society's General Conditions of Sale, 1980 ed, nor in the National Conditions, 20th ed. But each set contains a virtually foolproof special condition as to sale with vacant possession which should apply unless positively deleted in favour of sale subject to specified tenancies.

Apart from this both standard sets have long provided that the property is bought in its 'actual state and condition' (see National, No 13 (3), and Law Society's, No 5 (2) (*a*)). This, however, would not appear to extend to occupying persons, with or without a right (cf *Re Englefield Holdings Ltd and Sinclair's Contract* [1962] 1 WLR 1119), and would only extend to such physical impediments as are fixtures and not mere chattels (see *Cumberland Consolidated Holdings Ltd* v *Ireland* [1946] KB 264).

Nevertheless, a note should be taken that both sets may still contain a condition classifiable as an 'unjustifiable trap'. The National Conditions say that 'no error, misstatement or omission . . . in the sale plan or the Special Conditions shall annul the sale' (see No 17 (1)) and The Law Society's contain a condition in similar terms (see No 13 (2)). In *Curtis* v *French* [1929] 1 Ch 253, Eve J held this to cover the statement, which turned out to be a misstatement, that vacant possession would be given on completion, so depriving the purchaser of damages. In so far as vendors may rely on this to escape from damages, it is certainly a trap for purchasers, but any such reliance might yet turn out to be misplaced in view of the strong criticism which has been directed at the decision (see eg, Williams, *Sale of Land*, at p 129, note (x); Walford, *Sale of Land*, 2nd ed, at p 178). Thus in *Topfell Ltd* v *Galley Properties Ltd* [1979] 1 WLR 446 reliance was placed on various conditions of sale which appeared to put the purchaser on notice as to such matters as the one in issue, but Templeman J simply swept them aside:

In my judgment, these special and general conditions cannot be allowed to contradict the contractual obligation into which the vendors entered by virtue of the particulars and the contract, the contractual obligation to give vacant possession in the sense in which I have defined it of the ground floor to the purchasers

(p 450). Unfortunately, this judgment is directly contrary to the uncited decision of Whitford J in *Korogluyan* v *Matheou* (1975) 30 P & CR 309. So the efficacy of the trap remains obscure. But see generally Misrepresentation ante, p 55 et seq.

4 Possession before completion

Occasionally a purchaser may be allowed into possession of the property before completion. His particular position and the terms of his possession will depend primarily upon what has been agreed with the vendor (see, eg, *Cantor Art Services Ltd* v *Kenneth Bieber Photography Ltd* [1969] 1 WLR 1226, CA). For otherwise he has no right even of access, as opposed to possession, before completion, eg, to measure for carpets or curtains (but cp *Schindler* v *Pigault* (1975) 30 P & CR 328 where there were indications that a vendor not permitting access to a surveyor might be in default if completion be delayed in consequence). However, a few general propositions may be offered.

To start with the purchaser in possession before completion who pays a periodic sum for the privilege may be either a tenant or a licensee of the vendor. Under an open contract, such a purchaser will normally be regarded as a tenant (see *Francis Jackson Developments Ltd* v *Stemp* [1943] 2 All ER 601; cf *Dunthorne and Shore* v *Wiggins* [1943] 2 All ER 678) as also, apparently, will a purchaser who pays interest on the balance of the price in accordance with an arrangement made *after* the contract (*Finch* v *Thorpe* (1950) decided in a county court and reported in the *Law Journal*, vol 100, p 472). It is thought that the relationship of landlord and tenant does not arise if such interest is paid *pursuant* to the contract, since then the payment appears referable only to the relationship of vendor and purchaser and should not be regarded as rent.

Both The Law Society's Conditions of Sale (1980 ed, No 18), and the National Conditions (20th ed, No 8 (1)), provide that if the purchaser is let into occupation before completion he will be there as the licensee and not the tenant of the vendor. The intention is to prevent the purchaser obtaining protection under the Rent Acts which would otherwise be possible despite his failure to complete (see the cases cited in the previous paragraph). These general conditions expressly do not apply where the purchaser was already the vendor's tenant. They are also inapplicable to an agreement to grant a lease where rent in advance has been paid on possession being taken (*Joel* v *Montgomery & Taylor* [1967] Ch 272).

In conclusion, brief cross-references may be made to the collected consequences of a purchaser taking possession before completion. Firstly, it may indicate acceptance of the vendor's title (see p 130). Secondly, if the title is registered the purchaser acquires an overriding interest (s 70 (1) (g) of the Land Registration Act 1925; see *Bridges* v *Mees* [1957] Ch 475), and so also might the vendor if his right to interest counts as 'receipt of the rents and profits' within para (g) (cp s 3 (xxv) of the 1925 Act). Thirdly, the vendor's duties as a trustee cease and he will have a lien on the land until paid (see pp 170–172). Fourthly, interest becomes payable on the balance of the purchase price (see p 193). Fifthly, delay will not be a bar to an action for specific performance (see p 215). Sixthly, either taking or allowing possession might constitute a sufficient act of part performance (see p 48). Seventhly, if the purchase price happens to be payable by '*three* or more instalments' then there will be a 'rental purchase agreement' within the protective discretion conferred by the Housing Act 1980, s 88. Finally, vendors must not forget that a purchaser in possession may feel less pressure for an early completion and may indeed fail to complete, returning the property after damaging it. For example:

> So far as I was concerned Leatherslade Farm was a perfectly straightforward purchase . . . There was a certain amount of bargaining over the price . . . and it was finally agreed at £5,500. [The purchaser] was very keen to get the deal finished. He paid the deposit in cash, but the purchase was of course never completed, though it was arranged with the vendor to have possession before completion. And of course because it was not completed I did not get any fees. The next thing I knew was that the farm had been found to be the train robbers' hideout

(per John Denby Wheater in the *Sunday Telegraph*, 6 March 1966). A less dramatic illustration occurred where under a contract for the sale of a farmhouse and adjoining land the purchaser, without completing, had gone into possession, carried on his business of plastic manufacturer and caused such extensive alterations that the land, allegedly, was useless for agricultural purposes, the only permitted use under the planning legislation (*Maskell* v *Ivory* [1970] 1 Ch 502). The vendor sought an order that the purchaser, who had accepted title, lodge the balance of the purchase price in court but only obtained an order which gave the purchaser an option of going out of possession (ibid). Conversely, a person allowed into possession as purchaser under a contract for sale which subsequently turns out to be void (eg, for uncertainty) may be entitled to equitable relief in respect of expenditure on repairs or improvements to the property (such a claim was made but on the facts did not succeed in *Lee- Parker* v *Izzet (No 2)* [1972] 2 All ER 800; see also *Lee-Parker* v *Izzet* [1971] 1 WLR 1688; cf *Lloyd* v *Stanbury* [1971] 1 WLR 535, post, p 214). So caveat vendor!

IX TIME

THE preceding chapter considered the term implied if not expressed into contracts for the sale of land that vacant possession should be given on completion. Next one may well wonder when completion should take place.

If the time element is left open, then as Roxburgh J once said:

> It is, of course, well understood that, if a contract fixes no date for completion, the law implies that completion is to take place within a reasonable time. What is a reasonable time has to be measured by the legal business which has to be performed in connection with the investigation of the title and the preparation of the necessary conveyancing documents

(in *Johnson* v *Humphrey* [1946] 1 All ER 460, at p 463). However, this is insufficiently certain for practical purposes and times or dates will almost invariably be agreed by means of general conditions for each of the steps leading up to completion itself. Even so, the two standard sets of conditions of sale in their current editions are annoyingly out of step as to time-limits. Thus the differences for steps to be taken in any ordinary transaction may be tabled as follows (referring to the 20th ed of the National Conditions of Sale and the 1980 ed of the Law Society's):

Completion	26th working day after contract or later delivery of abstract (National, No 5 (1)); first working day 5 weeks after contract (Law Society's, No 21 (1)).
Abstract of title, delivery	11 working days after contract (National, No 9 (1)); 'forthwith' upon exchange of contracts (Law Society's, No 12 (1)).
Requisitions on title	11 working days after delivery of abstract (National, No 9 (3)); 6 working days after receiving abstract (Law Society's, No 15 (2)).
Observations on replies	6 working days (National, No 9 (3)); 4 working days (Law Society's, No 15 (3)).
Draft conveyance, delivery	6 working days before completion date (National, No 19 (3)); 12 working days before completion date (Law Society's, No 17 (1)).
Engrossment	3 working days after draft returned approved (National, No 19 (3)); 5 working days before completion date (Law Society's, No 17 (2)).
Notice to complete within	16 working days (National, No 22 (2)); 21 ordinary days (Law Society's, No 23 (4)).

So, despite differences, generally speaking one will not have to wonder for long

179

when completion should take place. But what if it does not then take place? This poses a problem which has long plagued practitioners.

A ALTERNATIVE COURSES

If there is delay in completion, the delay*ee* (to coin one of a pair of bad words) will want—when he eventually makes his mind up—one of two alternatives, either to hold the delay*or* to his contract (ie, specific performance) or else to escape from the contract himself (ie, rescission), plus in the latter case return or forfeiture as appropriate of the deposit, plus perhaps in any case damages. These alternatives strictly involve pursuing quite inconsistent courses, yet paradoxically a course towards the latter in practice may often lead the more speedily to the former.

1 Specific performance

If the delay*ee* wants the sale to go through, logically he should issue a writ claiming specific performance. *This he could do at once.* In other words, contrary to the views of the many, there is here no time of the essence nonsense (see per Vaisey J in *Marks* v *Lilley* [1959] 1 WLR 749, at p 753). Thus in a case where the purchaser dramatically tore the contract up a few minutes after signing it and the vendor instituted proceedings *before* the completion date, the Privy Council rejected a defence of prematurity saying that:

> the fallacy . . . consists in equating the right to sue for specific performance with a cause of action at law. In equity all that is required is to show circumstances which will justify the intervention by a court of equity

(in *Hasham* v *Zenab* [1960] AC 316, p 329; see also *Eva* v *Morrow*, an unreported decision noted at (1966) 116 NLJ 1657, where a writ for specific performance was successfully issued after service but before expiry of a notice to complete; and per Buckley J in *Manchester Diocesan Council of Education* v *Commercial & General Investments Ltd* [1970] 1 WLR 241, at p 249).

Now it is true that in *Hasham* v *Zenab* the Privy Council added that actual performance before the contract date would not be compelled ([1960] AC 330) and that one learned writer has somehow inferred that this means not before a date as to which time has been made of the essence (see (1960) 24 Conv (NS) 150). It is equally true that in *Marks* v *Lilley*, Vaisey J thought that the plaintiff had 'in a sense . . . acted rather precipitately' and agreed that 'it seems like a futile proceeding in a way'. Nonetheless more truth for the conveyancer may lie in the facts of the former case that (1) the purchaser was actually put into possession within seven days of issuing his writ, and (2) he obtained an order for his costs of the abortive action to be paid by the vendor (this was what the case was about). On top of these, there is now a (3): issue of a writ for specific performance before the contractual completion date has been held not to preclude relief by way of damages for delay in completion (*Oakacre Ltd* v *Claire Cleaners (Holdings) Ltd* [1982] Ch 197).

2 Rescission

If the delay*ee* wishes to escape from the contract by way of rescission he will have to show a breach by the delay*or* of 'one of his main duties under the contract' (see Williams, *Sale of Land*, at p 121). Delay, however, will not be a sufficient breach of the contract unless either the delay has been unreasonable or else time was of the essence (see dicta in *Stickney* v *Keeble* [1915] AC 386 and *Raineri* v *Miles* [1981] AC

1050). Where there has been such delay by one party he will then apparently be taken without any argument to have failed in one of his main duties, to have committed 'the breach of a term which went—to use an expression commonly used by common-law lawyers—to the root of the contract' (per Greer LJ in *Harold Wood Brick Co Ltd* v *Ferris* (1935) 153 LT 241, at p 242, omitted from [1935] 2 KB 198). Thus the other party, being defaultless, will be enabled to regard himself as discharged from the contract, retaining the deposit if the vendor, and obtaining its return if the purchaser (see the cases cited). But the first question is: when will a delay become unreasonable or time be of the essence?

B OF THE ESSENCE

Since waiting for a delay to cross the Rubicon to unreasonableness tends to be trying in its uncertainty, the question much more often asked is when the exceeded time can be said to be of the essence. That is really to ask what the exceptions are to the general rule—which has spread from equity via statute to the law—that stipulations as to time are *not* deemed to be or to have become of the essence of a contract for the sale of land (see *United Scientific Holdings Ltd* v *Burnley BC* [1978] AC 904, and s 41 of the Law of Property Act 1925). Because if the general rule itself applies, then for rescission rather than damages the contract must be regarded as reading that completion should take place on the specified date 'or within a reasonable time thereafter' (per Maugham J in *Re Sandwell Park Colliery Co, Field* v *Sandwell Park Colliery Co* [1929] 1 Ch 277, at p 282; also per Harman J in *Smith* v *Hamilton* [1951] Ch 174, at p 183; followed by Danckwerts J in *Re Barr's Contract, Moorwell Buildings Ltd* v *Barr* [1956] Ch 551, at pp 556-7; and per Russell LJ in *Hargreaves Transport Ltd* v *Lynch* [1969] 1 WLR 215, at p 220; and see *Williams* v *Greatrex* [1957] 1 WLR 31, where a 'thereafter' of ten years was held not unreasonable). This rubric would, of course, put us back where we were, ie, in uncertainty, so let us enquire about the exceptions.

These have been summarised in *Halsbury's Laws of England*, 4th ed, vol 9, para 481, p 338, as follows:

> Time will not be considered to be of the essence unless: (1) the parties expressly stipulate that conditions as to time must be strictly complied with; or (2) the nature of the subject matter of the contract or the surrounding circumstances show that time should be considered to be of the essence;

(quoted as correct by Lord Simon of Glaisdale in *United Scientific Holdings Ltd* v *Burnley BC* [1978] AC 904, at p 944; also by Lord Fraser of Tullybelton, at p 958).

1 Expressly

The first exception involves nothing more than construing the contract to see whether or not the parties have expressed in it their intention that time shall be of the essence. If they say so explicitly, then that is that. More often, however, the construction must be directed to the implicit, for which judicial precedents are of little utility. Nonetheless, an illustration or two may be given. Where a contract, having specified two different completion dates applying in differing circumstances, continued 'but the purchase shall in any event actually be completed not later than' a third date, this last was held of the essence (*Harold Wood Brick Co Ltd* v *Ferris* [1935] 2 KB 198; see also *Rickards (Charles) Ltd* v *Oppenheim* [1950] 1 KB 616, completion 'in six, or, at the most, seven months' originally of the essence).

Following from this, mention may be made of a possible trap only too often fallen into in practice.

Not uncommonly one will find special conditions providing for completion to take place '*on or before*' a specified date. The trap is that this pious hope, inserted mostly as a sop for those clients who think the agreed period too long, may make time of the essence. This result would be only consistent with the construction in the cases last cited and was clearly indicated by Grove J as his view in a case where later words affected the construction (see *Patrick* v *Milner* (1877) 2 CPD 342, at p 348); also it was apparently taken for granted by Maugham J construing 'on or about' which had been substituted for 'on or before' (in *Lock* v *Bell* [1931] 1 Ch 35, at p 43). In a more modern 'on or before' case, however, the obiter opinion of the Court of Appeal was that 'one may assume that, purely as a matter of construction of the contract, completion on the day agreed was not of the essence of the contract' (in *James Macara Ltd* v *Barclay* [1945] KB 148, at p 156), but it was added that 'that does not mean that the agreed date may be disregarded for all purposes' (loc cit; see also per Lord Fraser of Tullybelton in *Raineri* v *Miles* [1981] AC 1050, at p 1089 as to the wording 'on or before' a specified completion date limiting the available elasticity). So the trap may or may not be set, but there is still the danger to be avoided in practice that it could be accidentally sprung (see a note at (1956) 20 Conv (NS) 347). Thus similarly where the agreement was that both parties 'would use their best endeavours to complete the purchase by [a specified date]' Megarry V-C held that time was of the essence (*Pips (Leisure Productions) Ltd* v *Walton* (1980) 260 EG 601).

2   Circumstantially

This second exception involves enquiring as to the circumstances from which a court of equity would infer an intention of the parties that the time for completion of their sale and purchase should be of the essence. Again, however, this is more a matter for illustration than precedent. Most of the cases have concerned contracts for the sale of land together with the assets of a going business, and these cases are what Greer LJ spoke of as:

> those authorities which seem to have the effect that if, though in form the sale is a sale of land, it in reality is the sale of a business enterprise, then the equitable rule about time not being of the essence of the contract will not apply, either in the Chancery Court or in the courts of the common law

(in *Harold Wood Brick Co Ltd* v *Ferris* (1935) 153 LT 241, at p 242, omitted from [1935] 2 KB 198, at p 203, as to a brickfield with the tools of the trade carried on there; see also *MacBryde* v *Weekes* (1856) 22 Beav 533, as to working-mines). The commonest example of this has been the sale of public houses as going concerns, although shops and other businesses have been squeezed in (see *Coslake* v *Till* (1826) 1 Russ 376, where one day's delay discharged the contract; *Cowles* v *Gale* (1871) 7 Ch App 12; *Powell* v *Marshall, Parkes & Co* [1899] 1 QB 710; and *Lock* v *Bell* [1931] 1 Ch 35). The reason for inferring an intention that time should be of the essence in these matters has been said to be:

> When the subject-matter, which is to be bought and sold, is in its very nature, exposed to daily variation, time must necessarily form a very material ingredient in the contract

(per Gifford MR in *Coslake* v *Till*, ante, at p 379; see also per Morris LJ in *Williams* v *Greatrex* [1957] 1 WLR 31, at p 43, and cf *Hare* v *Nicoll* [1966] 2 QB 130).

Apart from sales of businesses and a few cases concerning wasting properties (see *Hudson* v *Temple* (1860) 30 LJ Ch 251, a nearly expired leasehold, also *Withy* v

Cottle (1823) Turn & R 78, a life interest), as Harman J has observed:

> it would need very special circumstances to make time of the essence of the contract on a sale of an ordinary private dwelling-house with vacant possession

(in *Smith* v *Hamilton* [1951] Ch 174, at p 179). Indeed in everyday conveyancing the only circumstances are that the vendor wants the money, perhaps to buy another house, and the purchaser wants to move in. But are these not special in any sense? In an early case, time was held to be of the essence where the circumstances were that:

> At the date of the contract [the purchaser] had then recently sold his own residence and was obliged to find another within a very short period; that he bought consequently with a view to immediate occupation by himself and that [the vendor] knew this

(per Rolt LJ in *Tilley* v *Thomas* (1867) LR 3 Ch App 61, at p 70; see also per Lord Atkinson in *Stickney* v *Keeble* [1915] AC 386, at p 401). These 'special' circumstances, of course, are hardly out of the ordinary at all, and indeed quite recently Lord Edmund-Davies dropped a parenthetical hint that the matter might be arguable (*Raineri* v *Miles* [1981] AC 1050, at p 1082).

Readers may at this point be conveniently reminded of two 'circumstances', already discussed, in which time is or may be of the essence, albeit not as to completion. First, there is the alleged rule that any stipulated time for delivery of requisitions will always be of the essence (see p 121). Secondly, the Privy Council has pronounced that the specified date for performance of any condition of a contract:

> must be strictly adhered to, and the time allowed is not to be extended by reference to equitable principles

(in *Aberfoyle Plantations Ltd* v *Cheng* [1960] AC 115, at pp 124–5; see p 30).

C   WAIVER

Even where time has been made of the essence, parties to contracts tend not to exact their pound of flesh but to allow some delay, provided it is only a little one. Yet even a little delay will be enough for a waiver by conduct:

> if the time is once allowed to pass and the parties go on negotiating for the completion of the purchase, then time is no longer of the essence of the contract

(per Malins V-C in *Webb* v *Hughes* (1870) LR 10 Eq 281, at p 286; see to the same effect *Luck* v *White* (1973) 26 P & CR 89, where time had been made of the essence by a notice to complete and had expired but discussions continued about a completion appointment). This means that the consequence of courtesy would be as if time had never been of the essence, involving either waiting for an unreasonable delay or else taking steps to make a later time of the essence (see *Rickards (Charles) Ltd* v *Oppenheim* [1950] 1 KB 616, wherein incidentally Denning LJ at p 623 described the waiver 'as a particular application of the principle which I endeavoured to state in *Central London Property Trust Ltd* v *High Trees House Ltd* [1947] KB 130').

However, this consequence as quoted should be contrasted with that in a case where, time having been originally of the essence, delay to a particular date is allowed: that later date automatically becomes of the essence instead (*Lock* v *Bell* [1931] 1 Ch 35; see to the same effect *Buckland* v *Farmar & Moody* [1979] 1 WLR 221, CA, where, after the expiry of a notice to complete, two fixed date extensions had allowed. Contrast too the case where, three days after time had run out, the vendors told the purchasers that there could be an extension provided the purchasers agreed to a sizeable increase in price; this was held to be not a waiver of delay but an effective rescission plus a fresh offer of sale (*Prosper Homes Ltd* v *Hambros Bank Ltd* (1979) 39 P & CR 395). Post-contract gazumping! Note now that The Law Society's Conditions (1980 ed, No 23 (8)) somewhat inconsistently contemplate extensions 'by agreement or implication' being followed by rein-vocation as a ten-days' notice to complete.

Is an oral extension of time, whether or not amounting to waiver, effective? The contention that written evidence is required, both to satisfy s 40 (1) of the Law of Property Act 1925 and because it is not possible to vary a written contract by an oral agreement, was referred to but not decided by Templeman J in *Clearbrook Property Holdings Ltd* v *Verrier* [1974] 1 WLR 243, at p 245.

D   (RE)MAKING OF THE ESSENCE

If time was not of the essence originally (the usual case) or no longer is, what can the delay*ee* do about it? The rule, notwithstanding loose language in books and judgments, seems to be that strictly time cannot be made of the essence after the contract, but the delay*or*'s delay can be made clearly unreasonable. The following passage puts the position:

> What right then had one party to limit a particular time within which an act was to be done by the other? It appears to me that he had no right so to do, unless there had been such delay on the part of the other contracting party as to render it fair that, if steps were not immediately taken to complete, the person giving the notice should be relieved from his contract. It has been argued that there is a right in either party to a contract by notice so to engraft time as to make it of the esssence of the contract where it has not originally been of the essence, independently of delay on the part of him to whom the notice is given. In my view there is no such right. It is plain on principle, as it appears to me, that there can be no such right. That which is not of the essence of the original contract is not to be made so by the volition of one of the parties, unless the other has done something which gives a right to the other to make it so. You cannot make a new contract at the will of one of the contracting parties. There must have been such improper conduct on the part of the other as to justify the rescission of the contract *sub modo*, that is, if a reasonable notice be not complied with. That this is the law appears to me abundantly plain.

This was actually said by Fry J in *Green* v *Sevin* (1879) 13 Ch D 589, at p 599, but enjoys impressive endorsement: thus in *Cumberland Court (Brighton) Ltd* v *Taylor* [1964] Ch 29, at p 37, Ungoed-Thomas J, believe it or not, quoted Danckwerts J in *Re Barr's Contract, Moorwell Buildings Ltd* v *Barr* [1956] Ch 551, at p 557, quoting Harman J in *Smith* v *Hamilton* [1951] Ch 174, at p 181, quoting what Fry J said! Much the same has also been said, but in his own words, more recently by Lord Simon of Glaisdale in *United Scientific Holdings Ltd* v *Burnley BC* [1978] AC 904, at pp 946–7. Yet one is always seeing such things said as the delay*ee* is 'entitled to give a reasonable notice making time of the essence of the matter' (per Denning LJ in *Rickards (Charles) Ltd* v *Oppenheim* [1950] 1 KB 616, at p 624) or that on delay 'if either side wanted to bring the other up to the mark, all he had to do was to give him reasonable notice requiring him to complete' (per Denning LJ again in *Williams* v *Greatrex* [1957] 1 WLR 31, at p 35). So there may be some sense in examining precisely what the delay*ee* can do.

1   Wait

The first thing for the delay*ee* to do is to be patient: he cannot, it seems, give any effective notice to the delay*or* immediately the completion date has passed (see per Harman J in *Smith* v *Hamilton* [1951] Ch 174, at p 181: cf per Croom-Johnson J, per incuriam perhaps, in *Phillips* v *Lamdin* [1949] 2 KB 33, at p 42 that notice may be given 'during the progress of the negotiations *towards* completion'). He must wait, it is said, until there has been a sufficient delay. But that delay which will be sufficient has been variously described in the cases—as 'unnecessary' (per Langdale MR in *Taylor* v *Brown* (1839) 2 Beav 180, at p 183, also per Lord Parker in *Stickney* v *Keeble* [1915] AC 386, at p 418), as 'great and improper' (per Langdale MR in *King* v *Wilson* (1843) 6 Beav 124, at p 126, see also *Pegg* v *Wisden* (1852) 16 Beav 239), and as 'gross, vexatious and unreasonable' (see *Wells* v *Maxwell* (1863) 33 LJ Ch 44); also reference has been made to the delay*or* being 'guilty of delay' simpliciter (per Lord Parmoor in *Stickney* v *Keeble* [1915] AC 386, at p 423).

Now recalling the proposition that if the delay really is unreasonable, no notice need be given, one may well wonder at these various descriptions. Does the delay*ee* have to wait until the delay is nearly unreasonable and then push it over the cliff with a notice (see Danckwerts J in *Re Barr's Contract, Moorwell Buildings Ltd* v *Barr* [1956] Ch 551, at p 556)? There appear to be two related reasons for giving a notice to complete: first, even if the delay*or* is thought to be already in breach, the notice will lend some certainty by setting a time limit (see per Stone V-C in *Manning* v *Turner* [1957] 1 WLR 91, at p 98); and, secondly, if the delay*or* is not yet in breach, the notice will create a circumstance indicating an unreasonable delay (cf per Romilly MR in *MacBryde* v *Weekes* (1856) 22 Beav 533, at p 543). This latter reason, however, has led to the common approach, of judges as well as of writers, of considering as two separate questions what might perhaps be better thought of as one. An example of this bi-partite approach would be to continue as follows:

> The court may still find that the notice stipulating a date for performance was given prematurely and/or that the date fixed for performance was unreasonably soon in all the circumstances

(per Lord Simon of Glaisdale in *United Scientific Holdings Ltd* v *Burnley BC* [1978] AC 904, at p 946). Nonetheless, the present writer feels that logically the delay*ee* ought to be able to give notice either immediately after the completion date specifying 'the reasonable time thereafter' or else after that reasonable time without limiting any further time (a view now canvassed with clarity by CT Emery at [1978] Conv 144–160). Accordingly in a disreputable case where there was no completion date at all in the contract, the sole question was said to be whether a reasonable time had elapsed after the contract; an informal agreement between solicitors was held to be ineffective to fix a completion date and the service of a notice to complete was treated as virtually irrelevant, but that agreement plus the fact that the solicitors were ready to complete was regarded as strong if not conclusive evidence of the expiry of reasonable time (*Inns* v *D Miles Griffiths Piercy & Co* (1980) 255 EG 623; see also an article by Angela Sydenham entitled 'Unreasonable Delay—Something of a Long-Stop on the Failure of a Notice to Complete?' at [1980] Conv 19–26).

So, the bi-partite approach is illogical but it is also established. This appeared to be both recognised and explained by Lord Simon of Glaisdale (loc cit) as follows:

> After the lapse of a reasonable time the promisee could and can give notice fixing a time for performance. This must itself be reasonable, notwithstanding that ex hypothesi a reasonable time for performance has already elapsed in the view of the promisee. The notice operates as evidence that the promisee considers that a reasonable time for performance has elapsed by the date of the

notice and as evidence of the date by which the promisee now considers it reasonable for the contractual obligation to be performed.
Let us accept the evidently inevitable and proceed.

2   Notice

Taking the rule, therefore, to be that 'once the right to serve a notice of the kind in question has arisen, the time allowed by the notice must be a reasonable time' (per Danckwerts J in *Re Barr's Contract, Moorwell Buildings Ltd* v *Barr* [1956] Ch 551, at p 556), the question once again is: what time will be reasonable? The answer is that it all depends:

> What constitutes a reasonable notice and a reasonable time to be fixed in it must depend upon the contract and the circumstances of each case

(per Romilly MR in *MacBryde* v *Weekes* (1856) 22 Beav 533, at p 543). So the question once again is: what circumstances?

The principal circumstance would appear to be indicated in Earl Loreburn's dictum: 'when I am asked to say that this time was insufficient I must see what had to be done within the time' (in *Stickney* v *Keeble* [1915] AC 386, at p 397). Thus, Vaisey J has doubted whether a twenty-one days' notice given by vendors twenty-one days after the completion date was long enough where the draft conveyance had yet to be submitted by the purchasers for approval (in *Re Engall's Agreement* [1953] 1 WLR 977, at p 979). In contrast, Goff J has held adequate a twenty-one days' notice when the title had by then been accepted, the conveyance engrossed and it only remained to pay the price and complete (*Re Martin's Bank Ltd's Contract* (1969) 113 SJ 980).

However, the court will also consider any other circumstances of the case:

> No doubt what remains to be done at the date of the notice is of importance, but it is by no means the only relevant fact. The fact that the purchaser has continually been pressing for completion, or has before given similar notices which he has waived, or that it is specially important to him to obtain early completion, are equally relevant facts

(per Lord Parker in *Stickney* v *Keeble* [1915] AC 386, at p 419; followed in *Ajit* v *Sammy* [1967] AC 255, where on the facts a notice to complete within six days was regarded as reasonable). In this, however, facts of concern to only one of the parties—the delay*ee*—may be observed. Are factors affecting the receiver rather than the giver of the notice equally relevant? Danckwerts J has held that they are, saying that:

> It is true that conveyancing difficulties may be some of the circumstances; but it seems to me that in naming a period which suddenly makes a definite requirement for completion and makes time of the essence in this way, regard must be had to all the circumstances of the case, and to the practical considerations of the ability in the circumstances of the purchaser to find the money, having regard to reasonable behaviour as well as to mere conveyancing matters, though it is quite true that conveyancing difficulties may be some of the circumstances

(in *Re Barr's Contract, Moorwell Buildings Ltd* v *Barr* [1956] Ch 551, at p 558). Yet, with respect, this seems a pernicious extension—surely the purchaser's financial arrangements should be purely his own affair? True, in the case, the vendor knew the purchaser was relying on a substantial sub-sale which had fallen through, and that without any such knowledge he would not have been restricted in selecting the period of his notice (see also as to this *Re Roger Malcolm Developments Ltd's Contract* (1960) 176 EG 1237; noted in *The Law Society's Digest*, Fourth

(Cumulative) Supplement, at p 21, and commented on at (1961) 25 Conv (NS) 260). But even so, why should a purchaser be able as of right to gain more time by the simple expedient of telling the vendor his hard-luck story (cp *Universal Corporation* v *Five Ways Properties* [1979] 1 All ER 552 CA)? What is more, as it stands the whole extension appears irreconcilable with the earlier holding of the House of Lords that a purchaser giving notice:

> was not bound to await the convenience of his vendors in carrying out their transactions with other people, unless he had either agreed to do so or led his vendors to believe that he would do so by his own statements or by his own conduct

(per Earl Loreburn in *Stickney* v *Keeble* [1915] AC 386, at p 398). What was sauce for the purchaser, should be sauce for vendors too.

Assuming that the notice, in all the circumstances, does limit a reasonable time, the party giving the notice must take care that he is himself at all times ready and able to complete. For if he is not the erstwhile delay*or* can turn the tables, being apparently able to choose *either* to rescind, recovering or returning the deposit, on the ground that time has been made of the essence by notice (see *Finkielkraut* v *Monohan* [1949] 2 All ER 234) *or* else simply to treat the notice as ineffective (see *Horton* v *Kurzke* [1971] 1 WLR 769; also *Re Prestbury Investments' Contract* (1961) 177 EG 75; noted in *The Law Society's Digest*, Fourth (Cumulative) Supplement at p 18). So a party contemplating making time of the essence by notice, just as originally, must beware of being caught in his own trap.

E CONDITIONS OF SALE

What must have emerged from the foregoing, if nothing else, is that a delay*ee* desiring to drive the delay*or* to complete or die deserves second sight. He has to guess and gamble on what the court will hold, in all circumstantial uncertainties, to be a reasonable time, whether in total or before and after notice. Consequently the standard sets of conditions of sale would obviously serve their clientele well were they to deal with this 'time of the essence' aspect. Let us see how far they do, remembering the the clientele mentioned generally means solicitors acting for *vendors*.

First, an incidental inference at least can be taken from any of the sets of general conditions that the completion date fixed in the special conditions is *not* of the essence. Thus The Law Society's Conditions (1980 ed, No 15) expressly provide that the time for delivery of requisitions, etc, should be of the essence, from which 'the inference is that in no other respect is time of the essence of the contract' (per Harman J in *Smith* v *Hamilton* [1951] Ch 174, at p 181), whilst the National Conditions (20th ed, No 5 (2)) put the point beyond argument by expressly providing that the time for completion 'shall not be of the essence of the contract' unless the special conditions are to the contrary.

Going to the other extreme, conditions of sale have been known to confer on the vendor a power to forfeit the deposit and re-sell immediately the purchaser was in default without any notice. The question then arising is whether such a power would apply immediately the specified completion date had passed. This has been mentioned but left open by Fry J (in *Howe* v *Smith* (1884) 27 Ch D 89, at p 105), and by Slesser and Roche LJJ (in *Harold Wood Brick Co Ltd* v *Ferris* [1935] 2 KB 198, both at p 208). Apart from these, Greer LJ has thought that such a power indicated that the time for completion was to be of the essence (ibid, pp 204–5), whilst Harman J has held that such a power would not apply until the purchaser was in default in not completing on the specified date *or* within a reasonable time thereafter (in *Smith* v *Hamilton* [1951] Ch 174, at p 183). In the result, therefore, the efficacy of such a power is uncertain, so that its absence from the standard sets of conditions (in their current editions) is perhaps fortunate. What is not present in each of these sets, however, does at last seem extremely efficacious.

After earlier unsatisfactory attempts, the National Conditions of Sale, in its 17th ed, hit the nail on the head with General Condition No 22 which has, not surprisingly, been reproduced with the same number and very slight amendments in the current 20th ed. The draftsman has also been paid the great compliment of having this condition adopted in substance for the 1970 ed of The Law Society's Conditions (No 19, retained as No 23 in 1980 ed). The successful condition No 22 in its current wording provides:

(1) At any time on or after the completion date, either party, being ready and willing to fulfil his own outstanding obligations under the contract, may (without prejudice to any other right or remedy available to him) give to the other party or his solicitor notice in writing requiring completion of the contract in conformity with this condition.

(2) Upon service of such notice as aforesaid it shall become and be a term of the contract, *in respect of which time shall be of the essence thereof*, that the party to whom the notice is given shall complete the contract within sixteen working days after service of the notice (exclusive of the day of service); but this condition shall operate without prejudice to any right of either party to rescind the contract in the meantime.

(The condition in each standard set then proceeds to deal in some detail with the consequences of non-compliance with such a notice).

This drafting, particularly the words which the writer has italicised, must have been inspired by the beginning of a sentence, in the judgment of Danckwerts J in *Re Barr's Contract, Moorwell Buildings Ltd* v *Barr* [1956] Ch 551 (where he found the condition's predecessor a failure). This sentence was: 'Apart from the provisions of any plain and clear conditions of sale, the law about making time of the essence of the contract for the purpose of completion, as I think is accepted on both sides, is subject to the following conditions' (ibid, p 556; the learned judge proceeded to state the 'reasonable notice after a reasonable time' requirements, applying where there is *no* plain and clear condition of sale). With the present condition, therefore, both the parties will have agreed that time is to be of the essence, so there seems no reason for waiting before giving notice and the number of days is no longer a minimum; the condition is akin to but more flexible than the provision for completion on one date 'but in any event not later than' a second date, approved in *Harold Wood Brick Co Ltd* v *Ferris* [1935] 2 KB 198. Nonetheless, the relevant explanatory note with the 17th ed was not over-optimistic, cautiously recommending 'that a party, who has himself occasioned delay, should make reasonable allowance for that delay before operating the condition'.

In fact, the condition has received resounding ratification in the courts. Thus Ungoed-Thomas J has held that 'time automatically became of the essence of the contract' under the condition, so making it unnecessary for him to go into all the circumstances of the case to see whether the notice was reasonable (in *Cumberland Court (Brighton) Ltd* v *Taylor* [1964] Ch 29, at p 38). Again, Buckley J has also held that 'it was open to the parties to make time of the essence ab initio' and the condition made it 'irrelevant to consider whether the conduct of the purchaser had been such that it was reasonable for the vendors to attempt to rescind the contract by giving notice to complete making time of the essence' (in *Innisfail Laundry Ltd* v *Dawe* (1963) 107 SJ 437). Accordingly where the notice to complete was served immediately on the completion date the Court of Appeal treated its efficacy as clear beyond argument (*Hooker* v *Wyle* [1974] 1 WLR 235). So there can be no doubt that this condition does confer the certainty sought for so long by conveyancers. What is more, no particular formalities are requisite for it to be called into play (see *Babacomp Ltd* v *Rightside Ltd* [1974] 1 All ER 142, CA, where National Condition 22 had been varied to stipulate fourteen days instead of the then twenty-eight days and solicitors had simply written: 'Please treat this letter as Notice to Complete in accordance with its terms').

Nevertheless, such conditions have not proved completely foolproof. Invalid notices to complete can still be encountered, as in *Woods* v *Mackenzie* [1975] 1 WLR 613 (where the notice was not served by all three of the vendors), *Rightside Properties Ltd* v *Gray* [1975] Ch 72 (where a one-day-short period was specified) and *Singh* v *Nazeer* [1979] Ch 474 (where notices to complete had been precluded by an order for specific performance). The biggest pitfall in practice lies in the stipulation that only a 'ready and willing' party can serve a notice to complete ('able' as well in The Law Society's Condition; cp *Horton* v *Kurzke* [1971] 1 WLR 769). Thus a vendor in breach of his contractual obligations, eg, because of a misdescription or failure to deliver an abstract of title, will not be within the condition (*Pagebar Properties Ltd* v *Derby Investment Holdings Ltd* [1972] 1 WLR 1500; see also *Re Stone and Saville's Contract* [1963] 1 WLR 163 where the vendor had neglected to answer a requisition on title). Being 'ready to complete' for the purpose of serving an effective notice to complete means that the vendor (or his solicitor) must have satisfied himself on every 'matter of substance' although he need not also have made all the necessary administrative arrangements for completion (see *Cole* v *Rose* [1978] 3 All ER 1121, where the vendor's solicitors had indicated that they were not able to give any undertaking as to the discharge of certain charges: this was treated as a matter of substance as opposed to a completion statement and the actual discharge of a mortgage in the ordinary case which would be merely administrative). See further notes at [1978] Conv 326–8 and [1979] Conv 161–3 querying the discharge of mortgages, which are now covered by The Law Society's Conditions, 1980 ed, No 23(3)(*b*).

Incidentally, it is not entirely clear from the wording of the conditions, but a notice to complete once served will bind the server as well as the receiver (see *Quadrangle Development and Construction Co Ltd* v *Jenner* [1974] 1 WLR 68, CA, applying to National Condition No 22 the decision in *Finkielkraut* v *Monohan* [1949] 2 All ER 234). In other words, the party serving a notice to complete must himself be ready both at the time of service and at the time of expiry, or else it may be a case of the biter bit. Accordingly another query which occasionally occurs is whether a notice once served can be unilaterally withdrawn. Probably not but the standard conditions are not explicit.

Finally, it may be noted with regret that in *Pagebar Properties Ltd* v *Derby Investment Holdings Ltd* [1972] 1 WLR 1500, at p 1505, Goulding J blurred somewhat the certainty of National Condition No 22 by accepting a contention that even where the notice was valid, if a purchaser without any fault on his part only discovered the existence of a breach by the vendor on the last day allowed for completion, and at the moment of attempted completion, then 'the framework of the conditions or the principles of equity demand' that he must have a reasonable opportunity to consider the matter. In the case, this merely meant taking instructions over a weekend, but one cannot always predict what will amount to a reasonable opportunity.

F   REPUDIATION

Apart from any conditions of sale, brief mention may be made that the delay*ee* need not concern himself with time being of the essence where the delay*or* not only delays but also repudiates the contract, for:

> If one party indicates by his conduct that he is unable or unwilling, whatever time is given to perform his contract, that is sufficient to justify an acceptance of the repudiation

(per Greer LJ in *Harold Wood Brick Co Ltd* v *Ferris* [1935] 2 KB 198, at p 205, see also per Roche LJ at ibid, p 208). This however, is no more certain than making time of the essence for it turns once again on the circumstances, the evidence, as to whether there really has been a repudiation (compare *Farrant* v *Olver* (1922) 91 LJ Ch 758, persistent and long refusal to perform the contract, with *Thorpe* v *Fasey* [1949] Ch 649). Even what the delay*or* actually says may have to be carefully construed. Thus where a purchaser's solicitors wrote that she had 'had some difficulty in connection with the proposed mortgage and that, therefore, it will not be possible to complete the purchase on the date fixed by the contract,' Harman J delivered himself of the following:

> If that letter had said: "I shall not complete", or "I cannot complete", or "Heaven knows when I may be able to complete" that would perhaps have entitled the vendor to deliver an ultimatum. But in my judgment the letter [mentioned above], which merely said that she was very sorry but she could not complete just at the moment, was far from being an anticipatory breach of the contract

(in *Smith* v *Hamilton* [1951] Ch 174, at p 182). In this connection, a diverting twist occurred where a vendor was held, in effect, to have repudiated the contract by serving a notice to complete when there was a still outstanding requisition (in *Re Stone and Saville's Contract* [1962] 1 WLR 460, at p 466; upheld on appeal [1963] 1 WLR 163; cp *Horton* v *Kurzke* [1971] 1 WLR 769). Again a vendor's letter treating the contract as off in pursuance of an invalid notice to complete has been treated as amounting to a wrongful repudiation of the contract so that the purchaser was entitled to damages (*Rightside Properties Ltd* v *Gray* [1975] Ch 72). But compare a case of purported rescission in reliance, albeit erroneously, upon a term of the contract: this should not amount to a repudiation (*Woodar Investment Development Ltd* v *Wimpey Construction UK Ltd* [1980] 1 WLR 277, HL).

G   DAMAGES

Lastly, a desirable remedy other than, or as well as, specific performance or rescission may be indicated (but only indicated, for remedies as a whole must be another matter), namely the recovery of damages. In the last edition of this book the proposition was put that in most ordinary conveyancing transactions any delay at all (whether or not unreasonable) past the date fixed for completion should lead to liability in damages at the instance of the other party (whether vendor or purchaser): citing CT Emery at [1978] Conv 144–60. The damages instanced would include the cost of hotel accommodation for the purchaser and his family and of storage of furniture where the vendor failed to complete on the fixed date although doing so within the period of a notice to complete; the damages for such delay might also be increased to cover any distress, anguish and inconvenience suffered (cf a note at ibid, pp 325–6). The House of Lords has since held that the proposition was correct (*Raineri* v *Miles* [1981] AC 1050). The case concerned, in effect, a contract for the sale of a house incorporating The Law Society's Conditions of Sale (1973 rev) where time had not been made of the essence but completion was fixed for 12 July 1977; on 11 July the vendor told the purchaser that completion could not take place on 12 July; on 13 July, the purchaser served a twenty-eight days' notice to complete and completion took place on 11 August. Recovery of the cost of temporary accommodation was sought as damages. It was held that a clause providing for completion on a specified day could not, unless there was a clear context to the contrary, be construed as meaning that completion could take place within a reasonable period thereafter. Accordingly, there was a breach of contract when the vendor failed to complete on the contractual date, and although equity would not allow rescission without a notice to complete or unreasonable delay, this did not negative the vendor's common law liability in damages. Further, the service of a notice to complete making time of the essence and giving new rights and remedies made no difference to the then existing breach of contract.

However, in the Court of Appeal, Templeman LJ observed ([1981] AC 1050, at p 1064) that, 'In a good many cases a short delay will not cause damage and if sufficient warning is given a purchaser will be able to mitigate or prevent any damage and is under a duty to do so. But where, as in the instant case, damage cannot be avoided, a vendor who chooses not to complete must take the consequences'. This would appear to present difficulties in practice as to the extent of the duty to mitigate, the question being what reasonable steps should be taken by the innocent party. On behalf of the party in delay, it is clearly advisable that an early warning of the prospect of delay (not amounting to a repudiation) should be given so as to require mitigation of loss by the other party.

In consequence of this case, practitioners could well consider the inclusion of a special condition of sale excluding, limiting or at least quantifying the measure of any damages for delay. Here reference should be made to Condition 22 of the 1980 ed of The Law Society's Conditions providing procedures for calculating compensation for delay which do not appear easy to operate in practice. Contrast Condition 5 (2) of the 20th ed of the National Conditions which is expressly without prejudice to 'the right of either party to recover from the other damages for delay in fulfilling his obligations under the contract'.

Compare the position, where instead of a late completion, a purchaser's breach by delay discharged the vendor: the vendor was entitled to resell the property and recover from the purchaser his loss, the difference between the resale price and the original sale price (*Harold Wood Brick Co Ltd v Ferris* [1935] 2 KB 198). See also the detailed provisions of National Conditions, 20th ed, No 22 (3), and The Law Society's Conditions, 1980 ed, No 23 (5)–(7) and cp *Talley v Wolsey-Neech* (1978) 38 P & CR 45, CA (a vendor who chose to exercise his rights under No 19 (4) (c) of The Law Society's 1973 revision was only entitled to recover the liquidated damages defined by it and was not, therefore, entitled to recover as further damages any rate of interest on the purchase price; the 1980 ed incorporates an apparently appropriate modification).

X APPORTIONMENT AND INTEREST

IT is not unknown—to put it mildly—for completion to take place on some other date than that specified in the contract. The more serious consequences of delay have already been considered. Now a thought may be spared for the less serious but more frequent irritant involved in adjusting the rights of the parties in respect of the period between the contractual completion and actual completion—the adjustment necessarily being made retrospectively by way of increase or decrease in the sum payable by the purchaser. In essence this is simplicity itself: equity looks on that as done which ought to be done, so the purchaser enjoys the income and suffers the outgoings of the property and the vendor is entitled to interest on the price, each as if the completion had taken place on the contractual date. Like any other proposition in principle, however, this warrants a closer scrutiny.

A APPORTIONMENT

This is almost self-explanatory. First, as to income, the vendor must account to the purchaser for all the rents and other profits of the property accrued due since the contractual completion (see, eg, per Lord Eldon in *Paine* v *Meller* (1801) 6 Ves 349, at p 352, and *Plews* v *Samuel* [1904] 1 Ch 464). Secondly, as to outgoings, the purchaser must repay to the vendor that proportion of the outgoings of the property—rents, rates, etc—paid by him in respect of the same period (per Romilly MR in *Carrodus* v *Sharpe* (1855) 20 Beav 56, at p 58; *Barsht* v *Tagg* [1900] 1 Ch 231).

In addition if the vendor is also the occupier, so that the property produces no income, he should pay a fair occupation rent for the period between the contractual and the actual completion date (as to fixing this, see per Knight-Bruce and Turner LJJ in *Sherwin* v *Shakspear* (1854) 5 De G M & G 517, at pp 532 and 538–9, respectively, also *Metropolitan Railway Co* v *Defries* (1877) 2 QBD 189, 387). Apparently he only escapes from this liability where the delay is due to the purchaser's default, the vendor having therefore had to remain in occupation to his own inconvenience (*Dakin* v *Cope* (1827) 2 Russ 170, at pp 181–2; *Leggott* v *Metropolitan Railway Co* (1870) 5 Ch App 716). Yet the writer wonders how often in modern practice anyone has thought to claim this rent for a purchaser in answer to a demand for interest (see per Parker J in *Halkett* v *Dudley* [1907] 1 Ch 590, at p 606). But perhaps the practical difficulties of quantification have seemed insuperable without litigation.

The standard sets of conditions of sale largely do no more than confirm all the above as being the general rule (see National Conditions, 20th ed, No 6; The Law Society's Conditions, 1980 ed, No 19; also Statutory Conditions, No 3). However, various qualifications of the rule, both at common law and under the conditions, are indicated in the following pages. But note here that neither set of conditions makes any provision about the vendor paying a fair occupation rent; in the absence of any such provision, it appears that the vendor would be liable to pay such a rent whether or not the delay was his fault (see above).

Ordinarily, the apportionments will all be calculated and paid or allowed, as already indicated, on actual completion by way of adjustment to the purchase price without waiting for later payments or receipts (cf ss 3 and 4 of the Apportionment Act 1870). However, The Law Society's Conditions, 1980 ed, No 19 (6) provides for sums such as service charges under leases to be apportioned subsequently when quantified; cp the National Conditions, 20th ed, No 6 (5) which provides for apportionment in such cases to be at completion on a 'best estimate' basis with appropriate adjustments later.

B INTEREST

It is clear, as Wilberforce J has said that:
> on general principle it is not right that the purchaser both should have the income of the property from the date of the contract [sic] and in addition should be relieved from paying interest on the purchase money

(in *Re Hewitt's Contract* [1963] 1 WLR 1298, at pp 1301–2). The interest is calculated on the balance of the purchase money, any deposit being treated as a payment on account (*Bridges* v *Robinson* (1811) 3 Mer 694).

The rate has usually been assumed to be that applicable to all equitable apportionments, namely, 4 per cent per annum (see, eg, per Leach V-C in *Esdaile* v *Stephenson* (1822) 1 Sim & St 122, at p 123, and per Parker J in *Halkett* v *Dudley*, ante). This rate is now rather unrealistic—an inducement to delay might be seen—and it tends to be expressly increased. Thus the standard sets of conditions of sale all permit the insertion of a special condition specifying a different, no doubt higher rate, to discourage any delay in completion on the part of the purchaser (see, eg, *Talley and Talley* v *Wolsey-Neech* (1978) 38 P & CR 45, CA—15 per cent specified).

However, there is now authority indicating that the low rate of 4 per cent per annum may no longer be treated as the appropriate equitable rate: in *Wallersteiner* v *Moir (No 2)* [1975] QB 373, CA, following a breach of fiduciary obligations, interest was awarded at the rate of 1 per cent above official bank rate or minimum lending rate in operation from time to time. Further, in *Bartlett* v *Barclays Bank Trust Co Ltd (No 2)* [1980] Ch 515 Brightman LJ recognised that the former 4 per cent rate had become unrealistic for a court of equity and held that the proper rate of interest following a breach of trust would be that allowed from time to time on the court's short-term investment account established under s 6 (1) of the Administration of Justice Act 1965 (see also a note at [1982] Conv 93–5).

Where there is no special provision for an interest rate, under The Law Society's Conditions, 1980 ed, No 1(a), the rate of interest will be 4 per cent above 'Bank of England minimum lending rate from time to time in force'. Inconveniently, this lending rate ceased to be in force on 20 August 1981. Leading counsel's opinion has been taken to the effect that the courts would substitute 'the prevailing London clearing bank base rate'. Sed quaere: it appears arguable that the courts would instead adopt the equitable rate as in *Bartlett* v *Barclays Bank Trust Co Ltd,* supra. The National Conditions (20th ed, Nos (4) and (7)) avoid this uncertainty by referring to the rate of interest 'prescribed from time to time under Land Compensation Act 1961'.

A special condition stating merely that interest shall be paid at a certain rate is not inconsistent with standard conditions (such as those in The Law Society's and National forms) incorporated so far as they are not inconsistent: in such circumstances the special condition fixes the rate but interest is payable only in accordance with the general conditions (*Re Debenham and Mercer's Contract* [1944] 1 All ER 364).

1   Vendor at fault

If, however, the delay is due to the wilful default of the vendor and the interest would exceed the income of the property, then the purchaser may keep the interest and the vendor keep any income, no one being permitted to profit by his own wrong (see per Leach V-C in *Esdaile* v *Stephenson* (1822) 1 Sim & St 122, at p 123; also *North* v *Percival* [1898] 2 Ch 128).

On their face the standard sets of conditions of sale have seemed merely to confirm this, with some slight extensions, eg, to cover the default of the vendor's mortgagee or Settled Land Act trustees (see eg, National Conditions, 20th ed, No 7 (2); also *The Law Society's Digest*, 1954, Opinion 70 (*b*) and (*c*) in Fourth (Cumulative) Supplement). In fact, however, they have been found to go unfairly far. They provided first for the purchaser to have the net income as from the contractual completion date; then for the vendor to have interest from that date unless the vendor is in default; and lastly for the vendor to elect to keep the net income instead of interest. This structure of the conditions has been held:

> clearly to link the right to income (less outgoings) with the right to receive interest, and to make it plain that the vendor can exercise the option to take the income of the property only in a case where, if he did not exercise the option, he would have been entitled to interest

(per Wilberforce J in *Re Hewitt's Contract* [1963] 1 WLR 1298, at p 1302). To put it another way, but not nicely, if the delay is due to the vendor's default, then under these conditions of sale the purchaser can both keep the interest and claim the income; the vendor loses both ways. This is not fair, but as the learned judge explained:

> the condition, to my mind, is quite clear and I do not think that I have any right to import into this contract the general rules of equity, however well established, which apply in cases where there is no express provision

(ibid, p 1303). The case concerned the 17th ed of the National Conditions, but the structure and substance of the condition has somewhat surprisingly survived into the present 20th ed (No 7). However, The Law Society's Conditions, 1980 ed, No 22 contains a radically different provision for compensation for late completion involving an option between claiming damages or claiming interest on the balance of the purchase money. It has yet to be seen how, if at all, this novel condition will work in practice.

2   Wilful default

Having said what happens when the delay is due to the wilful default of the vendor, consideration must now be given to the meaning of 'wilful default', The most quoted definition fell from Bowen LJ who having said that 'the term "wilful default" . . . is not a term of art,' continued:

> Default is a purely relative term, just like negligence. It means nothing more, nothing less, than not doing what is reasonable under the circumstances—not doing something which you ought to do, having regard to the relations which you occupy towards the other persons interested in the transaction. The other word which it is sought to define is "wilful" . . . it generally, as used in courts of law, implies nothing blameable, but merely that the person of whose action or default the expression is used, is a free agent, and that what has been done arises from the spontaneous action of his will

(in *Re Young and Harston's Contract* (1885) 31 Ch D 168, at pp 174–5). As a definition, this has often been quoted with approval in the courts (eg, *Re Woods and Lewis' Contract* [1898] 1 Ch 433, at p 435, per Romer J and 2 Ch 211, at p 215, per Collins LJ). At least, it indicates that a default may be 'wilful' notwithstanding 'that moral delinquency, intentional delay, wilful obstruction on the part of the vendor may all be absent' (per Lindley LJ in *Re Hetling and Merton's Contract* [1893] 3 Ch 269, at p 281). Incidentally, it may be remarked that the National Conditions of Sale, 20th ed, No 7 (2), refers to the vendor's 'default' without adding the word 'wilful' and without appearing to lose anything of substance.

As to 'default' itself, however, the definition has more recently been accorded less respect, with Wilberforce J after quoting the first sentence, proceeding to say:

> That, with great respect, does not seem to me to enlighten the matter to any great extent. It simply transfers the basic interpretation to another set of considerations, namely what one ought to do. One is still faced with the question of deciding what in fact the vendor ought to do in relation to this matter

(in *Re Hewitt's Contract* [1963] 1 WLR 1298, at p 1303). The learned judge then drew a distinction, in effect, between difficulties foreseen by the vendor who hoped but failed to overcome them and unforeseen occurrences, only delay caused by the former being due to wilful default (following dicta of Lindley LJ in *Re Hetling and Merton's Contract* [1893] 3 Ch 269, at p 281). His judgment does not directly contemplate the unforeseen but foreseeable occurrence, although the inference can be taken that he, like Bowen LJ, would extend the vendor's default to the reasonably foreseeable difficulty or occurrence causing delay. Thereafter, as in the tort of negligence, what is reasonably foreseeable 'can only be solved by consideration of the circumstances of each particular case' (Williams, *Sale of Land*, p 85, note (*k*)). Accordingly, a few illustrations of what has or has not been held, on the facts, to be a 'wilful default' on the part of the vendor, may be found helpful.

On the one hand, going abroad just before completion (*Re Young and Harston's Contract* (1885) 31 Ch D 168); failure to get an estate in from mortgagee-trustees (*Re Hetling and Merton's Contract* [1893] 3 Ch 269, mistake of law as to ineffective power of attorney); neglect to obtain certain necessary concurrences (*Re Stafford and Maples* [1896] 1 Ch 235); refusal to deliver an abstract of title (*Re Pelly and Jacob's Contract* (1889) 80 LT 45, misinterpretation of conditions of sale as to purchaser's entitlement); and semble insisting on a form of conveyance to which not entitled (*Bennett* v *Stone* [1903] 1 Ch 509, per Vaughan-Williams and Stirling LJJ, cp Cozens-Hardy LJ and also Buckley J at [1902] 1 Ch 226) have all been held to constitute wilful default.

On the other hand, a misstatement of the title in the conditions of sale (*Re London Corporation and Tubbs' Contract* [1894] 2 Ch 524, sed quaere, since the misstatement was careless, although honest, ie, prima facie reasonably foreseeable); failure to remove a defect in title only detectable with extreme vigilance (*Re Woods and Lewis' Contract* [1898] 2 Ch 211); and a mistake of fact (*Bennett* v *Stone* [1903] 1 Ch 509, semble unless persisted in) have all been held not to amount to wilful default.

Before passing on, mention may be made that, just as with the tort of negligence the damages must result from the breach of duty, so in this context what one has to look to 'is not necessarily solely, was there wilful default, but was the wilful default the causa causans of the delay' (per Buckley J in *Bennett* v *Stone* [1902] 1 Ch 226, at p 236; affirmed at [1903] 1 Ch 509). The delay in completion must be *due* to the vendor's wilful default.

3   Purchaser depositing

Additionally the purchaser may mitigate his liability to pay interest by appropriating the balance of the purchase money and giving notice of this to the vendor; the appropriation involves making the money available at a bank, usually by way of deposit. If the purchaser does this, then the vendor will only be entitled to the interest, if any, thereafter received by the purchaser from the money (see per Romilly MR in *Regent's Canal Co* v *Ware* (1857) 23 Beav 575, at p 587; also per Cozens-Hardy LJ in *Bennett* v *Stone* [1903] 1 Ch 509, at p 524). The standard sets of conditions of sale sometimes reiterate this right to mitigate by deposit (National Conditions, 20th ed, No 7 (1), proviso (ii); cp The Law Society's Conditions, 1980 ed, No 22, which does not).

In truth, this mitigating resource is no more than a recognition of the reality that if the purchaser is properly prepared to complete, his money must necessarily be lying idle and virtually interest-less. Even with this being so, interest will be payable by a purchaser whose act or default caused the delay in completion (see *De Visme* v *De Visme* (1849) 1 Mac & G 336; *Pearlberg* v *May* [1951] Ch 699); this too is confirmed by the conditions of sale just cited (and see *The Law Society's Digest*, No 73 (*b*) in Fourth (Cumulative) Supplement). Nor is the resource available to a purchaser where his contract expressly confers a right to interest on the vendor (see *Re Riley to Streatfield* (1886) 34 Ch D 386), but this is only the better opinion (see *Re Golds' and Norton's Contract* (1885) 52 LT 321, to the contrary), and the sets of conditions cited, of course, expressly preserved the resource.

4   Vendor's option

Again the purchaser will not be liable to pay interest to the vendor where the contract confers an option on the latter which he duly exercises to keep the income, if any, of the property (less outgoings) up to actual completion instead of interest (see National Conditions, 20th ed, No 7 (1), proviso (i); *The Law Society's Digest*, Opinion No 70 (*a*) in Fourth (Cumulative) Supplement). That this option under the cited conditions is not open to a vendor in default has already been noticed (see *Re Hewitt's Contract* [1963] 1 WLR 1298); nor is it open where the purchaser has duly deposited the purchase money, (see *The Law Society's Digest*, Opinion No 70 (*d*) in Fourth (Cumulative) Supplement).

C   PURCHASER IN POSSESSION

A purchaser will have to pay interest even before the contractual completion date has arrived if he has entered into possession of the property:

> The act of taking possession is an implied agreement to pay interest: for so absurd an agreement, as that the purchaser is to receive the rents and profits to which he has no legal title, and the vendor is not to have interest as he has no legal title to the money, can never be implied

(per Grant MR in *Fludyer* v *Cocker* (1805) 12 Ves 25, at p 27). This will be so even where the possession taken hardly amounts to a beneficial occupation and there is no income from the property (*Ballard* v *Shutt* (1880) 15 Ch D 122, purchaser put up a notice board on vacant land). It will also be so even though completion be delayed by the vendor's default (ibid). What is more, a purchaser in possession cannot avoid paying interest by depositing the purchase money (see *Re Priestley's Contract* [1947] Ch 469, but cp *Kershaw* v *Kershaw* (1869) LR 9 Eq 56).

All this is confirmed by the standard sets of conditions of sale (see National Conditions, 20th ed, Nos 8 (1) (ii) and (iv) and 7 (1), proviso (ii); The Law Society's Conditions, 1980 ed, No 18 (4)). However, it appears probable that the operation of these conditions will be confirmed to cases in which the purchaser has been *lawfully* allowed into occupation before completion (see *Cantor Art Services Ltd* v *Kenneth Bieber Photography Ltd* [1969] 1 WLR 1226, CA). In any other case, where a purchaser is let into possession by the vendor before completion, some express agreement as to terms would undoubtedly be reached.

XI COMPLETION

THE completion ceremony could be called the Mecca for all good conveyancers in each of their transactions. When completion should occur has already been discussed, now the questions are what and where.

A MEANING

What *is* meant by the 'completion' of a contract for the sale and purchase of land? There can be no doubt that the usual meaning is 'the complete conveyance of the estate and final settlement of the business' (per Stable J in *Killner* v *France* [1946] 2 All ER 83, at p 86; see also *Lewis* v *South Wales Railway* (1852) 10 Hare 113, at p 119). More recently Pennycuick V-C considered the meaning of the expression 'at the date of the completion of the said sale' and said:

> It seems to me that those words are themselves quite unambiguous and can only denote the date at which the sale of Church Farm is completed, in accordance with the ordinary meaning of that word in the language of conveyancing, namely, the execution of a conveyance and the payment of the purchase price

(in *Re Atkins' Will Trusts* [1974] 1 WLR 761, at pp 765–6). Thus in *Maktoum* v *South Lodge Flats Ltd* (1980) *The Times*, 22 April, a purchaser of certain underleases at a purchase price of £1,221,100 which she had paid in full, being allowed to take possession, was held not to have complied with a notice to complete. Judge Mervyn Davies was reported as saying that '"completion" meant "final settlement of the business". Here there had been no such final settlement because final settlement included constituting the purchaser as owner of the legal estate, by the vendor executing and the purchaser accepting the appropriate deed of assurance.' Compare, however, *D'Silva* v *Lister House Development Ltd* [1971] Ch 17 as to there being an effective grant of a lease by a duly executed deed, ie, by the lessor unilaterally without need of acceptance by the lessee (see further a note at [1982] Conv 2–4). Nevertheless, in principle completion signifies that what equity has long looked on as done (Vendor as Trustee, p 167) must actually be done—the vendor gets the money and the purchaser the land.

If the idea emerges of two suspicious solicitors sitting on either side of a table, one pushing forward the title deeds (including a conveyance duly executed by the vendor) and the other the purchase money (or the balance thereof after adjustment of accounts), with completion taking place suddenly by snatch and swop, then this idea is not entirely erroneous:

> It is a fundamental principle that the payment of the purchase money and the delivery of the conveyance are to be performed interchangeably

(per Vaisey J in *Palmer* v *Lark* [1945] Ch 182, at pp 194–5). Yet the completion ceremony tends to be a friendly affair with the fundamentals obscured by detail— the inspection of documents and receipts for rates and rents, the undertakings as to the unavailable or overlooked, the release of the deposit, the signing of schedules, the licence to assign, even the keys—and there may be four not two solicitors, the supernumeraries representing either side's mortgagees (strictly theirs are trans-actions separated by a scintilla temporis: see *Church of England Building Society* v *Piskor* [1954] Ch 553).

What is more, or maybe worse, nowadays there may be no completion ceremony at all because the practice of completing by post instead of in person has apparently become widespread enough for official sanction: see practice note published in (1978) *The Law Society's Gazette* vol 75, p 111, which essentially assumes that the purchaser's solicitor instructs the vendor's solicitor to effect completion as his agent (for hyper-critical comments, see [1978] Conv 88–91 and 180–3; cp The Law Society's Conditions, 1980 ed, No 21 (1), (3) and also the National Conditions, 20th ed, No 5 (4), both of which contemplate postal completions in terms not entirely consistent with those assumed above, ie, no agency is involved). But in theory completion must still occur, albeit by lonely non-ceremony, in the sense already indicated of exchanging money for documents.

B   REGISTERED LAND

As envisaged by statute, sales of registered land are completed in practice by payment of the purchase money on receipt (or deposit) of the vendor's land certificate and a duly executed form of transfer (see s 110 (6) of the Land Registration Act 1925; also *R* v *Edwards, ex parte Joseph* [1947] KB 392). The theoretical flaw in this is that the legal estate will not be vested in the purchaser unless and until his name appears on the proprietorship register (ss 19 (1) and 22 (1) of the Act, and r 83 (2) of the Land Registration Rules 1925 as amended in 1978; see *Smith* v *Express Dairy* [1954] JPL 45 and *Lever Finance Ltd* v *Needleman's Trustee and Kreutzer* [1956] Ch 375). Accordingly the late T Cyprian Williams submitted that 'except by special stipulation the vendor has no *right* to require the purchase money to be paid to him before the time of registration of the transfer' (*Sale of Land*, p 80, note (*s*)). He suggested instead no less than four other methods of completion, involving completing at the office of the Land Registry, or procuring a priority notice, or a provisional registration, or an actual registration of the purchaser (loc cit). Although his book was published in 1930 (introduction dated 13 June), he overlooked altogether the priority conferred by the purchaser's official search (introduced by the Land Registration Rules 1930, dated 26 March, see now the Land Registration (Official Searches) Rules 1981). It is in this search, of course, that sufficient safety is found for the practice of paying the purchase money before registration. Indeed, on the strength of this search, the authorities still say that:

> By analogy with the present law of unregistered conveyancing under which a purchaser is not bound to complete [sic] till he gets a conveyance, he is not, under the system of registration, bound to part with his purchase-money until *the vendor puts him in a position to be* registered as proprietor

(Ruoff and Roper, *Registered Conveyancing*, 4th ed, p 341, italics supplied).

The present writer still wonders, notwithstanding the efficacy of an official search, whether the true analogy does not involve deleting the italicised words, for without registration there has not been 'the complete conveyance of the estate' (see above). In other words the question is still strictly not the safety of the practice but the *rights* of the vendor and purchaser (and remember that it is the date of registration which is relevant for overriding interests: *Re Boyle's Claim* [1961] 1 WLR 339). As the late Professor Potter said:

> Whether in the absence of any specific stipulation a purchaser could insist upon depositing the purchase money in a bank or with a stakeholder pending

completion of registration is an open question. In practice, it is well to specify the form that completion shall take

(*Registered Land Conveyancing*, at p 332). Nevertheless such special stipulations certainly have not become the practice.

C THE PURCHASE MONEY

Strictly cash should be used for the completion. A purchaser of land, like any other person tendering payment, should do so in legal currency (see Currency and Bank Notes Act 1954, s 1, and Coinage Act 1971, ss 2 and 3). The vendor will not be bound to accept a cheque, or any other negotiable instrument, in payment of the purchase money (see *Blumberg* v *Life Interests and Reversionary Securities Corporation* [1897] 1 Ch 171; [1898] 1 Ch 27 and *Johnston* v *Boyes* [1899] 2 Ch 73). He may, of course, waive objection to the form of tender, for example, by asking for payment only by cheque (see *Cubitt* v *Gamble* (1919) 35 TLR 223), but only the unduly optimistic would expect the vendor's solicitor to accept payment by cheque, for if he does so without his client's authority and it bounces after the title deeds and conveyance have been handed over, he will be liable for any loss (see *Papé* v *Westacott* [1894] 1 QB 272). Indeed the pronouncement has actually been made that it is improper practice even to ask a vendor's solicitor to accept a cheque ((1969) *Law Society's Gazette* vol 66, at p 406). All this applies equally in theory to banker's drafts, which indeed are neither cheques nor bills of exchange having no distinct drawer and drawee (see *Capital and Counties Bank Ltd* v *Gordon* [1903] AC 240). Nevertheless, in practice, payment is nowadays almost invariably made and accepted in the non-bounceable form of a banker's draft, which has been pronounced proper although the definition of such a draft has had to be left to the discretion of the individual practitioner (see (1969) *Law Society's Gazette* vol 66, at pp 406, 761 and (1970) vol 69, p 603).

The acceptable methods of paying the purchase price are stipulated in both The Law Society Conditions (1980 ed, No 21 (2)) and the National Conditions (20th ed, No 5 (3) (ii)). Each set particularly includes banker's drafts but the former restricts these to those of London Clearing Bankers, trustee savings bank or National Girobank, whilst the latter extends to the drafts issued by any bank 'designated by the Chief Registrar under Building Societies Act 1962, s 59' (for a list, see (1981) 125 SJ 800).

D PLACE

Since deeds and money have each been thought too valuable to be parted with save by simultaneous swop, completion has been carried out comparatively rarely by post in the past (but see now the practice note adverted to ante, p 199). According to orthodoxy, completion should be effected in person by the solicitors acting, who must obviously get together in some place. But what place? If the contract is open on the point it would seem, in the absence of authority, that the vendor may name any place he likes for the completion (see to this effect Walford, *Sale of Land*, 2nd ed, p 24; Williams, *Sale of Land*, p 48, note (*r*)). The reason for saying this is simply the rule that any person bound to make tender—as the purchaser is of both the purchase money and the engrossed conveyance for execution—must seek out the tenderee to do so (see per Slesser LJ in *Reading Trust Ltd* v *Spero* [1930] 1 KB 492, at pp 513–14). The only legal limitation on the rule would appear to be that the place where the vendor, like the mountain, awaits the Mahomet-like purchaser has to be within England or Wales (loc cit; also *Re Young and Harston's Contract* (1885) 31 Ch D 168).

However, a practical limitation may be argued by analogy to the place for production of documents (p 126) that the vendor must meet any extra expense caused to the purchaser by completion elsewhere than 'at the vendor's own residence, or upon or near the property sold, or in London'. To these places there can be little, if any, doubt that practice has added the office of the vendor's solicitor, perhaps even to the exclusion of all other places (this seems to be the view from on high, see *The Law Society's Digest*, Opinions Nos 165–8 and 172, and 174 (*a*) in the Fourth (Cumulative) Supplement). Awkwardly, however, economics dictate that a good many completions should actually occur at a place strictly improper as between vendor and purchaser, namely at the office of the vendor's mortgagee's solicitor. In addition, there is still the remote possibility of a purchaser insisting, or trying to insist, that a sale of registered land be completed at HM Land Registry (see p 199).

All this could be inconvenient to either party so that not unexpectedly the standard sets of conditions of sale do provide for the place of completion, either 'at the office of the vendor's solicitors, or, if required by the vendor at least five working days prior to actual completion, at the office of the vendor's mortgagee or his solicitors' (The Law Society's Conditions, 1980 ed, No 21 (1)) or simply 'at such office or place as the vendor's solicitor shall reasonably require' (National Conditions, 20th ed, No 5 (4)). In the result, when completion is required by the vendor at a place according with incorporated conditions of sale, there seems nothing else to say save that the purchaser must bear any extra expense himself (see *The Law Society's Digest*, Opinion No 170). However, the National Conditions now contain a novel provision whereby the purchaser may insist upon vacant possession being handed over to him or his representative 'on, or immediately before the time of, completion . . . at the property' (No 5 (4) proviso). Presumably this will not mean that completion must take place actually at the property so long as the solicitors acting can by telephone obtain confirmation of the handing over of possession.

E MERGER

The general rule is that after completion no action can be brought on the contract for sale:

> It is well settled that, where parties enter into an executory agreement which is to be carried out by a deed afterwards to be executed, the real completed contract is to be found in the deed. The contract is merged in the deed . . . The most common instance, perhaps, of this merger is a contract for the sale of land followed by conveyance on completion. All the provisions of the contract which the parties intend should be performed by the conveyance are merged in the conveyance, and all the rights of the purchaser in relation thereto are thereby satisifed

(*Knight Sugar Co* v *Alberta Railway & Irrigation Co* [1938] 1 All ER 266, at p 269). For example the vendor's contractual obligations as to title (p 83) are replaced by his covenants for title (see p 258). This general rule applies also to sales of registered land save that the merger depends on both execution of the transfer and registration (*Knight Sugar Co* v *Alberta Railway & Irrigation Co*, ante, where the Privy Council were concerned with the slightly peculiar provisions of the Land Titles Act 1906 of

Alberta; see case notes at (1937–8) 2 Conv (NS) 262, and at [1962] BTR 388).

However, as indicated in the passage quoted, merger is not an absolute doctrine but depends entirely upon the intention of the parties (see *Barclays Bank Ltd* v *Beck* [1952] 2 QB 47). As Bowen LJ has variously explained:

> It is true that the execution of the conveyance puts an end to all contractual obligations which are intended to be satisfied by the execution. But that doctrine does not apply to cases where the contractual obligation is of such a kind that it cannot be supposed to have been the intention of all the parties that it should be extinguished by the conveyance

and:

> When one is dealing with a deed by which the property has been conveyed, one must see if it covers the whole ground of the preliminary contract. One must construe the preliminary contract by itself, and see whether it was intended to go on to any and what extent after the formal deed had been executed

(in *Clarke* v *Ramuz* [1891] 2 QB 456, at p 461 and in *Palmer* v *Johnson* (1884) 13 QBD 351, at p 357, respectively. An obvious example of non-merger would be the warranty given by a vendor of a house in the course of construction that it should be fit for human habitation (see *Hancock* v *BW Brazier* [1966] 1 WLR 1317 and cases there cited; but cp *Greswolde-Williams* v *Barneby* (1900) 83 LT 708). Less obvious examples would be a provision for compensation for any misdescription (see in *Palmer* v *Johnson,* ante), a provision for indemnity against tenant's claims (conceded in *Eagon* v *Dent* [1965] 3 All ER 334) or a provision for vacant possession on completion (see *Hissett* v *Reading Roofing Co Ltd* [1969] 1 WLR 1757).

Since cases can easily occur on the borderline between merger and non-merger, the practical desire for certainty should dictate that the parties express their intentions as to merger. This indeed is often done by special condition, especially where the matter is of importance, when a part of the purchase money may advisedly be withheld pending performance. The standard sets of general conditions of sale, however, no longer have anything to say on the subject.

XII DEPOSIT

ESTATE agents expect every purchaser to do his duty by paying a deposit. We have all got the message. But is there a duty? The very first term of an open contract for the sale of land, as stated by the late great T Cyprian Williams, is that:

> No part of the purchase money shall be payable as a deposit or otherwise until the proper time for completion of the purchase

(*Sale of Land*, p 27, with reference to *Binks* v *Rokeby* (1818) 2 Swanst 222, at pp 225–6, and *Doe d Gray* v *Stanion* (1836) 1 M & W 695, at p 701). Yet, notwithstanding this negative implication, there will almost invariably be found in any formal contract a positive provision for the payment of a deposit of 10 per cent of the purchase price (often by special condition, but also by The Law Society's Conditions, 1980 ed, No 9 and National Conditions, 20th ed, No 2). This is rarely, if ever, queried on behalf of purchasers. Whether it should be, would largely turn, of course, on the advantage to vendors of requiring a deposit. So what is this advantage?

As Lord Macnaghten has said:

> Everybody knows what a deposit is. The purchaser did not want legal advice to tell him that. The deposit serves two purposes—if the purchase is carried out it goes against the purchase money—but its primary purpose is this, it is a guarantee that the purchaser means business

(in *Soper* v *Arnold* (1889) 14 App Cas 429, at p 435). The question, therefore, is how the deposit acts as a guarantee. The short answer is that 'if the contract is not performed by the payer [the deposit] shall remain the property of the payee' (per Fry LJ in *Howe* v *Smith* (1884) 27 Ch D 89, at p 101; see also per Cotton and Bowen LJJ ibid, at pp 95 and 98, respectively). This calls for closer consideration, but first one need hardly mention that where it is the vendor who is in default, the purchaser is entitled to recover his deposit and that with interest (see per Cotton LJ in *Soper* v *Arnold* (1887) 37 Ch D 96, at p 100; affirmed (1889) 14 App Cas 429, also *Jacobs* v *Revell* [1900] 2 Ch 858, at p 869).

A FORFEITURE

The rule is that if a purchaser be so much in default as to discharge the vendor from the contract, the purchaser as a punishment will lose and the vendor as a consolation will gain the deposit (ibid, and see *Sprague* v *Booth* [1909] AC 576, at p 580). In colloquial conveyancing, the vendor may rescind the contract and forfeit the deposit (forfeiture is expressed in The Law Society's Conditions of Sale, 1980 ed, No 23 (5) (*b*) (i), and in the National Conditions, 20th ed, No 22 (3), but in each case only as a consequence of non-compliance with a notice to complete). The vendor may do this even without any express enabling provision in the contract—it is implied from the primary purpose of paying a deposit (see *Hall* v *Burnell* [1911] 2 Ch 551). He may also forfeit the deposit where the purchaser resists the enforcement by action of the contract as not observing the evidential requirements of s 40 of the Law of Property Act 1925 (see *Monnickendam* v *Leanse* (1923) 39 TLR

445, also *Low* v *Fry* (1935) 51 TLR 322), but not where he himself resists enforcement on this ground (*Gosbell* v *Archer* (1835) 2 Ad & El 500), nor, of course, where there has never been any concluded contract at all to enforce in any way (eg, agreement 'subject to contract,' see *Chillingworth* v *Esche* [1924] 1 Ch 97). What is more, the vendor has been held entitled to keep the deposit although it may exceed any loss he has suffered (see *Hinton* v *Sparkes* (1868) LR 3 CP 161).

All this springs directly from the primary purpose of requiring a deposit and is hardly to be doubted. Yet the present writer in all conscience must confess his difficulty in seeing how equity came to tolerate this. Why, in other words, was it not relieved against as a '*penalty*'? After all, deposits and penalties do have precisely the same purpose, namely to secure performance through fear of loss (compare Bowen and Fry LJJ in *Howe* v *Smith* (1884) 27 Ch D 89, at pp 98 and 101, with Lopes LJ in *Law* v *Redditch Local Board* [1892] 1 QB 127, at p 132, and Lord Dunedin in *Dunlop Pneumatic Tyre Co* v *New Garage & Motor Co Ltd* [1915] AC 79, at pp 86–8). And there are other similarities, for example, as with a penalty but not as with liquidated damages, the vendor may sue the purchaser for any loss he actually suffers beyond the deposit (see *Icely* v *Grew* (1836) 6 Nev & MKB 467). Thus one may reflect on the true test of a penalty, namely, any sum which is not a genuine pre-estimate of damage (see Lord Radcliffe's judgment in *Bridge* v *Campbell Discount Co Ltd* [1962] AC 600); the traditional 10 per cent on a sale of land represents pure practice and is never even a perfunctory pre-estimate.

Possibly a distinction between the two could be seen in the fact that deposits unlike penalties are paid in advance of any breach, so that repayment rather than relief against payment is in issue. Nevertheless some authority could be found for the availability of equitable relief in respect of sums already paid. This consists of cases concerning not deposits but contracts providing, in effect, for payment of the price by instalments and for forfeiture on breach of anything then already paid (*Re Dagenham (Thames) Dock Co, ex parte Hulse* (1873) 8 Ch App 1022; *Steedman* v *Drinkle* [1916] 1 AC 275; *Musson* v *Van Diemen's Land Co* [1938] Ch 253—all three sales of land; *Stockloser* v *Johnson* [1954] 1 QB 476, sale of goods; and *Galbraith* v *Mitchenall Estates* [1965] 2 QB 473, hire of caravan). From these cases, it emerged that the equitable principles were only similar, not identical: the court should look to see whether it would be unconscionable for the sums to be retained rather than oppressive for them to be obtained (affirmative relief was, in fact, given only in *Steedman* v *Drinkle*, ante). A variation was played on this theme in *Starside Properties Ltd* v *Mustapha* [1974] 1 WLR 816, where a contract for the sale of a house for £5,950 stipulated that a deposit of £1,250 should be paid by instalments (ie, £350 down and £16 per month, the purchaser being in possession) and provided for rescission and forfeiture on any payment being fourteen days late. The Court of Appeal considered the cited cases and held that there was jurisdiction to grant relief against such a penal provision if the justice of the case so required. Unfortunately this decision is not too helpful for present purposes, largely because the purchaser was not seeking recovery of instalments of the deposit paid but only time to pay the balance, and also because the matter was remitted to the county court judge to decide upon the merits.

Beyond these decisions, modern obiter dicta can also be discovered directly indicating that deposits may be treated as penalties even on a sale of land (see per Denning LJ in *Stockloser* v *Johnson* [1954] 1 QB, at p 491, giving the exaggerated example of a 50 per cent deposit plus re-sale at a profit, and per Lord Radcliffe in *Bridge* v *Campbell Discount Co Ltd* [1962] AC 600, at p 624). Nevertheless, it would still be over-optimistic to expect an equitable attack to succeed against the traditional 10 per cent. Thus such an attack failed dismally in *Windsor Securities* v

Loreldal and *Lester* (1975) *The Times*, 10 September, despite the circumstances that the sum forfeited totalled £235,000 and that a potential profit of £150,000 on resale was alleged. According to Oliver J, 'There was nothing in the facts of the present case to show that the forfeiture was unreasonable or in the nature of a penalty.'

B   SECTION 49 (2)

Apart altogether from any equitable principles affecting deposits, statute now provides that:

> Where the court refuses to grant specific performance of a contract, or in any action for the return of a deposit, the court may, if it thinks fit, order the repayment of any deposit

(s 49 (2) of the Law of Property Act 1925). Considering the constant threat of forfeiture in practice, there has been a remarkable scarcity of decisions involving this subsection. What few there were rather suggested a limited application (see, eg, *Hunt (Charles) Ltd* v *Palmer* [1931] 2 Ch 287 and *James Macara Ltd* v *Barclay* [1944] 2 All ER 31, on appeal [1945] KB 148). Now, however, we have received some different and authoritative-seeming judicial guidance.

First, in *Schindler* v *Pigault* (1975) 30 P & CR 328, at pp 336-7, Megarry J expressed the wide view that the statutory discretion was to be exercised where justice required it and was not confined to cases where the vendor's conduct had been unconscionable but was 'exercisable on wider grounds than that, including a general consideration of the conduct of the parties (and especially the applicant), the gravity of the matters in question and the amounts at stake'. Accordingly he was prepared to order the return of a deposit where the vendor had been indirectly responsible for the purchaser's inability to complete on time (ie, through failure to arrange for inspection by a sub-purchaser).

Then in *Universal Corporation* v *Five Ways Properties Ltd* [1979] 1 All ER 552, at p 555, Buckley LJ approved this wide view, namely that the subsection is 'designed simply to do justice between vendor and purchaser', adding, 'I take the word "justice" to be used in a wide sense, indicating that repayment must be ordered in any circumstances which make this the fairest course between the two parties'. He rejected the narrower view taken at first instance that a purchaser could only succeed 'if the vendor's conduct has been open to criticism in some way . . . having some mark of equitable disfavour attached to it' (loc cit; Eveleigh LJ was a little less confident at p 556; and cp *Cole* v *Rose* [1978] 3 All ER 1121, at p 1130, for a surprisingly narrow reading of Megarry J's view). Nevertheless the discretion must still be 'exercised judicially and with regard to all relevant considerations including the very important consideration of the terms of the contract into which the parties have chosen to enter' (loc cit). Accordingly, it was held that where a purchaser, unable to complete for lack of available funds, claimed repayment of his deposit, there was necessarily a triable issue. In addition and purportedly without attempting to prejudge that issue, Buckley LJ thought that it might be found 'more just to order repayment of the deposit, leaving [the vendor] such remedy in damages as may be available to it, than to allow it to retain the very substantial deposit which was paid in this case' (at pp 555-6, referring to 10 per cent of £885,000). Consider too *Maktoum* v *South Lodge Flats Ltd* (1980) *The Times*, 22 April, in which return of a deposit (10 per cent of £1,250,000) was ordered under the subsection as conferring an unrestricted discretion to adopt the fairest course in all the circumstances (apparently resale at a profit was possible). Quaere: is contracting-out of s 49 (2) possible? Unlikely!

This wide view of the subsection can only encourage purchasers not to give up their deposits without a battle. The statutory discretion looks at least as equitable and uncertain as equity's jurisdiction to grant relief in respect of penalties. Nevertheless one last restrictive point may perhaps stand untouched by the recent decisions: Vaisey J once observed that the subsection does not appear to cover anything other than the whole of the deposit, ie, the repayment ordered must be all or nothing (in *James Macara Ltd* v *Barclay* [1944] 2 All ER 31, at p 32, instancing the return of a deposit less the vendor's reasonable expenses as being fair but unauthorised).

C NON-PAYMENT OF DEPOSIT

What is the position if a purchaser fails to pay the deposit on exchange of contracts? As a starter, the vendor's solicitor may be liable in negligence for leaving his client with nothing to forfeit (*Morris* v *Duke-Cohan & Co* (1975) 119 SJ 826). But what is the effect on the contract itself? Where there is an express term for payment of a deposit but the purchaser fails to comply there is authority for the proposition that in general such payment constitutes a condition precedent to a binding contract: *Myton Ltd* v *Schwab Morris* [1974] 1 WLR 331 (where the purchaser's cheque was not met). However, in that case, Goulding J held in the alternative that non-payment merely entitled the vendor to rescind for breach of a fundamental term (see also *Pollway Ltd* v *Abdullah* [1974] 1 WLR 493, CA, indirectly supporting this view and notes at (1975) 39 Conv (NS) 313–5, and [1979] Conv 85–9). And now Warner J has reconsidered the cases and concluded that a provision for payment of a deposit is not a condition precedent but in general a fundamental term (*Millichamp* v *Jones* [1982] 1 WLR 1422). Readers should appreciate that the consequences of these alternatives are disconcertingly different: in substance, with the former the purchaser would have the choice of avoiding the formation of any contract by simply failing to make payment, whilst with the latter the vendor can choose to enforce the contract via remedies for breach. In the *Millichamp* case enforcement by the vendor would have involved treating the contract as discharged and suing for damages. However, on the out-of-the-ordinary facts, his lordship found that the non-payment had been a mere oversight not amounting to a breach of contract and that the vendor should have notified the purchaser and given him an opportunity of paying (the case concerned exercise after ten years of an option to repurchase when neither side had given the deposit a thought). On ordinary facts non-payment would be an immediate breach of contract without need of warning shots.

In addition to any such case, the question arises of whether the vendor can sue on the contract for the unpaid deposit, ie, as well as rescinding and forfeiting. There is one modern first instance decision which says not: *Lowe* v *Hope* [1970] Ch 94 (concerning the balance of a deposit), but this depended entirely upon an application of certain principles as to the effect of rescission which have since been destroyed by the House of Lords in *Johnson* v *Agnew* [1980] AC 367 (see p 210). Therefore properly to be preferred today should be the older case of *Dewar* v *Mintoft* [1912] 2 KB 373 in which, inter alia, Horridge J 'ruled that [the purchaser] could not put himself in a better position by refusing to pay the deposit than if the deposit had in fact been paid, in which case it could be retained by the seller . . . and . . . directed the jury that the damages should be [calculated accordingly]' (at pp 387–8; the actual loss was less than the deposit). And indeed this preference was duly shown by Warner J in *Millichamp* v *Jones*, supra, where he took the view, obiter in the end, that the vendor would have been entitled to sue for damages for breach of contract including the amount of the unpaid deposit.

Incidentally, in practice a deposit would rarely if ever be payable to the vendor or paid in cash, but would be received by an agent (or stakeholder) by cheque. Acceptance of a cheque here cannot be compelled but does seem to be allowed (see *Johnston* v *Boyes* [1899] 2 Ch 73 and *Farrer* v *Lacy, Hartland & Co* (1885) 31 Ch D 42; cp a note at [1979] Conv 90–1). As a result non-payment of a deposit normally involves a stopped cheque. In *Pollway Ltd* v *Abdullah* [1974] 1 WLR 493 the Court of Appeal held that the vendor's agent could sue on such a cheque notwithstanding rescission of the contract. Assuming, therefore, that the purchaser is not a man of straw, payment of a deposit appears obtainable for forfeiture in a roundabout way. Note too that each of the standard sets of conditions of sale in its current edition anticipates bouncing cheques and provides suitable remedies for a vendor (see National, 20th ed, No 2 (2) and The Law Society's, 1980 ed, No 9).

D DEPOSIT-HOLDER

Of course, a purchaser will rarely pay his deposit directly to the vendor, paying it instead to some third party, such as an estate agent or even a solicitor. The first thing of note is that this makes no substantial alteration at all to 'the nature of the deposit, or the implied terms upon which the money is paid by the purchaser' (per Eve J in *Hall* v *Burnell* [1911] 2 Ch 551, at p 554). What needs to be considered, however, is the capacity in which the third party receives the deposit for this does affect the rights of the vendor and purchaser. In other words, is the deposit held by a stakeholder or the vendor's agent?

In the absence of any expressed capacity, the implications as to the deposit-holder's capacity seem fairly clear. Thus prima facie the vendor's solicitor will not be a stakeholder but an agent for the vendor (*Edgell* v *Day* (1865) LR 1 CP 80; *Ellis* v *Goulton* [1893] 1 QB 350; also *The Law Society's Digest*, Opinion No 61), although in practice he may well express himself to be a stakeholder (see *Wolf* v *Hosier & Dickinson Ltd* [1981] Com LR 89). Again an auctioneer will impliedly hold any deposit payable to him as a stakeholder (*Furtado* v *Lumley* (1890) 54 JP 407). The estate agent, the most common holder, has done so ambivalently, but it is now established that he does *not* take a deposit as the vendor's agent (*Sorrell* v *Finch* [1977] AC 728, HL; see also Estate Agents (Accounts) Regulations 1981).

If the third party is expressly or impliedly a stakeholder this means that he is the agent of both parties, unable to pay the deposit to either party without the other party's consent unless and until 'the event of the contract' be decided (see Williams, *Sale of Land*, p 104, explained per Cross J in *Skinner* v *Reed's Trustee* [1967] Ch 1194, at p 1200; see also *Collins* v *Stimson* (1883) 11 QBD 142, at p 144). In practice, therefore, the vendor will obtain on completion a letter from the purchaser to the stakeholder releasing the deposit on which letter the stakeholder will act (after deducting, if an estate agent, his commission on the sale). If the parties come to blows, the court tends eventually to declare that one or other party can give a good receipt to the stakeholder who no doubt acts on this (see, eg, *Smith* v *Hamilton* [1951] Ch 174).

If the third party is expressly or impliedly the vendor's agent, as a general rule he must pay the deposit to the vendor on demand and any action by the purchaser to recover it can only be brought against the vendor (*Edgell* v *Day* (1865) LR 1 CP 80; *Ellis* v *Goulton* [1893] 1 QB 350). However, this rule does not hold true in respect of the period before a binding contract is concluded: here, the agent is deemed to be authorised by the vendor to pay the deposit over to the purchaser on, in effect, a simple demand after which it becomes money had and received to the use of the purchaser (*Goding* v *Frazer* [1967] 1 WLR 286).

In addition, as a general rule, an agent is accountable to the vendor for any profit he may make, in the way of interest or otherwise, out of the deposit (see per Tenterden LCJ in *Harington* v *Hoggart* (1830) 1 B & Ad 577, at p 586). The stakeholder's position has always been accepted as different. 'He puts the interest earned by the stake into his pocket. That is his reward for holding the stake' (per Harman J in *Smith* v *Hamilton* [1951] Ch 174, at p 184, see also per Tenterden LCJ in *Harington* v *Hoggart,* ante, at pp 586-7; and *The Law Society's Digest,* 1954, Opinion No 63). Notwithstanding doubts, this established proposition as to retention of interest has been applied to an estate agent holding a pre-contract deposit expressly as stakeholder even though no contract for sale was ever concluded (*Potters* v *Loppert* [1973] Ch 399).

Incidentally, there is something to be said for having the deposit paid to an agent rather than a stakeholder—after contract the vendor can get hold of the deposit (with any interest) and look out for loss himself, whilst the purchaser not only has rights against the vendor in all cases but also the protection of a lien on the land for the amount of the deposit plus costs (*Whitbread & Co Ltd* v *Watt* [1902] 1 Ch 835), which lien he does not apparently have when the deposit is paid to a stakeholder (*Combe* v *Swaythling* [1947] Ch 625). But against this can be put the point that a purchaser is entitled to have a deposit in the hands of a stakeholder applied first in discharge of any outstanding incumbrances on the property sold which the vendor has a duty to discharge; only after this does the deposit belong to the vendor, so that the purchaser's entitlement will enjoy priority over any liens of third parties, such as auctioneers (*Skinner* v *Reed's Trustee* [1967] Ch 1194). In that case, it was indicated without a decision that the position might very well be different if the deposit were held as agent for the vendor, ie, that an auctioneer's lien would have priority.

Finally the question used to be asked whether a fiduciary vendor, whatever the preference of the parties, must insist on any deposit being paid to his agent to avoid personal liability for loss, ie, because the deposit is trust money which must be within the trustee's sole control (see, eg, *Gibson's Conveyancing*, 19th ed, at p 112; cp 20th ed, at p 127). However the plain better view now is that there is no substance in the point: *Edmonds* v *Peake* (1843) 7 Beav 239 may be cited as sufficient approbation for allowing stakeholders to hold anyone's deposit.

XIII REMEDIES

THAT attention which has already been directed to the performance of a contract for the sale of land (see Completion, p 198) may now be turned to the position on *non*-performance. In other words, a look must be taken at the remedies arising on breach of contract, concentrating, of course, on those aspects peculiar to the sale of land and largely assuming the rest. However, readers may be reminded of the relevance, incidentally, of other parts of this book, particularly the chapters dealing with the Deposit and Time (pp 179, 203), but also those sections concerned with Misdescription, Misrepresentation and Non-disclosure (pp 52, 55 and 62).

Also, before proceeding, mention should be made of a couple of novel remedies which go beyond the more familiar topics of rescission, damages and specific performance and which appear available in particular for cases where the breach of contract involves sale of the land to a third party. First, in *Lake* v *Bayliss* [1974] 1 WLR 1073, a purchaser was allowed the equitable remedy of 'tracing' the land as trust property in the trustee-vendor's hands in its changed form of money, ie, the proceeds of sale (see further p 170; cp *Butler* v *Broadhead* [1975] Ch 97). Second, a tortious novelty, in *Esso Petroleum Co Ltd* v *Kingswood Motors Ltd* [1974] 1 QB 142, which concerned the transfer of legal title to the site of a petrol station in breach of a solus agreement for the supply of petrol, various injunctions were sought including a mandatory injunction to re-transfer. The defence inter alia argued that this would contravene the policy of the legislature, as embodied in the Land Charges Acts and Land Registration Acts, that only registered interests and overriding interests should bind purchasers of land. Bridge J rejected this argument and granted an injunction against the transferee as a tortfeasor personally liable to undo the consequence of his tort, namely conspiracy to induce breach of a contract. However, this tort requires deliberate inducement, which necessarily involves some knowledge or intentional disregard of the existence of the contract to be breached: see *Smith* v *Morrison* [1974] 1 WLR 659, at pp 676–7, where in effect the second purchaser's lack of an ulterior motive and honest doubt about the validity of the first purchaser's claim meant that there was no tortious liability found (adopted by Walton J in *Pritchard* v *Briggs* [1978] 2 WLR 317, at p 342). See further RJ Smith, 'The Economic Torts: Their Impact on Real Property' at (1977) 41 Conv (NS) 318–29.

A   RESCISSION

The question of the meaning and significance of 'rescission' in relation to a contract for the sale of land was reconsidered very recently by the Court of Appeal in *Buckland* v *Farmar & Moody* [1979] 1 WLR 221. As Buckley LJ put it (at pp 231–2):

> The word "rescind" may be used to describe the effect of the sort of relief that is normally granted where a contract has been obtained by fraud, misre-presentation or on some other ground which vitiates its character as a contract, where the court thinks it right to annul a contract in every respect so as to produce a state of affairs as though the contract had never been entered into.

But it is often used to describe the consequence of acceptance by one party to a contract of a repudiation of the contract by another party by breach of some essential term of the contract.

Accordingly he rejected a contention that the word should be read in 'its primary and strict meaning, that is to say annulment'; in his view 'there is no primary meaning' (at p 232). He even added: 'The word is capable of alternative meanings and is frequently used in alternative senses. It may be that it is capable of more than two meanings but it is not necessary to investigate that for present purposes' (loc cit). All this enjoyed more authority than it did novelty. Thus, a quarter of a century ago a solicitor, Mr A Bate, writing at (1955) 19 Conv (NS) 116–20 had with reasonable precision pointed out that 'rescission' has three fundamentally different meanings, namely (1) 'the setting aside of the contract in equity (in or out of court) for misrepresentation, duress or undue influence'; (2) 'the discharge at common law of the innocent party by the other's breach'; and (3) 'rescission by agreement'. Nevertheless Lord Wilberforce still thought it important 'to dissipate a fertile source of confusion' by drawing and indeed underlining the distinction between 'rescission ab initio, such as may arise for example in cases of mistake, fraud or lack of consent' and the 'so-called "rescission" . . . [i]n the case of an accepted repudiatory breach' (in *Johnson* v *Agnew* [1980] AC 367, at pp 392–3, where he also seemed unsure how to classify cases of a contractual right to rescind).

It had long been thought to be an established proposition that a party who elected for rescission of a contract could not also recover damages for loss of bargain but only forfeiture of any deposit and restitution and indemnity in respect of sums paid and expenses incurred (see per Megarry J in *Horsler* v *Zorro* [1975] Ch 302, at pp 309–12, also *Barber* v *Wolfe* [1945] Ch 187). Now, however, with the utmost authority, it has been determined that this is so only in cases of rescission ab initio (ie, the first of the meanings given above) and not where one party has treated the other's repudiation or breach as discharging the contract: in this latter case, rights under the contract remain intact and damages can be recovered (see per Goff LJ in *Buckland* v *Farmar & Moody* [1979] 1 WLR 221, at pp 237–8, thoroughly endorsed per Lord Wilberforce in *Johnson* v *Agnew* [1980] AC 367, at pp 393–9, where the cases to the contrary were overruled).

If there has been an effective rescission ab initio, then the rule is restitutio in integrum. Each party must disgorge any gains (money or property) gotten, ill or otherwise, under contract (save perhaps for any deposit paid, see p 203). This means, on the other side of the coin, that each party may also recover any money or property parted with under the contract (see, eg, *Mayson* v *Clouet* [1924] AC 980). In short, 'there ought to be a giving back and a taking back on both sides' (per Bowen LJ in *Newbigging* v *Adam* (1886) 34 Ch D 582, at p 595).

Additionally the party rescinding, not therefore being in breach, is entitled to be indemnified against obligations already assumed under the contract, provided that they were necesarily created by the contract (see per Bowen LJ in *Newbigging* v *Adam*, ante, at p 594). This proviso appertains to the difficult distinction between indemnity and damages (see the baffling illustration in *Whittington* v *Seale-Hayne* (1900) 82 LT 49, which all the books give). The only all-purpose example of indemnity items on a sale of land appears to be the expenses incurred by a purchaser in investigating title or by a vendor in proving title (see Williams, *Sale of Land*, p 122, note (*p*)).

If the purchaser does the rescinding, then he will have an equitable lien on the land to encourage due disgorgement and indemnity by the vendor as above (see *Whitbread & Co* v *Watt* [1902] 1 Ch 835 and *Kitton* v *Hewett* [1904] WN 21). Otherwise, where the vendor rescinds he will hold his land free again from any contract and may, therefore, resell for his own benefit just as any other owner (see per Fry LJ in *Howe* v *Smith* (1884) 27 Ch D 89, at pp 104 and 105, and per Eve J in *Hall* v *Burnell* [1911] 2 Ch 551, at p 555; as to forfeiture also of any deposit, see p 203). Without a rescission the only logical view is that the vendor has no right to resell merely because the purchaser is in breach of contract (but cp per Bacon V-C in *Noble* v *Edwardes* (1877) 5 Ch D 378, at p 388).

Apart from rescission at the election of one party as a discharge or avoidance of the contract, there may be rescission arising out of the agreement of both the parties. First, the parties may simply contract anew not to complete their old contract—so long as neither had performed his part of the old contract, no consideration beyond mutual releases would be required, and the new contract would not be called on to comply with s 40 of the Law of Property Act 1925 (see *Morris* v *Baron & Co* [1918] AC 1; cf *Goss* v *Nugent* (1833) 5 B & Ad 58 as to a variation rather than a rescission). This need detain us no longer here, the result of the rescission depending entirely on what the new contract says.

Secondly, the parties may at the outset agree that in certain circumstances their contract may be rescinded with stipulated consequences. Examples of this which have already been met are rescission in the face of unwelcome requisitions (p 122), or in the absence of a licence to assign leaseholds (p 140), or on non-compliance with a notice to complete (p 184). This last, however, calls for closer examination in that the conditions providing for it may apply to any non-performance of the contract (ie, not just delay) and also cater fully for the consequences (see National Conditions, 20th ed, No 22; The Law Society's Conditions, 1980 ed, No 23).

In essence the consequences of non-compliance by a purchaser with an effective notice to complete are not only that any deposit may be forfeited (see p 203), but also that the vendor may resell at the purchaser's peril. At the purchaser's peril, for the case is one of 'heads I win, tails you lose' in the vendor's favour. If the resale is at a higher price, the vendor keeps the profit (this would be implied if not expressed, see per Eldon LC in *Ex parte Hunter* (1801) 6 Ves 94, at p 97). If the resale is at a lower price (and within one year), then the purchaser must make up the difference, after receiving credit for any deposit (which last would also be implied anyway: see *Shuttleworth* v *Clews* [1910] 1 Ch 176). In addition, the vendor may recover the expenses of the resale (and, under The Society's Conditions, of 'any attempted resale'). Presumably a vendor is under a duty not only to act in good faith but also to take reasonable care when reselling to obtain the true market value of the property (cf *Cuckmere Brick Co Ltd* v *Mutual Finance Ltd* [1971] Ch 949).

The vendor's rights arising from a resale at a lower price are expressed by the two standard sets of conditions referred to above. However, the suggestion has been made that the difference in price plus expenses could be recovered from the purchaser by implication from the express right of resale (Williams, *Sale of Land*, p 92, note (*q*), citing *Lamond* v *Davall* (1847) 9 QB 1030, at p 1032, *Ex parte Hunter* (1801) 6 Ves 94, at p 97, and *Oakenden* v *Henby* (1858) EB & E 485). Yet the point has since been mentioned but left open by the Court of Appeal, which indicated instead that the vendor would be able to recover a similar amount by way of damages (in *Harold Wood Brick Co Ltd* v *Ferris* [1935] 2 KB 198).

B DAMAGES

Instead of restitution, an election may be made, in effect, to enforce a broken contract through damages. If so, the measure or amount thereof is governed by the general rule that:

where a contract is broken, the injured person is, so far as money can do it, to be placed in the same position with respect to damages as if the contract had been performed

(per Blackburn J in *Lock* v *Furze* (1866) 15 LT 161, at p 162; also *Engell* v *Fitch* (1869) LR 4 QB 659, at p 666).

In pursuance of this general compensatory rule, the assessment is normally as at the date of the breach:

But this is not an absolute rule: if to follow it would give rise to injustice, the court has power to fix such other date as may be appropriate in the circumstances. In cases where a breach of a contract for sale has occurred, and the innocent party reasonably continues to try to have the contract completed, it would to me appear more logical and just rather than tie him to the date of the original breach, to assess damages as at the date when (otherwise than by his default) the contract is lost

(per Lord Wilberforce in *Johnson* v *Agnew* [1980] AC 367, at p 499, where the relevant date was held to be that on which the vendor's remedy of specific performance aborted).

This 'contract lost' approach was actually applied in *Domb* v *Isoz* [1980] Ch 548, CA: damages were assessed as at the date on which the plaintiff-purchasers elected to pursue the remedy of damages in lieu of the remedy of specific performance. The facts that that date came in mid-hearing of the appeal and that after the trial the purchasers had bought another house were not material here. Lord Wilberforce's approach was also considered, but to different effect, in *Techno Land Improvements Ltd* v *British Leyland (UK) Ltd* (1979) 252 EG 805: this case concerned the breach in 1974 of a contract to take a long-term lease (35 years) at an annual rent of £61,000: originally, the plaintiff sought specific performance but in 1976 found short-term licensees and elected to seek damages only: then in 1977 the plaintiff found long-term tenants (25 years) at an annual rent totalling £52,000. The plaintiff claimed that the contract was 'lost' in 1976 when licences were granted so that damages should be assessed as in that year. However it was held that the plaintiff had been under a continuing duty to take reasonable steps to mitigate his loss and had done so by re-letting in 1977; accordingly the defendant was entitled to have this taken into account so that damages should be assessed as in 1977. The judge (Goulding J) added (ibid, p 809) that problems of financial instability and in particular of inflation might make it necessary in the future to reconsider and possibly qualify the principles on which he had relied in assessing compensation for loss. See further as to mitigation and inflation in relation to deferred structural repairs to tortiously damaged premises, *Dodd Properties (Kent) Ltd* v *Canterbury CC* [1980] 1 WLR 433, CA; also *Jarvis* v *T Richards & Co* (1980) 124 SJ 793 and *Zakrzewski* v *Chas J Odhams & Sons* (1980) 260 EG 1125 (where the state of the market at the date of breach had not permitted the purchase of a substitute property in mitigation of damage).

The general rule, however, is always subject to qualification by the rules as to remoteness of damage: in short, liability may not be for all the loss caused by the breach but only for the loss reasonably foreseeable, either objectively or subjectively, at the date of the contract (*Hadley* v *Baxendale* (1854) 9 Exch 341, as illuminated by *Victoria Laundry (Windsor) Ltd* v *Newman Industries Ltd* [1949] 2 KB 528). These propositions, capable of Parkinsonian expansion, happily are of general application and by no means peculiar to contracts for the sale of land. That they do apply also to these contracts was illustrated in a case where a purchaser was held unable to recover the profit obtainable by converting the property since, in the absence of special circumstances, no knowledge will be imputed to a vendor that the purchaser intends to use the property in any particular manner—ie, the loss was not reasonably foreseeable, objectively or subjectively (*Diamond* v *Campbell-Jones* [1961] Ch 22). This last case should be contrasted with *Cottrill* v *Steyning & Littlehampton BS* [1966] 1 WLR 753, where the vendor was shown to have known that the disappointed purchaser had intended to develop the land for profit, so that damages were assessed on this basis. Also with *Wadsworth* v *Lydall* [1981] 1 WLR 598; there, in effect, a vendor recovered interest and costs incurred in respect of a second mortgage entered into in consequence of the purchaser's default in paying the full balance of the price and so as to enable completion of the purchase of a new property. As to mental distress being reasonably foreseeable following breach of a contract for the sale of land, see *Buckley* v *Lane Herdman & Co* [1977] CLY 3143 and a note at [1978] Conv 325–6.

1 Vendor

In ordinary objective circumstances, therefore, what the parties may recover in the way of damages is fairly obvious, being basically the difference between the contract and market prices of the land. To put it more precisely, a vendor is entitled to the excess (if any) of the contract price over the value of the land left in his hands when regarded as a security for the money he would have received on specific performance of the contract, ie, the expenses of realisation (resale) have to be taken into account (see Parke B in *Laird* v *Pim* (1841) 7 M & W 474, at p 478, and *Noble* v *Edwardes* (1877) 5 Ch D 378, at p 385); the better view seems to be that the expenses of the original sale cannot be recovered by the vendor (see Williams, *Sale of Land*, p 126, note (1)), and any deposit must also be brought into account (see p 203).

The damages recoverable by a vendor will equal the full purchase price, however, where the vendor has executed a conveyance and let the purchaser into possession (*Laird* v *Pim*, ante; also, of course, if for some reason the net market value of the land is nil). This being so, there seems no reason in principle why a vendor who really wants the contract price, wants to be rid of the land and wants not to be bothered with the market values could not simply disregard any breach or repudiation by the purchaser and quickly complete on his own, thereafter suing for the price (relying on the implications of *White & Carter (Councils) Ltd* v *McGregor* [1962] AC 413, HL; cp *Hounslow London BC* v *Twickenham Garden Developments Ltd* [1971] Ch 233, also the terms of the orders made by Vaisey J in *Palmer* v *Lark* [1945] Ch 182, and by Stamp J in *Maskell* v *Ivory* [1970] 1 Ch 502). If he did this, he would not have parted too rashly with his security, for he would always enjoy an equitable lien as an unpaid vendor (see, eg, *Mackreth* v *Symmons* (1808) 15 Ves 329).

2 Purchaser

Conversely, a purchaser prima facie may recover from a vendor in breach the difference (if any) between the contract price and the higher market value of the land at the date of the breach (see *Diamond* v *Campbell-Jones* [1961] Ch 22; also *Engell* v *Fitch* (1869) LR 4 QB 659, where the purchaser's sub-sale at a higher price evidenced the land's value; cp *Ford* v *White & Co* [1964] 1 WLR 885, where a purchaser had wrongly thought he was buying a plot free from building restrictions but since the contract price was in fact equivalent to the market value subject to restrictions, the measure of damages was nil). In *Strutt* v *Whitnell* [1975] 1 WLR 870 a house was conveyed on sale to a property developer and there was a breach of the contract in that vacant possession could not be given; the measure of damages, being the difference in value of the house with and without vacant possession, had been assessed at £1,900. However, the vendor contended that he had immediately offered to buy back the house at the contract price so that the purchaser's damages, had he accepted, would have been nil. The Court of Appeal held that a purchaser was not obliged to mitigate his damages by reconveying the property to the vendor in such a case; he was entitled to retain the property and pursue his remedy at law by suing for damages for the breach.

A purchaser who does recover such damages—ie, where there is a difference— cannot also claim any conveyancing costs incurred in the abortive transaction for these would have been incurred anyway (see *Day* v *Singleton* [1899] 2 Ch 320, where the headnote is inaccurate; also per Sargant J in *Re Daniel, Daniel* v *Vassall* [1917] 2 Ch 405, at p 412). Consistent with this it is arguable that any costs not yet incurred but which would have had to be incurred had the contract been completed (eg, stamp duty) ought to be deducted from the damages. Indeed the Court of Appeal has conceded that this might be an appropriate deduction in some cases although on the facts disallowing such a deduction (*Ridley* v *De Geerts* [1945] 2 All ER 654).

Against all this, however, a purchaser who cannot recover such damages, ie, because no difference is shown between the contract price and market value, can claim instead his conveyancing costs fruitlessly incurred (*Wallington* v *Townsend* [1939] Ch 588). He will also, of course, in any case recover any deposit paid with interest (see p 203). In addition, in *Lloyd* v *Stanbury* [1971] 1 WLR 535, Brightman J held that the damages which such a disappointed purchaser was entitled to recover included expenditure incurred prior to the contract representing not only legal costs of approving and executing the contract, but also the costs of performing an act required to be done under the contract notwithstanding that the act was performed in anticipation of the execution of the contract. The learned judge added that, on general principles, the purchaser would be entitled to damages for any loss which ought to be regarded as within the contemplation of the parties, but subject to an important limitation: a purchaser allowed into possession before completion who elected to repudiate the contract could *not* recover money spent on improvements to the property. This decision has since been approved by the Court of Appeal in *Anglia Television Ltd* v *Reed* [1972] 1 QB 60 (which did not itself relate to a sale of land).

3 Defective title

At this point a peculiarity in the position of a purchaser of land is encountered. Hitherto the assumption has been that the general rule applies, enabling him to recover as damages any difference between the contract price and higher market value of the property, this representing his loss of bargain. This assumption is falsified to the extent that there may be applied 'an anomalous rule based upon and justified by difficulties in showing a good title to real property in this country' (per Sargant J in *Re Daniel, Daniel* v *Vassall* [1917] 2 Ch 405, at p 409). As was said in the leading case:

> It is recognised on all hands that the purchaser . . . is not to be held entitled to recover any loss on the bargain he may have made, if in effect it should turn out that the vendor is incapable of completing his contract in consequence of his defective title

(per Lord Hatherley in *Bain* v *Fothergill* (1874) LR 7 HL 158, at p 210; the House of Lords approved the rule as laid down in *Flureau* v *Thornhill* (1776) 2 Wm Bl 1078).

Consequently, if the vendor is in breach of his duty to show a good title, prima facie the purchaser may only recover nominal damages for his loss of bargain plus, however, the deposit with interest and his conveyancing costs incurred (*JW Cafés Ltd* v *Brownlow Trust Ltd* [1950] 1 All ER 894). This is affected neither by the vendor's knowledge of his defective title nor by his representations as to title, *except* that these may themselves give rise to an action for substantial damages in tort, ie, deceit or perhaps negligent misstatement or even under the Misrepresentation Act 1967 (see *Watts* v *Spence* [1976] Ch 165).

The vendor will not, however, be able to escape via this anomaly from paying substantial damages for loss of bargain where his breach is due not merely to his defective title but also to his own fault. In other words, the vendor must have done everything within his power to enable completion of the contract (see *Day* v *Singleton* [1899] 2 Ch 320 and *Re Daniel, Daniel* v *Vassall*, ante, failure respectively to obtain a licence to assign and to redeem a mortgage). Further, the onus is on the the vendor to prove his inability to carry out his contractual obligations, and this involves showing positively that he had used his best endeavours so to do (*Malhotra* v *Choudhury* [1980] Ch 52, CA, where evidence was lacking that an unenthusiastic vendor had ever attempted to induce his wife's concurrence in the sale, requisite because of a joint tenancy). Again, Megarry J has held that the statutory charge in favour of a spouse arising under the Matrimonial Homes Act 1967, being imposed generally and in no way dependent on the vicissitudes of a particular title to property, did not fall within the spirit and intendment of the rule in *Bain* v *Fothergill* (*Wroth* v *Tyler* [1974] Ch 30). Accordingly, a husband, unable to perform his contract to sell a house with vacant possession because his wife, having statutory rights of occupation, would not concur, was held unable to rely on the rule to limit the measure of damages (ibid). Thus one way or another uncooperative spouses seem especially expensive (see also *Watts* v *Spence,* ante). Further reference for the cons and pros of this anomalous rule in *Bain* v *Fothergill* may be made to articles by Angela Sydenham and CT Emery at (1977) 41 Conv (NS) 341–48, and [1978] Conv 338–45, respectively.

C SPECIFIC PERFORMANCE

The equitable relief of specific performance will be decreed in those cases only where damages at common law would not afford an adequate remedy (see, eg, *Flint* v *Brandon* (1803) 8 Ves 159, also *South African Territories* v *Wallington* [1898] AC 309 and, indeed, *Beswick* v *Beswick* [1968] AC 58). Since the subject-matter of every contract for the sale of land—be it terrace-house or flat—is unique in the eyes of equity, specific performance of such contracts will be available almost as of right (see per Grant MR in *Hall* v *Warren* (1804) 9 Ves 605, at p 608; also per Farwell J in *Hexter* v *Pearce* [1900] 1 Ch 341, at p 346, and in *Rudd* v *Lascelles* [1900] 1 Ch 815, at p 817). What is more, directed by a desire for mutuality, equity will equally allow a vendor to seek specific performance even though damages would be adequate consolation to him for the loss of the purchase price—so he can 'thrust the property down the purchaser's throat' (per Lindley LJ in *Hope* v *Walter* [1900] 1 Ch 257, at p 258). True the decree, as always in equity, depends on the discretion of the court, but this is predictable, not arbitrary, being exercised on settled principles (see eg, *Holliday* v *Lockwood* [1917] 2 Ch 47, at pp 56 and 57). Thus it can be said that 'in unexceptional cases this remedy will be accorded as a matter of course' (Williams, *Sale of Land*, p 133; for a modern example of a decree against a vendor flagrantly in breach of contract, see *Jones* v *Lipman* [1962] 1 WLR 832). The exceptional cases, in which specific performance may not be ordered, will involve some established objection such as hardship (see *Wroth* v *Tyler* [1974] Ch 30) or prejudice to third party rights (as in *Warmington* v *Miller* [1973] QB 877, CA) or illegality (cp *Ailion* v *Spiekermann* [1976] Ch 158) or even want of mutuality (but see *Price* v *Strange* [1978] Ch 337, CA, as to this merely being a matter to be taken into account as at the hearing).

The only point appearing to require particular mention here in connection with the discretionary nature of specific performance is the effect of delay. The normal six-year period of the Limitation Act 1980 (s 5) expressly applies neither to actions for specific performance (s 36 (1)) nor to the exercise of equity's discretion to refuse relief (s 36 (2)). Consequently, the equitable doctrine of laches—delay defeats equities—flowers forth once again (see, eg, per Cranworth LC in *Eads* v *Williams* (1854) 4 De GM & G 674, at pp 691–2; also *MEPC Ltd* v *Christian-Edwards* [1981] AC 205, HL, wherein the doctrine was thought undoubtedly applicable to a 66-year old contract for the sale of land). Therefore if there is delay in seeking a decree of specific performance, no decree may be obtainable; this has usually been taken to mean that an action must be commenced within one year (*Huxham* v *Llewellyn* (1873) 21 WR 570). However, the position appears to have changed; in *Lazard Brothers & Co Ltd* v *Fairfield Properties Co (Mayfair) Ltd* (1977) 121 SJ 793 an order for specific performance was made despite a period of nearly two years before issue of a writ, and Megarry V-C was reported as saying:

If specific performance was to be regarded as a prize, to be awarded by equity to the zealous and denied to the indolent, then the plaintiffs should fail. But whatever might have been the position over a century ago that was the wrong approach today. If between the plaintiff and defendant it was just that the plaintiff should obtain the remedy, the court ought not to withhold it merely because the plaintiff had been guilty of delay. There was not ground here on which delay could properly be said to be a bar to a degree of specific performance.

See also the same learned judge in *Wroth* v *Tyler* [1974] Ch 30, at p 53. An illustration of this approach, presumably, would occur where the purchaser, having an equitable right to do so, has taken possession under the contract:

All that needs to be done is for the legal title to be perfected. In such a case, laches or delay is not a bar

(per Denning LJ in *Williams* v *Greatrex* [1957] 1 WLR 31, at p 36; the purchaser there was held entitled to specific performance notwithstanding a ten-years' delay). Here it used to be thought that after twelve years' delay the purchaser's title would, in effect, become perfect because the vendor's title would be barred under the Limitation Act (now 1980, Sched 1, para 1) and authority supporting this thought could be seen in *Bridges* v *Mees* [1957] Ch 475. However, the Court of Appeal has now thought otherwise: without citation of any such relevant authority it was held that a would-be-purchaser under an *un*rescinded contract could not be in adverse possession and so should not acquire title by adverse possession: *Hyde* v *Pearce* [1982] 1 WLR 560.

Attention may also be drawn to the provision of s 2 of the Chancery Amendment Act 1858 (Lord Cairns' Act) that:

In all cases in which the Court of Chancery has jurisdiction to entertain an application . . . for the specific performance of any covenant, contract or agreement, it shall be lawful for the same court, if it shall think fit, to award damages to the party injured, either in addition to or in substitution for such . . . specific performance, and such damages may be assessed in such manner as the court shall direct.

In *Price* v *Strange* [1978] Ch 337, at p 369, Buckley LJ stated:

Two points are clear, First, the court is invested with the discretion whenever it has jurisidction to entertain a claim for specific performance, but not otherwise. Secondly, the discretion is not confined to cases in which damages could be recovered at law.

As to the first point, he proceeded to suggest that the section's discretion must always be available with sales of land since claims for specific performance would always be entertained even if sometimes refused (loc cit). Further he indicated that damages could be awarded under the section even though there might actually be some matter, eg, want of mutuality, which would have caused the court to exercise its discretion against specific performance (loc cit). An example of this second point could be found with a contract not evidenced by writing but supported by a sufficient act of part-performance (see per Goff LJ, ibid, p 358).

Lastly, note that it has now been made clear that, where there is non-compliance with a decree of specific performance, damages can be recovered in effect for breach of contract, either at common law or under Lord Cairns' Act (*Johnson* v *Agnew* [1980] AC 367, HL).

D VENDOR AND PURCHASER SUMMONS

In conclusion of this chapter, mention may merely be made that many minor matters impeding the parties are open to solution by way of a vendor and purchaser summons (a procedure introduced by s 9 of the Vendor and Purchaser Act 1874, and extended by s 49 (1) and (3) of the Law of Property Act 1925; see generally *Emmet on Title,* 18th ed, pp 266–7, and also, as to what may be determined on such a summons, *Wilson* v *Thomas* [1958] 1 WLR 422, applied in *Horton* v *Kurzke* [1971] 1 WLR 769). This summary procedure had been authoritatively described as 'a simple and inexpensive method of settling disputes between vendor and purchaser' (*Emmet on Title*, 14th ed, vol 1, p 121). Against this, however, other authority had said of the summons that 'It is supposed to be expeditious and cheap: it is neither' (see an editorial note at (1961) 25 Conv (NS) 90). The present writer prefers the latter view, and in particular feels that the truth shines forth from a statement following shortly after the expression of that view, namely:

> Most minor points of dispute are resolved by one side giving way because he sees no alternative; he cannot wait weeks or months before he can move into the house he has bought, or, as the case may be, before he gets his money which he needs to complete the purchase of another house

(loc cit).

Reference may also be made to *MEPC Ltd* v *Christian-Edwards* [1981] AC 205— contract for sale in April 1973, title queried in June 1973, vendor and purchaser summons in August 1975, first instance decision in May 1977, reversed on appeal in May 1978 and finally affirmed by the House of Lords in November 1979. Simple and inexpensive? And with the thought that there are no sharp sure remedies on a sale of land but only some that may prove worse than the disease, the writer moves on.

BOOK TWO

CONTENTS OF A CONVEYANCE

XIV INTRODUCTORY

CONVEYANCING is much like marriage; each transaction is bipartite. First comes the contract for sale, or, euphemistically, engagement, preceded only by certain preliminary enquiries and more or less close local searches. Then, after an investigation of title or publishing of banns, the transaction is solemnly completed.

The purpose of this second book is to examine the form and contents of the instrument by which the parties to a conveyance of land both formally express and achieve their intentions. The common failure to appreciate the nature of the binding obligations entered into on the solemnisation of holy matrimony is, today, all too frequently bewailed in the divorce courts and elsewhere. Equally a failure always to grasp the full significance of completing a conveyance is felt to be not uncommon. True the relationship of these parties, causing less heat, also causes less litigation. Nonetheless, there may still be some justification for offering to their potential advisers a closer consideration of the whys and wherefores of the traditional parts of a purchase deed. The more so since tradition may lead to allegiance without thought; after all no self-respecting draftsman should use any form of words, no matter how sanctified by long usage, without understanding the precise legal reason and purport.

Admittedly, this is a view not necessarily shared by all. Thus that now notorious lay conveyancer, Mr SG Carter, once told the police, so it was alleged, that,'You don't need all that legal guff the solicitors put in' *(Director of Public Prosecutions* v *Carter* (1967) 111 SJ 785, at p 786; see also *Carter* v *Butcher* [1966] 1 QB 526). What is more, this approach has been adopted by those who should, indeed did, know better: some surely enlightened solicitors produced a collection of precedents deliberately discarding traditional forms and phraseology (Parker, *Modern Convey-ancing Precedents*). Such sacrilege can only be condemned when perpetrated by the ignorant: it remains essential to appreciate—as Mr Parker doubtless did—what, if anything, will be lost and gained in the process of modernisation.

Additionally, the now familiar register office marriage has its counterpart in conveyancing. Accordingly the instrument of transfer of land under the Land Registration Acts and Rules throughout shares in the present consideration by way of comparison and explanation. This is felt to gain in significance since registration of title is of increasing importance; it has already embraced much of and is now the inevitable fate of the whole of England (which indeed was the real reason why the 1925 property legislation endeavoured to simplify conveyancing: see Cmnd 424 (1919), Appx, at p 34). True, in registered conveyancing, the draftsman has been warned to 'try to disregard the many familiar yet unnecessary phrases and clauses which he is accustomed to use in unregistered conveyancing because otherwise the resultant instrument may turn out to be what the Rules call "improper in form or substance"' (Ruoff, *Land Registration Forms,* 2nd ed, p 2). Despite this, too complete a disregard for the traditional may have its dangers even in registered conveyancing.

A   WHAT IS A 'CONVEYANCE'?

1   Ordinary meaning

First, notice that here the ordinary meaning of the word 'conveyance' as used by lawyers is being considered; the physical transport or haulage sense of everyday speech is irrelevant (cf *Neal* v *Gribble* [1978] RTR 409 as to the offence of taking a conveyance without consent within s 12 of the Theft Act 1968 being directed towards artefacts rather than animals). Second, notice that the word is merely an alternative, more modern substitute for the older 'assurance', both words enjoying the same ordinary meaning (see Earl Jowitt, *Dictionary of English Law*, vol 1, at pp 171, 485–6).

After this, three judicial definitions may be offered:

> The term "conveyance" is well-known to conveyancers as meaning an instrument which passes a freehold interest in property

(per Lopes LJ in *Rodger* v *Harrison* [1893] 1 QB 161, at p 169; see also per Kay LJ at p 172). The restriction to freehold interests alone was too narrow; any interest in property will suffice (see, eg, *Chesterfield Brewery Co* v *IRC* [1899] 2 QB 7, also *Grey* v *IRC* [1960] AC 1).

> An "assurance" is in reality something which operates as a transfer of property

(per Kay LJ in *Re Ray* [1896] 1 Ch 468, at p 476).

> The word "conveyance" means what it says. I find in Wharton's Law Lexicon that he defines it as "an instrument that transfers property from one person to another." That is all

(per Lord Halsbury in *Eastbourne Corporation* v *A-G* [1904] AC 155, at p 156).

From these quotations it emerges that a 'conveyance' cannot be oral (see also *Rye* v *Rye* [1962] AC 496, HL), ie, that it should *not* be taken in the loose sense of the transaction itself, but to connote a document. Nor, it appears, is a 'conveyance' strictly an instrument by which an interest in property is created as opposed to merely transferred (see *Re Sanders* [1896] 1 Ch 480, also *Re Stirrup* [1961] 1 WLR 449).

Therefore, the word 'conveyance' in its ordinary meaning may be defined as follows: namely, an instrument which operates to pass an interest in property from one person to another.

2   Statutory definition

The ordinary meaning of 'conveyance' is often extended or modified by definition for particular statutory purposes. However, only the definition in the Law of Property Act 1925 (s 205 (1) (ii)), will be commented on here, both as being the most relevant to a number of topics discussed later in this book and since the same principles of construction do apply in other cases. In fact, the other statutes of the 1925 property legislation contain substantially similar definitions (see s 20 (1) of the Land Charges Act 1972; s 55 (1) (iii) of the Administration of Estates Act 1925; s 117 (1) (v) of the Settled Land Act 1925) with the exception of the Trustee Act 1925, where the definition differs radically (s 68 (3)), and the Land Registration Act 1925, which contains no general definition (but see s 123 (3), ante, p 143). For the definition of 'conveyance on sale' in the Stamp Act 1891 see *Emmet on Title*, 18th ed, p 1105 et seq.

Section 205 of the Law of Property Act 1925 provides (writer's italics) that:
(1) In this Act *unless the context otherwise requires,* the following expressions
have the meanings hereby assigned to them respectively, that is to say:—

*　　*　　*　　*　　*

(ii) "Conveyance" *includes* a mortgage, charge, lease, assent, vesting
declaration, vesting instrument, disclaimer, release and *every other
assurance of property or of an interest therein by an instrument,* except a
will; "convey" has a corresponding meaning.

Where the word *'includes'* appears in a definition clause, it is in construction to be
replaced by the phrase 'in addition to its ordinary meaning means' (see per Lord
Esher MR in *Rodger* v *Harrison* [1893] 1 QB 161, at p 167; per Lord Watson in
Dilworth v *Commissioner of Stamps* [1899] AC 99, at p 195; and per Somervell and
Denning LJJ in *Deeble* v *Robinson* [1954] 1 QB 77, at pp 81-2 and 82-3 respectively).
Therefore, prima facie, s 205 enlarges the ordinary meaning of 'conveyance' (see per
Lord MacDermott in *Rye* v *Rye* [1962] AC 496, at p 507) and the only question is:
how far?

In this connection it will have been noticed that the concluding 'omnibus'
description employs a word—*'assurance'*—synonymous with the word being
defined. Also the House of Lords has decided that the words *'by any instrument'*
relate to the whole of the clause thus connoting documents and excluding
transactions (*Rye* v *Rye* [1962] AC 496; cf *Re Eicholz* [1959] Ch 708, at p 728).
Accordingly, any alteration of the ordinary meaning of 'conveyance' is only to be
found either where the context of the Act otherwise requires or else amongst the
instruments specified. Most of these latter, in fact, are within the ordinary meaning
as defined above (even an assent since 1925: see s 36 (2) of the Administration of
Estates Act 1925 and cp *Kemp* v *IRC* [1905] 1 KB 581), and all of them would be if
the ordinary meaning extends beyond the passing to the creation of interests in
property. Examples of the context otherwise requiring are ss 76 (5) and 77 (3) of the
Law of Property Act 1925 excluding leases at a rent, and s 72, which permits a
conveyance to oneself despite there being no passing of an interest in property (eg,
assents by personal representatives to themselves beneficially or as trustees: see *Re
King's Will Trusts* [1964] Ch 542; see also s 68 of the Settled Land Act 1925;
however, a lease to oneself or selves, a contractual relationship, is not permitted:
Rye v *Rye* [1962] AC 496).

3　Passing an equitable interest

An instrument which both formally purports to and does pass only an equitable
interest in land may be a 'conveyance' (see p 222). But an instrument which
purports, but is ineffective, to pass a legal estate in land and which operates only in
equity (eg under *Walsh* v *Lonsdale* (1882) 21 Ch D 9; see *Zimbler* v *Abrahams* [1903]
1 KB 577; or under *Re Rose* [1952] Ch 499) is clearly *not* 'a conveyance'. This is so
whether one is considering the ordinary meaning (for authority see per Lord Esher
MR and Kay LJ in *Rodger* v *Harrison* [1893] 1 QB 161, at pp 167 and 170
respectively; also *IRC* v *Angus* (1889) 23 QBD 579) or the definition in the Law of
Property Act 1925 (see per Maughan J in *Borman* v *Griffith* [1930] 1 Ch 493, at pp
497-8). Indeed this appears to be a proposition of universal application (see *Rose
Hall Ltd* v *Reeves* [1975] AC 411, at pp 419-20, where the Privy Council applied it for
Jamaica).

4   Land Registry transfers

Is a Land Registry transfer of registered land a 'conveyance'? It is certainly an instrument, but is it an instrument which operates to pass an interest in the land from one person to another? Only (*a*) an equitable interest or (*b*) the legal estate in the land are capable of being passed (see s 1 of the Law of Property Act 1925) and only these two need to be considered.

(*a*) Normally the beneficial equitable interest in the land will be passed to the tranferee independently of the execution of the transfer by virtue of a prior specifically enforceable contract for sale plus payment (see *Lysaght* v *Edwards* (1876) 2 Ch D 499; *Rayner* v *Preston* (1881) 18 Ch D 1; *Bridges* v *Mees* [1957] Ch 475; and *Re Birmingham* [1959] Ch 523; but cf per Lord Jenkins in *Oughtred* v *IRC* [1960] AC 206, at pp 238-41). But even if the transfer does operate to pass an equitable interest, since it purports to pass a legal estate, it will not be a 'conveyance' unless it is effective to pass a legal estate (see the preceding section of this chapter).

(*b*) The legal estate in registered land clearly passes only on registration, that is, when the transferee's name is entered in place of the transferor's name on the proprietorship register: ss 19 (1) and 22 (1) of the Land Registration Act 1925 (see also *Smith* v *Express Dairy* [1954] JPL 45 and *Lever Finance Ltd* v *Needleman's Trustee and Kreutzer* [1956] Ch 375; cf *R* v *Edwards* [1947] KB 392). More accurately, the legal estate is passed retrospectively as on the day on which the application for registration was deemed delivered to HM Land Registry: see rr 83 and 85 of the Land Registration Rules 1925 as substituted in 1978. But *what* operates to pass it is perhaps less clear.

There appear to be two choices; either the legal estate is passed by the Land Registry transfer when completed by the mere formality of registration or else it is passed simply by the registration itself. The former choice was preferred by the last editor of vol 3 of *Key & Elphinstone's Precedents in Conveyancing* (15th ed, at p 139), who expressly differed from the distinguished author of that volume, the late Professor Harold Potter, and stated that a Land Registry transfer is a conveyance of a legal estate since it 'is an instrument by which a legal estate is passed notwithstanding that a further step, viz, registration, is necessary before it attains its intended effect.' However, the present writer plumps firmly for the other choice in view of the specific provisions of the Land Registration Act 1925 as to the effect of registration.

In particular s 69 (1) provides that a proprietor of land whenever registered 'shall be deemed to have vested in him *without any conveyance,* where the registered land is freehold, the legal estate in fee simple in possession . . .' See also, however, ss 20 (1) and 23 (1), which prescribe the effect of registration of a disposition of, respectively, a freehold and a leasehold estate (bear in mind that the 'disposition' referred to in these sections is the transaction: ss 18 (5) and 21 (5)). Significant, too, is the complete absence of any such provision as that considered in *Knight Sugar Co* v *Alberta Railway Co* [1938] 1 All ER 266; namely s 51 of the Land Titles Act 1906 of Alberta which provided that 'so soon as registered, every instrument shall become operative according to the tenor and intent thereof, and shall thereupon create, transfer, surrender, charge or discharge, as the case may be, the land or estate or interest therein mentioned in the instrument.' This provision, which would lend unqualified authority to the last *Key & Elphinstone* choice, alone caused the Privy Council to hold a transfer of registered land in Alberta 'to differ in no relevant respect from an ordinary conveyance of unregistered land' (at p 270). But we have no such provision! Additional support and comfort for the writer's choice may be derived from the paragraph headed 'Statutory Magic' in Ruoff and Roper,

Registered Conveyancing, 4th ed, at p 64, and from the judgments in *Morelle* v *Wakeling* [1955] 2 QB 379, CA (particularly at p 412), and *A-G* v *Parsons* [1956] AC 421, HL (particularly per Earl Jowitt at p 441). See also an article by RC Connell in (1947) 11 Conv (NS) 188 and 232, and one by S Robinson in (1971) 35 Conv (NS) 21 (especially at p 42).

In other words, the writer's view is that a Land Registry transfer, unlike a conveyance, operates not in rem but only in personam to create rights enforceable inter partes and to authorise an entry on the register. It is not within the ordinary meaning of 'conveyance' and it is not specified in s 205 (1) (ii) of the Law of Property Act 1925 (cf per Lord Morton in *A-G* v *Parsons* [1956] AC 421, at p 445). This, indeed, appears to have been recognised by the draftsman of the Land Registration Act 1925, since certain provisions of the Law of Property Act 1925 relating solely to conveyances have been expressly incorporated into the registered system (see ss 19 (3), 22 (3) and 38 (1)). However, since a Land Registry transfer is capable of being everything that an unregistered conveyance is, *except* actually being a conveyance, it stands in practice in the same central position in the transaction and the two instruments should be considered together.

Finally, however, observe three points: First, all ascertainable published opinions hitherto have agreed that a Land Registry transfer *is* within s 205 (1) (ii) of the Law of Property Act 1925 (see, eg, Brickdale and Stewart-Wallace, *Land Registration Act 1925* (4th ed), at p 100; also Ruoff and Roper, *Registered Conveyancing,* 4th ed, at p 565). Unfortunately only in two places are any reasons at all given in support; the one in *Key & Ephinstone* has been dealt with above, and the other, in Potter, *Registered Land Conveyancing*, at p 78, was that 'an equitable interest is conferred' and it has since been demolished by *Borman* v *Griffith* [1930] 1 Ch 493 (see above). Second, the registration which divests the transferor and vests the legal estate in the transferee does so by operation of law and would not appear itself to be within the ordinary meaning of 'conveyance' (see *Re Calcott & Elvin* [1898] 2 Ch 460, but cf s 52 (2) (g) of the Law of Property Act 1925). And third, a conveyance on sale of *un*registered land in an area of compulsory registration does operate to pass the legal estate although subject to provision for it to re-pass: s 123 of the Land Registration Act 1925 (see p 142).

B   IS A DEED NECESSARY?

First, s 51 (1) of the Law of Property Act 1925 renders an instrument of grant entirely sufficient to convey interests in land by finally abolishing the older forms of conveyancing (ie, by livery or livery and seisin, by feoffment, or by bargain and sale). Then s 52 (1) of the same Act goes on to make a deed necessary by providing that:

> All conveyances of land or of any interest therein are void for the purpose of conveying or creating a legal estate unless made by deed.

However, subs (2) of this latter section sets out seven exceptions from the section, of which two only will be briefly noticed here, namely 'assents by a personal representive' and leases 'not required by law to be made in writing'. The former must nonetheless be 'in writing, signed by the personal representative' and must also 'name the person in whose favour it is given' in order to be 'effectual to pass a legal estate' (s 36 (4) of the Administration of Estates Act 1925). The latter exception refers to leases within s 54 (2) of the same Act which may be created by parol provided they (i) take effect in possession (not, eg, in nineteen days' time: see *Foster* v *Reeves* [1892] 2 QB 255, at p 257), and (ii) do so for a term not exceeding three years (eg, a periodic tenancy: *Re Knight* (1882) 21 Ch D 442; cp *Kushner* v *Law Society* [1952] 1 KB 264), and (iii) do so at the best rent which can be reasonably obtained without taking a fine (ie, premium; see *Hughes* v *Waite* [1957] 1 WLR 713, where advance payment of rent as a lump sum was held to be a fine). However, the legal assignment of such a lease, even though oral, must still be by deed (*Botting* v *Martin* (1808) 1 Camp 317). Further the combination of ss 52 (2) and 54 (2) does *not* make a valid oral lease into a 'conveyance': an instrument is still required (*Rye* v *Rye* [1962] AC 496).

Lastly, it should be mentioned that an instrument void as a conveyance of a legal estate because not a deed may still operate in equity as an agreement for a conveyance and for many purposes be as good as a conveyance under the doctrine of *Walsh* v *Lonsdale* (1882) 21 Ch D 9 (see *Zimbler* v *Abrahams* [1903] 1 KB 577). This will particularly be so if an 'estate contract' has been registered (s 2 (4), Class C (iv), of the Land Charges Act 1972, and see s 49 (1) (*c*) of the Land Registration Act 1925), or if possession has been taken of registered land so as to constitute an overriding interest (s 70 (1) (*g*) of the latter Act).

What form a Land Registry transfer has to take and whether it is a deed are both discussed later.

C   WHAT IS A DEED?

The formalities necessary to constitute a deed at common law, authoritatively stated in the sixteenth century, still apply. In *Goddard's Case* (1584) 2 Co Rep 4*b*, at 5*a*, it was said:

> for there are but three things of the essence and substance of a deed, that is to say, writing in paper or parchment, sealing and delivery.

To these s 73 of the Law of Property Act 1925 has now added:

> Where an individual executes a deed, he shall either sign or place his mark upon the same and sealing alone shall not be deemed sufficient.

(For corporations see s 74 of the same Act.)

The 'writing' referred to in *Goddard's Case*, ante, provided it is legible (ie, admits 'of a character being given to the handwriting'), may apparently be made in any way at all (*Geary* v *Physic* (1826) 4 LJ (OS) KB 147 (pencil); *R* v *Middlesex Registers* (1845) 7 QB 156 (lithograph); *Foster* v *Mentor Life Assurance Co* (1854) 23 LJQB 145 (print)). Against this, however, it seems that only 'paper or parchment' will suffice:

> For if a writing be made upon a piece of wood, or upon a piece of linen, or on the bark of a tree, or on a stone, or the like, etc, and the same be sealed and delivered, yet it is no deed, for a deed must be written either in parchment, or paper, as before is said, for the writing upon these is least subject to alteration and corruption

(Co Litt 35*b*; 229*a*).

The paper or parchment need only be signed, sealed and delivered by one of the parties to it in order for it to be a deed (see per Hawkins J in *IRC* v *Angus* (1889) 23 QBD 579, at pp 581 and 582). These three formal requirements of execution are considered in a later chapter (p 318), but note here that to them *Norton on Deeds* (2nd ed 1928, at p 3) would add, clearly correctly, the requirement of substance that the writing must be one:

> whereby an interest, right or property passes, or an obligation binding on some person is created, or which is in affirmance of some act whereby an interest, right, or property has passed.

This requirement would exclude such documents as degree or share certificates (see per Clauson J in *South London Greyhound Racecourses Ltd* v v *Wake* [1931] 1 Ch 496, at p 503) and whether or not it is satisfied is primarily a question of the parties' intention. Thus Wilberforce J has said (in *Re Stirrup* [1961] 1 WLR 449, at p 454) that:

> provided the sole formal requirement of being under seal is complied with, any document, since 1925, at any rate, is effective to pass a legal estate, provided the intention so to pass it can be ascertained.

Of course, a seal is not the *sole* formal requirement and the 'any document' is too wide (eg, a legal estate would not be passed to an infant or, in registered land, by any document), but the idea emerges.

Since a Land Registry transfer will be a properly executed writing (see the prescribed forms in the Schedule to the Land Registration Rules 1925) and will also create an obligation binding on some person (ie, contractually in personam), it will be a deed even though it may not be a conveyance. In fact, a Land Registry transfer has been judicially stated to be clearly a deed (by Vaisey J in *Chelsea and Walham Green Building Society* v *Armstrong* [1951] Ch 853, at p 857).

XV CONVEYANCE AND TRANSFER

A FORM

FINGS ain't what they used to be:

> . . . until quite recently the supreme piece of effort involved in conveyancing was the preparation of the deed itself. Years ago when people prided themselves on their use of legal English and perhaps were paid by the folio as well, conveyances were lengthy documents constructed with the greatest care. Now it may be that they are easier to prepare and their drafting is less important, but even so . . .

(per Widgery LCJ in *Green* v *Hoyle* [1976] 1 WLR 575, pp 580–1).

1 Tradition

The form of a conveyance of unregistered land is still dictated largely by tradition. Conveyancing practitioners are in general a conservative lot (note the small 'c' in the present context). Their motto might well be 'Do as you have done before'; they are never happier than when they are able to follow precedent; they are pleased in inverse proportion to the necessary alterations and additions. This is understandable and far from reprehensible. As a student, cribbing is cheating; as a practitioner, failure to crib may be professional negligence. Memories are to be trusted neither as to the law nor as to forms. Only rarely is a conveyancer met who would contemplate drafting any document without first searching for the nearest possible precedent or combination of precedents, either from past transactions in which he has acted or from one of the well-known published collections of precedents.

As a result the outline and order of the parts of a conveyance have become almost invariable and, as will be seen, have acquired some legal significance. In addition the traditional formulae, which appear in capital letters in conveyances and other deeds, perform an elementary but useful function apart altogether from any meaning which they may or may not have. Their function is to act as landmarks, or rather 'deedmarks', by which every conveyancing practitioner knows where one part of a deed begins and another ends (see also per Ungoed-Thomas J in *British Railways Board* v *Glass* [1964] 1 WLR 294, at p 303, affirmed at [1965] Ch 538). Of course, this could be achieved in other ways, say by breaking the deed down by means of sub-headings, which would accord more with the streamlining of conveyancing often advocated for this latter half of the twentieth century. Indeed, once one embarks upon purported rationalisation of the form and contents of deeds, it becomes well nigh impossible to stem the slaughter of dearly loved though archaic clichés.

At this point, the obvious observation must be made that the traditional need not be treated as mandatory. The essence of the exercise is the achievement of the parties' intentions through use of the English language.

> Ideally, a legal document and a poem have both got to be "right"—accurate, useful, unpadded, elegant

(per Roy Fuller, poet before professor after solicitor, at (1969) 113 SJ 662). Choice of form is for the purchaser, the consumer so far as concerns the conveyance, and he has actually been offered the opportunity of departing from tradition and using instead modern language and new lay-outs (ie, Parker's *Modern Conveyancing Precedents*, 1964). The commendable motive behind this publication was to make 'conveyancing documents more easily understood by the clients who sign them' (ibid, p 3; cp the welcome accorded to another new collection of forms as being 'worded in language which conveyancers can still understand': RGR reviewing Hallett's *Conveyancing Precedents* at (1965) 29 Conv (NS) 414). Certain detailed criticisms of this approach have been made, perhaps too trenchantly, elsewhere ('Unprecedented Precedents', (1964) 108 SJ 273; see also *Solicitor Quarterly* (1965) vol 4, pp 76–9). All that can be indicated here, as a general proposition to be borne in mind, is the peril to be evaded by those who leave the beaten path (cf (1970) *Law Society's Gazette* vol 67, p 643). Thus Lord Romer once began his speech as follows:

My Lords, if the gentleman who attends to the conveyancing side of the respondent's business had been a little more familiar with the terms usually employed by the practitioners in that art, it is, I think, at least possible that your Lordships would never have been troubled with this case. It is, indeed, one that furnishes a remarkable illustration of the confusion which may result from the use of inaccurate language

(in *Hughes* v *Utting & Co Ltd* [1940] AC 463, at p 475; all directed at a form of 'purchase by way of lease' so-called). The whole argument for the traditional has been captured in the following more authoritative words than the present writer's:

The common forms used by conveyancers are public documents. They have been brought into their present shape by the efforts of generations of conveyancers and while they have been modified from time to time in consequence of changes in the law, they remain substantially what they were many years ago. It follows that where a draftsman wishes to express a meaning which can be expressed by a common form, he should always employ it, for all lawyers will put a correct interpretation on his language without hesitation, while, if he endeavours to express the same meaning in a different form of words, he raises a presumption against the meaning, owing to his employment of unusual language, and he causes an unnecessary expenditure of time and labour to the person using the draft

(Elphinstone, *Introduction to Conveyancing*, 6th ed, p 29). Some overstatement may be detected, but the inference clearly can be taken that a conveyance is comparable to a doctor's prescription in that intelligibility to the layman, client or patient, is not of prime importance (see, for example, per Sachs LJ in *Caerphilly Concrete Products Ltd* v *Owen* [1972] 1 WLR 372, at p 376, as to the advantages of a formula being well-known to trained conveyancers outweighing any trap it may constitute for others).

Against this it must equally be borne in mind that too slavish an allegiance to tradition can also be dangerous. Those timorous practitioners who fearfully and thoughtlessly follow precedent, in case the magic fails to work, run risks all of their own making. Thus several modern cases were caused by this very fault. In *Golden Lion Hotel (Hunstanton) Ltd* v *Carter* [1965] 1 WLR 1189 in the conveyance of a freehold reversion to the lessee the customary express declaration of merger was included so inadvertently extinguishing not only the lease but also certain restrictive covenants by the lessor binding neighbouring land; Cross J accurately described this as 'faulty conveyancing'. In *Tophams Ltd* v *Sefton* [1967] 1 AC 50, where a short question of construction went all the way to the House of Lords, Lord Wilberforce remarked:

The covenants in the conveyance were presumably designed to give [Lord Sefton] satisfactory and secure protection. The method chosen, however, was in some ways unfortunate; for what the draftsman did was to carry over into the conveyance the covenants in the lease of 1929 with only some minor changes, and he may not have appreciated that covenants contained in a conveyance of the freehold by their nature operate quite differently from similar covenants contained in a lease, especially as regards purchasers

(at p 78). Thirdly *Whishaw* v *Stephens* [1970] AC 508 concerned the certainty of a particular clause in a settlement; in the Court of Appeal Winn LJ observed ('speaking,' as he said, 'as one utterly ignorant of trust law and practice') of the clause:

> The only real trouble here, I venture to think, is that the learned draftsman of this precedent was so soaked in Latinity, and it may well be also in the Germanic tongue, that he sought to force his verb to the end of the sentence and thereby produced complexity and some violence to English grammatical form

(sub nom *Re Gulbenkian's Trusts* [1968] Ch 126, at pp 138–9); and in the House of Lords, Lord Reid said:

> This clause does not make sense as it stands . . . But the client must not be penalised for his lawyer's slovenly drafting. Under modern conditions it may be necessary to relax older and stricter standards. If I adopt methods of construction appropriate for commercial documents and documents *inter rusticos* I must consider whether underlying the words used any reasonably clear intention can be discerned

(at [1970] AC 517; cp Lord Upjohn, at ibid, p 522). How damning! How awful! Yet the clause enjoyed a respectable provenance; Lord Denning MR said:

> We are told this clause was drafted by a very experienced conveyancer, Mr AH Withers, many years ago and was included in precedents published by *The Conveyancer* (1948–49) vol 13, pp 569, 570. It appears, I believe, also in Key and Elphinstone. It was used no doubt in many settlements. So its validity is of some importance

(in the Court of Appeal at [1968] Ch 132).

And finally in recent years we have witnessed a luxurious rash of cases concerning landlords' attempts to live with inflation. As Roskill LJ observed:

> The rent revision clauses which have come up for consideration are immensely varied in their terms. Their draftsmanship has been almost uniformly condemned judicially, not without justification . . . though in fairness to some of the draftsmen it is to be observed that some clauses have emanated, with or without modification, from well-known precedent books

(*United Scientific Holdings* v *Burnley BC* [1976] Ch 128, at p 146; on appeal [1978] AC 904; see also per Sir Eric Sachs in *CH Bailey Ltd* v *Memorial Enterprises* [1974] 1 WLR 728, at p 735).

The moral simply is that one must know precisely what one is doing when following precedents whether old or new. Let us turn now to a topic where the forms are infallible.

2   Registered land forms

The principles governing choice of form on a dealing with registered land render necessary a style entirely different from that of a deed not relating to registered land (cf generally 'Registered Conveyancing Technique' by Harold Potter at (1942–43) 7 Conv (NS) 24). In the first place, the important principle to remember is that the estate for the time being vested in the registered proprietor is only capable of being disposed of or dealt with in an authorised manner: s 69(4) of the Land Registration

Act 1925. By virtue of r 74 of the Land Registration Rules 1925 the forms set out in the Schedule to those Rules must be used in all matters to which they refer or are capable of being applied or adapted. Any alterations or additions which are necessary or desired may be made only if allowed by the registrar or the Rules (see, eg, r 117 and *Re King* [1962] 1 WLR 632).

A number of additions to the scheduled forms are certainly desirable, if not also necessary, since the forms are generally only skeletons of the completed instrument. For example, a receipt clause, the appropriate words in order to introduce the covenants for title implied under s 76 of the Law of Property Act 1925, a certificate of value and covenants generally are usually inserted. These, with others, which are, in practice, always allowed by the registrar, will be discussed later when dealing with each particular part of deeds relating to unregistered land. However, it may be said now that the printed forms of transfer of land obtainable from HMSO (not free of charge: r 318 was revoked by r 7 of the Land Registration Rules 1930) or from law stationers, in fact already contain most of the additions mentioned.

The Land Registration Rules incidentally provide (r 308) for the form of documents which are to be filed otherwise than in point of content. Thus such documents (other than maps or plans) must be printed, typewritten, lithographed, or written (what else was contemplated?) on stout paper, foolscap size, and a sufficient stitching margin must be allowed so that they may be conveniently bound. This provision has not always been strictly enforced in practice.

The scheduled forms apply to a variety of dealings with registered land. Starting at forms 19 and 20 with transfers of freehold land (whole and part respectively), they range via forms relating to settled land (forms 21–4), mines and minerals (forms 25–30), the exercise of a power of sale contained in a registered charge (form 31), leasehold land (forms 32–4), companies (form 35), charities (form 36), small holdings (forms 37–9—obsolete), the imposition of restrictive covenants (form 43), exchanges (form 44), to forms relating to charges and rentcharges (forms 45 et seq).

Although there are scheduled forms for transfers of leasehold land, there is no scheduled form for the grant of a lease of registered land, but s 18(1)(*e*) of the Land Registration Act 1925 provides it may be done 'in any form which sufficiently refers, in the prescribed manner, to the registered land.' Further, although there is a scheduled form of charge, by virtue of s 25(2) of the Land Registration Act 1925, a charge may be in any form, provided (*a*) that the land is clearly identified (ie, by reference to its title number) without reference to any other document, and (*b*) that the charge does not refer to certain other interests (ie, unregistered prior interests not being overriding interests). In practice, therefore, ordinary unregistered forms of leases and charges are not infrequently used with the usual Land Registry heading together with appropriate alterations to the parcels clause in order to comply with ss 18(1)(*e*) and 25(2) ante. Further, it is expressly contemplated by r 99 and form 21 of the 1925 Rules that in a transfer into settlement the parties may wish to make additions.

In the event of a transaction being undertaken for which no form is provided or to which the scheduled forms cannot conveniently be adapted, the instrument must be in such form as the registrar shall direct or allow, the scheduled forms being followed as nearly as circumstances will permit: Land Registration Rules 1925, r 75.

The sanction for preparing an instrument which appears to the registrar to be improper in form *or substance* (or to be not clearly expressed—a warning to draftsmen) rests also with the registrar. Under r 78, he may decline to enter the instrument in the register, either absolutely or subject to approved modifications. Alternatively, with the applicant's consent, he may settle the form of the entry to be made.

An instrument will be improper in form if it fails to comply with the principles upon which the register is kept. Thus an instrument which refers to other unregistered instruments, to trusts, or to the past history of the title will normally be rejected unless the offending reference is deleted (see also r 199 as to the mention of trivial, obvious or inconvenient matters). It was, however, decided by the Court of Appeal in *Morelle* v *Wakeling* [1955] 2 QB 379, at pp 415–16 (overruled, in effect, on other points by the House of Lords in *Attorney-General* v *Parsons* [1956] AC 421), that if the registrar, who has a discretion to allow a departure from the scheduled forms (see r 322(1)), registers a transfer which is not in a scheduled form, his acceptance of it must be taken as conclusive evidence of the sufficiency of the form used.

One fact emerges inescapably: the registrar has an enormous discretion, whilst the parties have little freedom as to the forms to be used. It is without doubt for practical purposes both simpler and better to accept the registrar's decision, which is unlikely to be unreasonable. In any case, it appears doubtful whether an appeal to the court from the registrar's decision can properly be made. Despite the provision of the Land Registration Rules 1925, r 299, that 'any person aggrieved by an order or decision of the registrar may appeal to the court,' Clauson J suggested obiter in *Dennis* v *Malcolm* [1934] Ch 244, at p 252, that no appeal lay in matters of an administrative character where the registrar has made no 'order or direction' (sic). The rather odd implication of this decision appears to be that no appeal would lie if the registrar were to decline to register an instrument (r 78), but that an appeal would lie if he were to direct a form to be used (r 75).

B COMMENCEMENT

What is the proper beginning of a conveyance of land? How should it be described? The old practice was to begin with 'This Indenture . . .' but now the law is that a deed may be called a deed or conveyance or whatever name appears appropriate to the intended transaction (s 57 of the Law of Property Act 1925). Further, it hardly matters if an inappropriate name is used, since the clearly expressed intentions of the parties will prevail over inaccurate technical words (see *Re Stirrup* [1961] 1 WLR 449, also *Grangeside Properties* v *Collingwoods Securities* [1964] 1 WLR 139).

The distinction between an indenture and a deed poll was and is that the former is a document inter partes written out in duplicate on the same parchment or paper and divided into two parts by cutting through with an irregular edge, each party retaining one part which could be fitted to the other to show its genuineness. At common law only those named as parties to the indenture could take an interest as immediate grantee or the benefit of a covenant as covenantee (see now s 56(1) of the Law of Property Act 1925). A deed poll, on the other hand, is a deed with smooth— or 'polled'—edges, ie, not indented, and is unilateral. It used to be necessary to indicate which the deed was, an indenture or a deed poll, but not now (s 56(2) of the Law of Property Act 1925).

However, this distinction between indentures and deeds poll may not be of merely academic interest. It was raised by Vaisey J in *Chelsea and Walham Green Building Society* v *Armstrong* [1951] Ch 853, where he held that a Land Registry transfer is in the nature of a deed poll rather than a deed inter partes, from which it follows that a person who is not a party to such a transfer can sue upon a covenant contained in it. Three points were specified (at pp 857–8) by Vaisey J as indicating that a Land Registry transfer is in the nature of a deed poll: (*a*) there is no reference to parties at the beginning, (*b*) it is expressed in the first person, and (*c*) it is of a quasi-public character. The first two of these three points are questions of form and not necessarily present (see the statutory Note to Form 19 in the Schedule to the Land Registration Rules 1925). However, it should be noted that Denning LJ in *Drive Yourself Hire Co (London) Ltd* v *Strutt* [1954] 1 QB 250, at p 273, stated that the technical rule that no one could sue on an indenture unless named as a party to it had been abolished, with the result that the distinction between indentures and deeds poll could be treated as 'old learning'. But this is not a view that should be taken too seriously since the whole of the learned lord justice's observations in that case have since been rendered extremely dubious by the House of Lords in *Beswick* v *Beswick* [1968] AC 58 (see further p 238).

However, to return to the question of commencement, all the forms contained in the Schedule to the Land Registration Rules 1925 require the heading prescribed by form 19 for a Transfer of Freehold Land (Whole), but otherwise waste no time with niceties and wade straight in, usually with 'in consideration of —— pounds (£——), I *AB*, of, etc, hereby,' etc.

C DATE

All conveyancers agree that deeds should have a date on them but not all appear to regard the date as being of much importance and few appear to be aware of any principles governing the choice of date. 'Please do not date' is the customary instruction pencilled on a document sent to a client for execution, and a possible inference would be that the complex matter of inserting a date is not to be meddled with by the abominable layman. In fact, the idea behind the instruction is probably that until completion the date to insert will not be known, an idea which enjoys general acceptance in practice and which has been held sound for stamp duty purposes (*Terrapin International Ltd* v *IRC* [1976] 1 WLR 665, despite an escrow; but cp *Alan Estates Ltd* v *WG Stores Ltd* [1982] Ch 511, CA). Nevertheless this still leaves for examination at least two conveyancing questions: what is the correct date? and, is it important?

1 The correct date

The commencing presumption is that the date, if any, appearing on the deed is the correct date (*Browne* v *Burton* (1847) 17 LJQB 49), though this is a rebuttable presumption, Patterson J saying (ibid, p 50), 'but as soon as the contrary appears, the apparent date is to be utterly disregarded.' The rule is that a deed takes effect from execution being completed by delivery and the only correct date is the date of delivery. This is old-established: 'All deeds do take effect from, and therefore have relation to, the time not of their date but of their delivery; and this is always presumed to be the time of their date unless the contrary do appear': Shep Touch 72, and there is much supporting authority. Delivery by whom, however, is considered later.

A query will immediately spring to the alert mind as to the position where two deeds both bear the same date or were both executed on the same day, particularly when the usual rule is recalled that the law disregards fractions of a day. In the words of Fry J:

> I think the law stands in this way, that when two deeds are executed on the same day, the court must inquire which was in fact executed first, but that if there is anything in the deeds themselves to show an intention, either that they shall take effect *pari passu* or even that the later deed shall take effect in priority

to the earlier, in that case the court will presume that the deeds were executed in
such order as to give effect to the manifest intention of the parties
(*Gartside* v *Silkstone Coal and Iron Co* (1882) 21 Ch D 762, at pp 767–8). Thus in
Weg Motors Ltd v *Hales* [1962] Ch 49 an option agreement and a lease were treated
by the Court of Appeal as one single transaction, despite the lease being described in
the agreement as 'of even date with but executed after these presents'. This
treatment was accorded not only because the parties so intended but also because 'it
is in fact impossible to execute two documents at precisely the same time' (per Lord
Evershed MR at p 69). Is this latter reason always so? Certainly one cannot sign or
seal more than one document at a time, but why cannot deeds be delivered en
masse? See also, however, *Church of England Building Society* v *Piskor* [1954] Ch
553, CA, as to the presumed scintilla temporis between purchase and mortgage.
Accordingly, the position if unclear may be clarified by presumptions.

It follows from the above that the lack of a date does not affect the validity of a
deed, and parol evidence is admissible to show the correct date: *Morrell* v *Studd and
Millington* [1913] 2 Ch 648 (per Astbury J at p 658). Thus it was said in *Goddard's
Case* (1584) 2 Co Rep 4*b*, at p 6, that:

> the date of a deed is not of the substance of a deed; for if it hath no date, or hath
> a false or impossible date, as the 30th day of February, yet the deed is good.

All this may reinforce the first reaction that the insertion of a date in a deed, even
though incorrect, is a matter of little importance. However, the reaction is rendered
erroneous by the conflict between the fact that the correct date itself is occasionally
of great importance and the fact that the commencing presumption is that the date
inserted is the correct one. Circumstances may easily occur in which it is wished to
rebut this presumption but it is found difficult or impossible to do so (as, for
example in *Cumberland Court (Brighton) Ltd* v *Taylor* [1964] Ch 29, where a
conveyance free from incumbrances was inconveniently found to be dated two days
before the discharge of the then vendor's mortgage; see also *Grangeside Properties
Ltd* v *Collingwoods Securities Ltd* [1964] 1 WLR 139 and *Koppel* v *Koppel* [1966]
1 WLR 802).

2   Importance of date

Accordingly, before dealing further with what date is the correct one to insert (ie,
delivery by whom?), it is proposed to mention quite briefly some of the matters
which turn upon the date of the deed. The object of this is to indicate when the
correct date itself may be important and it will be confined for the sake of brevity
mainly to the date of a conveyance of land.

The *first*, most obvious, point is the basic rule governing priority of estates and
interests, namely, that they rank in order of creation. A person who obtains a legal
estate or interest in land is not concerned with *subsequently* created estates and
interests, whether legal or equitable, unless his priority is displaced by fraud,
estoppel or gross negligence in relation to the title deeds. The same rule applies to a
person who obtains an equitable interest so far only as subsequently created
equitable interests (or legal interests created without value) are concerned;
otherwise a bona fide purchaser for value of the legal estate will obtain priority
unless he takes with notice (bearing in mind the modern tendency to replace the
doctrine of notice by provisions for registration of rights).

Secondly, the word 'date' appearing in a deed is to be construed as meaning the
day the deed is dated and not that on which it was delivered (assuming the deed is
not undated): *Styles* v *Wardle* (1825) 4 B & C 908, per Bailey J at p 911. Care must,
therefore, be taken not to conflict with the actual intentions of the parties.

Thirdly, s 62(1) of the Law of Property Act 1925 as to implied rights applies to quasi-easements 'at the time of conveyance . . . enjoyed with . . . the land' (see as to this *Goldberg* v *Edwards* [1950] Ch 247).

Fourthly, there are a vast number of statutory provisions (particularly in Finance Acts) which only apply to instruments made before or after a certain date.

Fifthly, there are a number of time limits which are calculated by reference to the date of a deed. Thus, before completion, where a person has obtained an official certificate of search in the land charges register, he is not affected by any entry made after his search (unless it is already protected by a priority notice), provided the purchase is completed before the expiration of fifteen working days: see s 11(5), (6) of the Land Charges Act 1972. Again, after completion, despite the apparent theory of the Stamp Act 1891 that instruments should be stamped before execution, s 15(2) of that Act enables certain specified instruments (including a conveyance on sale) to be stamped or presented for adjudication without payment of a penalty within thirty days after they have been 'first executed'. This may be taken as referring to the date of completion (*Terrapin International Ltd* v *IRC* [1976] 1 WLR 665) or it may better be taken as the earlier date of a delivery in escrow (see *Alan Estates Ltd* v *WG Stores Ltd* [1982] Ch 511, CA, noted at [1981] Conv 321–2, also as to 'Escrows' post p 322 et seq). Also by virtue of s 123 of the Land Registration Act 1925, inter alia, every conveyance on sale (as therein defined) of freehold land in an area of compulsory registration of title becomes *void* 'on the expiration of two months from the date thereof', with certain exceptions, unless an application for first registration has been made (see p 142). The section also applies to assignments on sale of leasehold land 'held for a term of years absolute having not less than forty years to run *from the date of assignment*.'

Sixthly, finally, and rather frighteningly, by virtue of s 9(1)(*g*) of the Forgery and Counterfeiting Act 1981, 'An instrument is false . . . if it purports to have been made . . . on a date on which . . . it was not in fact made . . .' As to this, cp *R* v *Wells* [1939] 2 All ER 169, CA, where a solicitor-trustee was held criminally liable in respect of the ante-dating of an endorsement on a settlement to negative the effect of provisions in the Finance Bill 1936 in case they became law. Thus the deliberate adjustment of the date of a deed in order to comply with one or other of the time limits mentioned above may prove a dangerous practice, since an intention to deceive, if not to defraud, would be difficult to deny.

3 Delivery by whom?

Having indicated why inserting the correct date may be important and stated that the correct date is that of delivery, the question now arises: delivery by whom? The formalities attending the execution of deeds will not be discussed here; suffice it to say that every executing party not only signs and seals but also delivers the deed, and the odds are that they will do so on different dates. The result is that the standard rules and dicta previously cited as to the correct date may be of negligible assistance.

It is submitted as clear that the correct date of deed is the date on which it is 'made', which is the date on which it becomes operative and binding as what it purports to be: compare the decisions of the House of Lords as to the making of a contract of sale in *IRC* v *Muller's Margarine Ltd* [1901] AC 217 and of a will in *Berkeley* v *Berkeley* [1946] AC 555. Upon what the deed purports to do depends the number of the parties who have to execute the deed to make it complete. The suggestion that the parties must execute the deed in any particular order appears 'simply absurd and ridiculous' (per Joyce J in *Edmondson* v *Copland* [1911] 2 Ch

301, at p 306). The correct date of the making of the deed is therefore the date on which the last essential party delivers the deed (see *Bishop of Crediton* v *Bishop of Exeter* [1905] 2 Ch 455).

For example, in the simplest possible case of a conveyance of land, the deed is made when it is delivered by the grantor (donor or vendor) without any necessity for reference to execution by the grantee: *Naas* v *Westminster Bank Ltd* [1940] AC 366. If there are, say, two joint grantors, the deed of conveyance should be dated when it is delivered by the second of them. This will be so even though in the deed the grantee undertakes obligations, since he will not be permitted to approbate and reprobate: ibid; see also *Halsall* v *Brizell* [1957] Ch 169. Observe also that s 65(1) of the Law of Property Act 1925 provides that a reservation of a legal estate operates without execution of the conveyance by the grantee. Compare, however, *Sinclair* v *IRC* (1942) 24 TC 432, CA, where certain share transfers which required execution by both the transferor and transferee before they could be registered were held inchoate and not 'stampable deeds' until completed by execution by the transferee. This decision presumably will apply in the few cases in which a Land Registry transfer requires execution by the transferee.

4 Blanks

A trap in practice concerns the filling in of gaps in a deed by solicitors at or after completion, eg, numerous dates in mortgage deeds. Speaking generally, if there are material blanks in a deed, the deed is a nullity unless and until it is redelivered by the grantor after the blanks have been filled in, and then the correct date of the deed will be the date of redelivery: *Re Seymour, Fielding* v *Seymour* [1913] 1 Ch 475 (cf *Farrier-Waimak* v *Bank of New Zealand* [1965] AC 377).

However, the mere filling in of the correct date of a deed after its execution does not affect the deed's validity: *Keane* v *Smallbone* (1855) 17 CB 179. Thus in *Bishop of Crediton* v *Bishop of Exeter* [1905] 2 Ch 455, all except one of the essential parties executed a deed during 1899 and the deed had the day and month left blank but the year, 1899, written in; the last essential party executed the deed on 4 January 1900, and the blanks were then filled in and the year altered to 1900; Swinfen Eady J held that this alteration did not affect the validity of the deed because it was not material (following the rule in *Pigot's Case* (1614) 11 Co Rep 26*b*, as qualified in *Aldous* v *Cornwell* (1868) LR 3 QB 573). See also *Rudd* v *Bowles* [1912] 2 Ch 60, where a lease was not void, the parties being estopped from denying that the lease was executed on the date inserted.

5 Land Registry transfers

In accordance with the prescribed forms in the Schedule to the Land Registration Rules 1925 a Land Registry transfer must be dated and the above principles apply (and see the Land Registration Rules 1925, r 86, as to re-execution after alterations). However, the date on the transfer and the date of registration will rarely, if ever, be the same. It must always be remembered that the legal estate only passes on the date of registration: Land Registration Act 1925, ss 19(1), 22(1). Thus, prior to the date of registration, for example, a valid notice to quit cannot be served by a purchaser: *Smith* v *Express Dairy Co* [1954] JPL 45; and a receiver cannot be appointed by a transferee of a registered charge: *Lever Finance Ltd* v *Needleman's Trustee and Kreutzer* [1956] Ch 375 (see s 33(2) of the Land Registration Act 1925).

It is true that s 27(3) of the Land Registration Act 1925 provides that a registered charge 'shall take effect from the date of delivery of the deed containing the same', but it has been held that this only gives the chargee protection inter partes and not the legal estate (ie, no priority over a tenant by estoppel): *Grace Rymer Investments Ltd* v *Waite* [1958] Ch 831.

D PARTIES

1 Who should be joined

'This deed is made the —— day of —— between' — whom? Usually, of course, there is no difficulty whatsoever in deciding who should be joined as a party to any particular deed. However, as with all the contents of a deed, there are general principles of law which should govern the decision and which are worth discussing. It is not proposed to deal here with the rules relating to the capacity of parties.

The basic principle is straightforward in statement: all necessary parties should be joined, but no unnecessary parties even though willing to join: *Corder* v *Morgan* (1811) 18 Ves 344. Which parties are necessary? The answer to this depends almost entirely on the intended function of the particular deed. Apart from its proper execution, in order to be a deed a document must (*a*) create a binding obligation, or (*b*) transfer property, or (*c*) confirm an act which transferred property. The general rule is, first, that only a person who is a party to a deed can be bound or benefited by an obligation intended to be created by that deed, and second, that property cannot be transferred by deed to a person who is not a party thereto. Therefore, all these persons should be made parties, that is the covenantor and covenantee, and the grantor and grantee.

At this point, it may prove convenient to explain that the traditional form still used for deeds of conveyance establishes at the outset who are the parties by expressly naming persons as such. Thus the deed will state that it is made—'between AB of —— [address and description] (hereinafter called "the Vendor") *of the one part* and CD of —— [address and description] (hereinafter called "the Purchaser") *of the other part*' (see Form 1, *Hallett's Conveyancing Precedents*, p 191). No matter that someone else may be mentioned or identified elsewhere in the body of the deed, as a grantee or covenantee, he will not be a party to it; this remains true although that someone else may even execute the deed. The words which the writer has italicised should not be regarded as functionless verbiage: they indicate that the document is an indenture inter partes, rather than a deed poll (for this, see p 232), and also name once and for all who are the parties (see the discussion and cases cited by Lord Upjohn in *Beswick* v *Beswick* [1968] AC 58, at pp 102–3; cp Parker, *Modern Conveyancing Precedents*, at p 6).

2 Exceptions to the general rule

There are, of course, numerous exceptions to the rule prohibiting persons who are not parties to a deed from enforcing it. Examples of these exceptions arise in the cases of agency (execution under a power of attorney), deeds poll, privity of estate, the benefit of covenants at common law, the benefit and burden of restrictive covenants in equity, trusts, policies of assurance under s 11 of the Married Women's Property Act 1882, and many other statutory exceptions. In substance, most of these exceptions simply allow enforcement by non-parties, though some of them in effect extend the number of original parties.

Section 56 of the Law of Property Act 1925—In particular the provisions of s 56(1) of the Law of Property Act 1925 should be noted, namely, that:

> A person may take an immediate or other interest in land or other property, or the benefit of any condition, right of entry, covenant or agreement over or respecting land or other property, although he may not be named as a party to the conveyance or other instrument.

This subsection is so widely worded that it could easily be taken as going so far as to abolish the otherwise established doctrine of privity of contract (see, eg, per Denning LJ in *Drive Yourself Hire Co v Strutt* [1954] 1 QB 250, at p 271 et seq). However, the subsection has long been restrictively regarded as directed against the rule mentioned ante, p 232, prohibiting persons who are not parties in the strict sense indicated above from benefiting under an indenture: see per Greene MR in *White v Bijou Mansions Ltd* [1938] Ch 351, at p 365. It was held in this case that it is not sufficient that the deed confers a benefit on the person seeking to enforce it, but that in order to be enabled so to do by s 56 'he must be a person who falls within the scope and benefit of the covenant according to the true construction of the document in question': per Simonds J [1937] Ch 610, at p 624; see also *Stromdale & Ball Ltd v Burden* [1952] Ch 223. Earlier, in *Re Ecclesiastical Commissioners' Conveyance* [1936] Ch 430 it had been held that such person must be both identifiable and in existence at the time of the deed.

Now these rather vague statements of the extent of s 56(1) have been approved and crystallised, with as much precision as one can expect from five speeches, by the House of Lords in *Beswick v Beswick* [1968] AC 58. The case did not directly concern conveyancing at all, so the facts may be disregarded. Nevertheless, the following conditions for the application of the subsection did emerge more or less clearly:

> First, the key expression 'land or other property' is to be construed in its context as confined to real property (ie, the history of the subsection prevailed over the statutory definition in s 205(1)(xx); cp per Lord Upjohn at p 105).

> Secondly, the conveyance or other instrument must purport to contain a covenant with, or to make a grant to, the particular non-party.

> Thirdly, the expression 'conveyance or other instrument' is limited to documents under seal.

> And fourthly, such documents to be within the subsection must be strictly inter partes.

These last three conditions were propounded only by Lord Upjohn (at pp 106–7), although he had the concurrence of Lord Pearce (at p 94), and can be described as obiter dicta (see p 102). Nonetheless, these views rest on, and clearly will carry, considerable authority. Yet so long as there may be any uncertainty about the application of s 56(1), the safest method in practice is to ignore the section and to join as parties so far as practicable every conceivable covenantee and grantee.

Section 63 of the Law of Property Act 1925—The 'all-estate' clause implied by s 63 of the Law of Property Act 1925 will only be dealt with here in order to answer the question which arises when the party conveying holds several estates and interests in the land conveyed but in different capacities. For example, if the grantor is entitled to one estate in the land as trustee and to another as beneficiary, does it matter in which capacity he is joined as a party to the conveyance? The effect of s 63 is that (subject to the contrary being expressed in the conveyance) conveyances made after 1881 will pass every estate or interest of the grantor even though it is not vested in him in the capacity in which he is joined as a party: *Taylor v London and County Banking Co* [1901] 2 Ch 231 (see further p 302).

Section 204 of the Law of Property Act 1925—By virtue of s 204 of the Law of Property Act 1925 any lease, sale or other act under an order of the High Court is not invalidated so far as a purchaser is concerned by reason, inter alia, of want of any concurrence, consent, notice or service, and the purchaser's notice of such want is irrelevant. At first sight it might appear that this section would enable land to be conveyed without joining the owner as a party. However, despite the wide wording of the section, it has been held that a purchaser is entitled to have joined in his conveyance all persons having a legal interest in the land (*Mostyn* v *Mostyn* [1893] 3 Ch 376), and that the court cannot convey the property of a person not a party to the proceedings, thinking it to belong to someone else: *Jones* v *Barnett* [1900] 1 Ch 370.

3 Nominees

A purchaser is entitled to insist upon conveyance to his nominee, for example, to a sub-purchaser (in any number of lots, provided that the purchaser pays any additional expenses), unless the purchaser's personal qualifications are material (and unless the contract expressly provided otherwise). Where a nominee is brought in, if the conveyance is subject to obligations, the vendor can compel the purchaser to join as a party to the conveyance in order to guarantee observance of the obligations: *Curtis Moffat Ltd* v *Wheeler* [1929] 2 Ch 224, at p 237. As to whether a sub-purchaser can compel the purchaser to join in the conveyance, see a note at [1979] Conv 1–3. Also notice that The Law Society's Conditions, 1980 ed, No 17(6), provides that the vendor may 'on reasonable grounds' decline to convey to a person other than the purchaser.

4 Trustees, and oneself

Apart from the grantor and grantee or covenantor and covenantee, it may be that consideration money arising must be paid to some third person (or persons). For example, where land is the subject of a vesting instrument under the Settled Land Act 1925 and there has been no deed of discharge then capital money arising must be paid to not less than two trustees (or to a trust corporation or into court): Settled Land Act 1925, s 18(1)(*b*), (*c*). In such a case the appropriate third person (or persons) should be joined in the deed to give a receipt for the consideration money.

Prior to the property legislation of 1925, a person could only convey freehold property to himself by way of a conveyance to uses under the Statute of Uses 1535. This statute has been repealed (s 207 of, and Sched 7 to, the Law of Property Act 1925) and the position is now governed by s 72 of the Law of Property Act 1925. By virtue of this section, any person or persons may convey to or vest in himself or themselves, alone or jointly with a third party, any property. This section was considered by the House of Lords in *Rye* v *Rye* [1962] AC 496, in which the majority based their decision on the ground that it is still not possible in law, despite the section, for one person to grant a lease of land to himself, or for two or more persons to grant a lease of land to themselves in any circumstances, largely because of the contractual nature of a lease. However, although one may not be able to covenant with oneself alone, a covenant by a person with himself and one or more other persons (eg, by a continuing trustee with new trustees) which would have been completely void before 1926 (*Napier* v *Williams* [1911] 1 Ch 361) is now to be construed as a covenant with the other person or persons alone (s 82 of the Law of Property Act 1925). Accordingly, a lease in such circumstances would be valid (see s 72(4) of the same Act). Further, it has actually been held possible for a person with different capacities to contract in his representative capacity with himself as an individual (*Rowley, Holmes & Co* v *Barber* [1977] 1 WLR 371).

5   Unnecessary parties

Having discussed the necessary parties to a deed of conveyance in accordance with the basic principle stated at the beginning of this section, it is appropriate now to mention the unnecessary parties. If any person owns an interest in the estate which is the subject-matter of the conveyance and that estate is to be conveyed free from the interest, then whether or not the owner of the interest must be joined as a party depends on whether or not his interest can be overreached.

Thus, if a mortgagor sells and the mortgage is not to be discharged before completion (assuming no satisfactory undertaking to discharge is given), then the mortgagee should be joined to release the estate conveyed. This assumes that a purchaser would otherwise take subject to the mortgage, eg, that, if it is registrable as a land charge, it has in fact been registered. Similarly, the owners of any other legal estate or interest (see s 1 of the Law of Property Act 1925) which cannot be overreached should be joined if the property is to be conveyed free therefrom.

However, it is clear that a person whose interest will be overreached by the conveyance, whether he concurs or not, is an unnecessary party. Such overreaching of equitable interests in land, and their attachment to the proceeds of sale, will occur where a tenant for life for the purposes of the Settled Land Act 1925 conveys, or where trustees for sale convey, though equitable interests having *priority* to the settlement or trust for sale must be distinguished from those taken *thereunder* (although certain of such equitable interests may be overreached by an ad hoc settlement or trust for sale: s 21 of the Settled Land Act 1925 and s 2 of the Law of Property Act 1925).

It follows logically from the preceding paragraph that a contractual stipulation that a purchaser (for money or money's worth) of a legal estate in land is to accept a conveyance made with the concurrence of any person entitled to an overreachable equitable interest should be void: s 42(1), (9) of the Law of Property Act 1925. However, so far as the parties are concerned, a purchaser may, of course, accept a conveyance made with such concurrence if he wishes. Also, if the vendor has both the legal estate and the equitable interest he may contract to convey both instead of overreaching the equitable interest, eg, a tenant for life under the Settled Land Act 1925 who has taken an assignment of the remainder.

6   Description of parties

It is usual in a deed to describe the parties thereto by both their first name (baptismal, Christian or otherwise) and their surname when they are first mentioned, and to add their address and occupation. Also, of course, the formula '(hereinafter called ——) of the —— part' will be added; the words in brackets merely facilitate a shorter description in the rest of the deed (as to the final words, see p 237).

However, it is not all that uncommon for parties to be incorrectly described, by accident or otherwise. Where a mistake has occurred, on evidence thereof being given, the court will correct any misdescription: see *Alexander Mountain & Co* v *Rumere* [1948] 2 KB 436 and *Etablissement Baudelot* v *RS Graham & Co* [1953] 2 QB 271. Even if the misdescription is intentional, it is:

> a very familiar principle of law, that where you are dealing with a grantee, you may describe that grantee in any way which is capable of ascertainment afterwards: you are not bound to give him a particular name; you are not bound to give his Christian name or his surname; you may describe him by any description by which the parties to the instrument think it right to describe him

(per Lord Halsbury in *Simmons* v *Woodward* [1892] AC 100, at p 105).

It may even be true that misdescriptions of parties matter less here than with the initial contract for sale. Thus, in the leading 'non est factum' case, Lord Hodson, having pronounced that to support the plea there must be a fundamental difference between documents, proceeded:

> Where, as in this case, there is an error of personality it may or may not be fundamental; the question cannot be answered in isolation. There is a distinction between a deed and a contract in that the former does not require consensus and the latter does. Hence in the case of deeds error of personality is not necessarily so vital as in the case of contracts

(in *Saunders* v *Anglia Building Society* [1971] AC 1004 at p 1019; cf *F Goldsmith (Sicklesmere) Ltd* v *Baxter* [1970] Ch 85, ante, at p 39).

This freedom of description should not, however, be abused.

> There can be no doubt that parol evidence as to the identity of a party to a deed is always admissible, but in considering such evidence it is of paramount importance to bear in mind the indicia of identity afforded by the deed itself

(per the Privy Council in *Fung Ping Shan* v *Tong Shun* [1918] AC 403, at p 406). Further, the use of a fictitious name could constitute the crime of forgery where as here the identity of the maker of the document is a material factor (cp *R* v *Gambling* [1975] QB 207; see a note 'Improper Names' at (1975) 39 Conv (NS) 6–7, also Forgery and Counterfeiting Act 1981, s 9(1)(*h*)).

Another reason for precision in naming the parties to a conveyance of land, a reason which cuts right across Lord Halsbury's 'very familiar principle', lies in the registration of land charges against a name rather than against the land (Land Charges Act 1972, s 3(1)). Thus for the purposes of registration and search the true names of successive estate owners assume an undue importance. This was farcically illustrated in *Oak Co-operative Building Society* v *Blackburn* [1968] Ch 730, reversing [1967] Ch 1169: a certain Miss *C* having agreed to purchase a property from a person who carried on business under the name of 'Frank David Blackburn' registered an estate contract against that name; subsequently her vendor, whose true name was 'Fran*cis* David Blackburn', mortgaged the property to the plaintiff society which had obtained a clear certificate of search against the names 'Francis Davi*s* Blackburn'. Both Ungoed-Thomas J and the Court of Appeal held that the society's search was not conclusive as against the true name. The former also held that Miss *C's* registration was equally ineffective since the statute contemplated only registration in the estate owner's 'proper formal names and not in any pet, familiar, nick or common forms of those names or any other names by which he may from place to place or time to time be known' [1967] Ch 1178). On appeal, however, it was said that if there were registration 'in what may be fairly described as a version of the full names of the vendor, albeit not a version which was bound to be discovered on a search in the correct full names, we would not hold it a nullity against someone who does not search at all or who (as here) searches in the wrong name' (per Russell LJ giving the judgment of the court, at [1968] Ch 743).

The practical difficulties attending this approach are only too obvious. However, it should be added here that by 'true' or 'correct' names in this last cited case was meant the names appearing on the title, in particular in the conveyance to the estate owner in question. In this respect the case has since been applied by Foster J who held that in the absence of evidence to the contrary the court should assume that the proper names of a person are those in which the conveyancing documents had been taken (*Diligent Finance Co Ltd* v *Alleyne* (1971) 23 P & CR 346, where a deserted wife had registered a Class F land charge against her husband but unfortunately forgot his middle name). So, although such names need not necessarily be true or correct or proper in other contexts, their selection and use for conveyancing purposes do call for some care.

7   Registered land

The above principles generally apply equally to the parties to dispositions of registered land (except, of course, for the observations relating to the Land Charges Act 1972). The most apparent difference is formal, not substantial; in the usual form of registered disposition the parties are not set out at the head of the instrument but are brought in as required. It is not '. . . made. . .between *AB* of, etc (hereinafter called "the Vendor") of the one part and *CD* of, etc. . .,' but instead '. . . I, *AB* of, etc . . . hereby transfer to *CD* of, etc. . .' Following from this the opinion of Vaisey J, expressed in *Chelsea and Walham Green Building Society* v *Armstrong* [1951] Ch 853, at pp 857–8 (mentioned earlier at p 232), will be recalled that a Land Registry transfer is a deed poll. It may also follow that s 56(1) of the Law of Property Act 1925 is not applicable to a Land Registry transfer (see p 232), except perhaps in the comparatively rare case of the parties being set out in the usual unregistered way (which is actually allowed 'where more convenient' by the statutory note to Form 19 in the Schedule to the Land Registration Rules 1925).

E   RECITALS

The word 'WHEREAS' in a deed traditionally denotes that here beginneth the recitals. It appears to the writer that in practice the use and effect of this part of a deed is either under-estimated or over-estimated, and the present purpose is, therefore, to consider some of the reasons for and the results of the inclusion of recitals. Whilst doing so, however, it should always be borne in mind that recitals are not an 'operative part' of a deed, which part traditionally commences after the recitals with 'NOW THIS DEED WITNESSETH . . .' However, it is *not* true to say, as did Lord Holt, that:

> the reciting part of a deed is not at all a necessary part either in law or equity . . . it hath no effect or operation

(*Bath* v *Montague* (1693) 3 Cas in Ch 55, at p 101; cp per Lord Warrington in *IRC* v *Raphael* [1935] AC 96, at p 135).

1   The general purpose

Recitals have the general purpose of stating 'how the vendor holds and sells', and so recitals which do this have been classified into two types, respectively narrative and introductory recitals. Narrative recitals deal with matters relating to the entitlement to the land of the grantor (ie, the vendor or donor). Introductory recitals are 'a preliminary statement of what the maker of the deed intended should be the effect and purpose of the whole deed when made' (per Lord Halsbury in *Mackenzie* v *Duke of Devonshire* [1896] AC 400, at p 406). Thus introductory recitals explain the purpose of the deed, that is, how and why the existing state of affairs is to be altered, the commonest example being a recital of the agreement for sale between the parties.

At one time, as all who investigate title to unregistered land appreciate, recitals used to be lengthy. Nowadays the sensible fashion is to have short recitals. This shortening could be achieved to a large extent by using the provision of s 58 of the Law of Property Act 1925 that an instrument expressed to be supplemental to a previous instrument is to be read and to have effect, as far as may be, as if the supplemental instrument contained a full recital of the previous instrument. This section gives no right to an abstract or production of the previous instrument, and a purchaser may accept the same evidence that the previous instrument does not affect the title as if it had merely been mentioned in the supplemental instrument.

However, the section, passed in accordance with one of the basic ideas of the 1925 property legislation, namely, of shortening conveyances, is not as much used in practice as it might be, possibly because of the inherent inconvenience of any cross-referencing. As a result, the shortening of recitals is usually achieved either by omitting them altogether in a simple case, or else by strictly avoiding any statement of the history of the grantor's present entitlement. For reasons of estoppel, discussed below, it is thought that recitals should not be omitted altogether and that the irreducible minimum recital will be something like 'Whereas the vendor is seised of the property hereinafter described in fee simple in possession free from incumbrances', to which one often adds: 'and has agreed with the purchaser for the sale thereof to him at the price of £——'.

Two points on the wording just quoted may be made. First, in view of the provisions of s 1(1) of the Law of Property Act 1925 as to legal estates in land capable of subsisting or of being conveyed or created, strictly the words 'for an estate' should be inserted before, and the word 'absolute' after, the words 'in fee simple'. Second, the word seised is still technically correct in respect of a freeholder notwithstanding the abolition of conveyancing by 'livery and seisin' (s 51(1) of the Law of Property Act 1925).

2 Incidental purposes

Apart from the general purpose of recitals already stated, there are a number of consequences or side-effects or incidental purposes, as you wish, which may result from the content or wording of recitals and which may be taken advantage of and therefore need to be watched in practice.

(1) *Estoppel*—It seems superficially convenient to proceed from mentioning the recital of the grantor's title to a discussion of the topic of estoppel by deed:

> If a distinct statement of a particular fact is made in the recital of a bond or other instrument under seal, and a contract is made with reference to that recital, it is unquestionably true that as between the parties to that instrument and in an action upon it, it is not competent for the party bound to deny the recital

(per Parke B in *Carpenter* v *Buller* (1841) 8 M & W 209, at p 212). The statement that the recital should be of 'a particular fact' is important:

> A general recital will not operate as an estoppel, but the recital of a particular fact will have that effect

(per Lord Lyndhurst LC in *Bensley* v *Burdon* (1830) 8 LJ (OS) Ch 85, at p 87). The reason for this rule was clearly stated by Bowen LJ in *Onward Building Society* v *Smithson* [1893] 1 Ch 1, at p 14:

> It would be dangerous to extract a proposition by inference from the statement in a deed and hold the party estopped from denying it; estoppel can only arise from a clear definite statement.

Thus a recital that the vendor is 'seised of or *otherwise* well entitled to' property would not operate as an estoppel (*Heath* v *Crealock* (1874) LR 10 Ch 22), and the covenants for title implied under s 76 of the Law of Property Act 1925 would not be sufficiently clear statements to estop the covenantor showing the true position: *Onward Building Society* v *Smithson*, ante.

Who is estopped—Of course, all the world is not estopped even if the recital is of a particular fact. First of all there must be an action founded on and not collateral to the deed. Then, a person who is a stranger to the parties to the deed cannot be estopped from denying any statement in that deed: cf *Lady Bateman v Faber* [1898] 1 Ch 144. Contrast, however, the position of persons claiming by, through, under or in trust for, a party to the deed, who are equally estopped with that party: *Poulton v Moore* [1915] 1 KB 400.

Whether or not all the parties to a deed are estopped by any particular recital is a question of construction. Only those parties who on a proper construction of the deed make the statement contained in the recital are estopped:

When a recital is intended to be a statement which all the parties to a deed have mutually agreed to admit as true, it is an estoppel upon all. But when it is intended to be the statement of one party only, the estoppel is confined to that party, and the intention is to be gathered from construing the instrument

(per Patterson J in *Stroughill v Buck* (1850) 14 QB 781, at p 787). Thus, an obvious example is that, where there is a recital of title, estoppel only operates against the vendor, not against the purchaser (cf per Lord Maugham in *Greer v Kettle* [1938] AC 156, at p 170).

Equally, one might well have thought that only the mortgagor, and not the mortgagee, would be estopped by a recital of title in a mortgage deed. Yet a different view has been expressed judicially. In *Woolwich Equitable Building Society v Marshall* [1952] Ch 1, Danckwerts J observed:

It seems to me that a mortgagee who has inserted in the deed under which he acquires title a statement that the mortgagor is 'the estate owner in respect of the property' which is being mortgaged or charged to the mortgagee cannot object if that statement is taken to be true

(ibid, at p 9). This view was incidentally adopted in *Church of England Building Society v Piskor* [1954] Ch 553 by Evershed MR saying (at p 559) that 'the mortgagees may well be said to be unable to complain of the truth of the recital which they, no doubt, caused to be inserted in their own mortgage'.

However, this appears to approach the estoppel effect of recitals in the wrong way: the party estopped should surely not be the one who drafted the deed (ie, purchaser or mortgagee) but rather the one who makes the recital according to the deed's operation (ie, vendor or mortgagor). However perhaps the quoted views can be confined to the question being considered of determining the chronology of identically dated purchase deeds and mortgage deeds by reference to internal evidence (a question for which a well-known rule of thumb answer has now been provided, independently of recitals, by the latter case).

As to the benefit of estoppel, it has been said that the doctrine of estoppel 'can have no operation except in the case of third parties who are innocent of fraud and have become owners for value' (*General Finance, etc, Co v Liberator Society* (1878) 10 Ch D 15, at p 24). Thus taking the benefit of an estoppel does not depend on executing, or even being a party, to the deed containing the recital or other statement; the principle is that estoppel operates in favour of those persons, such as successors in title, who are intended to and do act on the faith of the misrepresentation (*Re King's Settlement* [1931] 2 Ch 294, where the immediate grantee knew the truth). Of course, a person who is a complete stranger to the parties to the deed would not be entitled to act upon a recited statement without enquiry (*Trinidad Asphalt Co v Coryat* [1896] AC 587).

Feeding the estoppel—The consequence of an estoppel operating in respect of a recital of title, where there is in fact absence of title, is twofold and flouts the nemo dat quod non habet rule. First, the grantor cannot, as against other parties to the deed, deny that he had the title recited. Second, if the grantor subsequently acquires, by any means, the recited title (ie, the interest which he has purported to convey for valuable consideration), then since the grantor cannot deny that he had that title at the time of the conveyance, it can be claimed by and is passed automatically to the grantee without any further conveyance (*Re Bridgwater's Settlement, Partridge* v *Ward* [1910] 2 Ch 342). The estoppel is fed, to the advantage of the grantee, and this is one good reason why a recital of title, such as that given above (on p 243), should be insisted on by a purchaser as the irreducible minimum, assuming the facts are appropriate. Such a recital is necessary because, leases apart, no such estoppel arises out of the grant itself: *Re Maddy* [1901] 2 Ch 820; *Re Harper's Settlement, Williams* v *Harper* [1919] 1 Ch 270 (cf the peculiar twist in *Woolwich Equitable Building Society* v *Marshall* [1952] Ch 1, where the estoppel arising out of the grant of a lease was held good only because of the estoppel by recital in a later mortgage deed; see now *Church of England Building Society* v *Piskor* [1954] Ch 553).

The beneficial application of this doctrine was well illustrated not so long ago. In *Cumberland Court (Brighton) Ltd* v *Taylor* [1964] Ch 29 an abstract of title disclosed that a receipt endorsed on a legal charge was dated two days after the date of the conveyance by the original mortgagor to a purchaser from him; the result of this was that the receipt operated not to discharge the charge but to transfer it to the original mortgagor by virtue of s 115(2) of the Law of Property Act 1925. However, the conveyance by the original mortgagor had contained the common form recital that he was 'seised in fee simple in possession . . . free from incumbrances'. Accordingly, Ungoed-Thomas J held that the original mortgagor, who had become the mortgagee, would be estopped (as would anyone else) from enforcing the charge. Thus the title was good, the inconveniently dated receipt being cancelled out by the recital.

Freedom from incumbrances—A recital that the grantor is seised '. . . free from incumbrances' is, as indicated above, in practice commonly included in conveyances prepared on behalf of the purchaser. It is thought to be the better view that, if the vendor has contracted to convey free from incumbrances (in the absence of the contrary, this is implied), he cannot reasonably object to such a recital. But if the words 'free from incumbrances' were to be included in the operative part of the draft conveyance, the vendor should object to them since they would imply an absolute warranty going further than the qualified covenants for title usually implied under s 76 of the Law of Property Act 1925.

In practice, it is both customary and wise to treat the word 'incumbrance' as having the widest possible meaning, ie, as covering any right in favour of a third person which detracts from absolute ownership (but cp the 'money' meaning given by s 205(1)(vii) of the Law of Property Act 1925, also as to leases Danckwerts J in *District Bank Ltd* v *Webb* [1958] 1 WLR 148, at p 149, and Lord Radcliffe in *Fairweather* v *St Marylebone Property Co* [1963] AC 510, at pp 540–1).

Incorrect recitals—Finally on the topic of estoppel, it is presumably unnecessary to emphasise that a party is entitled to, and should refuse to execute a deed containing incorrect recitals (*Mansfield* v *Childerhouse* (1876) 4 Ch D 82). For there will be in such a case 'a presumption that the parties in entering into a deed have truly set forth the causes which led to its execution; [although] . . . collateral evidence can be adduced to rebut this presumption, provided that it is strong enough to do so' (per Foster J in *Beattie* v *Jenkinson* [1971] 1 WLR 1419, at pp 1424–5). However, there will be no estoppel in relation to incorrect recitals where the deed is illegal or fraudulent, in law or in equity, or where the recitals or other statements are themselves open to rectification (see per Lord Maugham in *Greer* v *Kettle* [1938]

AC 156, at p 171; applied in *Wilson* v *Wilson* [1969] 1 WLR 1470; see also *Allie* v *Katah* [1963] 1 WLR 202, as to the presence of any element of undue influence). Further, if the recital is correct but only so far as it goes, estoppel will not prevent proof of the whole truth: *Lovett* v *Lovett* [1898] 1 Ch 82. Also, in case you can envisage uncertain cases, it has been said that the doctrine of estoppel will not be extended: *General Finance Co* v *Liberator Society* (1878) 10 Ch D 15, per Jessel MR at pp 24–5.

(2) *Notice*—One natural consequence if not purpose of reciting any fact is to give notice thereof to future perusers of the deed with a resultant raising of appropriate requisitions on title which often proves a nuisance (as most recently with the ancient contract recited in *MEPC Ltd* v *Christian-Edwards* [1981] AC 205, HL). In particular, it is necessary to consider the position arising when, in a deed forming part of the title, there appears a recital of a trust, for example, that the vendors, whether past or present, hold the property on trust for one or more other persons. Such a recital will give notice of the trust, but today a purchaser is not bound to see to the destination of the money he pays, provided he pays it to at least two trustees (unless the trustee is a trust corporation), ie, he is not concerned with the beneficial interests: s 27 of the Law of Property Act 1925 (as amended by the Law of Property (Amendment) Act 1926); see also ss 18(1) and 110(2) of the Settled Land Act 1925, and compare *Re Soden and Alexander's Contract* [1918] 2 Ch 258. The result of the above is also that it is not normally necessary or permissible for a purchaser to enquire whether the trustees conveying were duly constituted. Further, it has long been accepted that a purchaser is not affected with notice of matters which he could not have learned without questioning the truth of the recitals or other contents of the documents of title: *Earl of Gainsborough* v *Watcombe Terra Cotta Clay Co Ltd* (1885) 54 LJ Ch 991.

Therefore, the position where a recital of trust appears, is usually as stated by Cozens-Hardy MR in *Re Chafter and Randall's Contract* [1916] 2 Ch 8, at p 18:

> I do not entertain any doubt that a recital that the owner of a legal estate is trustee for *AB* under a will or under a deed affects the purchaser with notice of the contents of the deed or of the will. But that doctrine has no bearing upon a case where there is nothing more than a statement that he holds on trust for *AB*. Such a statement is an admission against interest by the owner of the legal estate.

The practical consequence is that, when recitals are drafted to keep trusts off the title, reference should not be made to the document constituting the trust, but only to the existence of the trust itself (see further p 102).

It may not, of course, be safe to omit all mention of any trust in a conveyance of land. In *Re King* [1931] 2 Ch 294 a conveyance to grantees was expressed to be in consideration of love and affection but in reality the land was to be held on trusts declared by the grantees by a deed poll of the same date. The grantor held the deed poll and the grantees the conveyance. Farwell J held that, as the conveyance misrepresented the grantees to be absolute owners, the beneficiaries, including the grantor, were postponed to certain equitable incumbrances created by the grantees.

The practice should be to recite not too little (see the preceding paragraph) and not too much. If too much is recited a purchaser may well lose any statutory protection he may have. The danger of unnecessary recitals is well illustrated by *Re Duce and Boots Cash Chemists (Southern) Ltd's Contract* [1937] Ch 642, where a recital in an assent contained details of the will which showed that the land was settled within the Settled Land Act 1925, the conveyancing machinery of the Act having clearly not been observed; Bennett J held that the purchaser could not accept the assent as 'sufficient evidence' of its own propriety under s 36(7) of the Administration of Estates Act 1925.

(3) *Construction*—It has already been stated that part of the general purpose of recitals is introductory, to explain the purpose of the deed. From this the question arises, can such explanation affect the effecting of the purpose? The relationship of recitals to the construction of a deed is not really subject to any special rules, as appears sometimes to be suggested, but is governed by the ordinary general rule of construction, which was well stated by Sir John Romilly MR in *Re Strand Music Hall Co Ltd, ex parte European & American Finance Co Ltd* (1865) 35 Beav 153, at p 159, as follows:

> The proper mode of construing any written instrument is to give effect to every part of it, if this be possible, and not to strike out or nullify one clause in a deed, unless it be impossible to reconcile it with another and more express clause in the same deed.

It is true that the three apparently special rules enunciated by Lord Esher MR in the so-called leading case of *Ex parte Dawes, re Moon* (1886) 17 QBD 275, at p 286, are usually treated as the best statement of the law. These three rules were, in effect, as follows: first, if the operative part is ambiguous, clear recitals govern the construction; second, if the recitals are ambiguous, the operative part, being clear, governs; and third, if both the recitals and the operative part are clear but inconsistent, the latter governs. Presumably, if both the recitals and the operative part are ambiguous Lord Esher would have agreed as a fourth rule that Sir John Romilly's statement should be adopted. However, much to be preferred to these three rules is his earlier and simpler statement (as Brett LJ) in *Leggott* v *Barrett* (1880) 15 Ch D 306, at p 311, as follows:

> If there is any doubt about the construction of the governing words of that document, the recital may be looked at in order to determine what is the true construction; but if there is no doubt about the construction, the rights of the parties are governed entirely by the operative part of the writing or the deed.

This statement is in accord with the general rule of construction.

Creating a covenant—Whether or not a covenant is created by the wording of recitals is a question of construction, but that it is possible by law is well established:

> Where words of recital or reference manifested a clear intention that the parties should do certain acts, the courts have from these inferred a covenant to do such acts

(per Lord Denman CJ in *Aspdin* v *Austin* (1844) 5 QB 671, at p 683). For example, it was held in *Mackenzie* v *Childers* (1889) 43 Ch D 265 that a recital that the vendors intended to create restrictive covenants may operate as if it were a formal covenant contained in the operative portion of the deed; and in *Re Weston, Davies* v *Tagart* [1900] 2 Ch 164 a recital in a deed of separation that the husband and wife had agreed to live apart implied a covenant by the wife to live apart. However, in accordance with the general rule of construction given above, recitals cannot create a covenant if there is an express covenant in the operative part: *Dawes* v *Tredwell* (1881) 18 Ch D 354, at p 359.

3 Statutory purposes

As already stated, certain statutory provisions give rise to particular purposes for which recitals should be included in a deed of conveyance in appropriate circumstances. It is proposed to mention only the following four statutory provisions as being the most important, though there are others:

(*a*) *Section 45(6) of the Law of Property Act 1925* provides that recitals contained in deeds twenty years old at the date of the contract are to be sufficient evidence of their own truth until proved inaccurate. This provision is, of course, more of assistance to those presently investigating title than a compelling reason to insert recitals with a view to the fairly distant future. Of the provision, the Law Commission has observed that it:

> owes its origin in 1874 to the fact that, before the 1925 legislation, it was often necessary to investigate facts (such as pedigree) which were not readily ascertainable from the records kept in earlier times. These conditions no longer exist. There is little difficulty in obtaining proof of the facts relevant to investigation of title and there is no obvious justice in providing a statutory presumption (which may be incorrect) as to the accuracy of statements made as recently as twelve years ago. A provision of this kind would not be introduced in modern conditions if it did not already exist: there is much to be said for abolishing it altogether

(*Interim Report on Root of Title to Freehold Land*, 1967, para 44). In fact, instead of abolition, the Land Commission recommended that the provision be left as it is to die of obsolescence in view of the recommended reduction in the period of title. See further and generally p 94.

(*b*) *Section 45(1) of the Law of Property Act 1925* contains certain provisions, in effect, preventing the purchaser from requiring investigation of title prior to the commencement of title under the contract, apart from three specified cases. One of the provisions is that the purchaser is to assume, unless the contrary appears, that recitals contained in abstracted instruments of any document forming part of the prior title are correct and give all the material contents and that every such document was duly executed. Again, this provision is clearly intended to assist vendors in showing title, with the object, as always in the property legislation of 1925, of simplifying conveyancing.

(*c*) *Section 36(6) of the Administration of Estates Act 1925* provides that a statement in writing (eg, a recital) by a personal representative that he has not given or made an assent or conveyance in respect of a legal estate is, in favour of a direct purchaser (but without prejudice to any previous disposition made in favour of another purchaser, direct or indirect), to be sufficient evidence that no such assent or conveyance has been given or made (unless notice thereof had been placed on or annexed to the probate or administration). In the section, 'purchaser' means a purchaser for money or money's worth (s 36(11)), so that a mere voluntary assentee is not only unable to rely on s 36(6) for protection (so that the recital may as well be omitted) but may also be defeated by a subsequent purchaser. Further, s 36(6) proceeds with a fairly remarkable provision to the effect that, where personal representatives first voluntarily assent to the vesting of the legal estate in land (so that they no longer have the legal estate) and later purport to convey that legal estate to a purchaser who accepts the conveyance on the faith of a recital as above mentioned, then the conveyance operates by divesting the voluntary assentee of the legal estate and vesting it in the purchaser.

(*d*) *Section 38 of the Trustee Act 1925* provides in effect that certain recitals as to the reasons for a vacancy in a trust contained in an instrument appointing a new trustee in respect of land are, in favour of a purchaser of a legal estate, to be conclusive evidence of their own truth. See also s 35(3) of the Settled Land Act 1925 which is to much the same effect in respect of settled land. It is to be noted that in these two statutory provisions, unlike the others mentioned above, the evidence is 'conclusive', not just 'sufficient'.

4 Registered land

The official Land Registry view apparently is that in registered conveyancing recitals are out. Thus in his useful little book, *Land Registration Forms*, a former Chief Land Registrar (Mr Theodore B F Ruoff) laid down certain rules as to 'Unsuitable Instruments' including the following:

> For the same reason [ie because otherwise the resultant instrument may turn out to be what the Rules call "improper in form and in substance"] the draftsman will do well to eschew the use of recitals. Those dealing with the past history of title are forbidden (because the register shows the current position) and those dealing with present intentions are unnecessary

(2nd ed, p 2; see also Land Registration Rules 1925, r 78, and r 96, as to the necessity of deeds off the register by reason, inter alia, of lengthy recitals).

This view is thought to represent too absolute a bar. Of the two general purposes of recitals (dealt with in the first part of this section), narrative and introductory, the inclusion of either may on occasion be desirable. Thus, although narrative recitals are generally unnecessary because the history of the title since registration appears sufficiently from the register, such a recital would, for example, be useful and is usual where a personal representative or purchaser who has not been registered as proprietor transfers land (ie, under s 37(1) of the Land Registration Act 1925). Again, introductory recitals are not usually included in the interests of simplicity, but they might well be useful, for example, where only part of the land comprised on a title is being transferred. Another particular example where recitals might well be called for in a number of transfers of registered land would be in order to demonstrate the existence of a building scheme (see S Robinson at (1974) 38 Conv (NS) 107–9).

Further, as regards the so-called incidental purposes of recitals and the statutory purposes of recitals (both considered above), it is thought that recitals in Land Registry transfers could in appropriate circumstances serve the same purpose as in unregistered conveyancing and that it might therefore sometimes prove useful to include them.

F PREMISES

Hitherto what are usually regarded as the *non*-operative parts of a deed have been considered, namely, the commencement, the date, the parties and the recitals, all of which, as has been shown, are in fact operative at least to some extent. After these naturally comes the operative part, introduced familiarly with the words of the testatum: 'NOW THIS DEED WITNESSETH . . .' The apparently impartial word 'deed' is appropriate here: the description in the Commencement (p 232) should indicate the operation of the document; that in the testatum should indicate the nature of the document (and see the statutory forms in Law of Property Act 1925, Sched 5). In registered conveyancing, apart from the heading and date, the prescribed form of transfer (see Form 19 in the Schedule to the Land Registration Rules 1925) contains nothing but the operative part.

Strictly speaking, the premises are all the operative part of a deed coming before the habendum ('TO HOLD . . .'), including the implied covenants for title ('As beneficial owner'), the operative words ('HEREBY CONVEYS . . .') and the parcels ('ALL THAT . . .'). Thus Coke said (Co Litt 6a):

> The office of the premises of the deed is twofold: first, rightly to name the feoffor and feoffee; and secondly to comprehend the certainty of the lands or tenements to be conveyed by the feoffment.

A slightly different explanation, although to similar effect, was given by Lord Goddard in *Gardiner* v *Sevenoaks Rural District Council* [1950] 2 All ER 84, at p 85):

> "Premises" is, no doubt, a word which is capable of many meanings. How it originally became applied to property is, I think, generally known. It was from the habit of |conveyancers| when they were drawing deeds of conveyance referring to property and speaking of "parcels". They set out the parcels in the early part of the deed, and later they would refer to "the said premises", meaning strictly that which had gone before, and gradually by common acceptance "premises" became applied, as it generally is now, to houses, land shops, or whatever it may be, so that the word has come to mean generally real property of one sort or another.

Compare Lord Wilberforce's view that 'premises' is a word strictly of 'conveyancing jargon' which has passed into the 'quasi-legal vernacular' as referring to property 'but not with any precise connotation' (in *Maunsell* v *Olins* [1975] AC 373, at p 386).

Be that as it may, the word 'premises' is in this book used in relation to deeds of conveyance to indicate the part coming immediately before the operative words and after the recitals, and containing, apart from the testatum, only the statement of the consideration and the receipt clause, both of which are extremely important and well worth discussion.

1 Consideration

The first point to remember on consideration is that it is not essential to a deed: a legal estate may be passed and any covenant contained in a deed enforced at law even though the transaction is entirely voluntary (*Pratt* v *Barker* (1828) 1 Sim 1). However, this does *not* mean that a gratuitous or voluntary deed can always be accepted without question. In appropriate circumstances, a voluntary deed may suffer from any one of a number of consequences which not infrequently in practice constitute serious defects. By way of illustration the following points may be mentioned.

(1) *Root of title*—A voluntary conveyance less than fifteen years old will only be a good root of title if its nature is fully stated in the contract for sale: see p 101 et seq.

(2) *Covenants for title*—The covenants for title implied by s 76(1)(A) and (B) of the Law of Property Act 1925 on the part of a person who conveys and is expressed to convey as beneficial owner are only implied in a conveyance for valuable consideration. Again a covenantor under s 76(1)(A) is only liable for the acts and omissions of those through whom he claims otherwise than for value. Also the covenants implied in conveyances subject to rents by s 77 of the Law of Property Act 1925 are only implied where there is valuable consideration unless there is an express reference to the section (s 77(4)).

(3) *'Purchaser'*—The 1925 property legislation contains a vast number of provisions relating to and generally protecting a 'purchaser'. The ordinary meaning of 'purchaser' is simply one who acquires title to land by a lawful act (eg, conveyance, gift, or devise), rather than by a wrong (eg, disseisin), or by operation of law (eg, descent, dower, curtesy, inclosure, or partition). In other words, payment of a price is not a necessity. However, the definitions of 'purchaser' in the Law of Property Act 1925 (s 205(1)(xxi)), the Land Registration Act 1925 (s 3(xxi)), the Administration of Estates Act 1925 (s 55(1)(xviii)), and the Land Charges Act 1972 (s 17(1)), all have 'valuable consideration' as an essential element. In the

Settled Land Act 1925 (s 117(1)(xxi)), 'value' rather than 'valuable consideration' is made part of the definition of 'purchaser', but without, it is thought, any difference in meaning. The Trustee Act 1925 contains no definition of 'purchaser', although in s 17 thereof, by which the Act affords protection to purchasers and mortgagees dealing with trustees, a payment or advance of money is a requisite (compare ss 13, 27(2)(a) and (b) and 38 of the same Act, where the word 'purchaser' is used without any such requisite).

It is to be observed that s 17 of the Trustee Act 1925 refers to 'money'. In the definitions of 'purchaser' in the Law of Property Act 1925 (s 205(1)(xxi)) and the Administration of Estates Act 1925 (s 55(1)(xviii)), it is stated that 'valuable consideration' includes marriage but does not include 'a nominal consideration in money'; in the Land Registration Act 1925, 'valuable consideration' is separately defined in the same way (s 3(xxxi)). It will be appreciated that 'marriage' means future marriage: *Attorney General* v *Jacobs Smith* [1895] 2 QB 341. Also, it is well known that a reference to 'money or money's worth' (as in Pt I of the Law of Property Act 1925 and s 157(2) of the same Act, and s 4(6) of the Land Charges Act 1972) excludes marriage, though it apparently includes an existing debt: *Thorndike* v *Hunt* (1859) 3 De G & J 563. Although the Land Charges Act 1972, s 4(6) thus excludes marriage, it does not conversely include a nominal consideration: *Midland Bank Trust Co Ltd* v *Green* [1981] AC 513. Accordingly Lord Wilberforce proceeded:

> This conclusion makes it unnecessary to determine whether £500 is a nominal sum of money or not. But I must say that for my part I should have great difficulty in so holding. "Nominal consideration" and a "nominal sum" in the law appear to me, as terms of art, to refer to a sum or consideration which can be mentioned as consideration but is not necessarily paid. To equate "nominal" with "inadequate" or even "grossly inadequate" would embark the law upon inquiries which I cannot think were contemplated by Parliament

(ibid, p 532).

Aside altogether from statutory provisions, equity's notorious darling, the *bona fide* purchaser *for value* without notice, must be mentioned. If such a person obtains a legal estate it is clear beyond doubt that he has priority over all comers (*Pilcher* v *Rawlins* (1872) 7 Ch App 259); not so a volunteer (*Re Nisbet and Potts' Contract* [1906] 1 Ch 386).

(4) *Sale by tenant for life*—Consideration is vital to one or two transactions which will be ineffective if it is lacking. Thus a conveyance by a tenant for life under a strict settlement of land must normally be 'made for the best consideration in money that can reasonably be obtained' (s 39(1) of the Settled Land Act 1925), and as he is a trustee (s 107(1)), he cannot solve his problem of obtaining the stipulated best selling price by selling at a valuation: *Re Earl of Wilton's Settled Estates* [1907] 1 Ch 50 (except as to timber and fixtures under s 49(2) of the Settled Land Act 1925). However, strangely contradictory to s 39(1), a purchaser from such a tenant for life has no similar problem since he is to be 'conclusively taken to have given the best price, consideration or rent, as the case may require, that could reasonably be obtained by the tenant for life' (s 110(1) of the Settled Land Act 1925; see further *Re Morgan's Lease* [1972] Ch 1).

(5) *Avoidance of voluntary dispositions*—There are some very well-known statutory provisions which, speaking broadly, may operate to upset a voluntary conveyance or settlement. These provisions, as they affect links in the chain of title, have been sufficiently discussed ante, p 106.

(6) *Specific performance*—The equitable remedy of specific performance, being

discretionary, is not available on breach of voluntary agreement, even though it is contained in a deed: *Jefferys* v *Jefferys* (1841) Cr & Ph 138.

(7) *Resulting trust*—It is possible that in the absence of consideration a resulting trust will arise. Since the repeal of the Statute of Uses 1535 (by s 207 of, and Sched 7 to, the Law of Property Act 1925), a legal estate of land can be conveyed by a voluntary conveyance without a statement that the land is both conveyed 'unto and to the use of' the grantee, ie, no resulting *use* of the legal estate in favour of the grantor can now be implied and immediately executed by operation of law. Whether or not a resulting *trust* in equity for the grantor would have been implied by a voluntary grant before 1926 was, oddly enough, never settled and there was much conflict of opinion. However, s 60(3) of the Law of Property Act 1925 now provides:

> In a voluntary conveyance a resulting trust for the grantor shall not be implied merely by reason that the property is not expressed to be conveyed for the use or benefit of the grantee.

Therefore, prima facie, a voluntary grant 'to *AB*' simpliciter will not imply a resulting trust. However, the subsection does contain the words 'merely by reason that'—ie, a resulting trust may be implied in a voluntary grant because of other circumstances, eg undue influence (and see *Hodgson* v *Marks* [1971] Ch 892, CA). Further, it appears that if the subject-matter of a voluntary grant is pure personalty, there will be a presumption that a resulting trust is intended (*Re Vinogradoff, Allen* v *Jackson* [1935] WN 68), although this may be rebutted, eg, by a presumption of advancement.

(a)   Extrinsic evidence of consideration

For all the reasons mentioned it is essential when investigating title (or perusing deeds for any other purpose) to note whether or not any of the deeds are voluntary. However, it may be that a deed which contains no statement of consideration was nonetheless made for some consideration. A fine of £10 is imposed by s 5 of the Stamp Act 1891 for executing *or preparing* a document which does not set out all the facts and circumstances affecting liability to stamp duty with intent to defraud Her Majesty. This liability will not, of course, arise if, as is often the case, the necessary information is given separately, since there is then no intent to defraud.

If objection is taken to an apparently voluntary deed, extrinsic evidence is normally admissible to show that in fact it was made for valuable consideration: see per Cozens-Hardy LJ in *Re Holland, Gregg* v *Holland* [1902] 2 Ch 360, at p 388. As a contrast, however, if some consideration is stated in the deed it may not be permissible to show that the consideration was wrongly stated. In the early case of *Peacock* v *Monk* (1748) 1 Ves Sen 127, Lord Hardwicke stated (at p 128) that, in a deed:

> where any consideration is mentioned as of love and affection only, if it is not said also "and for other considerations", you cannot enter into proof of any other: the reason is because it would be contrary to the deed.

Nearly a century later, this view seemed to be qualified:

> The rule is that, where there is one consideration stated in the deed, you may prove any other consideration which existed not in contradiction to the instrument, and it is not in contradiction to the instrument to prove a larger consideration than that which is stated

(per Knight-Bruce V-C in *Clifford* v *Turrell* (1845) 1 Y & CCC 138, at p 149 (affirmed (1845) 14 LJ Ch 390)).

Another century or so passed and in *Turner* v *Forwood* [1951] 1 All ER 746 the position was confused rather than clarified by the Court of Appeal. In that case evidence was, in fact, admitted to show that the true consideration for a deed was £1,215, although the consideration stated was only 10s (ie 50p). In reaching this decision, Lord Goddard CJ followed *Clifford* v *Turrell*, ante; Singleton LJ pointed out that the recitals to the deed made it clear that the whole arrangement between the parties was not set forth in the deed; and Denning LJ allowed proof of the contractual consideration because an obviously nominal consideration was inserted. Then after a mere quarter of a century, Graham J observed: 'I do not see why, when the parties have chosen to express a transfer as being for a nominal consideration, the court should seek to hold that the consideration was in fact otherwise than as agreed and stated', before proceeding on the assumption that there was valuable consideration (*Peffer* v *Rigg* [1977] 1 WLR 285 at p 293). Where does this leave us? In the writer's opinion, the general rule laid down in *Clifford* v *Turrell*, ante, and followed by Lord Goddard CJ should be followed (see also per Evershed MR in *Woods* v *Wise* [1955] 2 QB 29, at pp 39–40).

Assuming that the rule really is that *additional* consideration may be shown provided there is no contradiction in terms of the deed, it is somewhat odd that the converse is not necessarily so. The rule appears to be that, if the valuable consideration stated in a deed is displaced by evidence, the deed cannot then be supported on the ground of natural love and affection: see per Lord Redesdale in *Willan* v *Willan* (1814) 2 Dow 274, at p 282 (giving the reason that 'if it could, every agreement with a relation must be supported, however inadequate the consideration'). This rule may be thought meaningless since, as stated earlier, a deed normally requires no consideration and, when it does, natural love and affection are insufficient (*Hughes* v *Seanor* (1869) 18 WR 108). However, the rule may perhaps be given some meaning by the suggestion that a total failure of the consideration stated in the deed, being the consideration on which the deed was founded, might afford a good defence to an action on any contract contained in the deed: *Bunn* v *Guy* (1803) 4 East 190; *Rose* v *Poulton* (1831) 2 B & Ad 822 (but compare *May* v *Tyre* (1677) Free KB 447). Thus, more recently, in *Triggs* v *Staines UDC* [1969] 1 Ch 10, an option to purchase land had been granted by Mr Triggs to a local authority expressly in consideration of an ultra vires covenant; in the course of his judgment Cross J referred to the argument of counsel that:

> Mr Triggs granted the option by a document under seal which itself imports consideration. That, of course, is true and, had no other consideration been expressed, the grant might have been enforceable by reason of the seal. But I cannot think that the fact that the grant of the option was by deed can save it when all the expressed consideration is void

(ibid, p 19, following cases concerning a wife's covenant not to apply for maintenance). This last must be distinguished from a case where a deed is made for a stated consideration which is partly valid and partly a nullity, the deed then being nonetheless enforceable (*Newman* v *Newman* (1815) 4 M & S 66), although the enforceability may perhaps be subject to the gloss introduced by Cross J in *Triggs* v *Staines UDC*, ante, that the void part of the consideration should be subordinate to the valid part which might on its own have sufficed for a reasonable man.

(b) *Registered conveyancing and consideration*

The prescribed forms of transfer of land set out in the Schedule to the Land Registration Rules 1925 are with a few exceptions based on Form 19, which requires the consideration to be stated, since it commences: 'In consideration of ——pounds (£   ) . . .' There is no alternative form for a voluntary transfer. This being so, it is sometimes suggested, in practice and elsewhere, that when the transfer is voluntary a fictitious consideration should be stated. This suggestion is, on the general principles given above, thought to be undesirable. It is preferable to adapt the prescribed form of transfer, for example, on the lines either of the forms (Forms 21, 22 and 23) of transfer to a tenant for life or statutory owners under the Settled Land Act 1925 (which commence 'Pursuant to a trust deed of even date herewith, made between, etc'), or else of the form (Form 36) of a transfer of land for charitable uses (which simply omits any statement of consideration). Consider also Precedent No 34, on p 80 of Ruoff, *Land Registration Forms* (2nd ed), which commences 'In consideration of my natural love and affection for . . .' (surely one of the familiar yet unnecessary phrases of unregistered conveyancing which we are to try to disregard; see ibid, p 2).

A final point on consideration to notice in connection with registered conveyancing is the position of volunteers. A disposition made without valuable consideration is subject *so far as the transferee is concerned* not only to the entries on the register and overriding interests but also to minor interests (ss 20(4) and 23(5) of the Land Registration Act 1925). Apart from this, when registered, such a disposition has *in all respects* the same effect as if it had been made for valuable consideration (ibid). The apparent result of these strong provisions is that in registered conveyancing a purchaser need never ascertain whether his vendor was a transferee for valuable consideration or a volunteer. This is a great contrast with the position in unregistered conveyancing.

2   Receipt

After the statement in the premises of a deed of conveyance of the amount of the consideration and of who paid it to whom, one usually finds the receipt clause, appearing in brackets, in some such words as 'the receipt whereof is hereby acknowledged'. There are three main reasons for the inclusion in a deed of a receipt clause, which are contained in ss 67–9 of the Law of Property Act 1925.

(1) *Sufficient discharge*—The first reason, which applies as between the parties to the deed, is that, by virtue of s 67 of the Law of Property Act 1925, which applies to deeds executed after 1881:

A receipt for consideration money or securities in the body of a deed shall be a sufficient discharge for the same to the person paying or delivering the same, without any further receipt for the same being endorsed on the deed.

Prior to the Conveyancing Act 1881 it was the practice to endorse such a receipt on documents, and this should still be the practice today whenever the document in question is not a *deed*. It will be noted that the receipt clause is only a 'sufficient discharge' (cf *Re Duce and Boots Cash Chemists (Southern) Ltd's Contract* [1937] Ch 642 as to the meaning of 'sufficient evidence' in s 36(7) of the Administration of Estates Act 1925; 'sufficient' does not mean 'conclusive').

Further, the old common law rule was that a receipt clause was, with minor exceptions, conclusive that the money had been paid (cf *Deverell* v *Whitmarsh* (1841) 5 Jur 963). However, this was never the rule in equity, which always permitted proof of non-payment (*Wilson* v *Keating* (1859) 27 Beav 121), and the equitable rule now prevails in any case over the old common law rule by virtue of s 25(11) of the Supreme Court of Judicature Act 1873 (re-enacted by, now, s 49(1) of the Supreme Court Act 1981). Nor, needless to say, will a receipt clause ever be conclusive for such other purpose as taxation disputes (see per Lord Thankerton in *Harrison* v *John Cronk & Sons Ltd* [1937] AC 185, at pp 192–3).

(2) *Subsequent purchaser*—The second reason for inclusion of a receipt clause in a

deed is said to be to protect subsequent purchasers, but it will be shown that most often a receipt clause will, in fact, be irrelevant to such protection. On the one hand, as between the parties to a conveyance on sale, the inclusion of a receipt clause does not prevent the fact of non-payment being set up. On the other hand, however, as against a subsequent purchaser the position is essentially different.

Until the purchase money is paid and from the making of a binding contract of sale (see *Re Birmingham, Savage* v *Stannard* [1959] Ch 523), the vendor has a lien on the property (realty or personalty; *Re Stucley* [1906] 1 Ch 67), ie, the notorious unpaid vendor's lien. This lien is not, it will be appreciated, excluded from arising as between the parties simply by the inclusion of a receipt clause (see *Mackreth* v *Symmons* (1808) 15 Ves 329). The risk then which a subsequent purchaser runs, if the original purchaser has not yet paid up, is the possibility of taking the property subject to the original unpaid vendor's lien. As far as a subsequent volunteer is concerned, of course, the risk is not a possibility but a certainty: *Ex parte Hanson* (1806) 12 Ves 346.

In accordance no doubt with the policy of the 1925 property legislation of protecting purchasers, s 68 of the Law of Property Act 1925 (applying to deeds executed after 1881) provides that:

> A receipt for consideration money or other consideration in the body of a deed or endorsed thereon, shall in favour of a subsequent purchaser, not having notice that the money or other consideration thereby acknowledged to be received was not in fact paid or given, wholly or in part, be sufficient evidence of the payment or giving of the whole amount thereof.

The impression might well be gained from a first reading of this section that a purchaser (as widely defined in s 205(1)(xxi) of the Act) will be free from the risk of any unpaid vendor's lien provided both that he in fact relies on the receipt clause and that he bears in mind that 'sufficient' is not conclusive evidence.

Such a purchaser, what is more, need not necessarily have seen the original deed containing the receipt clause: it seems to suffice for s 68 if he has seen an accurate copy (whether photographed or typed) or even record of the deed containing the receipt (see *London and Cheshire Insurance Co Ltd* v *Laplagrene Property Co Ltd* [1971] Ch 499). Unhappily however first impressions cannot always be trusted and this particular one will usually be shown up as false in the light of conveyancing practice.

Since 1925, at any rate, a purchaser's freedom from the risk of an unpaid vendor's lien in respect of *land* rests not on the presence or absence of a receipt clause but on the modern doctrine of notice. There are only two possible situations: either the original unpaid vendor has, as one would somehow expect, retained the title deeds pending payment, or he has parted with them.

In the former situation, a subsequent purchaser will be put on enquiry and so have a constructive notice of the original vendor's rights, ie, his unpaid vendor's lien (*Spencer* v *Clarke* (1878) 47 LJ Ch 692). The original vendor's rights, arising out of possession of the title deeds, are expressly not prejudicially affected by the Law of Property Act 1925 (s 13). In addition to this, not only is a purchaser within s 68 required by definition (s 205(1)(xxi)) to be 'in good faith', but the section only protects a purchaser 'not having notice . . .', and 'notice' by definition (s 205(1)(xviii)) includes constructive notice (and see also s 199(1)(ii) of the same Act). Since the lien is protected by possession of the title deeds it is not capable of registration under the Land Charges Act 1972 (s 2(4), Class C(iii)), and so does not come within s 199(1)(i) of the Law of Property Act 1925. Therefore, if an unpaid vendor retains the title deeds, a subsequent purchaser will take subject to the lien whether or not he relies on any receipt clause.

In the latter situation, where an unpaid vendor parts with the title deeds, the position depends on the post-1925 substitute for notice, namely, registration. An unpaid vendor's lien is usually accepted as within the meaning of 'a general equitable charge' in the Land Charges Act 1972 (s 2(4), Class C(iii)). Thus if the lien is neither 'secured by a deposit of documents' nor registered under the Land Charges Act 1972 it will be void against a subsequent purchaser for valuable consideration (not necessarily in money or money's worth) of any interest in the land (s 4(5); and see also s 199(1)(i) of the Law of Property Act 1925).

Again the risk of a subsequent purchaser taking subject to an unpaid vendor's lien is decided quite independently of reliance on a receipt clause. The conclusion is that the purported protection provided by s 68 of the Law of Property Act 1925 (ie, where there is a reliance on a receipt clause) will in the normal conveyancing case of a purchase of an interest in land prove either illusory or redundant.

(3) *Payment to solicitor*—The third reason for inclusion of a receipt clause is that, by virtue of s 69 of the Law of Property Act 1925 (applying whenever the consideration was paid or given):

> Where a solicitor produces a deed, having in the body thereof or endorsed thereon a receipt for consideration money or other consideration, the deed being executed, or the endorsed receipt being signed, by the person entitled to give a receipt for that consideration, the deed shall be a sufficient authority to the person liable to pay or give the same for his paying or giving the same to the solicitor, without the solicitor producing any separate or other direction or authority in that behalf from the person who executed or signed the deed or receipt.

Much reliance is, of course, placed in practice upon the authority of this section. However, it may come as a surprise to some practitioners to learn that a great deal of this reliance is misplaced. The section applies 'where a *solicitor* produces a deed,' etc. It apparently does not apply where a managing clerk does the producing (*The Law Society's Digest*, Opinion No 163), but has anyone ever refused to pay completion money to a managing clerk or legal executive (never mind to an articled clerk, secretary or office boy) in the absence of a separate authority, or even enquired whether or not they were paying a solicitor? Further, it is not just any solicitor who is within the section, but only that solicitor who is acting for the person giving the receipt (*Re Hetling and Merton's Contract* [1893] 3 Ch 269), and this does not, apparently, include the London agent of that solicitor (*Law Society's Digest*, Opinion No 164). If the Council of The Law Society are to be believed, as no doubt they are, the section could in practice prove to be a broken reed.

Also the section requires production of a *deed*, so that if the document in question is not under a seal, a separate authority to receive payment will be required. Since a conveyance of a legal estate in land must generally be made by deed (s 52(1) of the Law of Property Act 1925). This point will rarely upset conveyancing practice. However, it should be borne in mind and there are seven exceptions (see s 52(2) of the same Act) to the requirement of a deed. If advantage is taken of one of these exceptions (eg, reconveyance of mortgage by endorsed receipt under s 115 of the Law of Property Act 1925), then it follows that advantage cannot also be taken of s 69 of the Law of Property Act 1925. The position is the same where interests in land, other than a legal estate, are conveyed by signed writing (see s 53 of the Law of Property Act 1925).

Three final points on s 69 of the Law of Property Act 1925 may be mentioned. First, in accordance with practice, payment under the section should be tendered in cash or by banker's draft, not by cheque (see p 200). Second, again the word 'sufficient' is used, here as to authority; see the comments above on 'sufficient discharge' in s 67 of the Law of Property Act 1925. And third, the solicitor must actually *produce* the deed; ability to produce it is not equivalent to production: *Day v Woolwich Equitable Building Society* (1888) 40 Ch D 491. However, if all the conditions are satisfied s 69 can provide potent protection (see, eg, *King v Smith* [1900] 2 Ch 425).

(4) *Form*—In order to come within any of the three sections discussed above, although no particular form of words need be used, there must be an express acknowledgment of receipt of the consideration. It would be insufficient for this purpose merely to state that the consideration had been paid (*Renner v Tolley* (1893) 68 LT 815). However, a mere statement of payment will probably be sufficient to raise an estoppel against the vendor (see per Farwell J in *Rimmer v Webster* [1902] 2 Ch 163, at p 173), so that a subsequent purchaser may thereby receive a similar protection to that which s 68 of the Law of Property Act 1925 purports to provide.

The meticulously vigilant reader will have noticed that, of the three sections of the Law of Property Act 1925 discussed, only s 69 actually stipulates that the deed must be executed by the person entitled to give the receipt. Presumably for the other two sections to apply, the person who should receive the consideration must at least be a party to the deed. A discussion of who, in accordance with this, has power to give a receipt in any particular case is not within the scope of this book. It may be mentioned in passing that, in the case of capital money arising under a disposition on trust for sale of land or under the Settled Land Act 1925, the receipt must be given by at least two trustees, a trust corporation, or a personal representative. All these latter can (by virtue of s 23(3) of the Trustee Act 1925) make use of the provisions of s 69 of the Law of Property Act 1925.

(5) *Receipts in registered conveyancing*—The prescribed form of transfer of land (Form 19 in the Schedule to the Land Registration Rules 1925) contains no receipt clause. Since such a transfer is a deed, the inclusion of a receipt clause could theoretically bring any of ss 67–9 of the Law of Property Act 1925 into play. Accordingly, for the like reasons which apply in unregistered conveyancing, it may be useful to include a receipt clause, and in fact the published forms of transfer do include the words 'the receipt whereof is hereby acknowledged' (in italics often for easy deletion). However, there happens to be authority which suggests that such inclusion may be superfluous in all cases and pointless in most cases.

In question in *Rimmer v Webster* [1902] 2 Ch 163 was a statutory form of transfer of mortgage (from the Schedule to the Commissioners Clauses Act 1847) which, like Form 19, commenced 'In consideration of £——' and contained no receipt clause. Farwell J held (at pp 173–4) that such a transfer, simply by virtue of the statement of consideration, would bring into play the predecessor of s 68 of the Law of Property Act 1925 (ie, s 55 of the Conveyancing Act 1881), on the ground that this was presumably what the statute intended. The same reasoning applies equally to ss 67 and 69. Nevertheless, safety first probably should prevail in practice over superfluity to demand continued inclusion of a receipt clause.

Against this, it is clear that s 68 of the Law of Property Act 1925 will only operate where a purchaser has relied on the receipt clause which involves at least seeing the deed containing it or an accurate copy or record of that deed (*London and Cheshire Insurance Co Ltd v Laplagrene Property Co Ltd* [1971] Ch 499). But it simply is not the practice for a purchaser to investigate the instruments of transfer (containing any receipt clauses) to his vendor and to previous proprietors; such an investigation would offend the principles of registration of title. True, there may be a statement of 'the price paid' entered on the register itself (ie, under the Land Registration Rules

1925, r 247, as amended in 1976, 'if the proprietor so requests') and a purchaser should eventually see a copy of this. Unfortunately this statement has been held not to amount to a receipt clause but rather merely to indicate the amount payable (*London and Cheshire Insurance Co Ltd* v *Laplagrene Property Co Ltd* [1971] Ch 499, see especially at p 511, where Brightman J derived support for his view that 'price paid' here means 'cost price' from the absence of any receipt clause in Form 19). Accordingly, despite the potential applicability of s 68 in registered conveyancing, it seems that a purchaser of registered property would rarely if ever be able to surmount the first hurdle of showing reliance on a receipt clause.

Bad luck, but never mind, s 68 of the Law of Property Act 1925 is no loss: it beats just as much air here as in unregistered conveyancing. To be of any concern to subsequent purchasers, the unpaid vendor's lien requires protection by deposit of the land certificate or by notice on the register as well (see s 66 of the Land Registration Act 1925 and r 239 of the Land Registration Rules 1925), or even as an overriding interest if the vendor remained in occupation (ie, within s 70(1)(*g*) of Land Registration Act 1925; as in *London and Cheshire Insurance Co Ltd* v *Laplagrene Property Co Ltd* [1971] Ch 499). Reliance on any receipt clause is still entirely neither here nor there.

G   COVENANTS FOR TITLE

The covenants about to be discussed constitute in the writer's opinion not only an unsatisfactory part of a deed of conveyance but by far the most unnecessarily complex part. After the words of the receipt clause, the operative part of a conveyance customarily continues with the words 'the vendor as beneficial owner hereby conveys unto the purchaser'. It is proposed to deal with the significance of the words of grant (ie, 'hereby conveys') later. In the present section will be discussed the purpose and effect of the short expression of the vendor's capacity.

This is an example of legal shorthand, by means of incorporation by reference: the insertion of the three little words 'as beneficial owner' may imply into a conveyance covenants for title containing over 500 words. The implication now takes place by virtue of s 76(1) of the Law of Property Act 1925, and under this subsection certain alternative covenants for title may be implied by the expression of other capacities of the person conveying, namely, 'as settlor', 'trustee', 'mortgagee', 'as personal representative', 'as committee', 'as receiver', or 'under an order of court'. Section 76(1) itself refers to Sched 2 (Pts I to VI) to the Act for the terms of the covenants to be implied.

Although the fact of covenants for title being implied into conveyances by the use of certain appropriate expressions is surely familiar to most if not all conveyancing practitioners, experience suggests that the precise effect of such implication is not equally familiar. Apart altogether from the parties' desire for speed, conveyancing pays the more, the quicker the turnover. It must, therefore, be the rare conveyancer who, for example, pauses over the reflex action of filling in the blank in Special Condition D of The Law Society's Conditions of Sale, 1980 ed, which reads that: 'The vendor shall convey as . . .' The immediate practical consequence of this action is that later the vendor will be expressed in the conveyance itself to convey as stated in that Special Condition and almost never will any further question arise. However, the covenants for title will be thereby incorporated and will be available in case of need, that is if some defect in title turns out to have been overlooked, to protect the purchaser by imposing liability on the vendor. The contract for sale itself will no longer afford any protection after completion since, as to matters within the scope of the covenants for title, the intention certainly will be for there to be merger in the conveyance (see p 201). Equally the investigation of title by or on behalf of the purchaser cannot be relied on as necessarily revealing all defects in the vendor's title. Apart from the general acceptance of uncertainty as reasonably inherent in the complexities of land law (see p 5), there are such particular points as the prohibition of searching requisitions (p 117) and the problem of proving negatives (p 125). The covenants for title purport to provide a protection which is the logical corollary to these limitations. As Russell LJ put it: 'Conveyancing is conducted generally on a basis of good faith with something of a long stop in the shape of covenants for title' (in *Hodgson* v *Marks* [1971] Ch 892, at p 932).

Accordingly, in a client's and perhaps one's own interests, it might be desirable to pause over the Special Condition for at least a moment to consider, on the one side, whether sufficient protection is provided for a purchaser and, on the other side, whether too great a liability is imposed on the vendor. Indeed, it may be asserted with some confidence that not infrequently the protection will be found illusory or the liability unexpectedly extensive. A solicitor's own interests will not directly turn on this consideration, since by s 182(1) of the Law of Property Act 1925 the covenants implied under that Act in any instrument are to be deemed proper and a solicitor is not to be liable for failure in good faith to negative them. Nonetheless, this subsection does not provide compulsory blinkers: on the one hand, it remains sloppy practice to allow words in a deed of conveyance without fully appreciating their effect; on the other hand, lack of any action under the covenants for title could produce instead an action for professional negligence (see p 275).

It was early customary to express in a deed of conveyance a warranty or covenant for title, to provide a purchaser with contractual protection against a defect in title subsequently appearing. The practice, unfortunately, was for elaborate covenants for title to be set out at great length (in the interest of profit costs, which then depended upon the length of the document prepared), and well before the nineteenth century standard forms had become settled. Then, with the object of shortening conveyances and thereby simplifying conveyancing, it was provided by s 7 of the Conveyancing Act 1881 that the use of certain short expressions should, in effect, save the trouble until then expended in fully setting out the covenants. This trouble was saved because the use of the appropriate expression simply incorporated into the conveyance covenants for title in the settled standard forms. Section 7 of the Act of 1881 has now been replaced (with slight amendments) by s 76 of the Law of Property Act 1925, and the result is that we, in the twentieth century, still look to the nineteenth century standard forms of covenants now set out in Sched 2 to the latter Act. Therefore, not only are the implied covenants for title couched in 'extremely difficult words' (per Harman J in *Pilkington* v *Wood* [1953] Ch 770, at p 777), but very many old cases decided on express covenants are applicable (for an extremely interesting account of the growth of statutory implied covenants for title, see MJ Russell (1962) 26 Conv (NS) 45).

Before proceeding to give further and better particulars, it should be generally noted that s 76 of the Law of Property Act 1925 does not confine its operation to conveyances of land nor anywhere to deeds (though this latter seems to be assumed), but does restrict the wide definition of the word 'conveyance' (in s 205(1)(ii)) by never including a lease at a rent (s 76(5)), sometimes excluding a mortgage (s 76(1)(A) and (B)), and only including assents since 1925 (s 76(8); see also s 36(3) of the Administration of Estates Act 1925). In addition, reference may be made to *Curragh Investments Ltd* v *Cook* [1974] 1 WLR 1559, where it was contended unsuccessfully that non-compliance by a foreign company with certain provisions of the Companies Act 1948 rendered the covenants for title illegal or unenforceable, and to *Butler* v *Broadhead* [1975] Ch 97, where the equitable remedy of tracing was sought, again unsuccessfully, in respect of breach of the covenants for title. See a note in (1975) 39 Conv (NS) 4, 5.

1 'As beneficial owner'

The most convenient order in which to discuss the covenants for title is to take in turn those implied by each of the specified expressions of capacity, starting with the expression 'as beneficial owner', since this implies the maximum number of covenants. Incidentally, in passing, it may be recalled that use of the expression 'as beneficial owner' can now serve the additional purpose of bringing into play the Law of Property (Joint Tenants) Act 1964 (see s 1(1)).

By virtue of para (A) of s 76(1) of the Law of Property Act 1925 there is deemed to be included in a conveyance for valuable consideration (other than a mortgage) 'a covenant [sic] by a person who conveys and is expressed to convey as beneficial owner.' The terms of this covenant are set out at obscure length in Pt 1 of Sched 2 to the Act and for the purposes of comprehension may be sorted out, in essence, into the following four covenants:

(1) That the grantor has (with the concurrence of any person conveying by his direction) full power to convey the subject-matter as expressed.

(2) That such subject-matter shall be quietly enjoyed by the grantee without any lawful disturbance.

(3) That such subject-matter shall be received by the grantee freed from or indemnified against all incumbrances.

(4) That the grantor will do anything reasonably requested in order further or more perfectly to assure (or convey) such subject-matter to the grantee.

Leasehold property—If the conveyance happens to be an assignment of leasehold property (but is otherwise the same as before), then by para (B) of s 76(1), a further covenant is implied in the terms of Pt II of Sched 2 to the Act, which again may be resolved, in essence, into the following two covenants:

(5) That the lease is valid and subsisting.

(6) That the rent reserved by and the covenants contained in the lease have been paid, observed and performed.

These further covenants are necessary on account both of the usual restrictions on the investigation of title to leaseholds (see s 44(2), (3), (4) and (11) of the Law of Property Act 1925), and of the usual assumptions following from production of the receipt for the last payment due for rent (see s 45(2), (3) and (10) of the Law of Property Act 1925). See further p 131. Note also the mutual covenants implied by s 77 of the Law of Property Act 1925 and s 24 of the Land Registration Act 1925 (see r 109 of the Land Registration Rules 1925), in conveyances and transfers of land subject to rents.

It will be appreciated that the six covenants for title are given by virtue of s 76 only by the assignor on the sale of an existing lease, and not by the lessor on the grant of a new lease unless in consideration only of a premium (see ss 76(5) and 205(1)(xxiii) of the Law of Property Act 1925). However, it will also be appreciated that the relationship of lessor and lessee at common law automatically implies on the part of the former a covenant for quiet enjoyment (see an article by MJ Russell at [1978] Conv 418–31).

By way of mortgage—If the conveyance happens to be by way of mortgage or charge (but is otherwise the same as before, ie, 'as beneficial owner'; nothing is implied by 'as mortgagor'), then by paras (C) and (D) of s 76(1) the covenants in the terms set out in Pts III and IV of Sched 2 to the Act are implied (and see *Mornington Permanent BS* v *Kenway* [1953] Ch 382, at p 386). Although these covenants are substantially the same as covenants (1) to (6) above, there are four differences obviously attributable to the nature of the transaction concerned, which should be noted. First, covenant (2)—for quiet enjoyment—only arises on the mortgagee taking possession after a default by the mortgagor in paying principal or interest. Second, so long only as the mortgagor's equity of redemption subsists, performance of covenant (4)—for further assurance—is to be at the cost of the mortgagor-covenantor. Normally performance of this covenant is to be at the cost of the covenantee, the person requesting its performance. Third, in a mortgage of leasehold property, there is implied an additional covenant:

> (7) That the rent reserved by and the covenants contained in the lease *will*, so long as any money remains owing on the security of the mortgage, be paid, observed and performed.

Fourth, all the covenants are in terms absolute and not qualified as they are in any other conveyance to the extent and in the manner considered in the next part of this section.

2   Qualified covenants

Although the benefit of the implied covenants for title may be said to run with the land (see s 76(6) of the Law of Property Act 1925 and p 274), the only person who can be sued for damages in respect of a breach of any of the covenants given above is the grantor, as the covenantor. In other words, the burden of the covenants is personal and does not pass to the covenantor's successors in title—indeed, unlike restrictive covenants, it is by no means inherent that the covenantor should retain any land for the covenant to run with and it hardly runs with the 'valuable consideration' which must be given.

However, the covenantor's liability in damages is not absolute (except in the case of a mortgage, ante) but is qualified to extend only to a breach of the covenants caused by the acts or omissions of any of the following persons:

> (*a*) the covenantor,
>
> (*b*) anyone 'through whom he [the covenantor] derives title' otherwise than by purchase for value,
>
> (*c*) any person conveying by the covenantor's direction or 'claiming by, through or under' either the covenantor or a person within (*b*), and
>
> (*d*) any person claiming (sic) in trust for the covenantor

(see per Lindley LJ in *David* v *Sabin* [1893] 1 Ch 523, at p 532). Needless to say this list does not appear anywhere in the terms of the covenants but is gleaned from the wording of each of them. Also, of course, the qualification of liability varies as appropriate to each of the covenants. Thus, covenant (1), being entirely past, relates only to the acts or omissions of persons within classes (*a*) or (*b*) above. However, since such variations are entirely appropriate to the particular covenant, it is convenient and adequate to treat the above list as applying to all the covenants.

Short illustrations serve best to show how the qualification operates:

> (i) *A*, having incumbered land, conveys the fee simple to *B* for valuable consideration as beneficial owner; then *B* conveys it to *C* also for valuable consideration as beneficial owner. *B* will not be liable to *C* in respect of the incumbrance under the covenants for title, since he did *not* derive title through *A otherwise* than for value, but *A* will be liable both to *B* and to *C* since the benefit of the covenant runs with the land.
>
> (ii) Had *A given* the fee simple to *B*, the position would be reversed: *B* would

be liable to C for A's act (now within class (b) above), whilst A would be liable to nobody, since no covenants would have been implied on his part as he did not convey for valuable consideration (if he conveyed 'as settlor' any covenant (4)—for further assurance—would be implied: see later).

(iii) Had B conveyed to C as beneficial owner by way of mortgage, the facts otherwise being as in (i), then the covenants implied on the part of B would be absolute and he would be liable to C.

In connection with the qualification of the covenants, anyone who has courageously been studying the precise (or imprecise) terms of Pt I of Sched 2 may well be puzzled by the sense of the word 'notwithstanding'. It appears, for example, in covenant (1)—full power to convey—in the following context: 'That, notwithstanding anything by [the grantor] done . . . or omitted . . . [the grantor] has full power to convey'. This is somewhat ambiguous, and the suggestion in Megarry and Wade, *The Law of Real Property*, 4th ed, at p 608, *n* 88, that here 'notwithstanding' is used in the sense of 'to the extent of' does not seem to clarify. It is thought that the real answer is to read the covenant throughout not as positive but as negative, as follows: That nothing has been done or omitted by the grantor to cause the grantor not to have full power to convey.

As another consequence perhaps of nineteenth century drafting, the word 'through' appears to have a different meaning in each of the two phrases quoted respectively in (b)—'through whom he derives title'—and (c)—'claiming by, through or under' the covenantor—of the qualification list above. In (b) it covers predecessors in title in fee simple (assuming this to be the subject-matter) whilst in (c) it does not cover successors in title in fee simple but only persons with derivative interests such as lessees or mortgagees. Three examples will explain this: First, if T allows the acquisition of an easement by prescription and then gives the fee simple to V, who as beneficial owner sells it to P, then V will be liable for the omission of T, his predecessor in title in fee simple (T will not be liable to anyone as he will have given no covenants for title). Second, if V sells his land in fee simple, to T, who resells to V, having in the meantime granted a lease which he conceals, and V afterwards sells the fee simple to P as beneficial owner, then V will not be liable to P for T's act, although T was a person claiming through V. Third, if V grants a lease of his land to T, who surrenders the lease to V, having in the meantime granted a sub-lease which he conceals, and V afterwards sells the fee simple to P as beneficial owner, then V will be liable to P for the act of T, a person claiming a derivative interest through V. Of these examples, the second was based on an example given by Romer J and approved by A L Smith LJ in the leading case of *David* v *Sabin* [1893] 1 Ch 523 (at pp 530 and 544, respectively), and the third was based on the facts of that case.

On general principles, presumably, neither 'through' will cover squatters, at least on unregistered land. That is to say, a vendor whose title depends on adverse possession would not be liable for the acts or omissions of dispossessed predecessors in title since he would not derive title through them but would merely have extinguished their titles. Conversely, it follows, a vendor of land would not covenant to cover the acts or omissions of squatters since they would not be claiming 'by, through or under' him but rather, adversely to him. Oddly enough, however, none of this may hold true in registered conveyancing where the result of a successful squat is not extinction of the proprietor's title but simply a trust for the squatter—and a beneficiary surely does both derive title and claim through his trustee (see s 75 of the Land Registration Act 1925).

It is expressly stated in Pts I and II of Sched 2 that 'in the above covenant a purchase for value shall not be deemed to include a conveyance in consideration of marriage'. This is contrary to the general provision of the Law of Property Act 1925 (s 205(1)(xxi)), applying to s 76 itself, that valuable consideration does include marriage. An illustration of the resulting odd contrast would be the following: *A*, having created an incumbrance on land, then as beneficial owner gives the fee simple in the land to *B* in consideration of his marriage; later *B* as beneficial owner gives the fee simple in the land to *C* in consideration of his marriage; now the incumbrance is enforced against *C*. Since *B*'s conveyance to *C* was a conveyance for valuable consideration (s 205(1)(xxi) applying to include marriage) then by s 76(1)(A) a covenant was implied in the terms of Pt I of Sched 2. This covenant renders *B* liable, inter alia, for the acts or omissions of 'anyone through whom he derives title otherwise than by purchase for value' and, since here value expressly excludes marriage, *B* will be liable to *C* for *A*'s omission. It may be noted that *A* is equally liable to *B*. However, this illustration may be unlikely to occur in practice because both *A* and *B* would almost certainly not have conveyed as beneficial owners, but, if anything, as settlors, which will be discussed later.

3 Burden of proof

A potentially devastating addendum to the qualification of the covenants has been laid down by the courts in accordance with the general rule of evidence that he who alleges must prove. A plaintiff bringing an action for breach of the covenants for title must show an act or omission by a person mentioned in the list (*a*) to (*d*) above. Therefore, if the precise origin of the defect in title cannot be established, then no one can be made liable under the covenants. An interesting example is provided by the facts in *Stoney* v *Eastbourne Rural District Council* [1927] 1 Ch 367. Some time after the Duke of Devonshire, as beneficial owner, had sold a farm in fee simple to the plaintiff an undisclosed public right of way over the farm was established. Title to the farm had been vested in persons through whom the Duke derived title otherwise than for value since 1782. In other words, that was the date of the last conveyance for valuable consideration, the farm having remained in the Duke's family until the sale to the plaintiff. Therefore, to render the Duke liable on the covenants, the plaintiff had to show that the right of way was dedicated after 1782, whilst to avoid liability the Duke had to show a dedication before 1782. Neither could be sufficiently shown. The Court of Appeal decided that the words 'otherwise than by purchase for value' were not an exception from but part of the covenant, so that the burden of proof of breach was not on the Duke to show that he was within an exception but was on the plaintiff, and the action accordingly failed. A comparable decision had earlier been reached by the Court of Appeal in *Howard* v *Maitland* (1883) 11 QBD 695, where in the absence of evidence no inference had been taken that a grant of a right of common must have been by a predecessor in title of the plaintiff, these words not extending to 'every person in possession of this property since the foundation of the world' (per Lindley LJ at p 703).

4 The four basic covenants

Having briefly stated the seven covenants for title which may, by virtue of s 76(1) of the Law of Property Act 1925, be implied by a vendor conveying 'as beneficial owner', and having then fully discussed how these covenants are qualified, it will now be appropriate to consider certain important aspects of each of the four basic covenants implied when the property conveyed is *not* leasehold. Further fascinating reading upon these and other aspects may be found in another instalment in depth on this topic from MJ Russell at (1970) 34 Conv (NS) 178.

(1) *Full power to convey*—This covenant will be broken if the property conveyed is found to be subject to any defect in title not expressly excepted from the conveyance, provided that the defect was caused by a person within the qualification of the covenant. This proviso contains an important point to notice, namely, that the vendor does not covenant that he *has* any title but only that the title has not been made defective by the acts or omissions of either himself or the persons through whom he derives title otherwise than for value. In other words, the vendor or such predecessors in title must once have had the title; the covenant does not provide a purchaser with a remedy on eviction by title paramount. For example, if a squatter who has not acquired a title by adverse possession sells the fee simple in land as beneficial owner, and the purchaser is later evicted by the proper owner, then the squatter will not be liable under this covenant. This is an aspect that did not commend itself to a former editor of the *Conveyancer and Property Lawyer*, who typically complained:

> A purchaser's position would undoubtedly be more secure if every vendor gave unqualified covenants for title. If a vendor sells a Rolls-Royce that does not belong to him, the purchaser on being dispossessed can get his money back . . .; why should the position be different if the vendor sells a labourer's cottage?

(at (1964) vol 28, p 188). The answer appears to lie in the established approach that a vendor of land, unlike a vendor of goods, cannot be expected to have any confidence that his title is good (see p 5). One consequence of this was explained by Erle CJ in *Thackeray* v *Wood* (1865) 6 B & S 766, as follows:

> Upon a sale of real property it is for the purchaser to ascertain what the title of the vendor is, and to satisfy himself that he has a good title. The vendor then makes a conveyance and usually covenants that he has done no act to affect or derogate from his title. If the vendor has no title at all to the property conveyed, there would be no breach of such a covenant.

However, if the vendor knew that he had no title, then an action in tort by the immediate purchaser (it will not run with the land) for fraudulent misrepresentation might well succeed. Alternatively, it may be that such a purchaser can find a remedy under the Misrepresentation Act 1967 (see further pp 58, 120). Otherwise the covenants for title will be looked to in vain for recompense.

With the above may be contrasted the position where the vendor (or one of the predecessors in title for whom he is responsible) originally had title to all the land sold but has since allowed a squatter to obtain a title to some or all of it by adverse possession. That this is an omission for which the vendor will be liable under the covenants if he purports to convey all the land was decided by the House of Lords in *Eastwood* v *Ashton* [1915] AC 900 (for the suggestion that the covering of omissions by the covenants for title was historically all a ghastly mistake, due to the inadvertent dropping of an initial 'c', read M J Russell at (1967) 31 Conv (NS) 268 et seq). The interesting problem which could arise where a period of adverse possession or of prescription has stretched over more than one ownership, perhaps with uncertainty as to when it began and as to which covenantor omitted to stop it running at the eleventh hour, is considered by A M Prichard at (1964) 28 Conv (NS) 206, note 6.

(2) *Quiet enjoyment*—The covenant for quiet enjoyment without lawful disturbance is more frequently encountered when implied automatically at common law by the landlord and tenant relationship. Since, generally speaking, the cases on the landlord's covenant apply equally to the present covenant and will be fairly familiar to readers, no good purpose would be served by dealing in detail with

them here. However, four of the more salient points may be made. First, it will be appreciated that quiet enjoyment involves absence not of noise (see *Jenkins* v *Jackson* (1888) 40 Ch D 71) but of *physical* disturbance (see *Howard* v *Maitland* (1883) 11 QBD 695, which held: no breach of the covenant where there had been a judicial decree that land was subject to a right of common but no entry in pursuance thereof). Second, for there to be a breach of the covenant the disturbance has also to be lawful. This is not a contradiction; if the disturbance is unlawful, remedies in tort are available (see *Malzy* v *Eichholz* [1916] 2 KB 308). Third, the question arises whether a breach of this covenant can possibly be caused by the activities of the vendor on adjoining land, eg, interfering with the access of light to the purchaser's land. This is not, of course, a defect in title. The position appears to be that, on the one hand, if the adjoining land was acquired by the vendor *after* the conveyance in which the covenant is implied, then there can be no breach of the covenant, on the ground that to hold otherwise would be to enlarge the original grant (*Davis* v *Town Properties Investment Corporation Ltd* [1903] 1 Ch 797). On the other hand, if the vendor owned the adjoining land at the time of the conveyance, then the answer would really depend upon whether the activities amounted to a derogation from the original grant rather than to a breach of this covenant (see *Harmer* v *Jumbil (Nigeria) Tin Areas* [1921] 1 Ch 200, which extended the doctrine since there was no physical disturbance: cf *Port* v *Griffith* [1938] 1 All ER 295, at p 298). Fourth, again this covenant provides a purchaser with no remedy in the case of a vendor (or any predecessor for whom he is responsible) who has never had any title, since it does not cover eviction by title paramount: see *Baynes & Co* v *Lloyd & Sons* [1895] 2 QB 610.

(3) *Freed from incumbrances*—Those readers who are following this exposition by referring to the text itself (ie, Pt I of Sched 2 to the Law of Property Act 1925) may have noticed that this present covenant, embodied in the second paragraph of the full covenant, has no main verb. Indeed, grammatically the sense here is, to say the least, obscure. The paragraph begins: 'And that, freed and discharged . . .' and continues with this sub-clause right to the end of the paragraph. It seems that the paragraph can only be construed by repeating in it the main verb from the preceding covenant (2), so that it would, in substance, read as follows: 'And that [the subject-matter shall be quietly enjoyed by the purchaser] freed and discharged . . .' In other words, although often treated as an independent covenant, covenant (3) is really no more than part of covenant (2). The significance of this is that the covenant can be seen to be not that the land *is* free from incumbrances but rather for indemnity in the event of any incumbrance actually being enforced. This is submitted to be the correct view despite the (incorrect) promotion by Joyce J of the subsidiary verbs 'freed and discharged . . .' to main verbs in *Turner* v *Moon* [1901] 2 Ch 825, at p 828, but reference should be made to the contrary reasoning by MJ Russell at (1970) 34 Conv (NS) 187–8 (although the authorities there cited tend to support the present view, as also does *Thompson* v *Thompson* (1871) IR 6 Eq 113, recently excavated by CK Liddle at [1979] Conv 93–6).

Also, it must be remembered that the vendor only covenants to indemnify the purchaser in respect of incumbrances due to the acts or omissions of the qualified list of persons mentioned earlier. An illustration which, though turning on unusual facts, is of general application occurred in *Chivers & Sons Ltd* v *Air Ministry, Queens' College, Cambridge, third parties* [1955] Ch 585. There, as a part of the transaction for value by which the vendor had acquired the land (in 1834 by exchange under the Inclosure Act 1833), a liability (for chancel repairs) had been imposed on the owner of the land for the time being. Wynn-Parry J held that, since the liability was imposed by a combination of the common law and statute, there was no act or omission for which the vendor was responsible, so that the purchaser had no remedy under the covenant.

However, this case should be contrasted with the decision in *Stock* v *Meakin* [1900] 1 Ch 683, where a vendor was held liable to indemnify a purchaser in respect of a statutory charge on the land (the expenses of private street works), which he could not have prevented from arising, on the ground that he had omitted to discharge it. The principle of the decision would appear conveniently to bring within the covenant the cases where a subsisting mortgage has been granted by the predecessor in title for value of the vendor, ie, the latter may be liable for omitting to discharge it. The principle would not, of course, extend to any planning order, such as a building listed as being of special architectural or historic interest, about which the vendor (or any person for whom he is responsible) has done and could do nothing. On the other hand, if the vendor (or any person as before) has contravened any planning restriction with the result that an enforcement notice is served on the purchaser, then although this is not a matter of title, it is thought that there would be liability under this covenant, which is for freedom from all 'estates, incumbrances, *claims, and demands*', which is very wide.

(4) *Further assurance*—In form this covenant is that the vendor *and* any of the qualified list of persons for whom he is responsible will at all times execute and do anything reasonably requested in order to perfect the conveyance. An example of a deed of further assurance is provided by Form No 7 in Sched 5 to the Law of Property Act 1925. However, the only person who is bound by and can be sued under the covenant is the vendor. Therefore, so far only as compliance with the request is within the vendor's own power, the remedy for breach of the covenant will be an order for specific performance; otherwise it will be an award of damages for non-compliance as with the other covenants. It should be noted that the costs of any further assurance are expressly to be borne by the person making the request (unless, it will be recalled, the conveyance was by way of mortgage and the equity of redemption still subsists).

Under this covenant, the vendor can be compelled to convey to the purchaser (or the successor in title making the request) any outstanding estate or interest necessary to give effect (and no more: *Re Repington, Wodehouse* v *Scobell* [1904] 1 Ch 811) to the conveyance, even if that estate or interest was later acquired for valuable consideration: *Otter* v *Vaux* (1856) 26 LJ Ch 128. A common illustration of the operation of the covenant used to be the request that an entail be barred where an owner of a base fee had purported to convey the fee simple (see *Bankes* v *Small* (1887) 34 Ch D 415; 36 Ch D 716). A more practical illustration, although not common under this covenant, is the request that the Settled Land Act conveyancing machinery be complied with or that an outstanding mortgage or charge be discharged (see per North J in *Re Jones, Farrington* v *Forrester* [1893] 2 Ch 461, at p 471). Another modern example might be a formal assent or confirmatory conveyance where there had been reliance on an implied assent by personal representatives in their own favour (ie, prior to the decision in *Re King's Will Trusts* [1964] Ch 542; see a precedent published at (1965) 29 Conv (NS) 750).

Lastly it may be mentioned that the need to enforce a covenant for further assurances in respect of an outstanding legal estate may be obviated by the arising and feeding of an estoppel in respect of it. Thus in *Cumberland Court (Brighton) Ltd* v *Taylor* [1964] Ch 29, outlined ante, p 245, reference was made to this covenant for title in the pleadings as covering the inadvertently transferred and preserved legal charge, but no support was sought from the covenant in the judgment itself.

5 Conveyance on the direction of another person

If a person conveys on the direction of another person and that other person is in the conveyance expressed to direct as beneficial owner, then the same covenants for title are implied as if that other person had himself conveyed and been expressed to convey as beneficial owner (s 76(2) of the Law of Property Act 1925). The most useful example of the operation of this should occur in the case of a sub-sale without an intermediate conveyance. The same covenants are implied on the part of the purchaser with the sub-purchaser whether the conveyance is in the full form:

> the vendor as beneficial owner at the direction of the purchaser hereby conveys unto the sub-purchaser and the purchaser as beneficial owner hereby conveys and confirms unto the sub-purchaser etc,

or the only slightly more concise form:

> the vendor as beneficial owner at the direction of the purchaser as beneficial owner hereby conveys unto the sub-purchaser, etc.

However, whether the sub-purchaser is entitled to insist on either form so far as the vendor is concerned is open to doubt. As against the sub-purchaser, the vendor is merely a bare trustee for the purchaser and not a beneficial owner (see further (1962) 106 SJ 132; contrast Form 3 on p 18 of Parker, *Modern Conveyancing Precedents*, which rather oddly has a vendor convey as beneficial owner and a 'sub-vendor' convey as trustee).

6 Husband and wife

The traditional legal view that a man keeps a dangerous wife at his peril appears also in this topic. If a husband and wife both convey as beneficial owners, then in addition to the normal covenants there are implied on the part of the husband, first, covenants as if he directed the wife to convey (see the preceding paragraph), and second, covenants in the same terms as those implied on the part of the wife (s 76(3) of the Law of Property Act 1925). Thus, for example, the husband would be liable for a breach of the covenant (1)—full power to convey—if the wife were an infant (*Nash* v *Ashton* (1682) T Jones 195). Normally, however, being necessarily trustees of the legal estate for themselves (see ss 34 to 36 of the Law of Property Act 1925), they would convey 'as trustees' (see below).

7 'As settlor'

There is implied in a conveyance by way of settlement by a person who conveys and is expressed to convey as settlor only, covenant (4) above—for further assurance (s 76(1)(E) of, and Pt V of Sched 2 to, the Law of Property Act 1925). Naturally, valuable consideration is not made a requisite for the implication of the covenant. It should be noted that here the covenant is qualified much further even than is the covenant when a beneficial owner conveys: a settlor only gives the covenant for himself and the person subsequently deriving title under him.

However, even generous settlors, especially if voluntary, should beware of too readily entering into this covenant for further assurance. As mentioned earlier, the covenant may involve not only conveying an interest acquired later for valuable consideration (*Otter* v *Vaux* (1856) 26 LJ Ch 128), but also discharging outstanding incumbrances (see per North J in *Re Jones, Farrington* v *Forrester* [1893] 2 Ch 461, at p 471; and per Chitty LJ in *West* v *Williams* [1899] 1 Ch 132, at p 147).

8 'As trustee', etc

Where a person conveys (whether or not for value) and is expressed to convey as trustee, mortgagee, personal representative, or under an order of the court, then only one covenant is implied (s 76(1)(F) of, and Sched 2, Pt VI to, the Law of Property Act 1925 as amended by the Mental Health Act 1959, Sched 8, Pt I). This covenant is, in effect, that the person so conveying has not personally created any defect in title, ie, that he has not himself incumbered the land. It is important to notice that this covenant expressly extends only to such a person's own acts. Accordingly, no liability attaches where there has not been active participation in the creation of the incumbrance, mere notice being insufficient (*Woodhouse* v *Jenkins* (1832) 9 Bing 431). An example of the breach of this covenant occurred in *Wise* v *Whitburn* [1924] 1 Ch 460, where the defendants had been expressed to convey 'as personal representatives', although they had, by virtue of a prior implied assent, become trustees of the estate. It was held that the defendants were liable under the covenant because they had by their own act, ie, the implied assent, created a defect in title in that they rendered themselves unable to deal with the estate in their expressed capacity. Since the appearance of s 36(7) of the Administration of Estates Act 1925 (assent to be 'sufficient evidence' of its own propriety) a modern version of this example of liability would arise where a personal representative had failed to endorse on the probate or letters of administration a memorandum of a previous assent or conveyance for money or money's worth.

Although, as compared with the covenants implied into a conveyance 'as beneficial owner', the protection here provided for a purchaser is much less, the purchaser is *not* entitled where trustees are selling in exercise of a trust for sale to insist on having the beneficiaries joined to give the full covenants for title: *Cottrell* v *Cottrell* (1866) LR 2 Eq 330. This may well be thought unjust where, as with the common example of dwellinghouses owned by husband and wife, the trustees are themselves the sole beneficiaries. Normally, the contract will state that the vendors sell as trustees and the purchaser, relying as he must on the powers of overreaching, will not concern himself with the beneficial position (see s 27(1) of the Law of Property Act 1925). It is, of course, possible for a prospective purchaser from co-owners to enquire before contract whether or not the vendors are beneficially entitled and then to amend the contract accordingly. On the other hand, a tenant for life under the Settled Land Act 1925, whatever the extent of his beneficial interest, should convey 'as trustee', since he is by statute a trustee not only of the legal estate but also in respect of the exercise of his powers (ss 16 and 107 of the Settled Land Act 1925; cf *Weston* v *Henshaw* [1950] Ch 510).

There appears to be some doubt as to the capacity in which a mortgagee should be expressed to transfer the mortgage (ie, on a sale not of the mortgaged land but of the benefit of the mortgage). Thus Form No 1 in Sched 3 to the Law of Property Act 1925 has him do so 'as mortgagee', as also does Form 35 on p 692 of Hallett, *Conveyancing Precedents*. However, in Form 89 on pp 159–60 of Parker, *Modern Conveyancing Precedents*, the mortgagee is expressed to transfer 'as beneficial owner' with the clearly quite correct comment that the mortgagee 'is beneficial owner of the mortgage and should transfer [ie, covenant] accordingly'.

Ex abundante cautela, presumably, it is expressly provided that the above covenant may be implied in an assent by a personal representative 'in like manner as in a conveyance by deed' (see also s 36(6) of the Administration of Estates Act 1925). This is unnecessary since a conveyance by the Law of Property Act 1925 definition (s 205(1)(ii)) includes an assent and may be 'by any instrument'. Also it is provided elsewhere (s 115(6) of the Law of Property Act 1925) that the covenant is implied into a discharge or reconveyance receipt endorsed on a mortgage without the mortgagee being expressed to do so as mortgagee.

9 General considerations

There are several important general considerations applicable to all the covenants for title.

Joint or several?—First, a short point which may arise where the covenants are implied into a conveyance by or to more than one person. Apart from the wording of s 76, the liability of the covenantors might be joint or several or joint and several, and the rights of the covenantees might simply be either joint or several, not both, all with differing consequences which need not be rehearsed now. However, on the one hand, subs (1) of s 76 provides that in a conveyance *by* more than one person the covenants are implied 'by each person who conveys'. Since 'each' is probably a word of severance (see *Collins* v *Prosser* (1823) 1 B & C 682), it follows that the liability of the covenantors is several, ie, there are independent causes of action. On the other hand, the subsection provides that in a conveyance *to* more than one person the covenant is implied 'with the persons jointly, if more than one, to whom the conveyance is made as joint tenants, or with each of the persons, if more than one, to whom the conveyance is (when the law permits) made as tenants in common.' If the subject-matter of the conveyance is a legal estate in land it must, of course, be made to joint tenants (ss 1(6) and 34 of the Law of Property Act 1925) and the rights also will be joint, so that both covenantees must sue as plaintiffs to enforce the covenants—not an advantage. In other cases, 'when the law permits' and the conveyance is in fact to tenants in common, then the rights will be several and each covenantee can sue separately.

Date of breach—It will have become apparent from the earlier consideration of the terms of each of the various covenants for title that they may very easily overlap. For example, if a still outstanding mortgage had been created by a vendor of land before conveying the fee simple as beneficial owner and thereafter enforced, the purchaser in the meantime having unsuccessfully requested its discharge, then there will be a breach of all four of the vendor's implied covenants. In such a case the purchaser's choice of which covenant to pursue may, when appropriate, be governed by lapse of time. The length of the limitation period for all the covenants, assuming the normal case of a conveyance of an interest in land under seal (see s 52 of the Law of Property Act 1925), is twelve years, and otherwise six years, in the absence of any extensions (ss 2 and 8 of the Limitation Act 1980). However, the point is that the period can run from a different date for each of the covenants, so that one or more may be statute-barred.

This means simply that the covenants may be treated as breached on different dates in respect of the same defect in title. Therefore, even where the periods of limitation are not crucial, a later date of breach may be desirable as determining the date for assessing (inflated) damages: see *Conodate Investments Ltd* v *Bentley Quarry Engineering Co Ltd* (1970) 216 EG 1407.

Taking the still-outstanding mortgage example given above as a theme, the covenants are breached and time begins to run as follows:

(1) The covenant that the vendor has full power to convey will be broken by the mere existence of the mortgage as at the date of the conveyance: *Spoor* v *Green* (1874) LR 9 Ex 99, at p 110. (Incidentally, this is so also, as to other defects, with the leasehold property covenants as to valid lease and as to covenants observed, and with the trustee's, etc, covenant of not having himself incumbered.)

(2) The covenant for quiet enjoyment is not broken until the lawful disturbance—the enforcement of the mortgage—actually occurs, which may, of course, be years later (see *Conodate Investments Ltd* v *Bentley Quarry Engineering Co Ltd*, ante, where the conveyance had been in 1962 but third party rights were not asserted until 1967). In *Spoor* v *Green*, ante, Bramwell B (loc cit at p 111), also added the distinction that the first covenant of full power to convey can only be broken or not once and for all at the date of the conveyance, whilst the second covenant for quiet enjoyment will be broken anew by each and every disturbance. If one envisages a right of way over the land sold with occasional user over the years, one can see that here time may never stop running. This fact greatly strengthens the protection provided for a purchaser.

(3) If it is accepted that the covenant for freedom from incumbrances is merely a subsidiary of the covenant for quiet enjoyment (see the submission made at p 265), then the breach will occur as in (2), above. However, it was held by Joyce J in *Turner* v *Moon* [1901] 2 Ch 825 in no uncertain terms that, like the covenant of having full power to convey, the covenant for freedom from incumbrances is broken, if at all, as at the date of the conveyance and time runs from that date (see also per Harman J in *Pilkington* v *Wood* [1953] Ch 770, at p 777). Preferred to this is the view of Neville J in *Nottidge* v *Dering* [1909] 2 Ch 647, at p 656 (affirmed by the Court of Appeal at [1910] Ch 297), concerning a similarly worded express covenant, that there must be actual interruption of enjoyment to justify action.

(4) The covenant for further assurance is broken when a request to execute or do anything under the covenant—to discharge the mortgage—has been both made and refused (*Jones* v *King* (1815) 4 M & S 188), which may be a later date again.

It may also be noticed here that the material date for calculating the damages resulting from breach of one of the covenants is also the date of the breach, ie, the date from which the time runs (see *Turner* v *Moon*, ante).

Actual capacity—Only on the part of a person 'who conveys *and* is expressed to convey' in one of the specified capacities are the various covenants for title implied by s 76(1) of the Law of Property Act 1925 (italics supplied; cp s 77(1)B(ii), D(ii) and (4) where is said 'who conveys *or* is expressed to convey'—much significance of construction can be deduced from this difference). Does this ambivalent phrase mean that the person conveying must not merely be expressed to have a particular capacity but must also actually have that capacity? What, for example, is the position with regard to the covenants for title if a vendor conveying the fee simple in land 'as beneficial owner' is a trustee (as indeed in *Weston* v *Henshaw* [1950] Ch 510), or has previously conveyed elsewhere so that in fact he does not convey at all, never mind 'as beneficial owner'? (This last should be contrasted at once with the example discussed at p 264, where the vendor has *never* had any title, when there will be no breach of the *qualified* covenant of having full power to convey, assuming that it is implied, although the possible alternative remedy of an action for misrepresentation applies to both examples.)

The raison d'être of s 76, as we have already seen, was simply to shorten deeds of conveyance by obviating the setting out in full of express covenants for title. The actual capacity of the covenantor would, of course, be irrelevant if the covenants were set out in full and it should follow, since no alteration of the law was intended, that the position is the same under s 76. In other words, the phrase 'conveys and is expressed to convey' should be construed as 'expressly purports to convey'. Unfortunately, the phrase quoted has given rise to comparatively recent statements of contrary judicial views and some consequent uncertainty. Thus Clauson LJ in

Fay v *Miller, Wilkins & Co* [1941] Ch 360 (at p 366), said in relation to the expression 'as personal representative' (s 76(1)(F)):

It must, however, be borne in mind that the implication of covenants by a conveyance in that form is effective only if the conveying party is not only expressed so to convey, but in fact does convey as personal representative.

In the same case, Greene MR had already (at p 363), more definitely but less quotably uttered the same view, which was later cited as authority by Harman J in *Pilkington* v *Wood* [1953] Ch 770 (at p 777), for saying '. . . it being a *sine qua non* that the covenantor must be in fact, as well as being expressed to be, the beneficial owner'. Since then Megarry J also has indicated unqualified acceptance of this view (in *Re Robertson's Application* [1969] 1 WLR 109, at p 112).

However, the decision in *Fay* v *Miller, Wilkins & Co*, ante, concerned the liability of an auctioneer for breach of implied warranty of authority and that in *Pilkington* v *Wood*, ante, concerned the quantum of damages for professional negligence, so that the above judicial views were clearly obiter dicta. Further, not only do these views conflict with the raison d'être of s 76, but also with what was the existing trend of more direct authority, none of which was considered in either case. Thus, the covenants for title had been implied without question where a tenant for life (a trustee) was expressed to convey 'as beneficial owner' (*David* v *Sabin* [1893] 1 Ch 523 and *Re Ray* [1896] 1 Ch 468, see per Kay LJ at p 475), where trustees were expressed to convey 'as personal representatives' (*Wise* v *Whitburn* [1924] 1 Ch 460), and where personal representatives were expressed to convey 'as beneficial owners' (*Parker* v *Judkin* [1931] 1 Ch 475).

It may well be that, despite the view of Greene MR, Clauson LJ and of Harman J a decision on the point after full argument would hold actual capacity to be irrelevant. But this now seems unlikely and is hardly satisfactory to practitioners who must base themselves as far as possible on certainty (see the ubiquitous MJ Russell at (1968) 32 Conv (NS) 123). It may be suggested with some force that if a vendor contracts that he sells, say, as beneficial owner, but on investigation of his title it appears that he has not that capacity, then the purchaser is nonetheless entitled to have the covenants for title appropriate to a conveyance as beneficial owner and should insist on their express incorporation. However, this does depend on the investigation of title revealing, as it may not, the actual capacity (consider, eg, a sale by the survivor of beneficial joint tenants where there has in fact been a severance—will the words 'as beneficial owner' operate for the Law of Property (Joint Tenants) Act 1964 but not for s 76(1) of the 1925 Act?). A more foolproof practice, adoption of which might well be considered, is to by-pass the unfortunate phrase 'conveys and is expressed to convey' in every case by invariably incorporating expressly the covenants for title. Conveyances need be lengthened only negligibly: for example, instead of the words 'as beneficial owner' there could simply appear, elsewhere, the words 'the vendor hereby covenants with the purchaser in the terms set out in Part I of the Second Schedule to the Law of Property Act 1925'.

Contract provisions—On the one hand, as just mentioned, a purchaser is entitled to have the vendor enter, in the conveyance, into the covenants for title appropriate to the capacity in which the vendor contracted to sell, but not more than such covenants: *Worley* v *Frampton* (1846) 5 Hare 560. The purchaser's entitlement where there is no contract, the sale being compulsory, is now settled. On principle one might have thought that the vendor should not be obliged to enter into *any* covenants for title (compare *Baily* v *De Crespigny* (1869) LR 4 QB 180). However, comparatively recently in *Re King* [1962] 1 WLR 632 (on appeal as to other points only: [1963] Ch 459), Buckley J decided that in this respect a compulsory purchase must stand in the same position as a contractual purchase under an open contract (ibid, at p 651; see also *Harding* v *Metropolitan Railway Co* (1872) 7 Ch App 154). Nonetheless, it is worth noticing that the point of this decision was to allow the vendor not to enter into any more onerous covenants than those implied by conveying 'as personal representative', with the result that a provision could be inserted by him into the transfer excluding s 24(1)(*a*) of the Land Registration Act 1925 (this otherwise would automatically imply a like covenant to the covenant (6) above implied under s 76(1)(B) of the Law of Property Act 1925 into a conveyance of leaseholds 'as beneficial owner').

On the other hand, however, a provision in the contract may entitle the vendor to exclude the covenants for title from, or modify them in, the conveyance. The covenants may be excluded by simple omission to include: if the grantor is not expressed to convey in one of the specified capacities then no covenants for title on his part are implied: s 76(4) of the Law of Property Act 1925. Again, it is expressly provided (s 76(7)) that the covenants may be varied or extended, but only by deed or assent, and will then operate exactly as if implied by the section. A common but not obvious example of a vendor's right to modify the covenants for title occurs on the sale of leaseholds. Usually the contract will provide that the purchaser shall take the property 'as it is' or 'as it stands'. In such a case the vendor is entitled to modify covenant (6) above, ie, that the covenants contained in the lease have been observed and performed, in order to exclude his liability to the purchaser for any breaches of repairing covenants. This question was decided in *Butler* v *Mountview Estates Ltd* [1951] 2 KB 563, and is now expressly provided for by condition 11(7) of the National Conditions of Sale (20th ed), and condition 8(4) of The Law Society's Conditions of Sale, 1980 edition. Also the vendor would in such a case presumably always be able to exclude the similar covenant in s 24(1)(*a*) of the Land Registration Act 1925 (see *Re King* [1962] 1 WLR 632, at p 655; on appeal [1963] Ch 459).

However, it should be noted that apparently a modification of the covenants for title must not go so far as to destroy liability altogether. If it does, it will be repugnant and void: see *Watling* v *Lewis* [1911] 1 Ch 414. The proper procedure is to omit the covenants for title. Also it may be noticed that if the covenants for title implied in the conveyance do not conform to the parties' entitlement under the contract, there can be rectification: *Stait* v *Fenner* [1912] 2 Ch 504 and *Butler* v *Mountview Estates Ltd*, ante. Of course, if the purchaser has contracted to buy subject to something such as a mortgage or easement, which would otherwise be a defect in title, then the result of making the conveyance expressly subject thereto is that the covenants for title will not apply even in the absence of variation. This is because the covenants expressly relate only to the subject-matter of the conveyance as expressed to be conveyed.

Words of limitation—A trap which a purchaser must be careful to avoid is caused by this fact that the covenants for title are only implied into a conveyance 'as far as regards the subject-matter . . . expressed to be conveyed' (s 76(1) of the Law of Property Act 1925). It follows from this that, when a vendor conveys only such title as he has, the purchaser takes it for better or for worse and cannot complain under the covenants for title when he later discovers that the title the vendor had was defective: see *May* v *Platt* [1900] 1 Ch 616 (where with this object it was unsuccessfully claimed that a conveyance should be rectified by the insertion of 'if any' after 'all the estate term and interest') and *Smith* v *Osborne* (1857) 6 HL Cas 375 (see also *Fowler* v *Willis* [1922] 2 Ch 514 as to the contractual position). Obiter observations supporting this lack of liability may more recently be found in *George*

Wimpey & Co v *Sohn* [1967] Ch 487, per Harman LJ at p 505 and per Russell LJ at p 509.

The purchaser will be equally disappointed in the more likely event of his allowing the vendor simply to convey freehold land without any words of limitation, eg, by omitting to add 'in fee simple'. In such a case the conveyance operates to pass to the purchaser 'the fee simple *or other* the whole interest which the grantor had power to convey in such land' (s 60(1) of the Law of Property Act 1925). If it later turns out that the vendor had no power to convey the fee simple or indeed any interest in the land, then again there can be no liability under the covenants for title. See further MJ Russell at (1970) 34 Conv (NS) 180–3, where the suggestion is also made that the covenants for title will not cover any implied rights carried by the conveyance; again these are not part of 'the subject-matter . . . *expressed* to be conveyed'.

Despite knowledge—If any reader was surprised at the absence of liability just mentioned, he may be even more surprised by the presence of liability in the following circumstances. It appears clear that there can be no breach of the covenants for title in respect of any incumbrance or other defect to which the conveyance is expressly made subject. However, it is equally clear that the covenants do cover incumbrances and defects fully known to the purchaser at the time of the conveyance, even covering those appearing by recital on the face of the conveyance: *Page* v *Midland Railway* [1894] 1 Ch 11; *Great Western Railway Co* v *Fisher* [1905] 1 Ch 316 (and see per Stamp J in *Hissett* v *Reading Roofing Co Ltd* [1969] 1 WLR 1757, at p 1759; also MJ Russell at (1970) 34 Conv (NS) 194–6). With this may be compared the stricter rule for contracts that a purchaser who knows of an irremovable defect in title cannot therefore refuse to complete (*Ellis* v *Rogers* (1885) 29 Ch D 661; *Timmins* v *Moreland Street Property Co Ltd* [1958] Ch 110; and further ante, p 62).

Chain of protection—It was remarked at the very outset of this section (p 259) that covenants for title were available in case of post-completion discovery of a defect in title 'to protect the purchaser by imposing liability on the vendor'. Later it was observed that the benefit of the covenants runs with the land (s 76(6) of the Law of Property Act 1925), although the burden is personal to the covenantor and also extends only to the acts and omissions of a qualified list of persons. The result of the benefit running is that the protection provided for a purchaser goes far beyond an action for damages against his immediate vendor. Under normal practice, a purchaser of land obtains the benefit of a chain of protection consisting of the covenants for title given by each of the previous vendors of the land conveying 'as beneficial owner'. Since such vendors assume liability for the acts and omissions, inter alios, of anyone through whom they derive title otherwise than for value, the covenants for title extend back to cover intermediate donors, testators and intestates (who will not, of course, have given the full, if any, covenants), stopping short only at the preceding vendor. Thus the chain is not broken by a voluntary change in title, and, though each vendor gives only qualified covenants, the total should amount to an absolute guarantee of title.

However, an absolute guarantee would be an ideal situation. In the first place, the purchaser, on whom rests the burden of proof (*Stoney* v *Eastbourne Rural District Council* [1927] 1 Ch 367), must choose the proper defendant, the particular vendor responsible. Success in this choice may still bring little joy if that vendor is, as may easily be the case, deceased and his estate distributed, or a man of straw in some other way. Then the chain may be broken by one of the previous vendors conveying otherwise than 'as beneficial owner' or by the covenants being either expressly modified to exclude liability for the defect in question or else simply omitted altogether. Again the incumbrance or other defect in title may have been imposed by someone for whom no previous vendor was responsible: see *Wyld* v *Silver* [1963] 1 QB 169, where a purchaser finding his land lumbered with an annual fair by virtue of an inclosure award made pursuant to a private Act of Parliament and 'with no hope of remedy under his ordinary qualified covenants for title', received Russell LJ's 'unqualified sympathy' but nothing more (at p 194). Yet a break in the chain of protection of this sort does not itself constitute a defect in title: *Re Scott and Alvarez's Contract* [1895] 1 Ch 596. An absolute guarantee, an unbroken chain of protection, is too much to expect.

Running with the land—The chain of protection for a purchaser is only capable of existing because the benefit of the covenants for title can be said to run with the land. In fact, the benefit must run with some estate or interest in the land. Section 76(6) of the Law of Property Act 1925 actually says that the benefit:

> shall be annexed and incident to, and shall go with, the estate or interest of the implied covenantee and shall be capable of being enforced by every person in whom that estate or interest is, for the whole or any part thereof, from time to time vested.

This seems irresistibly to suggest that only a person having the same estate or interest as the covenantee in the land can enforce the covenants. In other words, if the covenants are implied into a conveyance of the fee simple, then a subsequent purchaser of the fee simple could enforce them but a lessee could not. Somewhat surprisingly, it follows inevitably that such covenants could not be enforced by any mortgagee, even of the immediate purchaser. The point is that, since 1925, mortgagees can no longer take the same estate or interest as a purchaser of the fee simple; indeed they are no more than lessees (s 85(1) of the Law of Property Act 1925). It is true that a mortgagee will almost always have the benefit of absolute covenants for title from his mortgagor (see p 260), but unhappily this benefit is likely to prove valueless in that the insolvency of the mortgagor appears to be a predictable concomitant of the mortgagee's need for enforcement (see further AM Prichard at (1964) 28 Conv (NS) 205). However, arguably all this is not the position.

Covenants for title were an old established example of covenants the benefit of which ran with the land at common law (pre-dating in this respect *The Prior's Case* (1369) YB 42 Edw III Hil, Pl 15, f 3). Also at common law the benefit of such covenants was treated as annexed to and ran along with the same legal estate in the land that the covenantee had (see *Westhoughton Urban District Council* v *Wigan Coal & Iron Co* [1919] 1 Ch 159). Therefore, s 76(6) can be seen to do no more than state the common law position.

However, as from 1925 the common law position has been altered by s 78 of the Law of Property Act 1925, which provides that:

> A covenant relating to any land of the covenantee shall be deemed to be made with the covenantee and his successors in title *and the persons deriving title under him or them*, and shall have effect as if such successors and other persons were expressed.

Like s 76 itself, this provision might have been taken to have the object simply of shortening conveyances and other deeds, but it has been held by the Court of Appeal to alter the common law by virtue of the italicised words (*Smith and Snipes Hall Farm Ltd* v *River Douglas Catchment Board* [1949] 2 KB 500, followed in *Williams* v *Unit Construction Co Ltd* (1951) 19 Conv (NS) 262, CA and both approved in *Federated Homes Ltd* v *Mill Lodge Properties Ltd* [1980] 1 WLR 594). In the *River Douglas* case, ante, a lessee was held enabled by s 78 to enforce a covenant made with a purchaser of the fee simple. Since there is nothing obvious which prevents s 78, as interpreted by the Court of Appeal's decision, from applying, it would seem to follow that a lessee, like a purchaser of the fee simple, unexpectedly obtains the benefit of the chain of protection provided by covenants for title. Rather less unexpectedly, this argument would mean that a mortgagee also gains the benefit of the chain. However, in the initial edition of this book this passage somewhat doubtfully concluded with the cryptic comment: sed quaere! Since then this very argument has been directly challenged for a number of separate reasons which together would amount to an entirely convincing rebuttal were they not substantially similar to the objections advanced against there being any such decision as that in the *Smith and Snipes Hall Farm* case itself. Anyway readers really must refer further to AM Prichard's article at (1964) 28 Conv (NS) 205 et seq, for the full flavour of his reasoning (and perhaps also to MJ Russell in (1979) 123 SJ 71).

Lastly, it may be mentioned that the ultimate beneficiary of the chain of protection strung by successive conveyances of unregistered land is likely, if present trends continue, to be the Chief Land Registrar. Once title to the land is registered, any hitherto undiscovered defects in title may well lead to rectification of the register. If this happens, instead of enforcing the covenants for title, a disappointed proprietor will probably seek indemnity under s 83 of the Land Registration Act 1925. If so, and successfully, then subs (10) of that section in effect provides that the benefit of the covenants for title runs on to the Chief Land Registrar.

10 Caveat solicitor

If the implied covenants for title satisfactorily fulfilled their object of protecting purchasers (which is very much a pious hope) they they would certainly further weaken the caveat emptor rule in the purchase of land. Nonetheless, the primary protection for a purchaser is afforded by the usual investigation of title. If a defect in the vendor's title is overlooked, the purchaser will seek recompense, but infrequently under the covenants for title. The defendant will normally be his solicitor and the cause of action professional negligence, although it is true that the period of limitation is less (six years rather than twelve years: ss 2 and 5 of the Limitation Act 1980), so that the purchaser may have no choice of defendants.

However, a plaintiff is under a common law duty to take all reasonable steps to mitigate any loss caused to him (see per Lord Haldane in *British Westinghouse Electric and Manufacturing Co Ltd* v *Underground Electric Railways Co* [1912] AC 673, at p 689). Could a solicitor who has negligently investigated title compel his client to mitigate his damages by pursuing his alternative remedy under the implied covenants for title? Harman J answered this question in *Pilkington* v *Wood* [1953] Ch 770, at p 777, as follows:

> I am of the opinion that the so-called duty to mitigate does not go so far as to oblige the injured party, even under an indemnity, to embark on a complicated and difficult piece of litigation against a third party . . . . It is no part of the plaintiff's duty to embark on the proposed litigation in order to protect his solicitor from the consequences of his own carelessness.

11 Registered conveyancing

In the previous parts of this chapter the extremely difficult topic of covenants for title (as implied by s 76 of the Law of Property Act 1925) has been considered at length but almost entirely in relation to *un*registered conveyancing. This concluding part merely adds some notes on that topic in relation to registered conveyancing, and as they are really no more than a postscript these notes are confined entirely to transfers of freehold land and to the implication of covenants by the expression 'as beneficial owner', although much of what is said will be of general application. Unfortunately, as will be seen, the complications of the topic are added to by the relevant provisions of the Land Registration Act and Rules 1925—not the best drafted of the 1925 property legislation—simply because these do not blend satisfactorily with provisions based on the *un*registered system of conveyancing.

Before considering the effect and therefore the value (if any) of the implied covenants for title in registered conveyancing, it is necessary first to see that they may in fact be implied therein. This is usually assumed without any comment other than a reference, by footnote, to s 38(2) and rr 76 and 77 of, respectively, the Land Registration Act and Rules 1925. This same assumption has even appeared in one reported case, although it was there rather vitiated by some apparent mispleading (see per Orr J in *Watts* v *Waller* [1973] 1 QB 153, at pp 171–2; cf also per Stamp J in *Hissett* v *Reading Roofing Co Ltd* [1969] 1 WLR 1757, at p 1759). The prescribed form of Transfer of Freehold Land (Form 19 of the Schedule to, and r 98 of, the Rules) leaves no place for insertion of the words 'as beneficial owner', but it is particularly provided by r 76 that for the purpose of introducing the covenants implied under s 76 of the Law of Property Act 1925 a person may be expressed to transfer as beneficial owner.

However, a theoretical difficulty can be discerned. By s 76 of the Law of Property Act 1925 the covenants for title may only be implied '*in a conveyance*', and at the very commencement of this book (p 222), for the reasons there given, the writer expressed his opinion that a Land Registry form of transfer is not a 'conveyance' as defined in the Law of Property Act 1925 (s 205(1)(ii)), but is primarily an authority to the Registrar to make certain entries on the register. Accordingly, the position might seem to be like that in *Guyot* v *Thomson* [1894] 3 Ch 388, where an exclusive licence to manufacture under a patent had been granted 'as beneficial owner'; Lindley LJ said (at p 398):

> I do not think that this is a conveyance within the meaning of the Conveyancing Act. But it does not follow that the introduction of the words "as beneficial owner" is unimportant. Those words show that the parties did not mean to treat this as a revocable licence.

So with a Land Registry transfer, at least the transferor impliedly covenants not to revoke his authority to the Registrar.

(a) *Effect and value of transfer 'as beneficial owner'*

Nonetheless, it would be very strange indeed to conclude that the assumption universally held which forms the basis of s 38(2) and r 77 (of, respectively, the Land Registration Act and Rules 1925) was unjustified. Accordingly, in the expectation that the courts would hold that the words 'as beneficial owner' inserted into a Land Registry form of transfer can have the same operation as if inserted into a conveyance of unregistered land, we may now consider whether anything is thereby gained. Remember that here again the contract for sale will probably merge in the transfer since it is a specialty even if not a conveyance (cf *Knight Sugar Co* v *Alberta Railway Co* [1938] 1 All ER 266).

In the first place, the implied covenants for title will be of obvious value if the freehold land transferred is registered with a possessory or qualified title, since protection may be required in case of rights and interests subsisting prior to or excepted from registration respectively (see ss 6, 7 and 20(2) and (3) of the Land

Registration Act 1925). Further, since a transferee of freehold land will take subject to minor interests if the transfer is made without valuable consideration (see s 20(4) of the same Act), it is still often stated that introduction of the implied covenants for title will then be desirable (eg, Ruoff and Roper, *Registered Conveyancing*, 4th ed, at p 288). However, this seems to overlook the point that the full covenants are only implied by conveying as beneficial owner for valuable consideration (s 76(1)(A) of the Law of Property Act 1925) and that, *if anything* (nothing is advised), the transfer will be made 'as settlor' (see s 76(1)(E) of the same Act).

Of more real importance is the less rare case of a transfer for valuable consideration of freehold land by a proprietor registered with an absolute title. Is there any point in inserting the words 'as beneficial owner'? The semi-official opinion appears to be that there is little, the past two Chief Land Registrars still subscribing to the following (in Ruoff and Roper, *Registered Conveyancing*, 4th ed, at p 270:

> . . . if the operation of the covenant (power to convey with quiet enjoyment) is compared with the effect of a transfer for value of freehold land registered with an absolute title, which is as watertight as a title can be, it appears to do no more than reiterate the legal position created by registration of the transfer and it may seem to perform no unperformed or useful function

(though this opinion is again completely contradicted, as to overriding interests, two pages later). The semi-classic opinion was to the same effect. In Brickdale and Stewart-Wallace, *Land Registration Act 1925*, 4th ed, it is suggested in a footnote (at p 257), that practice should continue to comply with the repealed s 16(3) of the Land Transfer Act 1897, under which a vendor with absolute title was not required to enter into covenants for title.

As far only as *registrable* interests are concerned, these two opinions, being based on the nature of an absolute title, are probably correct: the transferee should not be affected by such interests unless they are registered (but cp *Peffer* v *Rigg* [1977] 1 WLR 285 and *Lyus* v *Prowsa Developments Ltd* [1982] 1 WLR 1044, pp 161–162); if they are registered, then not only will the purchaser, in the usual way, have notice of their existence, but by r 77(1)(*a*) the implied covenants for title take effect as if the transfer was expressly made subject to them. Indeed, what is expressed to be transferred is 'the land comprised in the title above mentioned' (which must mean both the land physically and the estate and interest therein) and this amounts to incorporating by reference into the instrument of transfer all the entries on the register. Further, the actual transfer only takes effect on and by virtue of an appropriate entry on the register (s 19(1) of the Land Registration Act 1925). Nevertheless, a warning reference must be made here to *Watts* v *Waller* [1973] 1 QB 153, where damages actually were recovered from a vendor of registered land in respect of a land charge protected on the register, *but* r 77(1)(*a*) had not been relied on.

(b) Overriding interests

However, the difficult and controversial problem (to which the two opinions cited above do not appear to be directed) is whether the implied covenants for title afford protection against *overriding* interests, since these are neither entered on the register nor overreachable as minor interests (see s 3(xv) and (xvi) of the Land Registration Act 1925). The diverse list of overriding interests is set out in s 70(1) of the Act, and the fact that a transferee necessarily takes subject to any there may be even without notice (s 20(1)(*b*)) is one of the weaknesses of the system of registered conveyancing. The suggestion has been made and can be accepted that the only overriding interest to escape the covenants for title would be a right 'in course of being acquired under the Limitation Acts' (see MJ Russell at (1970) 34 Conv (NS) 190–1). Also the reader will no doubt have noticed that many of the decided cases on the implied covenants for title in *un*registered conveyancing arose out of what would have been overriding interests in registered conveyancing; eg, *Eastwood* v *Ashton* [1915] AC 900 (squatter's rights—s 70(1)(*f*) of the Land Registration Act 1925); *Stoney* v *Eastbourne Rural District Council* [1927] 1 Ch 367 (public right of way—s 70(1)(*a*)); *Chivers & Sons Ltd* v *Air Ministry, Queens' College, Cambridge, third parties* [1955] Ch 585 (chancel repairs—s 70(1)(*c*)). As illustrated by these cases, the existence of an overriding interest could be a breach of any one of the four covenants for title implied in a sale 'as beneficial owner' (Pt I of Sched 2 to the Law of Property Act 1925).

The practice in registered conveyancing is for a vendor to disclose any existing overriding interests known to him but not for these to be mentioned in the instrument of transfer. In *un*registered conveyancing mere disclosure such as this would not absolve a vendor from liability under the implied covenants for title (*Page* v *Midland Railway* [1894] 1 Ch 11; *Great Western Railway Co* v *Fisher* [1905] 1 Ch 316), but in registered conveyancing it does by virtue of r 77(1) of the Land Registration Rules 1925, which provides that the covenants:

> take effect as though the disposition was expressly made subject to:—
>
> (*b*) any overriding interests of which the purchaser has notice and subject to which it would have taken effect, had the land been unregistered.

This rule is not without its difficulties. What can 'notice' comprehend in this registered conveyancing context? What do the words beginning 'and subject to which . . .' mean? Why is the comma where it is? But the result seems clear: once again vive la différence between registered and unregistered conveyancing. Thus in a case where, after completion, property was found to be still subject to a tenancy and the purchasers recovered damages for failure to give vacant possession, Stamp J remarked:

> Alternatively, the [purchasers] claimed damages for breach of the implied covenant for quiet enjoyment and title. Had the land not been, as in fact it was, registered land, the [purchasers] could, so it appears, subject to proof of the facts on which [they] rely, have succeeded in their alternative claim on the implied covenants, notwithstanding that they knew of the [tenant's] presence on the property at the time of the conveyance; but having regard to the terms of the relevant Land Registration Rules 1925 counsel for the [purchasers] felt unable to argue before me that this was not fatal to the [purchasers'] claim which accordingly was not proceeded with

(in *Hissett* v *Reading Roofing Co Ltd* [1969] 1 WLR 1757, at p 1759).

In view of r 77(1)(*b*), therefore, the present question is the position where there are existing overriding interests *not disclosed* (or otherwise known) to the transferee. The facile answer has been suggested that it follows from the provision in r 77(1)(*b*) itself, that all such other overriding interests must be covered by the covenants for title (Law Commission, Published Working Paper No 37, para 31(*c*)). But can the answer really be so disappointingly simple? Must the long discussed, divergent views expressed by very learned writers all be dismissed as beside the simple point?

First, in 1934, the late Professor Harold Potter, in his classic though ill-written *Registered Land Conveyancing*, stated (at p 69) that the implied covenants for title probably would *not* be effective in the case of an undisclosed overriding interest, giving the reason (inadequately) that 'the transfer by registration only confers upon the transferee the estate of the proprietor subject to the overriding interests, if any, affecting the estate.' He therefore recommended and drafted an express proviso extending the implied covenants in this respect. In 1941, Potter used his book substantially unaltered as the preliminary section of his vol 3 of *Key and Elphinstone, Precedents in Conveyancing* (14th ed of the whole, but the first volume on Registered Conveyancing). In the same year Mr R E Megarry (as he then was), reviewing that edition of *Key and Elphinstone* in 57 LQR 564, jumped heavily on Potter's statement. Understandably taking Potter's contention to be that overriding interests are excluded from the implied covenants for title by the words 'other than those subject to which the conveyance is expressly made' (see para 2 of Pt I of Sched 2 to the Law of Property Act 1925) on the ground that it is expressly provided that a transfer is subject to all overriding interests, Megarry said (at p 566): '"Subject to which the conveyance is made" and "subject to which the conveyance is expressly made" are two different phrases.' In other words, as an instrument of transfer is not *expressly* made subject to overriding interests, the implied covenants for title are effective in this respect. The following year, however, Potter returned to the attack with a most abstruse article in reply (58 LQR 356).

In effect, Potter said that Megarry had failed to pick upon the primary reason for the view stated (which was hardly surprising since this reason was not itself stated). In this chapter, under the sub-heading 'Words of limitation' (at p 272), it was pointed out that the covenants for title are only implied into a conveyance 'as far as regards the subject-matter . . . expressed to be conveyed' (s 76(1) of the Law of Property Act 1925), so that they afford no protection where a vendor conveys only such title as he has or simply without words of limitation (referring to *May v Platt* [1900] 1 Ch 616, and s 60(1) of the Law of Property Act 1925). Potter's reasoning is based on applying this proposition of *un*registered conveyancing to the undoubted fact that no words of limitation appear in a transfer of registered land, all that is expressed to be transferred being 'the land comprised in the title above mentioned'. In other words, the transferor transfers only what he is registered with, which is indeed all he has. What is the proprietor of an absolute title in freehold land registered with? The answer is: the fee simple, subject, inter alia, to any overriding interests affecting the land (see ss 5(*b*) and 20(1)(*b*) of the Land Registration Act 1925). Therefore, a transferee cannot be heard to complain under the implied covenants for title if all he gets is what was expressed to be transferred to him.

Despite the very great respect accorded to any view expressed by Megarry, it does appear to the present writer that the reasoning of Potter's reply is absolutely logical, sound and to be preferred. Further, it gains indirect support from the decision in *Re Chowood's Registered Land* [1933] Ch 574, that no loss is caused, and so no indemnity available, when the register is rectified to give effect to an overriding interest (see also *Re Boyle's Claim* [1961] 1 WLR 339). Accordingly, Megarry's view, expressed before Potter had fully stated his reasons, should perhaps be regarded as given per incuriam. In other words, the *implied* covenants for title are probably *not* effective protection in the case of undisclosed overriding interests. This being so, the inevitable conclusion would be that the mere insertion of the words 'as beneficial owner' in a transfer for value of freehold land registered with absolute title probably is pointless.

A more recent view on what may be called the Potter-Megarry controversy, though adding nothing, is somewhat ironical. In 1954 a new edition of vol 3 of *Key and Elphinstone's Precedents in Conveyancing* appeared (15th ed of the whole but only the 2nd ed of vol 3) under the editorship of Mr T I Casswell, a registrar of HM Land Registry. In this edition the view of the author (Potter) is explicitly dissented from by Mr Casswell (at p 128), who entirely accepts Megarry's view without apparently adverting at all to the author's convincing reply. However, the practitioner's guiding principle of safety first prevailed, and the proviso recommended by Potter expressly extending the implied covenants for title to cover overriding interests still found a place amongst the precedents (cl 1, Form IV, on p 408).

For further reading reference ought now to be made to PH Kenny at [1981] Conv 32–7, purporting to perceive Potter's fallacies, and to MJ Russell again at [1982] Conv 145–50, turning his attention to leasehold transfers too.

H   WORDS OF GRANT

In accordance with the scheme of this book of considering in turn the traditional parts of a deed of conveyance, the operative words (customarily 'the vendor as beneficial owner *hereby conveys* unto the purchaser . . .') have now been reached. The covenants for title implied by phrases such as 'beneficial owner' have already been dealt with at inordinate length. By happy contrast, dealing with words of grant requires less than a page. There are but three points worth mentioning.

First, what verb should be used in a conveyance to pass an estate or interest in land? The answer is: any verb you like. Section 51(2) of the Law of Property Act 1925 provides that: 'The use of the word grant is not necessary to convey land or to create any interest therein.' Thus any appropriate word may be used, such as the customary 'conveys' in a conveyance (which is indeed used in the forms in Scheds 4 and 5 to the Law of Property Act 1925) or, for example, 'assents' in an assent. Further, it appears that an *in*appropriate word such as 'assents' in a conveyance, or presumably 'conveys' in an assent, will be equally effective provided only that the intention of the parties to pass the estate or interest concerned from one to the other is apparent (see *Re Stirrup's Contract* [1961] 1 WLR 449, but cf *Hanbury* v *Bateman* [1920] 1 Ch 313, post, p 303).

Second, the Law of Property Act 1925, s 59(2), provides that: 'The word . . . "grant" does not, in a deed made after [1 October 1845] imply any covenant in law, save where otherwise provided by statute.' The only two statutes known to the writer otherwise providing are so remote from everyday realities that a passing reference is all they warrant: s 22 of the Queen Anne's Bounty Act 1838 and s 132 of the Lands Clauses Consolidation Act 1845. The covenants that these two sections imply by the use of the word 'grant' are substantially like those implied for title by s 76 of the Law of Property Act 1925.

Third and last, the prescribed Land Registry forms, of course, use the word 'transfer' (see, eg, Form 19 in the Schedule to the Land Registration Rules 1925). In the rare event of it being desired to use the word 'grant' to take advantage of one or other of the two sections referred to in the preceding paragraph, then the suggested formula is 'grant and transfer,' obtaining the best of both (see *Key and Elphinstone, Precedents in Conveyancing*, 15th ed, vol 3, at p 434).

I   PARCELS

The traditional form of conveyance of unregistered land after the operative words—'the vendor as beneficial owner hereby conveys unto the purchaser'—customarily continues with the *parcels clause*. The purpose of this clause, familiarly introduced by 'ALL THAT . . .', is simply to provide a physical description of the property conveyed. Whether any particular piece or parcel of land is within any particular description involves questions of construction and of fact (see *Goodtitle d Radford* v *Southern* (1813) 1 M & S 299). This has two consequences, first, precedents (judicial and otherwise) are of minimal assistance since what is the appropriate description will depend on and vary with the land in question. Secondly, the parcels clause strictly requires the most precise draftsmanship because it embodies the essential (or lay) object of the whole exercise. The practical difficulties presented by this have even received sympathetic recognition in the House of Lords, Lord Sumner saying (in *Eastwood* v *Ashton* [1915] AC 900, at p 916):

> Conveyancers, however, have to do the best they can with the facts supplied to them and it is only now and again that confusion arises.

As to the need for three-dimensional parcels clauses, see a note at [1977] Conv 297–8; also *Commissioner for Railways* v *Valuer-General* [1974] AC 328.

1   Plans

One neat method of solving the problem of framing a complete and accurate verbal description is to pass the buck by referring to a visual description by means of a plan. This saves work; frequently a satisfactory plan can be copied off either the abstract or the contract for sale, and if not the client can be made to pay a surveyor to produce a plan. This may not do the client much good. As the Report in 1979 of the Royal Commission on Legal Services incidentally emphasised in its chapter on Conveyancing (Vol 1, pp 284–5, para 21.10):

> Whether a title is registered or unregistered, one of the most fruitful sources of dispute and litigation relates to boundaries. Many conveyances have no plans. Some have plans which are too small. Some plans lack measurements. Some plans have measurements but do not reveal the point from which the measurement has been taken. Many plans depict the size, shape and extent of the property wrongly.

Further reference may be made to a note about 'Bothersome Boundaries' at [1980] Conv 162–4.

There is, to put it at its lowest, no reason why a plan should not be used. Plans are included in the definition of document in the Civil Evidence Act 1968 (s 10(1)), and are normally admissible in evidence (s 2). Of course, the plan should, as a general rule, be incorporated into the conveyance by some words of reference in the parcels clause; it is insufficient merely to annex a plan to the conveyance (see *Re Otway* (1862) 13 Ir Ch R 222; and *Wyse* v *Leahy* (1875) IR 9 CL 384; vice versa, it is good conveyancing practice also to have a reference on the plan to the conveyance into which the plan is incorporated, and also to have the plan signed by the parties: see *Law Society's Digest*, Opinion No 157). As an exception to this general rule, Cross J has held that a plan can be looked at even where there is no reference to it, provided *one* the verbal description in the conveyance is not clear, *and two* the plan physically forms part of the conveyance, as by being bound up with it or drawn on it (*Leachman* v *L & K Richardson Ltd* [1969] 1 WLR 1129). The suggestion has also been made that plans may become admissible in other cases as extrinsic evidence to explain the construction of ambiguities (by PVB at (1969) 85 LQR, pp 461–2) but more recently Buckley LJ contentedly confined himself within the four corners of the conveyance, looking outside only for comfort with a conclusion already reached (*Wigginton & Milner Ltd* v *Winster Engineering Ltd* [1978] 1 WLR 1462, at p 1474); no decision was found necessary as to how far regard could be had to extraneous matters (see ibid, at p 1475; cp *Willson* v *Greene* [1971] 1 WLR 635, regarding pegs in the ground, and *Neilson* v *Poole* (1969) 20 P & CR 909 concerning conveyances to adjoining purchasers).

However, assuming a plan is effectively used, shifting the work does not necessarily involve shifting responsibility; a solicitor has a duty to satisfy himself as to the identity of the property (see *Law Society's Digest*, Opinion No 127, which adds that the method of doing so is a matter for his discretion and that personal inspection is not, as a rule, necessary). The old dictum that lawyers cannot be expected to count may no longer be true (hence the Final Accounts Examination), but solicitors have as yet no map-reading badge to compete for and checking plans remains outside our professional competence. Nevertheless attention may justifiably be called to certain legal principles by which conveyancing by reference to plans should be tested.

General entitlement—By way of stating another general rule, a purchaser ought and is entitled to ensure that there is in the conveyance to him a description of the property which, first, is complete and accurate; secondly, identifies the land with that which he has agreed to buy; and thirdly, is sufficiently connected with the description in the title deeds if not identical (see, eg, per Swinfen Eady J in *Re Sansom and Narbeth's Contract* [1910] 1 Ch 741, at p 749). In achieving such a description, the purchaser has, of course, the initiative in that it is almost invariably his obligation to prepare the conveyance and submit a draft for the vendor's approval (see as to this Condition 19 of the National Conditions of Sale, 20th ed; Condition 17 of The Law Society's Conditions of Sale, 1980 edition). Indeed the purchaser's choice of form is not only his obligation but his privilege:

> Where it is simply a question of convenience to the purchaser, not involving any matter of substance affecting the vendor, it is idle for the vendor to raise objections as to the form of the conveyance

(per Wood V-C in *Cooper* v *Cartwright* (1860) Johns 679, at p 685; see also *Law Society's Digest*, Opinion No 146 and No 160(*c*) in Fourth Cumulative Supplement as to submission of a draft conveyance complete in itself—merely stating 'parcels as in contract' not sufficing).

However, although the purchaser may have the initiative, a vendor must not abandon all interest in the description of the property he is to convey. Whilst accuracy is the purchaser's right, it is the vendor's duty: it is a question of substance, as well as one of convenience. This is merely one aspect of the rule that a grant is to be construed most strongly against the grantor on the basis of no derogation from grant and what the vendor risks is breach of the covenants for title (see post p 289). Accordingly, choosing a final description should be in the nature of a joint endeavour.

Contract description—The first principle, then, in choice of description is that it must give effect to the contract for sale (*Monighetti* v *Wandsworth Borough Council* (1908) 73 JP 91). Since this is so, the importance of the contract description in fact representing the intentions of the parties will be readily appreciated. For example, if a purchaser tenders a conveyance with a plan in accordance with the contract plan, the vendor cannot object that it includes more land than he really intended (see *Re Lindsay and Forder's Contract* (1895) 72 LT 832, also *Lloyd* v *Stanbury* [1971] 1 WLR 535), nor can the purchaser complain that it includes less than he really thought (see *Gordon-Cumming* v *Houldsworth* [1910] AC 537).

What is more, the vendor may look in vain to qualifying words. Thus in *Re Lindsay and Forder's Contract* (1895) 72 LT 832, the contract plan bore a note that 'this plan is simply prepared as a guide to intending purchasers, and its accuracy in regard to area, measurement, abuttal or otherwise is in no way guaranteed', and it was held that, notwithstanding the note, it formed part of the contract, and that the purchaser was entitled to a conveyance of the whole of the land coloured on the plan. Similarly in *Re Freeman and Taylor's Contract* (1907) 97 LT 39 a contract plan had had on it: 'Note—This plan is for the purpose of delineation only', with the obvious intention, one might have thought, of weakening the plan's effect. However, Kekewich J held that the note meant that the plan was merely not drawn to scale, so that its lines and proportions had still to be taken as correct. Again in *Re Sparrow and James' Contract* [1910] 2 Ch 60, a plan was attached to the contract particulars with a caveat to the effect that it was for reference only and that no guarantee of the accuracy was given, although it was believed to be accurate. In the parcels clause of the draft conveyance submitted by the purchaser the premises were expressed to be 'delineated or shown on the plan drawn on the back of these presents', and that plan was a copy of the contract plan. The vendor proposed inserting 'by way of elucidation and not of warranty' before 'delineated'. Farwell J held that, since the purchaser was on the facts entitled to have a conveyance by reference to a plan, the vendor was not entitled to insert any qualifying words.

However, the caveat on the contract was not absolutely dismissed: there was a hint that it might enable the vendor to correct the plan on proper evidence if the purchaser was refusing to complete on the ground that the plan was inaccurate (ibid, p 63). But, as to this, compare *Jackson* v *Bishop* (1979) CA (noted at [1982] Conv 324–6); in that case there was a note on a developer's site plan that 'the plot boundaries as shown may be subject to adjustments'; this was held merely to mean that the vendors could alter their layout only

> until they had sold the plots off. But once they have represented to a purchaser that he is going to get a plot in accordance with their site plan, a scale plan which shows the position of his house and shows the nature and the shape of the plot that he is going to get, it cannot in my view lie in their mouths to say "We are not responsible for the fact that you are not getting what was represented on that plan at all; you are getting an irregularly shaped plot which bears little, if any, resemblance to the plot shown on the plan, and it was for your advisers to discover at the time when the contract was prepared whether the plan accurately represented the boundaries which we, the vendors, were able to convey to the purchasers"

(per Buckley LJ).

This last cited case also indicates that the vendor's duty here is not simply contractual: liability in negligence was imposed on the principle that an estate developer owes a duty of care to the purchaser to ensure that the site plan is accurately drawn, not only to scale, but 'in the sense that it can without difficulty be related as it stands to existing features on the land' (per Bridge LJ). There seems no good reason why this tort duty should not be extended to private vendors (cp *Hone* v *Benson* (1978) 248 EG 1013) but it may not actually require much greater accuracy than already contractually required. Thus in *Denny* v *Hancock* (1870) 23 LT 686 a professionally drawn plan deceived even a professional (another surveyor) into thinking that an apparent boundary (an iron fence) corresponded with the real boundary ('a line of some half-dozen low wooden posts sunk into the ground, which were scarcely visible, except on a careful inspection'). As the headnote put it, in such circumstances, 'it is the duty of the vendor not only distinctly to mark the real boundary on his plan, but to describe it so as to preclude mistakes in the particulars of sale.' Accordingly the purchaser was held entitled to resist specific performance.

Needless to say, any vendor caught in breach of duty here may well blame his professional advisers for letting him down and may even expect judicial encouragement. Thus in *Scarfe* v *Adams* [1981] 1 All ER 843, CA, at p 845, Cumming-Bruce LJ expressed the hope that:

> this judgment will be understood by every conveyancing solicitor in the land as giving them warning, loud and clear, that a conveyancing technique which may have been effective in the old days to convey large property from one vendor to one purchaser will lead to nothing but trouble, disputes and expensive litigation if applied to the sale to separate purchasers of a single house and its curtilage divided into separate parts. For such purposes it is absolutely essential that each parcel conveyed shall be described in the conveyance or transfer deed with such particularity and precision that there is no room for doubt about the boundaries of each, and for such purposes if a plan is intended to control the description, an Ordnance map on a scale of 1:2500 is worse than useless. The plan or other drawing bound up with the deed must be on such a large scale that it clearly shows with precision where each boundary runs. In my view the parties to this appeal are the victims of sloppy conveyancing for which the professional advisers of vendor and purchasers appear to bear the responsibility. We are not concerned in this appeal with determining or apportioning that responsibility. This court has to try to order the confusion created by the conveyancers.

Beyond boundaries, the vendor's duty goes further: his plan must not mislead the purchaser as to anything else either. Thus in *Dykes* v *Blake* (1838) 4 Bing (NC) 463, the plan had been so detailed as to suggest to prospective purchasers that it indicated every easement to which the property was subject. In fact there was one right of way not shown but which could have been discovered by inspection of a lease referred to in the particulars of sale. Tindal CJ held (at p 476):

> that the inspection of the plan would lull all suspicion to sleep, and that it was calculated, not simply to give no information, but actually to mislead. Particulars and plans of this nature should be so framed as to convey clear information to the ordinary class of persons who frequent sales by auction; and they would only become a snare to the purchaser, if after the bidder has been misled by them, the seller should be able to avail himself of expressions which none but lawyers could understand or attend to.

Accordingly the purchaser was entitled to rescind (cp *Faruqi* v *English Real Estates Ltd* [1979] 1 WLR 963 as to adequate disclosure, ante p 66). Again in *Bascomb* v *Beckwith* (1869) 20 LT 862, the framing and colouring on a plan misled the purchaser into believing that a nearby plot was part of a building estate sold subject to restrictive covenants whereas in reality it had been retained by the vendor. It was held that the vendor would not be entitled to specific performance unless he entered into a restrictive covenant covering the retained plot too. Compare, however, *Tucker* v *Vowles* [1893] 1 Ch 195, where a binding building scheme with restrictive covenants was not deduced from an estate plan, with *Whitehouse* v *Hugh* [1906] 2 Ch 283 where reliance on an estate plan as embodying a representation as to the existence of a road failed only because of a condition of sale allowing variations of the plan.

Further, choosing a description of the property sold should not mean passively lifting a parcels clause from the abstract of title. As Lord Kinnear has said (in *Gordon-Cumming* v *Houldsworth* [1910] AC 537, at p 547):

> it is the duty of the conveyancer in framing a disposition upon sale not to take for granted that he is to follow the exact terms of the description of the existing title, but to make full enquiry into the facts in order that he may be able to describe correctly the subject intended to be disponed.

An illustration of this occurred in *Wallington* v *Townsend* [1939] Ch 588, where there was a contract to sell land described by a plan which was an exact copy of the plan on the conveyance to the vendor. Unfortunately, it had been overlooked that in the meantime the vendor had also purchased the adjoining bungalow and made certain alterations. Consequently the contract plan contained part of the bathroom, lavatory, coal box and drains of the adjoining bungalow. Morton J held that this 'disputed strip' was in fact included in the contract, but, happily for the vendor's modesty, the case is only reported on the question of damages for breach of contract.

This sort of boundary alteration may be very difficult indeed for the conveyancer to discover by enquiry, as was well illustrated by *Hopgood* v *Brown* [1955] 1 WLR 213. There the conveyance to the purchaser had been by reference to a plan on an earlier conveyance. The vendor, however, had in the meantime permitted the next-door neighbour to build a garage which in fact substantially jutted over the proper dividing boundary, although neither had realised this. The Court of Appeal held that the vendor was estopped from denying that the proper boundary was as altered by the garage and that the purchaser as a successor in title was also estopped (cp *Penfold and Penfold* v *Cooke* (1978) 128 NLJ 736, CA). Earlier in *Bell* v *Marsh* [1903] 1 Ch 528 a like result had been reached with an encroaching greenhouse, but on the basis of adverse possession for the statutory period and despite a claim that the greenhouse's owner (a solicitor) and his successors were estopped by his negligence from claiming such a title. See also *Howton* v *Hawkins* (1966) 110 SJ 547 (where conveyances of freehold reversions were construed as including strips of land which the lessees had illegitimately incorporated into their gardens), and compare *Curtis* v *Chamberlain* (1969) 212 EG 277, CA (where leases of adjoining properties were renewed by reference to the original plans, disregarding intervening agreements, with the consequence of re-transferring a strip of land from one tenant to the other).

Further, where the boundaries are shown uncertainly in the title deeds, disputes as to their lines are sometimes sensibly settled by an agreement on the ground which determines the 'parcels' for the future. However, it appears that such an agreement needs neither evidence in writing nor registration as an estate contract to bind successors in title (see *Neilson* v *Poole* (1969) 20 P & CR 909). Again, how can the conveyancer possibly be sure of knowing all the relevant factors outside the title deeds?

Conveyance description—Assuming that the vendor had done his duty and described the property sold in a manner neither inaccurate nor misleading, it might be thought that that is that. Not so. Read the following passage from Seaborne, *Vendor and Purchaser*, 7th ed, p 405, which was quoted with express approval by Swinfen Eady J in *Re Sansom and Narbeth's Contract* [1910] 1 Ch 741, at p 747:

It is considered by some practitioners that a vendor may insist upon a repetition of the exact words of the contract, and may refuse to convey by any other description; but this is a misapprehension. The subject-matter of the contract is not words, but land; and if the purchaser considers that the words used in the contract do not describe the land which he intended to purchase with sufficient distinctness, he has a right to frame a new description, either by means of a plan or otherwise.

As to the right to a plan, see further p 286.

Assuming now that a fresh description is being framed, which is the better method: verbal or by reference to a plan? In the old leading case of *Eastwood* v *Ashton* [1915] AC 900 the conveyance in question contained four overlapping descriptions as follows:

All that farm called . . . Bank Hey Farm . . . containing 84 acres 3 roods and 4 perches or thereabouts and in the occupation of [names of two tenants] all of which premises are more particularly described in the plan endorsed on these presents and are delineated and coloured red in such plan.

The House of Lords rejected the first three descriptions, the first by name because there was no longer any farm so called, the second by acreage because it was only 'thereabouts' and anyway the disputed strip was of only one-twelfth of an acre, and the third by occupation because the tenants had sublet (the Court of Appeal, reversed, in fact had preferred this third description). It was accepted that 'the one accurate guide is this endorsed plan' (per Lord Parker of Waddington, at p 908), by which the disputed strip was included, although it was added that in such a case all four descriptions might have to be considered together to construe any one of them. This point that the court 'must have regard to the conveyance as a whole, including any plan which forms part of it' when ascertaining the property conveyed was recently restated by Buckley LJ in *Wigginton & Milner Ltd* v *Winster Engineering Ltd* [1978] 1 WLR 1462, at p 1473—the new leading case.

In view, perhaps, of this last point, it was also indicated in *Eastwood* v *Ashton* that one description alone is all that is required or necessary, Lord Sumner saying (at [1915] AC 916):

> If, however, several different species of description are adopted, risk of uncertainty at once arises, for if one is full, accurate and adequate, any others are otiose if right, and misleading if wrong.

The case by no means says that description by plan is always better, but it does demonstrate the possible inadequacy of verbal descriptions (see also per Stamp LJ in *Wallis's Holiday Camp* v *Shell-Mex* [1975] QB 94, at p 105). Thus in one modern case where the precise extent of land sold was in dispute, Brightman J observed:

> If there is a moral to this unfortunate story, it is the danger of dispensing with a plan to a contract of sale, particularly where natural boundaries are not obvious and the vendor is selling part only of his land

(in *Lloyd* v *Stanbury* [1971] 1 WLR 535, at p 544). In that case the moral was certainly thrust home to the vendor who suffered in damages, in effect, for failure to use a definitive plan. A good illustration of natural and obvious boundaries rendering a plan superfluous occurred with the conveyance of a named island in *Collector of Land Revenue, Singapore* v *Hoalim* [1978] AC 525, PC.

Right to a plan—However, assuming that the vendor has for some reason adopted only a verbal description in the contract for sale, what is the position if the purchaser submits a draft conveyance incorporating a plan which he has himself had prepared? In other words, can the vendor properly refuse to convey by reference to a plan?

Before considering any of the cases, three general principles may be restated: first, unless a question of substance is involved, the purchaser has choice of form; secondly, the form of the parcels clause is not in itself a question of substance, although its accuracy (whatever the form) is; and thirdly:

> The vendor is not at liberty to say that he does not know the boundaries of his own land, or does not know what he meant by the contract. It must be assumed that he does know, and if he knows he must be able to say whether the purchaser's description is correct or not; and he should either admit its correctness or point out where it is incorrect.

This passage was taken from Seaborne, *Vendor and Purchaser*, 7th ed, p 405, and approved by Swinfen Eady J in *Re Sansom and Narbeth's Contract* [1910] 1 Ch 741, at p 749 (see also per Farwell J in *Re Sparrow and James' Contract* (1902) [1910] 2 Ch 60, at p 62; and *Law Society's Digest*, Opinions Nos 148 and 151).

From these three principles it would clearly follow that a vendor is *not* entitled to refuse to convey by reference to a plan, if the purchaser wishes it, but is only entitled to correct the plan. However, the two most relevant cases hardly provide unqualified support for this proposition. In the first case, *Re Sansom and Narbeth*, ante, where the vendor (in fact his solicitors) refused to convey by reference to *any* plan, Swinfen Eady J said (at p 749):

> I consider that, *in all simple cases in which a plan would assist the description*, the purchaser has a right to have a plan on the conveyance. I am not, however, prepared to say that in every case a purchaser is entitled to have a description by plan.

This qualification, imported by the italicised words, of the purchaser's right on principle to a plan, is with respect very odd indeed. One might have thought that a plan would *only* assist the description in complicated cases. As to this, the learned judge was expressly influenced (also at p 749) by the consideration that, unless the case were simple, 'the form of the conveyance so far as regards the accuracy of the plan might lead to much litigation', and he referred in particular to the difficulty of defining the exact boundaries of a considerable estate. However, on this two comments may be made: first, that in making this qualification Swinfen Eady J appears to overlook the third principle above (despite having himself approved it), and secondly, that the difficulties which he had in mind are now in practice taken care of by the standard forms of contract (see Condition 13(2) of the National Conditions of Sale, 20th ed, and Condition 13(1) of The Law Society's Conditions of Sale, 1980 edition—'The vendor . . . shall not be required to define exact boundaries . . .').

In the second case, *Re Sharman and Meade's Contract* [1936] Ch 755, the vendor refused to convey by reference to the plan on the draft conveyance submitted by the purchaser unless it was checked by a surveyor at the purchaser's expense. This was such a simple case that a verbal description would have been sufficient. Farwell J referring to *Re Sansom and Narbeth*, ante, said (at p 758) that Swinfen Eady J had not intended a hard and fast rule that in *every* simple case a purchaser was entitled to a plan. So far so good, but he went on (at p 760) to lay down the purported rule that the duty of a vendor is simply to convey under a description which is 'a sufficient and satisfactory identification' of the property. Therefore in his judgment only if a plan is necessary for such a description is the purchaser entitled to one, since otherwise the vendor would be put unnecessarily to extra expense. In the case, the vendor's verbal description was held sufficient without a plan.

It will be noted that this purported rule is both. wider (not being confined to simple cases) and narrower (a plan being necessary to rather than just assisting the description) than that propounded by Swinfen Eady J (in *Re Sansom and Narbeth*, ante). In addition, it may be seen that the rules laid down in the two cases not only conflict with each other but also with the three general principles which were mentioned above and which were indeed recognised in the cases. For authority, both judges looked only to the earlier decision of Farwell J (senior) in *Re Sparrow and James' Contract* (1902) [1910] 2 Ch 60, where he enunciated similar rules to those in *Re Sharman*, although deciding on the facts that without a plan the description there would be insufficient.

What obviously weighed most heavily with Farwell J (father and son) was dislike of the thought that an unreasonable purchaser could compel a vendor to incur unnecessary expense. Not, of course, the expense of preparing the plan but of paying a surveyor to check its accuracy. However, surely this quite improperly overlooks the principle that a vendor must be taken to know what he is selling. After all, a vendor unquestionably must incur expense in showing title, ie, the quality of his ownership: why not also in showing the quantity?

Lastly, on this particular question, it should be noted that, whether or not a purchaser is generally entitled to insist on a plan, apparently a mortgagee or trustee can be called on to convey only by the words and descriptions by which the conveyance was made to him (see *Goodson* v *Ellisson* (1827) 3 Russ 583, at p 594).

Words of reference—Assuming that the property is to be described in the conveyance by a plan, does it matter what particular words of reference are used in the parcels clause to incorporate the plan? In *Eastwood* v *Ashton* [1915] AC 900 the words used were:

all of which premises are *more particularly described in* the plan endorsed on these presents *and are delineated* and coloured red *in* such plan.

Lord Wrenbury said (at p 920) that:

these words seem to me to mean that the previous description may be insufficient for exact delimitation, and that the plan is to cover all deficiencies, if any.

The words of reference italicised are obviously strong, and should be used whenever sole reliance is to be placed on a plan. Thus in *Wallington* v *Townsend* [1939] Ch 588, where the words of reference used were 'more particularly delineated in' the plan prevailed. Again in *Baxendale* v *Instow Parish Council* [1982] Ch 14 land comprising a foreshore had been conveyed as 'more particularly delineated and described in the plan' which was sufficient to rebut any possible presumption that a conveyance of a movable foreshore had been intended.

Turning to words of reference which may weaken the effect of a plan, in *Horne* v *Struben* [1902] AC 454 there had been a grant of a farm with the boundaries specified both verbally and 'as will further appear by the diagram framed by the surveyor'. An inconsistency between the two descriptions was resolved by the Privy Council against the plan by construing the words used as 'merely an appeal to the diagram for further elucidation of the text and not a subordination of the text to the diagram' (at p 458).

However, the qualifying phrase most commonly used today is 'for the purpose of identification only'. The effect is that the plan may be looked to for elucidation but not contradiction of the verbal description: *Wigginton & Milner Ltd* v *Winster Engineering Ltd* [1978] 1 WLR 1462. In that case, the Court of Appeal reviewed the earlier authorities and it is now clear that the idea must be abandoned that any plan incorporated by such a phrase could at most be looked to for rough guidance as to the geographical situation of the land. On the contrary, such a plan can be taken as indicating precise boundaries whenever the parcels clause itself merely uses words of general description, ie, insufficiently precise to be open to detailed contradiction (see per Bridge LJ ibid, p 1475). Nevertheless, this remains a weakening phrase in the sense that where the verbal description is sufficient, the plan must be treated as subordinate and to be disregarded in the event of any inconsistency (cp per Buckley LJ ibid, at p 1470 and at pp 1475–6). This general approach was adopted in *Spall* v *Owen* (1981) 44 P & CR 36 where the essential description was 'known as plot no 1 . . . all of which property is for the purpose of identification delineated on the plan . . . annexed hereto and therein edged red': this site plan was looked at and prevailed.

Whilst it is obviously wrong to use a combination of strengthening and weakening words of reference (such as '. . . which for the purposes of identification only is more particularly described in . . .'; cf *Neilson* v *Poole* (1969) 20 P & CR 909), this leaves the question of which should be used. There is a tendency for a vendor's solicitor to stick out, against the purchaser's solicitor's opposition, for inclusion of the weakening words, which on reflection is peculiar since a verbal description is at least as likely to give too much land as is a plan and is much less likely to enjoy the precision due to preparation by a surveyor.

Such a dispute as this was decided by Farwell J in *Re Sparrow and James' Contract* [1910] 2 Ch 60 (ante p 283) in favour of the purchaser, ie, no weakening words. However, the learned judge remarked (at p 62):

I am not aware of any decision which shows that a plan on a conveyance amounts to a warranty that the plan is accurate.

If this were truly so, it would not matter whether qualifying words were inserted or not. But surely the correct view is that, provided the plan is incorporated into the parcels clause (see p 281), then in the absence of qualifying words it must be treated as one with the rest of the conveyance (see per Buckley LJ in *Wigginton & Milner Ltd v Winster Engineering Ltd* [1978] 1 WLR 1462, at p 1475), and therefore construed against the vendor not as a warranty of accuracy but on the principle of no derogation from grant. Further, the covenants for title implied by s 76 of the Law of Property Act 1925 relate to 'the subject-matter expressed to be conveyed', so that there may in fact be covenants, albeit qualified, as to the accuracy of a plan (as, indeed, in *Eastwood v Ashton* [1915] AC 900; see also *Wilson v Greene* [1971] 1 WLR 635, where liability under these covenants was the question).

Construction—It was pointed out in the preceding paragraph that, if incorporated, a plan must be treated as one with the rest of the conveyance. Accordingly, looking at both verbal and plan descriptions contained in one parcel clause:

The proper mode of construing any written instrument is to give effect to every part of it, if this is possible, and not to strike out or nullify one clause in a deed unless it be impossible to reconcile it with another and more express clause in the same deed

(per Romilly MR in *Re Strand Music Hall Co Ltd, ex parte European & American Finance Co Ltd* (1865) 35 Beav 153, at p 159). If an inconsistency nonetheless appears between the two descriptions, the impasse may be resolved by reliance on the so-called rule falsa demonstratio non nocet (a false description does no harm), to which Lord Sumner has added (in *Eastwood v Ashton* [1915] AC 900, at p 914), cum de corpore constat (provided the thing is certain). All that this means is that if the court is able to decide that one of the descriptions is true it can then reject the other false description(s). No a priori guide exists at all as to which description is to prevail (see Lord Parker in *Eastwood v Ashton,* ante,.at p 912), and a contention that the rule can only apply where the false follows the true was rejected by the Court of Appeal in *Cowen v Truefitt Ltd* [1899] 2 Ch 309 (see at pp 311 and 313).

Plans not prevalent—In each of the leading cases, old and new (ie, *Eastwood v Ashton* [1915] AC 900 and *Wigginton & Milner Ltd v Winster Engineering Ltd* [1978] 1 WLR 1462) a plan easily prevailed over a verbal description. However, this is far from always being the case. Thus in *Willis v Watney* (1881) 51 LJ Ch 181 a yard included in the verbal description but not coloured in the plan was held to be passed. Again, a plan drawn on a scale too small for the boundaries to be accurately traced was not able to control a verbal description in *Taylor v Parry* (1840) 1 Man & G 604 (although note that in *Hopgood v Brown* [1955] 1 WLR 213 the Court of Appeal simply took as straight a dividing boundary not clearly shown on the plan).

Following upon this, reference may be made to *Maxted v Plymouth Corporation* [1957] CLY 243, CA, also reported in *The Times* of 28 March 1957, which illustrates that a plan boundary may be rejected under the falsa demonstratio rule even though the falsity was deliberate. This case concerned the ownership of half a Devon hedge, which consisted of a bank of earth and stones some feet wide and high topped with bushes, since whoever owned it was liable to the Plymouth Corporation for the cost of making up the street on to which the hedge fronted. The appellant's vendor had owned up to the middle line of the hedge and the question was: what was conveyed to the appellant? This involved construing the parcels in the conveyance to the appellant and these contained the words:

> all that piece and parcel of land forming the northernmost portion of a field situate at Efford in the city of Plymouth in the County of Devon numbered 109 on the ordnance map . . . which said piece of land is delineated on the plan drawn herein.

The appellant, apparently foreseeing the possibility of road charges, had his architect who prepared the plan draw the boundary at the foot of the hedge, thus deliberately excluding any conveyance of his vendor's half of the hedge. Denning LJ commented (see *The Times* report) that he:

> could not imagine that the man who sold this land would have ever intended to keep in his own hands that little strip of Devon hedge, and if it had been drawn to his attention he would surely have done something about it,

but he added:

> nevertheless, if that was the true construction of the conveyance the court would have to give effect to it.

Despite this latter comment, the Court of Appeal were able to uphold their all too apparent inclination to decide that the appellant's ingenious plan—in both senses— failed. They looked at the conveyance and plan as a whole, made a comparison with the Ordnance Survey map referred to, and found that the boundary on the plan had been put ('maybe by design,' as Denning LJ remarked), in the wrong place. Accordingly, the boundary on the plan was rejected as falsa demonstratio, so that the appellant got the whole of the land up to the middle of the hedge and was liable for road charges.

Projections—As an example of another principle of construction, in *Truckell* v *Stock* [1957] 1 WLR 161 an apparent conflict between a plan and a verbal description was resolved without rejecting either description as false. In essence, an owner of adjoining plots had conveyed one plot as follows:

> all that land, dwelling-house, office, garages, outbuildings and premises . . . delineated and coloured pink and red on the plan attached hereto.

In fact, the footings and eaves of the dwellinghouse projected beyond the coloured portion. Although stating that, had there been a conflict the description by plan would have prevailed, the Court of Appeal held that the projections were passed on the basis that the plan merely showed boundaries at ground level whilst the verbal description, particularly the word 'dwelling-house,' showed the actual physical thing conveyed.

However, not cited to nor dealt with by the Court of Appeal was the apparently inconsistent decision in *Laybourn* v *Gridley* [1892] 2 Ch 53, where the essential facts were the exact reverse of those in *Truckell* v *Stock*, ante. Again there had been common ownership of two premises, a portion of one overhanging the other. Here the latter, the overhung one, was conveyed as follows:

> . . . all that . . . together with the messuage, tenements . . . and which said hereditaments and premises, *with the dimensions, abuttals, and boundaries thereof, are more particularly delineated* in the map or plan drawn on these presents and thereon coloured green.

North J said (at p 58):

> What is conveyed is the piece of land coloured green, with all the buildings thereon; that, in the absence of anything else to the contrary, passes everything above and below.

Accordingly, he held that the overhanging portion of the adjoining premises had been passed by the conveyance. This decision must be regarded either as impliedly overruled by *Truckell* v *Stock*, ante, or else, preferably, as distinguishable as depending on the construction of the parcels clause in question, particularly of the italicised words.

Reference may also be made to the extreme case of hang-over (or under) which occurred in *Grigsby* v *Melville* [1974] 1 WLR 80, CA, where it was contended that, since the plan attached to a conveyance of a cottage was merely of the boundaries as they existed at ground level, a cellar wholly beneath the cottage was not conveyed. This contention was rejected, notwithstanding that the only practical access was from retained land and that easements and quasi-easements had been excepted and reserved to the vendor. But this was rather more than a mere projection case of the *Truckell* v *Stock*, ante, sort.

Land Registry transfers—Turning finally to registered conveyancing, it may first be said that this section is concerned only with plans, if any, on the instrument of transfer and not directly with plans or maps kept by HM Land Registry. (For details of these latter see rr 272–85 of the Land Registration Rules 1925 and consider a critically cadastral article by MM Barrett at [1981] Conv 257–68). Although s 76 of the Land Registration Act 1925 does provide generally how registered land may be described—'. . . regard being had to ready identification of parcels, correct descriptions of boundaries, and, so far as may be, uniformity of practice' (oh, counsel of perfection!)—parcels clauses are, in fact, included in the prescribed forms of transfer of registered freehold land.

If the *whole* of the land comprised in the title is transferred, then the short description prescribed is 'the land comprised in the title above referred to' (Land Registration Rules 1925, r 98 and Schedule, Form 19). This incorporates by reference the description contained in the property register of the title, which in turn refers to the general map or filed plan as well as having a short verbal description. Thus, although such transfers are invariably made by reference to a plan—indeed the plan is the very basis of registered conveyancing—the parties thereto never need to concern themselves with the questions of the preparation of and entitlement to a plan on the instrument of transfer which may arise in *un*registered conveyancing.

Further, in theory, no question of the correctness of the plan should arise, since, as Ruoff and Roper, *Registered Conveyancing*, in its detergent advertisement way still puts it (4th ed at p 43), the Registry plans are for every title 'accurate', 'revised to date', and 'clear and reliable', as against 'what is frequently a vague or inaccurate map endorsed upon an unregistered title deed'. However, it may be recalled in passing that the Registry plans are not always righter than right, as was demonstrated in *Lee* v *Barrey* [1957] Ch 251 (where the 'Brand X' plan on an earlier filed transfer actually prevailed with the Court of Appeal); see also *Re Boyle's Claim* [1961] 1 WLR 339. Whilst it is only fair to add that these were extremely rare occurrences it may be mentioned too that difficulties can be experienced in scaling-up Land Registry plans, since a millimetre's waver either way may make a four-foot difference (taking the normal scale of 1/1250 of the National Grid maps being used by the Registry). Such an error might be material (see *Bellotti* v *Chequers Developments Ltd* [1936] 1 All ER 89), but in practice these difficulties may be overcome by requesting the Registry to make or use a larger scale or more detailed plan (see *Registered Land Practice Notes*, 1982/83, p 24, F3).

Like questions to those arising in *un*registered conveyancing could perhaps arise as to any inconsistency between the verbal description in the property register of a title and the plan it refers to. Rule 285 of the Land Registration Rules 1925 provides that the Registrar 'shall decide any conflict between the verbal particulars and the filed plan or General Map'. However, it is arguable that the verbal particulars should always prevail since s 76 of the Land Registration Act 1925 concludes by providing that the filed plan, if any, or general map shall be used for assisting the identification of the land. In other words, the reference in the register to the filed plan is, in effect, 'for the purposes of identification only', an established qualifying phrase (see further, if not too far, an unhappy note at [1979] Conv 316–9).

If *part* only of the land comprised in a title is transferred, then the prescribed parcels clause is as follows: '. . . the land shown and edged with red on the accompanying plan and known as . . . [and—*if it is desired that a particular verbal description be entered on the Register*—described in the schedule hereto] being part of the land comprised in the title above referred to' (see Form 20, Schedule to the Land Registration Rules 1925). A note, much taken advantage of in built-up areas, is added to the effect that the special plan may be dispensed with if the verbal description is sufficient to enable the land to be identified on the Registry maps and plans. However, generally, a special plan must be incorporated into a transfer of part, so that the same questions of preparation and accuracy of (although not of entitlement to) a plan may arise as in *un*registered conveyancing (and see *Law Society's Digest*, Opinion No 1275).

Also there may again be inconsistencies between the verbal and plan descriptions but (although no qualifying phrase is prescribed or apparently permissible: *Registered Land Practice Notes*, 1982/83, p 15, C1), here the question will be for decision by the court and not by the Registrar under r 285 since here the conflict is not with 'the filed plan or General Map'. In such a case as this (whoever decides the conflict), the instrument of transfer can be seen to perform a dual function. First, it immediately provides the material for entries in the register, and secondly, it may in the future be the basis of a rectification of the register since it determines the rights between the parties. This consequence—resembling the situation in *Lee* v *Barrey* ante—even without any fault on the part of HM Land Registry, means simply that in such cases the register is not conclusive.

2 Presumptions

Any uncertainty caused by lack of precision in the parcels clause of a conveyance as to the position of boundaries may be cured by certain presumptions. In particular the presumptions relating to the following four sorts of boundary are worth mention, though the first three only briefly:

(1) *Roads*—The presumption is that the owner of land adjoining a road is the owner of the soil of one-half of the road (as to the surface, see *Attorney-General* v *Beynon* [1970] Ch 1). Therefore such soil is also presumed to be included in a conveyance of the land (see *London and North Western Railway Co* v *Mayor of Westminster* [1902] 1 Ch 269). This presumption applies to streets in towns as well as in the country (*Re White's Charities* [1898] 1 Ch 659), and to private roads (*Smith* v *Howden* (1863) 14 CB (NS) 398), but *not* to a railway (*Thompson* v *Hickman* [1907] 1 Ch 550) not semble to courtyards or squares.

Further, this presumption is rebuttable, not only expressly by precision in the parcels clause but also by an inference of a contrary intention on the part of the grantor which may be taken from the surrounding circumstances (see *Mappin Bros* v *Liberty & Co Ltd* [1903] 1 Ch 118). Thus, there will be a rebuttal if such circumstances show that the grantor purposes to use the soil for some particular purpose for which he needs to retain ownership (see *Leigh* v *Jack* (1879) 5 Ex D 264), eg, to lay out the roads of a building estate (see *Plumstead Board of Works* v *British Land Co* (1874) LR 10 QB 16; reversed on appeal on other grounds, ibid, p 203; but applied recently in *Giles* v *County Building Constructors Ltd* (1971) 22 P & CR 978).

(2) *Rivers*—The presumption again is that the owner of land adjoining a *non-tidal* river owns the bend of the river up to mid-stream (see per Bowen LJ in *Blount* v *Layard* [1891] 2 Ch 681*n*, at p 689*n*). Therefore again, if the parcels clause is not precise, half the bed will be presumed to be included in a conveyance of the land. If the river is *tidal* the bed belongs to the Crown at any point at which the water regularly flows and reflows unless granted away (*Attorney-General* v *Lonsdale* (1868) LR 7 Eq 377). As to the doctrine of accretion, see *Southern Centre of Theosophy Inc* v *State of South Australia* [1982] AC 706.

(3) *Fences*—Great faith but unhappily no authority supports a presumption that a wooden fence belongs to the owner of the land on the side where the supporting posts are. See much further the detailed discussion of this most troublesome boundary by JE Adams in (1971) *The Law Society's Gazette* vol 68, at pp 275 and 375.

(4) *Hedge and ditch*—Where two properties are separated by a hedge and single ditch there is a well-established presumption as to ownership:

> The rule is this: No man making a ditch can cut into his neighbour's soil, but usually he cuts it to the very extremity of his own land; he is, of course, bound to throw the soil which he digs out upon his own land; and often, if he likes, he plants a hedge on the top of it; therefore, if he afterwards cuts beyond the edge of the ditch, which is the extremity of his land, he cuts into his neighbour's land

(per Lawrence J in *Vowles* v *Miller* (1810) 3 Taunt 137, 138; see also *Weston* v *Lawrence Weaver Ltd* [1961] 1 QB 402).

For the rule to be applied, there must in fact be a ditch, ie, an artificial excavation. The presumption does not arise if there is a natural watercourse (*Marshall* v *Taylor* [1895] 1 Ch 641; cf *Jones* v *Price* [1965] 2 QB 618), nor if there is no ditch at all (*Collis* v *Amphlett* [1920] AC 271—no entitlement to 'ditch width'; see also *White* v *Taylor (No 2)* [1969] 1 Ch 160, where wasteland on one side was as good as a ditch for the purpose of preserving ownership of a hedge). Further, even if the presumption does arise it may be rebutted by evidence to the contrary, although since the presumption is a strong one, the rebutting evidence must be clear: *Henniker* v *Howard* (1904) 90 LT 157.

A modern illustration both of the non-arisal of the hedge and ditch presumption and of its rebuttal occurred in *Davey* v *Harrow Corporation* [1958] 1 QB 60, CA. In that case the plaintiff claimed damages for nuisance in respect of subsidence caused by the penetration of the roots of elm trees. The plaintiff alleged that the boundary to his plot was a concrete post and wire fence. This fence had been erected by the plaintiff's predecessor in title as close in as possible to the near side of certain bushes which bounded the plot on that side and which stood on a low bank on the far side of which was a ditch. The elm trees grew on the bank.

Thus, in the absence of evidence to the contrary, the stage was set for the application of the hedge and ditch presumption, and at first instance it was, in fact, applied by Sellers J, who held that the plaintiff had not proved that the elm trees belonged to the defendants. However, further evidence was admitted before the Court of Appeal, who, in a comparatively short judgment of the court read by Lord Goddard CJ (much of which judgment does not concern us), reversed Sellers J. In the first place, evidence was given of a meeting between the plaintiff's predecessor in title and a representative of the defendants at which it was agreed that the defendants should have the hedge and that the post and wire boundary fence should be as near thereto as possible. Thereafter the defendants always treated the hedge as theirs until the present action. It was held that this evidence effectively displaced the presumption based on the position of the ditch.

In the second place, and more important for present purposes, it was shown that in the various conveyances which formed the plaintiff's title, the parcels conveyed were always described by reference to the Ordnance Survey map. The point here is that there is no room for the hedge presumption if the correct position of the boundary can be established from the title deeds, for example, if the plans referred to therein are sufficiently precise. The evidence of an official from the Ordnance Survey Office was that the line on the map delineating the boundary in dispute indicated the centre of the existing hedge:

> This is in accordance with the invariable practice of the survey as was proved in *Fisher* v *Winch* [1939] 1 KB 666 and in our opinion, after that case and this, courts in future can take notice of this practice of the Ordnance Survey as at least prima facie evidence of what a line on the map indicates

(per Lord Goddard CJ at [1958] 1 QB 69; see also Cassels J in *Rouse* v *Gravelworks Ltd* [1940] 1 KB 489, at p 493).

Since parcels in unregistered conveyances are often described by reference to the Ordnance Survey map, or else to a plan based thereon, the latter point mentioned in *Davey* v *Harrow Corporation*, ante, is important as it would appear that in such cases the hedge and ditch presumption can never arise. At first sight, the point is of even greater importance in registered conveyancing than in unregistered conveyancing, since r 272 of the Land Registration Rules 1925 provides that 'the Ordnance Survey map shall be the basis of all registered descriptions of land'. Thus it appears to have been inferred from the above (eg, in a case note in 21 Conv (NS) 303; see also at (1958) 74 LQR 123) that the hedge and ditch presumption can therefore rarely if ever arise in registered conveyancing. This view overlooks the *'general boundaries rule'* contained in r 278 of the 1925 Rules, as follows:

> (1) Except in cases in which it is noted in the Property Register that the boundaries have been fixed, the filed plan or General Map shall be deemed to indicate the general boundaries only.

> (2) In such cases the exact line of the boundary will be left undetermined—as, for instance, whether it includes a hedge or wall and ditch, or runs along the centre of a wall or fence, or its inner or outer face, or how far it runs within or beyond it; or whether or not the land registered includes the whole or any portion of an adjoining road or stream.

> (3) When a general boundary only is desired to be entered in the register, notice to the owners of the adjoining lands need not be given.

> (4) This rule shall apply, notwithstanding that a part or the whole of a ditch, wall, fence, road, stream or other boundary is expressly included in or excluded from the title or that it forms the whole of the land comprised in the title.

This rule leaves the door wide open for reliance on all conceivable presumptions in the event of a boundary dispute relating to registered land (see as to a river bed, per Willmer, Diplock and Edmund Davies LJJ in *Hesketh* v *Willis Cruisers Ltd* (1968) 19 P & CR 573, at pp 575, 579 and 585, respectively).

J   EXCEPTIONS AND RESERVATIONS

Immediately after, although really as part of, the parcels clause in the traditional form of conveyance of land there comes, if at all, the phrase 'EXCEPT AND

RESERVING. . .' followed by a number of *things* (for want of a more imprecise term) which, in effect, the vendor wants for himself. Lumped together in this clause the technically minded may expect to find first, exceptions, second, reservations, and third, re-grants. For reasons which will appear, only the first of these three is properly placed after the parcels; the other two should be placed in the habendum (but cf Forms 5 and 6, Sched 5, Law of Property Act 1925).

Also amongst the so-called 'exceptions and reservations' one not infrequently finds out rights which have been reserved (or re-granted) on an earlier conveyance and subject to which the property is now being conveyed. This occurs generally because the draftsman has merely copied verbatim the earlier parcels clause. However, such rights should follow the habendum and be preceded by the words 'Subject to . . .' Otherwise the risk is run of creating new rights increasing the original burden (see *Scotson* v *Jones* (1961), unreported but noted at 231 LT News 187). However, the Court of Appeal has emphasised that the technical conveyancing phrase 'Excepting and reserving' is not necessarily of such significance that it will govern the construction of all that immediately follows it so as to convert existing rights into new grants (*Re Dances Way, West Town, Hayling Island* [1962] Ch 490; see per Lord Evershed MR at p 502, and per Upjohn J at p 506). Against this Buckley J has felt able to construe clauses beginning 'Subject to . . .' and following the habendum as extending to newly created rights (*White* v *Taylor (No 2)* [1969] 1 Ch 160). Note also the converse effect on 'subject to' of s 65(2) of the Law of Property Act 1925.

Incidentally, it should be noted that the use of capitals to introduce the exceptions and reservations may have some importance in construction. Thus Ungoed-Thomas J observed in one case:

> That this exception was not intended to be restricted (sic) in its scope to the immediately preceding words may be indicated by the capital letters in which "SAVE AND EXCEPT" is written

(*British Railways Board* v *Glass* [1964] 1 WLR 294, at p 303; affirmed on appeal at [1965] Ch 538). In fact the case concerned, not an exception, but strictly the re-grant of a right of way, which was accordingly held to be for all purposes and not confined to the matter mentioned immediately before in the conveyance. Thus what is indicated by capitals is whether the whole or only a part of the parcels clause is affected.

1 Distinguishing exceptions and reservations

The distinction between exceptions and reservations had received early seventeenth century statement by Coke in his *Commentary upon Littleton* as follows (1 Inst 47a):

> Note a diversitie betweene an exception (which is ever of part of the thing granted and of a thing *in esse*) . . . and a reservation which is alwaies of a thing not *in esse*, but newly created or reserved out of the land or tenement demised.

This distinction is still valid. Thus, as to exceptions, prima facie a grant of land includes physically everything above and below its surface (see *Allaway* v *Wagstaff* (1859) 4 H & N 681), but the grantor may limit the physical extent of his grant by expressly excluding or excepting from it some part of the land, such as a field, a house, a flat, trees or mines and minerals. The effect is that the part excepted simply does not pass by the grant (see *Doe d Douglas* v *Lock* (1835) 2 A & E 705). As Lord Simonds has said, in another context:

> In the simplest analysis, if *A* gives to *B* all his estate in Wiltshire except Blackacre, he does not except Blackacre out of what he has given; he just does not give Blackacre

(in *St Aubyn* v *Attorney-General* [1952] AC 15, at p 29, a death duty case). Any provisions added as to what the grantor shall or may do in relation to the part excepted generally operate only as covenants (see per Scrutton J in *Jones* v *Consolidated Anthracite Collieries Ltd* [1916] 1 KB 123, at p 135). Again the nature of a reservation may be inferred from Coke's words 'out of' and 'demised'. Denning LJ explained both this and the distinction from a re-grant more recently in a case concerning a so-called 'reservation' of sporting rights (*Mason* v *Clarke* [1954] 1 QB 460, CA, at p 466; reversed on appeal at [1955] AC 778, HL, without affecting this aspect) as follows:

> A "reservation" is only properly admitted of services to be rendered by the tenant, such as paying rent or providing a beast (heriot), whereas a right to come and kill and carry away wild animals is only a liberty or licence—a *profit à prendre*—which can take effect only by grant and not by exception and reservation. Words of reservation of sporting rights operate therefore, not by way of reservation proper, but by way of re-grant by the tenant.

In other words, today only a rent (whether rent service or rentcharge) issuing out of the land can properly be reserved, whilst incorporeal rights over the land (such as easements or profits à prendre) have strictly to be re-granted. Rarely, however, is this distinction appreciated even judicially; for example, Scrutton J said that he understood:

> a reservation in its technical sense to be the re-grant out of the subject-matter conveyed of something not previously existing, as a rent or an easement

(in *Jones* v *Consolidated Anthracite Collieries Ltd* [1916] 1 KB 123, at p 135). Nonetheless, it will be seen that this distinction between re-grants on the one hand and exceptions and reservations (properly so-called) on the other hand may be of importance with regard, at least, to construction and execution.

Thus the distinction and one important consequence were illustrated in *Johnstone* v *Holdway* [1963] 1 QB 601, where a vendor had contracted to sell certain land to a company and the company had directed a conveyance from the vendor to a purchaser of part of the land. Giving the judgment of the court, Upjohn LJ said:

> During the argument before us a point emerged that the exception and reservation of the mines and minerals was to the vendor, that is the legal owner, but the exception and reservation of the rights of way was to the company, the equitable owner. If the reservation of a right of way operated strictly as a reservation, then as the company had only an equitable title it would seem that only an equitable easement could have been reserved; but it is clear that an exception and reservation of a right of way in fact operates by way of regrant by the purchaser to his vendor, and the question, therefore, is whether as a matter of construction the purchaser granted to the company a legal easement or an equitable easement

(at pp 612–13). In fact, it was held that a legal easement had been granted but without, somewhat surprisingly, any reference being made to s 65(1) of the Law of Property Act 1925, which would, it is thought, have substantially supported the court's approach (see p 299).

2 'Except and reserving . . .'

In practice, as indicated, no attempt is ever made to separate the wheat from the chaff: exceptions, reservations and re-grants are all lumped together after the parcels clause. This in itself hardly matters, since if any question should arise the court will do the separating and decide which is which according to their substance rather than to what the parties have (mis)named them. Thus in *Attorney-General for NSW* v *Dickson* [1904] AC 273, PC, the clause read:

> reserving to [the grantor] all such part of the said piece or parcel of land hereinbefore described as may be within 100 feet of highwater mark

and it was held (at p 277) that 'the word "reserving" would operate as an exception'.

Again, a grant of land 'reserving. . . the liberty of working coal' was construed by the House of Lords in *Hamilton* v *Dunlop* (1885) 10 App Cas 813 (a Scottish case, but the decision was not apparently confined to Scottish law) as an exception of that estate in the coal which had been vested in the grantor at the date of the conveyance. This case was distinguished, however, in *Duke of Sutherland* v *Heathcote* both by Vaughan Williams J at [1891] 3 Ch 504 and by the Court of Appeal at [1892] 1 Ch 475. There land had been granted 'saving and reserving nevertheless . . . full and free liberty . . . to search for, get, dig, drain, and carry away the coal, ironstone, and minerals'. At first instance the ground of distinction was that, as the grantor had been exercising a power of appointment, he had himself had no estate in the coal, etc, at the date of the conveyance. On appeal the grounds of distinction were first that, unlike the earlier case, no intention to except had been shown on a proper construction and, second, that the decision of the House of Lords was confined to Scottish law. Accordingly, the clause was held to operate as a re-grant of a profit à prendre.

However, more recently, the general words: 'Except and reserving unto the vendor such rights and easements or quasi-rights and quasi-easements as may be enjoyed in connection with the . . . adjoining property', were *not* construed as excluding from the conveyance of a cottage the cellar underneath even though it had been used for storage in connection with the adjoining property (*Grigsby* v *Melville* [1974] 1 WLR 80, CA). See also *Pallister* v *Clark* (1975) 30 P & CR 84, CA, as to the words 'It is hereby agreed and declared' introducing the re-grant of an easement.

3 Construction of exceptions

Making the distinction between exceptions, reservations and re-grants is thus primarily a question of construction. Equally, the point of making the distinction is also primarily one of construction. In *Savill Bros* v *Bethell* [1902] 2 Ch 523 CA, there had been a grant 'save and except and reserving' a piece of land of uncertain position. Treating this as an exception, Stirling LJ giving the judgment of the court, stated (at pp 537–8) that:

> It is a settled rule of construction that, where there is a grant and an exception out of it, the exception is to be taken as inserted for the benefit of the grantor, and to be construed in favour of the grantee. If, then, the grant be clear, but the exception be so framed as to be bad for uncertainty, it appears to us that, on this principle, the grant is operative and the exception fails.

An example of this settled rule occurred in *Pearce* v *Watts* (1875) LR 20 Eq 492, where a provision that 'the vendor reserves the necessary land for making a railway' (ie, not just a right of way over the land) was held to be an exception and void for uncertainty. Again this rule explains why there can never be an implied exception: *Mitchell* v *Mosley* [1914] 1 Ch 438, CA.

4 Construction of reservations

This rule of construction against grantors (including lessors) was early applied to the construction of reservations proper (ie, of rents, etc), in *Lofield's Case* (1612) 10 Co Rep 106*a*. But where there is only a reservation so-called (ie, of an incorporeal right, such as an easement or profit à prendre), the rule, long accepted and now established, is the opposite: in cases of doubt, the reservation of a right should be construed against the purchaser as being strictly the (re)grantor: *St Edmundsbury and Ipswich Diocesan Board of Finance* v *Clark (No 2)* [1975] 1 WLR 468, CA (disapproving a contrary view derived from the words 'without . . . any regrant' in s 65(1) of the Law of Property Act 1925; see post, also a note at (1975) 39 Conv (NS) 384–6).

An example occurred in *South Eastern Railway* v *Associated Portland Cement Co* [1910] 1 Ch 12, where an agreement that a vendor might construct a tunnel under a proposed railway line was construed as a re-grant of a right of way and held valid since the vendor would be able to cure any uncertainty by himself selecting the position. Also in *Foster* v *Lyons* [1927] 1 Ch 219 a demise 'reserving, nevertheless, to the lessor . . . full right to build to any height on adjoining land . . . notwithstanding such buildings may obstruct any light on the land hereby demised' was construed as a grant by the lessee amounting to an agreement within s 3 of the Prescription Act 1832 and as such preventing him from acquiring a right to light by prescription. Again it is quite consistent with this rule of construction that implied reservations so called, ie, re-grants, should be possible, although admittedly rare as being inconsistent with the other more potent rule of no derogation from grant (see per Thesiger LJ in *Wheeldon* v *Burrows* (1879) 12 Ch D 31, at p 49).

5 Execution

Apart from the question of construction, it used to be necessary to distinguish exceptions and reservations proper from reservations so-called to decide whether or not the conveyance required execution also by the purchaser. An exception, being merely an expressed omission from the grant, has always had full effect despite non-execution by the grantee, as has a reservation proper (ie, of rents, etc: see Co Litt 143*a*). However, since a purported reservation of an incorporeal right operated as a re-grant and since a person could not grant to himself, in order to be effective *in law* execution by the purchaser used to be requisite (see per Stirling J in *Thellusson* v *Liddard* [1900] 2 Ch 635). Despite this, if the purchaser failed to execute the conveyance, he would nevertheless have been bound *in equity* to give effect to the intended easement or profit à prendre and his successors in title would likewise be bound since they would be put on notice by the terms of the purported reservation provided contained in a document of title (see *May* v *Belleville* [1905] 2 Ch 605).

Although non-execution by the purchaser was thus never a very serious defect, an ingenious conveyancing device was adopted from 1881 to 1926 in order to render such a purported reservation effective in law, as well as in equity, despite non-execution by the purchaser. The vendor would convey land to the purchaser and his heirs to the use that the vendor should have a legal easement or profit à prendre and subject thereto to the use of the purchaser and his heirs. By s 62 of the Conveyancing Act 1881 the use relating to the easement or profit à prendre would, without more, be duly executed (*not* meaning signed, sealed and delivered). Previously, this would not have been so, the purchaser not being seised in the sense required by the Statute of Uses 1535.

After 1925 this conveyancing device became obsolete for two reasons. First, both the Statute of Uses 1535 and the Conveyancing Act 1881 were repealed by the Law of Property Act 1925 (s 205 and Sched 7). And second, s 65(1) of the 1925 Act provided that:

> A reservation of a legal estate shall operate at law without any execution of the conveyance by the grantee of the legal estate out of which the reservation is made, or any re-grant by him, so as to create the legal estate reserved, and so as to vest the same in possession in the person (whether being the grantor or not) for whose benefit the reservation is made.

Accordingly, the ordinary practice whereby a purchaser does not execute a conveyance unless it contains covenants or declarations on his part is now in this respect legally effective. Incidentally, it will be noticed that the subsection failed to distinguish reservations proper from re-grants.

Less incidentally, the subsection is expressed to operate in favour of 'the person (*whether being the grantor or not*) for whose benefit the reservation is made' and is thus a statutory application of the otherwise sadly restricted s 56(1) of the Law of Property Act 1925. More important, the subsection only operates where there is a reservation of a *legal estate* which, as defined in s 1 of the Law of Property Act 1925, would include a profit à prendre (eg, in *Mason* v *Clarke* [1955] AC 778, a right to rabbit) but not if only reserved for life, which occasionally is the case with sporting rights (but see s 149(6) of the same Act as to leases for lives).

More surprisingly, the subsection apparently vests the legal estate *in possession* in all cases. For example, an easement for a term of years absolute may be granted now to take effect in the future (eg, in nineteen days' time: see *Foster* v *Reeves* [1892] 2 QB 255, at p 257; cf s 149(3) of the Law of Property Act 1925 as to reversionary leases) and in doing so it will nonetheless be a legal estate. But a purported reservation, ie, a re-grant, of such a reversionary easement will on the face of it be simply vested in possession, and not at all in reversion, by s 65(1).

Assuming next that an easement is intended to be reserved as a legal estate, then the normal rule is that to be a legal estate it must be created (apart from creation by statute or prescription) by deed: s 52 of the Law of Property Act 1925. This is even so, it seems, if the creation is for a term not exceeding three years (see *Hewlins* v *Shippam* (1826) 5 B & C 221, at p 229; *Wood* v *Leadbitter* (1845) 13 M & W 838, at p 843; cf s 54(2) of the Law of Property Act 1925). From this it might be thought that s 65(1) would only operate on a reservation contained in a deed and not on one contained in one of the exceptions to s 52, such as a valid lease under hand. However, *Mason* v *Clarke* [1955] AC 778 concerned just such a reservation (see per Denning LJ at [1954] 1 QB 466) and nowhere in the various judgments was there any suggestion made that s 65(1) did not apply for this reason. The inherent assumption, if correct, would represent an illogical but convenient extension.

Lastly, on execution, it may be suggested that the practice, although legally correct, ought *not* to be to dispense with execution by a purchaser. It is surely much simpler in the long run to have him execute a duplicate than to rely on an acknowledgment for production.

6 Time

On the one hand, a so-called reservation of an incorporeal right, such as an easement or profit à prendre, since it operates as a re-grant, must comply with the rule against perpetuities to be valid (see *South Eastern Railway* v *Associated Portland Cement Co* [1910] 1 Ch 12; *Sharpe* v *Durrant* (1911) 55 SJ 423; *Dunn* v *Blackdown Properties Ltd* [1961] Ch 433; also *Newham* v *Lawson* (1971) 115 SJ 446).

On the other hand, an exception *cannot* by its very nature be touched by the perpetuity rule. The reason is that 'a valid exception operates immediately, and the subject of it does not pass to the grantee'. This was stated by the Privy Council in *Cooper* v *Stuart* (1889) 14 App Cas 286, at p 289, where it held invalid the purported exception 'of a right to *resume* any quantity of land, not exceeding 10 acres in any part of the said grant'. A clearer illustration had occurred much earlier in *Horneby* v *Clifton* (1567) 3 Dyer 264*b*, where the grant was of 'the messuage or tenement in Fleet Street, called "The Three Conies" with all the chambers, cellars *and shops*, etc, excepting and reserving [to the grantor] *the shops* for his own sole use and occupation'. This exception (as it was treated) was held void as repugnant to the grant.

7 Registered conveyancing

Hitherto discussion in this section has been confined to *un*registered conveyancing. Since an exception is simply an omission from the grant (or transfer) no special provisions in the Land Registration Act 1925 were really requisite. In fact, the Act (ss 18(1) and 21(1)) expressly empowers a registered proprietor to transfer 'the land or any part thereof' specifically mentioning the transfer of mines and minerals apart from the surface and vice versa (this was probably unnecessary in view of the partitioning definition of 'land' in s 3(viii) of the Act, which includes the words 'whether the division is horizontal, vertical or made in any other way'). Also, which probably was necessary, a registered proprietor is expressly empowered by the Act to transfer the land subject to reservations (ss 18(1)(*d*) and 21(1)(*c*)—here again re-grants are not distinguished although there is reference to the creation of easements, etc).

Generally, the considerations relating to exceptions and reservations (proper and so-called) in registered conveyancing are the same as those which arise in *un*registered conveyancing. The only question, therefore, which will be mentioned is whether s 65(1) of the Law of Property Act 1925 applies equally to Land Registry transfers. It will be remembered that that subsection renders a reservation effective at law 'without any execution of the *conveyance* by the grantee *of the legal estate* . . .' The present writer, for the reasons given earlier in this book, considers that a Land Registry transfer is not a conveyance at all; the late Professor Harold Potter, not going quite as far as this, did take the view that such a transfer is not a conveyance of the legal estate within the subsection mentioned (see his *Registered Land Conveyancing*, at p 79). In other words, according to these views, execution of the transfer by the transferee cannot be dispensed with under s 65(1). It should perhaps also be said that the editor of the last edition of vol 3 of *Key & Elphinstone, Precedents in Conveyancing*, at p 139, expressly differing from Professor Potter (who originally wrote the volume), states that a Land Registry transfer *is* a conveyance of a legal estate within s 65(1) since 'it is an instrument by which a legal estate is passed notwithstanding that a further step, viz, registration, is necessary before it attains its intended effect'. He adds that HM Land Registry is unlikely to object to a reservation on the ground of non-execution by the transferee, which is a good practical point. A better practical point might appear to be that of safety first: more certainty may be achieved for the transferor by insisting on execution by the transferee, particularly since the reservation, if it does operate only in equity, may not create an overriding interest (see s 70(1)(*a*) of the Land Registration Act 1925). In any case, however, the reservation, being an express re-grant, would require completion by registration to operate in law (see s 19(2) of the same Act).

K GENERAL WORDS

Since certain of the *express* provisions, found in the traditional form of conveyance, which relate to the property conveyed have already been discussed in some detail (see ante, sections I and J), certain of the *implied* provisions relating to such property may now be little more than mentioned.

At one time, the practice in drawing conveyances of land was to add on at the end of the parcels clause a number of *general words*, such as:

> Together with all and singular fences hedges ditches ways passages waters watercourses lights privileges easements advantages and appurtenances whatsoever to the said piece or parcel of land and premises belonging or appertaining

(taken from a deed of indenture dated 1870). As regards any rights already legally appendant or appurtenant to the land conveyed, these added words were of no effect, apart from precluding arguments as to intention, since such rights automatically passed with the land without any mention at all (see per Joyce J in *Godwin* v *Schweppes Ltd* [1902] 1 Ch 926, at p 932). However, such general words were capable of having a very potent, not to say creative, effect as regards 'quasi-easements'. This was illustrated by Fry LJ in *Bayley* v *Great Western Railway* (1884) 26 Ch D 434, at p 457, as follows:

> If one person owns both Whiteacre and Blackacre, and if there be a made and visible road over Whiteacre, and that has been used for the purpose of Blackacre in such a way that, if [the] two tenements belong to several owners there would have been an easement in favour of Blackacre over Whiteacre, and the owner aliened Blackacre to a purchaser, retaining Whiteacre, then the grant of Blackacre either "with all rights usually enjoyed with it" or "with all rights appertaining to Blackacre" or probably the mere grant of Blackacre itself without any general words, carries a right of way over Whiteacre.

Here there is reference not only to the significance of the 'general words' but also to the creation of easements by implication from the mere grant itself. This latter implication would be by virtue of what is usually known as the rule in *Wheeldon* v *Burrows* (1879) 12 Ch D 31 (per Thesiger LJ at p 49).

Three distinctions may be noted between the old 'general words' and the latter rule as they operate on quasi-easements. First, the former creates legal easements *expressly*, ie, by the wide terms of the conveyance, whilst the latter does so impliedly on the broader principle of no derogation from grant. This distinction has, however, become blurred. In order simply to shorten conveyances, s 62 of the Law of Property Act 1925 (replacing s 6 of the Conveyancing Act 1881), provides that conveyances 'shall be deemed to include and by virtue of this Act shall operate to convey' in effect all the old 'general words'. Thus the 'general words' are now implied into the conveyance, but if they then operate to create any easements, strictly they still do so expressly (see per Sargant LJ in *Gregg* v *Richards* [1926] 1 Ch 521, at pp 534–5). The second distinction is that in a conveyance the 'general words' can only operate by way of grant whereas *Wheeldon* v *Burrows* may exceptionally also permit a reservation or re-grant to be implied. And the third distinction relates to registered conveyancing: the implied 'general words' are specifically applicable (see Land Registration Act 1925, s 19(3), also s 20(1), and Land Registration Rules 1925, r 251) but no clear equivalent provision is available for '*Wheeldon* v *Burrows*' rights.

Beyond this merest mention of the acquisition of easements and profits à prendre by implication, readers are required to remember their real property law, with refreshing reference if needs be to, say, Megarry and Wade, 4th ed, pp 827–41.

L   THE 'ALL-ESTATE' CLAUSE

At one time the practice, where a conveyance was of the fee simple (or else of the whole interest, whatever it might be, of the grantor), was to insert in the parcels clause after the 'general words', something which was known as the 'all-estate' clause, in some such words as:

> And all the estate right title interest use trust benefit property claim and demand whatsoever both at law and in equity of him the said [grantor] therein and thereunto

(taken from a deed of indenture dated 1870). Whether the 'all-estate' clause was ever really worth its keep is doubtful, but its express insertion is now certainly unnecessary. In accord with the general motive of shortening instruments of conveyance, s 63(1) of the Law of Property Act 1925 (replacing s 63 of the Conveyancing Act 1881) provides that:

> Every conveyance is effectual to pass all the estate, right, title, interest, claim and demand which the conveying parties respectively have, in, to or on the property conveyed, or expressed or intended so to be, or which they respectively have power to convey in, to or on the same.

1   Contrary intention

Prima facie, this section, unlike s 62 (implied 'general words'), does not merely provide that an additional clause is to be read into conveyances, but instead states how effectual 'every conveyance' is to be. In other words, the appearance of the section is of one relating to substance rather than to form. If so, the section could be far more potent than the clause it supersedes, since the word 'conveyance' is widely defined for the purposes of the Act (s 205(1)(ii)) to include instruments, such as leases, in which the old 'all-estate' clause would not, for obvious reasons, have been inserted. However, the section yields not only to an expressed contrary intention but also to the other terms and provisions of the conveyance (s 63(2)). Therefore a lease, even without any express exclusion of the section, will not pass the fee simple since this would be inconsistent with its habendum (Co Litt 183a: *Buckler's Case* (1597) 2 Co Rep 55). Accordingly, express exclusion is not only unusual but also unnecessary if the intention of the parties can be gathered from 'the whole scope of the instrument as to which special regard is to be had to what I call introductory recitals' (see per Chitty LJ in *Williams* v *Pinckney* (1897) 67 LJ Ch 34, at p 40). In this last-mentioned case, for example, a mortgage which was not mentioned in a deed purporting to settle 'all the estate', etc, of the settlor, was held not to be included in the settlement. See also *Public Trustee* v *Duchy of Cornwall* [1927] 1 KB 57 (tithe rentcharge not passed without express mention as not being an interest in the land itself).

2   Use of clause

Nonetheless, subject to the above, the 'all-estate' clause may be useful where, as with the old practice, the conveyance is of the fee simple or other whole interest. For example, the clause will pass all the estates and interests of a conveying party despite their not all being vested in him in the capacity in which he was made a conveying party (see per Lord St Leonards in *Drew* v *Earl of Norbury* (1846) 3 Jo & Lat 267, at p 284, and also *Taylor* v *London and County Banking Co* [1901] 2 Ch 231). After all, the statement of a party's capacity in a conveyance is not normally intended to qualify or explain the operative word. Thus, as Danckwerts J observed of a tenant for life who had charged the land as beneficial owner:

> He was not in fact "beneficial owner"; but, of course, the words "as beneficial owner" are merely words implying covenants for title and not in themselves necessary

(in *Weston* v *Henshaw* [1950] Ch 510, at p 516; he also held the deed not to be thereby a forgery: ibid, p 518; see also per Buckley J in *Re Pennant's Will Trusts* [1970] Ch 75, at p 81). Accordingly, if personal representatives convey part of their deceased's land and express themselves to do so 'as beneficial owners' or 'as trustees' without first making a formal written assent in their own favour, the conveyance will nonetheless effectively operate to pass the legal estate in the land to the purchaser despite the strictly inaccurate statement of capacity (see *Parker* v *Judkin* [1931] 1 Ch 475 and *Re Stirrup's Contract* [1961] 1 WLR 449; distinguish *Re King's Will Trusts* [1964] Ch 542 since, even assuming the decision to be correct, there was no such conveyance in question but only an appointment of new trustees). However, this operation may not be so if the result would be a breach of trust (see *Fausset* v *Carpenter* (1831) 2 Dow & Cl 232) although one might have thought that notice on the part of the grantee should be necessary for this restriction (see, to this effect, *Parker* v *Judkin*, ante).

Other illustrations of the use of the clause occurred in *Thellusson* v *Liddard* [1900] 2 Ch 635 and *Price* v *John* [1905] 1 Ch 744. In the former, an equitable term, which had probably merged at law but which the parties concerned had treated as still subsisting in equity, was passed by the clause. And in the latter, where a husband who had a rentcharge issuing out of his wife's land joined with his wife to convey part of the land, the clause operated to release that part of the land from the rentcharge.

3 Construction

Much more recently, in *Re Stirrup* [1961] 1 WLR 449, Wilberforce J was able to state that the section (ie, s 63), in conjunction with the wide definition of 'conveyance' in s 205(1)(ii) as including an assent, seemed:

> to produce the result that an assent, provided that it is under seal, is effective to pass whatever estate the conveying party has.

Not apparently cited to the learned judge was the decision in *Hanbury* v *Bateman* [1920] 1 Ch 313 that the section's predecessor (ie, s 63 of the Conveyancing Act 1881) did not convert an instrument expressed to be a conveyance into a power of appointment despite the fact that 'conveyance' was then defined as including an appointment (s 2(v) of the 1881 Act; cf the different wording in this respect of s 205(1)(ii) of the 1925 Act). Sargant J in this case took the view (at p 320) that the section should be read 'every *conveyance* is effectual to *convey* all', etc, or 'every *appointment* is effectual to *appoint* all', etc, and so on, and should not be read mutatis mutandis, that is, not 'every *conveyance* is effectual to *appoint* all', etc. However, the decision in *Re Stirrup*, ante, was more firmly grounded on the common law principle of the parties' intentions prevailing over formal defects (see, eg *Cholmondeley* v *Clinton* (1820) 2 Jac & W 1, at pp 91–3 also *Re Pennant's Will Trusts* [1970] Ch 75; cp *Re King's Will Trusts* [1964] Ch 542).

Even more recently, the Court of Appeal in contrast adopted a construction so restrictive as to deprive the section of most of its potential. In *Cedar Holdings Ltd* v *Green* [1981] Ch 129, CA, spouses were joint tenants of a house; the husband and another woman executed a legal charge of the house; the charge clearly could not affect the legal estate but a declaration was sought that it did affect the husband's beneficial interest. The declaration was refused on the ground that the property charged was land and not the proceeds of sale under the statutory trusts (reference was made to *Irani Finance Ltd* v *Singh* [1971] Ch 59, CA). However, in *Williams & Glyn's Bank Ltd* v *Boland* [1981] AC 487, HL, at p 507 Lord Wilberforce stated in parenthesis that he considered *Cedar Holdings* to have been wrongly decided. Accordingly, on materially identical facts, Bingham J has refused to follow *Cedar Holdings* and instead held that a valid equitable charge of the husband's beneficial interest had been created: *First National Securities Ltd* v *Hegarty* (1982) *The Times*, 2 November.

4 Registered conveyancing

The wording of ss 20(1) and 23(1) of the Land Registration Act 1925 which provide that registration should confer the legal estate together with 'the appropriate rights and interests which would, under the Law of Property Act 1925, have been transferred if the land had not been registered', clearly extends to the 'all-estate' clause implied by s 63 of the Law of Property Act 1925. Less clear, however, is the possible application of the 'all-estate' clause to the system of registered conveyancing.

The general principles of this system demand that registration should pass neither more nor less than the estate or interest of which the transferor was registered as proprietor (or which he had power to convey under s 37 of the Act). Despite this, ss 20(1) and 23(1) of the Act appear to permit as an exception the operation of the implied 'all-estate' clause. Nonetheless, it is thought that when (if ever) the clause does operate to enlarge the expressed effect of the transfer (which is to pass 'the land comprised in the title above mentioned', the title stating the transferor's estate and interest) then the interest by which the effect is enlarged will either be equitable and not registrable or else, in any case, equitable until entered on the register. Fortunately this speculation is largely if not entirely academic; the implied 'all-estate' clause has comparatively rarely had any operation in *un*registered conveyancing and is much less likely to operate in registered conveyancing.

M HABENDUM

'TO HOLD the same unto the Purchaser in fee simple' are the words which traditionally follow the parcels clause in a deed of conveyance of unregistered land and which thus mark the end of the *premises* of the deed. The clause is invariably called the habendum although technically this is not quite correct. In the heyday of conveyancing, the clause used to commence 'To have and to hold . . .' (as now in the Church of England Form of Solemnisation of Marriage) meaning 'to have an estate of inheritance and to hold the same of some superior lord' (Co Litt 5*a*). To 'have', the habendum proper, has been abandoned since the Conveyancing Act 1881, leaving the 'to hold,' the tenendum, alone and known by the company it used to keep.

1 Purpose

After stating the office of the premises, Coke continued 'The habendum hath also two parts, viz: first to name again the feoffee, and, secondly, to limit the certainty of the estate' (Co Litt 6*a*). Thus, just as it is the function of the parcels clause to determine the quantum physically of land passing, the purpose of the habendum is to determine the quantum of the *estate* in that land which the grantee or purchaser will take. This merely means that normally the estate to be taken will be delimited by the words of limitation used in the habendum, such as 'in fee simple' (which have now—since 1881—largely replaced 'and his heirs' in conveyances of freehold land).

It should be mentioned that immediately after the habendum and probably to be treated as part of the same clause, two further matters are found when appropriate. These are, first, some cross-reference (beginning 'Subject to . . .') to the reservations, if any, already made in the premises of the same or of an earlier deed of conveyance and which it was indicated earlier (p 294) should properly appear in the habendum rather than be coupled with exceptions in the parcels clause (see also MJ Russell at (1970) 34 Conv (NS) 191–2). And second, if the grantee is not taking for his own benefit then a reference to the trusts upon which he is to hold the land will at this point be introduced. Both these matters are in a sense within the purpose of the habendum of limiting the quantum of the estate to be held by the grantee.

Performance of any of these purposes by the habendum, rather than elsewhere in a deed of conveyance, is purely traditional and not essential: if there is no habendum at all, the quantum of estate specified, eg, in the premises, will be taken (see per Abbott CJ in *Goodtitle d Dodwell* v *Gibbs* (1826) 5 B & C 709, at p 717). Since 1925, if no words of limitation are used anywhere, and no contrary intention appears, then a conveyance of freehold land will pass to a purchaser 'the fee simple or other the whole interest which the grantor had power to convey in such land': s 60(1) of the Law of Property Act 1925. This is a convenient provision in case of accidental omission, but for at least two reasons it should in practice never be deliberately relied on. First, the provision is insufficiently certain in that a contrary intention may always inconveniently appear. And second, the omission of words of limitation apparently renders nugatory the usual implied covenants for title (cf *May* v *Platt* [1900] 1 Ch 616).

2   Relation to premises

Certain rules have been enunciated from time to time for deciding cases where there is a conflict between the premises and the habendum of a deed of conveyance. Before indicating these rules, it may be noticed that they are, as always, subject to the primary principle governing the construction of any deed, which is 'to give effect to every part of it, if this be possible, and not to strike out or nullify one clause in a deed, unless it be impossible to reconcile it with another and more express clause in the same deed' (per Romilly MR in *Re Strand Music Hall Co* (1865) 35 Beav 153, at p 159). However, if reconciliation proves impossible, then the following a priori rules govern the position.

(1) *Different grantee*—This unlikely aspect may be taken briefly. Where a person is named as grantee in the premises, another person named as grantee in the habendum and not in the premises takes no interest in the land—'it is but a nugation' (per Manwood J in *Anon* (1573) 3 Leonard 32, lx; and see *Reynold* v *Kingman* (1587) Cro Eliz 115; premises to *A*, habendum to *A* and *B*; whole estate passed to *A* and nothing to *B*). Contrast the position where no person is named as grantee in the premises, when the person named in the habendum will take: *Butler* v *Dodton* (1579) Cary 86, at p 122.

(2) *Different estate*—If words of limitation are unnecessarily included not only in the habendum but also in the premises and, worse, the words of limitation differ, then Blackstone stated his view that the habendum could '*lessen*, enlarge, explain *or qualify*, but not totally contradict or be repugnant to the estate granted in the premises' (2 Bl Com 298). This view is not entirely acceptable as to the italicised

words. The better view appears to be that 'the habendum never abridges the estate granted by the premises of the deed' (per Verney MR in *Kendal* v *Micfield* (1740) Barn Ch 46, at p 47) although 'it may indeed alter or vary it' (ibid) or 'construe and explain the sense in which the words in the premises should be taken' (per Lord Davey in *Spencer* v *Registrar of Titles* [1906] AC 503, at p 507). In effect, therefore, the habendum can do almost anything provided it does not cut down or abridge the estate expressly granted by the premises.

For example, where the estate granted in the premises was to *A* and his heirs, and in the habendum to *A* for life, the latter was held to be void as an attempt to limit a smaller estate than that already granted and so being repugnant: *Throckmerton* v *Tracy* (1555) 1 Plow 145. Where the converse occurred, ie, in the premises a grant to *A* for life and in the habendum to *A* and his heirs, *A* again got the fee simple since there was no question of the habendum abridging the premises: *Kendal* v *Micfield*, ante. An apparent infringement of the no abridgement rule occurred in *Altham's Case* (1610) 8 Co Rep 150*b*, where the grant was to *A* and his heirs (ie, the fee simple) and the habendum to *A* and the heirs of his body (ie, an entail which is a lesser estate). It was held that *A* got only the latter, the estate tail, on the ground that the habendum explained what heirs were intended by the premises. Contrast with the above the position, most usual in practice, where 'by your premises you have given no certain or express estate than that otherwise the law would give' (ie, in the absence of words of limitation there would be implied by law in an intended conveyance of freehold land, before 1926, a life interest and after 1925 generally the fee simple) for then 'you may alter and abridge, nay, you may utterly frustrate it by the habendum' (*Stukeley* v *Butler* (1614) Hob 168).

(3) *Different property*—Therefore, although the habendum may not abridge the estate, if any, expressly limited by the premises, it may explain and so extend or vary it. The reason is that that is really the habendum's sphere of operation to determine the quantum of the estate granted, so that the premises in a sense trespass if they also deal therewith. However, the property itself, which is properly described only in the parcels clause, is not the concern at all of the habendum. Accordingly, if the habendum purports to repeat the parcels then 'the habendum shall be construed as if there had been no such recital' since it does 'something which is not its office and is superfluous and therefore all that recital shall be of no effect' (per Manwood CB in *Carew's Case* (1585) Moore 222, at p 223). Thus, it is clear that the habendum not only cannot abridge the parcels but also cannot extend or vary them (Shep Touch 75). Nonetheless it does appear that the expression in the habendum of what would in any case be implied into the premises (eg, by s 62 of the Law of Property Act 1925), may serve under the general rules of construction to make the parties' intentions clear (see per Warrington LJ in *Gregg* v *Richards* [1926] 1 Ch 521, at p 533).

3 Registered conveyancing

No habendum is included in the prescribed form of transfer of registered freehold land (see Form 19 in the Schedule to the Land Registration Rules 1925). Indeed words of limitation of the estate taken by the grantee do not need to be incorporated into such a transfer. What is expressed to be transferred is 'the land comprised in the title above mentioned'. This in fact means the fee simple, *not* because of the operation of s 60(1) of the Law of Property Act 1925 (see ante) but simply because any freehold land will be comprised in such title, and the statement of the estate of the grantor is incorporated by reference into the transfer. The prescribed form of transfer of leasehold land (see Form 32) follows exactly that for freehold land, with the sole addition of 'for the residue of the term granted by the registered lease'. Accordingly, the effect of the habendum in registered conveyancing is much simplified by its absence.

N   DECLARATION OF TRUST

Joint or co-purchasers are nowadays often encountered in practice, especially in the case of residential property, where, due no doubt to 'women's lib', the names of both spouses tend to be wanted on the title. Then, if title to the land is unregistered, some such clause as the following will very often be found in the conveyance to them, making its appearance immediately after the habendum:

The Purchasers hereby declare as follows:

(*a*) The Purchasers shall hold the said property upon trust to sell the same with power to postpone the sale thereof and shall hold the net proceeds of sale and other money applicable as capital and the net rents and profits thereof until the sale upon trust for themselves as joint tenants;

(*b*) Until the expiration of twenty-one years from the death of the survivor of the Purchasers [eighty years from the date hereof] the trustees for the time being of this deed shall have power to sell mortgage charge lease or otherwise dispose of all or any part of the said property with all the powers in that behalf of an absolute owner.

Of course, if the purchasers, presumably after appropriate advice, elect to take in equity not jointly but in undivided shares, para (*a*) of the clause will simply conclude instead with: 'as tenants in common in equal shares [*or as the case may be*].'

When the clause is used, one of its first functions is to puzzle any intelligent laymen there may be about. Not many clients, thank God, have the temerity to question their professional advisers, but a few do dare the devil and then the barrage begins: 'We don't want to sell, we want to live there—what's a trust anyway—we're not tenants, we're buying the freehold—why can't we sell twenty-one years after we're dead—aren't we actually absolute owners—what's it all for?' Let us see, not generally, space prohibits, but with the particular position of husband and wife as joint purchasers in mind.

In the first place, sub-clause (*a*) only expresses what is implied by statute. The conveyance to *H* and *W* without words of severance will create a statutory trust for sale in essentially the same terms as sub-clause (*a*) (see s 35, reached via s 36 and s 34, also s 25 (1), of the Law of Property Act 1925).

But a query remains. Are the words 'for themselves as joint tenants' vital, the statutory machinery only operating where land is 'beneficially limited' to joint tenants (see s 36 of the 1925 Act)? This may be argued (it has been, fully, see (1944) 9 Conv (NS) 72 et seq), but even if *H* and *W* turned out to be beneficial tenants in common the courts apparently would not be discouraged in the slightest from finding a statutory trust for sale (see *Re Buchanan-Wollaston's Conveyance* [1939] Ch 738, also *Bull v Bull* [1955] 1 QB 234 and *Williams & Glyn's Bank Ltd v Boland* [1981] AC 487, HL). Ought any subsequent purchaser to enquire beyond the conveyance to *H* and *W*? At worst (ie, no statutory trust for sale, eg, a bare trust), he would probably enjoy the protection accorded to 'equity's darlings' (*Pilcher v Rawlins* (1872) 7 Ch App 259; otherwise see s 23 of the Law of Property Act 1925). Nonetheless, his requisitions should perhaps be humoured in anticipation where sub-clause (*a*) is to be omitted, by simply tacking a 'beneficially' on to the habendum, thus calling for minimal explanation all round.

So far, then, sub-clause (*a*) seems to serve no purpose. But pause a moment: we are envisaging spouses as joint purchasers of residential property, so the possibility of ferocious disputes as to exact entitlement should be anticipated. Consequently, the conveyancer's instinctive need for quiet certainty ought to be met by the incorporation of an express declaration of the beneficial interests: that such a clause should prove conclusive, short of rectification, now appears exceedingly well supported by authority (see quite recently per Buckley LJ in *Pink v Laurence* (1977) 36 P & CR 98, at p 101; also *Brykiert v Jones* (1981) 125 SJ 323, CA). In addition, the cautious conveyancer must insist upon the joint purchasers executing the conveyance, in substance as settlors, in order to render the declaration effective beyond argument (see notes and correspondence at (1977) 41 Conv (NS) 78–9 and 365–6 and [1979] Conv 5–7).

To begin with, of course, *H* and *W* do actually have all the powers of an absolute owner by virtue of their beneficial entitlement. Nevertheless, since exercise of such inherent powers could only be in the capacity of beneficial owners, not as trustees (see *Green v Whitehead* [1930] 1 Ch 38), reliance on them is probably better avoided as risking bringing the equities on to the title. In other words, the exercise of any powers by *H* and *W* should not be accepted by a purchaser unless *either* the equitable interests have been investigated to see that they remain the beneficial owners (ie, as with the survivor of beneficial joint tenants before the Law of Property (Joint Tenants) Act 1964), *or else* the exercise would be within the powers of trustees who are not also the beneficial owners. Hence, in the interests of purchasers, express powers are conferred by sub-clause (*b*), but is this expression necessary?

As trustees for the sale of land, *H* and *W* 'have all the powers of a tenant for life and of the trustees of a settlement under the Settled Land Act 1925, including in relation to the land the powers of management conferred by that Act during a minority' (s 28 (1) of the Law of Property Act 1925; whether or not there is a minority: *Re Gray* [1927] 1 Ch 242). So extensive are these powers—including selling, exchanging, granting options, leasing, and mortgaging, as well as wide managerial ability—that we need only think of how they fall short of the powers of an absolute owner and how far in a way which matters for practical purposes. Bear in mind, however, that giving a trustee the powers of an absolute owner does not quite mean what it says: these powers, like all a trustee's discretions, must nonetheless be exercised honestly and reasonably in the interests of the beneficiaries. Any act patently unreasonable for trustees, such as giving the property away, should in any case be objected to by subsequent purchasers, when explanation would bring in the equitable title.

The statutory powers of disposition are subject generally to more or less pernickety regulations (just see Pt II of the Settled Land Act 1925). The most essential of these is obtaining the best consideration, price or rent, but this will neither inconvenience unduly *H* and *W* nor concern a purchaser who is conclusively taken to have complied with this and indeed all the other regulations (s 110(1), ibid; see also *Re Morgan's Lease* [1972] Ch 1; cf *Davies v Hall* [1954] 1 WLR 855, as to good faith).

Apart from regulations, the statutory powers have two major limitations. The first and lesser of these is that an ordinary lease cannot be granted for more than a fifty-year term (s 41, ibid); but this is largely mitigated in practice by the wide meaning of building leases, which can be granted for a 999-year term (see ss 44 (1) and 117 (1) (i), ibid). The second more important limitation is that mortgages may be granted for certain purposes only (s 71, ibid; see also s 16 of the Trustee Act 1925). These purposes, though mostly concerned with the welfare of the land, do *not* include raising the initial purchase price (cf *Re Suenson-Taylor's ST* [1974] 1 WLR 1280). This limitation, which would seriously hinder much day-to-day practice may well not do so, since mortgagees do not, and probably need not, look for protection any further than to a *purported* exercise by the mortgagors of their statutory powers (s 17 of the Trustee Act 1925), whilst the beneficiaries, *H* and *W*, are unlikely to complain of a breach of trust.

However, these two major limitations, particularly the latter, cannot be completely talked away: mortgagees may be taking a risk and may object; other beneficiaries are possible in the future and may complain. And there are other minor limitations with their own irritation value: the power to grant options has shortcomings (s 51 of the Settled Land Act 1925; not extending, semble, to rights of pre-emption); there is no power of disposition at a consideration to be ascertained by valuation or arbitration (*Re Earl of Wilton's SE* [1907] 1 Ch 50); and having sold all the land, *H* and *W* would find themselves strictly unable to purchase further land (*Re Wakeman* [1945] Ch 177; only if they cannot determine the trust by distributing the proceeds, eg, if *H* has vested his beneficial interest in an infant daughter, could this limitation become acute).

Accordingly, the conscientious conveyancer, with a wise eye to the remotely conceivable and touching the stone of safety first, may well still wish to extend the statutory powers of the trustees ('for the time being' *is* otiose: s 18(1) of the Trustee Act 1925). If so—and his attitude is eminently understandable—he may be relieved also to know that he will not necessarily be acting improperly in extending the statutory position (s 182 (2), (3) of the Law of Property Act 1925). Against this, however, the pushed practitioner may foresee, reasonably, that the pinch of the limitations will too rarely be felt after a common or garden husband and wife purchase. If he therefore leaves *H* and *W* to rest on the statutory powers, he may be even more relieved to know that he 'shall not be deemed guilty of neglect or breach of duty, or become in any way liable' (s 182 (1), ibid).

A case, not entirely convincing, can thus be made out for dropping the clause quoted at the outset of this chapter from conveyances of *un*registered land to beneficial joint tenants. If the case is accepted, we will all be able to keep up with that ever-expanding neighbour, registered conveyancing practice. Here one past Chief Land Registrar under the sub-head 'Unsuitable Instruments', has exhorted us: 'Do not attempt to paint the lily', his horrid example of which being 'a provision that the trustees for sale or other joint owners are to have the same powers of mortgaging and leasing as an absolute owner' (Ruoff, *Land Registration Forms*, 2nd ed, p 2). Expressing the trust for sale itself, surprisingly, still passed muster (ibid, Precedent No 90, p 161). His exhortation accorded closely with the statutory note to Form 19 in the Schedule to the Land Registration Rules 1925: 'Where the transfer is to two or more jointly, no addition need be made to the form' (execution by the transferor alone is also indicated). However, in 1974, the same Chief Land Registrar actually promulgated a new printed form of transfer to joint proprietors—Form 19(JP)—containing a declaration as to whether or not the survivor of the transferees is able to give a valid receipt for capital money and with a consequential provision for the deed to be executed by them (see (1975) 39 Conv (NS) 152). In effect this caters for equitable entitlement (ie, joint if the receipt can be given) and presumably nothing more was thought remotely requisite. Nevertheless a few practitioners do still remain liable to excommunication for the heresy of including in transfers of registered land, as in conveyances of unregistered land, the whole shoot of expressing the trust for sale, and of extending the powers of the trustees to those of an absolute owner during the perpetuity period. But is this heresy or revelation? If the conscientious conveyancer does not accept the case for dropping the clause in *un*registered conveyancing, how is it that he does so in registered conveyancing and without qualms?

The reason, as the big book puts it (Ruoff and Roper, *Registered Conveyancing,* 4th ed, at p 377), is because:

> it is fundamental that any registered proprietor or proprietors can exercise all or any powers of disposition unless some entry on the register exists to curtail or remove these powers. Thus, in order to deprive registered proprietors of full powers of mortgaging or leasing, for example, there would have to be a restriction on the register expressly preventing them from exercising these powers and the normal obligatory restriction (statutory form 62) deals only with the payment of capital money. If, however, a trust deed expressly limits the powers of the trustees, it is their duty to apply for the entry of an appropriate restriction.

Yet with respect, does this not slightly confuse the position of the trustees with that of the purchaser? Probably a purchaser need only look for restrictions on the register and in their absence assume that his vendors have full powers, no person dealing with registered land ever being affected with notice of any trust (s 74 of the Land Registration Act 1925)—'probably' only, because the contrary has been argued (see *Key and Elphinstone*, 15th ed, vol 3, pp 255–8, also (1958) 22 Conv (NS) 14 et seq, and even Ruoff and Roper themselves at ibid, p 390). But surely the powers of the trustees are not really extended by provisions protecting purchasers. Although a purchaser may get a good title, there will still be a breach of trust if the vendors exceed their ordinary powers as trustees. Consequently, should not trustees for sale strictly apply for the entry of an appropriate restriction whenever the trust deed does not extend their powers to those of an absolute owner?

Assuming that the conscientious conveyancer can in no way resist declaring, in a conveyance to beneficial joint tenants, that 'the trustees for the time being of this deed shall have all the powers of an absolute owner', need he also restrict them to the perpetuity period? Or is the customary precursor, 'until the expiration of twenty-one years from the death of the survivor of the purchasers', a part of the clause which is not excellent?

The older precedent books used to intimate that this restriction was included anyway ex abundanti cautela, the perpetuity rule not being infringed because it 'applies only to vesting in interest of a limitation, not to its determination, and is a breach of the Law of Public Policy and not a legal fetish' (*Key and Elphinstone,* 15th ed, vol 1, p 15 note (*b*)). But since the passing of the Perpetuities and Accumulations Act 1964 such caution has become pathological. Section 8(1) of that Act provides:

> The rule against perpetuities shall not operate to invalidate a power conferred on trustees or other persons to sell, lease, exchange or otherwise dispose of any property for full consideration, or to do any other act in the administration (as opposed to the distribution) of any property . . .

In conclusion, it can only be commented that the draftsman acting for joint purchasers, particularly spouses, needs to think pretty carefully which parts, if any, of the standard declaration of trust he keeps and which he jettisons.

O COVENANTS

In accordance with the traditional format of a deed of conveyance, after the habendum and any declaration of trust there will be inserted any covenants which are to be entered into by any of the parties. Thus here would appear the grantor's covenants for title were they still expressed rather than implied by the statement of his capacity in the operative words. An almost infinite variety of covenants is possible, since they are after all merely agreements made under seal. Precisely *which* covenants any of the parties may be required to enter into is, of course, a matter entirely of contract, although in a conveyance of freehold land, the central fact of this book, the likely variety is limited (covenants for indemnity apart) to covenants involving acts, positive or negative, in relation either to the land sold or to land retained. Nonetheless, even with the variety thus limited, any attempt to deal at all adequately with the construction and operation of particular covenants would call for inordinate space. Nor it seems can sufficient justification be seen for continuing to outline here the principles prescribing the enforceability of such covenants: look back to your land law (see, eg Megarry and Wade, *Real Property*, 4th ed, Chapter 12, pp 720–75).

P   ACKNOWLEDGMENT AND UNDERTAKING

> [Counsel] says we are dealing here with honourable people. I have not the faintest doubt that is the case, but a little experience in these courts leads one to suppose that that is not always the case in dealing with land. The vendor who likes to keep and refuse to hand over a document of title when he is under no obligation to hand it over is a very common creature. That is why in conveyances there is always an undertaking to produce documents and so on

(per Lord Greene MR in *Eccles v Bryant* [1948] Ch 93, at p 100).

Accordingly, to deal with such common creatures, in the customary form of a deed of conveyance, immediately after the positive and/or restrictive covenants on the part of the purchaser, not infrequently encountered is a statutory acknowledgment and undertaking on the part of the vendor. Generally it goes something like this:

> The Vendor hereby acknowledges the right of the Purchaser to the production of the documents specified in the Schedule hereto (the possession of which is retained by the Vendor) and to delivery of copies thereof and hereby undertakes with the Purchaser for the safe custody thereof.

The object and result of including a clause in this form is to enable s 64 of the Law of Property Act 1925 to impose an obligation (*not* to create a covenant), in effect, to comply with both the acknowledgment and the undertaking in accordance with the terms of that section.

The old practice (ie, prior to the Conveyancing Act 1881) was to take a covenant from the vendor for the production and safe custody of any document not handed over and to do so by a separate deed rather than in the conveyance itself. Then on subsequent dealings the covenant was kept off the abstract in order to preclude requisitions as to any documents mentioned in it but prior to the root of title. This is no longer a consideration since s 45 (1) of the Law of Property Act 1925 in any case precludes such requisitions. There is therefore today generally no reason for a separate deed, although s 64 does appear to envisage and certainly also applies to a separate 'writing'. The covenant under the old practice created difficult questions as to whether or not its benefit or its burden ran respectively with the land and with the documents. Additionally, the continuing personal liability of the original covenantor was unpopular. As will be seen, these problems are not present with the statutory acknowledgment and undertaking, so that since they first appeared (in s 9 of the 1881 Act) they have superseded, without prohibiting, the old practice.

1   The obligations

As s 64 of the Law of Property Act 1925 is far too long to be reproduced with advantage here, only an outline of the two branches of obligations which it may impose (either jointly or separately) will be given together with a discussion of any points arising. As to the first branch of the obligation, ie, as to production and copies of documents, subs (4) (i) provides that production is to be, one, at all reasonable times, and, two, for the purpose of inspection and of comparison with abstracts or copies. Could any more be asked? Certainly it could; the right to make one's own copies or even abstracts is *not* included. Here subs (4) (iii), which only obliges the *delivery* of true, attested or unattested, copies or extracts, may be compared with s 96 (1) of the same Act which gives a mortgagor with a subsisting equity of redemption the right 'to inspect and *make* copies or abstracts of or extracts from' the documents of title in the hands of the mortgagee. In addition subs (4) (ii) of s 64 provides for production in any court (semble anywhere in the world) or elsewhere in the United Kingdom in connection with proving title. Also to be noted however, is the practical restriction on extravagant requests for either production or copies which appears in subs (5)—all the costs and expenses of performance are to be paid by the requestor.

The second branch of the obligations, imposed by the undertaking for safe custody, is more straightforward; by subs (9) of s 64 the obligation is 'to keep the documents safe, whole, uncancelled and undefaced'. Lest this seems too high an obligation—title deeds do tend to be vulnerable—performance of the undertaking (as also of the acknowledgment) is provided with an escape-hole: 'unless prevented from so doing by fire or other inevitable accident' (subss (9) and (2); cp *Barrett v Brahms* (1967) 111 SJ 35, where the defendant to a summons for production of documents of title gave evidence that 'he had lost or mislaid the documents and that it was possible that they had been stolen from him whilst he was in Israel', but there is no reported suggestion that he might be within the escape-hole; it is incidentally amusing to note that the plaintiff only brought the action because his own title deeds had been lost in the post). Also each branch of the obligations may be modified by the expression of a contrary intention (subs (13)) provided that the modification is not actually repugnant to the obligations (see *Watling v Lewis* [1911] 1 Ch 414), in which case complete omission is the proper course.

2   How they run

Put shortly, the burden of the statutory obligations runs with the documents and the benefit with the land. More particularly, subss (2) and (9) of s 64 provide that the persons having possession or control of the documents from time to time have the burden of and are bound by both branches of the obligations *but* so long only as they have possession or control. Thus, unlike the position under the old practice of giving a covenant, even an original giver of the acknowledgment and undertaking ceases to be liable once he has parted with the documents and therefore he has no need to take any covenant for indemnity from the recipient. Consequently, too, an original giver has no inducement (there is no obligation) to notify the person having the benefit that he has parted with the documents. Accordingly in practice the benefit of a statutory acknowledgment and undertaking tends to become illusory simply because the current possessor of the documents cannot be traced. In this respect the old practice was superior since the original covenantor and his successors, having personal liability (either original or under a covenant for indemnity), would normally give notice of a change in possession of the documents.

Whilst subs (3) of s 64 provides that the benefit of the acknowledgment is in the person to whom it was given and all his successors in title (not being lessees at a rent), there is no similar provision in that section for the running of the benefit of the undertaking. Nonetheless, it does appear generally to be assumed that the benefit of the undertaking also runs, if only under s 78 of the Law of Property Act 1925 (as to covenants relating to the land of the covenantee). However, this, poses a problem: does a possessor of documents bound by an undertaking for safe custody who negligently destroys them become successively liable to every future owner of the land? If so, and there seems no logical reason why not, the consequences could be serious since liability for breach is in damages (subs (10)). The case would be different with the acknowledgment since liability there only involves specific performance (subss (2) and (7)) and expressly not damages (subs (6)), so that impossibility of performance due to negligent or even (semble) deliberate destruction of the documents would appear effectively to defeat any person otherwise entitled to require production. This is distinctly odd, particularly when it is recalled that the escape clause is restricted to 'fire or other inevitable accident', but presumably the section, like equity and nature, can do nothing in vain (cf per Cowper LC in *Seeley v Jago* (1717) 1 P Wms 389; and see *Turner v Clowes* (1869) 20 LT 214).

3   Purchaser's entitlement

Subsections (8) and (11) of s 64 provide that the statutory acknowledgment and undertaking satisfy any liability to give a covenant either for the production and delivery of copies of documents or for the safe custody of documents. Under the general law a liability to give such a covenant existed whenever a vendor retained documents of title subsequent to the commencement of title (see *Cooper v Emery* (1844) 1 Ph 388). Section 64 enables but does not compel a vendor in such a case to give the statutory acknowledgment and undertaking in place of the covenant to which the purchaser would otherwise be entitled. The vendor could still opt to give the covenant, but would be foolish to do so since the covenant would create a more onerous liability. The statutory acknowledgment and undertaking are to be prepared at the expense of the purchaser whilst the vendor bears the expense of perusal and execution thereof by himself and by any other necessary parties other than the purchaser (see s 45 (8) of the Law of Property Act 1925). All of this paragraph is subject to any contrary intention being expressed in the contract.

Originally, trustees (and personal representatives and mortgagees) retaining documents of title were not, as a matter of practice, required to give any covenant as to documents retained at all. Later it became usual for them to give the same covenant as a non-fiduciary vendor, but 'so as not to create any liability for damages'. Since this limitation of liability would probably be repugnant to the obligations imposed by the statutory undertaking, and so void (see *Watling v Lewis* [1911] 1 Ch 414), the position now is that fiduciary vendors normally give only the statutory acknowledgment. However, this position is not based on any rule of law but only on conveyancing practice; General Condition 17(5) of The Law Society's Conditions of Sale, 1980 ed, provides for the practice, but the National Conditions of Sale, 20th ed, now no longer have any such provision.

The apparent reason for the present practice as to fiduciary vendors is that:

> The general rule is that a trustee does not covenant except for his own acts, and ought not to be asked to guarantee the safety of documents which might be lost without his personal neglect, as, for instance, by his solicitor on a journey, when properly removing them

(*Wolstenholme & Turner's Conveyancing*, 3rd ed, p 44, cited by counsel in *Re Agg-Gardner* (1884) 25 Ch D 600, at p 603, but not referred to in the judgment). The present writer does not find this a convincing reason: even a trustee should select his agents with care, and in case of any such loss either he would have a remedy in an action for professional negligence or misconduct, or else he would be within the escape hole of 'fire or other inevitable accident' mentioned earlier. Further, trustees, whether they like it or not, might well find the burden of a statutory undertaking imposed on them in the ordinary course of their trust simply by acquiring possession or control of documents with which such a burden runs (see s 64 (9)). If so, no complaint could be raised, so why should one be raised against the initial giving of an undertaking? Additionally, if fiduciary vendors do not give the statutory undertaking they unfairly deprive the purchaser of rights which he would otherwise have against subsequent possessors of the documents. Thus there does appear to be, at least, an argument for suggesting that the present practice is not only not binding in law but unreasonable and ought not to be followed (see further RC Fitzgerald (1947) *The Solicitor*, at p 28). Nevertheless it should be noted that the practice has received The Law Society's supposed seal of approval (*Law Society's Digest*, Opinion No 191).

Finally as to a purchaser's entitlement, probates and letters of administration should be included in the statutory acknowledgment and undertaking since endorsements may be made on them under s 36 (5) of the Administration of Estates Act 1925. In other words, grants of representation are, because of that subsection and since 1925, not just documents of record but muniments of title (see *Re Miller & Pickersgill's Contract* [1931] 1 Ch 511).

4 When retained

The statutory acknowledgment and undertaking can only impose obligations on a vendor where he '*retains* possession of documents' (s 64 (1) and (9) of the Law of Property Act 1925), hence the words in brackets in the example wording given at the beginning of this section which are intended to forestall subsequent enquiries as to retention. Accordingly, if the documents are not retained by a vendor but, eg, by his mortgagee, there is no point at all in the vendor giving the statutory acknowledgment and undertaking (although he should procure that the mortgagee gives an acknowledgment; see below). In such a case, not uncommon, resort should be had by the purchaser to the old practice by having the vendor give a covenant for production and copies and safe custody to operate when he recovers possession of the documents on paying off the mortgage (see *Re Pursell and Deakin* [1893] WN 152 and General Condition 17 (5) of The Law Society's Conditions of Sale, 1980 ed, see for further suggestions RG Rowley at (1962) 26 Conv (NS) 453–5).

Occasionally, a purchaser is required by the contract for sale to give to the vendor an acknowledgment and undertaking on completion of the sale. Then the question may arise whether a person who receives documents can be said to be a person who '*retains* possession of documents' within s 64. Generally, it is assumed that he can, but some doubt does exist.

5 Custody

Hitherto the purchaser's rights have been discussed on the assumption that he does not on completion get the documents in question because they are retained by the vendor. Now it may be considered who, as between vendor and purchaser, is entitled to possession of any of the documents. The general rule is that the vendor should on completion hand over *all* documents, however ancient, in his possession or control relating to the land—'the purchaser shall have all the charters, deeds and evidences, as incident to the lands . . . for the evidences are, as it were, the sinews of the land' (Co Litt 6*a*; see also *Re Duthy and Jesson's Contract* [1898] 1 Ch 419, and of *Re Knight's Question* [1959] Ch 381). If the documents are not in the possession of the vendor but are in his control, he must obtain them for the purpose of handing over at his own expense: *Re Duthy and Jesson's Contract,* ante (contrast the earlier expense of obtaining them to verify the abstract which falls on the purchaser: s 45 (4) of the Law of Property Act 1925). Of course, if any of the documents since the root of title are not in the possession or control of the vendor when they should be, the purchaser will be put on notice (see *Oliver v Hinton* [1899] 2 Ch 264, and s 13 of the Law of Property Act 1925).

It will be appreciated, therefore, that the statutory acknowledgment and undertaking can only come into play, as between vendor and purchaser, where an exception to the above general rule applies. Assuming there to be no contractual stipulation on the point, a vendor is only entitled to retain documents of title where (*a*) he retains any part of the land to which the documents relate; or (*b*) the documents consist of a trust instrument or other instrument creating a trust which is still subsisting, or an instrument relating to the appointment or discharge of a trustee of a subsisting trust (s 45 (9) and (10), proviso, of the Law of Property Act 1925). Only three points need to be noticed here.

The first is the wide definition of 'land' contained in s 205 (1) (x) of the Law of Property Act 1925. Thus, a vendor has been held entitled to retain documents of title which, inter alia, showed title to an easement formerly appurtenant to the land sold but since deliberately extinguished by unity of possession: *Re Lehmann and Walker's Contract* [1906] 2 Ch 640. Compare *Re Williams and Newcastle's Contract* [1897] 2 Ch 144, where a vendor was held not entitled to retain documents relating to both a freehold property and an insurance policy, although only the former was sold since the latter was not 'land'.

The second point to notice is that exception (*b*) above would appear to apply where a trust relating to the land sold continues in respect of the proceeds of sale. Thus on a sale of land by co-owners, who are necessarily trustees first to sell the land and then to hold the proceeds on the 'statutory trusts' (see ss 34–6 of the Law of Property Act 1925) and where there is no separate trust instrument (a very common position), the purchaser strictly should *not* be entitled to (though in practice he most often will) receive the conveyance to the vendors.

Thirdly, it is arguable that a grant of probate which does not include any other land should strictly be handed over to a purchaser from the executor, although for good practical reasons it never is.

6 Equitable right

So far discussion has been based on the two alternatives of a vendor either handing over all the documents of title on completion or else retaining one or more of them and so himself giving the statutory acknowledgment and undertaking. What, however, is the position where a vendor neither hands over nor retains documents of title? It seems (but is not certain) that the vendor is liable nonetheless to procure, if he can, an acknowledgment for production and copies (but not an undertaking for safe custody) from the person who has possession of the documents (see *Re Pursell and Deakin* [1893] WN 152; but cf *Re Jenkins' Contract* [1917] WN 49). The vendor may be able to satisfy this liability by showing that the benefit of an earlier statutory acknowledgment will run at law with the land to the purchaser (see s 64 (3) of the Law of Property Act 1925). Otherwise the vendor may well be faced with an insurmountable obstacle if the documents in question are lost, or if the possessor of the documents will not co-operate by giving an acknowledgment (query: could this be compelled under the usual implied covenant for further assurance? see p 266). In *Barclay v Raine* (1823) 1 Sim & St 449, the resulting position was held to be that a vendor could not force his title on a purchaser unless he was able either to hand over the documents of title or to give a covenant for their production. In theory at least this decision has been modified by, now, s 45 (7) of the Law of Property Act 1925, which provides that:

> The inability of a vendor to furnish a purchaser with an acknowledgment of his right to production and delivery of copies of documents of title or with a legal covenant to produce and furnish copies of documents of title shall not be an objection to title in case the purchaser will, on completion of the contract, have an equitable right to the production of such documents.

Therefore, the question is: when will the purchaser have an equitable right to production? The answer, however, is not at all certain (see the full discussion by 'ABC' in (1954) 98 SJ 102, 121 and 138; also by EO Walford in (1949) Conv (NS) 354). Probably it is correct to say that such an equitable right arises against any vendor (and his successor in possession, but see below) who retains documents of title on selling the whole or any part of the land and in favour of the purchaser and his successors in title. But possibly it only arises where land held under one title is divided, the right being against the owner of one part (he possessing the documents of title) in favour of the owners of the remainder (see *Fair v Ayres* (1826) 4 LJ (OS) Ch 166, incidentally deciding that production cannot be required under the usual covenant for further assurance). In any case, being only an equitable right, and so depending on notice, it may be defeated on the documents being acquired by a bona fide purchaser for value without notice thereof. However, it is arguable that such a purchaser will necessarily be fixed with constructive notice of the right, since the documents of title themselves will show the basic fact that a part of the land to which they related has been sold off. Against this, it is also arguable, though with little confidence, that an equitable right to production of documents is registrable as an equitable easement under the Land Charges Act 1972, s 2 (5), Class D (iii), and so void unless protected by registration (s 4 (6)).

However, the inevitable conclusion from this uncertainty appears to be that it will normally be impossible for a vendor, who is unable to hand over documents of title or to procure an acknowledgment, to show positively that the purchaser will have an equitable right to production. Accordingly, the decision in *Barclay v Raine*, ante, should still apply so that the purchaser will in such circumstances be able to object to title and refuse to complete. Neither General Condition 12 (3) of the National Conditions of Sale 20th ed, nor General Condition 17 (5) of The Law Society's Conditions of Sale, 1980 ed, as to documents not in the possession or control of the vendor, his mortgagees or trustees, are in the writer's opinion quite apt to prevent this objection.

7 'To another'

Turning to a more minor point, in order for s 64 of the Law of Property Act 1925 to impose obligations capable of binding documents and being enforced it is necessary that the vendor retaining possession of the documents *'gives to another'* the acknowledgment and undertaking. Thus the section probably cannot operate (eg, as to the grant of representation) where a personal representative assents to himself (as trustee or beneficially) even if a purported statutory acknowledgment and undertaking be given in the assent (cf *Re Skeats' Settlement* (1889) 42 Ch D 522). This will not, of course, concern the personal representative/assentee but it might penalise his successors in title to whom the benefit would otherwise have run. In such a case, then, care should be taken to see that a statutory acknowledgment and undertaking are given in a subsequent conveyance. If they are not, possibly there may still be the equitable right of production on which to rely, but the availability of this right does appear to be particularly doubtful in respect of the grant of probate or letters of administration, especially if no other land was included in the grant (see *Law Society's Digest*, Opinion No 199).

However, it is thought that an acknowledgment and undertaking given by a person to other persons including himself should be validated by s 82 of the Law of Property Act 1925. Further, in *Rowley, Holmes & Co v Barber* [1977] 1 WLR 371 it was held that a personal representative had power to enter into a contract in his representative capacity with himself in a different (individual) capacity. By parity of reasoning, a personal representative should perhaps be regarded as able to give an effective acknowledgment or covenant in an assent in his own favour.

8 Registered conveyancing

Needless to say, no clause of acknowledgment or undertaking is included in the prescribed forms of transfer of registered freehold land (see Forms 19 and 32 in the Schedule to the Land Registration Rules 1925). Nonetheless, there is really no doubt that one could be included if wished, the only question is: would there be any point in doing so? The semi-official view is dogmatic: to do so would be 'mere verbiage' (Ruoff and Roper, *Registered Conveyancing*, 4th ed, p 327). Although this view may be accepted as normally correct in cases where the transferor is registered with an absolute or good leasehold title, two exceptions to it are even semi-officially recognised (p 328). First, where the transferor has only a possessory title, an acknowledgment and undertaking will be necessary with regard to pre-registration documents, as in unregistered conveyancing. Second, when part of the land comprised in a leasehold title is transferred, an acknowledgment and undertaking will be necessary in respect of the lease itself.

In addition to these two exceptions, three other cases have been suggested (see Potter, *Registered Land Conveyancing*, pp 69–70) in which an acknowledgment and undertaking would be necessary or at least useful. One is if documents relating to overriding interests are retained. The second is if documents relating to interests referred to in the Charges Register are retained. And the third exception suggested is in respect of the grant of representation where personal representatives of a deceased proprietor transfer without first themselves obtaining registration (which is common enough under the authority of s 37 of the Land Registration Act 1925). The reason given for this last is that the grant becomes a link in title as in unregistered conveyancing since such a transfer can only be made if the personal representatives were in fact entitled themselves to be registered. In such a case, the grant has to be lodged in order for the application for registration to succeed (under r 170 (4) of the 1925 Rules; in practice only a photostat or a certified copy will be lodged) and it is said that it is as well to be able to call for it. Ruoff and Roper, however, make the point (op cit, at p 594) that 'not only would a personal representative who refused to deposit the grant (or evidence of it) at the Land Registry to enable an assent to be registered be acting in derogation of his assent, but he also could be made to produce the grant, regardless of whether he had given an acknowledgment.' Although this point might well appear reasonable, it is unfortunately not supported by any authority; note that s 36 (5) of the Administration of Estates Act 1925 only enables production to be required to prove that the transferee's own notice has been endorsed on the grant, and that the implied covenants for title do not assist (see s 76 (1) (F) of the Law of Property Act 1925, also *Fair v Ayres* (1826) 4 LJ (OS) Ch 166). The better practice is surely that suggested by the last editor, Mr TI Casswell, of vol 3 of *Key & Elphinstone, Precedents in Conveyancing* (15th ed), namely, that deposit of the grant at HM Land Registry before completion should be required unless a solicitor's undertaking to make the deposit after completion is forthcoming. And perhaps the best practice of all would be for purchasers to insist upon personal representatives procuring their own registration as proprietors before transferring (see s 110 (5) of the Act).

Q   CERTIFICATE OF VALUE

The next clause which is now invariably found (where the circumstances are appropriate) in both a conveyance of unregistered land and a Land Registry transfer is known as the 'certificate of value'. This is included for a purely revenue reason and very little will be said about it here. This reason is that stamp duty under the heading 'Conveyance or Transfer on Sale' in Sched 1 to the Stamp Act 1891 will be charged at a reduced rate where the consideration does not exceed a specified amount *and the instrument is certified at* that amount (see s 55 (1) of the Finance Act 1963, and now Finance Act 1982, s 128 (1)). These italicised words mean that the instrument:

> contains a statement certifying that the transaction effected by the instrument does not form part of a larger transaction or series of transactions in respect of which the amount or value, or aggregate amount or value, of the consideration exceeds that amount

(s 34 (4) of the Finance Act 1958). The object of this is to restrain the evasion of stamp duty by the artificial splitting up of a transaction into a number of smaller ones, each expressed to be for a consideration low enough to qualify for a reduced rate. Whether or not a certificate of value can properly be given in any particular case is really a question of fact, not of law, although guiding principles have from time to time been laid down (see the leading case of *Attorney-General v Cohen* [1937] 1 KB 478, CA). Despite there being the sanction of a fine under s 5 of the Stamp Act 1891, the restraining influence of a certificate of value in practice rests entirely on the bona fides of the parties and their solicitors (cf *Eva v Morrow* (1966) 116 NLJ 1657). The subject may be pursued further in works on the law of stamp duties (and see [1962] BTR 36 as to the stamp duty attracted by a Land Registry transfer).

R   EXECUTION

1   Testimonium

Traditionally the ultimate part of every deed (of conveyance or otherwise) is the testimonium:

> IN WITNESS whereof the parties hereto have hereunto set their hands and seals the day and year first before written

—which, to some extent, speaks for itself. These words, it is true, equally traditionally will be followed by an attestation clause (dealt with later) but this latter clause is strictly not *part* of the deed.

Before considering the requirements for due execution of a deed, one preliminary question following on from the testimonium should be mentioned. This question is: need a person who is joined more than once as a party to one deed (ie, in different capacities) set his hand and seal to it more than once? For example, in *Young v Schuler* (1883) 11 QBD 651, a person who both had an interest in the property being conveyed and was an attorney for another party, only executed the deed once. This was held sufficient, but it was emphasised in the case (at p 655), that the better practice is to have execution in each capacity. The reason is that, if such a person only executes once, whether or not he is bound in all his capacities depends entirely on evidence of his intention so to be bound being available and, if available, also admissible (ie, it must not contradict the terms of the deed).

Contrast the case of a person who, rather than having more than one capacity, has several interests in the property conveyed and who intends to pass all of them. The position is that a person having more than one interest in property conveyed will, by executing the conveyance, pass all his interests *unless* a contrary intention is shown; this is by virtue of s 63 of the Law of Property Act 1925 (which implies the 'all estate' clause into conveyances made after 1881). In other words, here, unlike a person with more than one capacity, the presence of the necessary intention does not have to be shown, but only the absence of an expressed contrary intention. Accordingly, execution only once is clearly quite sufficient (see *Drew v Earl of Norbury* (1846) 3 Jo & Lat 267).

2   Signed

The requirements of a deed at common law have, as already remarked, long been established:

> . . . for there are but three things of the essence and substance of a deed, that is to say, writing in paper or parchment, *sealing and delivery* . . .

(*Goddard's Case* (1584) 2 Co Rep 4*b*, at 5*a*). As a preliminary to these requirements (which are really only formal and not properly described as 'of the essence and substance'), s 73 of the Law of Property Act 1925 has added that 'where a person executes a deed [after 1925] he shall either sign or place his mark upon the same and sealing alone shall not be deemed sufficient'. By this, what had already become the practice of conveyancers became the law.

However, it does appear that what will amount to a signature may perhaps differ very little from a seal. Thus in *Barrett v Brumfitt* (1867) LR 3 CP 28, in which a notice of objection rubber stamped with a facsimile signature was held validly 'signed' as required, Bovill CJ said (at p 31):

> The ordinary mode of affixing a signature to a document is not by the hand alone, but by the hand coupled with some instrument, such as a pen or a pencil. I see no distinction between using a pen or a pencil and using a stamp, where the impression is put upon the paper by the proper hand of the party signing. In each case it is the personal act of the party, and to all intents and purposes a signing of the document by him. If the objector here had used a pencil or a paint brush, it would hardly have been contended that he had not signed the notice.

Again, less anciently, in *Goodman v Eban* [1954] 1 QB 550 the Court of Appeal held a bill of costs rubber stamped with a facsimile of the plaintiff solicitor's signature to be 'signed' as required by s 65 (1) of the Solicitors Act 1932 (previous Acts had required bills to be 'subscribed with the proper hand of the attorney'; see now s 69 of the Solicitors Act 1974). Denning LJ, it is true, delivered a convincing dissenting judgment, in which he observed (at p 561) that:

The virtue of a signature lies in the fact that no two persons write exactly alike and so it carries on the face of it a guarantee that the person who signs has given his personal attention to the document.

Nevertheless, the case has since been referred to with approval by the Court of Appeal in *LCC v Agricultural Food Products Ltd* [1955] 2 QB 218 (see also per Walton J in *Graddage v Haringey LBC* [1975] 1 WLR 241, at p 246, and per Michael Davies J in *R v Brentford Justices, ex parte Catlin* [1975] QB 455, at p 462; but contrast restrictive dicta per Denning LJ in *Lazarus Estates Ltd v Beasley* [1956] 1 QB 702, at p 710, and per Sellers LJ in *Plymouth Corporation v Hurrell* [1968] 1 QB 455, at p 461).

The majority based their decision in *Goodman v Eban,* ante, on the plaintiff's patent intention by the stamp to authenticate his bill. Nonetheless, they were not prepared to commit themselves to the logical implications of this basis. Lord Evershed MR queried (at p 559), whether a document bearing a typed or printed representation, *not* a facsimile, of a signature could be said to be 'signed' simply because the requisite intention to authenticate was present.

However, the majority in *Goodman v Eban*, ante, looked for support to the cases on the provision in s 9 of the Wills Act 1837 that a will 'shall be *signed* at the foot or end thereof'. Thus this provision has been held satisfied by a stamping with an instrument on which the testator had had his usual signature engraved (*Jenkins v Gaisford* (1863) 3 Sw & Tr 93). But, of more present interest, this provision has also been held satisfied by the affixing of a seal stamped with the testator's initials (*In the Goods of Emerson* (1882) 9 LR Ir 443) although sealing alone is clearly not enough (cf *Wright v Wakeford* (1811) 17 Ves 454). Could a deed of conveyance, then, be both signed and sealed at one fell swoop by the affixing of a seal bearing a person's initials *or mark* (see s 73 above)? Logically it could, provided the requisite intention to authenticate is present; practically, of course, this argument should only be relied on in retrospect if endeavouring to cure an otherwise defective execution.

3   Sealed

This next requirement, namely, that 'no writing without a seal can be a deed' (Shep Touch 56) dates from the days of general illiteracy when a personal seal was the only way of authenticating a document. Typically of English law, the rule remains although the raison d'être has gone:

> a seal nowadays is very much in the nature of a legal fiction. The seal is no longer a wax impression of a man's crest or coat of arms; it is usually no more than an adhesive wafer attached by the law stationer [or copy typist] when the document is engrossed. It is the party's signature, and not his seal, which in fact authenticates the document

(per Lord Goddard, *Sixth Interim Report of the Law Revision Committee* 1937, Cmd 5449, p 35).

Thus the conveyance will normally be signed with the wafer present but largely ignored (except, that is, on copies of the document where must appear the letters 'LS'—locus sigilli: the place of the seal). The ceremony of sealing has withered away but fortunately the customary token gesture suffices:

> Meticulous persons executing a deed may still place their finger on the wax seal or wafer on the document, but it appears to me that, at the present day, if a party signs a document bearing wax or wafer or other indication of a seal, with the intention of executing the document as a deed, that is sufficient adoption or recognition of the seal to amount to due execution as a deed

(per Danckwerts J in *Stromdale & Ball Ltd v Burden* [1952] Ch 223, at p 230).

However, although this formal requirement of sealing has lost not only its raison d'être but also its solemnity, it is not yet legally pointless. Apart from the seal being a substitute for consideration, the absence of a seal renders a conveyance of land void at law (s 52(1) of the Law of Property Act 1925). What then if the law stationer or copy typist overlooks the wafer (or, not an uncommon occurrence, it comes unstuck)? Danckwerts J, it will have been noticed, required at least some 'indication of a seal' for adoption but he also held that the time-worn formulae 'this deed witnesseth' and the parties 'set their hands and seals' amounted to a clear estoppel as to sealing.

This decision was more recently accepted by the Court of Appeal in *First National Securities Ltd v Jones* [1978] Ch 109 (where the earlier apparently inconsistent authorities were reviewed). It was held that a document which had no wax or wafer seal attached but which did have a printed circle containing the letters 'LS' was capable of being a deed. Two members of the court expressly regarded it as of importance that the document contained an attestation clause and also that the signature of the executing party was in fact placed across the circle (see per Buckley LJ at p 118, and per Goff LJ at p 120): the third member of the court considered that no further formality should be required than the signature opposite the words 'Signed, sealed and delivered' (see per Sir David Cairns at p 121). See also the application and exposition of the resultant rules in, of all places, Stockport County Court: *Commercial Credit Services v Knowles* [1978] CLY 794.

4 . . . and Delivered

'After a deed is written [signed] and sealed, if it be not delivered, all the rest is to no purpose' (Terms de la Ley). The formal requirement of delivery is not normally mentioned in the testimonium although the setting of hands and seals is. This practice is inconsistent; surely all or, more logically, none of the requirements should be mentioned:

the order of making a deed is, first to write it, then to [sign and] seal it, and after to deliver it; and therefore it is not necessary that the [signing] sealing or delivery be mentioned in the writing, for as much as they are done after

(*Goddard's Case* (1584) 2 Co Rep 4*b*, at 5*a*).

Although this final act of delivery is an essential formality, the manner in which it may be performed is not subject to precise definition. Clearly, on the one hand, actual physical delivery, a handing-over, of the document as of a chattel, is sufficient without the necessity for any words, formal or otherwise (*Thoroughgood's Case* (1612) 9 Co Rep 136*b*). But on the other hand, delivery may be effected by words alone without any physical handing-over:

the efficacy of a deed depends on its being [signed] sealed and delivered by the maker of it; not on his ceasing to retain possession of it

(per Lord Cranworth in *Xenos v Wickham* (1866) LR 2 HL 296, at p 323). Thus more recently Lord Denning MR has pronounced:

The law as to 'delivery' of a deed is of ancient date. But (sic) it is reasonably clear . . . 'Delivery' in this connection does not mean 'handed over' to the other side. It means delivered in the old legal sense, namely, an act done so as to evidence an intention to be bound. Even though the deed remains in the possession of the maker, or of his solicitor, he is bound by it if he has done some act evincing an intention to be bound, as by saying: 'I deliver this as my act and deed'

(in *Vincent v Premo Enterprises (Voucher Sales) Ltd* [1969] 2 QB 609, at p 619; cf per

Winn LJ at ibid, p 623, suggesting that modern life should require more concentration on the physical movement of the document; see further DEC Yale at [1970] CLJ 52 et seq, demonstrating historically that the law as pronounced is neither very ancient nor in the old legal sense).

Accordingly, delivery may now be widely defined as an act and/or words by the maker of a deed adopting it as his. The traditional way of performing this formality, as the Master of the Rolls indicated, was (and with some still is) to have the maker place a finger on the seal and say: 'I deliver this as my act and deed.' It matters not (except in point of proof) that no-one else is present. Delivery is entirely unilateral; no acceptance of it by any other party is necessary, so that if the deed is one of conveyance it will operate to vest the property in the grantee although only unless and until the grantee disclaims when the property will revest in the grantor (*Mallott v Wilson* [1903] 2 Ch 494).

However, apart altogether from any act or words, delivery may simply be an inference from the conduct of the parties, whether at the time of execution or afterwards (*Keith v Pratt* (1862) 10 WR 296). Delivery has even been inferred from the mere facts of signing and sealing (*Hall v Bainbridge* (1848) 12 QB 699). Nonetheless, the possibilities of inference are not unlimited:

> No case has ever been decided that because a man knew that people had been acting on a blank deed as if it were perfect it must therefore be inferred that he knew that the deed was filled up, that he knew how it was filled up, and that he must be taken to have redelivered it. That is carrying the doctrine far beyond any case that can be referred to

(per Kay LJ in *Powell v London & Provincial Bank* [1893] 2 Ch 555, at pp 555–6).

Here it needs to be emphasised that chronologically delivery is the last requirement of a deed. If anything, whether the signing or the sealing or the filling in of material blanks comes after, then the deed must be redelivered: *Tupper v Foulkes* (1861) 9 CB (NS) 797. Thus delivery, being the final formality, tends in law to overshadow the other requirements. However, on the one hand, a written instrument is not constituted a deed by delivery alone (*Goodright v Gregory* (1773) Lofft 339) and, on the other hand, delivery may not be a requirement at all where execution is by a corporation (ie, sealing probably imports delivery: see per Buckley J in *D'Silva v Lister House Development Ltd* [1971] Ch 17, at pp 29–30, referring to s 74 of the Law of Property Act 1925).

5   Escrows

In considering the final formal requirement for execution of a deed, it is vital to appreciate that:

> There are two sorts of delivery, and two only, known to the law, one absolute, and the other conditional, that is an escrow to be the deed of the party when, and if, certain conditions are performed. If the deed operated as a complete delivery, cadit quaestio; if it did not, then it must be either in escrow or a nullity

(per Farwell LJ in the leading case of *Foundling Hospital v Crane* [1911] 2 KB 367, at p 377; see also per Lord Cranworth in *Xenos v Wickham* (1866) LR 2 HL 296, at p 323). Common conditions on which there is delivery as an escrow are payment of the money consideration (see per Romilly MR in *Walker v Ware Railway Co* (1865) 35 Beav 52) or the execution of a counterpart (as in *Beesly v Hallwood Estates Ltd* [1961] Ch 105), but almost any condition will serve.

Almost any condition, because two, perhaps three, limitations on the conditions do appear from the cases. First, the condition of the delivery must be beyond the unilateral control of the grantor or maker of the deed (per Farwell LJ in the *Foundling Hospital* case, ante, at p 379; see also the *Windsor Refrigerator* case [1961] Ch 375, CA). Therefore, after delivery as an escrow, the grantor is irretrievably committed; he cannot resile or recall the document but can only await performance of the condition by, more often than not, the grantee. Here it may also be noted that it has long been established that not even the death of the grantor prevents the subsequent performance of the condition and consequent operation of the deed (*Perryman's Case* (1599) 5 Co Rep 84a; see also per Cross J in the *Windsor Refrigerator* case, at [1961] Ch 88, at p 99).

At this point a fairly recent obiter dictum uttered in the House of Lords, in a stamp duty case, must be mentioned, but only sotto voce. Lord Denning MR in the Court of Appeal had put the case of a conveyance which is executed by the vendor but delivered in escrow, saying that so soon as the condition (payment of the price) were performed the sale was complete: *Cory (Wm) & Son Ltd v IRC* [1964] 1 WLR 1322, at p 1341. But in the course of allowing an appeal Lord Reid expressly referred to this instance of an executed conveyance delivered in escrow and shortly said: 'In my understanding there would then be nothing binding: both parties would have a *locus poenitentiae*' [1965] AC 1088, at pp 1107–8). However, in view of all the earlier established authorities, none of which were apparently cited, and even with the greatest respect, this can only be disregarded as per incuriam pending a direct consideration by the House of Lords (but see also Diplock LJ dissenting in the Court of Appeal at [1964] 1 WLR 1322, at p 1346, explained by JGM at [1964] BTR 285). In the meantime these dicta have been referred to by Walton J in *Terrapin International Ltd v IRC* [1976] 1 WLR 665, at pp 669–70. He rejected Lord Reid's quoted view as being 'quite clearly a total misunderstanding of the doctrine of an escrow' but nevertheless accepted Diplock LJ's equally erroneous analysis. But see further now *Alan Estates Ltd v WG Stores Ltd* [1982] Ch 511, CA (post p 327).

Secondly, the delivery of a deed disposing of the grantor's own property cannot be made conditional on the death of the grantor, because this would be necessarily testamentary and so must be duly executed as a will (see per Farwell LJ in *Foundling Hospital v Crane*, ante, p 379; cf donatio mortis causa, not applying to realty or leaseholds). And a third limitation may be that the condition should never be offensive to the policy or purposes of a statute. Thus in *Plymouth Corporation v Harvey* [1971] 1 WLR 549, Plowman J held ineffective a surrender of a lease delivered in escrow by a tenant to a third party, the condition of the escrow being the tenant's failure to comply with certain covenants in the lease. This was treated as being merely a device to circumvent the provisions of s 146 of the Law of Property Act 1925 and as remaining in substance a forfeiture within that section (see further the editorial observations at (1971) 25 Conv (NS) 141–2). In the light of this decision, a slightly sideways glance has to be directed at the example of an escrow visualised as a real transaction by Winn LJ in *Vincent v Premo Enterprises (Voucher Sales) Ltd* [1969] 2 QB 609, at p 621, with a condition, in effect, that an impending budget should impose no adverse tax consequences.

(a)   Proof of escrow

Yet again, it has long been established that it is a question of fact depending upon all the circumstances of the transaction whether a document has been delivered as a deed to take effect from the moment of delivery or as an escrow not to operate until a certain condition is performed (see *Murray v Stair* (1823) 2 B & C 82). No formal act or express form of words is necessary to constitute an escrow and the mere signing, sealing and using of words of delivery which are absolute in form is not conclusive against an escrow (*Christie v Winnington* (1853) 8 Exch 287; and see *Thompson v McCullough* [1947] KB 447, CA).

It used to be thought that delivery to the grantee himself was conclusive against an escrow, delivery to a third party (akin to a stakeholder) instead being required. That this is not so was decided by the Court of Appeal in *London Freehold and Leasehold Property Co v Suffield* [1897] 2 Ch 608; it remains a question of fact. However, where a document appears to be executed as a deed and is in the grantee's (or other proper) custody, then a heavy onus of proving delivery as an escrow is on the party so asserting (*Rowley v Rowley* (1854) Kay 242). Alternatively, if the grantee has possession, this in itself may be evidence of the performance of the condition on which delivery was to become absolute (*Hare v Horton* (1883) 5 B & Ad 715).

Now an aspect of an absolute execution may be considered which resembles but is to be distinguished from delivery as an escrow. Frequently in practice a grantor executes a deed in the expectation that it (or a duplicate or counterpart) will be executed also by some other person. Thus in *Luke v South Kensington Hotel Company* (1879) 11 Ch D 121 it was stated by Jessel MR (ibid, at p 125), that:

> it is well settled that if two persons execute a deed on the faith that a third will do so, and that is known to the other parties to the deed, the deed does not bind in equity if the third refuses to execute.

But this statement was unanimously denounced by the House of Lords in *Lady Naas v Westminster Bank Ltd* [1940] AC 366 as being obiter, based on no authority and too wide. Viscount Maugham suggested (ibid, at p 376) that the statement would reflect the law if the words 'and that is known to the other parties to the deed' were deleted and the words 'and with the intention that the two persons will not otherwise be bound' substituted. The result of this amendment, and indeed of the decision of the House of Lords, is that in the absence of delivery by the grantor as an escrow proper (ie, unless the execution is found as a fact to be conditional on execution by the other person) a deed will operate immediately to vest the beneficial interest in the grantee which interest can only then be divested by disclaimer.

(b) Effect of escrows

Hitherto in this section, the execution of deeds has been dealt with in general terms. Now the discussion is to be related more particularly to the delivery of conveyances in everyday practice. According to such practice, a vendor's solicitor will almost invariably have his client sign the conveyance (thereby adopting the wafer seal on it) and return it to him ('undated please') some time before completion. The position resulting from these actions, recalling that the final formality of delivery is required, depends entirely upon the intention of the vendor himself, *not* of the vendor's solicitor (see per Buckley J at first instance in *Beesly v Hallwood Estates Ltd* [1960] 1 WLR 549, at p 562).

Four resulting positions only appear possible. First, there may be no delivery at all, absolute or conditional, in which case the vast majority of conveyances during the last couple of centuries would strictly be invalid. This is clearly not worth pressing further here. Second, there may be an absolute delivery of the conveyance, passing the legal estate then and there without anything further (eg, without even payment of the price). This result, although possible (see eg, *Macedo v Stroud* [1922] 2 AC 330), has been judicially stigmatised as 'monstrous' (per Romilly MR in *Walker v Ware Railway Co* (1865) 35 Beav 52), and is so unlikely to be intended by any vendor that it too need not be pursued further here. Third, the vendor may merely intend to put his solicitor in a position to deliver the conveyance for him in exchange for the purchase price on the due completion date, unless in the meantime contrary instructions are given. This, it is thought, will normally be the under-standing of the lay vendor (and perhaps of his solicitor), namely that nothing irrevocable is effected by simply signing and returning the conveyance. Unfor-tunately, this understanding cannot, at least under present conveyancing practice, stand comparison with the law:

> There are certain things in the law which are well settled, and whether you like it or not, and one is that an authority to an attorney to deliver a deed on behalf of another can only be conferred by an instrument under seal duly executed by the principal

(per Joyce J in *Re Seymour* [1913] 1 Ch 475, at p 481; see also per Bowen LJ in *Powell v London & Provincial Bank* [1893] 2 Ch 555, CA, at pp 562 and 563; and generally now s 1 (1) of the Powers of Attorney Act 1971). Therefore, the vendor's solicitor can only deliver the conveyance for the vendor on completion if he has a power of attorney by deed so to do, and this rarely, if ever, will he have. Only one unusual and probably inconvenient exception to the above rule exists, namely for the conveyance to be delivered in the presence of the vendor, when the authority so to do can be given orally or even by signs (*R v Longnor* (1833) 4 B & Ad 647), but again this is unlikely. In other words, it would again follow that if this third position is intended by the vendor, then the vast majority of conveyances during the last couple of centuries have still been invalid.

Obviously, therefore, the fourth possible position must be fallen back on, simply so that the vendor may not be taken to have intended a solemn farce. This position is to say that the vendor, by returning the conveyance signed and sealed to his solicitor, then delivered it as an escrow on the obvious condition (there may be others) of payment of the purchase price (see, eg, the terms of the order made in *Palmer v Lark* [1945] Ch 182; note also the suggestion made in *Gibson's Convey-ancing*, 20th ed, p 254, that the conveyance be returned by a vendor to his solicitor *expressly* as an escrow in order to avoid completely the second possible position mentioned above). Accordingly, all the ordinary rules as to the effect of escrows apply and need to be considered as vitally relevant to day-to-day conveyancing practice. This consideration is particularly important since the effect of escrows, little appreciated generally it is thought, does have perhaps unsuspected and possibly serious consequences.

(1) *Irrevocable* —One effect of delivery of a conveyance as an escrow has already been mentioned in passing, namely, that it is necessarily quite irrevocable on the part of the vendor:

> if you do deliver a document as an escrow it is your act and deed and is not recallable

(per Harman LJ in *Beesly v Hallwood Estates Ltd* [1961] Ch 105, at p 118). As a result the purchaser's position is thereafter very much strengthened if only in that, if the vendor fails or refuses duly to complete, he need not rely on his contractual remedy of specific performance, with its all too familiar limitations, but has the alternative course of simply tendering the balance of the purchase money in cash (this being normally the only condition of the escrow, see *Coupe v Collyer* (1890) 62 LT 927). Thus in *Kingston v Ambrian Investment Ltd* [1975] 1 WLR 161, CA, the sole issue on appeal was upon what condition the defendants had delivered the transfer as an escrow: the defendants contended that the condition was that the plaintiffs paid the balance of the price and costs 'promptly' (according to the county court judge, within seven days). The Court of Appeal rejected this and held that in all the circumstances the plaintiffs were still entitled to have the executed transfer handed over on tender of appropriate payment.

Again in *Glessing v Green* [1975] 1 WLR 863, CA, the parties had come to terms on a sale price for certain land with an option to repurchase, but no concluded contract was ever established; so far as material, the vendor signed and sealed an agreed form of conveyance, the purchaser made no payments at all and the vendor served a notice to complete and sought vacation of the registration of an estate contract. Sir John Pennycuick (giving the judgment of the court) restated the position in general conveyancing practice as to delivery in escrow and found that in the circumstances the condition manifestly intended by the vendor was twofold: payment of the purchase price and also execution by the purchaser, this being necessary because of the option to repurchase (see at p 867). Then he stated (at p 868c):

> We think it clear that where a conveyance is executed in escrow there must be a time limit within which the implied condition of the escrow is to be performed and that the purchaser cannot insist on the right to perform the condition free from any such limit.

In considering what the time-limit should be, however, some disapproval was expressed of calling in aid equitable principles of imprecise application (as had been indicated in *Beesly v Hallwood Estates Ltd* [1961] Ch 105, per Harman LJ at p 118, and per Lord Evershed MR at p 120). Further, a practical resource for vendors caught in an escrow situation was outlined as follows (at p 869 c/d):

> Where there has been an antecedent contract and after execution of the conveyance by the vendor the purchaser fails to complete, and the vendor then serves notice making time of the essence, the expiration of this notice seems plainly the appropriate point beyond which it could not be said that the sale would be capable of completion in due course within the meaning of the condition. Where there has been no antecedent contract the expiration of a comparable notice by the vendor if given should, we think, be treated by analogy as the appropriate point.

In this case it was clear that any due or reasonable time had long expired, but otherwise it appears a remarkable suggestion that, where there is no binding and enforceable contract for sale (as there was not in either the *Kingston* or the *Glessing* case) and therefore no relevant conditions of sale, a vendor has justification for serving a notice to complete designed to make time of the essence of a contract. It is the more surprising in the context of this latter decision, since such a notice to be effective depends on the test condemned as imprecise, namely the passing of reasonable periods. What is more, where there is no contract, the purchaser on performance of the condition of the escrow (usually payment of the price) becomes entitled to delivery of the executed conveyance or transfer, but will not enjoy any of the other contractual rights ordinarily exercised by a purchaser on or before completion (eg, as to inspection of documents and even discharge of mortgages). Whilst there may be remedies available under the covenants for title, this is hardly satisfactory for the purchaser or his mortgagee.

(2) *Not equitable*—Beyond the above, from the moment the vendor delivered the conveyance as an escrow, the purchaser, to the detriment of any innocent third parties, will apparently have had more than a mere equitable interest under the contract requiring to be protected by registration under the Land Charges Act 1972. The strength of the purchaser's position, and the paralysis of the vendor's, was well illustrated over a century and a half ago in *Hooper v Ramsbottom* (1815) 6 Taunt 12. There the vendor, having handed to his solicitor both the title deeds and the conveyance as an escrow conditional on payment of £330, the balance of the purchase money, later persuaded his solicitor to release the title deeds and deposited them with his bankers, who were without notice, to secure an overdraft of several thousand pounds. Then, the vendor having become bankrupt, the purchaser

claimed and was held entitled to receive the title deeds on payment of the £330 which had been regularly tendered to the bankers, since the vendor had had no rights at all over the title deeds, but merely the duty at law to hold them until the purchaser paid the £330.

(3) *Retrospective*—It is of the essence of delivery as a escrow that the document is not operative as a deed until the condition on which it is delivered is performed *(Degoze v Rowe* (1591) Moore KB 300). On performance of the condition, however, the deed is to be treated as having been duly executed retrospectively as at the date of delivery as an escrow *(Graham v Graham* (1791) 1 Ves 272). Accordingly, the legal estate is passed retrospectively as at that date (per Farwell LJ in the *Foundling Hospital* case [1911] 2 KB 367, at p 377) and the grantor must *then* have had capacity so that, for example, an infant will not be bound even if he comes of age before the condition is fulfilled (see per Cross J in the *Windsor Refrigerator* case [1961] Ch 88, at pp 102–3). Cross J, in the case last mentioned, went on to quote the view expressed in *Williams on Vendor and Purchaser* (3rd ed, pp 1184–5) that:

> if a man delivers a conveyance of land as an escrow at a date when he has not got the legal estate conveyed but subsequently obtains it before the condition is fulfilled, the deed will not carry the legal estate to the grantee on the fulfilment of the condition.

But, with respect, this view must be regarded as expressed per incuriam since it appears to overlook and is inconsistent with the well-known cases on the doctrines of 'estoppel, tenancy by and feeding the' (see *Church of England Building Society v Piskor* [1954] Ch 553, and cases there cited).

Further the retrospective effect was considered in *Security Trust Co v Royal Bank of Canada* [1976] AC 503, PC, and the general principles outlined as follows:

> On fulfilment of the condition subject to which it was delivered as an escrow, a deed is not taken to relate back to the date of its delivery for all purposes, but only for such purposes as are necessary to give efficacy to the transaction—*ut res magis valeat quam pereat* (see *Butler and Baker's Case* (1591) 3 Co Rep 25a). Thus the fact that the grantor has died before the condition of an escrow is fulfilled does not entail the consequence that the disposition fails. If and when the condition is fulfilled the doctrine of relation back will save it, but notwithstanding the relation back for that limited purpose the grantee is not entitled to the rents of the property during the period of suspense or to lease it or to serve notices to quit (see Sheppard's Touchstone, 7th ed, (1820), p 60: *Thompson v McCullough* [1947] KB 447).

This seems to suggest that the retrospective operation will not validate other, intermediate transactions (such as mortgages) by the purchaser even though occurring after delivery in escrow. However, any such transaction by the vendor would apparently be invalidated as against the purchaser on the basis of being in derogation of his grant (see *Hooper v Ramsbottom* (1815) 6 Taunt 12).

Lastly reference really must be made to a thoroughly modern consideration of this 'relic of mediaeval times' by the Court of Appeal in *Alan Estates Ltd v WG Stores Ltd* [1982] Ch 511 (see per Lord Denning MR at p 520). There a lease and counterpart were exchanged by way of delivery in escrow on 1 November 1976; the condition of the escrow was fulfilled on 18 November 1977; the lease provided that rent was payable 'from the date hereof' but no date had been inserted in the blanks left for the purpose in either document. By a majority decision (Ackner LJ dissenting) allowing an appeal it was held that the relevant date was the earlier date (ie in accordance with the retrospective operation indicated above and not applying *Terrapin International Ltd v IRC* [1976] 1 WLR 665). Lord Denning MR restated the effect of delivery in escrow as follows (ibid, pp 520–1):

The question in this case is: what is the effect of an escrow before the conditions are fulfilled? One thing is clear. Whilst the conditions are in suspense, the maker of the escrow cannot recall it. He cannot dispose of the land or mortgage it in derogation of the grant which he has made. He is bound to adhere to the grant for a reasonable time so as to see whether the conditions are to be fulfilled or not. If the conditions are not fulfilled at all, or not fulfilled within a reasonable time, he can renounce it. On his doing so, the transaction fails altogether. It has no effect at all. But if the conditions are fulfilled within a reasonable time, then the conveyance or other disposition is binding on him absolutely. It becomes effective to pass the title to the land or other interest in the land from the grantor to the grantee. The title is then said to 'relate back' to the time when the document was executed and delivered as an escrow. But this only means that no further deed or act is necessary in order to perfect the title of the grantee. As between grantor and grantee, it must be regarded as a valid transaction which was effective to pass the title to the grantee as at the date of the escrow: see *Perryman's Case* (1599) 5 Co Rep 84*a*. But this doctrine of 'relation back' does not operate so as to affect dealings with third parties: see *Butler and Baker's Case* (1591) 3 Co Rep 25*a*. So far as the grantee is concerned, whilst the conditions are in suspense, he gets no title such as to validate his dealings with third persons. He cannot collect rents from the tenants. Nor can he give the tenants notice to quit. He cannot validly mortgage the land, though, if he purports to do so, the mortgage might be 'fed' later when he acquires the title.

Sir Denys Buckley, agreeing, emphasised that on fulfilment of the condition the rights and liabilities of the parties (also semble the grant of the legal estate) should be ascertained as if the instrument had been delivered absolutely and not as an escrow in the first place (ibid, p 528).

6 Attestation

Invariably the execution of deeds (of conveyance or otherwise) is witnessed by one person who subscribes to an attestation clause—'signed, sealed and delivered by the said   in the presence of [name, address, occupation]'. However, such attestation is as a general rule strictly an *un*necessary formality, although there are a number of statutory exceptions.

The anticipated value of an attestation clause is obvious: if it is in proper form, even without production of the witness, or any recollection by him, it should be strong evidence of due execution (see *Hope v Harman* (1847) 16 QB 751*n*; also *Stromdale & Ball Ltd v Burden* [1952] Ch 223 and *First National Securities Ltd v Jones* [1978] Ch 109, CA). In this connection, it may be noted that a party to a deed is not a competent witness (*Seal v Claridge* (1881) 7 QBD 516). Traditionally, but totally without authority, this incompetence also applies to spouses of parties. However, it does not apply to persons (eg, directors) in whose presence the seal of a corporation is affixed (eg, under s 74 of the Law of Property Act 1925), since such persons are not treated as attesting merely as witnesses but as part of the act of sealing (*Shears v Jacob* (1866) LR 1 CP 513; see also the *Windsor Refrigerator* case [1961] Ch 375, CA).

Additionally, a person who is to take under a deed may well be concerned to know that it has been duly executed. Normally, of course, a purchaser relies on the vendor's solicitors and assumes an absence of forgery or fraud (see pp 85–86). And where mortgagees had not insisted on any especial witnessing of signatures on a charge, one of which turned out to be a forgery, Bingham J is reported as saying that 'he did not think that they had departed from normal practice' (*First National Securities Ltd v Hegarty* (1982) *The Times,* 2 November). But if there is any anticipatory suspicion, what rights has a purchaser? At common law prima facie a purchaser had *no* right to require the vendor to execute the conveyance in the presence of himself or his solicitor, but was entitled reasonably to require this in special circumstances (see, eg, *Ex parte Swinbanks* (1879) 11 Ch D 525). Since this was all a question of fact, there was often much uncertainty and the position now (since 1881) is, by virtue of s 75 of the Law of Property Act 1925 that:

> On a sale, the purchaser shall not be entitled to require that the conveyance to him be executed in his presence, or in that of his solicitor, as such; but shall be entitled to have, at his own cost, the execution of the conveyance attested by some person appointed by him, who may, if he thinks fit, be his solicitor.

The authoritative *Williams on Vendor and Purchaser* (3rd ed, p 689) advised that:

> Where the conveying parties and their solicitors are unknown to the purchaser or his solicitor, it is a prudent precaution to insist on the exercise of the right so conferred, in order to avoid all risk of forgery or fraud.

Much indignation would certainly be engendered by following this advice. It has never been the usage of the profession to make enquiry as to the genuineness of the signature or seal to any conveyance (see *Law Society's Digest*, Opinion No 125, dated 1859). Indeed, it has even been quasi-authoritatively pronounced not to be the duty of a purchaser's solicitor to call s 75 in aid in the absence of suspicious circumstances (ibid, Opinion No 162, dated 1892).

7 Omnia praesumuntur rite esse acta

If all else fails, it may often be possible to rely in practice on the presumption of due execution:

> When a deed comes from an unsuspected repository, the court, in the absence of evidence to the contrary, is bound to presume that, so far as the deed appears to have been executed by the parties to it, it was in fact executed by them—that is to say, executed under seal and delivered by them so as to be a complete deed

(per Kekewich J in *Re Airey* [1897] 1 Ch 164, at p 169; see also s 4 of the Evidence Act 1938). In addition, in appropriate circumstances time may be a substitute for any of the formal requirements of a deed: despite an apparently defective execution due execution may be presumed from long enjoyment (*Woolley v Brownhill* (1824) 13 Price 500).

8 Land Registry transfers

Land Registry transfers have been judicially stated to be deeds (per Vaisey J in *Chelsea and Walham Green Building Society v Armstrong* [1951] Ch 853, at p 857) which, inter alia, presupposes compliance with all the formal requirements of execution already discussed. In fact the prescribed form of transfer of freehold land (Form 19 in the Schedule to the Land Registration Rules 1925), which many of the other forms follow, specifies places for both the transferor's signature and a seal, and also has an attestation clause stating that the transfer has been 'signed, sealed and delivered'. Thus, apparently the usual formal requirements must necessarily be complied with. This would have been much more apparent had Form 19 simply concluded (as do Forms 48, 49 and 50): 'to be executed as a deed'. Further there might justifiably be thought to be some subtle distinction here since, for example, Forms 51, 52, 54 and 55 all conclude 'to be executed as Form 19', rather than 'as a deed'. However, the only two distinctions that the present writer can see are that Form 19 specifies, first, the inclusion of an attestation clause, so perhaps making attestation one of the necessary formalities, whilst ordinarily a deed does not in law require attestation, and second, the use of a signature, so perhaps excluding the ordinary alternative of making a mark (cp s 73 of the Law of Property Act 1925). Neither of these suggested distinctions seems likely to have any substance.

Apart from these distinctions, as far as execution is concerned, the same rules appear to apply equally to unregistered conveyances and to Land Registry transfers. Indeed s 38 (1) of the Land Registration Act 1925 provides that:

> The provisions as to execution of a conveyance on sale contained in the Law of Property Act 1925 shall apply, so far as applicable thereto, to transfers on sale of registered land.

This may well have been intended as a reference to ss 51–75 of the Law of Property Act 1925, which relate to 'conveyances and other instruments', and in fact such a reference is assumed in Ruoff and Roper, *Registered Conveyancing*, 4th ed, at p 271. However, the only provision as to execution of a *conveyance on sale* contained in the Law of Property Act 1925 is s 75, concerning the right of a purchaser as to presence at execution (discussed above) and it does not seem proper or necessary to give a more extended construction to s 38 (1) of the Land Registration Act 1925.

Three minor distinctions, the first two of which, as distinctions, are probably illusory, may in conclusion be mentioned. First, it is stated in Ruoff and Roper (loc cit), that:

> In unregistered conveyancing it is still sometimes considered that the husband or wife of a party to a deed is not a satisfactory attesting witness, but the Chief Land Registrar regards the rule—if it is a rule of practice—as anachronistic and he does not insist upon its observance.

Second, in dealings with part of the land comprised in a title, which must normally be accompanied by a plan, there is an additional formality of execution, namely, that the plan must be signed by the grantor and by or on behalf of the grantee (see rr 79 and 113 of, and Note to Form 20 in the Schedule to, the Land Registration Rules 1925). And third, although a Land Registry transfer may be delivered as an escrow, performance of the condition thereof can have no retrospective operation as to title; the legal estate will only pass on registration (ss 19 (1) and 22 (1) of the Land Registration Act 1925).

INDEX